YANKEE STADIUM

1923 | 2008

America's First Modern Ballpark

Edited by Tara Krieger and Bill Nowlin
Associate editors Len Levin and Carl Riechers

◀SABR▶

Society for American Baseball Research, Inc.
Phoenix, AZ

Yankee Stadium 1923-2008: America's First Modern Ballpark
Edited by Tara Krieger and Bill Nowlin
Associate editors Len Levin and Carl Riechers

Book Design: Rachael E Sullivan
Front and back cover photography by Scott Pitoniak.
Black and white images are from SABR/The Rucker Archive.

978-1-960819-00-0 Yankee Stadium ebook
978-1-960819-01-7 Yankee Stadium paperback
Library of Congress Control Number: 2023904812

CONTENTS

INTRODUCTION

For a franchise with 40 pennants and 27 World Series championships over the course of its 120-year history, the New York Yankees have been woefully underrepresented in book-length SABR publications. This oversight may have been purposeful, but not intentional – to put together an anthology about the Yankees, there have to be editors volunteering for projects, and interested editors often had other passions. SABR's Yankees books hitherto are limited to a book of biographies on the 1947 Yankees published by University of Nebraska Press in 2012 (a companion to a book about the 1947 Brooklyn Dodgers, both edited by Lyle Spatz), and a collection of essays about Babe Ruth published in 2019.[1]

So when Bill Nowlin approached me about resuming a project about the original Yankee Stadium in time for the 100th anniversary of its opening, the opportunity seemed obvious. The idea had first been conceptualized and preliminarily developed by SABR member Joe Wancho as a compilation of significant game stories at the Stadium, which opened in 1923 and closed in 2008. Although the book still includes 50 memorable major-league games that were played at the Stadium, it also contains 40 essays about the Stadium history.

We titled the book the first "Modern" Ballpark, because baseball had never seen anything like Yankee Stadium before it was built. It was the first ballpark to include three levels of seating, accommodating more fans by far than any other in the country. It was also intended from the outset to be used as a multipurpose venue. So inside this book are not only baseball-related essays, but also accounts of memorable football games, boxing matches, soccer seasons, track and field meets, and wrestling competitions, not to mention rodeos, concerts, and religious and political assemblies. Baseball events at the Stadium also didn't end with the Yankees – the field also hosted more than 200 Negro Leagues contests, Hearst Sandlot Classics for developing youth stars, and even an AAGPBL exhibition game. Readers will also notice articles on some of the topics they would expect – Stadium construction and renovation, concessions, the first groundskeeper, famous speeches and ceremonies, no-hitters, Monument Park, the Stadium on film, and much more, including reminiscences from some of the personalities who called the Stadium their home for work and play.

Following these essays are the games. As the goal of SABR publications is to encourage new research, 44 of the 50 games were written specifically for this book. But don't think of this as a list of the "50 Greatest Games"—many other memorable games have already been published with the SABR Games Project, and we have included a list of them, in the Appendix. Instead of the games here all being "Yankee Stadium's Greatest Hits," some may be that third-, fourth-, or fifth-best single on an album – also solid songs, but sometimes overlooked in anthologies.

We hope you enjoy these essays as much as we enjoyed putting them together, and that they help you understand what made the House that Ruth Built so special for 85 years.

—Tara Krieger

NOTES

1   The two SABR books edited by Lyle Spatz are *The Team That Forever Changed Baseball and America: The 1947 Brooklyn Dodgers* (2012) and *Bridging Two Dynasties: The 1947 New York Yankees* (2012). The Babe Ruth book is *The Babe*, Bill Nowlin and Glen Sparks, editors (Phoenix: SABR, 2019).

YANKEE STADIUM

By Vincent J. Cannato

The New York Yankees did not have an auspicious beginning as a franchise. Starting as the New York Highlanders, they played their home games at Hilltop Park in upper Manhattan from 1903 to 1912. In 1913 the Highlanders moved to the Polo Grounds and officially changed their name to the Yankees. (Before 1913, newspapers would often refer to the Highlanders with the nickname "Yankees" or "Yanks.")[1] The team played 10 uneasy seasons at the Polo Grounds, sharing the field with its owners, the New York Giants. From 1903 to 1915, the Highlanders/Yankees never won their division and had eight losing seasons.

In 1915 the Yankees were purchased by Jacob Ruppert, a beer magnate of German descent and a former congressman, and Tillinghast L'Hommedieu Huston, a wealthy engineer and contractor. They were determined to turn the Yankees into a winning franchise. To that end, they made two key decisions. First, they purchased the contract of Babe Ruth from the Red Sox in December 1919. Ruth had begun to revolutionize baseball by showing the possibilities of an offense geared toward the home run. In 1918, he led the league (with Tillie Walker) with 11 homers; in 1919 he led with 29 homers. In his first season with the Yankees, Ruth hit 54 home runs while playing his home games at the Polo Grounds.

With Ruth now a Yankee, Ruppert and Huston needed a new ballpark to showcase their star player. Attendance for Yankees home games more than doubled as the team began to outdraw the Giants, embarrassing the Giants owners, who made it clear that the Yankees should find a new home. That the Giants defeated the Yankees in both the 1921 and 1922 World Series did not lessen the fact that Babe Ruth proved a bigger attraction than the Giants.

Ruppert and Huston considered a number of locations for their new ballpark, including sites in Queens, the Inwood section at the northern tip of Manhattan, and 136th Street and Broadway in Manhattan. In the end, they settled on a 12½-acre lumber mill owned by the estate of William Waldorf Astor at 161st Street and River Avenue in the Bronx for which they paid $675,000. The site was directly across the Harlem River from the Polo Grounds. Ruppert and Huston relocated the franchise just as the population of the Bronx was exploding. Subway lines had begun to reach into the borough and with them came the building of apartments for the upwardly mobile middle class. The population of the Bronx increased from 200,507 in 1900 to 1,265,258 in 1930.[2]

The groundbreaking for the new stadium took place in May 1922. The ballpark was completed in less than a year. The Osborn Engineering Company designed it. "Ruppert and Huston made it clear that they wanted Osborn to do something that went beyond all previous ballparks," writes architectural historian Paul Goldberger. They wanted a stadium, not merely a ballpark, with a seating capacity bigger than any baseball venue in existence. Initially, the Osborn design called for a completely enclosed, circular stadium that would have looked like the multi-use ballparks of the 1970s. With decks completely surrounding the stadium, the

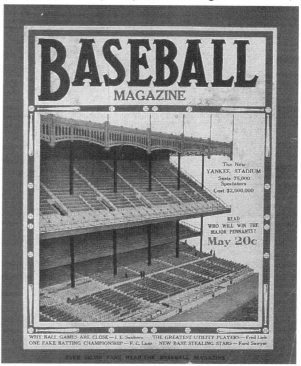

The May 1923 issue of Baseball Magazine showed off the Yankees' new $2.5 million stadium.

YANKEE STADIUM 1923-2008

plans called for a seating capacity of 80,000. In the end, the plans were modified and the upper decks ended at the flagpoles, allowing light and air to enter the stadium. The stadium cost the Yankee owners $2.5 million.[3]

White Construction Company was responsible for building the stadium, which required 30,000 cubic yards of concrete from Thomas Edison's concrete company, 2,500 tons of structural steel, 2½ million feet of lumber shipped from the Pacific coast, and 16,000 square feet of sod. The signature of the new ballpark began as a minor detail: a copper frieze, which hung down 16 feet from the roof of the upper deck. Along with pinstripe uniforms, the frieze (later painted white) became an iconic symbol of the Yankees.[4]

Yankee Stadium was not the first to be called a "stadium" – Griffith Stadium in Washington was built in 1911 and Harvard Stadium in Boston was built in 1903 – but it was certainly the largest and grandest. It was the first triple-decker ballpark, consisting of field level, upper deck, and a 19-row mezzanine in between. There were, however, obstructed views caused by the upper-deck support beams.

Opening Day was a cool afternoon on Wednesday, April 18, 1923. Commissioner Kenesaw Mountain Landis took the subway to the game, and Governor Al Smith threw out the first ball. John Philip Sousa, the March King, and his band provided the pregame patriotic music. The papers estimated a crowd of 70,000 that day, but that was most likely an exaggeration, as the new park could hold only 60,000. Whatever the exact number, it was far and away the largest crowd ever to turn out for a baseball game. The Yankees defeated the Red Sox, 4-1, on Bob Shawkey's three-hit complete-game win, but the day belonged to Babe Ruth. In the bottom of the third inning, with two runners on base, Ruth launched a home run into the right-field seats, the first home run in the new stadium. Sportswriter Fred Lieb dubbed the new stadium The House That Ruth Built. It was true in more ways than one, and the name stuck for more than eight decades.[5]

The stadium was built to accommodate the Yankees' star slugger. Originally, the right- and left-field foul poles were 255 feet from home plate. From there, the outfield fences shot out to 423 feet in right-center and 474 in left-center with dead center 487 feet away. The deepest part of the ballfield came to be known as "Death Valley," which began at 500 feet. The field benefited sluggers like Ruth who could hit the ball down the lines for a home run – although some argue that short foul poles cost Ruth homers, with

umpires calling some of his shots foul. In fact, it could be argued that the dimensions of the Polo Grounds were better suited for Ruth.[6]

The stadium remained a work in progress. For its second season, the right- and left-field fences were moved back to 280 (left field) and 295 (right field) feet. This helped reduce the so-called "Bloody Angle" between the right-field foul line and bleachers, which caused many difficult bounces. Death Valley was brought in to 490 feet. In the 1930s the Yankees closed down even more of the vast outfield expanse by moving center field in to 449 feet and left-center to 461 feet. Before the 1928 season, the Yankees added second- and third-level decks from the left-field foul pole to the bleachers; in 1937 the same was done from the right-field foul line. The changes in the outfield seating originally increased the number of seats in the stadium to just over 67,000 in the late 1920s and 71,679 in the late 1930s. When chairs replaced concrete benches in the bleachers, stadium capacity was reduced back to 67,000 by the late 1940s.[7]

To cap off a successful first year in their new ballpark, the Yankees defeated their Manhattan rivals, the New York Giants, for their first World Series championship. Ruth hit 41 home runs that season and was named American League MVP. In the first six years at their new stadium, the Yankees, led by manager Miller Huggins, won four pennants and three World Series titles. In 1927 the Yankees won 110 games with the Murderers' Row of Ruth, Gehrig, Tony Lazzeri, Earle Combs, and Bob Meusel, one of baseball's greatest teams of all time. Attendance at Yankee Stadium averaged about a million fans a year until the Great Depression reduced those numbers somewhat. Between 1923 and 1964, the Yankees had only one losing season. The Yankees now had both a monumental new home and a successful franchise worthy of their new stadium.

The new stadium was not without its tragedies. On May 19, 1929, the Yankees had taken a 3-0 lead against the Red Sox on homers by Ruth and Gehrig. The game had begun in sunshine but a few innings later clouds rolled in and brought a light drizzle. By the bottom of the fifth inning, the skies opened and the stadium was deluged in a massive downpour. Thousands of fans in the right-field bleachers – nicknamed "Ruthville" because so many of his homers had landed there – tried to make it to the stadium exits. In the mad rush to avoid the rain, two people were trampled to death and 62 people, many of them youngsters, were injured.[8]

Even from its earliest years, the Yankees were tied to tradition, and that sometimes made them slow to innovate. The first night game at Yankee Stadium did not come until 1946, 11 years after the first night game in the majors. "The Yankees were even slow in holding Ladies Day for their female fans," write Steve Steinberg and Lyle Spatz, with the first such event taking place in 1938.[9] More importantly, the Yankees were slow to embrace racial integration. Not until 1955, eight years after Jackie Robinson broke the game's color line, did the Yankees add their first African American, Elston Howard, to their roster.

Their slowness to integrate is ironic considering that the team had been welcoming Negro League games at the stadium for some time. The first Negro League game at Yankee Stadium took place on July 5, 1930, between the New York Lincoln Giants and Baltimore Black Sox. For the next two decades, Negro League teams regularly played games at Yankee Stadium. From 1940 to 1947, the New York Black Yankees called it home, but many other teams also used the stadium. From 1940 to 1946, a total of 145 Negro League games were played at Yankee Stadium, attracting 984,000 fans. For Negro League teams, playing games in Yankee Stadium meant prestige, large crowds, and, most importantly, bigger gate revenues, which helped keep those teams afloat.[10]

Ruppert died in 1939. Ed Barrow continued to run the team after Ruppert's death, and Joe McCarthy continued as manager, having taken over in 1931. (McCarthy would continue as manager until he resigned during the 1947 season. Bucky Harris managed the Yankees in 1947-1948.) In 1945 Del Webb, Dan Topping, and Larry MacPhail purchased the Yankees from Ruppert's estate for $2.8 million. (Webb and Topping bought out MacPhail two years later.) In 1947 George Weiss took over the operations of the team and in 1949 Casey Stengel became manager. In many ways, the postwar Yankees of Joe DiMaggio, Yogi Berra, Phil Rizzuto, Whitey Ford, and Vic Raschi were even more dominant than the prewar Yankees. From 1947 to 1964, the team reached the World Series in 15 out of 18 seasons, and won it 10 times.

Postwar exuberance brought attendance at the stadium to over 2 million, although, following larger trends, it dropped off in the 1950s. Even with that, attendance held steady throughout the 1950s and early 1960s, averaging about 1.5 million per season.

In 1953 Webb and Topping sold Yankee Stadium to Chicago businessman Arnold Johnson for $6.5 million. (Included in the deal was the Yankees' minor-league stadium in Kansas City.) Johnson then turned around and sold the rights to the land below Yankee Stadium to the Knights of Columbus for $2.5 million. The Knights then leased the land back to the Yankees in a 28-year deal under which the team would pay the Knights $182,000 per year.[11] When Johnson purchased the Philadelphia Athletics the following year, with plans to move the team to Kansas City, the commissioner's office forced him to sell Yankee Stadium to avoid any conflict of interest. John Cox, a friend and business associate of Johnson's, took ownership of the stadium and in 1962 would donate the stadium to his alma mater, Rice University – or at least it seemed that way. As was later discovered, Cox had only purchased an option to buy the stadium from Johnson, and did not actually own it. Therefore, as Jeff Katz writes, the "deed of gift from Cox to Rice was for *his option* to purchase stock, not outright stock."[12]

During the original Yankee Stadium's first 42 years in operation, it witnessed 27 World Series (of which the Yanks won 20) and two All-Star Games (1939 and 1960). Some of the most iconic figures in baseball history called the stadium home. It was where Babe Ruth set the single-season home-run record of 60 in 1927 (breaking his own record of 59 set in 1921) and where Roger Maris broke Ruth's record in 1961. It was where, on June 2, 1925, Lou Gehrig started at first base for Wally Pipp, the second game of his streak of 2,130 consecutive games. When Gehrig was too ill to play anymore, he bade farewell to fans on July 4, 1939, in one of the most memorable speeches in American history. Struggling with the effects of ALS, the disease that would kill him less than two years later at the age of 37, Gehrig called himself "the luckiest man on the face of the Earth."[13] The stadium also witnessed the only perfect game in World Series history when Don Larsen beat the Dodgers in Game Five of the 1956 World Series.

The Yankees also created what would become one of its greatest traditions. In 1947, the team held its first Old-Timers Day, featuring an exhibition game with retired players. Since then, it has been a way for the team and fans to honor those who once wore the pinstripes. Although other teams have held similar games, the Yankees are the only team to turn the event into a yearly celebration.

Though baseball was the heart and soul of the stadium, it was never just an arena for the nation's pastime. Fall and early winter meant football at Yankee Stadium. The football Giants called Yankee Stadium home from 1956 to 1973. It hosted three pre-Super

Bowl NFL championship games, including one of the most famous football games ever played, the 1958 championship game between the Giants and the Baltimore Colts, when the Colts defeated the Giants in overtime on Alan Ameche's one-yard touchdown run.[14]

College football also found a home at the stadium, most famously hosting 22 annual Army-Notre Dame games, which had been one of college football's greatest rivalries. New York University and Fordham University also used Yankee Stadium as a home field. In the 1960s Eddie Robinson, the football coach at Grambling State University, persuaded Yankees officials to allow historically Black colleges to play a championship game each year at the stadium. Beginning in 1968, the New York Urban League Football Classic featured the best Black college football teams facing off at Yankee Stadium.[15]

Mid-century America's other favorite sport was boxing. Over its 50-year history, the original stadium witnessed 29 title matches. Rocky Graziano, Sugar Ray Robinson, Rocky Marciano, and Floyd Patterson all fought to huge crowds in outdoor bouts. Perhaps the most famous fights at the Bronx ballpark were the two between Joe Louis and Max Schmeling. In 1936 the German fighter knocked out Louis in a victory that was celebrated in Nazi Germany. Two years later, Louis came back for a rematch and knocked out Schmeling, a victory widely celebrated in the African American community, helping turn Louis into a national hero.[16]

To see Yankee Stadium as purely a sports venue would be to miss another aspect of the monument's social value. To many Americans, it was also a place of prayer and worship. In fact, the largest crowd in Yankee Stadium history did not occur during a sporting event, but rather at the Jehovah's Witnesses Divine Will International Assembly on August 3, 1958. More than 122,000 people jammed into the stadium, filling both the stands and the outfield. Another 53,000 people assembled outside the stadium to listen on loudspeakers.[17] The year before, evangelist Billy Graham had attracted over 100,000 people to the stadium, including Vice President Richard Nixon, for a religious revival as part of his long-running New York Crusade.[18]

The Catholic Church also had strong ties to the stadium. The highlight was Pope Paul VI's visit on October 4, 1965, the first visit by a sitting pope to America. In addition to a speech at the United Nations and a visit to the Vatican Pavilion at the World's Fair in Queens, the pope held a nighttime Mass for 90,000 worshippers at Yankee Stadium. The pope told the crowd, and the national audience tuned in to watch on television, "You must love peace."[19]

As it entered its fifth decade of operation, Yankee Stadium had become one of the nation's top sporting monuments. However, the stadium itself was starting to show wear. And so was the Bronx. And so were the Yankees.

**

It seemed appropriate that the great four-decade Yankee dynasty would end just as the City of New York was beginning its slow decline that ultimately led to its near-bankruptcy with the 1975 fiscal crisis. The year 1964 marked the Yankees' last appearance in a World Series for the next 12 years. Attendance had already been declining. In 1961, 1.747 million had shown up to watch Mantle and Maris battle to beat Ruth's home-run mark. Five years later, the last-place 1966 Yankees played before only 1.124 million fans.

In 1964 Dan Topping and Del Webb announced that they were selling the team to CBS. Corporate ownership was something new for the Yankees, but it was also a curious purchase for CBS. Buying the Yankees was CBS head Bill Paley's attempt for status and prestige. "You certainly can't expect to be the toast of such friends if you keep putting on ... *The Beverly Hillbillies,*" an anonymous CBS executive explained. "On the other hand, if you own the Yankees ... you've arrived."[20]

CBS purchased the Yankees just as the team's on-field performance was beginning to decline. To make matters worse, the Yankees fired a number of iconic figures, including manager Yogi Berra and announcer Mel Allen. In 1966 announcer Red Barber was told that his contract would not be renewed, allegedly after Barber insisted on pointing out the abysmally small crowd at a late September game in the Bronx. With a paid attendance of only 413, Barber called it the "smallest crowd in the history of Yankee Stadium," noting that "the crowd is the story, not the game."[21]

By the mid-1960s, the once great Yankees dynasty had fallen hard. Mediocre teams and an aging ballpark helped tamp down attendance, but there was another reason for the troubles at Yankee Stadium. Crime was skyrocketing in New York. In 1960 there were 435 murders in the city, and by 1965 that figure had climbed to 681. By 1970, the city suffered 1,201 murders. Burglaries, robberies, and car thefts all saw similar increases during those years.[22]

Legitimate fears of crime were mixed with the anxiety of White New Yorkers about the racial changes occurring in the Bronx. Although the population of both the city and the borough remained flat during the 1950s and 1960s, New York saw a flight to suburbia of middle-class Whites who were replaced in the city by a near equal number of lower-income African Americans and Puerto Ricans. The Bronx had been almost 90 percent White in 1950; by 1970 African Americans and Puerto Ricans made up 46 percent of the borough's population.[23]

"There could be no denying that the Yankee Stadium neighborhood was changing," wrote Marty Appel, former public-relations director for the Yankees.[24] A symbol of the changes was the Grand Concourse, just three blocks east of Yankee Stadium. Long considered an elegant European-style boulevard, the Grand Concourse was beginning to fray by the mid-1960s. The Concourse Plaza Hotel at 161st Street, which for decades symbolized luxury and had once been home to many Yankees players, had by the late 1960s become a welfare hotel.[25]

In August 1970, at the annual Mayor's Trophy Game between the Yankees and Mets, New York Mayor John Lindsay was seated with Mike Burke, who ran the Yankees for CBS. "Look, we've really got to do something for the Yankees," Lindsay told Burke.

"Will you come to a meeting next week at my office?" It was Lindsay who first approached the Yankees.[26]

Lindsay, whose mayoralty seemed to bounce from one crisis to another, did not want to see the Yankees leave New York. The New York football Giants officially announced their move to New Jersey in August 1971, as Lindsay and the Yankees were negotiating the deal over Yankee Stadium. Burke, for his part, happily responded to Lindsay's offer by stating that the team's preference was first for a domed, multipurpose stadium, in keeping with the style of new stadiums at the era. Barring that, the Yankees wanted a modernized stadium with improved parking and traffic flow to better accommodate its largely suburban fan base.[27]

In a letter to City Hall a few months later, Burke made clear the growing concerns about crime. "Given the apprehension about personal safety that grips all citizens, it becomes imperative that sports fans be able to drive private cars with relative ease directly to Yankee Stadium and to park within full sight and easy walking distance for it," Burke wrote.[28]

Lindsay offered the Yankees a $24 million deal that would include the city acquiring both the land from the Knights of Columbus and the stadium from Rice University, as well as paying to renovate Yankee

Fans await the opportunity to purchase World Series tickets in 1952.

SABR/The Rucker Archive.

Stadium. The $24 million figure was what the city had spent a decade earlier to build Shea Stadium for the Mets.

In 1971 the city used the power of eminent domain to take both the stadium and the land on which it stood. It then proceeded to negotiate with Rice and the Knights for fair-value payment for their lost property. Meanwhile, the Yankees agreed to a 30-year lease with the city for the use of the new stadium.

Nobody believed that Lindsay's $24 million offer was anywhere close to what the project would cost. In April 1973, Lindsay admitted that an additional $7 million would be needed for the project, but in private his budget chief was putting the total figure at closer to $80 million. Once Lindsay had made the deal to acquire the stadium and complete the renovations, the city was going to be on the hook for whatever the final bill was.[29]

The city's generous offer was not enough to keep CBS interested in continuing its ownership of the team. Bill Paley had purchased the Yankees as a prestige project; now the Yankees had become more of an embarrassment. Paley quietly let it be known in the summer of 1972 that the team was for sale. Burke connected with a little-known Cleveland shipping executive, George Steinbrenner, and in January 1973 CBS announced that it had sold the Yankees to an ownership group headed by Steinbrenner for a cash deal of $10 million. CBS had bought the team for $13.2 million nine years earlier. While on paper it looked like an embarrassing loss for Paley and CBS, in reality with tax write-offs and depreciation, it turned out to be a wash.[30]

The last year in the old Yankee Stadium was 1973. The New York Giants, still waiting for their new Meadowlands stadium to be completed, played only their first two games of the 1973 season at Yankee Stadium before being forced to move to New Haven's Yale Bowl.

The last game at the old ballpark was played on Sunday, September 30. More than 32,000 fans came out to see the Yankees lose to the Detroit Tigers for a disappointing cap to another mediocre season as the Yankees finished in fourth place with an 80-82 record. As soon as the last out was made, bedlam erupted as "fans set about taking Yankee Stadium home with them," wrote Appel. "Those who didn't storm the field for pieces of sod wiggled their seats loose from the concrete. ..." At one point, first-base coach Elston Howard tussled with one of the unruly fans who was trying to grab first base out of Howard's hands.[31]

The city wasted no time in continuing what those fans had begun on the last day of the season. The next day Lindsay was at Yankee Stadium for the ground-breaking of stadium renovations, which began with gutting the insides of the park. For the next two years, Shea Stadium was home until a new chapter at Yankee Stadium could be opened.

* * *

The Yankees returned to their newly renovated stadium on April 15, 1976, with an 11-4 victory over the Minnesota Twins before a sold-out crowd of 52,613. Bob Shawkey, the Yankees pitcher who won the first game at Yankee Stadium in 1923, threw out the first pitch. The Yankees held a pregame ceremony connecting the thread of the greatest memories from old park to the new park. DiMaggio, Mantle, Berra, Frank Gifford, and Joe Louis, as well as the widows of Ruth and Gehrig, were in attendance. Despite the Yankees' win, it was Twins outfielder Dan Ford who hit the first home run in the renovated ballpark. (Newly named Yankee captain Thurman Munson became the first Yankee to homer in the ballpark, two days later.)[32]

By the time of the 1976 reopening, city officials were estimating that the stadium would end up costing the city at least $100 million, not including debt service, but they admitted that even that was not the final cost.[33] The ultimate price tag for the Yankee Stadium renovations was never disclosed but estimated to be close to $150 million, almost six times Lindsay's initial offer in 1971.

Whatever qualms there may have been about the public funding of the new ballpark, the newly renovated stadium was certainly an improvement. There was a 565-foot-long electronic scoreboard and escalators for the fans to reach the upper deck. There were no more obstructed views, since the old support posts were replaced by a cantilevered upper deck. There were fewer bleacher seats and the section of bleachers in dead center was blacked out so as not to distract batters. Not all of the changes were improvements. The famous frieze that lined the upper deck of the grandstand in the old ballpark was gone. All that remained was a replica frieze above the bleachers. Still, fans got more than 2,000 additional parking spots in a garage adjacent to the stadium, thus reducing the suburban fan's exposure to the surrounding neighborhood. Blue plastic seats, a few inches wider than in the old stadium, replaced the old wooden seats. One of the most striking additions was a 138-foot smokestack in the shape of a baseball bat outside the main entrance to the stadium. Weighing 45 tons and made of stainless steel and fiberglass, the bat became a designated meeting place for fans.[34]

The renovated stadium held fewer seats than the old ballpark. Before the renovations, the stadium could hold 65,000 fans; the new ballpark held 57,145. The left-field foul line was moved out 11 feet to 312 feet, while the right-field line was moved out 14 feet, to 310 feet. The rest of the fences were moved in, including the infamous Death Valley. The deepest part of the ballpark in left-center field had once been 490 feet before being brought in to 461 feet in 1937. In the renovated ballpark, Death Valley now measured 417 feet (and would be moved in even closer to 408 feet in the late 1980s).[35] In the old ballpark, Death Valley contained the monuments of Gehrig, Ruth, and Miller Huggins, which had stood in the field of play along with a flagpole. Now the monuments sat behind the outfield wall, paving the way for the creation of Monument Park. DiMaggio and Mantle received their own monuments there in the 1990s, with an additional 19 plaques going up between 1976 and 2008.[36]

The Yankees won three consecutive pennants and two World Series in their first three years in the new ballpark. A competitive team combined with a refurbished stadium with more parking in close proximity to the stadium helped draw more fans. Over 2 million people came to the Bronx ballpark in 1976, nearly double the crowds the Yankees drew in the old ballpark. By 1980, attendance had reached 2.6 million.

Despite the larger crowds, the situation in the Bronx had not improved. The borough lost 20 percent of its population during the 1970s. The South Bronx – the area immediately to the south of the stadium – was especially hit hard by waves of arson. During the 1970s, seven census tracts in the South Bronx lost more than 97 percent of their buildings to arson and abandonment; another 44 tracts had lost more than 50 percent of their buildings.[37]

This was brought home to baseball fans across the country on the night of October 12, 1977. It was Game Two of the World Series between the Dodgers and Yankees. Several times during the ABC telecast, cameras panned to a scene about a mile south of the stadium. A fiery blaze could be seen from the South Bronx – just one of the hundreds of fires that were decimating that section during the late 1960s and the 1970s. Announcers Howard Cosell and Keith Jackson discussed the fire at least five times during the game. Legend has it that Cosell said during the game: "Ladies and gentlemen, the Bronx is burning."

However, Cosell never actually said those words that night.[38]

Yet suburban fans were not deterred from coming to the Bronx to see baseball games. The question is what would happen when the Yankees stopped fielding competitive teams. The answer came during the 1980s and early 1990s. After the Yankees lost the 1981 World Series to the Dodgers, they failed to make the playoffs for the next 13 seasons. On top of that, crime continued to worsen during the crack epidemic of the late 1980s and early 1990s. Not surprisingly, attendance again tailed off, falling to 1.7 million by 1992.

Falling attendance at the stadium led Steinbrenner to make noises about taking his team elsewhere. A possible move to New Jersey was squashed in 1987 when that state's voters rejected by a 2-to-1 vote a $185 million bond measure to pay for a new Yankee Stadium.

There was some debate about whether Steinbrenner would have actually moved the team from the Bronx. There was too much history there, and the Yankees were nothing if not tied to tradition. Although fears of relocating the team lingered throughout the late 1980s and the 1990s, the team's changing fortunes in the mid-1990s quieted down such talk. After a 13-season drought, the Yankees finally made the playoffs in 1995, before losing to the Mariners in the Division Series. For 13 of the next 14 seasons, the Yankees made the playoffs, including winning the World Series in four out of five seasons from 1996 to 2000.

This mini-dynasty, led by the "Core Four" of Derek Jeter, Mariano Rivera, Andy Pettitte, and Jorge Posada as well as skipper Joe Torre, helped revive the franchise. Just as the decline of the Yankees in the mid-1960s tracked the decline of New York City, the success of the late 1990s/early 2000s Yankee team mirrored the renaissance of New York City under the mayoralties of Rudy Giuliani and Michael Bloomberg. Crime and public disorder plummeted. The city no longer faced either looming bankruptcy or fiscal austerity and budget cuts. Between 1990 and 2010, the city's population increased by more than 10 percent. The Bronx saw an even bigger increase in its population. These factors, plus the dominant Yankees teams of that era, brought more fans to the stadium. With 1.675 million fans in 1994, the stadium broke the 3 million mark in 2000 and the 4 million mark in 2005.

Despite all of this, Steinbrenner continued to make noises about moving his team out of the Bronx. In 1996 the architectural firm Hellmuth, Obata, and Kassabaum (HOK) produced a study listing four possible alternative sites for a new Yankee Stadium: 1) Van Cortlandt Park in the northern Bronx; 2) Pelham Bay Park in the eastern Bronx; 3) the West Side Rail Yards along the Hudson River in Manhattan; and 4) its current site in the Bronx, either with a renovated stadium or a new stadium across the street. HOK strongly endorsed the West Side Rail Yard as the Yankees' best option.[39]

The issue lay dormant for two years until April 13, 1998. A few hours before the Yankees were scheduled to play the Angels, a 500-pound concrete and steel beam fell and landed on Seat 7 in Section 22 of the loge level. No one was in the stadium at the time, but the games for that day and the following day were postponed. The fallen beam gave Steinbrenner ammunition to make his case for a new stadium.[40]

Steinbrenner was fortunate that Giuliani, who prided himself as the city's number-one Yankees fan, was mayor of New York. The mayor became Steinbrenner's key ally in finding the team a new stadium, keeping alive the idea of relocating the team to the West Side Rail Yards. Giuliani and Steinbrenner found little political support for a new stadium. Few believed that taxpayers should pay hundreds of millions of dollars to build a ballpark owned by wealthy private interests. The Yankees were also in the middle of what became one of the greatest seasons in franchise history in 1998. By the summer, perhaps recognizing the opposition to a new publicly funded stadium, Steinbrenner began to soften his stance. He opened up the possibility of the team paying some of the costs of a new stadium and said that if the city could guarantee 3 million fans per season, he would consider keeping the team in the Bronx.[41]

Giuliani had not given up on a dream of a new ballpark for the Yankees. Nothing more symbolized the close relationship between the Yankees and the Giuliani administration than when Deputy Mayor Randy Levine left his post at City Hall in 2000 to become president of the Yankees. In December 2001, a few days before he was set to leave office, Giuliani announced plans for two new stadiums, for both the Yankees and Mets. Both would have retractable domes. The stadiums were estimated to cost $1.6 billion each. The details of the financing were still not settled, but it was clear that the onus would fall on the city.[42]

Giuliani's successor, billionaire businessman Michael Bloomberg, nixed the plan shortly after he took office, calling it "corporate welfare." However, a few years later, a new stadium for the Yankees was back on the table. The city could either spend hundreds of millions of dollars to again renovate the stadium that it owned or it could find a way to get the Yankees a new stadium. In 2006 Bloomberg and state officials agreed on a plan for new stadiums for both the Yankees and Mets. Financing would come from a mix of city, state, and private funding. The new Yankee Stadium would be built across from the current stadium in Macombs Dam Park. Groundbreaking for the new stadium began in August 2006 and it was set to open in 2009.

The Yankees made 2008 a season-long celebration of the old ballpark. They drew a record 4.298 million fans that season, but the team missed the playoffs with a disappointing third-place 89-73 record. The final game took place on the night of September 21. An ailing 98-year-old Bob Sheppard, the Yankees' public-address announcer for 57 years, recorded the starting lineup earlier that day from his home to be played before the game. The pregame ceremonies featured Yankees stars from previous decades. The Yankees defeated the Orioles that night, 7-3. Catcher José Molina hit the final home run at the Stadium.[43]

When the last out was completed, the fans did not run on the field as they did in 1973. (After the 1970s, increased stadium security, including the use of New York City police, had prevented fans from storming the playing field.) Instead, in 2008 most fans remained in their seats as the Yankees took the field one last time. Derek Jeter gave an impromptu speech thanking fans. "It's a lot of tradition, a lot of history, a lot of memories," Jeter said of the 85 seasons at Yankee Stadium. "Now the great thing about memories is you're able to pass it along from generation to generation." Jeter tipped his cap to the fans and then led his teammates for one final lap around the field as Frank Sinatra's "New York, New York" played in the background.[44]

The refurbished, city-funded stadium had stood for 33 seasons from 1976 until 2008. During that time, it hosted 10 World Series (of which the Yankees won six) and two All-Star Games (1977 and 2008). This iteration of Yankee Stadium also had more than its share of baseball memories. In its first year, the stadium saw Chris Chambliss's dramatic walk-off home run in the bottom of the ninth inning of Game Five of the ALCS against the Royals to send the Yankees to their first World Series in 12 years. As Chambliss rounded the bases, hundreds of jubilant fans took to the field, almost preventing Chambliss from reaching home plate.[45] Another iconic game featured Reggie

Jackson's three home runs against the Dodgers in Game Six of the 1977 World Series.[46] Dave Righetti threw a Fourth of July no-hitter against the Red Sox in 1983,[47] and both David Wells and David Cone pitched perfect games, in 1998 and 1999 respectively. There were also controversies such as the 1983 "pine-tar incident," when the Royals' George Brett's home run off Goose Gossage was called back because of excessive pine tar on Brett's bat.[48] Another controversy occurred during the first game of the 1996 ALCS against the Orioles, when 12-year-old Jeffrey Maier reached out with his glove to catch Derek Jeter's fly ball to right field, yet the umpires ruled that Jeter had homered.

The renovated ballpark did not feature any NFL football, and the only college football was the Urban League Classic games between the best historically Black college football teams from 1976 to 1987. The renovated Yankee Stadium hosted, in 1976, the New York Cosmos soccer team, a team powered by superstars Pelé and Giorgio Chinaglia. (The old stadium had

actually hosted the Cosmos in their inaugural season back in 1971.) Boxing also played less of a role, with the exception of the September 28, 1976, heavyweight fight between Muhammad Ali and Ken Norton when Ali successfully defended his title in a controversial 15-round decision.

Although Yankee Stadium appeared in a few movies, the small screen was perhaps the site of its most famous appearance. The popular 1990s sitcom *Seinfeld* contained a recurring storyline in which George Costanza worked for the Yankees as the assistant to the traveling secretary. The exterior of the stadium was often featured on the show, which also included an over-the-top rendition of George Steinbrenner voiced by creator Larry David.[49]

World leaders continue to pay visits to Yankee Stadium. John Paul II celebrated Mass for 80,000 worshippers on October 2, 1979, while his successor Benedict XVI would make it three papal visits to Yankee Stadium with a Mass on April 20, 2008. In

SABR/The Rucker Archive.

Before a game, Yankees manager Casey Stengel gives a lesson in Stengelese to the Little League Champions from Monterrey, Mexico, who won back-to-back titles in 1957 and 1958.

June 1990 Nelson Mandela made the stadium the first stop on his American tour, just four months after being released from a South African prison. Wearing a Yankees cap and jacket, Mandela told the adoring crowd: "I am a Yankee."[50]

Music was an integral part of Yankee Stadium. Concerts had been absent until the Beach Boys played in 1988. Beginning in 1980, Steinbrenner chose Frank Sinatra's song "New York, New York" to be played over the loudspeakers after every home victory. Organ music was also an important part of Yankee games, with Eddie Layton playing the organ from 1967 to 2003. Robert Merrill, a longtime baritone for the Metropolitan Opera and a good friend of Steinbrenner's, also became a fixture at Yankee Stadium starting in 1969. Wearing a Yankee pinstripe jersey with the number 1½, Merrill sang the National Anthem at Opening Day, Old-Timers Day, and other special occasions.

Apart from music, no other sound defined Yankee Stadium as the voice of Bob Sheppard, who served as the public-address announcer from 1951 to 2007. After Sheppard retired, Derek Jeter asked him to record the Yankees captain's at-bat introduction to be used for every home at-bat. When the Yankees moved to their new ballpark in 2009, Paul Olden took over as the public-address announcer.

The terrorist attacks of September 11, 2001, affected the entire nation, but especially New York City. Eleven days after the attacks, Giuliani asked Steinbrenner if the city could use the Stadium as the site of an interfaith memorial service called "Prayer for America." Former President Bill Clinton, Oprah Winfrey, and singers Placido Domingo and Bette Midler were among the attendees.[51] On October 30, 2001, at the start of Game Three of the World Series between the Yankees and Diamondbacks, President George W. Bush arrived to throw out the game's first pitch. "What unnerved the fans was that they knew they were either in the safest place in the world at that moment or the absolutely most dangerous place in the world," wrote Tom Verducci, "but they had no way of ruling out either choice with any certainty." Wearing a blue FDNY jacket, Bush went to the pitcher's mound and threw a perfect strike.[52]

In the wake of 9/11, all major-league ballparks began to play "God Bless America" during the seventh-inning stretch. Most stadiums dropped the tradition the following season, but it has continued at Yankee Stadium. For a number of years, the Irish tenor Ronan Tynan sang "God Bless America" in person until he was let go by the Yankees for making an anti-Semitic remark.[53] The stadium also used a recorded version of Kate Smith's rendition of the song, but that was ended in 2019 because of complaints that other Smith songs contained racist lyrics.[54]

***

Built across 161st Street from the original stadium, the new Yankee Stadium was an enormous structure, bigger than the old stadium, which was still standing on Opening Day and was not fully demolished until the following year. Whereas the renovated stadium had been painted white, the new stadium made from limestone, was a distinguished light brown. Tall, narrow, windowed arches wrapped around the exterior. Just inside the exterior shell of the new stadium was a seven-story, 31,000-square-foot grand concourse called the Great Hall lined with retail space and with 20 banners of Yankees greats hanging on the wall.

The final price tag for the new stadium was more than $1.5 billion. The Yankees financed their end of the deal from city- and state-backed bonds. Unlike many new stadiums, the Yankees never sold naming rights. The city and state spent $400 million on parking, parks, and improvements to the surrounding neighborhood. This included, for the first time, a Metro North train station for suburban commuters.

The south side of 161st Street, where the old stadium was located, was converted into a new, multi-use Macombs Dam Park, which includes four basketball courts, handball courts, and the Joseph Yancey Track and Field, with synthetic turf in the middle for football and soccer. The new park also includes three ballfields: one for baseball, one for softball, and one for Little League. The baseball field occupies the footprint of the old stadium field. In 2020 the field was named in honor of former Yankee Elston Howard.[55]

Luxury was the operative word for the new stadium. No expense was spared for the players' clubhouse and training area. A high-end steakhouse was opened behind right field. High-definition video screens were everywhere. The new stadium had 56 luxury boxes. There were more than 4,000 premium field-level seats starting at $500 a ticket. The most expensive seats in the front rows cost $2,500 and included waiter service.[56]

However, not everything was perfect. The new stadium opened in the middle of a recession and the Yankees found it hard to sell all of their luxury boxes. Even worse, the front-row luxury seats were not filled for most games, with empty seats a common sight during televised games, forcing the team to cut the prices for all of their premium seats. There was another subtle difference between the ballparks. Verducci noticed that the new stadium was much quieter than the old one. The upper decks were sloped away from the field and did not feel on top of the ballfield as in the old stadium.[57] Players noticed it as well. Jeter said that the new ballpark "had a different feel," despite all the new amenities. The old stadium "was more intimidating," he said. "The fans were right on top of you." Mariano Rivera also complained that the new stadium "doesn't hold noise, or home-team fervor, anywhere near the way the old place did."[58]

Ruppert's original Yankee Stadium was designed to make money by selling baseball to the burgeoning middle class. By contrast, the new Yankee Stadium, a sports venue geared increasingly toward the needs of the affluent, would become an emblem of a New York that Mayor Bloomberg once called a "luxury city."

Ruppert's Yankee Stadium was nothing if not grandiose, but it was also an original piece of architecture that the Yankees were able to fill with decades of memorable sporting and historical events. The Yankees have successfully transferred their 85 years of history – Monument Park, Old-Timers Day, Sinatra's "New York, New York" – from the old ballpark to the new one. The question going forward is whether the new Yankee Stadium will be able to create traditions and memories of its own. If it does, then it too will become a national monument rather than a historical replica.

NOTES

1   Marty Appel, *Pinstripe Empire: The New York Yankees from Before the Babe to After the Boss* (New York: Bloomsbury, 2012), 18-19.

2   Robert Weintraub, *The House that Ruth Built* (New York: Little, Brown and Company, 2011), 23-32; Joseph Durso, *Yankee Stadium: Fifty Years of Drama* (Boston: Houghton Mifflin Company, 1972), 38-40; Paul Goldberger, *Ballpark: Baseball in the American City* (New York: Alfred A. Knopf, 2020), 116-117; Neil J. Sullivan, *The Diamond in the Bronx: Yankee Stadium and the Politics of New York* (New York: Oxford University Press, 2001), 35-37; Steve Steinberg and Lyle Spatz, *The Colonel and the Hug: The Partnership that Transformed the New York Yankees* (Lincoln: University of Nebraska Press, 2015), 198.

3   Goldberger, 119-121.

4   Weintraub, 53-55.

5   Weintraub, 35-47; Appel, 130-132.

6   Philip J. Lowry, *Green Cathedrals: The Ultimate Celebration of All Major League and Negro League Ballparks,* Fifth Edition (Phoenix: Society for American Baseball Research, 2019), 213-214; Appel, 127; Weintraub, 91.

7   Lowry, 213-214.

8   "Two Dead, 62 Hurt in Yankee Stadium as Rain Stampedes Baseball Crowd," *New York Times*, May 20, 1929: 1.

9   Steinberg and Spatz, 321.

10 For more on the Negro Leagues at Yankees Stadium, see Lawrence D. Hogan, "The Negro Leagues Discovered an Oasis at Yankee Stadium," *New York Times*, February 13, 2011, and James Overmyer, "Black Baseball at Yankee Stadium: The House That Ruth Built and Satchel Furnished (with Fans)," in John Graf, Duke Goldman, and Larry Lester, eds., *From Rube to Robinson: SABR's Best Articles on Black Baseball* (Phoenix: Society for American Baseball Research, 2020), 59-76.

11 Christopher J. Kauffman, *Faith and Fraternalism: The History of the Knights of Columbus* Revised Edition (New York: Simon & Schuster, 1992), 394.

12 Sullivan, 85-87; Jeff Katz, *The Kansas City A's & the Wrong Half of the Yankees* (Hingham, Massachusetts: Maple Street Press, 2007), 158-159.

13 Ray Robinson and Christopher Jennison, *Yankee Stadium: 75 Years of Drama, Glamor, and Glory* (New York: Penguin Studio, 1998), 54-55.

14 Durso, 125-129.

15 Alfred Santasiere III, "Home of Champions, Part II," MLB.com, November 1, 2013, https://www.mlb.com/news/yankee-stadium-college-football-history.

16 Durso, 90-94; "Memorable Fights at Yankee Stadium," *Sports Illustrated*, October 20, 2010. https://www.si.com/boxing/2010/10/20/20-omemorable-fights-at-yankee-stadium#gid=ci0255c8fba00024a5&pid=yuri-foreman-vs-miguel-cotto.

17 "Jehovah's Witnesses Rally 250,000 at Final Session," *New York Times*, August 4, 1958: 1. Another 77,000 Jehovah's Witness members gathered at the Polo Grounds at the same time, bringing the total at the two venues to over 250,000.

18 "100,000 Fill Yankee Stadium to Hear Graham," *New York Times*, July 21, 1957: 1.

19 "Ninety Thousand Amens," *New York Times*, October 5, 1965: SU2:1; *Fourteen Hours: A Picture Story of the Pope's Historic First Visit to America* (New York: Dell Publishing Co., Inc., 1965).

20 Sullivan, 124.

21 Barber quoted in Robinson and Jennison, 119.

22 Crime data comes from Kenneth T. Jackson, ed., *The Encyclopedia of New York,* Second Edition (New Haven: Yale University Press, 2010), 330.

23 Evelyn Gonzalez, *The Bronx* (New York: Columbia University Press, 2004), 110.

24 Appel, 360.

25 "Once-Grand Concourse: The Avenue, a Symbol of Prosperity Has Grown Old and Causes Concern," *New York Times*, February 2, 1965: 35; "Grand Concourse: Hub of Bronx Is Undergoing Ethnic Change," *New York Times*, July 21, 1966: 28; Young quoted in Tony Morante, "The Turbulent '70s: Steinbrenner, the Stadium, and the 1970s Scene," in Cecilia M. Tan, ed., *Baseball Research Journal New York, New York: Baseball in the Big Apple* (Phoenix: Society for American Baseball Research, 2017), 111.

26 Sullivan, 117-119; Joseph Durso, "The $24-Million Picnic," *New York Times*, April 5, 1971: 39.

27 Sullivan, 117.

28 Sullivan, 131-2.

29 "Memo Indicates City Obscured Stadium's High Cost," *New York Times*, February 3, 1976: 63.

30 Bill Madden, *Steinbrenner: The Last Lion of Baseball* (New York: HarperCollins, 2010), 9-13.

31 Appel, 394. The picture of Elston Howard and the fan fighting over first base can be found in *New York Times*, October 1, 1973: 50.

32 "Yankees Win First Game in Rebuilt Stadium," *New York Times*, April 16, 1976: 57.

33 "Stadium's Cost Now Seen as Loss," *New York Times*, April 15, 1976: 69.

34 "Stadium's New Big 'Bat' Proves a Hit in First Appearance Here," *New York Times*, July 27, 1975: 34.

35 Lowry, 159-160.

36 Chris Landers, "The Long and Winding Story Behind Yankee Stadium's Monument Park," MLB.com, July 24, 2018, https://www.mlb.com/cut4/how-yankee-stadium-s-monument-park-was-created-c286873704.

37 Megan Roby, "The Push and Pull Dynamics of White Flight: A Study of the Bronx Between 1950 and 1980," *Bronx County Historical Society Journal*, Vol. XLV, Nos. 1 & 2, Spring/Fall 2008, 34-55; Joe Flood, "Why the Bronx Burned," *New York Post*, May 16, 2010, https://nypost.com/2010/05/16/why-the-bronx-burned/.

38 Jonathan Mahler, *Ladies and Gentlemen, The Bronx Is Burning: 1977, Baseball, Politics, and the Battle for the Soul of the City* (New York: Farrar, Straus and Giroux, 2005), 330.

39 Sullivan, 165-166.

40 Murray Chass, "Beam May Be Lever for Steinbrenner's Case," *New York Times*, April 14, 1998: C1.

41 "As Gates Rise, Steinbrenner Softens on Bronx," *New York Times*, July 9, 1998; "Steinbrenner Foes Buoyed by His Recent Comments, *New York Times*, July 10, 1998; "In First, Steinbrenner Offers to Help Pay for a New Stadium," *New York Times*, July 29, 1998: B6; "Quit Whining and They Will Come," *New York Times*, July 10, 1998: A14.

42 "In Bottom of the 9th, Giuliani Presents Deal on Stadiums," *New York Times*, December 29, 2001: A1.

43 Appel, 552-556.

44 Appel, 556-7.

45 Joseph Wancho, "October 14, 1976: Chris Chambliss' Home Run Delivers Pennant to the Bronx," https://sabr.org/gamesproj/game/october-14-1976-chris-chambliss-home-run-delivers-pennant-to-the-bronx/.

46 Scott Ferkovich, "October 18, 1977: Reggie Becomes 'Mr. October' with 3 Home Runs in World Series," https://sabr.org/gamesproj/game/october-18-1977-reggie-becomes-mr-october-with-3-home-runs-in-world-series/.

47 Bill Nowlin, "July 4, 1983: Dave Righetti Tosses a No-Hitter on Fourth of July," https://sabr.org/gamesproj/game/july-4-1983-dave-righetti-tosses-a-no-hitter-on-fourth-of-july/.

48 Filip Bondy, *The Pine Tar Game: The Kansas City Royals, the New York Yankees, and Baseball's Most Absurd and Entertaining Controversy* (New York: Scribner, 2015), 127-154.

49 Peter Botte, "How Larry David Turned His Yankees Pain into 'Seinfeld' Gold," *New York Post*, April 11, 2020, https://nypost.com/2020/04/11/how-larry-david-turned-his-yankees-pain-into-seinfeld-gold/.

50 "Mandela Takes His Message to Rally in Yankee Stadium," *New York Times*, June 22, 1990: A21.

51 Appel, 517.

52 Tom Verducci, "It's Gone: The Passing of Baseball's Cathedral," *Sports Illustrated*, September 22, 2008, https://vault.si.com/vault/2008/09/22/its-gone-goodbye.

53 "Tenor Booted from Yankees Game after anti-Semitic Slur," *New York Post*, October 16, 2009, https://nypost.com/2009/10/16/tenor-booted-from-yankees-game-after-anti-semitic-slur/.

54 "Yankees Drop Kate Smith's 'God Bless America' After Being Told About Her Racist Songs," *USA Today*, April 19, 2019, https://www.usatoday.com/story/sports/mlb/yankees/2019/04/18/yankees-drop-kate-smith-god-bless-america-7th-inning-stretch/3510295002/.

55 New York City Department of Parks & Recreation, "Macombs Dam Park," https://www.nycgovparks.org/parks/macombs-dam-park/highlights/19804.

56 "Luxury Strikes Out," *Wall Street Journal*, March 6, 2009: W1; "Red-Faced Yanks Cut Elite Prices," *New York Post*, April 29, 2009: 5.

57 Verducci, "New Stadium an Instant Classic."

58 Chris Smith, "Derek Jeter Opens the Door," *New York Magazine*, September 21, 2014, https://nymag.com/intelligencer/2014/09/derek-jeter-private-photos.html; "Mo Rivera: Old Yankee Stadium Had Far Better Atmosphere Than New One Does," CBS News, May 7, 2014, https://www.cbsnews.com/newyork/news/mo-rivera-old-yankee-stadium-had-far-better-atmosphere-than-new-one-does.

THE BRONX ALWAYS BECKONED

By Bob Golon

The headline in the March 13, 1903, edition of the *New York Times* read "Baseball Grounds Fixed." The non-bylined article described an agreement, announced by American League President Ban Johnson, that a plot of rocky land was leased for the construction of a ballpark to be occupied by the newly minted New York American League Baseball Club. It was in an elevated section of upper Manhattan, at 168th Street and 11th Avenue, with a spectacular view of the Hudson River and the New Jersey Palisades when looking west. On it, Hilltop Park was built, becoming the home to the American League Baseball Club of New York, nicknamed the Highlanders (soon to be renamed the Yankees), for the next 10 years.

In this same article, Ban Johnson described how "legal issues" always seemed to rise as individuals with a vested interest against the establishment of a new club in New York somehow managed to convince the city to cut a street through the middle of a desired American League property. It was a veiled reference to the National League's New York Giants and their owners, primarily the former owner Andrew Freedman, whose Tammany Hall connections often enabled them to successfully block the progress of the Americans.[1] The negotiations for the hilltop were completed in secrecy and a successful lease arrangement was made, but, according to Johnson, an ace-in-the-hole always had to be at the ready, in case the agreement fell through at the last minute. Johnson described his contingency plan as such:

"Had there been a slip up on this property, we had everything shaped to the minute to sign a lease for the Astor estate at One Hundred and Sixty-first Street and Jerome Avenue (in the Bronx), in which event the American League would have conducted the club."[2]

In an irony of all ironies, this location in the Bronx was destined to become baseball's most famous address in 1923 as the site of the original Yankee Stadium.

As early as autumn 1902, before the Highlanders ever played a game, the Bronx was being mentioned as a possible home for the new club.[3] Proponents felt it was a fertile ground with an untapped fan base for baseball. However, the new interborough elevated and underground rail systems to the Bronx were still in the planning stages, raising a concern about the ability of Manhattan fans to reach the Bronx easily.

Highlanders owners Frank Farrell and Bill Devery were partial to a Manhattan location, but events quickly conspired to make Hilltop Park obsolete. First, before the beginning of the 1911 season, the wooden Polo Grounds in upper Manhattan burned to the ground, leaving the Giants without a home. In a grand gesture, Farrell offered the use of Hilltop Park to the Giants while the new concrete-and-steel Polo Grounds was being built. Concurrently, the Yankees' 10-year lease on the Hilltop Park property expired after the 1912 season, not to be renewed. Before his death, Giants owner John T. Brush offered the use of the new Polo Grounds to Farrell, returning the favor of the year before. It provided the Yankees a temporary home in Manhattan, but the Bronx still beckoned.

In 1911 Farrell turned his attention to a plot of land in the Kingsbridge section of the Bronx, at 221st Street and Broadway, for a new park for the Yankees. The site was just north of where the Harlem River bends and becomes the Spuyten Duyvill Creek. Farrell had plans for a 32,000-seat concrete-and-steel stadium, whose entrance on Broadway would be a short walking distance from the 225th Street subway station. He announced his plans with great fanfare, yet some problems still had to be resolved. Legal issues involving the existing owners of the property arose regarding the future transfer of ownership of the grounds. Additionally, the proximity to the river rendered the plot of land a swamp, causing Farrell to arrange for the digging of drainage tunnels and the grading of the land by importing considerable rock and gravel from the excavation site for Grand Central Terminal in Manhattan.[4] The dual legal and excavation expenses would be a blow from which Farrell's ownership would not survive, and by the end of the 1914 season, the Yankees were up for sale, still without a new ballpark of their own.

A Manhattan brewery magnate, Colonel Jacob Ruppert Jr., along with Captain T.L. Huston, expressed interest in the club, but a review of the

YANKEE STADIUM 1923-2008

Yankees' finances almost derailed the deal. In a 1931 article, Ruppert said, "I never saw such a mixed-up business in my life – liabilities, contracts, notes, obligations of all sorts. We went through it thoroughly, my lawyer and I. There were times when it looked so bad no sane man would put a penny into it."[5] A deal was struck, however, and it was immediately revealed that Ruppert and Huston had plans for a new ballpark … again, in the Bronx! The rumor had ground being prepared for a new stadium on Astor property along Westchester Avenue and Clason Point Road, east of the Bronx River.[6] This, too, was not to be. The next rumor had Ruppert interested in land in Long Island City, Queens, at the foot of the 59th Street Bridge,[7] as well as other sites in Manhattan. Ruppert then decided to focus on a long-term lease at the Polo Grounds,[8] as the gathering storm clouds of World War I served as a deterrent to any firm investment plans.

After the war's end, Ruppert set out in earnest to build his ballclub. In late 1919 he acquired pitcher Carl Mays from the Boston Red Sox. Mays was having disagreements with the Red Sox management, yet the purchase of Mays was viewed as "a serious breach of something or other," according to Ruppert. Ban Johnson suspended Mays, and Ruppert applied for a court injunction, which was allowed.[9] Johnson, who rarely had an associate with whom he didn't feud, turned his animosity toward Ruppert by plotting to revoke the club's charter if it did not have a stadium to play in. Johnson proceeded to pressure Charles Stoneham and John McGraw to evict the Yankees from the Polo Grounds, which the Giants were more amenable to do at this point. The Giants outdrew the Yankees by approximately 90,000 in 1919. In December the Yankees had purchased Babe Ruth and by mid-May they were outdrawing their landlords considerably, much to the Giants' chagrin. On May 14, 1920, Giants treasurer Francis X. McQuade announced that the Yankees would no longer be welcomed at the Polo Grounds after the 1920 season.[10]

This drew an immediate and well-planned response from Ruppert. Knowing that his team needed a place to play, Ruppert informed Johnson that he owned a parcel of land at Madison Avenue and 102nd Street, a single city block, much too small to accommodate a major-league ball field. Ruppert promised to build a small grandstand and field, playing games at a park where every fly ball would result in a home run, causing great embarrassment to Johnson. Johnson backtracked, intervened with the Giants ownership, and the eviction was called off.[11]

Ruppert later revealed that this situation, as well as the enormous popularity of the aforementioned Babe Ruth, convinced him that it was time to no longer be "a tenant ballclub." Although he said that he and the Giants' Charles Stoneham had a good relationship and there was no danger of any further eviction action,[12] Ruppert decided it was his time to build a triple-decked mega-structure to house not only the Bambino, but also the new legion of fans who followed Ruth and the suddenly competitive Yankees. The long-standing view of the Giants evicting the Yankees because of Babe Ruth's popularity, while perhaps plausible, was not the main reason for Ruppert's decision to leave the Polo Grounds and build his own ballpark. It was primarily a shrewd business move on the part of Ruppert, one of many successful decisions he made during his ownership. He had a hot product, and he sought to capitalize on it.

Ruppert's choice of land was that Astor property originally mentioned by Johnson as his fallback position in case the Hilltop Park deal fell through in 1903 – 161st Street and Jerome Avenue in the Bronx on the east bank of the Harlem River, directly opposite the Polo Grounds. The Bronx beckoning came full circle. What Ruppert built was an edifice described by writer F.C. Lane in the April 29, 1923, issue of *Baseball Magazine the following way: "From the plain of the Harlem River it looms up like the great pyramid of Cheops from the sands of Egypt."*[13] Or, less dramatically but far more popular, it was "The House That Ruth Built," the original version of which endured for the next 50 years. Yankee Stadium was not referred to in that way until Opening Day, April 18, 1923, when *New York Evening Telegram writer Fred Lieb surveyed the scene after the Babe*'s dramatic home run into the right-field stands. Lieb considered both the Ruth-friendly dimensions in right field, as well as the Babe's already proven ability to put people into the seats, and christened the ballpark as "The House That Ruth Built" in his game column.[14] Yet, according to Ruth, it was that Opening Day home run that gave Lieb's phrase its staying power.[15] Claire Ruth, Babe's wife, was quoted as saying, "I think that was the proudest moment of his life, and I think he believed that it would never have been 'The House That Ruth Built' if he hadn't hit that home run that day."[16]

After the City of New York renovated the original Yankee Stadium in 1974-75, many continued to refer to the new building as "The House That Ruth Built." Though it wasn't the same exact stadium, it was on the same footprint in the Bronx, the land that had beckoned since 1903. New challenges to the Bronx would emerge in the late 1980s when George Steinbrenner had serious discussions with the New Jersey Sports and Exposition Authority about moving the Yankees to the Meadowlands Sports Complex, adjacent to Giants Stadium.[17] The Bronx eventually won this challenge, too, and the new Yankee Stadium, which opened in 2009, sits directly across East 161st Street from the original site. The Yankees are synonymous with the Bronx, and will remain so for the distant future.

NOTES

1   Ray Robinson and Christopher Jennison, *Yankee Stadium: 75 Years of Drama, Glamor, and Glory (New York: Penguin Group, 1998)*, 2.

2   "Baseball Grounds Fixed," *New York Times, March 13, 1903.*

3   "American League Here," *New York Times, September 7, 1902.*

4   "Farrell's New Ball Park," *New York Times,* November 12, 1911.

5   Jacob Ruppert, "The Ten-Million-Dollar Toy," *Saturday Evening Post, March 28, 1931.*

6   "Yankees in the Bronx," *New York Times, May 13, 1915.*

7   "Yanks New Home Will Be in Queens," *New York Times, October 3, 1915.*

8   "Yankees Seek Lease," *New York Times, December 14, 1915.*

9   Ruppert, "The Ten-Million Dollar Toy."

10 "Yanks Lose Home at Polo Grounds," *New York Times, May 15, 1920.*

11 Steve Treder, *Forty Years a Giant: The Life of Horace Stoneham (Lincoln: University of Nebraska Press, 2021)*, 28-29.

12 Ruppert, "The Ten-Million-Dollar Toy."

13 Robinson and Jennison, *Yankee Stadium: 75 Years of Drama, Glamor, and Glory*, 2.

14 Robert Weintraub, *The House That Ruth Built: A New Stadium, the First Yankees Championship, and the Redemption of 1923 (New York: Little, Brown and Company, 2011)*, 22.

15 "The House That Ruth Built," www.baberuthcentral.com/babesimpact/babe-ruths-legacy/the-house-that-ruth-built/, accessed August 22, 2022.

16 "The House That Ruth Built."

17 Bob Golon, *No Minor Accomplishment: The Revival of New Jersey Professional Baseball* (New Brunswick, New Jersey: Rutgers University Press/Rivergate Books, 2008), 41.

YANKEE STADIUM:
THE GIANTS' GREATEST MISTAKE

By John Bauer

Wednesday, April 18, 1923, represents an important milestone in the history of the New York Yankees. When the Yankees opened the doors to their eponymous colosseum in the Bronx, the club achieved a level of permanence and stability previously lacking. From this ground of their own, the Yankees embarked on an unrivaled half-century of dominance over the American League and excellence in the World Series.

Original co-owners Frank J. Farrell and William S. Devery – a gambler/pool-hall owner and a former police superintendent – lacked the resources to equip the then-Highlanders for a sustainable pennant challenge. They managed to parlay political connections to secure a property lease in Upper Manhattan from the Institute for the Blind on Broadway between 165th

and 168th Streets, but could do no better than build a no-frills wooden facility known as Hilltop Park for the team's arrival in 1903. The club was left homeless when its lease expired at the end of the 1912 season, and the newly christened Yankees became tenants of the National League's New York Giants at the Polo Grounds starting in 1913.

Farrell and Devery lacked the finances to convert the Yankees into challengers to the Giants for the affections of fans in Manhattan. Farrell examined potential sites in the Bronx before and after accepting tenancy with the Giants, but never consummated a deal. The deeper-pocketed partnership of Jacob Ruppert and Tillinghast L'Hommedieu Huston acquired the Yankees in 1915. Ruppert had taken over the family

White Construction Company signed on as general contractor on April 18, 1922, a year to the day before the Stadium would open.

business from his father, and Jacob Ruppert Brewery was one of the most successful beer makers in the pre-Prohibition era. Huston was an engineer by training and a successful businessman.

A ballpark of the Yankees' own was intrinsic to turning around their fortunes. With his background, Huston took a particular interest in the ballpark project and even visited several potential sites before he and his partner assumed formal control.[1] They inspected several more sites in Manhattan, Queens, and the Bronx in the coming years. One site under consideration was near 42nd Street in Midtown Manhattan, and another was located at 145th Street and Lenox Avenue in Upper Manhattan. Next, Huston scouted a site in Queens easily accessible by railway, but Ruppert nixed the idea in favor of remaining in Manhattan.[2] Ruppert's brewery was located on the Upper East Side, and there was some thought to acquiring nearby land.

World War I paused efforts to build a new ballpark. In the meantime, Ruppert and Huston initiated building a team capable of challenging for the club's first pennant. With AL President Ban Johnson's support, Miller Huggins was hired from the St. Louis Cardinals as manager for the 1918 season. The acquisition of Babe Ruth before the 1920 season proved to be just one in a series of transactions with the Red Sox that provided the foundation for eventual pennant and World Series winners. The improvement of the Yankees began to grate on the Giants, in particular their pugnacious manager, John McGraw. During the 1920 season, the Giants served notice that the Yankees would be evicted after the campaign. Eventually, the Giants and Yankees agreed on a lease for the 1921 season, with an option for 1922. The Giants hiked the rent from $65,000 to $100,000, adding to the urgency to find a new home.

Ruppert and Huston, sometimes known collectively as "the Colonels" given their prior military experience, focused on a 10-acre plot of land just a short walk from the Polo Grounds across the Macombs Dam Bridge that linked Manhattan and the Bronx across the Harlem River near the Polo Grounds. Bounded by 157th and 161st Streets north to south, and Doughty Street and River Avenue west to east, the former lumberyard site was owned by the estate of William Waldorf Astor, who died in 1919.

Ruppert and Huston confirmed on February 5, 1921, that they planned to build their new arena at the Bronx location. They Colonels retained Osborn Engineering Company to design their stadium for a fee of $223,000.[3] The Cleveland-based firm had experience in stadium design as major-league clubs transitioned to steel and concrete structures with Navin Field and the Polo Grounds among their handiwork. Braves Field, which opened in 1916 and remained the most recent ballpark, was also an Osborn product. Artists' renderings depicted a fully enclosed stadium that included three levels with a middle mezzanine.[4] The mezzanine became a feature when the city's refusal to sanction a stadium taller than 108 feet required a more modest middle tier.[5] Another striking feature was the arched frieze that extended downward approximately 16 feet across the top of the grandstand. Originally planned to be made of a copper-iron alloy, the actual frieze was pure copper supplied by the U.T. Hungerford Brass and Copper Company.[6] The stadium was intended to seat 75,000, which would make it the largest ballpark in the country by tens of thousands.

Preparatory work hastened after the February announcement, although it took several months to close the real estate deal. Engineers arrived to begin filling and grading the land, and also studying drainage, the latter an important feature given the site's proximity to the Harlem River. Osborn engineers were "sinking test pits" in order to determine the type of foundation that could be supported by the soil.[7] Workers also cleared the land of boulders and the remnants of Astor's lumberyard. The Colonels handed over an initial deposit of $100,000 in March while attorneys conducted research to ensure a free and clear title. On May 16 Ruppert and Huston took formal possession when they paid an additional $500,000 in Liberty Bonds to Farmers' Loan and Trust Company, the Astor estate trustee.[8]

Some issues had to be resolved before actual construction could begin. First, clearing and preparation of the site needed to be completed. The process involved excavating 25,000 cubic yards of soil for the foundation and using 45,000 cubic yards of soil to fill and level the site.[9] Second, postwar supply shortages had created price inflation, and the Yankees opted to wait for costs to decline before awarding contracts for structural steel, concrete, and lumber. Finally, city authorities had to approve the closing of 158th Street and Cromwell Avenue, both of which ran through the proposed stadium footprint. The process had been expected to be a formality given Ruppert's connections with Tammany Hall. The powerful Board of Estimate took an initial favorable view of the proposal at a December public hearing. Osborn submitted plans to the Bronx Bureau of Buildings on January 15, 1922, and Huston was optimistic about breaking ground by

YANKEE STADIUM 1923-2008

March 1.[10] That date slipped, and the Board of Estimate deferred final approval of the application when Mayor John Francis Hylan unexpectedly requested additional information to ensure compliance with the terms of the street closure agreement. On March 31 Hylan provided his assent and the Board of Estimate's Sinking Fund Committee issued its formal approval.

While waiting for official word of the street closings, the Yankees began actively soliciting construction bids. Bids for steelwork were received in December 1921; reflecting inflated costs, they were higher than hoped.[11] On January 3, 1922, the Yankees issued a broader call for bids on all or part of the construction. The club's press statement read, "Tenders will be received on the following subdivision of work, but any one can bid on the work as a whole."[12] Through advertising in New York area newspapers and engineering publications, firms were invited to bid on a range of projects, including excavation, grading, reinforced concrete, tile work, painting, wooden bleachers, and toilets. The Yankees placed a priority on fan comfort, especially for female patrons. Designed with "potty parity" in mind years before sports venues considered such things in earnest, plans called for 16 "toilet rooms" with eight each for men and women.[13]

White Construction Company was selected on April 18, 1922, as the general contractor under Osborn's oversight. The parties executed the contracts on May 5 with an initial cost of $1.25 million, although the total price tag seemed likely to approach $3 million when the land, legal fees, and other work were factored in. White employed dozens of subcontractors, and its president, Charles Escher, committed to completing the job by November.[14] It was initially anticipated that enough construction could be complete to allow the Yankees to host the World Series at the new ballpark if they won the AL pennant. Lead engineer Bernard Green stated that "[T]he contractors will do their best to see that the park is ready for the big series. That's a fair enough proposition."[15] Such plans seem particularly aggressive given that twenty-first-century stadium construction often takes years rather than months, but White planned to utilize double shifts and as many as 500 workers on a daily basis to meet the deadline. Huston maintained a regular presence at the building site and also deputized his friend, Col. Thomas H. Birmingham, to work with Green in overseeing the construction. Huston and Birmingham's close involvement even extended to the selection of chairs to be used in the grandstand, a process that took two weeks before Huston found a seat to his satisfaction.[16]

From the outset, Ruppert insisted that the stadium would be named after the team rather than bear his moniker. "Yankee Field" had been one suggestion, but the grandness of the structure led the club to gravitate toward "stadium" in the name. For years, "the Yankee Stadium" (or even "the Yankees' stadium") was the convention before the article was later dropped in favor of simply "Yankee Stadium." Further, Ruppert and Huston had no intention of using the Stadium strictly for baseball. A colosseum so grandiose as to be named a "stadium" would be a playground for sports like boxing, football, track and field, and ice skating. For boxing, the ring would be placed over second base, under which a vault was constructed to store electronic communications equipment. Boxing promoter Tex Rickard, who later built the third Madison Square Garden and founded the New York Rangers, sought control of the venue's nonbaseball events.[17] For athletics, a running track was installed that ran through center and right fields approximately 30 feet from the bleachers and curved in such a way as to become an antecedent warning track in left field. The track included a feature by which it could be raised to add a curb for running and cycling events and then lowered to field level during ballgames. The track was the standard 400 yards in circumference and 24 feet in width, but the layout of the field led to an oblong shape with a 120-yard straightaway down the left-field foul line.

The ambition of the plans to have a functioning venue by fall 1922 came up against certain realities. Work commenced within weeks of contracts being signed, but strikes and supply shortages led to delays in the shipment and delivery of materials. White hired the American Bridge Company and Taylor-Fischer Steel Construction to erect the steel skeleton, and Edison Portland Cement Company (owned by Thomas Edison) to handle the concrete work. However, a railroad strike delayed arrival of the steel until July. In total, 2,500 tons of structural steel and 1,000 tons of reinforced steel created the skeleton with 30,000 cubic yards (or 140,000 bags) of concrete[18] forming the body.

The bleachers were the first part of the Stadium to be built, and were also the subject of one of the major changes to the original design. Various work orders and change orders contributed to increased costs and scheduling delays, and the bleachers were a significant contributor to that. Out of concern that the planned movable wooden bleachers would contrast negatively with the concrete grandstand, Ruppert and Huston invested another $136,000 to establish concrete footings and ensure that the exterior walls matched the rest of the stadium.[19] The left-field and right-field bleachers were built at right angles to each other, but they were positioned differently in relation to the playing field. The right-field bleachers rested at the top of an upward slope from the running track. Right-field bleacher patrons would enjoy a closer view of the field, as the left-field bleachers were about 100 feet farther from home.

By mid-September the stadium was 30 percent complete. The bleachers and concrete lower deck were in place and cranes were onsite to begin building the mezzanine and upper tier. Hosting the World Series was out of the question, and the Yankees and Giants squared off for the second straight postseason at the Polo Grounds. After the Giants took the Series in five games (with four wins and a draw), one commentator suggested that the Yankees had given the "most stupid exhibition ever furnished in a World's Series," potentially dampening fan enthusiasm.[20] "[S]ince New York will always be with a winner and never endure a loser, it seems that there will be a great many vacant seats in the new stadium next season."[21] The Colonels focused on completion in time for the 1923 season and received some help from the schedulers. With the Giants planning to expand the Polo Grounds to 55,000 seats, the AL and NL announced that the 1923 season would start one week later than would have been expected. The NL would open on Tuesday, April 17, and after some wrangling to appease Boston Red Sox owner Harry Frazee's desire to share in a weekend gate at the monstrous stadium, the AL would start on Wednesday, April 18, with Yankees-Red Sox headlining the day.

One aspect of the Stadium that was complete in 1922 was the installation of the grass field. Groundskeeper Phil Schenck, who also tended to the field at Hilltop Park, traveled through New England, New York, and Pennsylvania to find sod to his liking. He eventually settled on turf found from a Long Island location he refused to reveal, with 116,000 square feet shipped to the Bronx. Schenck's attention to detail included sifting the soil and dirt through a silk cloth to remove any rocks or pebbles.[22] On November 27, with Huston in attendance, the final piece of turf was placed into the field and snowflakes began falling within minutes. Schenck declared to Huston, "Sir, I have the honor to inform you that the playing field of this here place is absolutely finished and complete. ..."[23] Beneath the surface existed an extended network of pipes to ensure adequate drainage. A "weblike" arrangement of 16 pipes under the infield and 11 large pipes under the outfield, plus a concrete gutter in the front of the grandstand were employed to keep the field as dry as possible.[24]

In December, as Huston continued to oversee construction, he also announced his intention to sell out. Huston announced, "I'm old and tired. The Yankees are a good team and the stadium is nearly finished. It looks as if my work is about done."[25] The expectation was that Ruppert would buy out his partner's interest, but Huston made clear that other offers had been tabled. The new stadium factored into negotiations, both by enhancing the value of the franchise and by incurring debt and other liabilities associated with construction. When a stalemate was reached over such liabilities, and Huston balked at Ruppert's insistence on a condition that his partner not buy another team, the deal fell through in early January. The two put on brave faces with Huston declaring his plan to remain co-owner "for several years to come," and Ruppert offering that the two were "just as good friends as ever."[26] The matter was revisited within months.

Progress continued through a cold and snowy winter. On February 14 Ruth visited the stadium that Fred Lieb would credit him with "building." Wearing a tailored suit with a brisk wind around him, Ruth took some practice swings over a slush-covered home plate. Although the foul lines at Yankee Stadium were roughly the same distance as the Polo Grounds, the right-field bleachers were a more inviting target. The configuration of the bleachers was such that they were 20 feet closer to home plate (about 300 feet at right-center) than the concrete wall that formed the inside of the Polo Grounds horseshoe; fortunately, Ruth was not right-handed, as the distance to left-center was much farther at the new stadium.[27]

In fact, the playing field was intimate in some ways but expansive in others. Initially, first base and third base were only 36 feet from the lower grandstand box seats, 10 feet closer than the Polo Grounds.[28] Home plate was only 60 feet in front of the backstop, a distance considered too close by sportswriter Joe Vila.[29] While they would be adjusted after the inaugural season, the foul lines were 257 feet to left and 258 to right. Unlike right field, the left-field grandstand continued into left field with a sweeping curve that made for an expansive outfield in left and center. Dead center field was approximately 500 feet from home plate with a flagpole inside the bleachers that was considered in play. Also, the configuration of the left-field bleachers was such that there was an alley or gap, also considered in play, between the bleachers and grandstand.

YANKEE STADIUM 1923-2008

The scoreboard erected on top of the right-field bleachers provided fans with more information than they received at most major-league ballparks. Thirty feet high, 66 feet wide, and topped by a large clock, the scoreboard displayed the batting order of the Yankees and their opponents horizontally across the top. Across the bottom, the number of the batter as well as the numbers of balls, strikes, outs, and even the umpires were present. The bulk of the scoreboard was devoted to line scores for all major-league games, with AL games on the left and the NL on the right. The amount of information the Yankees sought to convey required three operators on days with a full slate of big-league games.

For fans attending games, Yankee Stadium could accommodate most preferred modes of transportation. The Yankees promoted the various subway lines from Manhattan to the ground, and the station at 161st Street and River Avenue was enlarged to handle expected large game-day crowds. For those choosing to travel by car, several thousand parking spaces were made out of the remainder of the land around the Stadium. Once fans arrived, there were several access points around the exterior, which was almost a half-mile in circumference. The main entrance was located at the southwest corner of the Stadium, at 157th and Doughty Street, with another major access point at the southeast corner near 157th and River Avenue. Other grandstand entrances dotted 161st Street. Ticket booths, 36 in all, featured at each entrance. To manage crowd flow, the Stadium had a system of scissor ramps behind the center and at the right end of the grandstand. Bleachers could be reached via entrances and exits along River Avenue, at 157th and 161st Streets.

In the final weeks before Opening Day, the finishing touches were applied. The final grandstand and bleacher seats were installed and painted green, and the sections and seats were assigned numbers. The club intended to move its offices from Midtown to the Stadium, but that was one part of the project that was not ready for the start of the season. Underneath the grandstand were the clubhouses and various storage rooms. The Yankees occupied the dugout on the third-base side, a difference from the Polo Grounds. Their clubhouse was located under the grandstand at street level, accessible from the dugout by a passageway and flight of stairs. The visitors clubhouse was also on the third-base side, which required opponents to walk across the field and through the Yankees dugout in order to reach it. Ruth opined that the arrangement might lead to tussles between opposing players.[30]

The Yankees received applications for Opening Day tickets throughout the winter, but tickets were not made available for public purchase until April 11. Even then, fans could buy tickets only at one of three Manhattan locations: the Yankees offices and the Winchester store, both in Midtown, and Spalding's sporting goods store on Nassau Street downtown. Most of the tickets, however, were held over for sale on game day. That is, approximately 50,000 tickets (30,000 in the grandstand and 20,000 in the bleachers) were held back until noon on April 18, just 3½ hours prior to first pitch.

On Opening Day, fans swarmed the area surrounding Yankee Stadium. Demand for tickets proved so great that an estimated 25,000 were turned away. Before the game, the Yankees and Red Sox players paraded to the center-field flagpole, where the American flag and AL pennant were raised. Governor Al Smith received the honor of throwing the first pitch, which he delivered cleanly into catcher Wally Schang's glove. The pitching matchup featured New York's Bob Shawkey against Boston's Howard Ehmke. Shawkey delivered the first official pitch to Chick Fewster at 3:31 P.M., one minute later than scheduled. The highlight of the game was provided by The Babe himself. In the third inning, Ruth delivered the moment the occasion required with a line-drive shot into the right-field bleachers, a three-run homer that provided the winning margin in the Yankees' 4-1 victory. The time of game was two hours and five minutes, and the attendance was officially stated as 74,200, a mark that bested by a considerable margin the former record of 42,620 who attended Game Five of the 1916 World Series between the Red Sox and Brooklyn Dodgers at Braves Field.

Other milestones occurred at Yankee Stadium in 1923. The Yankees hosted their first Sunday game on April 22 against Washington. With the legalization of Sunday baseball in New York in 1919, the Giants and Yankees recognized the potential for large gates, and jostling for Sabbath dates contributed to the conflict between the clubs. The Yankees could grab more of this market now, and the crowd of 65,000 against the Senators proved the concept. Days later, President Warren G. Harding became the first chief executive to grace the Stadium. An avid baseball fan, Harding chatted up Ruth before the game and kept score of the Yankees' first shutout in their new home. Tex Rickard indeed promoted the first boxing event at the Stadium on May 12 for the Milk Fund charity. The gates opened five hours before the opening bout of this boxing festival with the feature fight involving Jack McAuliffe against Luis Angel Firpo.[31] When the Milk Fund attendance was announced as 62,000, Yankees business manager Ed Barrow was forced to admit that the Stadium's capacity was not as large as advertised on Opening Day. College football debuted with a contest between Syracuse and Pittsburgh on October 20 with more games scheduled for that fall.

In February 1924 the Yankees announced several changes to the Stadium for the coming season. The most significant concerned the playing field and its effect on foul-line distances. The infield diamond was pushed out by 10 feet and tilted slightly to the right. In doing so, this move added foul territory but also extended the foul lines. Right fielders would have been pleased by the elimination of the so-called "bloody angle." In the 1923 season, the foul line met the right-field grandstand almost at its terminus. This feature created a pocket between the end of the grandstand and the start of the bleachers where balls took strange and challenging caroms and bounces. With the change, the right-field foul line connected with the bleacher wall, extending the length from 258 feet to 295 feet. In left field, the sweep of the grandstand with the reconfigured infield created an additional 24 feet of distance, from 257 feet to 281 feet.

The Stadium never became the fully-enclosed three-tier colosseum of its original designs, but later projects expanded the upper decks beyond the foul poles and into the outfield. In 1928, Ruppert hired L.M. Neckermann to add seven sections to the mezzanine and upper deck on the left-field side at a cost of $400,000. The same firm was retained to do similar work on the right-field side during the 1936-1937 offseason at a cost of $850,000.[32] This latest project also included the replacement of wooden areas in the Stadium – with particular attention to the bleachers – with concrete and steel, addition of curves to the fences to eliminate some of the sharper angles, and reconfiguration of the right-center-field bleachers to bring them almost 30 feet closer to the center-field flagpole.[33] With that project complete, Yankee Stadium achieved its familiar structural shape and reached a capacity of 72,000.

In addition to the milestones noted above, two additional events set the Yankees on the road to becoming the most successful franchise in major-league history. In May 1923 Ruppert bought out his partner for approximately $1.5 million. The deal was complete with Huston being relieved of any debt or other liabilities on the Stadium and Ruppert dropping his demand

that Huston stay out of baseball; however, Huston never re-entered the game in any significant capacity. In October the Yankees finally hosted a World Series in a ground of their own; Game One went against them when future Yankee manager Casey Stengel's ninth-inning inside-the-park home run decided the game in favor of the Giants. The Yankees recovered to win the first of 20 World Series at pre-renovation (1923-1973) Yankee Stadium. Their tenure at the original Stadium included the eventual departure from New York of the Giants, whom the Yankees more than eclipsed in a reversal of fortunes. Ruppert may not have foreseen California baseball at the time, but his words proved prescient in many ways: "Yankee Stadium was a mistake – not mine, but the Giants'."[34]

SOURCES

In addition to the sources cited in the Notes, the author reviewed baseball-reference.com, retrosheet.org, and several New York-area newspapers accessible through newspapers.com.

NOTES

1   Ron Amore, *A Franchise on the Rise: The First Twenty Years of The New York Yankees* (New York: Sports Publishing, 2018), 269.

2   Amore, 271.

3   Amore, 272.

4   "Yankees to Build Stadium in Bronx," *New York Times*, February 6, 1921: 20.

5   Amore, 273.

6   Amore, 274; Robert Weintraub, *The House That Ruth Built* (New York: Little Brown and Company, 2011), 46.

7   "Yanks Make First Payment for Land," *New York Times*, March 19, 1921: 16.

8   "Deal for Yankees' Home Completed," *New York Times*, May 17, 1921: 14.

9   "Size of Stadium Impresses Crowd," *New York Times*, April 19, 1921: 15.

10   James Crusinberry, "Yankee Owners Devoting Attention to New Stadium," *New York Daily News*, January 4, 1922: 20.

11   "Yankees Call For Bid On Stadium," *New York Times*, January 4, 1922: 15.

12   "Construction of New Yankee Stadium May Start Soon," *New York Evening World*, January 4, 1922: 23.

13   "Sizable Job, Making Last Word in Modern Ball Parks," *New York Daily News*, April 1, 1923: 51.

14   Amore, 276.

15   "Work Begins Today on Yankee Stadium," *New York Times*, May 6, 1922: Sports 8.

16   W.O. McGeehan, "Yankees Start to Build Big Park," *New York Herald*, April 1, 1922: 10.

17   "Yankee Ball Park Big Sports Arena," *New York Times*, August 30, 1922: Sports 11.

18   Weintraub, 54.

19   Weintraub, 55.

20   "Where the Real Blow Comes," *The Sporting News*, October 19, 1922: 2.

21   "Where the Real Blow Comes."

22   John Kieran, "Infield at Yankee Stadium Completed as Per Schedule," *New York Tribune*, November 28, 1922: 14.

23   Kieran.

24   "Sizable Job, Making Last Word in Modern Ball Parks."

25   "Huston to Sell Out His Yankee Interest," *New York Times*, December 12, 1922: 1.

26   "Ruppert Declares Huston Will Stay," *New York Times*, January 6, 1923: Sports 10.

27   "Yankees Announce Changes at Stadium," *New York Times*, February 3, 1924: Sec. 1, Part 2: 1.

28   "Yankees' New Park Almost Completed," *New York Times*, March 11, 1923: 1.

29   Joe Vila, "Faults Are Found With New Ball Park of the Yankees," *The Sporting News*, March 15, 1923: 1.

30   Marshall Hunt, "No Homers, Despite Low Grade Hurling," *New York Daily News*, February 15, 1923: 24.

31   "Rickard Inspects Yankee Stadium," *New York Times*, May 8, 1923: 13.

32   Weintraub, 368.

33   Marty Appel, *Pinstripe Empire: The New York Yankees From Before The Babe to After The Boss* (New York: Bloomsbury, 2012), 54.

34   Amore, 282.

PHIL SCHENCK: YANKEE STADIUM'S FIRST GROUNDSKEEPER

By Doug Vogel

November 27, 1922, was an overcast and chilly day, but the grounds crew finished laying the last pieces of outfield sod, pleasing the head groundskeeper. Phil Schenck stood with New York Yankees co-owner Colonel Tillinghast L'Hommedieu Huston admiring the view. Five months earlier, the jovial groundskeeper had promised to have the playing field finished before the first snow fell:

"Sir, I have the honor to inform you that the playing field of this here place is absolutely finished and complete. I herewith hand you the keys to the diamond."[1]

Schenck's handiwork stood out among the remaining unfinished construction at the new Yankee Stadium that was emerging on the banks of the Harlem River. Ten minutes later, it started to snow. By the time Huston and Schenck left the stadium, the turf was covered in a blanket of white powder.[2]

Phil Schenck had been employed by the franchise dating back to 1903, when they were known as the New York Highlanders. Schenck was hired to build and maintain the new playing field at Hilltop Park in the Washington Heights neighborhood of New York City. He worked tirelessly, maintaining and improving the ballfield for the next nine years, earning him the nickname of the Demon Groundskeeper.[3] The local baseball writers featured stories about his magical maintenance methods just as often as they wrote about Highlanders stars Wee Willie Keeler and Jack Chesbro. Schenck's outgoing personality and portly stature made good copy.

The team outgrew Hilltop Park and signed a 10-year lease to play at the Polo Grounds starting in 1913. On October 5, 1912, the Highlanders played their last game on a Phil Schenck-prepared field, outscoring the Washington Senators, 8-6.[4] The ballpark was demolished the following spring. Phil Schenck no longer had a field to maintain.

The New York baseball beat writers now jokingly referred to Schenck as the Groundless Groundskeeper and wrote that he was "the only major league groundskeeper without a ground to keep."[5] He went to work for Henry Fabian, who maintained the Polo Grounds. Schenck was very familiar with the ballpark, having worked there as a kid helping Old Johnny Murphy, Fabian's predecessor, maintain the place.[6] Schenck was now relegated to being a common crew member, but his good nature and strong work ethic were much appreciated.

Schenck was too valuable and too well-liked to be let go outright by the team now known as the Yankees. He remained with the organization and was kept busy as an equipment manager, handyman, and office gofer. When winter came around, Schenck was sent south to prepare the Yankees' spring-training sites every

Babe Ruth pitches in to help the grounds crew in The House That Ruth Built.

29

year, including fields in New Orleans, Shreveport, Brunswick (Georgia), and Jacksonville.[7] He faithfully served the team for the 10 years, and welcomed any work the Yankees gave him.[8]

Schenck's loyalty paid off in 1922, when he signed a contract to oversee the construction of the playing field for the new Yankee Stadium.[9] The groundless groundskeeper would soon have a brand-new baseball field to maintain that he could call his own. "I used to play around this very place when I was a kid," Schenck reminisced. "I used to swim right where the diamond is now. I was born in the Bronx, only six blocks from here."[10]

The construction of the new Yankee Stadium commenced on May 5, 1922,[11] and Schenck's first job was to assist the White Construction Company with installing the internal drainage of the playing field. Properly installed drainage would make the future playing field much easier for Schenck to maintain.[12] Some 2,200 lineal feet of four-inch terra cotta tiles radiated in 24 lines from the pitcher's mound. The tiles connected to the main drain lines leaving the stadium, ensuring a dry playing surface after a hard rain.[13] After completing the state-of-the-art drainage, it was Schenck's turn to fashion the remaining pile of rubble into a verdant, emerald green ballfield like the one his past reputation was built on.

Every detail that would ensure that the playing surface of the new Yankee Stadium was the best in the major leagues was overseen by Schenck. A dedicated staff of laborers whom Schenck would train to become his grounds crew was assembled. Their first task was to install the subsoil to cover the drainage system and create the base for the playing field. The quality of the soil on hand was not up to Schenck's standards. The crew labored for weeks to sift the piles to remove the large rocks, tree roots, and grass clumps before spreading it evenly across the future stadium floor. A two-ton roller firmed the hand-graded soil before a nine-inch layer of topsoil was spread on top of the base. Horse manure and limestone were tilled into the topsoil to enrich the growing medium. Fertilizer was carefully applied after hand grading and rolling was completed.[14] The field was now ready to transition from a flat, dirt construction site to a glorious baseball diamond.

The infield was built on Schenck's perfectly graded field. It was designed by the engineers of the Osborn Engineering Company.[15] Schenck called it the "turtle-back mound" because it looked like a shell of a large tortoise. He didn't like the height of the mound, and

he didn't like the turf beyond the track that ramped up to the outfield fence, either. He vowed to replace them both, but the big pimple would remain for now.[16]

Schenck visited five neighboring states searching for the perfect turf to cover his diamond. He chose the 160,000 square feet of sod for the infield and outfield from a secret source on Long Island.[17] The green squares were laid out, rolled for smoothness, and carefully watered daily to prevent desiccation until all the truckloads were unloaded and laid. Fresh grass seed was spread over the sod, raked in, and rolled again to ensure a thick, healthy playing surface.[18]

The final details were checked off the punch list one at a time. The infield skin was raked repeatedly until no stone bigger than a "mosquito's eye" remained.[19] The pitcher's rubber and home plate were set in concrete. A 1,000-pound gas-powered Coldwell Model H lawn mower that both cut and rolled the grass to help maintain a firm and true playing surface was purchased.[20]

The stadium also included a 400-yard, 24-foot-wide running track with red cinders that encircled the playing field and was an added feature for Schenck's crew to maintain. Designed by Frederick W. Rubien of the Amateur Athletic Union, it was the venue for track and field meets sometimes held when the Yankees were on road trips.[21] By late fall, Schenck's installation was complete. "I've worked night and day on it. I'm glad it's over," he said. "I'm going home to bed now and leave a call for February 4."[22]

The grand opening of the stadium was set for April 18, 1923, and Phil Schenck's reputation as the top groundskeeper in the major leagues was once again on full display. The tarp that covered Schenck's masterpiece over the winter was removed to reveal an emerald green turf, just as expected. The warmth from the tarp duped the grass into an early spring green-up, one of the many tricks the Demon Groundskeeper kept up his sleeve. The Yankees and the visiting Boston Red Sox both held brief workouts on the pristine sod the day before the grand opening. "So far, no spikes have dented the new turf carefully laid by Phil Schenck last fall," wrote Fred Lieb in the *New York Evening Telegram*.[23] Schenck would soon find out he would need all the tricks he could muster and learn a few more new ones to help in the maintenance of the new ballpark.

Wear and tear were Phil Schenck's greatest adversary, and it commenced on Opening Day. Participants in pregame festivities including John Philip Sousa and the Seventh "Silk Stocking" Regiment Band, local politicians, baseball dignitaries, the Yankees and Red Sox players, cameramen, and sportswriters all herded across the manicured turf.[24] The sellout crowd of 74,200 exited across the field after the Yankees handed the Red Sox a 4-1 loss featuring a three-run Babe Ruth stadium-christening clout.[25] The extra foot traffic was a cost of doing business for the opening of the grandest stadium ever built, and it was a welcome sight to Schenck, who was more than happy to make any repairs.

Maintenance of the new stadium wasn't going to be about preparing for just baseball games. Yankee Stadium was designed as a multipurpose stadium with the ability to generate revenue when the Yankees were away and during the offseason as well.[26] This greatly added to Schenck's workload. During the 1923 season, the assault on Schenck's masterpiece included 76 regular-season Yankees home games, three World Series home games, Tex Austin's Rodeo, championship boxing matches, AAU track and field events, and college and local football games. "I figure that a million and a half people scruff across this lot every year," Schenck said.[27]

The rodeo came to town on August 15 for a 10-day engagement and proved to be a huge headache for Schenck during the stadium's maiden season. "Matting at a cost of $25,000 was laid over the infield grass at the behest of the stadium management but at the rodeo's expense. When the matting was removed at the end of the rodeo, the all-important infield grass was seen to be a dried-out yellow swatch."[28] Schenck had five days to work his magic on repairing the field. The Yankees returned to the stadium after an extended 17-day, 12-game road trip to find Schenck applying a special tobacco-based fertilizer that he sourced from Scranton, Pennsylvania.[29] The "secret blend" jump started the greening-up process of the yellow turf. The rodeo never returned to the stadium during Schenck's tenure.

The 1923 World Series between the Yankees and the New York Giants provided Schenck the opportunity to showcase his field against his cross-river rival Henry Fabian of the Polo Grounds. Schenck had Yankee Stadium in as good shape as was humanly possible for Game One after seven months of baseball games and extracurricular wear and tear. Photos of the day show a well-worn but manicured field.[30] The Yankees won the deciding Game Six at the Polo Grounds, sparing Schenck's field the abuse of a championship celebration. For all his hard work, the players

voted Phil Schenck a $750 share of the World Series winnings.[31]

Proactive maintenance was the benchmark of Schenck's program: "After every baseball game and between periods of a football game my men hunt out every new scar and sprinkle it with a mixture of seed, humus, bone meal and sheep manure."[32] By the end of the grass-growing season, the continued use of the field took its toll, regardless of how much care was given. Schenck said, "During the fall, professional football teams practice here most every day, rain or shine, and they sure tear up the turf."[33] In spite of the grounds crew's herculean efforts, by the end of every football season, the field was always in need of new sod the following spring.

The spring of 1924 found Schenck eliminating what he felt was poor design. "Phil Schenck, the rotund Stadium ground keeper, has been busy all winter working on his new field," a sportswriter commented. "The open winter has been a big help to him. The diamond has been completely remodeled and rebuilt. The new diamond will not be the turtle-back in as far as of last season."[34] Schenck flattened the infield diamond and lowered the pitcher's mound. He installed red clay around home plate to keep the players from "digging in," a practice that left holes and created constant maintenance issues. After finishing the repairs to his field, Schenck's second task was to oil up and clean the large Seth Thomas clock on the stadium scoreboard. It sat dormant all winter until Schenck climbed up the bleachers and performed the annual winding. The Yankees didn't "officially" start their season until the clock was running.[35]

Everyone had a Babe Ruth story to tell, and Schenck was no different. He had plenty of them, but the one he liked to recount was the day The Babe hit an inside-the-park home run against the Cleveland Indians in 1924. Schenck and his friend Henry Fabian watched Ruth crush a Dewey Metivier pitch a claimed 592 feet to dead center field.[36] Fabian laughed, not at the ball that came up short of the fence, but at the divot that the ball sent flying. Ruth raced around the bases for the unlikely home run. Schenck gladly repaired the divot after the game.

Football games at the stadium were played in all weather, rain or shine. The concentrated wear of football cleats tearing up dormant turf put a yearly end to anything being associated with the field looking manicured. The 1926 season opener of the New York Yankees of the old American Football League became a nightmare for Schenck. The field had received

24 hours of rain the previous day and it continued throughout most of the game. Star Red Grange and the Yankees hosted the Los Angeles Wildcats. The Galloping Ghost was hampered by the soft field, mustering only two 15-yard runs as the field was reduced to a miniature swamp. "After a few minutes of scrambling around in the muck and mire of Phil Schenck's beloved ballfield, everyone was covered in mud and you couldn't read the numbers from one another," a sportswriter reported.[37] The football Yankees won 6-0.

The Jack Dempsey-Jack Sharkey boxing match held on July 21, 1927, in midseason, would prove to be Schenck's greatest challenge to repair. The Yankees were set to return for a doubleheader with the St. Louis Browns on July 26, giving Schenck five days to work his magic. "See the square where the border is a little light colored?" Schenck mentioned to a writer after the season. "That's where the ring was for the Dempsey-Sharkey fight. The reporters and excited fans in the ringside seats scraped their feet and wore off the grass. Wherever there were seats on the ground we found bare patches the next day."[38] To the delight of Schenck, the Yankees wore out only the basepaths, scoring 27 runs in the doubleheader.[39]

Twelve days before the 1928 home opener, the beloved Phil Schenck died suddenly at home.[40] The Yankees were in a pinch but had to look no farther than across the Harlem River and hired Walter Owens, the assistant groundskeeper of the Polo Grounds.[41] Owens had trained under the watchful eye of Schenck's good friend Henry Fabian and was more than qualified to fill Schenck's big shoes. His first task was to prepare Schenck's ballfield for the home opener against the Philadelphia Athletics. His preparations for his first game as a head groundskeeper included extra pregame grooming for the ring ceremony and championship banner raising of the 1927 World Series winners.[42] Owens labored with great success as the Yankees' head groundskeeper for the next 24 years. The Demon Groundskeeper's legacy was in good hands.

AUTHOR'S NOTES

The author would like to recognize the importance of reference librarians. The staff of the Wayne Township (New Jersey) library consistently fill obscure requests, provide any and all assistance needed, and do it with a smile. Also, a big thank you to Andy Stamm, librarian at the United States Golf Association Museum. His timely correspondence answered a lot of questions.

The terms groundskeeper and groundkeeper were both used by sportswriters during this period. Dan Cunningham, the current Yankee Stadium turfgrass expert, has the title of head groundskeeper.

Golf course architect William H. Tucker's obituary noted that he "put in the turf of the original Yankee Stadium."[43] In the book *The Architects of Golf* the authors wrote, "Tucker was a nationally known turfgrass expert and had been called upon to install the original turf at such sports facilities as Yankee Stadium and the West Side Tennis Club."[44] It is well documented that Phil Schenck installed the sod at the new Yankee Stadium. Tucker's name never came up connecting him to any phase of the project in any newspaper archives searched. His involvement remains a mystery.

NOTES

1   John Kieran, "Infield at Yankee Stadium Completed as Per Schedule," *New York Tribune*, November 28, 1922: 14.

2   James Crusinberry, "Yankee Diamond Tucked in for Winter Sleep," *New York Daily News*, November 28, 1922: 28.

3   W.O. McGeehan, "Pinochle Ousts Baseball in Camp of the Yankees," *New York Tribune*, April 12, 1919: 21. "Phil Schenck, the Demon Ground Keeper, will precede the team to each burg, by twenty-four hours and iron out the different diamonds."

4   1912 New York Highlanders Statistics, Baseball-Reference.com, baseball-reference.com/team/NYY/1912.shtml, Accessed July 17, 2022.

5   "Sure Sign of Spring," *Washington Times*, February 18, 1922: 9.

6   Will Wedge, "Yankee Clock Starts Ticking," *Baltimore Sun*, March 3, 1924: 33. Johnny Murphy was the groundskeeper before Henry Fabian.

7   W.O. McGeehan, "Hannah and Schneider Join at Jacksonville," *New York Tribune*, March 25, 1919: 19. Preparing spring training fields kept Schenck busy for various reasons. The circus wintered on the Southside Ballpark field before the Yankees' arrival. "Phil Schenck is still telling of the engineering feats he accomplished in filling the elephant tracks."

8   "Allen Russell Quits Yanks," *Paterson* (New Jersey) *Evening News*, July 18, 1918: 10. Schenck worked for the Yankees in multiple capacities after losing his Hilltop Park groundskeeper position. "Miller Huggins … had left word with Phil Schenck, the clubhouse man, to pack up his belongings and send them to Baltimore where Russell lives."

9   "Phil Schenck to Make New Diamond for Yanks," *Washington Times*, August 3, 1922: 16.

10 Wedge: 33.

11 Different starting dates found include May 6, 1922. Michael P. Wagner, *Babe's Place: The lives of Yankee Stadium* (Akron:48HrBooks, 2017), 15. "Limited construction didn't actually begin until May 6."

12 Harry C. Butcher, "Good Farm Practice Has Helped the Yankees Win Their Pennants," *Fertilizer Review*, October 1927: 10-11. Schenck remarked, "Our drainage system made it possible for us to play the fourth game in the World Series with Pittsburgh."

13 "Yankee Stadium, New York," *Architecture and Building*, May 1923: 49.

14 Butcher, 11.

15 "Fabian Dean in His Line," *Auburn* (New York) *Citizen*, August 15, 1928: 5. The Osborn engineers were simply copying what was a common construction technique of the era. "Henry Fabian, dean of the groundskeepers, constructed the first turtleback baseball field in Dallas in 1889." Other ballparks that Osborn Engineering built include Boston's Fenway Park and Chicago's Comiskey Park.

16 Frederick G. Lieb, "Yankee Diamond Has Been Moved," *New York Evening Telegram*, February 3, 1924: 14. "The new diamond will not be the turtleback affair of last season."

17 Kieran, 14.

18 Butcher, 11.

19 Kieran, 14.

20 "An Effective Power Mower," *American City Magazine*, July 1925: 113.

21 Al Copland, "News Marathon Track All Set for New Record," *New York Daily News*, April 24, 1923: 23. The Daily News Marathon of May 20, 1923, was the first track event held on the new Yankee Stadium track.

22 Kieran, 14.

23 Frederick G. Lieb, "Shawkey to Pitch Opening Contest," *New York Evening Telegram*, April 17, 1923: 4.

24 "Biggest Ball Park Opens Gates Today," *New York Daily News*, April 18, 1923: 22.

25 1923 New York Yankees Statistics, Baseball-Reference.com, baseball-reference.com/boxes/NYA/NYA192304180.shtml. Accessed July 24, 2022. Baseball-Reference.com lists the Opening Day crowd as 74,200 while most newspapers used the 75,000 official seating capacity in their reporting.

26 "Yankee Stadium, New York." "The field is also suitable for other athletic events and there is a cinder running track about it."

27 Butcher, 10.

28 Tom O'Connell, "Vet Rodeo Mgr. Frank Moore Eschews Tools of the Trade," *Billboard*, October 21, 1950: 58, 63.

29 Will Wedge, "Tobacco Fertilizer," *New York Sun*, March 3, 1925: 33.

30 1923 World Series Recap, MLB.com, mlb.com/news/1923-world-series-recap. Accessed October 1, 2022. Photo of Casey Stengel sliding into home during Game One at Yankee Stadium shows extensive wear to the home plate/baseline area.

31 "26 Yankees Each Receive $6,160.46," *New York Times*, October 17, 1923: 16.

32 Butcher, 10.

33 Butcher, 10.

34 Frederick G. Lieb, "Yankee Diamond Has Been Moved," *New York Telegram and Evening Mail*, February 3, 1924: 14.

35 Wedge, 33.

36 Will Wedge, "Ruth's Cruel Homer," *New York Sun,* July 21, 1924: 20. Ruth's blast of 592 feet is either a printing error or yellow journalism. The correct 1924 measurement was 490 feet to dead center. Yankee Stadium, Clem's Baseball, andrewclem.com/Baseball/YankeeStadium.html#diag. Accessed October 25, 2022.

37 Leonard Cohen, "New York Yankees Beat Wildcats, 6-0, on Tyron's Sprint," *New York Evening Post*, October 25, 1926: 15.

38 Butcher, 10.

39 1927 New York Yankees Statistics, Baseball-Reference.com, baseball-reference.com/teams/NYY/1927-schedules-scores.shtml. Accessed July 24, 2022

40 "Yankees First Groundkeeper Dies," *Syracuse Journal*, April 10, 1928: 13. The Yankees had initiated a spring-training regimen three years earlier to help the "rotund" Schenck lose weight. Will Wedge, "Phil Schenck in Training," *New York Sun*, February 4, 1925. "Phil Schenck, the sod shampooer of the Yankees, has been dispatched to St. Petersburg to prepare for the coming season. Schenck will not only prepare the ball yard for the Ruppert Rifles but he will also prepare himself physically. Doc Woods, Yankee trainer, will supervise Schenck's course of conditioning exercises." No formal obituary of Schenck made the papers.

41 Dr. Ken Kurtz, "An Inning From Our Past," *Sports Turf Manager*, July/August 2003: 7-14.

42 Frank Wallace, "Cobb's Ghost Covers Right Field," *New York Daily News*, April 21, 1928: 29. "Each Yankee received a blue diamond in a ring as a reward for winning the world series."

43 Obituary, *New York Times,* October 8, 1954: 23.

44 Geoffrey S. Cornish and Ronald E. Whitten, *The Architects of Golf* (New York: HarperCollins Publishers, Inc. 1993), 419.

WHITEY WITT – THE FIRST YANKEES HITTER TO COME TO THE PLATE AT YANKEE STADIUM

By Mike Richard

It was long before the days when the elegant voice of Bob Sheppard introduced the starting lineup at Yankee Stadium.

However, if there was a public-address announcer at the Bronx ballpark on the day it opened on April 18, 1923, before a baseball record 74,200 fans – and there wasn't – it may have sounded something like this …[1]

"… Leading off for the New York Yankees, the center fielder, Whitey Witt."

Witt was born Ladislaw Waldemar Wittkowski on September 28, 1895, in Orange, Massachusetts, and grew up in the nearby town of Winchendon.

But old-time baseball fans will remember him as Whitey Witt. He shared the outfield with Babe Ruth

Whitey Witt batted .301 as a Yankee, from 1922-1925.

Courtesy of the National Baseball Hall of Fame.

and Long Bob Meusel, playing that opening season for manager Miller Huggins.

"I made the major leagues because I could hit, I could field and I could run," Witt recalled in a 1985 interview, three years before his death. "That was my biggest asset there." The .287 lifetime hitter had three seasons batting over .300.[2]

The pregame festivities featured Governor Alfred E. Smith throwing out the first pitch, while fans arriving early to the game were serenaded by John Philip Sousa's Seventh Regiment Band.

Starting pitchers for the Stadium's inaugural game were Bob Shawkey for the Yankees and Howard Ehmke for the Boston Red Sox.

History notes that shortstop Chick Fewster of the visiting Red Sox was actually the first batter in Yankee Stadium history. However, in the bottom of the first, Witt led off for the Yankees and grounded hard to Fewster, who threw to George Burns at first for the out.

In the second inning, Red Sox first baseman Burns would earn the first hit in the history of the ballpark. However, when he also attempted to get the first stolen base, Burns was thrown out by catcher Wally Schang.

In the third inning, second baseman Aaron Ward had the first Yankees hit at Yankee Stadium, and after the game both he and Burns each received a box of cigars for their historic hits.[3]

Ruth hit the first home run at the Stadium, a three-run shot to right field in the third inning to help defeat his former team, the Boston Red Sox, 4-1. Witt was on base, having worked a walk. In the bottom of the fifth, Witt himself had a single to right-center.

"It was an amazing day," Witt recalled in a 1984 interview with Rich Westcott. "The new ballpark, the crowd, all the excitement. It was an experience that you could never repeat in a hundred years. We were in awe when we first saw the park. It seemed so big. Huge. At the time, there was nothing like it in baseball.

Looking around, it was enough to make your eyes pop out."[4]

Witt began his career in 1916 playing five years with Connie Mack's Philadelphia Athletics.

It was while playing for Mack that his lengthy name was shortened.

"Mack didn't want to write Wittkowski on the batting card every day, so he changed my name to Witt," he told Westcott. "Then, because I had blond hair, he called me Whitey."

Witt got what he called "the biggest break of my life" when he was sold to the pennant-winning New York Yankees on April 17, 1922.[5]

After the Yankees had won their first pennant the previous year, outfielders Babe Ruth and Bob Meusel ignored Commissioner Kenesaw Mountain Landis's ban on barnstorming, which was a popular postseason sidelight in those days. Landis slapped each player with a six-week suspension, which kept them out of the Yankees lineup until May 20, 1922, and the Yankees had to find some outfielders to pick up the slack.

When the suspended duo returned, Witt found himself in center field to comprise the outfield of Ruth in left and Meusel in right. At the time, the Yankees played their home games at the Polo Grounds when the New York Giants were on the road.

"Babe and I got along great because both of us drank," Witt said with a laugh in our 1985 interview. "The rest of the players used to call me his errand boy because when we'd get on the road and he wanted a bottle of whiskey, he'd say, 'Whitey, here's $20, go down to the desk' ... 'course this was during prohibition ... 'Go down to the desk and get me a bottle of whiskey.' Then we'd go up in his room and raise hell," Witt said.[6]

During one of their drinking sprees, an undercover detective learned of their carousing and blew the whistle on the ballplayers. Since Ruth was the big name, he was fined $5,000 while Witt was hit with a $500 fine.[7]

There was also an incident five days after The Babe returned from his barnstorming suspension in late May 1922: A fan began needling Ruth from the stands, and The Babe went after him. While the fan fled, it took several police and teammates to restrain Ruth.[8]

"Shortly after the incident in which Babe tried to get into the stands, (Giants owner) Charles Stoneham informed our owners that he wanted the Yankees out of the Polo Grounds," Witt said. "They didn't know that the Yankees already owned property within sight of the Polo Grounds and even before Stoneham realized it, the Yanks were starting to build."[9]

The Yankees swept all four games during that inaugural series against the Red Sox.

"I was a punch hitter and a good bunter," Witt told a reporter from his hometown newspaper, the *Winchendon Courier*. "I used to get 40 hits a year on bunts. Nowadays it seems the art of bunting is lost. Everybody is swinging for the fences."[10]

During that 1923 season, Witt helped the Yankees defeat the St. Louis Browns for the pennant, snapping back after being beaned by a bottle thrown from the stands into center field at the beginning of a crucial series with the Browns.

According to a story by Tim Quinn in *Today's Sunbeam* in 1983, Witt was going back on a ball in deep center field at Sportsman's Park when a bottle came out of the stands, hitting him in the head and knocking him out.

American League President Ban Johnson offered a reward for the information leading to the conviction of the bottle thrower.

"A popular account of the incident said a 10-year-old boy threw the bottle. The reward however, was finally awarded to a spectator who persisted in his claim that the bottle had been on the field already and Witt kicked it up into his face while giving chase to the fly ball," Quinn wrote.[11]

Quinn wrote that information – perhaps fabricated – emerged that Witt "was not struck by a thrown bottle, but rather the bottle had been thrown onto the field earlier and Witt unknowingly stepped on it. While in pursuit of the fly ball, the bottle bounded up and struck him above the eye."[12]

Regardless, the incident provided the Yankees with more inspiration to beat the Browns in 15 of the 20 games the two teams played during New York's pennant-winning season.

Witt came back in the series with several timely hits, drove in two runs – including the pennant clincher – and chased a long fly into deep center, making a dramatic leap into the stands to record the out. The St. Louis fans, apparently contrite after what had happened to him earlier in the series, gave him a tumultuous ovation.[13]

The Yankees center fielder also enjoyed his best offensive season in Yankee Stadium's first year with a .314 batting average and career highs in home runs (6), runs batted in (55), and runs scored (113). His .979 fielding average led American League outfielders.

In the 1923 World Series, Witt went 6-for-25 with two doubles and four RBIs. A year later, he batted .297 for the second-place Yankees, but his future with the team appeared on the wane.

Hitting just .200 as a backup outfielder, Witt was released in July 1925.

After baseball, Witt and his wife, Mary (McClain) Witt, owned a farm in Alloway Township, New Jersey. He also operated a tavern called Whitey's Irish Bar in nearby Salem, New Jersey, for some 17 years.

Witt was invited back to Yankee Stadium 14 times for annual OldTimers games, introduced as the first Yankee to come to bat at the Stadium.[14] Witt attended the 25th and 50th anniversaries of Yankee Stadium, and in 1973 he cut a cake at home plate with Ruth's widow to commemorate the golden anniversary of the ballpark.[15]

In his old age, despite his longtime absence from the game, Witt said he still received four or five fan letters per week, as well as baseball cards to autograph for young fans.[16] That lasted until his death at the age of 92 on July 14, 1988.

SOURCES

In addition to the sources shown in the notes, the author used baseball-reference.com, SABR.org, Newspapers.com, and www.retrosheet.org. for background information, and the following:

Schott, Arthur O. "The First Game at Yankee Stadium," SABR Research Journal Archive, http://research.sabr.org/journals/first-game-at-yankee-stadium.

Webb, Melville E., Jr. "Ruth's Homer Beats Sox Before 74,200," *Boston Globe*, April 19, 1923: 1.

NOTES

1   According to Frederick C. Bush's article "Babe Ruth Homers in Yankee Stadium's Grand Opening, Hinting at Franchise's Dynastic Future" for SABR's Games Project (https://sabr.org/gamesproj/game/april-18-1923-yankee-stadium-grand-opening-hints-at-franchises-dynastic-future/), the attendance for the day was exaggerated. Bush cited Robert Weintraub's comment that Yankees business manager Ed Barrow admitted he had added standing-room fans to his original estimate and amended his Opening Day figure to 62,200. Weintraub wrote that even this figure is "probably still exaggerated, but [it was] nevertheless by far the largest crowd in the sport's history." Robert Weintraub, *The House That Ruth Built: A New Stadium, the First Yankees Championship, and the Redemption of 1923* (New York: Little, Brown and Company, 2011), 17-18.

2   Author interview with Witt, July 1985. Hereafter cited as Witt interview.

3   Ed Cunningham, "Echoes from That Babe Ruth Swat," *Boston Herald*, April 19, 1923: 14.

4   Rich Westcott, "Whitey Witt," SABR BioProject. https://sabr.org/bioproj/person/whitey-witt/.

5   Witt interview.

6   Witt interview.

7   Jim Ogle, "The First Yankee to Bat at Yankee Stadium Returns," *Yankees Magazine*, August 1983: 15.

8   Ogle.

9   Tom Quinn, "Salem County's Major Leaguer: In Baseball's Golden Age, Whitey Witt Played Alongside the Greatest," *Today's Sunbeam* (Salem, New Jersey), 1983 (exact date unknown). While Witt said this incident happened in May of 1922, his dates were probably off since Yankee Stadium was likely already under construction by that time.

10 "Whitey Pays Visit to His Family Here," *Winchendon* (Massachusetts) *Courier*. December 30, 1970.

11 Quinn.

12 Quinn.

13 Quinn.

14 Quinn.

15 Quinn.

16 Witt interview.

WHEN HARRY MET THE BRONX BOMBERS: THE HISTORY OF YANKEE STADIUM CONCESSIONS

By Don Jensen

The 12-page official program of the new "Greater New York Base Ball Club of the American League" at its home opener on April 30, 1903, was published by Harry M. Stevens, who had built a concessions empire since the 1880s that extended from the Midwest to New England. Stevens had made a fortune in New York City the previous decade managing the concessions at the Polo Grounds, home of the National League Giants, the new club's now immediate rival; Madison Square Garden; and the upstate Saratoga Racecourse. The association of Stevens' firm with the new American League franchise (at first called the Highlanders) would enable Harry to become a key force in the emergence of the franchise as a dynasty in major-league baseball.[1]

The advertisements scattered throughout the inaugural program and scorecard, priced at 5 cents, reflected the goal of concessionaires everywhere: to enhance and profit from the fan experience at the ballpark. In addition to player rosters and space to keep score, the card included advertisements for Philip Morris cigarettes, Dewar's scotch, Coca-Cola, Horton's ice cream cones, Atlas motor oil and grease, Pommery champagne, and Henry Rahe's Café across the street. At Rahe's, fans could order Jac. Ruppert's Extra Pale, Knickerbocker, and Ruppiner beers. One ad tried another way to pique fan interest: "Any baseball player who will hit the 'Bull Durham' cut-out sign on the field with a fairly batted ball during a regularly scheduled league game will receive $50.00 in cash [almost $1,700 in 2022]."[2]

THE BUSINESS OF CONCESSIONS

But profits for the new franchise from selling scorecards and advertisements alone would be small. By contrast, catering to the fans' desire for refreshments during the game would provide the Highlanders' owners, gambler Frank Farrell and former New York

City Police Chief Bill Devery, with a vital source of revenue to supplement income from ticket sales. In selling concession rights to an experienced and shrewd entrepreneur like Stevens, the club could avoid the burden of procuring food and beverages, hiring cooks, vendors, and other salespeople, setting prices, and meeting fans' expectations for superior quality. (Some clubs at the time, such as the Chicago Cubs, sold concessions themselves.)

When the Highlanders opened for business at American League Park – soon after called the Hilltop due to its location on a ridge in northern Manhattan – the question of what food and drink to sell at ballparks already had a long and controversial history. Initially, baseball owners were slow to provide concessions

Courtesy of the National Baseball Hall of Fame.

Harry M. Stevens, shown at left with Yankees owner Jacob Ruppert, was the Yankees' official concessionaire through the 1963 season.

and other entertainment to fans. However, unauthorized bars, liquor booths, rum shops, and "restaurants" – saloons – often popped up near ballparks and siphoned off potential revenue from the teams. Gradually, clubs came to offer items such as cherry pie, cheese, chewing tobacco, tripe, chocolate, and onions, like food sold at fairs, racetracks, circuses, railway stops, and other outdoor venues. In the 1880s, Chris Von der Ahe, a German immigrant and later Stevens' mentor, bought a team, the St. Louis Browns of the American Association, to increase profits at his bar near Sportsman's Park, the Browns' home. He later added an amusement park with a Bavarian-style beer garden, a water flume ride, an artificial lake, and a racetrack near the outfield. The American Association, known as the "Beer and Whiskey League," prohibited gambling on its grounds and disapproved of the racetrack but permitted beer sales. In contrast, teams in the more established National League sought a more respectable clientele by having higher ticket prices and forbidding the sale of liquor at games.

The controversy over alcohol in ballparks raged well into the twentieth century when the growing temperance movement lobbied baseball clubs to eliminate bars and hard liquor, and to sell beer more discreetly. (Soft drink manufacturers marked their beverages as "temperance drinks" – often soda water sweetened with syrup.) However, it was impossible for the New York American League club to fully board the Prohibition bandwagon after Jacob Ruppert, who inherited a fortune in the family brewing business, purchased the team on January 11, 1915.

Harry M. Stevens set up shop at the Hilltop with a proven business model that improved on Von der Ahe's approach. Unlike Von der Ahe, Stevens put the fan experience of watching the game above everything else. Stevens may have been the first concessionaire to have his vendors patrol the stands during the games. He placed drinking straws in glass soft-drink bottles so spectators could watch the play as they sipped, and varied product offerings by the city to accommodate local tastes. Eventually, Stevens controlled so many venues that several items on his menu became standard ballpark fare, including peanuts, nonalcoholic beverages, and ice cream.

Later baseball legend credited Stevens with introducing hot dogs to ballparks, but there is no evidence that in 1903 he offered frankfurters on his menus, either at the Hilltop or elsewhere. Hot dogs, initially working-class street food, were first introduced to the United States by German immigrants who settled in the Midwest after the Civil War. Around 1867, Charles Feltman, a German-American restaurateur, began selling sausages in rolls at Coney Island. In the 1880s Von der Ahe introduced a "wiener wurst" in St. Louis, where they became a staple at Browns games. The food also may have grown in popularity in New York City with the arrival of Jewish immigrants from Eastern Europe in the early 1900s.

There is no information on the profits Farrell, Devery, and Stevens made from concessions sales in the early years at the Hilltop. However, circumstantial evidence from major-league clubs elsewhere suggests they were substantial. One team reported making more than $2,000 in 1908. Another earned an estimated $1,000 on Coca-Cola sales, with a cut of 40 cents on a case of 24 bottles selling at a nickel apiece. By 1910, Stevens had a son at Yale, rode around in a "swell" automobile, sat in a box at the theater, smoked dollar cigars, dined at swanky Sherry's restaurant, and lived in a series of fancy Midtown hotels.[3]

The best indicator that business was good was Harry Stevens' steady rise as a central player in the business affairs of the Highlanders and other clubs. With the money rolling in, Stevens became a dependable financier to whom owners could turn if they needed to meet a payroll or just the money to paint an outfield fence. Even as he developed his business with the Highlanders, he served on the New York Giants board of directors, with whom he had long been identified. Stevens considered becoming a partner with Brooklyn owner Charles Ebbets in 1908 and an owner of the Giants after the death of John T. Brush in 1912. Thus, when Jacob Ruppert and businessman Tillinghast L'Hommedieu Huston bought the New York American League team in 1915, the new owners awarded Stevens the concessions rights, no doubt partly due to his large bankroll.

HIGHLANDERS TO YANKEES

Stevens' position with the Yankees was bolstered after the 1920 season, when Ruppert and Huston hired Ed Barrow, Harry's longtime friend and former business partner, from the Boston Red Sox to become the business manager of the Yankees. Barrow had spent a lifetime in baseball as a minor-league manager, minor-league owner, minor-league president, and major-league manager. Before he joined the Yankees, Barrow had never won a pennant as a general manager. But with Ruppert's support, Barrow created one of the greatest dynasties in sports history. In his 24 years with the club, the Yankees won 14 American League championships and 10 World Series.[4]

Barrow and Stevens had been friends since the 1890s, when both men frequented the Pittsburgh sports scene. Barrow landed a job in a hotel that catered to sportsmen. Barrow and Stevens were partners, hawking scorecards, refreshments at the ballpark, and playbills to local theaters.[5] The partnership soon broke up amicably after Barrow decided to remain in baseball and not accompany Stevens to New York City to sell food and drink for the Giants. But they remained close.

Stevens came to hate Huston, who wanted to break the concessions contract with the Stevens family and install his son as the concessionaire at the Polo Grounds, which the Yankees shared with the New York Giants. Meanwhile, Barrow was caught in the middle of the squabbling between Huston and Ruppert over how to run the team, especially Huston's criticism of Miller Huggins' effectiveness as on-field manager. Huston in any case wanted out, and after negotiations for the sale of the club to a third party fell through,

he tried to find a purchaser for his half of the team. Ruppert did not want a new partner, so he bought out Huston himself. After completing the transaction, Ruppert offered Barrow the chance to buy 10 percent of the Yankees for $300,000. Barrow borrowed the money from Harry Stevens, intending to repay the loan with future dividends. Ruppert promoted Barrow to team treasurer and gave him a spot on the Yankees' board of directors. Stevens' contract with the Yankees was secure.

At this point in his career, Stevens styled himself as "publisher and caterer … from the Hudson to the Rio Grande" – the latter a reference to his racetrack in Juarez. With the opening of Yankee Stadium on April 18, 1923, the financial heart of Stevens' far-flung concessions empire shifted from the Polo Grounds across the river to the Bronx. The new facility was the largest in baseball and could accommodate about 60,000 hungry customers. (At the height of the Yankees' popularity in the 1920s and 1930s, about 80,000 fans could be squeezed in.) This size was not daunting to Stevens,

Courtesy of the National Baseball Hall of Fame.

Concession salesmen worked exclusively on commission, and sales were often dependent on the weather.

who was used to overseeing large crowds. (He catered the famous Dempsey-Carpentier heavyweight championship bout – an early "Fight of the Century" – in Jersey City in 1921, where almost 90,000 people attended.) It was said of his firm that it served up to 250,000 spectators at various ballparks and racetracks on summer afternoons. As Stevens' ties to the Yankees grew, Harry and his sons – especially Frank – became close friends with national idol Babe Ruth, who conspicuously consumed Stevens' frankfurters. Ruth gave the elder Stevens a signed picture of himself that read, "To my second dad, Harry M. Stevens." After he hit 60 home runs in 1927, Ruth presented Harry with a poster showing an image of every ball he hit out of the park. Each had the date of a blast, and they were numbered from 1 to 60.

THE BUSINESS OF CONCESSIONS

Concessions provided an important part of the Yankees' profits throughout the following years. In the 1929 season, the last before the great stock-market crash, about one-third of the team's net income – $271,028 – came from selling food and drink. This was higher than the crosstown Giants (whose concessions were still managed by the Stevens company) and the second highest in the major leagues.[6] During the Depression in 1933, the Yankees made $59,000 from concessions sales even though the team lost money overall.

In May 1934 Harry Stevens, 76 years old, died of pneumonia. Two of Harry's sons, Frank and Joe, who informally ran the company in their father's final years, formally took over. After that, business at Yankee Stadium remained profitable for the company and the club.[7] In the 1940s the Stevens empire operated not only in Yankee Stadium and at the Polo Grounds but at Ebbets Field in Brooklyn, Braves Field and Fenway Park in Boston, and high-profile racetracks like Churchill Downs, Pimlico, Belmont Park, Saratoga, Hialeah, and Narragansett. Stevens' venues also included minor-league parks, dog tracks, state fairgrounds, and polo fields. Other concessions networks operated around the country, most notably that of the Jacobs brothers, Sportservice, Inc., which had its headquarters in Buffalo and operated in venues not served by Harry M. Stevens. Several smaller, profitable chains prospered on the West Coast. But while concessions firms came and went, the Stevens empire seemed eternal, like Yankee Stadium itself.[8]

However, profit margins in the industry remained small. In 1942 a representative of Sportservice provided a cost itemization for each dime hot dog his company sold and from which his firm earned only half a cent.[9] Horse racing crowds had the highest average – one reason Harry Stevens controlled prestigious tracks around the country. Fans of track and field spent about 40 cents per capita. Baseball crowds spent 15 cents (22 cents at doubleheaders), and boxing and hockey crowds spent 8 cents. Football fans paid on average 10 cents in mild weather and 25 cents in bad weather. (They were not generally crowds who spent a lot of money, since they sat on their hands during a game and were unwilling to reach into their bulky overcoats for a dime.) Football fans spent more when it was cold: They clamored for hot food, paper rain hats, and unlimited coffee.[10]

Profits also depended on less predictable factors like fan moods and the weather. Experienced salespeople, who during the Great Depression were frequently older men, varied their sales pitch based on their assessment of crowd psychology. They worked exclusively on commission, getting from 10 to 20 percent of total sales. One veteran salesman at Yankee Stadium, who had refined his sales pitch, claimed he made $26 on a good day but only $3 on his worst. One of his less experienced colleagues usually pulled in $2 to $8. Sudden weather changes could be disastrous. Counting on a sweltering day, a concessionaire might prepare to sell copious quantities of ice cream and cold drinks only to find that unexpectedly cold weather might shift the demand to coffee, hot dogs, and soup.[11]

Managing an army of vendors at a facility as large as Yankee Stadium was complicated. Forgetting the company founder's belief in the importance of audience preferences, Stevens company executives came to produce concessions the way Henry Ford manufactured autos: They strictly rationed supplies and insisted on the uniformity of practices – coffee was made the same way every game, and vendors were trained how to put a hot dog in a roll and apply mustard with a minimum of motion. They kept track of coffee sales by counting the number of paper cups issued. Still, there were many opportunities for vendors to cheat. Most bags of peanuts contained 50 to 60 items, but a vendor could pick up empty bags around the ballpark and reapportion his stock to make it look as though he sold more. Harry Stevens did not make his employees sew up their pockets, as did the Jacobs brothers, but the firm carefully monitored the activities of all his employees. It required all vendors to wear the prices of their wares on a printed card in their hat so they could not overcharge customers.[12]

DECLINE

The Yankees opened the 1964 season without Harry M. Stevens as their concessionaire.[13] The team had replaced Stevens with National Concessions Service, a division of Automatic Canteen Company, a firm partly owned by the team's owners, businessmen Del Webb and Dan Topping. The menu now included novel items such as shrimp rolls, pizza, fish sandwiches, and milkshakes.[14]

Having the Yankee owners control the team and the Stadium's food and drink operation made good financial sense for the team. In any case, the formidable grip of the Stevens operation on the industry had long been weakening. The Stevens family continued to be reluctant to adapt to evolving audience tastes. (The Stevens company was the only major concessionaire to boil rather than fry its hot dogs, because the elder Harry insisted on cooking them that way.)[15] The reluctance to innovate was reinforced by the large scale of the Stevens holdings, which forced management to standardize its offerings with little variation "from the Hudson to the Rio Grande."[16] Finally, a company like Stevens, with a highly variable level of concessions profits as its core business, almost inevitably would have less resilience than a larger food conglomerate for which concessions were only a sideline.[17]

At Yankee Stadium, Automatic Canteen, under various names, managed concessions until the Stadium closed in 2008.[18] The Yankees then created a new firm in partnership with the Dallas Cowboys called Legends Hospitality.[19] That conglomerate focused on food, beverage, merchandise, retail, stadium operations, and entertainment venues like the San Francisco 49ers' Levi's Stadium and the Indianapolis Motor Speedway. Legends tentacles also stretched beyond food to helping teams operate stadiums and selling naming rights and personal seat licenses.

Harry M. Stevens could not have dreamed of culinary offerings at the new Yankee Stadium today. They include meatball parmesan sandwiches, egg creams, cheesesteaks, garlic fries, and Buffalo chicken quesadillas, along with Nathan's hot dogs. Nor could he have conceived of the video menu boards scattered throughout the ballpark. But he would be on more familiar ground reading the results of a Yankee Stadium concessions case study conducted by Legends in 2014. The report found that the most effective way of increasing concessions sales per capita was to increase the average number of dollars customers spend per transaction.[20] This was sound business practice, indeed, and one Harry Stevens pioneered more than a century ago.

NOTES

1   By 1911 the more headline-friendly "Yanks" or "Yankees" had largely supplanted "Highlanders" as the unofficial nickname of the American League Base Ball Club of Greater New York. But in the writer's view, a certain clarity is achieved by using "Highlanders" for the club during its tenure at Hilltop Park (1903-1912) and reserving "Yankees" for thereafter.

2   Marty Appel, *Pinstripe Empire: The New York Yankees from Before the Babe to After the Boss* (New York: Bloomsbury, 2012), 20-21.

3   David Quentin Voigt, *The League that Failed* (Lanham, Maryland: Scarecrow Press; Illustrated edition (June 1, 1998), 69.

4   Daniel R. Levitt, "The Making of Ed Barrow." *Base Ball*, vol. 1, No. 2, (Fall 2007): 67.

5   Levitt, 68.

6   The Chicago Cubs claimed $132,162 in net concessions in 1929, the highest in the major leagues.

7   After Stevens' wife, Mary, died in 1941, Harry's estate was valued at $1.2 million. https://vindyarchives.com/news/2013/apr/21/valley-relishes-harry-stevens/. Accessed November 21, 2022.

8   Howard Whitman, "Selling the Crowds," *Saturday Evening Post*, April 11, 1942: 25. Some independent firms worked on a single venue or with one partner only. Fred Kanen supplied $400,000 worth of food, drink, and programs to 2 million fans each year at Madison Square Garden. The Miller brothers, Frank, and Paul, had a "single plum," the Ringling circus, for which they Millers supplied 6 million fans and the Ringling's elephants.

9   The breakdown probably was similar for the frankfurters sold by the Stevens company at Yankee Stadium: meat, 3 cents; roll, 1 cent; vendor's commission, 1½ cent; cost of concession rights, 2½ cents; wastage ¾ cent; and overhead, ¾ cent. There was twice as much profit to be had by selling soft drinks: wholesale price per bottle: 3⅓ cents; breakage and handling costs: ¼ cent; ice: ½ cent; vendors commission: 1½ cents; costs of concessions rights: 2½ cents; overhead: ¾ cent; paper cup: ⅛ cent. These costs totaled 9 cents, leaving a penny profit. Whitman, 62.

10   Whitman, 62.

11   Whitman, 25.

12   Whitman, 25.

13   Appel, 350.

14   Appel, 350.

15   When Bob Lurie purchased the San Francisco in 1976, he wanted to introduce wine, but the Stevens Company was aghast, since it went against traditional ballpark fare.

16   That problem popped up in San Francisco as well in 1958 when the Stevens operation set up shop after the Giants move. Some local fans not only were reluctant to embrace their new club, but preferred the concessions their beloved, now-defunct Seals sold for decades.

17   Stevens took a major hit in the 1980s, when many cities forbade beer sales, a major moneymaker, before the end of the game.

18   Aramark acquired the Harry M. Stevens name in 1994.

19   Appel, 350.

20   Yankee Stadium Concessions Case Study: https://www.legends.net/hospitality/yankee-stadium-concessions-case-study#:~:text=Yankee%20Stadium%20Concessions%20Case%20Study%20CONCESSIONS%20GROWTH%20AT,growth%20for%20its%20stands%20without%20raising%20food%20prices. Accessed November 21, 2022.

BLACK BASEBALL AT YANKEE STADIUM

By James Overmyer

Yankee Stadium had been open for seven seasons by the summer of 1930. The home team, featuring Babe Ruth, whose slugging changed the way baseball was played, had brought its New York fans four pennants and three World Series championships in those years. When the Stadium wasn't being used by the Yankees, it hosted professional and college football games, prizefights, and the annual Knights of Columbus track and field meet. But it had never seen a game between Negro League teams.[1]

That changed on July 5, when New York's Lincoln Giants played a doubleheader at the Stadium against the Baltimore Black Sox. The Yankees, like other professional clubs, charged rent for the use of their ballpark. But this one was on the house, although the benefactor and recipient couldn't have been more unalike. The Yankees' millionaire owner, Jacob Ruppert Jr., was giving away his ballpark for the day to an organization headed by A. Philip Randolph, whose goal in life was to make other millionaires miserable.[2]

The Stadium, seating 62,000, was a gem among the revolutionary modern steel and concrete ballparks built since the turn of the century. Despite its enormous capacity, the Yankees were able to keep it full, thanks primarily to the slugger Ruth. The Babe homered on Opening Day in 1923, and sportswriter Fred Lieb labeled the ballpark "The House That Ruth Built."[3]

The recipient of Ruppert's "loan" of his fabled ballpark was the Brotherhood of Sleeping Car Porters, a five-year-old union seeking to represent the African American men who staffed the Pullman sleeping cars on the passenger trains that provided most of the intercity transportation of the day. The union had no other ties to baseball – this was just one of its several major entertainment-related fundraisers. And Ruppert, despite his gracious offer, had no other connections with the Brotherhood.

But the tradition of Black baseball at the Stadium begun through his beneficence continued for nearly 20 years, with a short interruption during the depths of the Great Depression. From the Porters' doubleheader on July 5, 1930, through the end of the 1948 season, when

Negro League ball began to fail, there were a total of 228 games with at least one (usually two) Black teams involved, putting money in the pockets of both the Negro Leagues and the Yankees organization.

Negro League teams, cut off from mainstream capital financing as were most Black businesses, usually couldn't afford to build their own ballparks. Instead, they rented grounds, often from a team in White organized baseball. Black ball's experience at Yankee Stadium, though, ranks at the top of all these real estate deals in all major ways (attendance, financial success, and the importance of the games, for example). The Stadium is rivaled only by Comiskey Park in Chicago, where the Negro Leagues' annual star attraction, the East-West All-Star Game, was played annually beginning in 1933.

The long-term relationship with Yankee Stadium was broad in scope. The Stadium served as a showcase for all African American big-league baseball, especially the Eastern teams in the second Negro National League. Twenty-one different Negro League teams, or squads considered to have been of equivalent ability in 1930 through 1932, the years when there was no Black major league on the East coast, took the field, as did several official and ad hoc Black all-star teams

Ruppert had taken over running the Jacob Ruppert Brewing Company from his father late in the nineteenth century. Under his control, the Manhattan brewery was making more than a million barrels of beer when Prohibition went into effect in 1920. Many breweries closed, but Ruppert stayed in business making legally allowable weak beer (with only 0.5 percent alcohol content) while riding out the nation's dry experience. For the lifelong bachelor and man about town, his favorite extracurricular activity was his ball team. In 1915 he bought a half-share in the Yankees and became sole owner before the 1923 season. At one time the National Guard aide de camp to New York's governor, he liked to be called "Colonel."[4]

Randolph, president of the Sleeping Car Porters union, had a nickname, too. An outspoken pacifist during World War I, he was called by someone in Woodrow Wilson's administration "the most dangerous Negro in America."[5] Neither Randolph nor his union looked threatening in 1930, though. It had been trying for five unsuccessful years to organize the porters since a group of Pullman veterans in New York City had founded it in 1925. Randolph became their first president after thrilling 500 members crowded into a Harlem Elks hall with a vision of what a strong union could do for them, and the Porters became more than a dream.[6] But it took 12 more years of hard work before it reached a labor agreement with the Pullman company.

The explanation for this strange matchup of Colonel Ruppert and the union involves the distinctive nature of New York City politics at the time. Ruppert had served four terms in Congress (from 1899 to 1907), backed by the city's Tammany machine. New York's political hierarchy was simple in those days. The Tammany Society controlled the Democratic Party from its Manhattan headquarters known as Tammany Hall, and the Democrats usually controlled the city. Tammany won the votes of the city's newcomers by catering to their needs for work, public relief in hard times, and validation as New Yorkers. New York's African Americans, many of them migrants from the South, were included in Tammany's outreach to potential Democratic voters.

Porters secretary-treasurer Roy Lancaster was a political creature who belonged to Tammany's Black wing and was regarded during this founding period as perhaps the second most important union leader after Randolph.[7] Lancaster worked his way through the Tammany hierarchy to get the Colonel to partner up for July 5, as he later told a fellow union official: "I remember Roy telling me [Ruppert's] name and that he couldn't be reached. No Negro seemed to have a chance to get anything put on in that park – for free, particularly. But Roy had enough connections to get that park."[8]

The success of the fundraiser depended on the selection of the teams. The Lincoln Giants, one of the best-known black ballclubs in New York, as the home team and the Baltimore Black Sox as the visitors fit the bill. They had been charter members of the Eastern Colored League and its successor, the American Negro League, the two Negro Leagues on the East Coast before going out of business, the first in 1928 and the second in 1929, as the Great Depression loomed.

Each squad had an eventual member of the National Baseball Hall of Fame at first base in John Henry Lloyd, who was also field manager for the Lincolns, and Jud Wilson for the Black Sox. The rest of the lineups were peppered with talent. Appropriately, the teams split the doubleheader. The Lincolns pounded Black Sox pitching in the first game for a 13-4 win. The Giants' Lloyd, right fielder Charlie "Chino" Smith, and third baseman Bill Riggins each had three hits – Smith's were two homers and a triple. Baltimore left fielder Rap Dixon ripped two home runs in the second game (and one in the first game), and right-hander Lamon Yokely pitched a complete-game 5-3 win.

The Porters also staged a small track meet between games for the fans' further diversion. Running champions competed, but the best-known entrant, at least to New Yorkers, had no medals to his name. Bill "Bojangles" Robinson, the actor and tap dancer of Broadway and movie fame, was given a 25-yard head start, and ran the rest of a 100-yard dash backwards. He beat the rest of the field, who had run the dash forward.[9]

The published attendance was as high as 20,000, a highly impressive turnout for a Black baseball game anywhere, except for the crowds in the 40,000-plus range at the annual All-Star Game in Chicago. The union announced a profit of $3,500, a share of the US gross domestic product equal to about $350,000 today.[10] Most of the press coverage of the doubleheader was about the games' heroics (and those of Bojangles and the other racers). However, William G. Nunn, the *Pittsburgh Courier* sports editor, called the afternoon's play at the Stadium a validation of Black baseball's importance: "In the days of our old age, we'll look back upon Yankee Stadium, July 5, 1930, as one of the red-letter days of our lives."[11]

The Stadium, in fact, had many more red-letter days for Black baseball in its future. Some were right around the corner. During the last week of September 1930, a 10-game matchup between the Giants and the Homestead Grays of Pittsburgh, the "race championship" of that year, included six games at the Stadium. Since league ball had folded in the East, no one could prevent any two teams from calling their competition a "championship series," though in fact these were clearly two of the strongest Black squads in the region. The Grays had won three of the four games played in Pittsburgh and Philadelphia, but the Lincoln Giants split each of the three Yankee Stadium doubleheaders on September 21, 27, and 28 to make the series competitive down to its very last innings.

The New York games were so razor-close that an injury to one of the Lincolns' stars in the final contest may well have tipped the series in the Grays' favor. The Giants had won the first game of the final doubleheader on September 28, 6-2, led by ace starter Bill Holland. They were trailing by only 1-0 in the fifth inning of the nightcap, looking to tie the series at five-all, when second baseman Walter "Rev" Cannady and right fielder Chino Smith collided on a short fly ball. Smith was hurt, and he was replaced in the lineup by Luther "Red" Farrell, a left-handed pitcher who played the outfield when not on the mound. Farrell was a prodigious slugger, but not a particularly adept fielder. With two out in the top of the eighth he misjudged a fly ball that Smith likely would have caught, which turned into a double. Then Homestead third baseman Judy Johnson ripped a triple between the lumbering Farrell and center fielder Clint Thomas, and the Grays were on their way to a four-run inning and the championship.

Ruppert was reportedly impressed enough by the Lincolns' play in the Porters' games to make his park available to them again. He may have admired the team, but a more likely explanation for the championship series landing at the Stadium was that Roy Lancaster served as "matchmaker" and promoter, taking away a share of the profits. Attendance ran to more than 10,000 for the first and third doubleheaders, both on Sundays, traditionally the big day for Black baseball attendance. Importantly for the future of Negro ball in the Bronx, the two teams and Lancaster walked away with a combined $9,098. The Yankees' share of $4,243 ($3,237 after paying for ticket printing and game-day payroll expenses), was 32 percent of the gross gate of $13,341. This was very good money for the Black franchises and a nice "bonus" for the Yankees for use of the ballpark while the team was on the road.[12]

Black ball at the Stadium was off to a good start for everyone. But the Depression loomed, and Negro baseball took a calamitous nosedive. The Yankee Stadium results reflected this. The Harlem Stars, a successor team to the Lincoln Giants, played three doubleheaders in 1931 that drew only about 13,000 fans in all. The final date, on August 16, was another Sleeping Car Porters benefit, which flopped. The final balance sheet showed the Porters had lost $187.97.[13]

After that debacle, there were no Black games at the Stadium until 1934. Then William A. "Gus" Greenlee, who had led the revival of league baseball by founding the second Negro National League in 1933, began to rent the Yankees' home. Greenlee had also spearheaded the annual East-West Games at Comiskey Park. Historian Neal Lanctot says that "perhaps more than any other owner, Greenlee realized the importance of presenting black baseball in a major league venue, transcending the usual white perception of black baseball as semi-professional in caliber."[14]

About 25,000 fans turned out for the return to the Stadium, a doubleheader on September 9. Unsurprisingly, Greenlee's Pittsburgh Crawfords were represented. They played the Philadelphia Stars to a 1-1 tie in the second game, called due to darkness. That game featured the Stadium debut of the best draw throughout Negro baseball's entire run there. Satchel Paige pitched for the Crawfords, dueling Stars ace Slim Jones.

From 1934 through 1938, Greenlee's Negro National League booked one or two doubleheaders a season, the dates usually serving as fundraisers for civic purposes that benefited New York's African Americans. The games were well attended, averaging from 15,000 to 20,000 fans per date, except when Paige came to town again on September 26, 1937. Satchel, who had been the pitching mainstay of Greenlee's Crawfords, deserted with other stars that spring for a rich offer from the Dominican Republic's summer league. The departure of Paige and the others was the beginning of the end for Greenlee and his Crawfords, who were out of business by 1938. But the defectors were still useful to Greenlee at the end of 1937. He paid $3,000 to the Yankees to stage a game between a team of Negro National League All-Stars and the "Santo Domingo Stars." As many as 30,000 fans attended as the Dominican stars won, 9-4, and a second game ended in a five-inning tie called by darkness.[15]

Although Greenlee faded from the Black big-league scene, his idea of playing Negro League games in Yankee Stadium persisted. His arrangement with the Yankees had one major drawback – the Yankees charged from $2,500 to $3,000 per date, substantially cutting into profits. But before the 1939 season, the Negro National League hired Philadelphia sports figure Ed Gottlieb as its booking agent for Stadium games. Gottlieb, although White, was a part-owner of the NNL's Philadelphia Stars. He also was one of the leading bookers of semipro games on the East Coast. He could walk into the Yankees' front office and work out a deal that reduced the rental charge in exchange for many more playing dates. Analysis of financial transactions from 1939 on appears to show that the Yankees changed their financially challenging flat rate to a rent of 25 percent of gross revenue, with a $1,000 minimum.[16]

The Yankees also offered the Ruppert Memorial Trophy, named after the recently deceased Colonel, to the Negro National League team winning the most games at the Stadium each year. The combination of Gottlieb's new deal and the trophy caused Black baseball at the park to leap to six dates, a total of 11 games, in 1939, with an estimated total attendance of about 79,000. And use of the Stadium just kept increasing. From 1940 through 1946, the financial heyday of the Black leagues, there were a total of 148 games played on 77 different dates, drawing just over a million fans. The World War II seasons were difficult for White professional baseball, but paradoxically the Negro Leagues never had it better in terms of attendance and profits. The turning of the mighty manufacturing sector in Northern cities into a defense industry drew new workers, including African Americans, from the less industrialized South, greatly increasing Black ball's fan base.

The Stadium was well located to attract the Black New York baseball fan, only four subway stops north of 125th Street, Harlem's commercial and entertainment center. The closer a Black ballgame in New York City was to Harlem, the better its chance of making money. The New York Giants' Polo Grounds, opposite Yankee Stadium on the Manhattan side of the East River, was one subway stop closer. Many games were played at the Polo Grounds when Negro League ball in the city was in its heyday during World War II. (Gottlieb said the Polo Grounds came into use when the Stadium couldn't meet the increased demand for dates.[17]) But the Negro National League usually turned to the Yankees in making up its New York schedule, certainly in part because of Gottlieb's close relationship with management there.

Negro League games at Yankee Stadium were mostly a showcase for the Negro National League, the only ones, for example, competing for the Ruppert Trophy. But as the annual number of games steadily increased, from 11 in 1939 to 31 (on 15 dates) in 1946, teams from the Negro American League, located in the Midwest and South, played the Stadium when they made Eastern barnstorming swings. The first appearance of the Negro American League was August 27, 1939, when the Negro Leagues staged a second East-West All-Star Game in New York, a money-making follow-up to the main East-West Game played in Chicago on August 6. The East team, composed of NNL stars, avenged an earlier loss in Chicago with a 10-2 victory. The attendance of 20,000 was the best for a Black game at Yankee Stadium that year.

The leagues would also occasionally use this big venue for important championship games.

The Baltimore Elite Giants beat the Grays, 2-0, on September 24, 1939, to wrap up the NNL pennant playoffs, and the Negro World Series, which was partially played in cities other than the homes of the contenders, visited the Stadium in 1942 and 1947. Individual NAL teams began to play there in the latter part of the 1940 season as the Memphis Red Sox took on the St. Louis Stars. The NAL was regularly appearing at the Stadium by 1941.

The most important Midwestern visitors were the Kansas City Monarchs. The Monarchs were one of the strongest teams in the NAL, but the real reason they were so welcome was that they brought Paige, a major drawing card all by himself, back to Yankee Stadium. The legendary Satchel made 20 starts there for Black teams. Crowds for those games averaged about 20,400 per date, nearly double the 11,600 averaged for the rest of the dates. His teams won 13 of his 20 starts (there were two ties and only five losses). Paige himself got credit for 11 wins, against only two defeats.

He was not the only Negro League workhorse at the Stadium. Little right-hander Dave Barnhill was the New York Cubans' staff ace in the early 1940s. The Cubans were the team with most of the good Black Latin American players in the NNL. But owner Alex Pompez would gladly sign US-born talent, too, as witnessed by his recruitment of North Carolinian Barnhill in 1941. From 1941 through 1943, Barnhill was the Cubans' regular starter for the coveted Sunday Stadium dates. He made 21 starts and one relief appearance in those three years, earning 10 wins against eight losses, plus a save. After recovering from an injury in 1944, and appearing more often at the Polo Grounds, more and more the Cubans' home park, he pitched in the Stadium again in 1946 and 1948. Then he split four more decisions for a career record there of 12-10. Barnhill finished 17 of his 24 starts, which included two two-hitters, two four-hitters, and three five-hitters.

Josh Gibson was another legendary Negro Leaguer who excelled at the Stadium. He made several appearances, the first in the championship series of 1930 and the last in August 1946. The Negro Leagues' most prolific home-run hitter, he crashed seven homers there. His second, on September 27, 1930, the next to last day of the big Grays-Lincoln Giants series, was among the longest shots there by any player. He was an 18-year-old rookie with the Grays and while he was the regular catcher, he hadn't yet graduated to the position of "main man" in the Homestead batting order. He batted sixth on this day. Gibson had hit an opposite-field homer to right in the first game, which the Lincolns won, 9-8. Homestead jumped right on Giants starter Connie Rector in the first inning of the nightcap, and the young catcher came up with two men on. Rector pitched, and Gibson launched a shot to left field that the *Chicago Defender* reporter pegged at 460 feet.[18] Gibson went out at the Stadium in 1946 with the same sort of flourish, bombing a 430-foot shot to center to help beat the Black Yankees, 7-0, in the May 26 game, and doubling in a run in his last appearance there, on August 30. Josh, who could still hit for power although his all-around skills were decaying at only age 34, was closer to the end than anyone imagined. He suffered a stroke in early January of 1947, and never played again.

The career path of Gibson, who reportedly was gravely disappointed in not being chosen to help integrate the White majors, parallels the late-1940s history of the Negro Leagues, which went into sudden and irreversible decline after the color barrier was broken in 1947. Black baseball at Yankee Stadium went down with it, as attendance plummeted to about 7,000 per date in 1947 and 8,000 in 1948.

The Negro National League went out of business after the 1948 season, with most surviving teams, including the New York Cubans, huddling in the Negro American League. Pompez, the Cubans owner, had become a scout for the New York Giants, and his team played at the Polo Grounds. Pompez, the Cubans owner, had become a scout for the New York Giants, and his team played at the Polo Grounds. From then on, the Negro League presence at the Stadium was intermittent, at best. By then opportunities for the best Black players were steadily becoming available in the formerly White major and minor leagues, and the one surviving Negro League, the American, could no longer be considered to have top-level ball.

Of the 456 team appearances at Yankee Stadium through the end of the 1948 season (the 228 games times two teams per game), 420, or 92 percent of the total, were Negro League or equivalent teams, plus the Negro League all-star teams. The two local teams that played there the most, the New York Black Yankees (48-51-5) and the Cubans (36-34-2), had only middling records. Among the regular Negro League competitors, the top won-lost marks were held by the Homestead Grays (26-11-1) and the Elite Giants from Nashville and then Baltimore (23-11-1).

In the last three years of high-quality Black games, lesser-ranked regional Black teams like the Richmond Giants, Jacksonville Eagles, and the Asheville (North Carolina) Blues played, usually in the preliminary game of a four-team Sunday doubleheader. Occasionally, a White team would provide an opponent. The 1946 season ended on October 4 and 6 with games between the Satchel Paige and Bob Feller all-star squads as the two well-known hurlers brought to New York their 20-game postseason barnstorming show, top Black players against top Whites. Although Feller's team had the better overall record, the Paige All-Stars won, 4-0, at the Stadium on the 6th. Feller's team had triumphed, 4-2, on the 4th.

The games at the Stadium added a great deal to the competitive nature of Negro baseball and helped popularize it in what was then the biggest city in the United States. But what were they worth financially to all involved? Anything approaching precise information on Negro League finances is sorely lacking today. Financial records were usually lost when the Black teams went out of business. But in two donations in 1955 and 1970, the Yankees gave the National Baseball Hall of Fame many of their old business and financial records, a run of data from 1913 to 1950.

The Yankee ledgers contain reports of cash receipts and expenditures for nearly all the Black games from 1930 through 1944. A combined look at the Yankees' data and newspaper coverage of the Negro Leagues allows tracking of all the Black games through 1948, when both leagues were playing and competition was at its highest.

Calculation of gross gate receipts and net profits from the Black games at the Stadium uses the Yankee financial records as a base, but also depends upon attendance figures to help reach financial results. After establishing an attendance figure for each date and making some assumptions based on what the average ticket price might have been, it appears that through 1944, the last full year of Yankees records, the collaboration brought in a gross amount of about $426,000. After subtraction of the federal 10 percent entertainment tax on each ticket sold and Stadium game-day expenses, there was a net of about $372,000. Of that amount, the Negro Leagues and the independent teams that sometimes played took away about 70 percent, $255,000. The Yankee organization kept about 30 percent. The $115,000 the Yankees made over 13 years isn't much for a team that was usually leading its league in attendance each season, but it was a nice windfall, a small profit made while the Stadium would otherwise be sitting idle.[19]

On the other hand, the money going to the Negro Leagues was a vital sum. During the heyday years of

1939 through 1944, the Black leagues had an estimated income from the Stadium of $32,500 per season. In comparison, the Newark Eagles, considered one of the higher-salaried Black teams, and one of the few clubs whose records survive, had an annual payroll of $22,500 toward the end of that period. So a relative handful of games at Yankee Stadium in the prime seasons cleared more than the entire Eagles payroll for players and other employees, with plenty left over.[20]

This makes the importance of Yankee Stadium as one of the most important venues for Negro League baseball quite clear. Paid attendance at Negro League games, which had no broadcast or licensing rights, was all important. In that respect the Stadium shares top honors with Comiskey Park, the site of the East-West games. From the first game in 1933 through 1948 the East-West game in Chicago drew an average of 36,500 per game. This was more than three times the average attendance at the Stadium's Black games, a figure from Chicago even more impressive considering how much greater the New York attendance was than for the average Negro League game. More people went to an East-West Game than attended a game at Yankee Stadium even when the matchless Paige was starting. And the East-West Game produced dozens of thrilling games and individual performances that have become part of Black baseball lore.[21]

But the Stadium games, held in the leading city in the United States, in the park of the leading baseball team, provided important prestige for the Negro Leagues in addition to a financial shot in the arm for the Black majors. Essentially, the title for most influential Negro League game of the year was regularly won by Chicago, while the crown for sustained influence rested in New York.

NOTES

1   The major Black teams playing at Yankee Stadium are called "Negro League" teams here, even though during the Great Depression the leagues were not always in continuous operation. The best teams and players were still playing as independent clubs and were of league-level ability.

2   Randolph was the driving force behind the union he organized, the Brotherhood of Sleeping Car Porters.

3   Michael Gershman, *Diamonds: The Evolution of the Ballpark* (Boston, New York: Houghton Mifflin, 1993), 138.

4   "Ruppert, Owner of Yankees and Leading Brewer, Dies," *New York Times*, January 14, 1939: 7; Dan Levitt, "Jacob Ruppert," SABR Baseball Biography Project, http://sabr.org/bioproj/person/b96b262d; Elizabeth L. Bradley, *Knickerbocker, the Myth Behind New York* (New Brunswick, New Jersey: Rivergate Books, 2009), 121-23.

5   Larry Tye, *Rising from the Rails: Pullman Porters and the Making of the Black Middle Class* (New York: Henry Holt and Company, 2004), 114.

6   Tye, *Rising from the Rails*, 112-13; "Randolph Leads Fight for Porters," *New York Amsterdam News*, August 26, 1925: 9; "500 Enthusiastic Porters Loudly Cheer Proposed Porters' Union," *New York Amsterdam News*, September 2, 1925: 9.

7   William Hamilton Harris, *Keeping the Faith: A. Philip Randolph, Milton P. Webster, and the Brotherhood of Sleeping Car Porters, 1925-1937* (Urbana: University of Illinois Press, 1977), 26, 73.

8   C.L. Dellums, interview by Joyce Henderson, oral history transcript for the Bancroft Library, University of California, Berkeley, at Online Archive of California (http:www.oac.cdlib.org); "Roy Lancaster 'Puts Over' Big Benefit Event," *New York Age*, July 19, 1930: 6.

9   "Thousands at Yankee Stadium," *New York Amsterdam News*, July 9, 1930: 13.

10 Lucien H. White, "Roy Lancaster 'Puts Over' Big Benefit Event"; "How Much Is a Dollar from the Past Worth Today?" Measuringworth.com, https://www.measuringworth.com/dollarvaluetoday.

11 William G. Nunn, "Diamond Stars Rise to Miracle Heights in Big Game at Yankee Bowl," *Pittsburgh Courier*, July 12, 1930: 14.

12 American League Base Ball Club records, National Baseball Hall of Fame Library and Museum, Cooperstown, New York.

13 William E. Clark, "A. Philip Randolph Explains Why Stars Got No Money from Porter's Benefit," *New York Age*, August 29, 1931: 6.

14 Neil Lanctot, *Negro League Baseball: The Rise and Ruin of a Black Institution* (Philadelphia: University of Pennsylvania Press, 2004), 38.

15 American League Base Ball Club records.

16 Art Rust Jr., *"Get that Nigger Off the Field!": a Sparkling, Informal History of the Black Man in Baseball* (New York: Delacorte Press, 1976), 55; American League Base Ball Club records.

17 Rust, 55.

18 "Homestead Grays Defeat Lincoln Giants 6 Out of 10 Games for Eastern Title," *Chicago Defender*, October 4, 1930: 8.

19 American League Base Ball Club records.

20 Newark Eagles Business Papers, Newark (New Jersey) Public Library.

21 Dick Clark and Larry Lester, eds., *The Negro Leagues Book* (Cleveland: Society for American Baseball Research, 1994), 242-254.

THE NEGRO LEAGUES EAST-WEST
ALL-STAR GAME AND THE TWO GAMES
HELD AT YANKEE STADIUM

By Thomas Kern

The White major leagues held their first All-Star Game on July 6, 1933, at Comiskey Park in Chicago. Taking place in conjunction with the Chicago World's Fair, the game was the brainchild of Chicago's Mayor Edward Kelly with help from the *Chicago Tribune* to hype the Fair and spur interest in baseball, whose fortunes had been declining during the Depression.

Around the same time, Pittsburgh writers Roy Sparrow and Bill Nunn met with Cumberland Posey of the Homestead Grays to discuss holding a Negro League all-star showcase in New York City. After no progress was made, the writers met with Gus Greenlee, owner of the Pittsburgh Crawfords, who helped initiate contact with Chicago American Giants owner Robert Cole to facilitate leasing Comiskey Park in Chicago for an all-star contest.[1] The game would be known as the East-West Classic, and its players chosen via fan voting (as was the case with the NL/AL All-Star Game) with ballots provided by prominent African American newspapers.

Some thought that a joint All-Star game might be in the cards, but with segregationist Commissioner Kenesaw Mountain Landis in charge of the White major-league game, a contest between the two leagues had no chance of success.[2] The East-West All Star Game organizers scheduled a September 10, 1933, matchup of their own Negro League stars in a game that led to nearly 40 contests in one format or another over 30 years.[3]

The inaugural game was all that had been hoped for – an 11-7 slugfest with the West team led by Mule Suttles' homer and three RBIs and Willie Foster's complete game.[4] In subsequent years, the game would bring together a who's who of Negro League greats and remind any follower of baseball of what might have been.

Fast forward to 1939. Black baseball's national showcase had taken place in six consecutive years (the East and West each winning three), all at Chicago's Comiskey Park. A June 1939 meeting in Pittsburgh of the boards of the Negro American and National Leagues approved the seventh All-Star Game to be played again in Chicago. No mention at that time was made of a second game. The August 6 contest saw the West (Negro American League) squad come from behind to win dramatically 4-2 over the East (Negro National League). The devastating loss by the East All-Stars prompted its owners to call for a rematch. According to Fay Young in the *Chicago Defender*:

> After the West defeated the East ... the owners in the Negro National League were not convinced that the West had a better team, therefore they issued a challenge to the Negro American League for a game to be played in New York on Sunday, August 27, at the Yankee Stadium, home of the New York American League club. ... The game in New York will not be a second East versus West Classic but will be a game between stars of the two leagues. Many of the same players who took part in the game in Chicago will be in action. In fact, the East can hardly produce a better lineup than what was on the field on August 6. True, the home run kings of the Eastern circuit fell down – but don't we all have off days?[5]

The idea of a second All-Star Game prompted by the intense rivalry of the two leagues was understandable, but why Yankee Stadium? Negro League teams in New York City had never succeeded in the way that teams in other East Coast cities had – Pittsburgh, Newark, and Philadelphia in particular. Perhaps a place like Pittsburgh, home of the Homestead Grays (and until 1938, the Pittsburgh Crawfords), would have been better. But New York was the mecca for the White major leagues and a platform from which to display the talents of Black baseball players and to confirm how deserving they were to play alongside their White peers.

In his work *Black Baseball's National Showcase*, Larry Lester wrote that "the last year of the [1930s] decade proved to be a pivotal year for baseball in America, particularly Black baseball. More attention than ever was focused on the integration issue … more and more press coverage, and more campaigns questioning the 'gentlemen's agreement' imposed by Major League owners [to exclude Blacks from their game], continued to be front page news."[6] Bringing the best of the Negro Leagues to New York was a palpable way to shine a light on their play. In fact, the game at Yankee Stadium saw eight future Hall of Famers (Oscar Charleston, Andy Cooper, Leon Day, Josh Gibson, Buck Leonard, Hilton Smith, Turkey Stearnes, and Willie Wells) either play, manage, or coach. And a case could be made that several others who appeared in the game should be in the Hall as well.

The Negro National League at that time included two teams from New York City – the New York Black Yankees and the New York Cubans – as well as one from across the Hudson River in Newark, the Eagles. The Black Yankees and Cubans finished third and seventh respectively in the Negro National League that year and three of their players, Bill Holland and Terris McDuffie of the Black Yankees and Cando López from the Cubans, were the only ones from New York teams selected. Each played in one of the two games.

Local newspapers lauded the arrival of the All-Star Game in New York, noting that "for the first time since its conception seven years ago, the East will have the opportunity to witness the Dream Game of Negro baseball, when the All-Star teams of the Negro National and American Leagues clash at Yankee Stadium Sunday, August 27th."[7]

If the Negro National League owners were looking for revenge at Yankee Stadium for their earlier loss at Comiskey, they got it. The *New York Daily Worker* wrote, "Led by Josh Gibson, whom many big leaguers have called the greatest catcher in the game today, the Eastern All-Stars of the Negro National League pounded out a 10-2 victory over the Western All-Stars before 20,000 fans at the Yankee Stadium yesterday."[8] Gibson drove in four runs along with Bill Wright's and Willie Wells' two each. Three pitchers for the East split the innings equally: Bill Byrd, Terris McDuffie (in front of his hometown crowd), and Newark's Leon Day. Although the West squad had seven hits (to the East's 10), they could muster only single runs off Byrd in the first and McDuffie in the sixth.

Dan Burley of the *New Amsterdam News* wrote after the game that it "served the purpose of placing two brands of ball played by the Negro leagues on display for the first time in the East. Out West, the boys rely on old time strategy, stolen bases, squeeze plays, bunts, and sacrifices. Out here [the East], it is knock the ball out of the park and be done with it."[9]

There was another element to the game at Yankee Stadium that perhaps only New York could bring. Burley wrote:

> The crowd was gay and colorful, counting in its bigwigs Elks, politicians, theatrical and nightlife celebrities plus a sprinkling of Alphas [Alpha Phi Alpha], Deltas [Delta Sigma Delta], and others. Henry Armstrong, welterweight titleholder, threw the first ball, John Henry Lewis, undefeated as light-weight champion, making the attempt to catch it but dropping the ball as it crossed the plate.[10]

Fay Young of the *Chicago Defender* offered his own postgame commentary on the bigger picture, lamenting the attendance and considering the causes for such poor numbers:

> New York had an East versus West game. The official paid attendance was a bit over a reported 20,000. … To have one game on a Sunday afternoon after several four team gala bills [Negro League owners would often schedule doubleheaders at venues like Yankee Stadium showcasing four different teams] naturally left the fans believing they would be paying a price for one half of what they had been getting [the ticket price was the same for one game as it had been for two and this affected attendance]. … The Chicago game taught the promoters a lesson. Of the 32,000 [in the stands at Comiskey], less than 1,500 were White baseball fans paying their way. In other words, the success of the game was made by Negro newspapers and the daily press. Even as liberal as [the White press] were here, it didn't put people in the gate.[11]

Young also asserted that Negro League owner Effa Manley of the Newark Eagles did not promote the game to the African American community as well as those in the Chicago area did for their All-Star Game, hence lower attendance from the Black community. The upshot? Grand plans for a showcase event at Yankee Stadium failed to come to fruition.

In 1948, nine years later, the East-West All-Star Game returned to Yankee Stadium. After the 1939 East-West Classic, Negro League owners paired the annual Comiskey Park game with a second contest in Cleveland (1942), Washington (1946), and the Polo Grounds in New York (1947).

The period between the two Yankee Stadium Classics may have been less than a decade, but in other ways, it was an eternity. Dan Burley of the *New Amsterdam News* wrote in early 1948, "When [Jackie] Robinson went into big league baseball, he took the Negro League attendance at all-Negro contests with him."[12] The long-awaited breaking of the color barrier in the White major leagues had the inevitable impact of lessening interest in the Negro Leagues among its primary customer base, African Americans. And although the talent drain took some time as Black stars and emerging talent began to take roster spots on American and National League teams and in their minor-league systems, the Negro League game itself suffered. Look no further than the number of future Hall of Famers who played or managed in the 1948 game compared with 1939. Eight appeared in 1939 and only two in 1948: Willard Brown and Pop Lloyd (as manager).

Unlike 1939, when the decision to play a second game was spur-of-the-moment, the *Chicago Defender* reported that in 1948 "the Negro American league club owners have decided on the players who will represent them in the 16th annual East vs. West game to be played at Comiskey Park, Sunday afternoon, August 22nd. … A second game between the East and West teams, called the "Dream game," will be played in New York that week."[13]

At the first game, in Chicago, the West defeated the East 3-0. Two days later, on Tuesday, August 24, substantially the same teams met again in front of an announced attendance of 17,928 at the Stadium. Once again, as in 1939, the East made up for its earlier loss in Chicago, winning easily, 6-1.

Players from the Negro National League's New York teams this time contributed heavily to the win. Minnie Miñoso of the hometown New York Cubans batted second and went 2-for-2. George Crowe of the Black Yankees played first and batted fifth, going 2-for-4 and scoring twice. Louis Louden (Cubans) and Marvin Barker (Black Yankees) made appearances and Dave Barnhill of the Black Yankees tossed a scoreless

middle three innings. John Henry "Pop" Lloyd, who had played and managed much of his career in the New York/New Jersey area, managed the East to victory.

Several compelling storylines emerged during and immediately after the 1948 games that suggested the handwriting was on the wall for the future quality of the All-Star Games and the Negro Leagues as a whole.

The ticket from the August 24 game at Yankee Stadium made it clear which league had superiority in the pecking order between the Negro and White major leagues. On it was written:

> "The Colored All-Star Game Dream Game is scheduled to be played on the Night of August 24th. In the event of RAIN, it will be played on the Night of August 25th. In the event the Yankee-Chicago [White Sox] game scheduled for the Night of August 23rd is rained out, the game will be played on August 24th, thereby postponing the All-Star Game to the Night of August 25th."[14]

Although not surprising, the notation on the ticket is reminiscent of the stark inequality of an earlier era, or at least those who controlled the pocketbook.

Before the game the *New Amsterdam News* had written that the game was expected to draw a crowd of about 40,000.[15] As it turned out, fewer than 18,000 attended, the lowest All-Star Game attendance outside of two games that had been played in Cleveland and Washington.[16]

The August 28 edition of the *Chicago Defender* noted:

> Baseball fans and the general public are blaming the slump in the East versus West game attendance to politics and ticket scalping. Last year 48,112 watched the classic. Sunday 42,099 was the attendance although it was reported a few minutes before as 37,099. Leroy "Satchel" Paige drew 51,000 in the same park on Friday night August 13th. On that night fully 15,000 were unable to get inside the park. Sunday, at the East vs. West game there weren't 15,000 on the outside.[17]

African Americans had now turned their eyes to the small number of Black ballplayers in the American and National Leagues. Exorbitant ticket prices and ticket scalping also drove away cost-conscious fans.[18] As a result, the game's showcase lost its luster.

The *Defender's* Satchel Paige reference spoke to the exodus of its better players to Organized Baseball. In fact, Paige had pitched on Friday, August 20, in Cleveland before 78,383 fans. The *Indianapolis Star* wrote, "Ageless Satchel Paige shut out the Chicago White Sox with three hits last night. ... The fabulous Negro hurler now has won all three of his major league starts and has a season record of five victories and only one loss. A total of 201,829 customers have jammed their way into the stands to watch Paige in his three major league starts."[19] The African American community were voting with their feet. They cared about Black baseball players, following their stars as they now competed head-to-head with their White counterparts.

On September 4, the *Defender* observed:

[T]he crowd was asked to stand in silent tribute to the late George Herman "Babe" Ruth [Ruth had died on August 16, eight days earlier]. No mention was made of the last Negro baseball men's death – namely Josh Gibson [January 20, 1947], hero of many an East vs. West game; Candy Jim Taylor, manager of the East nine and of the Chicago American Giants [April 3, 1948]; Cum Posey, Homestead Grays and former secretary of the Negro National League [March 28, 1946]. Maybe they didn't amount to much in the eyes of the owners and promoters of the game, but baseball fans wondered why.[20]

The lack of respect accorded to the Negro Leagues in situations like this was at least somewhat mitigated by the slowly increasing number of its players who were afforded an opportunity to help integrate the previously White major and minor leagues. However, the breaking of the color barrier brought about conflicted feelings within the African American community about Negro League baseball, its role, and its future.

In a September 1948 editorial titled "Don't Let Negro Baseball Die!" a writer for the *Pittsburgh Courier* wrote:

I pride myself on being a staunch supporter of Satchel Paige, Jackie Robinson, Larry Doby, and Roy Campanella. I'm praying that Don Newcombe, Dan Bankhead, and Sammy Jethro[e] get major league calls next year, but – for God's sake, fans, don't let Negro baseball die! ... The way I see it, Negro fans are doing Negro baseball, future Negro

stars and potential major leaguers a great injustice by withdrawing their support. For if the Negro teams are forced to curtail their activities due to inability to meet expenses, the hopes of hundreds of Negro aspirants for major league careers will be doomed. How will major league scouts be able to look over Negro material if there are no Negro teams playing?"[21]

In the twenty-first century, all agree that the national pastime is in a better place than it was before Jackie Robinson's trailblazing. The 1948 East-West All-Star Game at Yankee Stadium may have helped shine a light on how much was still to be done to repair the fracture of segregation, both for baseball and beyond.

It is worth noting that in Larry Lester's significant work on the East-West All-Star Game that in 1958 and 1961, the Negro American League, weakened now to independent minor-league status, held All-Star games at Yankee Stadium. The league disbanded after 1962.

SOURCES

Larry Lester's *Black Baseball's National Showcase* serves as the primary source of the All-Star Game statistics, supported by Seamheads.

NOTES

1   Cumberland Posey, "Posey's Points," *Pittsburgh Courier*, August 15, 1942: 16.

2   Chester Washington of the *Pittsburgh Courier* wrote on June 17, 1933, of a proposed "interracial" All-Star Game between the White and Negro Leagues that would "not only settle a lot of arguments, but would probably draw one of the biggest turnouts of Negro and Nordic fans in the history of the game." Chester Washington, "Sez Ches," *Pittsburgh Courier*, June 17, 1933: 15.

3   Larry Lester, *Black Baseball's National Showcase: The East-West All-Star Game, 1933-1962*, Expanded Edition (Kansas City: NoirTech Research, Inc., 2020), 400-401.

4   Lester, 33.

5   Fay Young, "The Stuff Is Here ... Past-Present-Future," *Chicago Defender*, August 19, 1939: 17.

6   Lester, 116.

7   "All Star East West Game at Yank Stadium, August 27," *New Jersey Herald News*, August 19, 1939.

8   "Gibson Leads Attack as East beats West, 10-2," *New York Daily Worker*, August 28, 1939.

9   Dan Burley, "Power Crushes West 10-2," *New Amsterdam News*, September 2, 1939: 17.

10   Burley.

11   Fay Young, "Fay Says," *Chicago Defender*, September 9, 1939: 17.

12   Dan Burley, *New Amsterdam News*, January 3, 1948: 16.

13   "West Selects Players for the Big Game, August 22," *Chicago Defender*, July 31, 1948: 24.

14   Lester, 298.

15   Swig Garlington, "40,000 Expected at Dream Game," *New Amsterdam News*,
      August 21, 1948: 16.

16   Larry Lester, *Black Baseball's National Showcase: The East-West All-Star
      Game, 1933-1953* (Lincoln: University of Nebraska Press, 2001), 321.
      The Cleveland game was the second of two in 1942, two days after the
      Comiskey Park contest that the East had won with 45,000 fans in attendance.
      The game at Municipal Stadium drew just under 11,000 with the East
      winning again. Griffith Stadium in Washington hosted the first of the two
      All-Star Games in 1946, drawing a little over 16,000 compared with 45,000
      at Comiskey. The East and West split the two games with each side winning
      in its respective region.

17   Morgan Holsey, "Scalpers and Politics Mar East-West Game," *Chicago
      Defender*, August 28, 1948: 24.

18   Holsey.

19   "78,382 Fans See Paige Pitch Another Cleveland Shutout," *Indianapolis Star*,
      August 21, 1948: 16.

20   "Second East versus West Game Draws 17,928," *Chicago Defender*,
      September 4,1948.

21   Don't Let Negro Baseball Die," *Pittsburgh Courier*, September 4, 1948: 10.

SATCHEL PAIGE AT YANKEE STADIUM

By Nick Malian

Yankee Stadium is considered baseball's biggest stage, a modern marvel of concrete and steel. The fashionable frieze that encircled the top of the exterior walls added regality and panache not seen in other stadiums. Yankee Stadium was expansive enough to host larger-than-life characters like Babe Ruth, Reggie Jackson, and George Steinbrenner, yet be intimate enough for an emotional send-off for the "luckiest man on the face of the earth." The perpetual success of the New York Yankees between the 1920s and 1960s elevated Yankee Stadium to celebrity status in popular culture and became the place to be seen for fans and players, White and Black.

Yankee Stadium was also an important venue for Black baseball by showcasing elite Black baseball players to larger, mostly White crowds. In 1934 the Negro Leagues began hosting fundraising events, exhibition games, and the Negro League World Series games at the Stadium. Playing there gave credibility, prestige, and financial support to Black baseball players.[1] With this new opportunity for Black baseball players in New York, baseball's showman took advantage of baseball's biggest stage.

Leroy "Satchel" Paige authored one of the most legendary careers in baseball history. He was born on July 7, 1906, and his journey from abject poverty in Mobile, Alabama, to Cooperstown, New York, is as improbable as it was mythical.[2] Beginning in 1926, his professional career spanned four decades in which he traveled across the Americas, pitching for whichever team paid the most. Aside from the longevity of his career, Paige is most often remembered for his showmanship and iconic style. It paired well with his godlike precision and otherworldly speed that dominated professional baseball. Joe DiMaggio called him "the best and fastest pitcher I ever faced."[3]

Paige commanded the attention of fans like no other player of his time. During his barnstorming games in the 1930s and 1940s, the reported attendance in games Paige pitched averaged 20,668.[4] fans. In comparison, the average attendance in the same time frame for Yankees games was just 15,000.[5] Fans were not only admirers of Paige's talent and success.

It was reported that he singlehandedly grew Negro League ticket sales to 200,000 a season[6] and as such grew the salaries of Black baseball players from the increase in gate receipts.[7]

The legend of Satchel Paige grew through his barnstorming tours and Negro League games, and it was Yankee Stadium that helped to bring his legend to the masses. He made 34 pitching appearances at the ballpark between 1934 and 1953. Paige started 20 of the games as a Negro Leaguer and barnstormer between 1934 and 1937. Scant newspaper accounts indicated that he pitched 107 innings, had 90 strikeouts, gave up 81 hits and 16 walks and was credited with an 11-3 record. As a relief pitcher for the Cleveland Indians and St. Louis Browns between 1948 and 1953, Paige made 13 relief appearances and one start. He pitched 33 innings, struck out 17 and gave up 22 hits and 11 walks, a WHIP of 1.00. He finished with an 0-3 record

In his four appearances at Yankee Stadium with the 1952 St. Louis Browns, Satchel Paige had a 2.55 ERA in 17 2/3 innings.

and five saves. Chronicling these games offers insight into his lifestyle and career as one of the most dominant and iconic pitchers of all time.

THE NEGRO LEAGUES AND BARNSTORMING AT YANKEE STADIUM

Paige pitched for the first time at Yankee Stadium on September 9, 1934, as a member of the legendary Pittsburgh Crawfords. The game was part of a four-team doubleheader fundraiser for Harlem's Colonel Charles Young American Legion Post. Over 30,000 people, including hundreds who scaled the bleacher fences, were treated to a pitchers' duel between Paige and Slim Jones of the Philadelphia Stars. At the time it was the largest crowd to watch Black baseball in New York.[8]

The story of his first game at Yankee Stadium began in typical Satchel Paige barnstorming fashion. Determined to arrive at the ballpark on time, Paige drove all night from Pittsburgh. He arrived in New York with little time to rent a hotel room, so he parked his car near the Stadium and slept the remainder of the evening. In the morning he was awakened by the batboy, who had been summoned by the Crawfords manager to find Paige. "I got into my uniform just in time to get that first pitch over the plate," Paige recounted in his autobiography, *Maybe I'll Pitch Forever*.[9]

The Stars took an early 1-0 lead and Slim Jones sustained it until the eighth inning, when he fielded a bunt with runners on first and second and made the out at first instead of taking the lead runner, Oscar Charleston, who moved to third base. The next batter, Leroy Morney, drove in Charleston to tie the game. In the ninth inning, with one man on, Paige walked two batters.[10] He then proceeded to strike out the final two batters, including Ameal Brooks on three swings and misses. Chester Washington recounted in the *Pittsburgh Courier*, "It was one of the most momentous occasions in Satchel's life and fans gave him a real ovation for his never-say-die spirit. ..."[11] Paige finished the complete game with 12 strikeouts and three walks. The game was called because of darkness, ending in a 1-1 tie.

Three weeks later, on September 30, a crowd of 35,000 was treated to a rematch between Paige and Jones in another Negro League doubleheader. The game remained scoreless through six innings. The Stars scored their only run in the top of the seventh, then the Crawfords capitalized on two fielding errors

and won, 3-1. Paige was sensational. He pitched a complete game and struck out seven, gave up five hits and did not issue a walk.[12]

Paige returned to Yankee Stadium in the fall of 1937 as member of the Paige All-Stars. Originally named the Santo Domingo Stars, this was a team of ex-Negro Leaguers who left the United States at the beginning of 1937 for better pay and societal freedom in the Dominican Republic. Paige was the ringleader of the move and recruited his Crawfords teammates, including Cool Papa Bell, Leroy Matlock, Sam Bankhead, and Josh Gibson. In a hasty response, Crawfords owner Gus Greenlee banned Paige and his team from organized Black baseball,[13] only to reinstate the group in 1938.[14]

The Paige All-Stars traveled across the United States throughout 1937 and made their way to Yankee Stadium on September 26, in a rematch from a game the week before. On September 19 the Paige All-Stars had lost, 2-0, to young Johnny "Schoolboy" Taylor and a team of Negro League All-Stars at the Polo Grounds. Taylor threw a no-hitter; Paige gave up eight hits.

The rematch at Yankee Stadium was important to Paige, as whispers had begun to circulate that he was no longer considered the best pitcher in baseball. So in front of more than 25,000 spectators on September 26, 1937, Paige put on a clinic "with his dazzling fire-ball, baffling the Leaguers all afternoon."[15] He struck out seven over nine innings and went 1-for-4 at the plate, earning the 9-4 win. That was his last game at Yankee Stadium until 1941.

By 1941 Paige had been pitching professionally for 15 years, and the wear and tear on his arm began to show. While barnstorming through Latin America, Paige experienced a "dead arm" that forced him to return to the United States for medical treatment. He thought his career was over until the owner of the Kansas City Monarchs, J.L. Wilkinson, resurrected it.

Wilkinson had been following Paige's career for several years. He first hired Satchel to pitch for the Kansas City Monarchs when they played against the Chicago American Giants on September 22, 1935, in Chicago. However, Paige was expected to pitch at Yankee Stadium that same day for the Pittsburgh Crawfords, the team that held his contract, but chose a bigger payday. This decision, along with several others over the next three years, would further complicate Paige's relationship with the Crawfords and his future with the team.

In 1938 Crawfords owner Gus Greenlee was forced to sell many of his assets, including Paige, whom he offloaded to the Newark Eagles. Despite the agreement with owners Abe and Effa Manley, Paige did not report to the Eagles.[16] He spent the next three years barnstorming in Mexico, the United States, and Puerto Rico, absent from the public eye, but became the center of the latest Negro League controversy upon his return.

When Paige returned to the United States in 1941, Wilkinson hired him to play for his traveling team, the Baby Monarchs, with the ultimate expectation that he would play for the Kansas City team. Not surprisingly, the Manleys were furious over Wilkinson's move, because Paige was still under contract. The Manleys retaliated by poaching Negro American League players who were under contract. Paige remained with the Monarchs, and the Manleys were allowed to keep the less-talented players they poached as compensation.

Since Paige had been away from Negro League baseball for half a decade, Wilkinson decided that his return to the Negro Leagues required much fanfare and attention. Wilkinson enlisted New York playwrights Moss Hart and George S. Kaufman to craft a momentous return for Paige. They agreed that the stage of Yankee Stadium was befitting for a man of his stature. Thus, Wilkinson loaned Paige to the New York Black Yankees for the Negro National League season opener on May 11, 1941, at Yankee Stadium.[17] Mayor Fiorello LaGuardia threw out the first pitch in front of 20,000 mostly Satchel Paige fans. It was estimated that a quarter to half of the crowd was White despite the New York Giants playing at the Polo Grounds, reinforcing Paige's influence on baseball and his ability to attract fans.[18]

Paige earned the complete-game victory, 5-3, for the Black Yankees. He struck out eight and gave up five hits, relying on a newly developed curveball rather than his blistering fastball to dismantle the Philadelphia Stars.

Two months later, on July 20, 1941, Paige returned to Yankee Stadium, this time as a member of the Kansas City Monarchs. The matchup was against Dave Barnhill and the New York Cubans in the first game of a Negro League doubleheader. In front of an estimated 27,000 fans, the largest crowd at Yankee Stadium that year to watch Black baseball, Paige and the Monarchs dominated the Cubans both offensively and defensively. He struck out three and went 1-for-2 at the plate but had to exit the game in the eighth inning after being hit by a pitch. The Monarchs won, 7-2.[19]

Paige's final appearance at Yankee Stadium in 1941 was on August 24 against the Newark Eagles. The game would have been otherwise a normal outing for the Monarchs and Eagles had it not been for the contentious history between Paige and the Manleys. Paige was exceptional, pitching five scoreless innings and striking out seven. He was 2-for-3 at the plate with a run scored as the Monarchs beat the Eagles, 6-1.[20]

Paige and the Monarchs returned to Yankee Stadium in 1942 for two games, against the New York Cubans and the Homestead Grays. A crowd of 30,000 watched Paige and teammate Hilton Smith shut out the Cubans, 9-0, on August 2; the game was called in the seventh by agreement due to the lopsided score. Paige gave up the only hit in the fourth inning and was replaced by Smith in the fifth.[21]

Game Three of the Negro League World Series was played at Yankee Stadium on September 13, 1942. Paige and the Monarchs had built a 2-0 series lead against the Homestead Grays, winning convincingly in Washington, 8-0, and Pittsburgh, 8-4. Mayor LaGuardia was in attendance once again among a crowd of 25,000.[22] This was Paige's third pitching appearance in as many games, and it showed. He was in a jam early, giving up a two-run home run to Howard Easterling, and was replaced in third inning by Jack Matchett. The Monarchs amassed 16 hits that propelled them to a 9-3 victory and a commanding 3-0 series lead. Paige and the Monarchs went on to win the Negro League World Series, four games to one.[23]

In 1943 Paige and the Monarchs faced Dave Barnhill and the New York Cubans on three occasions at Yankee Stadium. On June 27 Paige coasted through five shutout innings, scattered four hits, and struck out five. The game was tied going into the seventh inning when the Monarchs scored three runs. The Monarchs won the game, 6-3, in front of 22,000 fans, the largest crowd to see Black baseball at Yankee Stadium that year.[24]

As was usual for Black baseball games, the reported attendance varied depending on the source. In game two of a three-game series, an estimated 20,000[25] or 34,000[26] spectators watched Paige face off against Dave Barnhill on August 8. Paige was not his usual self, giving up eight hits over three innings. Jack Matchett replaced him in the fourth inning, but the Cubans were relentless and won, 8-5.

The rubber match at Yankee Stadium was held on September 12. It was a masterful pitchers' duel that capped off the Negro National League season. In the second game of the day for New York, the Cubans shut out Kansas City, 2-0. Barnhill and Paige both pitched complete games, which was uncommon for Paige late in his career. Barnhill gave up just two hits and struck out seven; Paige scattered 10 hits and struck out eight in the loss.[27]

In his only appearance at Yankee Stadium in 1944, Paige pitched in front of 28,000 against the New York Cubans in the second game of a doubleheader on August 26. It was promoted as the rematch between Paige and Johnny "Schoolboy" Taylor from seven years earlier. It was also the first game since Taylor's return to Negro League baseball after he spent the previous two years working in a defense factory. Paige pitched five solid innings and struck out five to earn the 4-2 win.[28]

In 1945 Paige pitched twice at Yankee Stadium. On June 17, against the Philadelphia Stars, he threw six scoreless innings and retired 11 men in a row but did not factor in the decision, a 3-1 win.[29] Two months later, on August 12, Paige pitched another gem, striking out eight Black Yankees and giving up four hits over six innings to lead the Monarchs to a 4-1 win.[30]

In 1946, his 20th year pitching professionally, Paige continued to defy Father Time, especially while pitching at Yankee Stadium. At this point in his career, Paige did not pitch complete games, but he was able to put together meaningful and efficient outings with his fastball and pitch location.

"Paige Sparkles, But Mates Lose to N.Y." read the headline in the *Pittsburgh Courier* for the July 7, 1946, game between the Black Yankees and Monarchs.[31] Paige pitched five innings, held the Black Yankees to two hits, struck out six, and did not give up a run. He was replaced in the sixth by Hilton Smith, who gave up four runs. Kansas City lost the game, 4-3, in 10 innings.

Three weeks later, on August 1, Paige and the Monarchs had their revenge, blanking the Black Yankees, 10-0. It was Yankee Stadium's first Negro League night baseball game.[32] Paige was sensational and efficient; in five scoreless innings, he faced 18 batters, had five strikeouts, and did not issue a walk.[33] On September 15, 1946, in the final season game at Yankee Stadium, the Black Yankees won, 3-1. Paige pitched three scoreless innings in front of 11,000 fans.[34]

At the end of the major-league baseball season, on October 6, 1946, Bob Feller and his All-Stars battled Paige and his All-Stars before a crowd of 27,463 at Yankee Stadium. Paige and Feller each pitched five innings, and it was Paige who triumphed. He struck

out four batters to Feller's none and gave up three hits, blanking the Feller All-Stars, 4-0.[35]

In 1947 Paige and the Monarchs were walloped, 8-3, by the New York Cubans on August 8. Paige gave up three hits and one unearned run.[36] The Monarchs returned to Yankee Stadium on August 24 to take on the New York Black Yankees in the second game of a Black Yankees doubleheader. The teams played to a scoreless tie that was called by agreement in the 10th inning.[37]

HIS TIME HAS COME

It seemed like a publicity stunt at the time, but when Bill Veeck signed Satchel Paige for the Cleveland Indians on July 7, 1948, on Paige's 42nd birthday no less, he did it to give his youthful pitching staff veteran experience. Veeck said, "We are convinced he is the best available player who has a chance to help us win the pennant."[38] And that he did. Paige played a pivotal role in the 1948 World Series championship season for Cleveland and was called upon three times to pitch in relief against the Yankees at Yankee Stadium.

By July 21, the Indians were in first place in the American League, 3½ games ahead of the fourth-place Yankees. New York hosted Cleveland in a doubleheader. In game one, the Yankees won, 7-3, on Eddie Lopat's complete game. In game two, run production was plentiful, and by the bottom of the sixth inning, when Paige entered the game, the Yankees were ahead 8-4. Paige was spectacular in one inning of work, holding Tommy Henrich, Yogi Berra, and Joe DiMaggio to a strikeout, a groundout, and a fly out respectively. In the top of the seventh, Cleveland cut the deficit to 8-7 and then won the game, 12-8, tying the series at one game apiece.

In the rubber match the next day, the Yankees scored six times off Bob Feller and took a 6-5 lead into the bottom of the sixth, when Paige came in. He gave up a single to Tommy Byrne and then retired Snuffy Stirnweiss, Tommy Henrich, and Charlie Keller. In the bottom of the seventh, Paige struck out DiMaggio, but DiMaggio reached first on an error by catcher Jim Hegan. Paige then retired the next three Yankees. However, Cleveland came up short and lost, 6-5.

On August 27, 1948, Cleveland visited New York for a doubleheader that was created by a rainout in May. Cleveland was a half-game ahead of the third-place Yankees and a half-game behind the first-place Red Sox. Cleveland routed New York, 8-1, in game one, and New York returned the favor in game two. Paige pitched in the bottom of the eighth inning of the second game with the Indians down 7-1 and retired the side on two fly-ball outs and a strikeout. Cleveland scored just once more in the top of the ninth and lost 7-2.

In the 1949 season, the defending World Series champions were in fourth place by June 18 when Paige made a rare start against New York ace Vic Raschi. This decision proved costly for Cleveland, which had won six games in a row. Paige walked three of the first four batters and gave up five hits and three earned runs. The *Brooklyn Daily Eagle* wrote that his performance "left a lot to be desired for."[39] But the loss was not squarely on Paige; the Cleveland offense failed to produce as Raschi held them to seven hits and drove in a run of his own with a triple off Paige. Paige was replaced in the sixth and suffered his fourth loss of the season.

Cleveland faced New York on July 25 riding a four-game winning streak. Paige relieved Early Wynn in the bottom of the eighth and got six consecutive fly-ball outs, securing a 4-2 victory and his fourth save of the season. This was an important game for Cleveland; the win put the Indians three games behind the Yankees. This was the last game Paige pitched at Yankee Stadium for a World Series and pennant contender. Bill Veeck sold the Indians after the 1949 season, and the new ownership offered Paige one-quarter of his 1949 salary for the coming season. Paige declined and left the majors to barnstorm.

In 1951 Paige had been receiving offers to return to major-league baseball and consulted his friend Bill Veeck for advice. Veeck asked Paige to hang tight as he had something in the works. By midsummer, Veeck had purchased the St. Louis Browns, and within a week Paige was signed. Reported attendance nearly doubled, from 293,790 in 1951 to 518,796 in 1952 after Paige's first full season with the team, despite the Browns being the worst team in baseball.

However, when the Browns returned to Yankee Stadium with Paige on September 11, 1951, they swept the doubleheader against the eventual 1951 World Series champion Yankees, 4-3 and 6-3. In the second game of the doubleheader, Paige relieved ex-Yankee Tommy Byrne in the sixth inning. He pitched 3⅓ innings of one-hit ball and secured the 6-3 victory and his fifth save of the season.

Paige pitched in four games at Yankee Stadium in 1952. His appearances ranged from less than one inning of work to a seven-inning outing that included extra innings. The Browns were still at the bottom of

the league, but when Paige pitched at Yankee Stadium, the games were competitive.

Paige's first pitching appearance in 1952 at Yankee Stadium was on April 30. He replaced Bob Cain in the bottom of the seventh with the Browns up 8-4 and a runner on first base. Paige retired Gene Woodling, Yogi Berra, and Johnny Mize to end the inning. In the bottom of the eighth, with two outs, Paige gave up a single to Mickey Mantle, then struck out Joe Collins. He continued his dominant performance in the ninth inning, shutting down the Yankees and earning his first save of the season in the 9-4 victory. Paige allowed one hit and one walk and struck out two in three innings. On June 7 the Browns lost to the Yankees, 2-1. Paige uncharacteristically walked two Yankees in the bottom of the eighth but did not give up a run.

In his longest pitching appearance at Yankee Stadium since he pitched a complete game in a loss to Dave Barnhill on September 12, 1943, Paige replaced Stubby Overmire in the bottom of the fourth of a 4-4 game on July 12. He pitched spectacularly for seven innings as the game went into extra innings, but the Yankees offense ultimately proved too much for the lanky veteran.

In the bottom of the 11th inning, Yogi Berra singled off Paige and went to second on a bunt single to third by Gil McDougald. Gene Woodling singled to load the bases. Pinch-hitter Johnny Mize popped out to the shortstop. Then pitcher Allie Reynolds hit a single to center field that scored Berra to end the game, 5-4. It was Paige's fifth loss of the season.

Paige made his final 1952 appearance at Yankee Stadium on August 26, another heartbreaking walk-off loss. In the ninth, with the game tied 3-3, the Browns intentionally walked Mantle, a lifetime .500 hitter in eight at-bats against Paige, to pitch to Joe Collins. Collins was 2-for-9 against Paige with three strike-outs and no home runs until he belted a line drive into the right-field stands with two Yankees aboard. It was Paige's ninth loss of the season.[40]

Paige called his 1953 season the worst he ever had.[41] He finished with a 3-9 record and a 3.53 ERA. It was his last full major-league season. Veeck sold the Browns in the offseason; the new ownership moved the team to Baltimore and let Paige go.

Paige made four relief appearances at Yankee Stadium in 1953 that included his shortest outing. On May 17 he replaced Don Larsen in the bottom of the ninth with two outs and the game tied, 4-4. He walked Gil McDougald, then was replaced by Virgil Trucks, who got a groundout to end the inning. The Yankees won, 6-5, in extra innings.

A month later, on June 16, Paige and the Browns defeated the Yankees, 3-1. The win ended both the Browns' 14-game losing streak and the Yankees' 18-game winning streak. After the game Paige said, "There's no team I like to beat better than them Yankees."[42] He pitched 1⅔ innings of shutout ball to secure the win for the Browns and earn his sixth save of the season. Paige was especially proud of this outing, saying, "I had that Mantle kid so confused he tried to bunt on a third strike. Imagine a fool thing like that. A home run hitter to bunt with two strikes on him."[43]

Two days later, on June 18, Paige was not as sharp when he replaced Bob Cain in the seventh inning with the Browns down 1-0 and Yankee runners on first and second. Paige gave up an inherited run on a single by Billy Martin with the bases loaded. His afternoon was done the following inning when he was pinch-hit for. The Yankees blanked the Browns, 3-0.

Paige's final appearance at Yankee Stadium, on September 16, 1953, came more than 19 years after his first. He replaced Duane Pillette in the bottom of the sixth with one out, the bases loaded, and a 4-1 lead. He gave up a single to Willy Miranda that scored Hank Bauer, but Johnny Mize was thrown out trying to score from second to end the inning.

Paige breezed through the seventh inning but was challenged in the eighth and ninth. The Yankees scored with two outs in the bottom of the eighth on a pinch-hit single by Mantle. Then Don Bollweg flied out. In the top of the ninth, Paige helped his cause by hitting a fielder's choice grounder that scored Jim Dyck and increased the Browns' lead to 5-3. In the bottom of the ninth with one out, Bill Renna hit a double to right field. Andy Carey flied out to deep center but Renna did not tag. Paige walked Irv Noren, then got Hank Bauer fly out, ending the game. It was Paige's 11th and final save of the season and the last time he pitched at Yankee Stadium.

Paige is immortalized in the annals of baseball history for his showmanship, blistering fastball, pinpoint accuracy, and a number of apocryphal tales of his playing days. He pitched in a plethora of sandlots and ballparks throughout his career that paled in comparison to the vaunted Yankee Stadium. Each of Paige's 34 appearances at Yankee Stadium contributed to his legendary career and demonstrated his versatility as a pitcher and tenacity as an athlete. But what stands out the most when Paige pitched in Yankee Stadium was his ability to draw a crowd and entertain the masses. The greatest showman in baseball deserved the greatest stage. And there was no greater stage in baseball than Yankee Stadium, and no greater showman than Satchel Paige.

SOURCES

In addition to the sources cited in the Notes, the author consulted Baseball-reference.com, https://www.baseball-almanac.com/teams/yankatte.shtml, and the following:

Sullivan, Neil J. *The Diamond in the Bronx: Yankee Stadium and the Politics of New York* (New York: Oxford Press, 2008).

NOTES

1   James Overmyer, "Black Baseball at Yankee Stadium: The House That Ruth Built and Satchel Furnished (with Fans)," SABR.org, https://sabr.org/journal/article/black-baseball-at-yankee-stadium-the-house-that-ruth-built-and-satchel-furnished-with-fans/, accessed June 2022.

2   Paige's birthdate has been reported differently at times. We use the date as provided by Seamheads.com.

3   Joe Posnanski, *The Baseball 100* (Avid Reader Press: New York, 2021), 707.

4   The average attendance for games Paige pitched at Yankee Stadium was determined conservatively, using the newspaper reported attendance cited in Notes 8, 12, 15, 18-22, 24, 25, 27-32, 34-37 and dividing by 20, for the number of games pitched.

5   Average attendance at Yankee Stadium for New York Yankee games was determined from https://www.baseball-almanac.com/teams/yankatte.shtml.

6   Larry Tye, *Satchel The Life and Times of An American Legend* (New York: Random House, 2009), 63.

7   Tye, 63.

8   William E. Clarke, "30,000 Attend Four-Team Double Header at Yankee Stadium," *New York Age,* September 15, 1934: 5.

9   Leroy (Satchel) Paige, *Maybe I'll Pitch Forever* (South Orange, New Jersey: Summer Game Books, 2018), 67.

10 Paige was known to intentionally walk the bases loaded for show. However, this was not the case in this game.

11 Chester L. Washington, "Paige Fans 12 to Shade Jones in Hot Mound Duel," *Pittsburgh Courier,* September 15, 1934: 14

12 C. Augustus Austin, "35,000 Fans See Black Yankees and Pittsburgh Crawfords Defeat Chicago and Phila. At Stadium," *New York Age,* October 6, 1934: 5.

13 Tye, 110-111.

14 Tye, 117.

15 "25,000 Watch Satchel Get Revenge Over All-Stars in Yankee Stadium," *Pittsburgh Courier,* October 2, 1937: 16.

16 In *Maybe I'll Pitch Forever*, Paige said of Greenlee and the trade "Only he was selling a piece of paper and not the real stuff. Whatever happened, I didn't pay much attention to it down in Mexico." *Maybe I'll Pitch Forever,* 105.

17 Tye, 146.

18 "18,000 Thrilled as Satchel Paige Returns in Triumph in N.Y.," *Pittsburgh Courier,* May 17, 1941: 16.

19 Maurice Dancer, "27,500 See KC and Paige Defeat Cubans," *Chicago Defender,* July 26, 1941: 23.

20 St. Clair Bourne, "Monarchs Trounce Eagles, 6-1; Cubans Top Philadelphia, 4-3," *New York Amsterdam Star-News*, August 30, 1941: 18.

21 "Paige in Form Before 30,000 Fans," *Greenville* (Ohio) *Daily Advocate*, August 3, 1942: 5.

22 "25,000 See Monarchs Defeat Grays, 9 to 3," *New York Times,* September 14, 1942: 21.

23 Dave Barr, "The 1942 Negro Leagues World Series – A Story That's Hard to Tell," MLB.com/blogs, October 29, 2013, accessed August 30, 2022, https://nlbm.mlblogs.com/the-1942-negro-leagues-world-series-a-story-thats-hard-to-tell-b085462d2a41.

24 Wendell Smith, "Paige Stars as Monarchs Win in Yankee Stadium," *Pittsburgh Courier*, July 3, 1943: 18.

25 Wendell Smith, "'Satch' Is Blasted Before 20,000 Fans at Yankee Stadium," *Pittsburgh Courier*, August 14, 1943: 18.

26 Daniel, "Cuban Stars Defeat Monarchs and Philly," *New York Amsterdam News,* August 14, 1943: 15.

27 "Barnhill Gives Up 2 Hits; Beats Satchell, 2-0," *New York Amsterdam News*, September 18, 1943: 20.

28 Wendell Smith, "28,000 See Cubans Top Barons: Lose to K.C.," *Pittsburgh Courier,* September 2, 1944: 12.

29 "14,000 Witness Paige Score Four Hits At Yankee Stadium, Sun," *New York Age,* June 23, 1945: 11.

30 Haskell Cole, "Paige Sparkles as Kansas City Triumphs," *Pittsburgh Courier,* August 13, 1945: 12.

31 Haskell Cole, "Paige Sparkles, But Mates Lose to N.Y.," *Pittsburgh Courier*, July 13, 1946: 16.

32 "Paige Halts Black Yanks: Stars as Monarchs Triumph in Stadium Night Game, 10-0," *New York Times*, August 2, 1946: 25.

33 "Paige Halts Black Yanks."

34 "Black Yankees Beat Monarch Nine by 6 to 1," *New York Amsterdam News*, September 21, 1946: 13.

35 "Paige's All-Stars Rout Feller's, 4-0," *New York Times,* October 7, 1946: 25.

36 "Cubans Triumph by 8-3," *New York Times,* August 9, 1947: 8.

37 "Black Yanks Win and Tie," *New York Times* August 25, 1947: 20.

38 Associated Press, "Indians Sign Fabulous Satchel Paige," *Syracuse Post-Standard,* July 8, 1948: 14.

39 "Raschi Subdues Indians for No. 11," *Brooklyn Daily Eagle,* June 19, 1949: 22.

40 Associated Press, "Tribe Beats A's; Yanks Win 6-3," *Waco News-Tribune,* August 27, 1952: 12.

41 *Maybe I'll Pitch Forever,* 233.

42 Ben Phlegar (Associated Press), "Brownies Elated at Yank-Kill," *Mt. Vernon* (Illinois) *Register News*, June 17, 1953: 10.

43 Joe Reichler (Associated Press), "Satchel Confesses He's Best Relief Pitcher in Game Today," *Alton* (Illinois) *Evening Telegraph,* June 19, 1953: 16.

LOU GEHRIG'S FAREWELL SPEECH

July 4, 1939

By Paul Hofmann

Lou Gehrig played his final game for the New York Yankees on April 30, 1939. Though only 35 years old, the Iron Horse, who played in 2,130 consecutive games, had been diagnosed with amyotrophic lateral sclerosis (ALS).[1] To honor their stricken star, the Yankees held Lou Gehrig Appreciation Day on July 4, 1939.

The Independence Day doubleheader pitted the sixth-place Washington Senators, who entered play with a 28-42 record, 24½ games off the pace, and the three-time defending World Series champion New York Yankees, who were 51-16, 12½ games clear of the second-place Boston Red Sox. The games were overshadowed by the ceremony that took place between them. It was Lou Gehrig Appreciation Day and 61,808 fans jammed into Yankee Stadium to pay homage to the Yankees' ailing star.

While Gehrig dressed in the clubhouse, some of his old teammates dropped in to say hello, including Mark Koenig, Wally Schang, Herb Pennock, Bob Shawkey, Benny Bengough, George Pipgras. Tony Lazzeri, Earle Combs, Joe Dugan, Waite Hoyt, Bob Meusel,

A packed crowd of 61,808 fans heard Lou Gehrig make his "Luckiest Man" speech between games of a doubleheader against Washington.

Everett Scott, and Wally Pipp, who faded away as the Yankees' first baseman the day Gehrig took over back in 1925.[2] Missing from the clubhouse was Babe Ruth. Ruth had yet to arrive and, given Ruth and Gehrig's relationship, everyone wondered whether the Bambino would show up.

Ruth and Gehrig couldn't have been more different. Ruth was a brash and boorish free spirit who had a casual and often defiant way of dealing with authority. He was also fun-loving and charismatic, with an ego that craved the spotlight. By contrast, Gehrig was modest and reserved, avoiding public attention. He was the consummate company man. Given these differences, it seemed unlikely that a relationship beyond the playing field would have materialized.[3] However, a close relationship between the two did develop and from the very beginning it was complicated.

In the early years, Ruth was a mentor whom Gehrig idolized. Columbia Lou never believed that he could be Ruth's equal. "The only real home run hitter that has ever lived," Gehrig once said in reference to Ruth. "I'm fortunate to be even close to him."[4] The two developed a close relationship. Sharing confidences, eating, traveling and barnstorming together, playing cards, swapping batting tips, fishing and golfing together, Ruth and Gehrig should have grown closer with the passing years.[5] Instead they grew apart and the relationship entered a period of estrangement, when each refused to speak to the other.

In the opener of the doubleheader, the Senators scored two first-inning runs in support of right-hander Dutch Leonard (8-2), who limited the Yankees to six hits and helped his own cause with a sixth-inning RBI single. Right-hander Monte Pearson (7-2) suffered the loss for Yankees, who managed a single run in the third and another in the ninth on a one-out home run by right fielder George Selkirk as the Senators hung on for a 3-2 victory.

Ruth arrived in plenty of time for the ceremony, wearing a cream-colored suit and looking tanned and rested. By the late 1930s, Ruth had ballooned to 270 pounds and was beginning to experience some health problems of his own.[6]

After the first game, microphones were set up behind home plate for the ceremony. Sid Mercer, dean of beat reporters covering the Yankees, served as emcee for the event. New York Mayor Fiorello La Guardia officially extended the city's appreciation of the service Gehrig had given to his hometown. The mayor praised Gehrig as "the greatest prototype of good sportsmanship and citizenship."[7] Postmaster

General James Farley, also in attendance, concluded his remarks with "for generations to come, boys who play baseball will point with pride to your record."[8]

Ruth then took a turn at the microphone. Though their relationship had been troubled, Ruth never held a grudge and seemed happy to be reunited with his old friend. In his own blustering style, Ruth gave his unqualified opinion that the 1927 Yankees were better than the 1939 edition. Summarizing his belief, Ruth said, "In 1927 Lou was with us, and I say that was the greatest ballclub the Yankees ever had."[9] The Sultan of Swat continued, "I know Lou is going to keep that stiff upper lip and he's gonna keep on going."[10]

Mercer then introduced Gehrig to the huge throng in attendance and millions listening on radios across the country. Head bowed, Gehrig stood silent until he privately whispered something to Mercer, who returned to the microphone and told the crowd and listening audience, "Lou has asked me to thank you all for him. He is too moved to speak."[11] The response to Mercer's remark was chants of "We want Gehrig!" throughout the ballpark.[12]

As the chants continued, Gehrig took a handkerchief from his pocket, wiped away his tears and moved toward the microphones once again. Head bowed, he spoke slowly and evenly as he delivered the most memorable farewell speech in baseball history. While no complete recording or transcript of the speech is known to exist, one commonly accepted version is as follows:

> "Fans, for the past two weeks you have been reading about the bad break. Today I consider myself the luckiest man on the face of the earth. I have been in ballparks for seventeen years and have never received anything but kindness and encouragement from you fans.
>
> "When you look around, wouldn't you consider it a privilege to associate yourself with such a fine looking men as they're standing in uniform in this ballpark today? Which of you wouldn't consider it the highlight of his career just to associate with them for even one day? Sure, I'm lucky. Who wouldn't consider it an honor to have known Jacob Ruppert? Also, the builder of baseball's greatest empire, Ed Barrow? To have spent six years with that wonderful little fellow Miller Huggins? Then to have spent the next nine years with that outstanding leader, that smart student of psychology,

the best manager in baseball today, Joe McCarthy? Sure, I'm lucky.

"When the New York Giants, a team you would give your right arm to beat, and vice versa, sends you a gift – that's something. When everybody down to the groundskeepers and those boys in white coats remember you with trophies – that's something. When you have a wonderful mother-in-law who takes sides with you in squabbles with her own daughter – that's something. When you have a father and a mother who work all their lives so you can have an education and build your body – it's a blessing. When you have a wife who has been a tower of strength and shown more courage than you dreamed existed – that's the finest I know.

"So I close in saying that I might have been given a bad break, but I have an awful lot to live for. Thank you."[13]

Like many in attendance, Ruth was moved to tears by Gehrig's brief speech. The Babe went over to shake his old friend's hand but impulsively put his arm around Gehrig and hugged him – ending the long-standing and petty feud between them.[14] It was the first time Gehrig cracked a smile all day. As they embraced, a tearful Ruth couldn't have imagined he would be facing a similar crowd under very similar circumstances less than a decade later.

After the ceremony, Gehrig returned to the clubhouse, where he saw right-hander Steve Sundra, who was slated to start the nightcap for the Yankees. Gehrig went to Sundra and said, "Big Steve, win the second game for me, will ya?"[15]

Sundra (5-0) delivered a six-hit complete game and the Yankees scored six runs in the first three innings off Venezuelan rookie right-hander Alex Carrasquel (4-6) on their way to an 11-1 victory. Selkirk paced the Yankees' hitting attack with three hits, including a home run, while second baseman Joe Gordon drove in four runs for the Yankees. Right fielder Taffy Wright accounted for the Senators lone run with a second-inning home run.

On June 2, 1941, Gehrig died at his home.

SOURCES

In addition to the sources cited in the Notes, the author consulted Baseball-Reference.com and Retrosheet.org.

NOTES

1   Amyotrophic lateral sclerosis, commonly known as ALS or Lou Gehrig's disease, is an incurable fatal neuromuscular disease. The disease attacks nerve cells in the brain and spinal cord. Motor neurons, which control the movement of voluntary muscles, deteriorate and eventually die. When the motor neurons die, the brain can no longer initiate and control muscle movement. Because muscles no longer receive the messages they need in order to function, they gradually weaken and deteriorate, resulting in paralysis.

2   John Drebinger, "61,808 Fans Roar Tribute to Gehrig: Chief Figure at the Stadium and Old-Time Yankees who Gathered in His Honor," *New York Times,* July 5, 1939: 21.

3   Jonathan Eig. *Luckiest Man: The Life and Death of Lou Gehrig* (New York: Simon & Schuster, 2005), 97.

4   Eig, 100.

5   Ray Robinson, "Ruth and Gehrig: Friction Between Gods," *New York Times*, June 2, 1991: 394.

6   Ruth experienced the first of two heart attacks while playing golf in 1939.

7   Drebinger, "61,808 Fans Roar Tribute to Gehrig."

8   Drebinger.

9   Eig, 315.

10   July 4, 1989-Tigers vs. Yankees (WPIX-Part 2), www.youtube.com/watch?v=uhUL-ff8NQw (accessed August 15, 2022).

11   Rosaleen Doherty, "Wife Brave, Lou Shaken as 61,000 Cheer Gehrig," *New York Daily News,* July 5, 1939: 120.

12   Doherty.

13   Transcript adapted from "Farewell Speech," lougehrig.com/index.php/farewell-speech/.

14   Robert Creamer, *Babe: The Legend Comes to Life* (New York: Simon & Schuster, 1974), 415.

15   "Pages Out of the Past," *Atlantic City Evening Union,* January 18, 1952, as cited by David Skelton, "Steve Sundra," SABR BioProject, https://sabr.org/bioproj/person/3c2f6fad.

SAFE AT HOME: BABE RUTH AT THE "HOUSE THAT RUTH BUILT," 1939-1948

By Dan Neumann

The story of Yankee Stadium cannot be told without telling the story of Babe Ruth. His home-field exploits during his playing days are well covered, but a study of his later appearances at the Stadium is equally valuable. Each unique its own way, these appearances provide valuable insight into Ruth as a player, a teammate, a celebrity, and an American icon.

The Babe left the Yankees after the 1934 season, playing one year in Boston before retiring as a player in 1935. His relationship with the Yankees was strained in the ensuing years, and he did not formally return to Yankee Stadium until the famed Lou Gehrig Day in 1939. For the next decade, until his death in 1948, Ruth appeared at the Stadium on several occasions, each time to thundering ovations from throngs of adoring fans.

LOU GEHRIG DAY (JULY 4, 1939)

Ruth left the Yankees after the 1934 season, spending a few months with the Boston Braves in 1935 before quitting as a player. Frustrated at his lack of managerial opportunities, Ruth kept his distance from the game, and was rarely seen at Yankee Stadium during the latter half of the 1930s. In 1936, when Ruth asked for tickets to Opening Day, he was instructed to send a check to the team offices.[1] By the late 1930s, the relationship between the team and its most legendary player was clearly a strained one.

Ruth and Lou Gehrig were teammates on the Yankees from Gehrig's debut in 1923 until Ruth left the team. The had not spoken in five years, with the cause of the rift never definitively determined. The two had even traded barbs in the press a few years earlier.[2] In early 1939 Gehrig announced his retirement after being diagnosed with amyotrophic lateral sclerosis, the illness that would eventually take his life. The Yankees organized a Lou Gehrig Day in Gehrig's honor between games of a doubleheader against the Detroit Tigers on July 4. The 1927 Murderers Row team was invited to return to the Stadium and honor their captain. Attendees included future Hall of Famers Tony Lazzeri, Waite Hoyt, Earle Combs, and Herb Pennock, as well as Wally Pipp, the first baseman whose injury famously made a place for Gehrig in the Yankees lineup. Retired pitcher George Pipgras was also there, although the trip was less arduous for him than for the others. Pipgras was now an American League umpire and was assigned to work that day's doubleheader.[3]

Ruth arrived late to the proceedings, dressed in a white suit and two-tone shoes, and sporting a dark tan.[4] Several men gave speeches paying tribute to Gehrig, including Mayor Fiorello La Guardia, Postmaster General James Farley, and Yankees manager Joe McCarthy.[5] Ruth then gave a brief speech praising Gehrig and expressing his belief that, even in 1939, he and his former teammates would defeat the present-day team.[6] The two men shook hands, and Ruth wrapped his arms around Gehrig in an embrace. Gehrig then delivered his famous "Luckiest Man" speech.[7]

The Ruth/Gehrig hug has been the source of debate in the ensuing years. The day (and Ruth's gesture) is often cited as bringing an end to the feud between the two men. Biographer Robert Creamer writes that the embrace "ended the long antagonism" between the two men.[8] Others, including Hall of Fame catcher Bill Dickey, were more skeptical. Discussing a picture of the two on that day, Dickey said that "if you look close, Lou never put his arm around the Babe. Lou just never forgave him." The two, Dickey claimed, were "never friends again."[9] Pictures from that day do show Gehrig's arm around Ruth, albeit with a grasp much looser than the Babe's. Gehrig's grin is rather sheepish, compared to the beaming Babe. Whether or not this evidences a dislike for Ruth would be impossible to determine. Gehrig's personality was naturally less gregarious than Ruth's, even when putting aside the emotion of the day and Gehrig's natural sadness and exhaustion accompanying his illness and the end of his career.

The two were photographed together at the 1939 World Series in Yankee Stadium, but it is unclear how often (if at all) the two visited prior to Gehrig's death in June 1941.[10]

RUTH BATS AGAINST WALTER JOHNSON TO BENEFIT THE WAR EFFORT (AUGUST 23, 1942)

With American entry into World War II, Ruth frequently donated his time to raising money for the war effort. He played a series of golf matches against Ty Cobb to benefit war charities and bowled against New York Giants football star Ken Strong for the same purpose.[11] He visited veterans hospitals and sent recorded messages to the troops.[12] Ruth's part in the war was not limited to his roles as a fundraiser and a morale booster. A widely circulated story at the time told of Japanese soldiers shouting "To hell with Babe Ruth!" as they attacked American soldiers. Upon hearing this, Ruth angrily destroyed most of the souvenir items he had brought back from his barnstorming trip to Japan a decade earlier.[13]

In 1942 Ruth returned to a more familiar sport in a charity benefit at Yankee Stadium. Donning the Yankees uniform for the first time since 1934, Ruth batted against legendary pitcher Walter Johnson in a fundraiser for the Army-Navy Fund. Ruth hit Johnson's fifth pitch into the right-field stands. The 20th pitch was driven into the upper deck, although just foul. This was good enough for the Babe, however, as he circled the bases, doffing his cap to the crowd of over 70,000.[14] "I knew I couldn't top that," Ruth said later.[15] Together Ruth and Johnson raised more than $80,000 for the Army-Navy Fund.[16]

While clearly the highlight of the fundraiser, the matchup between the two legends was only part of the day's special activities. Yankees and Senators players took part in several athletic competitions. Senators George Case and Johnny Sullivan were victorious in a sprint over Tuck Stainback and Johnny Lindell. The two also joined Mickey Vernon and Ellis Clary on a victorious sprinting team over Charlie Keller, Tommy Henrich, Joe Gordon, and George Selkirk. Washington Senator Al Evans won the accuracy throwing contest for catchers (defeating Bill Dickey among others) and tied for the lead in a "barrel pitching" contest. Only Yankees pitcher Norm Branch was victorious in an event. He won the fungo-hitting contest with a distance of 376 feet.[17]

RUTH'S LAST "GAME" IN YANKEES PINSTRIPES (JULY 28, 1943)

Pitcher Johnny Sain is perhaps best known as one half of the "Spahn and Sain" duo on the Boston Braves of the late 1940s. He won 20 games four times for the Braves and was a three-time World Series winner with the Yankees of the early 1950s. He is also the

On September 28, 1947, the Bambino made an appearance before a game benefitting his Babe Ruth Foundation – later recognized as the first Old-Timers Day.

answer to a somewhat misleading trivia question, as he is cited as the first pitcher to face Jackie Robinson in the major leagues, and the last to pitch against Babe Ruth in an organized game.[18]

The Robinson piece is true enough, as Sain was the starting pitcher for the Braves against the Brooklyn Dodgers on April 15, 1947. The Ruth piece is a bit more misleading. In July 1943, while serving in the military, Sain was pitching in an exhibition game at Yankee Stadium against a team managed by Ruth. Ruth inserted himself as a pinch-hitter against Sain, hitting one long foul before walking.[19] "Between me and the ump, we walked the Babe," Sain said years later.[20] Ruth initially refused a pinch-runner, and the next batter singled. After coming up "lame and puffing," in the words of biographer Robert Creamer, Ruth submitted to the pinch-runner and jogged off the Yankee Stadium field. It was his last appearance in a formal game at Yankee Stadium.[21]

BABE RUTH DAY (APRIL 27, 1947)

Hospitalized and diagnosed with throat cancer in late 1946, Ruth had less than 18 months to live by the time the 1947 baseball season began. Commissioner Happy Chandler declared April 27 to be Babe Ruth Day in all major-league ballparks, with the minor leagues soon following suit. No baseball figure had been honored with a national commemoration day since Harry Wright in 1896.[22] Only two years after the end of World War II, when Japanese soldiers were shouting "To hell with Babe Ruth!" the Bambino was also honored with ceremonies in Tokyo and Osaka.[23]

The ceremony that day lasted only 10 minutes, with speakers including Cardinal Francis Spellman and Commissioner Happy Chandler. Chandler was loudly booed by the New York fans because of his recent one-year suspension of Dodgers manager and one-time Ruth roommate Leo Durocher for associating with gamblers.[24]

With his voice ravaged by cancer, Ruth began his speech by noting that "you know how bad my voice sounds, well it feels just as bad."[25] He had not prepared a speech, and his extemporaneous remarks were largely a tribute to the game he loved: "You know this baseball game of ours comes up from the youth. That means the boys. And after you've been a boy and grow up to know how to play ball, then you come to the boys you see representing themselves today in our national pastime. The only real game in the world, I think, baseball."[26] The speech, which was broadcast to every ballpark in the major leagues where a game was being played that day.[27] brought tears to the eyes of the 58,339 assembled fans. Longtime Yankees general manager Ed Barrow, who had also managed Ruth with the 1918 Red Sox, had retired earlier that year but attended the ceremonies at Yankee Stadium that day. He refused to go down onto the field. "I never did like to cry in public," Barrow told a reporter.[28]

THE "OTHER" BABE RUTH DAY (SEPTEMBER 28, 1947)

Largely forgotten between the Babe Ruth Day of April 1947 and the Babe's final appearance of June 1948 is the second "Babe Ruth Day," held in September 1947 to benefit the Babe Ruth Foundation. Ruth had established this foundation earlier in 1947 to benefit underprivileged children.[29] In the months since his April appearance, doctors had begun treating Ruth's cancer with an experimental drug. He had improved rapidly and had begun traveling the country doing promotional work on American Legion baseball for the Ford Motor Company.[30] So remarkable was Ruth's improvement that he hoped to pitch an inning during the September game. In actuality, the "miraculous recovery" was merely a temporary remission of the Babe's cancer. By late September his health was in decline again and he was forced to watch the game from the stands.[31]

Ruth's former teammates and adversaries traveled to Yankee Stadium to attend or play in the game. These included future Hall of Famers Waite Hoyt, Earle Combs, Harry Hooper, Tris Speaker, Jimmie Foxx, Charlie Gehringer, and even the 80-year-old Cy Young.[32] A contemporary newspaper account described the event as "one of the most remarkable pageants ever seen in a baseball arena."[33] The most memorable performance came from Ty Cobb, who was flown from Nevada to New York on Yankees owner Del Webb's private plane.[34] Cobb, now 60 years old, led off the game in the first inning. He turned to catcher Wally Schang and said, "Would you mind backing up a bit? I'm an old man now, and I can barely hold on to this bat. I am worried I will hit you with it."[35] Schang respectfully obliged, only for Cobb to lay down a bunt and attempt to beat it out for a hit. He missed by only a step. After the game, Cobb and Ruth were photographed together for the last time. In his book on the relationship between the two men, author Tom Stanton writes, "Whether from pain or medication or emotion, Ruth's eyes were wet when Cobb laid his hand on Ruth's right shoulder. The moisture caught the flash of the camera."[36]

A few days later, Ruth, Cobb, and Young attended Game One of the 1947 World Series at Yankee Stadium. The fans stood and applauded Ruth after the National Anthem. Wearing an oversized camel's-hair coat and smoking a cigar, Ruth gingerly stood and waved to the crowd.[37]

RUTH'S FINAL YANKEE STADIUM VISIT AND NUMBER RETIREMENT (JUNE 13, 1948)

To celebrate the 25th anniversary of Yankee Stadium, the Yankees scheduled a celebration on June 13, 1948. The centerpiece of this celebration was the retirement of Ruth's number 3. Nearly ubiquitous in twenty-first-century American sports, number retirements had not yet attained their place in the American consciousness. Only Gehrig and Giants pitcher Carl Hubbell had been so honored in baseball, joined by a handful of players in the NFL and NHL.[38] In the decade and a half since Ruth left the team, the number had been worn by journeymen like Bud Metheny, Eddie Bockman, Roy Weatherly, Allie Clark, and Frank Colman.[39] The current wearer was outfielder Cliff Mapes, who switched briefly to number 13 before settling on 7, a number he wore until he was traded to Detroit in 1951. Later that same year, Mickey Mantle donned number 7, making Mapes one of the last Yankees to wear 7 before *it* was retired.[40]

The cool, rainy weather set the stage for what one Ruth biographer has described as a "maudlin ceremony."[41] Several of Ruth's teammates had died young, including future Hall of Famers Lazzeri, Pennock, and Gehrig.[42] Members of the 1923 team (the first to call Yankee Stadium home), participated in a two-inning exhibition against "old-timers" from later Yankees teams. Participating members of the '23 team included Waite Hoyt, Wally Pipp, Carl Mays, and Wally Schang, who was likely glad Ty Cobb was not playing in this game.[43] The latter-day team included Red Rolfe, Mark Koenig, and the still-active Joe Gordon, a former Yankee then a member of the visiting Cleveland Indians. Far from an old-timer, Gordon was an All-Star in 1948 and would help lead the Indians to a World Series victory a few months later. "Once a Yankee, always a Yankee," said Hoyt.[44]

Mel Allen, who broadcast games for the Yankees until 1985, emceed the proceedings. Ruth waited in the clubhouse until it was nearing the time for his name to be announced. Moving into the dugout, he spotted a fielder's mitt and picked it up. "You could catch a basketball with this," he quipped.[45] His name finally announced by Allen, Ruth "walked out into the cauldron of sound he must have known better than any man," in the words of sportswriter W.C. Heinz.[46] He spoke only briefly, expressing his pride at having hit the first home run in Yankee Stadium history. After the ceremony, Ruth sat in the locker room drinking a beer with his friend and former teammate Joe Dugan. "How are things, Jidge?" Dugan asked, using the nickname (a variation of George) common among Ruth's teammates. "Joe, I'm gone," Ruth replied. The two men began to cry.[47] The Babe never returned to Yankee Stadium in his lifetime.

The most enduring image of that day is a photograph of Ruth, standing on the third-base side of home plate, with Bob Feller's bat in his hand to support himself, his number 3 jersey on his still broad shoulders. The Yankees had dressed on the third-base side clubhouse during Ruth's playing days but had moved to the first-base side prior to the 1946 season. Since Ruth's old locker had not been moved, he dressed in what was now the visitors' clubhouse, and entered the field through the Indians' dugout. First baseman Eddie Robinson, who would one day play for the Yankees and lived long enough to start his own podcast prior to his death in 2021, worried about Ruth's stability in climbing the dugout stairs. "He just looked wobbly," Robinson later recalled.[48] Robinson handed the Babe a bat to steady himself, one that belonged to Bob Feller.[49]

Later titled "The Babe Bows Out," the picture was taken by Nat Fein, a substitute photographer for the *New York Herald Tribune*. While most photographers had positioned themselves in front of Ruth on the baseline, Fein chose to photograph the Babe from the back. "The number 3 was the thing I was interested in," Fein would say. "I felt the only way to tell the story of Babe retiring was from the back."[50] The picture appeared on the front page of the *Herald Tribune* the next day and was awarded a Pulitzer Prize. *Life Magazine* would describe it as "one of the greatest pictures of the 20th Century."[51]

THE BABE'S FUNERAL (AUGUST 17 AND 18, 1948)

The Babe succumbed to cancer on the evening of August 16, 1948. The original suggestion had been to hold Ruth's wake at the Universal Funeral Home on Lexington Avenue in Manhattan, but the Babe instead would lie in state at Yankee Stadium for two days, on August 17 and 18.[52] Ruth's daughters had originally objected to the plan, based both on Ruth's treatment by the Yankees after his retirement, and on a desire to protect their father's image. "Poor Daddy, he looked so awful," his daughter Julia would say. "I hated to think of all those people going by and seeing him looking like that. He looked so old, so sad."[53]

Ruth's casket arrived at the Stadium in the mid-afternoon of August 17. His wife, Claire, and her daughter, Julia, whom Ruth adopted as his own, attended. Dorothy Ruth, the Babe's biological daughter from a previous relationship, did not. She was estranged from her stepmother and stepsister.[54] Speaking of that day, Julia later said, "It was quiet. As quiet as you could get in New York City. And bare. Absolutely bare. There were flowers. There was light."[55] The gates opened at 5:00 P.M., and while they were originally scheduled to close at 10:00 P.M. (reopening the next morning), an announcement was soon made that the gates would remain open all night to allow all mourners their chance to bid the Babe goodbye.[56]

The next morning, charter buses arrived from Maryland, Delaware, Massachusetts, Rhode Island, and Connecticut. Vendors sold hot dogs and pictures of the Babe.[57] VIPs included entertainer Bill "Bojangles" Robinson and Hank Greenberg and Leo Durocher.[58] A 26-year-old man who had lost his leg in World War II told reporters that when he was a student at St. Joseph's Orphanage in Poughkeepsie, New York, Ruth had taken him and 250 of his classmates to a game at Yankee Stadium.[59] Also among the mourners was 3-year-old Harry Escobar, wearing a full Yankees uniform and a black armband his father had taped around his left sleeve. Young Harry's picture adorned the picture of the *New York Daily News* the next day, with a headline reading: "Ruth's Last Gate, His Greatest."[60]

The Stadium that Ruth played in stood for another quarter-century after his death, before undergoing a major renovation in the 1970s. The renovated park was finally torn down in 2009, replaced by the current version of Yankee Stadium. Many American heroes would appear at Yankee Stadium through the years, not just in baseball but in other sports and other walks of life. Yet Babe Ruth remains the only one to lie in state at the Stadium, the only one given credit for "building" the iconic ballpark. The outpouring of love for him over those two days in August of 1948 is evidence of his singular place in the hearts of Yankees fans then and now.

NOTES

1   Robert Creamer, *Babe: The Legend Comes to Life* (New York: Penguin, 1988), 405.

2   Jonathan Eig, *Luckiest Man: The Life and Death of Lou Gehrig* (New York: Simon & Schuster, 2005), 223.

3   Frank Graham, *The New York Yankees: An Informal History* (New York: Putnam, 1947), 252.

4   Leigh Montville, *The Big Bam: The Life and Times of Babe Ruth* (New York: Doubleday, 2006), 354.

5   Eig, 315.

6   Paul Hofmann, "Lou Gehrig Appreciation Day: Ruth and Gehrig End Feud," in Bill Nowlin and Glen Sparks, eds., *The Babe* (Phoenix: Society for American Baseball Research, 2019), 296.

7   Tara Krieger, "Babe Ruth and Lou Gehrig," in *The Babe*, 93.

8   Creamer, 415.

9   Krieger in *The Babe*, 93.

10   Krieger, 93.

11   Montville, 355.

12   Ruth's message to the troops, which accompanied a highlight film of the 1943 World Series, can be found at https://www.youtube.com/watch?v=z8VOUh1aoKU.

13   Montville, 355.

14   Jane Leavy, *The Big Fella: Babe Ruth and the World He Created* (New York: HarperCollins, 2018), 431.

15   Henry Thomas, *Walter Johnson: Baseball's Big Train* (Washington: Random Press, 1995), 342.

16   Leavy, 431.

17   James Dawson, "Ruth, Johnson Turn Back Clock; Fans See What Made Them Click," *New York Times*, August 24, 1942: 19.

18   Matt Schudel, "Pitcher Johnny Sain, 89, Hurled His Way into History," *Washington Post*, November 9, 2006. Accessible online at: https://www.washingtonpost.com/archive/local/2006/11/09/pitcher-johnny-sain-89-hurled-his-way-into-history/2c37bf0a-7705-4b88-acd7-0fe3f5e7dbc1/.

19   Creamer, 417.

20   Schudel, "Pitcher Johnny Sain, 89."

21   Creamer, 417.

22   Marty Appel, *Pinstripe Empire: The New York Yankees From Before the Babe to After the Boss* (New York: Bloomsbury, 2012), 260.

23   Joe Schuster, "Babe Ruth Day," in *The Babe*, 299. (Ruth was in New York and did not attend the ceremonies in Japan.)

24   Schuster, 299.

25   Montville, 359.

26   Creamer, 419.

27   Schuster, in *The Babe*, 299.

28   Appel, 261.

29   Creamer, 420.

30   Creamer, 420.

31   Creamer, 420.

32   Stanton, 235.

33   " Old-Timers Game Goes to Yankees," *New York Times*, September 27, 1947: 25.

34   Tom Stanton, *Ty and the Babe: Baseball's Fiercest Rivals: A Surprising Friendship and the 1941 Has-Beens Golf Championship* (New York: Thomas Dunne Books, 2007), 235.

35   Joe Posnanski, *The Baseball 100* (New York: Avid Reader Press, 2021), 736.

36 Stanton, 236.

37 Kevin Cook, *Electric October: Seven World Series Games, Six Lives, Five Minutes of Fame That Lasted Forever* (New York: Henry Holt and Company, 2017), 100.

38 Appel, 269.

39 Appel, 269.

40 Appel, 269.

41 Montville, 363.

42 Montville, 363. Gehrig died at 37 in 1941, Lazzeri at 42 in 1946, and Pennock at 53 in 1948.

43 Appel, 269.

44 Appel, 269.

45 Montville, 363.

46 Glen Sparks, "Babe Ruth Makes Final Visit to Yankee Stadium," in *The Babe,* 302.

47 Creamer, 423.

48 Leavy, 455.

49 Leavy, 455.

50 Sparks, in *The Babe,* 303.

51 Sparks, in *The Babe,* 303.

52 Montville, 366.

53 Leavy, 468.

54 Leavy, 469.

55 Leavy, 469.

56 Leavy, 469.

57 Leavy, 469.

58 Leavy, 471.

59 Leavy, 469.

60 Leavy, 472.

YANKEE OLD-TIMERS DAY – A LONG-RUNNING TRADITION

By Ralph Peluso

The original Yankee Stadium, with its majestic triple-deck structure, was impressive. Jerry Coleman, ex-Yankee, World Series MVP winner, and broadcaster, recalled the ballpark with awe: "That stadium ... that huge triple deck with the façade up there ... my God, it was like going to a cathedral, really."[1] Memorable moments thrilled fans over the years: a seventh-game World Series win, Ruth's 60th, Maris' 61st, Mantle's 500th.

Yankee Stadium, rebuilt in 2009, was a special place for memorable events. One such event was the long-running Old-Timers Day.[2]

Although the Yankees have maintained the tradition of the old-timers games the longest, John Thorn, Major League Baseball's historian, noted that the recognition of former players playing exhibition games dated back to 1875. The "Old Duffer" Knickerbockers of the 1840s and 1850s played the "Youngsters" of the 1860s.[3]

Yankee Stadium Old-Timers Day roots can arguably be traced to two moments that honored dying ballplayers. The first was on July 4, 1939, Lou Gehrig Appreciation Day. On hand were Gehrig's 1920s teammates, including Mark Koenig, Wally Schang, Herb Pennock, Wally Pipp, Bob Shawkey, Benny Bengough, George Pipgras, Tony Lazzeri, Earle Combs, Joe Dugan, Waite Hoyt, Bob Meusel, Everett Scott, and Babe Ruth. The unforgettable part of that day was Gehrig's iconic goodbye, his "Luckiest Man on the Face of the Earth" speech.[4]

The second was on April 27, 1947. Babe Ruth Day was proclaimed across professional baseball by Commissioner Happy Chandler to honor The Babe.[5] On that day Larry MacPhail, the Yankees general manager, announced that the Yankees would host their first Old-Timers Day on September 28.[6] This event would include an exhibition game between former players.

Red Patterson, the Yankees' publicity director, continued the tradition in homage to Ruth.[7]

Regardless of the day one selects as the origin, the Yankee Old-Timers Day tradition has continued with its pomp, revelry, and circumstance for either 75 or 83 years, with a two-year interruption (2020-21) because of the COVID pandemic. Following are some Old-Timers Day events with significant themes.

RECOGNITION OF THE BABE AND THE FIRST OFFICIAL OLD-TIMERS DAY (1947)

The Yankees had clinched the American League pennant two weeks earlier, but still a crowd of 25,085 attended the Yankees' final game of the regular season on September 28, 1947. The one-time very familiar Bambino batting stance was not seen this day. A frail, visibly ill Ruth appeared, his camel-hair coat collar turned up and buttoned to his chin.[8] Barely able to speak, Ruth waved to the roaring crowd.[9] Ruth could not suit up for the game. He posed for pictures with other immortals like Ty Cobb and Tris Speaker. Yankee greats there included Frank Baker, Herb Pennock, Bob Meusel, Earle Combs, Waite Hoyt, Lefty Gomez, and Red Ruffing. Philadelphia Athletics owner-manager Connie Mack managed a squad of non-Yankee former stars including Speaker, Al Simmons, George Sisler, Jimmie Foxx, Mickey Cochrane, Lefty Grove, Chief Bender, Cy Young, Ed Walsh, and Ty Cobb. Twenty current or future Hall of Famers played or attended. Combs sealed the win with an inside-the-park home run over Tris Speaker's head. The quip of the day may have been uttered by Hoyt who, after throwing out Ty Cobb said, "They had been trying to do that for 40 years."[10]

All gate receipts were donated to the Babe Ruth Foundation, which had recently been founded to aid underprivileged youth.[11] The event reportedly raised about $45,000.[12]

SILVER ANNIVERSARY CELEBRATION OF THE STADIUM (1948)

Silver Anniversary Day, June 13, 1948, was festive, cast in emotional celebrations: the 25th anniversary of Yankee Stadium, the retirement of Ruth's number 3, and recognition of some of the most storied players.[13] On a bittersweet note, it was Ruth's last appearance at the Stadium.[14]

Yankees President Dan Topping presented Ruth with a pocket watch with the inscription "Silver Anniversary 1923-1948, the House That Ruth Built." Former general manager/club President Ed Barrow, who greeted Ruth at the plate, also received an inscribed pocket watch. Ruth thrilled fans when he assumed his familiar once-feared stance and took a mighty cut.[15]

American League President Will Harridge accepted the Ruth uniform and proclaimed that "it would never again be worn here or on the road."[16] That Ruth uniform remains on display at the National Baseball Hall of Fame in Cooperstown, New York.

Before the player introductions, memorial wreaths were placed on the Lou Gehrig, Jacob Ruppert, and Miller Huggins monuments. Bob Shawkey, Huggins' successor as Yankees manager, placed the wreath on his monument; Barrow, on Ruppert's; and Bill Dickey, on Gehrig's.[17]

Players from the 1923 team squared off against a collection of former Yankees. New York Mayor William O'Dwyer threw out the first pitch; Governor Al Smith had used the same ball for the Stadium's inaugural toss in 1923.[18] Yankees players in the Old-Timers game included Joe Sewell, Tiny Bonham, Hank Borowy,[19] Red Rolfe, George Selkirk, Lefty Gomez, Tom Zachary, Bill Dickey, and Mark Koenig. The '23 team, anchored by Pipp, Meusel, Bullet Joe Bush, Carl Mays, Shawkey, Hoyt, and Dugan, prevailed, 2-0. The

SABR/The Rucker Archive.

Mickey Mantle and Joe DiMaggio (center top) and Claire Ruth, the Babe's widow (center bottom) were frequent Old-Timers Day guests.

Yankees All Stars were managed by Ruth with help from Chuck Dressen. Meusel drove in Dugan and Pipp on a blooper misplayed by Rolfe.[20]

DIMAGGIO'S FIRST OLD-TIMERS DAY (1952)

On August 30, 1952, Joe DiMaggio returned for the first time in what would be a very long Old-Timers Day run for him.[21] He returned every year until his death before the 1999 season, except for 1988, when he was recovering from abdominal surgery.[22] That span of 46 years was the second-longest number of appearances by any Yankees old-timer. Hector Lopez holds the record with 53 appearances (1967-2019).

The Yankees commemorated their 50th year by honoring living members among the greatest Yankees of all time as voted by the baseball writers.[23] Joe DiMaggio managed the cast of "All-Timers." Honorees included Bill Dickey, Phil Rizzuto, Earle Combs, Lefty Gomez, Red Ruffing, Wally Pipp, Frank Crosetti, and Home Run Baker, who managed the "Yankee All Stars." The All-Timers prevailed, 3-0.

Special recognition was given to Clark Griffith, pitcher and manager of the 1903 team, then known as the Highlanders, by American League President Will Harridge, with a little help from Supreme Court Justice Tom Clark, Connie Mack, and Ed Barrow. Others from Highlanders days included Dave Fultz and Elmer Bliss.

The Yankees held a reunion dinner at the Ruppert Brewery.[24]

SECOND DECADE OF OLD-TIMERS DAYS BEGINS (1957)

On July 27, 1957, 30 former Yankees stars and 25 Detroit Tigers notables compiled this installment of Old-Timers Day. In perhaps an ironic moment, Home Run Baker and Joe DiMaggio were captured giving home run tips to Mickey Mantle. Mantle was the Triple Crown winner in 1956, with 52 homers that year – a mark neither DiMaggio nor Baker ever reached.

Other notable attendees: recent Hall of Fame inductee Wahoo Sam Crawford, Mickey Cochrane, Ty Cobb, and Earle Combs.

DIMAGGIO'S TAINTED AT-BAT (1965)

On July 31, 1965, before a crowd of 42,170, Al Schacht, known as baseball's Clown Prince and noted for his comedic antics on the diamond, played a big part in the DiMaggio at-bat. Schacht served as a guest umpire, and his generous rules interpretations victimized former Cincinnati Reds star pitcher Bucky

Walters. Schacht allowed a DiMaggio at-bat to continue, twice.[25] Disappointed fans groaned when Jim Hegan caught the Yankee Clipper's foul pop. Sighs turned into cheers when Hegan "dropped" the ball. Walters looked in and smiled. DiMaggio hit another popup, near third. Monte Irvin made a backhanded grab. As DiMaggio started to walk away, Schacht ruled the backhanded catch "illegal." DiMaggio did not disappoint; on the next pitch, he smacked a line drive into the left-field stands.[26]

NEW AND OLD OLD-TIMERS (1969)

Old-Timers Day on August 9, 1969, was themed the Yankee All-Timers and the opponent All-Timers. For the first time since October 5, 1951 (Game Two of the World Series), Mickey Mantle and Joe DiMaggio played together.[27] A fan vote selected the all-timers. The outcome was odd: Two active Yankees were selected as Yankee All-Timers, Mel Stottlemyre and Joe Pepitone. The under- or near 40-year-old contingent included the newly retired Mantle, Whitey Ford, Tony Kubek, Bobby Richardson, and Bill Skowron. The Yankees roster included Bill Dickey, Joe Dugan, Waite Hoyt, Lefty Gomez, Charlie Keller, and Gil McDougald. Yankees opponents included Carl Furillo, the Bronx-born Rocky Colavito, and Hall of Famers Monte Irvin and Dizzy Dean. The largest ovations went to the newly elected Hall of Fame members Roy Campanella and Stan Musial.[28] The game ended in a 0-0 stalemate.

GOLDEN ANNIVERSARY OF FIRST PENNANT (1971)

On July 10, 1971, the Yankees celebrated the 50th anniversary of their first pennant, in 1921, when the Yankees were tenants in the Polo Grounds. At least one member of all 29 pennant-winning teams was on hand. From the 1921 team were Whitey Witt, the first Yankee to take a turn at the plate in 1923 at Yankee Stadium, and Roger Peckinpaugh, who managed the Yankees for 20 games as a 23-year-old in 1914 and anchored shortstop for the Yankees for nine seasons.[29]

The two-inning affair was capped off with an unlikely inside-the-park home run by Elston Howard off Ralph Terry. It was the only run of the game.[30] Throughout the game there was remarkable fielding, including a leaping grab by Gil McDougald off a hot smash by Tommy Byrne, and a running catch by Charlie Keller on a ball hit to deep left field by Hank Bauer. Pitchers were relieved after nearly every hitter, which enabled nearly all the attendees to participate.

Of the 56 players on hand, the lone non-Yankee was a recent Hall of Fame inductee, Satchel Paige. Casey Stengel was the brunt of a press-box joke attacking his wisdom: "He has DiMaggio batting third and [Tommy] Henrich fourth."[31] Tom Tresh was the youngest Old-Timer, at 32.

MICKEY'S FINAL HOMER AT THE OLD YANKEE STADIUM (1973)

Longtime Yankees broadcast Mel Allen, the author of the widely recognized home-run call "It's going, going, gone!" announced the Yankee Old-Timers Day on August 11, 1973.[32] Whitey Ford took the mound. No strange sight for Yankee fans. Into the batter's box came Mickey Mantle. Ford and Mantle were not only former teammates and close friends, but roommates for a time.

The stadium buzz turned loud. Over 46,000 fans watched this moment unfold, future Hall of Famers and Yankees immortals squaring off.

Ford readied and wasted no time. With the count 1-and-1, Mantle took an awkward cut, topping the pitch foul. With a better swing, he hit the next offering hard, a liner foul. Ford grooved the next pitch. Mantle hit it a long way into the upper deck, but foul. George Selkirk, coaching at third base, encouraged Mantle. Mel Allen gleefully implored, "Straighten it out, Mick." With those words still hanging in the air, Allen continued, "[The pitch is] down the alley. There it goes; going, going, gone!"[33] Mantle had launched a majestic fly that landed about 25 rows back in the lower left-field stands. In his prime, that ball most likely would have reached the upper deck. Fans cheered wildly as Mantle began the familiar head-down trot around the bases. He moved more slowly now with a more pronounced limp. This was Mantle's final homer at the original Yankee Stadium. Renovation plans had been announced, and for the next two years, the Yankees played in Shea Stadium.

The Old-Timers team was divided between the Stengels and the Houks. The Stengels included Ford, Witt, Rizzuto, Johnny Mize, DiMaggio, Hector Lopez, and Andy Carey. The Houks included Mantle, Nick Etten, Irv Noren, Howard, Vic Raschi, Allie Reynolds, and Ryne Duren.[34]

"BILLY MARTIN WILL RETURN" (1978)[35]

Just five days after "quitting," Billy Martin was rehired to take the reins again with the start of the 1980 season at Old-Timers Day on July 29, 1978.

The theme of this game was the silver anniversary of the amazing run of five straight World Series championships (1949-1953). According to John Sterling, announcing from the radio booth, this may have been the greatest assemblage of former players. The game marked Roger Maris's first Yankee Old-Timers event. Joe Pepitone caught fans' attention with two batting-practice blasts into right field. After the second, he pranced around the bases in his home-run trot. Harmon Killebrew and Elston Howard smashed several batting-practice drives into the left-field seats.

After the announcements like "the crafty chairman of the board" (Ford), "the greatest switch-hitter of the game" (Mantle), and "the greatest living player" (DiMaggio), Yankees' PA announcer Bob Sheppard, announced that manager Bob Lemon had signed a new five-year contract with the club.[36] He would manage through 1979 and then work as general manager through 1983. Fans booed. Sheppard quieted the crowd with his gentle but firm voice as only he could do. "Please, please … managing the Yankees in 1980 and for many more beyond then, number 1 …"[37] Applause erupted, rocked the stadium and continued for seven minutes.[38] Billy was coming back.[39]

ONE RETURNS, TWO REUNITED, SNUBBED EX-PLAYER SATISFIED (1982)

On August 7, 1982, introductions for the great Yankees teams ranged from some lesser-known players like Marius Russo and Ed Wells to legends occupying their customary last and next-to-last spots in the introduction order, DiMaggio and Mantle, respectively.[40]

There were two notable reunions at the event this year. Joe DiMaggio took the field with his brother Dom, a Boston Red Sox star who had not put on a uniform for an old-timer event since 1971. Dom declined playing in the game due to a medical problem with his eyes. The other, Ray Fisher, the oldest Yankee at the time at 94, was rolled onto the Yankee Stadium field in a wheelchair for the first time. During his career with New York, he played at Hilltop Park and the Polo Grounds, but he was banned from baseball over a contract dispute before the 1921 season. Fisher's lifetime banishment from baseball was lifted by Commissioner Bowie Kuhn in 1980.[41]

Reports of the Old-Timers Game in the next day's newspaper were brief: The American League All-Stars defeated the Yankee Stars, 2-1; Billy Pierce bested Whitey Ford; singles by Bob Allison, Vic Wertz, Steve Whitaker, and Roy Sievers produced the runs for the All-Stars, and the Yankees scored on singles by Irv Noren, Hector Lopez, and Jake Gibbs.[42]

Jim Bouton, a pitcher with the Yankees from 1962 to 1968, received more press with his reminiscent *New York Times* piece about his omission from Yankees invitees. The missed invitation stemmed from his controversial 1970 book, *Ball Four*, which revealed some of the players' on- and off-the-field antics that previous writers would not dare print.[43] In retrospect, Bouton felt he'd laughed last; defying baseball norms about speaking out, he was ahead of his time.

LITTLE RAY AND THE RETURN OF THE PRODIGAL YANKEE (1998)

For the 52nd Old-Timers Day, on July 25, 1998, Frank Messer, a former Yankees broadcaster who began serving as emcee for Old-Timers Day in 1988, manned the microphone. The game would feature players from the Yankees and Dodgers teams from the 1970s.[44] His first two introductions were important. First, he welcomed Little Ray Kelly, who sat in the dugout on April 18, 1923, Yankee Stadium's Opening Day, and served as Babe Ruth's mascot until the early 1930s.[45] Messer also recognized Jim Ogle, the 25-year director of the Yankees Alumni Association.[46]

Then, the announcement of the return of the "prodigal Yankee"; Messer welcomed back Jim Bouton, the hat-flying phenom with 21 victories in 1963. He referred to Bouton as an accomplished author. Fans roared. Bouton slyly smiled as he walked out, all the controversy from his book forgotten, thanks to a letter written by Bouton's son Michael to the *New York Times* asking that the Yankees forgive his father.[47]

Copyright Jerry Coli / Dreamstime.

The 2007 Old-Timers Day included Whitey Ford (16), Yogi Berra (8), Reggie Jackson (44), Don Mattingly (23), Ron Guidry (49), Moose Skowron (14), Don Larsen (18), Graig Nettles (9), Bobby Murcer (1), Goose Gossage (54), Paul O'Neill (21) Scott Brosius (18), Joe Pepitone (25), and Chris Chambliss (10).

Dodgers in attendance included Ralph Branca, the pitcher who in 1951 yielded "The Shot Heard Round the World" to Bobby Thomson that gave the rival Giants the pennant. Other Dodgers there were Tommy Lasorda, Willie Davis, Steve Howe, and Tom Niedenfuer.

Mel Allen was posthumously honored as the "forever and legendary voice of the Yankees," with a plaque in center field.[48]

Willie Randolph hit a walk-off homer as the Yankee Old-Timers bested the Dodgers again.

CELEBRATING A RUBY JUBILEE (2001)

On July 21, 2001, while Billy Crystal collected autographs in the dugout, the familiar voice of Bob Sheppard set the stage for the 55th Old-Timers Day celebration. He introduced the co-emcees, radio broadcasters John Sterling and Michael Kay. Sterling referred to Yankee accomplishments as magical and somewhat mythological, saying, [S]everal of the greatest moments in baseball history have been right here on this sacred field." Michael Kay reminded the crowd that the Yankees had won four out of the last five World Series and were currently atop the AL East, meaning the fans should expect great Old-Timers Days in the future.[49]

Specific historical mention went to Ron Blomberg (baseball's first designated hitter) and Rick Cerone, who was in the unenviable situation of following Thurman Munson behind the plate in the 1980 season.

After a pause to recognize the passing of former Yankees since the previous Old-Timers Day, accolades were given to Don Larsen for his 1956 World Series perfect game and to Hank Bauer, record holder for the World Series consecutive-game hitting streak (17). Then members of the 1961 Yankees were introduced. Yogi Berra and Whitey Ford received the loudest ovations. Posthumous honors were paid to Elston Howard, the first African American to play for the Yankees; and Roger Maris and Mickey Mantle, by their sons Kevin Maris and David Mantle. Mantle and Maris combined for 115 homers in 1961 in the pursuit of Ruth's record of 60. Acgor Billy Crystal, creator of the movie *61**, described Mantle and Maris as humble but the heart and soul of the '61 team. He imagined what Mantle would respond: "Aw shucks, Whitey won 25 games, our catchers hit 64 home runs and we had the best defensive infield in baseball. We had a pretty good year."[50]

The last introductions were Reggie Jackson[51] and player/broadcaster Phil Rizzuto.

POMP, COMMEMORATION, AND IMAGE (2004)

For the 58th Old-Timers Day event, on July 10, 2004, former players once again gathered from an array of eras. Player ages ranged from the not very old to the aged.

Old-Timers Day by this time had become the Yankees' most elaborate promotional event. And with it came the need for extensive and careful planning.[52] The emphasis on an Old-Timers game had lessened.

Debbie Tymon, who in 2022 was the Yankees' senior vice president of marketing and had been with the organization for nearly four decades, has headed this effort for much of that time. She and the team spend several months on a list of tasks, including deciding the invitees and that year's commemorations, as well as travel and accommodations, the pre-event dinner, and the post-event wrap party.

There were two honorees in 2004. Honoring Red Ruffing, a plaque was added in center field's Monument Park. Ruffing holds the Yankee record for complete games (261).[53] Ruffing had allowed the most hits as a Yankee pitcher, 2,995. Catcher Thurman Munson was also honored; August 2 marked 25 years since his death.

The Yankees provide every Old-Timer in attendance with a new uniform. "I don't want to hear at 12:30 that day that someone has forgotten their uniforms," explained Tymon as to why players did not bring their own.[54] As of 2004, each player also received a commemorative Louisville Slugger for his participation.

Every aspect of Old-Timers Day is well-orchestrated right down to the introduction order of invitees. By 2004, Yogi Berra and Phil Rizzuto, the senior statesmen, were fully entrenched in DiMaggio's former closing spot in the roll call. Rizzuto even mimicked DiMaggio's over the head two-handed salute to the crowd.

On this day other Yankee greats on hand included Reggie Jackson, Don Mattingly, Bill Skowron, and Hank Bauer. Luis Sojo hammered a walk-off home run off Ron Guidry. Sojo performed his best Reggie Jackson imitation – Jackson was recovering from knee surgery and didn't play – as he rounded the bases.[55]

OLD-TIMERS BID FAREWELL TO THE ORIGINAL CATHEDRAL (2008)

On Saturday, August 2, 2008, the largest contingent, more than 70 Old-Timers, including 18 for the very first time, were at the original Yankee Stadium for its final Old-Timers Day celebration. The doors to the new Yankees home opened on April 3, 2009, on the north side of 161st Street and River Avenue.[56]

Each of the last 16 Yankees World Series championship teams since 1947 was represented at the 2008 event by at least one player. Yankees alumni in uniform included Hall of Fame members Yogi Berra, Wade Boggs, Whitey Ford, Reggie Jackson, Dave Winfield, and 2008 inductee Rich "Goose" Gossage.[57] Baseball's all-time stolen-base leader Rickey Henderson made his first Yankee Stadium Old-Timers Day appearance. The loudest and longest welcome of the afternoon went to Willie Randolph, unceremoniously dumped as Mets manager in June.[58] The standing ovation lasted several minutes.[59] Lesser-known players were also on hand. One such player who had experienced a magical season in pinstripes was Aaron Small. He compiled a remarkable 10-0 record for the 2005 AL East champions. Prior to that, he had won 15 games in seven seasons. Perhaps the least-recognized player there was Mickey Klutts, a Yankees veteran of eight games from 1976-78.

The 1996 World Series winners were well represented. Tino Martinez (then a special assistant to the general manager), Pat Kelly, Jimmy Key, Graeme Lloyd, Ramiro Mendoza, Jeff Nelson, and Tim Raines were all on hand, as were other Yankees including Mike Stanley, David Wells, current pitching coach Dave Eiland, former manager Buck Showalter, and former coach Jeff Torborg. First-time attendees included Don Baylor, Tony Fernandez, Wayne Tolleson, and YES Network broadcaster Al Leiter.

The widows of five legendary Yankees were also present – Arlene Howard, widow of Elston Howard; Helen Hunter, widow of Jim "Catfish" Hunter; Jill Martin, widow of Billy Martin; Diana Munson, widow of Thurman Munson; and Cora Rizzuto, widow of Phil Rizzuto.

The greats and the ordinary gathered in uniform, each with their memories and sentiments, and said goodbye to the great stadium in the Bronx.

NOTES

1   Associated Press, "Yankee Stadium: Remembering a Baseball Cathedral," ESPN.com, July 3, 2008. http://www.espn.com/espn/wire/_/section/mlb/id/3472343. Accessed December 14, 2022.

2   A great deal of information regarding Old-Timers Days at Yankee Stadium may be found at this site: http://www.ultimateyankees.com/oldtimersday.htm. Date accessed October 31, 2022.

3   John Thorn, https://twitter.com/thorn_john/status/1567886317484130305. Accessed October 31, 2022.

4   John Drebinger, "61,808 Fans Roar Tribute to Gehrig," New York Times, July 5, 1939: 1.

5   Robert W. Creamer, Babe: The Legend Comes to Life (New York: Simon & Schuster, 1992), 418-419.

6   Jane Leavy, The Big Fella (New York: Harper, 2018), 444.

7   Leonard Koppett, "Yankee Old Timer Fans Get a Run for the Money," New York Times, July 11, 1971: S 1. Red Patterson was the first publicity director for a major-league baseball team, joining the Yankees in 1946. Patterson is credited with many innovations promoting fan interest during his 45-year career in professional baseball. See Ross Newhan, "Red Paterson Dies of Cancer," Los Angeles Times, February 11, 1992: C2.

8   Sports Century: Babe Ruth Sports Century: ESPN Classic, available at https://www.youtube.com/watch?v=5GkZRw21kho. Accessed October 31, 2022.

9   Hy Turkin, "Ruth Whispers His Gratitude to Cheering Fans," New York Daily News, April 28, 1947: 3.

10 Jim McCulley, "Ancients Turn Back Clock – 2 Inns," New York Daily News, September 29, 1947: 43.

11 "Babe Ruth Foundation Set Up to Aid Underprivileged Youth; Famous Player Makes Initial Gift to the Organization," New York Times, May 9, 1947: 27.

12 McCulley.

13 "25 Years of Glorious Deeds in Stadium Revived by Babe Ruth and Host of Other Yankee Stars," New York Times, June 14, 1948: 26.

14 Joe Trimble, "Number 3 Brings Down House That Ruth Built," New York Daily News, June 14, 1948: C17.

15 Babe Ruth's Last Appearance at Yankee Stadium, YouTube, https://www.youtube.com/watch?v=nmcjCQNGzDY. Accessed November 4, 2022.

16 Trimble.

17 Trimble.

18 "25 Years of Glorious Deeds in Stadium Revived by Babe Ruth and Host of Other Yankee Stars."

19 Bonham and Borowy were still active players at the time.

20 "25 Years of Glorious Deeds in Stadium Revived by Babe Ruth and Host of Other Yankee Stars."

21 "Old Timers Day Today at Stadium," New York Times, August 30, 1952: S 7.

22 Dave Anderson, "Reggie a No-Show; Billy Draws Cheers," New York Times, July 17, 1988: S3.

23 "Old Timers Day Today at Stadium."

24 "Old Timers Day Today at Stadium." See also "Yankee Stars Through 50 Years Thrill 41,558 at Stadium," New York Times, August 31, 1952: S 1, 2.

25 Mark Leepson, "Of Al Schacht and a Cracker Jack Afternoon," New York Times, October 21, 1984: S2.

26 "DiMaggio Hits One for Auld Lang Syne at Yankee Stadium," New York Times, August 1, 1965: S1.

27 John Drebinger, "Yanks Win, 3 to 1, Tie Series; Lopat Holds Giants to 5 Hits." New York Times, October 6, 1951: 1.

28 "New Old Timers Steal the Show," New York Times, August 10, 1969: Sports S1.

29 "74,200 See Yankees Open New Stadium: Ruth Hits Home Run," New York Times, April 19, 1923: 1, 15.

30 Leonard Koppett, "Yankee Old Timer Fans Get a Run for the Money," New York Times, July 11, 1971: S 1.

31 "Yankee Old Timer Fans Get a Run for the Money."

32   Mickey Mantle 1973 – His Last Home Run in Yankee Stadium, OTD, 8/11/1973, YouTube, https://www.youtube.com/watch?v=I9fNcMLaW_A. Accessed October 15, 2022.

33   Mickey Mantle 1973 – His Last Home Run in Yankee Stadium, OTD, 8/11/1973.

34   Gerald Eskenazi, "Old Yankees Visit Their Past," *New York Times*, August 12, 1973: Sports 1.

35   *New York Daily News* front-page headline, July 30, 1978.

36   On DiMaggio, see "Baseball's Centennial 'Greatest Players Ever' Poll," nationalpastimemuseum.com, September 12, 2019, https://www. thenationalpastimemuseum.com/article/baseballs-centennial-greatest-players-ever-poll. Accessed December 14, 2022.

37   Bob Sheppard 1978 – Billy Martin to Return as Manager Speech, 7/29/1978, YouTube, https://www.youtube.com/watch?v=KQf2BYjnkRw. Accessed December 6, 2022.

38   Murray Chass, "Martin Will Rejoin Yanks as Club's Manager in 1980," *New York Times*, July 30, 1978: S5 1, 3.

39   Martin never managed the Yankees in 1980. On June 18, 1979, the Yankees fired Bob Lemon after the club got off to a slow start. Martin rejoined the Yankees then. On October 29, 1979, Martin was once again fired for a fight in Minneapolis. The Martin saga continued, with Martin ultimately hired and fired five times as Yankees manager before his death in 1989.

40   1982 New York Yankees Old Timers Game (revised), YouTube, https://www. youtube.com/watch?v=LPkWAUEhVyc. Accessed December 4, 2022.

41   Jacob Pomrenke, "A Rose by Another Name; Ray Fisher's Ban from Baseball," the nationalastimemusuem.org. January 4, 2020. https://www. thenationalpastimemuseum.com/article/rose-another-name-ray-fishers-ban-baseball-0. Accessed December 14, 2022.

42   Murray Chass, "Trading Dent for Mazzilli," *New York Times*, August 8, 1982: S5 1, 5.

43   Jim Bouton, "Outside Looking In: An Uninvited Guest Gets Last Laugh," *New York Times*, August 8, 1982: Sports 2.

44   1998-07-25: New York Yankees Old Timers Day, YouTube, https://www. youtube.com/watch?v=lvGyJT_D5nI. Accessed December 4, 2022.

45   Richard Goldstein, "Ray Kelly, 83, Babe Ruth's Little Pal, Dies," *New York Times*, November 14, 2001: A25.

46   1998-07-25: New York Yankees Old Timers Day.

47   Dave Anderson, "Return of the Prodigal Yankee Old-Timer," *New York Times*, July 26, 1998: Sports 1.

48   1998-07-25: New York Yankees Old Timers Day.

49   2001-07-21: Old Timer's Day – Tribute to the 1961 New York Yankees, YouTube, https://www.youtube.com/watch?v=BGfug-RkNxE. Accessed December 1, 2022.

50   2001-07-21: Old Timer's Day – Tribute to the 1961 New York Yankees.

51   Reggie Jackson becomes Mr. October during the 1977 World Series | Yankees-Dodgers: An Uncivil War, YouTube, https://www.youtube.com/ watch?v=DzEavV_Q29U. Accessed December 1, 2022.

52   Richard Sandomir, "Sports Business: Yankees Plan to Make Old-Timers Look New," *New York Times*, July 9, 2004: D 6.

53   Andrew Marchand, "Yanks Honor Ruffing," *New York Post*, July 11, 2004.

54   Sandomir.

55   Sojo Wins 2004 Old Timers' Day with a Walk-Off Homer, YouTube, https:// www.youtube.com/watch?v=DH8j4iWMSOE. Accessed December 1, 2022.

56   Tyler Kepner, "Amenities and Expectations at Yankee Stadium Opening," *New York Times*, April 4, 2009: S 1.

57   Reggie Jackson, recovering from knee surgery, did not play in the Old-Timers Day game.

58   Billy Altman, "Yankee Greats, and Not-So-Greats, Celebrate the End of Many Eras," *New York Times*, August 3, 2008. Digital Access December 1, 2022.

59   Yankees Old Timers Day 2008 Willie Randolph, YouTube, https://www. youtube.com/watch?v=7QftffrazT8. Accessed December 1, 2022.

"WE WERE THE ONLY GIRLS TO PLAY AT YANKEE STADIUM"

By Tim Wiles

Between 1923 and 2008, Yankee Stadium hosted 6,746 American League and related professional baseball games, including 161 postseason games and four All-Star Games. More than 200 Negro League games have also taken place there. On August 11, 1950, the ballpark hosted its first and only game between two teams of female professional baseball players, when the Chicago Colleens and the Springfield Sallies of the All-American Girls Professional Baseball League (AAGPBL) played a three-inning exhibition before that day's contest between the Yankees and the Philadelphia Athletics.[1]

The *New York Times* called the game "a spirited exhibition," noting that the "Colleens, managed by Dave Bancroft, famed Giant shortstop of thirty years ago, won by a score of 1-0."[2] The *New York Herald Tribune* saw the game differently, noting that the Colleens won, 3-0. "Umpires were provided by the Yankees: Ralph Houk at home plate. Gene Woodling at first, Ed Lopat at second and Allie Reynolds at third."[3]

At present, we do not know who got on base, scored, or drove in runs in this historic game, as no box score, scorecard, or narrative game account has yet been found. We do know the name of the first woman to throw a pitch at Yankee Stadium, though: "No other woman had ever pitched off that mound before me," said Gloria 'Tippy' Schweigert, the 16-year-old who started that day for the Colleens.[4] This source credits her with throwing a no-hitter in the start, though no game account confirms that.[5]

In November 2022, this author spoke to all three of the surviving players who took the field that day: Joanne McComb, Mary Moore, and Toni Palermo. All expressed difficulty recalling much beyond the honor of playing in the House That Ruth Built.

"I played first base, I know that," recalled McComb. "I was more impressed with the surroundings. The game itself, to me, was just another game."[6]

Mary Moore played second base and recalled hitting a ball into the infield and running toward first base, where she took a spill on wet grounds after veering off to the right, muddying her bright white uniform. She can't recall if she was safe or out, but "I would think that I would remember if I was safe."[7]

Toni Palermo played shortstop, recalling that Phil Rizzuto loaned her his glove – and she used it in the game. She also could not recall game details, but noted, "I just know that I really enjoyed it, that I had his glove and I felt like a star out there. I was a confident player. I wanted every ball hit to me, no matter what the situation, and with his glove, I felt even more powerful."[8] Palermo also recalled Casey Stengel working with her on double plays before the game, teaching her to time the approaching ball, get it on the hop she wanted, and to just kick the corner of the bag. "And it made a difference," she recalled.[9] None of the three could confirm the game score.

Beyond the lack of a box score, another intriguing loss for history is the fact that, according to Merrie Fidler, the Yankees organization wrote an enthusiastic letter to the AAGPBL after the game, which included the sentence "The game was carried in its entirety on television and there has been a great deal of interesting comment around the city since."[10] This footage has not survived.

Playing in Yankee Stadium was a source of pride for many of the players that day, as they often gave that as their favorite memory when asked on questionnaires, by reporters, and at panel discussions.

"Imagine, if you will, back then, being a girl and playing professional baseball on the field at Yankee Stadium. Think what it must feel like to us, walking and running around the outfield, standing in the same batter's box where the likes of Babe Ruth, Phil Rizzuto, and Joe DiMaggio had stood. It was truly amazing and exciting for us," recalled pitcher Pat Brown in her autobiography *A League of My Own*.[11]

The Yankees and A's players were friendly with the female players, and there was much interaction on the field and in the dugouts. Said Jane Moffet, "I ... found myself in the dugout with several of the Yankees ball players, I was with Yogi, Whitey Ford, Casey Stengel,

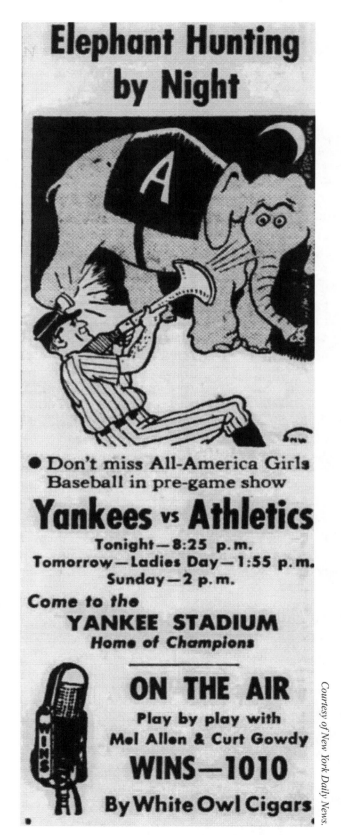

The three-inning exhibition between the Chicago Colleens and Springfield Sallies on August 11, 1950, marked the only time the AAGPBL played at Yankee Stadium.

Courtesy of New York Daily News.

and others. Casey and Yogi were very friendly and stayed with us in the dugout talking baseball. I went out and warmed up the pitcher, and we played our three-inning game. Then we stayed for the game. I have been a devoted Yankee fan ever since. All in the life of a rookie."[12]

Joanne McComb recalled Johnny Mize: "He was a character. He sat on the bench with us during the game, and offered to trade us chewing tobacco for bubble gum."[13]

McComb listed the game as her favorite baseball memory and recalled, "The Yankee players acted as our bat boys in the dugout with us."[14] Mary Lou Kolanko mentioned that "I warmed up playing catch with Phil Rizzuto."[15]

Barbara "Bobbie" Liebrich, who along with Pat Barringer was one of the two player-manager-chaperones on the touring teams, remembered that "[a]fter the game I and the other manager (Barringer) were on Paul and Dizzy Dean's TV show."[16] Liebrich and Barringer were also the keepers of the excellent set of three tour scrapbooks and a photo album documenting the annual tours, which is housed at the National Baseball Hall of Fame Library in Cooperstown.

"I'm just sorry I broke my ankle, because after that, the teams went up and played at Yankee Stadium, and I missed that game," lamented Shirley Burkovich.[17]

"I remember the game at Yankee Stadium," said Jacqueline "Jackie" Mattson. "What a thrilling experience it was to meet Yogi Berra. His offer to let me use his bat was hilarious. What a club it was! It had a thick handle and was very heavy at the end. I was 5'5" tall and weighed one hundred pounds. If I had swung Yogi's bat, it would have spun me in a circle, once or twice around. Needless to say, I used my own evenly balanced bat with its nice thin handle."[18]

"We were the only girls to play at Yankee Stadium," Mattson said. "That was an experience in itself. The stadium was the hugest thing that you'd ever seen."[19]

Pat Brown, who was in the A's dugout, said: "We were all talking to the (A's) players who had come into our dugout, and, at the same time, were cheering for our team playing out on the field. Suddenly everyone became very, very quiet, and we all looked toward the entry to the dugout. A tall thin man with white hair and a nice smile had just entered the dugout. We all knew who he was, and we respectfully waited for him to speak. It was Connie Mack, the manager of the Athletics, a man who was indeed a legend in baseball."[20]

"Everybody was in awe," she said.[21] "It turned out that this was to be his last year managing. In 1956, when I read in the paper that he had died, I remembered him as that very special person who took the time to come into the dugout and say hello to some women professional players. Some things you can never forget."[22]

"What a thrill! We even met Mr. Connie Mack, wearing his customary vested suit and his straw hat," recalled Pat Courtney.[23] "I was so impressed with Connie Mack – his demeanor, and always so well dressed," remembered Joanne McComb.[24]

"We did play in Yankee Stadium which was a *great* thrill," recalled player Mary Moore in a 2004 interview with AAGPBL historian Merrie Fidler. "Walking onto that field was like in a movie. It just was so beautiful – manicured. It was – I mean words just can't describe it, actually. We played very good ball at the time and you could just hear the crowd 'oooh' and 'aaah' and it was just awesome. It's really – you can't even describe it. You know, when we were touring around the country, we played at some nice places and then some of them they were almost like cow pastures."[25]

The game in Yankee Stadium came roughly midway during the 1950 traveling exhibition schedule conducted by the two teams. From 1948 to 1950, the Colleens and Sallies toured through much of North America in order to promote the league, generate revenue, and recruit new players.[26] The Colleens and Sallies were also considered farm teams, not just scouting the available talent at their many stops, but also refining the skills of those players already on their rosters, in preparation for call-ups to the established, fixed location teams in Midwestern cities like Rockford, South Bend, Peoria, and Kalamazoo.

"We had good, good crowds because half the proceeds would go to some local charity," noted Mary Moore. "Murray Howe, our public relations guy, he was always ahead of us and he had press coverage and we had to take turns giving interviews on radio in each town that we went into. So we did have good advance publicity."[27]

The Liebrich-Barringer scrapbook collection reveals fundraisers to raise money for swimming pool construction; the Fresh Air Fund; a high-school band that needed funds to pay expenses to Chicago to play at the Lions International convention; a scholarship fund for a young pianist to the New England Conservatory; polio benefits; police and fire departments; Boys Club Building Fund; Optimist Club's Boys Work program; funds for needy families; Community Chest funds;

and a city playground fund.[28] Admission was usually $1 for adults and 50 cents for children. A few locations had discounted bleacher seats, and at least one Southern venue, Duncan Park in Spartanburg, South Carolina, offered "Colored Bleachers" for 50 cents.[29]

Between June 3 and September 4, the players traveled by bus through Illinois, Ohio, West Virginia, and points southward, including Roanoke, Asheville, Macon, Knoxville, and Hazard, Kentucky. Then it was over to Hagerstown, Maryland, and then up through New Jersey, New York, Pennsylvania, then back south for games in Washington (where they played two games at Griffith Stadium), Virginia, Maryland, and Delaware. Then it was New York again, Massachusetts, Connecticut, Maine, New Hampshire, Vermont, and games in Sherbrooke and Montreal, Quebec. They finished up by working their way west across New York and Ohio.[30] The teams scheduled 95 games in that stretch, playing 83, with 12 rainouts.[31]

The players were mostly in their late teens or early 20s, and only one, Canadian center fielder Joan Schatz, was married at the time.[32] The bus rides were long, often conducted overnight, with players assembling on the bus after their postgame showers. "The bus driver, Walt, loved to sing along with those songs, he had a beautiful voice, we traveled at night, and Wimp (Baumgartner) would stand up in front of the bus with him, and we'd sing songs all night. We had good singers on those teams!" recounted Isabel Maria Lucila Alvarez de Leon y Cerdan, also known as Lefty Alvarez. "The days were ours to do with whatever we wanted. We had to do laundry, and catch up on our sleep, and do letter-writing. But in a couple of places, like New York, we went to Radio City Music Hall and Coney Island. It was a beautiful experience to get to do that and travel all over. We played through all the South, the East, the New England states and Canada, so there are places I would have never gotten to see, to do all this *and get paid for it* was really nice."[33]

Speaking of the 1949 tour, Jane Moffett reminisced: "We traveled 26,000 miles that first summer in a bus. We played every day and prayed for rain because that was the only way we got time off. We could play a game and the next stop could be 200 miles away. A lot of police departments, fire departments and organizations would sponsor us as a fundraiser and we got called frequently to be on radio shows."[34] Anna Mae O'Dowd added, "There was a lot of singing and a lot of jokes on the bus. It was fun. Of course, you got very tired too. I remember that well."[35]

Mary Moore, who led the Sallies in games played (77), hits (75), total bases (96), home runs (3), runs scored (65), and RBIs (48) in 1950, recalled, "We toured 21 states and Canada that first year. On the farm team level, we got $25 a week and $21 for meals that wasn't taxable, plus all of our travel and housing expenses taken care of."[36]

Many of these young women had never been away from home, and the opportunity to see the country, and Canada, was educational. Massachusetts native Pat Brown was surely not the only player whose eyes were opened to segregation: "I learned a lot that summer of 1950 while traveling through the segregated South. I had never seen such signs before as 'Colored Only,' or 'White Only.' Even some of the posters announcing our games advertised separate seating for 'Colored.' I was only a teenager, but after what I had seen, nobody had to tell me that segregation was wrong; I just knew it. Those images and other situations stayed with me, and I became a firm believer in civil rights and equality. Even today, I cannot erase those images from my mind."[37]

A week before the Yankee Stadium game, the AAGPBL made national news when former Yankee star Wally Pipp called 26-year-old Rockford Peaches first baseman Dottie Kamenshek, a perennial all-star who was hitting .343 at the time, the "fanciest-fielding first baseman I've ever seen, man or woman."[38] Shortly thereafter, Kamenshek and AAGPBL President Fred Leo were contacted by officials with the Fort Lauderdale team and the Florida International League, offering to buy her out. Both Kamenshek and Leo turned down the offers. Kamenshek thought the offer was not sincere, and Leo said, "Rockford couldn't afford to lose her. I also told them we felt that women should play baseball among themselves and that they could not help but appear inferior in athletic competition with men."[39]

When asked about Pipp's comments, Bancroft replied that "Kamenshek was 'an extraordinary player,' but that he leaned against any woman being able to play in the major leagues. But he also added, 'Remember, it was only a short time ago that most major league players, managers, and sportswriters rejected the idea of Negroes ever playing the big top. Time marches on.'"[40]

Of managing the women's teams, Bancroft told writer Will Wedge, "It's fun here, mixed with the usual headaches of a skipper, and it pays better than the minors. And it sure comes under the head of new experiences, and even at 57, and as gray-haired as I am, I can be attracted by novelty.

"But don't get me wrong. This girls baseball is more than a novelty, because it is good brisk baseball, and we give the customers a fast show, the games running only about an hour and a half. And I'm telling you that the adeptness of 99% of these dolls simply amazes me and their sport has caught on well in the Midwest. ... These girls just can't get enough baseball. They want to bat for an hour before the game, but after twenty minutes on the mound, I've had more than enough exercise."[41]

Historian Merrie Fidler has also discovered that the AAGPBL planned, but apparently never held, another game in Yankee Stadium in the 1950 season. According to an article she found in a Scranton newspaper, "The (Kenosha) Comets and (Racine) Belles are scheduled in a nine-inning exhibition as a preliminary to the regular American League scheduled contest between Chicago and the Yankees. ... Considerable interest has been evidenced throughout the East in the game played by the AAGPBL after barnstorming tours by farm clubs last year. The two teams will fly by a chartered airliner to New York, and will return by air in time to resume their scheduled games at Fort Wayne and South Bend."[42]

In myriad interviews conducted over the last 30 years, since the film *A League of Their Own* was released, a trope emerges that these young women used their high salaries and newfound freedom to blaze new trails for their gender, which often involved higher education – at that time not at all common for young women. Pat Brown's autobiography repeats that pattern.

In a related article, Brown sums up, as no other player has done, the value of playing in the AAGPBL. This is the list of "Lessons from Pat Brown's Baseball Life" that she wrote about: "Toughness, assertiveness, teamwork, belief in self, independence, broader perspective, acting under pressure, and courage."[43] One quality she did not list was confidence. But she addressed it elsewhere: "I myself was only 17, 18 when I went out there to play. I was very shy, quiet through high school. The league changed me. It gave me confidence, it built me up. I finally realized that I wasn't a freak because I was athletic. Before I started playing, people said to me, 'It's wrong that you want to play baseball. It's okay when you're a little kid, when you're a tomboy.' Once I became a professional baseball player, I felt vindicated."[44]

Pat Brown went on to earn not just her master's in library science, but also her law degree and a master's in divinity.[45]

The entire tour was a rare opportunity for young women to expand their horizons through travel, athletic achievement, and making good money while enlightening crowds and opening eyes all across North America. We'll give the last word to Mary Moore: "Playing and getting to see the country like that and getting paid for it was more than you could ever dream of – I mean it was a dream come true – what else? You loved to play ball and you're seeing the country and you're traveling and everything and you couldn't ask for anything more."[46]

Women did have one more chance to play at Yankee Stadium, in a Negro American League doubleheader on July 11, 1954, between the Kansas City Monarchs and the Indianapolis Clowns. A newspaper article in advance of the game said, "The girls take a back seat to no one on the field either. They both really play baseball and Miss Toni Stone of the Monarchs, and Miss Connie Morgan of the Clowns have displayed plenty of ability."[47] While advance publicity had both women slated to play second base, the lack of a box score makes it currently impossible to know if either actually played.

AUTHOR'S NOTE

The author is grateful for research help from Merrie Fidler, official historian of the AAGPBL Players Association; Brian Richards, senior museum curator of the New York Yankees; Cassidy Lent and Rachel Wells of the National Baseball Hall of Fame library; former players Joanne McComb, Mary Moore, and Toni Palermo; Adam Berenbak of the National Archives; and historians Carol Sheldon and Ryan Woodward.

NOTES

1   John Drebinger, "Yanks Bench DiMaggio, Stagger to 7-6 Victory Over Athletics," *New York Times*, August 12, 1950.

2   Drebinger.

3   Untitled *New York Herald Tribune* article dated August 12, 1950, retrieved from Liebrich-Barringer AAGPBL Tour Scrapbooks (MSS 10, 1-D-2), National Baseball Hall of Fame Library, Cooperstown, New York, September 30, 2022.

4   W.C. Madden, *The Women of the All-American Girls Professional Baseball League: A Biographical Dictionary* (Jefferson, North Carolina: McFarland & Company, 1997), 220.

5   Madden, 220.

6   Joanne McComb, telephone interview, November 22, 2022.

7   Mary Moore, telephone interview, November 6, 2022.

8   Toni Palermo, telephone interview, November 6, 2022.

9   Palermo interview.

10 Merrie A. Fidler. *The Origins and History of the All-American Girls Professional Baseball League* (Jefferson, North Carolina: McFarland & Company, 2006), 110.

11 Patricia I. Brown, *A League of My Own: Memoir of a Pitcher for the All-American Girls Professional Baseball League* (Jefferson, North Carolina: McFarland & Company, 2003), 66.

12 Kat D. Williams, *Isabel "Lefty" Alvarez: The Improbable Life of a Cuban American Baseball Star* (Lincoln: University of Nebraska Press, 2020), 59.

13 McComb interview.

14 Joanne McComb. Player questionnaire in the research files of the National Baseball Hall of Fame, 1997.

15 Joanne McComb, *Touching Bases*, the newsletter of the AAGPBL Players Association, January 2005.

16 Mary Lou Kolanko, *Touching Bases*.

17 Madden, 148.

18 Brown, 173.

19 Andy Horschak, "Brewers, ex-Comet Preserve the Legacy of the AAGPBL," undated clipping, likely from the *Kenosha News*, retrieved from Liebrich-Barringer AAGPBL Tour Scrapbooks.

20 Brown, 67.

21 Dennis Daniels, "Move over Cobb, Ruth & Williams!" *Boston Herald*, October 12, 1988: 31.

22 Brown, 67.

23 Brown, 162.

24 McComb interview.

25 Mary Moore, interview with AAGPBL historian Merrie Fidler, conducted by phone in March 2004. Interview transcript provided by Merrie Fidler.

26 https://www.aagpbl.org/history/league-history. Retrieved October 21, 2022.

27 Moore interview.

28 Numerous articles from the AAGPBL Tour Scrapbooks.

29 Numerous newspaper game advertisements from the AAGPBL Tour Scrapbooks.

30 Tour schedule and results from the AAGPBL Tour Scrapbooks.

31 Typescript of schedule and results, AAGPBL Tour Scrapbooks.

32 Mary Hayes, "Yank Stadium to Queen City: Diamond Damsels Hit With Patrons," *News* (city unidentified) from AAGPBL Tour Scrapbooks.

33 Jim Sargent, *We Were the All-American Girls* (Jefferson, North Carolina: McFarland, 2013), 281.

34 Jessica Driscoll. "Former Pitman Resident Honored as Baseball First," *Gloucester County Times* (Woodbury, New Jersey), July 5, 2010.

35 Katie Sartoris. "Annie O'Dowd Recalls Time Spent in All-American Girls Professional Baseball League," *Villages Daily Sun* (The Villages, Florida), May 31, 2013.

36 Pat Andrews. "Female Star Returns Downriver: LP Grad Depicted in 'A League of Their Own,'" *Heritage Newspapers/News-Herald* (Taylor, Michigan), October 25, 1995: 4-C.

37 Brown, 70-72.

38 Fidler, 223.

39 Ed Sainsbury (United Press), "Florida Nine Tries to Sign Woman Player," unknown newspaper, August 3, 1950, AAGPBL Tour Scrapbooks.

40 Will Wedge, "Setting the Pace," *The New York Sun*, August 5, 1948, AAGPBL Tour Scrapbooks.

41 Wedge.

42   "Girl Ball Teams in Stadium Game: Jean Marlowe to Play in New York July 17," *Scranton* (Pennsylvania) *Times Tribune,* May 31, 1950: 41.

43   Patricia I. Brown and Elizabeth M. McKenzie, "First Person … A Law Librarian at Cooperstown," *Law Library Journal*, Volume 93:1. Winter, 2001.

44   Liz Galst, "The Way It Was: A Real Professional Ballplayer Looks at League," *Boston Phoenix*, July 3, 1992: Arts Section 7.

45   Carol Sheldon, "Patricia Brown," *Boston Herald.* Player profile provided at AAGPBL website. https://www.aagpbl.org/profiles/patricia-brown-pat/219. Retrieved November 22, 2022.

46   Mary Moore interview.

47   "Clowns-KC Monarchs at Stadium Sunday: Bitter Rivalry for NAL Girl Players in Focus," *New York Amsterdam News,* July 10, 1954: 23.

BATS, BALLS, BOYS, AND DREAMS:
THE HEARST SANDLOT CLASSIC
AT YANKEE STADIUM, 1959-1965

By Alan Cohen

Jim Spencer had 36 major-league home runs at Yankee Stadium during his 15-year career, the first coming on August 6, 1969. However, his first Yankee Stadium homer came on August 12, 1963, in a tune-up game for the annual Hearst Sandlot Classic. Spencer was on the United States All-Stars, who defeated the Eastern Pennsylvania All-Stars, 10-6. On August 17, 1963, he took the field in the 18th annual Hearst Sandlot Classic.

The Hearst Classic was a national showcase for young ballplayers. The annual game, played between the New York Journal-American All-Stars and the U.S. All-Stars, was first contested in 1946 at the Polo Grounds. The New York team was the cream of the New York sandlot leagues, and the US team represented cities in which the Hearst newspaper chain had publications. In 1959 the game, known to locals as the Journal-American Game, was moved to Yankee Stadium.

From the games held at Yankee Stadium between 1959 and 1965, 30 players advanced to the major leagues. At least one Hearst player was in each All-Star Game from 1954 through 1978.

The games were played during a time of change. In 1960, the US presidential election to choose a successor to Dwight Eisenhower was three months away, and the spy trial of U-2 pilot Francis Gary Powers was making headlines. In 1961 Cold War tensions were high. In the *New York Journal-American*, a headline read, "If War Comes to New York: Shelters Can Save Millions of Lives." In 1962 newspapers spoke about the stars in the sky being joined by something called Telstar, the first of a series of communications satellites that would dot the skies in coming decades. In 1964 Lyndon Johnson was in his first summer in the White House and the Warren Commission was investigating the assassination of President John F. Kennedy.

AUGUST 18, 1959: US ALL-STARS 13; JOURNAL-AMERICAN ALL-STARS 4

The US All-Stars erased an early three-run deficit to win 13-4 as 14,098 looked on. The starting pitchers were Larry Bearnarth for the New Yorkers and Richard Donaldson of Pittsburgh for the US All-Stars. The US All-Stars had 10 hits and took advantage of eight Journal-American All-Star errors.

Bearnarth pitched two shutout innings but came out of the game after walking the bases full in the third inning. The US All-Stars scored four runs in the frame and took a lead they did not relinquish. After completing his studies at St. John's in 1962, Bearnarth signed with the Mets and made his debut on April 16, 1963. In four seasons with the Mets, he went 13-21.

Donaldson pitched a scoreless first inning, but a throwing error by shortstop Ernie Fazio on a potential double-play ball in the second inning led to three runs. Donaldson was replaced by Boston's Wilbur Wood, who stopped the bleeding and his mates provided ample run support. He got the win and had the biggest career success of anyone who played in the 1959 game.

The US team was led by manager Ossie Vitt and coach Buddy Hassett. New York manager Tommy Holmes and his assistant, Steve Ray, put the Journal-American players through their drills.

Players partook in the activities that were essential to the program. They toured the Empire State Building; took a trip to West Point for the Cadet dress parade and lunch; and went to Bear Mountain for a steak dinner. They took the Circle Line boat trip around Manhattan, and they saw ballgames at Yankee Stadium.

On Monday, August 17, the US team drilled at the soon-to-be demolished Ebbets Field and received their uniforms. That evening, there was a banquet in the Terrace Room at the Hotel New Yorker (where the US players stayed during their week in New York), followed by a visit to the Radio City Music Hall, where everybody saw the movie *North by Northwest*.

AUGUST 18, 1960: US ALL-STARS 6; JOURNAL-AMERICAN ALL-STARS 5

In a thriller, the US All-Stars prevailed, 6-5. The New Yorkers took the early lead on a two-run inside-the-park homer by Rickie Stancavage, which US All-Star pitcher John Vergare remembered was misplayed by one of his outfielders.

Howie Kitt, who had completed his freshman year at Columbia University, was the starting pitcher for the New Yorkers. In three innings, the left-hander allowed no hits. His seven strikeouts (six were consecutive) set a Hearst Classic record. He received the Lou Gehrig Award as the game's MVP and signed with the Yankees for an $80,000 bonus. He later graduated cum laude with a degree in economics from Hofstra University. In 1965, with his fastball gone and his once great prospects but a memory, he accepted a fellowship from Columbia and went on to earn a PhD in economics His career took him to the top echelons of antitrust and trade regulation matters.

After Kitt left the game, the US All-Stars mounted a charge and took a 4-2 lead on a two-run homer by San Antonio's Joel Tigett. Texas's *Seguin Gazette* proclaimed that "Tigett's booming bat was heard throughout the entire U.S. during the All-Star game in New York last August 18. The fourth inning was the occasion when the entire baseball world stood up and took a startled look at Seguin and Joel. That's when Joel simply strode up to the plate and blasted a 415-foot home run into the 20th row behind left field at Yankee Stadium."

The starting catcher for the US All-Stars was Bill Freehan, representing the *Detroit Times,* and his double drove in the first run for the visitors. He came around to score the tying run on a single by Baltimore's Charlie Bree, who scored on Tigett's two-run homer. In 14 full seasons with the Tigers, Freehan was named to 11 All-Star teams, including 10 in succession from 1964 through 1973

Mike Marshall, a natural shortstop from Adrian, Michigan, also represented the *Detroit Times*. He entered the game in the sixth inning to play right field. He went to the mound in the bottom of the eighth with two outs. The New Yorkers had already scored a run to make the score 6-5 and were threatening to do more damage. Marshall secured the final out of the inning and retired the side in order in the ninth inning to save

the win. It was in Los Angeles that Marshall gained a share of immortality. Dodgers manager Walter Alston bought in to Marshall's desire to work often to maintain his strength. In 1974 Marshall appeared in 106 games, posted a 2.42 ERA, was credited with 21 saves, made the NL All-Star team, and won the National League Cy Young Award.

Center fielder Brian McCall of the US All-Stars had completed his junior year of high school. The Long Beach, California, lad signed with the White Sox for $50,000 in 1961. The program handed out at the game in New York noted that McCall was a gifted cartoonist and illustrator. McCall got his first taste of the big leagues in 1962. On September 28, 1962, in his third game, he singled for his first major-league hit. At breakfast prior to the final game of the season, McCall introduced his mother to a couple of the White Sox coaches. The 19-year-old wound up starting the game against the Yankees and became one of the youngest players to have a multiple home-run game. In the third inning, he hit his first big-league homer off Bill Stafford. His seventh-inning homer off Ralph Terry was the icing on the cake as Chicago won 8-4. After baseball, McCall became a successful artist.

AUGUST 24, 1961: US ALL-STARS 6; JOURNAL-AMERICAN ALL-STARS 3

A five-run fifth inning propelled the New Yorkers to the 6-3 win.

Davey Johnson had completed his first year at Texas A&M. He was very highly thought of by Buddy Hassett, who commented, "I like his wrist action and the way he whips the bat around so fast." Two long homers, one of which sailed to the upper deck at the Bronx ballpark, were particularly impressive. Johnson remembers rooming with fellow San Antonian Jerry Grote during their stay in New York. Johnson remembered Grote having him sit on Grote's shoulders when the future Mets catcher was doing pushups, so as to strengthen his arms.

Johnson signed with Baltimore for a $25,000 bonus after his sophomore year of college. He secured a guarantee that he could finish college. He was named to four American League All-Star teams and won three Gold Glove Awards. He went on to a successful career as a manager.

Shaun Fitzmaurice of Wellesley, Massachusetts, the substitute center fielder for the US All-Stars, finished in a second-place tie in the MVP voting. He banged out an inside-the-park homer to deepest center field with Grote on base in the ninth inning at Yankee Stadium on that August evening to cut the New York lead to 6-3, but the US team could not close the gap any further.

Larry Yellen started for the New Yorkers and struck out five batters in three scoreless innings. In the summer of 1962, he signed with Houston for $55,000. He was called up late in the 1963. Houston planned to use him in a game on September 27. The idea was to field a team of their youngest players. However, that year, Yom Kippur Eve was on September 27, and Yellen is Jewish. General manager Paul Richards acquiesced to Yellen's request not to play on September 27, and the youngster was handed the ball on the prior day.

AUGUST 16, 1962: US ALL-STARS 4; JOURNAL-AMERICAN ALL-STARS 4

Eddie Joost took over the reins as US manager in 1962.

The game was tied 4-4 and stopped by curfew after 11 innings and more than four hours of play. It was the only tie in the history of the series. The game's MVP, New York shortstop Joe Russo, made some sparkling plays in the field, including robbing Boston's Tony Conigliaro of a hit, and went 2-for-4 with an RBI. In the last inning, writer Morrey Rokeach of the *Journal-American* went to the New York team's dugout and informed Russo that he had been chosen MVP. Russo graduated from St. John's University and was a baseball coach at the school for 27 years, 23 as head coach.

A blurb in the game program over Conigliaro's picture said that he "could be best prospect on US All-Star squad." In the third inning, he singled in a run and eventually scored during a three-run rally. On his first visit to Yankee Stadium, he was in awe of the place. "I'm going to be here (playing for some big-league club)," said Conigliaro to his Boston teammate and longtime friend Bill "Skip" Falasca. Conigliaro was signed by the Red Sox for $20,000. In 1964 he made his major-league debut. After going 1-for-5 in his first game, played at Yankee Stadium, he hit a home run on the first pitch he saw at the Boston home opener at Fenway Park. His career was affected by a beaning incident in 1967.

In practices held at Yankee Stadium, Baltimore's Ron Swoboda homered, but in the game itself, a very nervous Swoboda went 0-for-4. The kids saw a Mets game during their time in New York. Swoboda signed with the Mets before the 1964 season. He is best remembered for his game-saving catch in fourth game of the 1969 World Series.

AUGUST 14, 1963: US ALL-STARS 4; JOURNAL-AMERICAN ALL-STARS 0

The US All-Stars won 4-0 in front of 15,432 spectators. The teams pitchers were dominant, registering 14 strikeouts in the shutout.

The MVP trophy went to Joe Gualco of San Francisco. He excelled in relief, striking out six of the eight players he faced. Entering the game with his team leading 3-0, he allowed only one hit and a walk. After college, he went into education and was named the head baseball coach at George Washington High School in San Francisco in 1981. He served in that post for 13 years.

San Antonio's Freddie Patek stood only 5-feet-5 but packed a wallop. During a practice at St. John's, he slammed a couple of balls out of the park at the 390-foot mark. He is best remembered for his years with the Kansas City Royals. He was named to three All-Star teams and was part of three consecutive divisional champions that lost in the American League Championship Series to the Yankees.

Jim Spencer of Baltimore had just completed his sophomore year in high school and did not turn 16 until four days after his selection was announced. In 1978 he returned to Yankee Stadium as a member of the Yankees and once again was on the same field with 1963 teammate Fred Patek in the Bronx during the American League Championship Series.

Fran Healy was just thrilled to be a part of the scene at the Hearst Classic: "Even if I play here in a World Series some day – and don't get me wrong, I'm not a fathead or anything – I don't think the thrill could ever be bigger than it is right now." In 1964 Cleveland offered Healy a bonus and allowed him to complete his second year at American International College in Springfield, Massachusetts, and report to his minor-league team after the semester was complete. After his playing career (his best years were with the Kansas City Royals), he went into the announcing booth working with the Yankees and Mets and produced the Emmy Award-winning *Halls of Fame* television series.

Skip Lockwood and his parents, made their way to New York in a "beat-up old Buick." He was led around to the sights in New York by his mother, who in her younger days, had been a Radio City Music Hall Rockette. Lockwood contributed to his team's win with a fourth-inning RBI single. He was signed as an infielder by Kansas City for $135,000 in 1964. In five seasons with the Mets, whom he joined in 1975, he saved 65 games and had a 2.80 ERA.

AUGUST 19, 1964: JOURNAL-AMERICAN
ALL-STARS 2; US ALL-STARS 1

The New York World's Fair was housed in Flushing, across from the new home of the Mets, and was added to the stops made by the youngsters participating in the Hearst game. The Polo Grounds, home to so many Hearst games, had been demolished.

A crowd of 14,189 came to Yankee Stadium on August 19. The New Yorkers won the game, 2-1. The low-scoring affair saw strikeout records galore. New York pitchers fanned 16 and limited the opposition to three hits. The 11 strikeouts registered by the US All-Stars pitchers produced a game total of 27, a record for the event.

Don Balsamo started and struck out a record eight during his three innings on the mound for the New Yorkers. He attended Long Island University and played ball in the Atlantic Collegiate Baseball League in 1967, pitching the first no-hitter in the history of the four-team summer league on July 29. He did not play in Organized Baseball.

For two innings, the New Yorkers were shut out by Joe Coleman. Coleman struck out two batters in his two innings of work. He was the first-round draft pick of the Washington Senators in 1965 and made his debut at the end of the season. His best years were with Detroit. He went 88-73 in six years in the Motor City, had two 20-win seasons, and was named to the American League All-Star team in 1972.

Ron Thomas of Los Angeles pitched the third and fourth innings for the US team, striking out seven batters. (One of the batters reached base when the catcher mishandled the pitch in the third inning.) Thomas thus set single-inning and two-inning strikeout records. In the fourth inning, he yielded the second of MVP Steve Frohman's doubles, and allowed the New York first baseman to score the run that knotted the score at 1-1. Frohman signed with the Cardinals, but never got beyond Class A.

AUGUST 21, 1965: US ALL-STARS 9;
JOURNAL-AMERICAN ALL-STARS 3

The US All-Stars exploded for six runs in the 10th inning to win in front of 16,191 fans at Yankee Stadium.

The MVP was first baseman Pete Koegel of Seaford, New York, who had two hits, including a towering 450-foot fourth-inning triple off the auxiliary scoreboard in left field. He was signed by Kansas City in 1965. It took six years and many stops, but on September 1, 1970, Koegel arrived in the majors with the Milwaukee Brewers. He appeared seven games in 1970, mostly as a pinch-hitter. On September 25 he had his only major-league homer. In all, he played in 62 major-league games.

Although more than 90 percent of the players in the Hearst Sandlot Classic never got to the majors and most never played professionally, they had memories and stories to share.

John Salmon of Malden, Massachusetts, played the entire 1965 game, went 3-for-6 with an RBI on a suicide squeeze and was runner-up in the balloting for the Gehrig Award. Salmon remembered Koegel's triple. At first, he thought that left fielder Mike Houck had a chance at the ball, and did not hustle on the play. Houck, though, was a pitcher-first baseman whose first and only game in left field was in the tune-up at Shea Stadium on August 19. He did not have a realistic chance to catch the ball. Salmon got a master's degree in business from Babson College in Wellesley, Massachusetts. He pursued a career in sales and then went on to work in probations for the Boston court system. Houck played briefly in the Baltimore Organization.

What else do they remember? After a tune-up game on August 19, the players visited the World's Fair, and that evening they had dinner at Mama Leone's. John Salmon of Boston and Mike Houck of Albany, New York, would never forget that dinner.

SOURCES

In addition to the sources cited in the notes, the author used Baseball-Reference.com and interviewed the following people about the Hearst Games from 1959 through 1965:

Tim Cullen, August 29, 2014; Ernie Fazio, March 14, 2015; Shaun Fitzmaurice, March 15, 2015; Joe Gualco, July 23, 2016; Fran Healy, July 1, 2021; Jim Henneman, July 7, 2014; Mike Houck, April 20, 2016; Davey Johnson, March 10, 2015; Howie Kitt, May 19, 2016; Skip Lockwood, April 24, 2015; Mike Marshall, March 4, 2015; Brian McCall, June 5, 2015; Jim McElroy, June 6, 2014; Joe Russo, January 22, 2015, and May 27, 2017; John Salmon, January 19, 2016; Ron Swoboda, January 7, 2014; Steve Thomson, July 2, 2016; John Vergare, November 26, 2014.

CORRESPONDENCE:

Bob Nash (1963 US All-Stars)

Other articles about the Hearst Sandlot Classic:

Cohen, Alan. "The Hearst Sandlot Classic: More than a Doorway to the Big Leagues," *Baseball Research Journal* (Society for American Baseball Research, 2013), 21-29.

Cohen, Alan. "When They Were Just Boys: Chicago and Youth Baseball Take Center Stage," *The National Pastime* (Society for American Baseball Research, 2015), 74-77.

Cohen, Alan. "Bats, Balls, Boys, Dreams and Unforgettable Experiences, Youth All-Star Games in New York, 1944-1965," *The National Pastime* (Society for American Baseball Research, 2017), 85-88.

Cohen, Alan. "From Sandlot to Center Stage: Pittsburgh Youth All-Star Games, 1944-59," *The National Pastime* (Society for American Baseball Research, 2018), 60-63.

NOTES

1   The format was devised by *New York Journal-American* sports editor Max Kase who in 1945 had launched the Journal-American Sandlot Alliance. The Alliance became the Greater New York Sandlot Athletic Alliance after the Hearst program ceased in 1966 and as of 2022 remained active under the leadership of Victor Feld.

2   The selection process for the US All-Stars varied. It included a series of baseball schools and tryouts culminating in big games in Boston and San Francisco; All-Star Games in Baltimore, Detroit, Los Angeles, Milwaukee, Pittsburgh, San Antonio, and Seattle; and a poll of area writers and coaches in Albany, New York.

3   The Polo Grounds was not well-maintained after the New York Giants moved to San Francisco after the 1957 season. By 1958 the facility was being used for stock-car races and the track around the field made play difficult when the Hearst game was held there in 1958. The logical choice was to move the game to Yankee Stadium in 1959.

4   The 1965 game was the last Hearst Sandlot Classic. The demise of the game was hastened by several factors including two New York City newspaper strikes. The first lasted 114 days from December 8, 1962, through March 31, 1963. The second lasted for 23 days between September 13 and October 8, 1965, and the losses from this strike were such that it effectively shut down the *New York Journal-American,* which was the force behind the game. The *Journal-American* ceased publication on April 28, 1966.

5   The 30 players who advanced to the major leagues are Wilbur Wood, Larry Bearnarth, Fritz Fisher, Darrell Sutherland, Bill Ott, Bob Guindon, Glenn Beckert, Ernie Fazio, Tim Cullen, Mike Marshall, Brian McCall, Bill Freehan, Mike Ryan, Shaun Fitzmaurice, Jerry Grote, Davey Johnson, Joe Foy, Larry Yellen, Tony Conigliaro, Ron Swoboda, Don Mason, Fran Healy, Skip Lockwood, Fred Patek, Jim Spencer, Sonny Ruberto, Terry Crowley, Joe Coleman, Pete Koegel, and Mike Jorgensen.

6   Dan Brigham, "If War Comes to New York: Shelters Can Save Millions of Lives," *New York Journal-American,* August 16, 1961: 25.

7   "S.F.'s Fazio to Start at Short in Hearst Game," *San Francisco Examiner,* August 18, 1959: III, 4. The annual visit to Radio City allowed the boys to see the floor show including the Rockettes and the following films: *North by Northwest* (1959), *Song Without End* (1960), *Fanny* (1961), *That Touch of Mink* (1962), *The Thrill of It All* (1963), and *The Unsinkable Molly Brown* (1964).

8   "Antitrust and Trade Regulation Specialist Howard Kitt Joins CRA International's New York Office; Founder of NERA's Antitrust Consultancy Offers Wealth of Experience," Business Wire, June 2, 2005.

9   "Tigett Wallop Gives Seguin Greatest Sports Moment," *Seguin* (Texas) *Gazette:* October 12, 1960: 3, 1.

10   Morrey Rokeach, "Vitt Impressed by Star Nine's Power, Speed," *New York Journal-American,* August 19, 1961: 15.

11   Rokeach.

12   "17th Annual Hearst Classic: United States All Stars vs. N.Y. All-Stars: Yankee Stadium, Aug. 16, 1962." Official Program.

13   Bill Nowlin, "Tony Conigliaro," SABR BioProject, https://sabr.org/bioproj/person/tony-conigliaro/.

14   Jeff Cohen, "All 5 N.E. Boys Make Hit in N.Y. Sandlot Classic," *Boston Record American,* August 16, 1963: 72.

15   "Gualco MVP in Hearst Classic," *San Francisco Examiner,* August 15, 1963: 51, 55.

16   Bill McSweeney, "Hearst Sandlot Classic Wednesday," *Boston Record American,* August 12, 1963: 40.

17   Garry Brown, "From MLB to TV Interviews, Holyoke's Fran Healy Remains Pride of the Paper City," *Springfield Republican,* October 28, 2019. https://www.masslive.com/living/2019/10/from-mlb-to-tv-interviews-holyokes-fran-healy-remains-pride-of-the-paper-city.html.

18   Author interview with Skip Lockwood, April 24, 2015.

19   Bill Nowlin, "Skip Lockwood," SABR BioProject, https://sabr.org/bioproj/person/Skip-Lockwood/.

LIVE FROM YANKEE STADIUM: A BRIEF HISTORY OF THE YANKEES ON RADIO

By Donna L. Halper

For New York Yankees fans, Wednesday, April 18, 1923, was a momentous occasion: That was the day the brand-new Yankee Stadium made its debut. More than 74,000 fans were in attendance, and thousands more tried (and failed) to get in.[1] There was national interest in the game, thanks in large part to the popularity of Babe Ruth; as a result, the press box was crowded with reporters from a wide range of publications. But one group was absent from the day's events: radio broadcasters.

That really wasn't surprising. Commercial radio was not even two years old, and remote broadcasts were still in their infancy. But in addition to technological challenges, one other factor kept the home opener off the air – opposition from the Yankees management, the baseball writers, and the Western Union Telegraph Company. Yankees management believed that allowing the games to be broadcast would cut into attendance. The writers worried that broadcasting the game, or even giving the scores, would cut

Radio broadcasts of Yankees games in the 1920s were sparse, but Graham McNamee (shown here with Babe Ruth) often called the few that did make the air.

into sales of newspapers.[2] And Western Union had established strong business ties with the newspapers, offering exclusive access to scores and summaries of games from all over the country. If radio stations could broadcast the games, the telegraph company's importance would be diminished.[3]

While it might have been courteous for the Yankees to broadcast the sold-out 1923 home opener, the fans probably weren't expecting it, given how new radio broadcasting was. Meanwhile, a few radio stations were beginning to broadcast scores and brief summaries, and these reports were welcomed by the listeners, especially fans eager to know how Babe Ruth had done that day.[4] There was also a new sports commentary program, one of the first of its kind. It was hosted by William J. "Bill" Slocum, then of the *New York Tribune*; he had covered the Yankees for nearly a decade. Even Slocum's fellow beat reporters enjoyed listening to his radio show, with his anecdotes about games he had seen, and players he knew – including Babe Ruth.[5] (Slocum was also Babe Ruth's ghostwriter, something most fans probably did not realize.[6])

During the regular season in 1923, there were no broadcasts of Yankees games, but arrangements were made to put the World Series between the Yankees and the Giants on the air, on stations WJZ and WEAF, live from Yankee Stadium and the Polo Grounds. It wasn't the first time World Series baseball was broadcast live, nor the first time that a Yankees game was broadcast. A year earlier, anyone with a radio had heard the Yankees play the Giants in the 1922 World Series, but since Yankee Stadium had not yet been completed, the games originated from the Polo Grounds, with sportswriting legend Grantland Rice doing the play-by-play.

The announcers for the 1923 World Series were Major J. Andrew White, editor of a radio magazine, *The Wireless Age*, on WJZ, and Graham McNamee, a former vocalist and now an up-and-coming announcer, on WEAF. The broadcasts almost didn't happen; the owners did not want to grant their permission, but Commissioner Kenesaw Mountain Landis stepped in and overruled them.[7] Interestingly, some of the same baseball writers who had expressed opposition to broadcasting any games, including the president of the Baseball Writers Association, Fred Lieb, and fellow baseball writers Bozeman Bulger and Hugh Fullerton, went on the air to offer commentary during the Series.[8]

But if the fans expected more Yankees baseball on the air in 1924, they were disappointed. All that was available were nightly scores provided by some local stations. The World Series was broadcast again, but the Yankees were not part of it, since they didn't win the pennant. The next time a Yankees game was broadcast was Opening Day 1925, when the World Series champion Washington Senators came to Yankee Stadium. Unfortunately for Yankees fans, the game was only broadcast by a Washington station, WRC, and it was not broadcast live. It was a re-creation, originating from the broadcasting studio of the *Washington Times* newspaper. Charles Matson was the announcer, and he narrated the story of the game "just as it [was] telegraphed from Yankee Stadium by R.D. Thomas of the *Times* sports staff."[9]

It wasn't until 1926 that another Yankees game was broadcast live. On April 13, 1926, Boston Red Sox owner Bob Quinn, who had also kept the games off the radio, relented and permitted the home opener against the Yankees to be broadcast live from Fenway Park,[10] with *Boston Traveler* baseball writer Gus Rooney doing the play-by-play on station WNAC.[11] Then, on April 21, the Yankees also broadcast their home opener, against the Red Sox, with Graham McNamee at the microphone, over WEAF.[12] There is no available evidence that suggests this was coordinated by the Red Sox and Yankees; rather, it appeared to be a coincidence. Quinn made his decision so suddenly that even the Boston sportswriters were surprised – when they received the press release, they didn't even know who would be doing the play-by-play.[13] As for the Yankees, team management was convinced there was no need to broadcast more than one game, and the home opener seemed a good choice. At that time, teams received no revenue from putting a game on the air, and ballclubs like the Yankees that already had good attendance saw little incentive to allow any broadcasts.[14] Thus, while the 1926 home opener got on the air, no other Yankees games were broadcast until the team reached the World Series.

Throughout 1926, a growing number of radio stations were linking up to broadcast certain important current events, like political conventions, presidential speeches, or the World Series. There was no national network yet (though the National Broadcasting Company would soon make its debut), but by October 1926, the World Series games were scheduled to air on stations in 22 cities; announcers Graham McNamee and Phillips Carlin opened the Series live from Yankee Stadium as the Yankees played the St. Louis Cardinals.[15] (Carlin and McNamee were becoming a popular sportscasting duo. Since Carlin joined WEAF in November 1923, they had collaborated on coverage of numerous sporting events, including college football and major-league baseball.)

By 1928, it was finally possible to hear the World Series from coast to coast, thanks to NBC, and a second network, CBS (then known as Columbia). Both networks had announcers at Yankee Stadium on October 4: McNamee and Carlin handled the games for NBC, and at Columbia, it was the team of Edward "Ted" Husing and J. Andrew White. White, a veteran sportscaster, was now the president of Columbia; Husing had worked for WJZ as a staff announcer for musical programs but had transitioned to covering sports, including World Series broadcasts. In 1929 both networks also broadcast the home opener between the Yankees and Red Sox, on April 18, live from Yankee Stadium. McNamee did the play-by-play for NBC affiliates, and Ted Husing was behind the microphone for Columbia stations.[16]

Many Yankees fans undoubtedly enjoyed listening to the network announcers; although there were no ratings services yet, there was growing evidence that listeners approved of baseball play-by-play, and radio stations were receiving fan mail and phone calls saying so. For example, Harry Hartman, sports commentator at WFBE in Cincinnati, noted that the broadcasts were turning more people into baseball fans. He said that "women and children have become more acquainted with [baseball], and are eager to accept when invited to attend a game."[17] The belief that the radio broadcasts were helping to create new fans was echoed by Bob Quinn of the Red Sox, Sam Breadon of the Cardinals, and several other owners and executives who had previously objected to putting the games on the air.[18]

But Yankees management did not agree. Other than Opening Day, no other Yankees games were available in 1929. And there was little indication that that policy would change. Ed Barrow, secretary of the Yankees, said in early 1930 that no games would be broadcast except for Opening Day because he continued to believe more broadcasts would have a negative impact on attendance.[19] Meanwhile, the Yankees were increasingly becoming outliers: By 1930, a growing number of major-league teams were relaxing their "no radio" policy and allowing more broadcasts during the season. As further proof that the owners were no longer unified on the subject, when major-league owners gathered in early December 1931 for their winter meetings, an attempt by some owners to ban all broadcasts in 1932 was quickly blocked; Chicago Cubs President William L. "Bill" Veeck (the elder)

was among the faction that strongly supported broadcasting the games.[20]

But the Yankees ownership held firm.[21] In 1931 and 1932, just the home opener got on the air. The Yankees won the pennant in 1932, and in late September, the networks began broadcasting the World Series, with the Yankees playing the Chicago Cubs. And the night before Game One, New York listeners heard "The Old Maestro," bandleader Ben Bernie, offering something for baseball fans during his popular WEAF and NBC program. He was joined by Yankees manager Joe McCarthy and Cubs manager Charlie Grimm, each telling listeners why their team was going to win.[22] (It was McCarthy whose prediction was right – the Yankees swept the Cubs in four games.)

However, to the dismay of Yankees fans, even the Opening Day games ceased to be broadcast during the mid-1930s. The only option was network coverage if the Yankees made it back to the World Series (which they did again in 1936). By now, baseball was on the air in an ever-increasing number of cities, and it was even sponsored – stations were making money from airing the games. And rather than depressing attendance, it was keeping fan interest high – something Bill Veeck had been saying since 1927.[23]

In April 1938 things finally changed, thanks in part to Bill Slocum. He had retired from sportswriting and was hired by General Mills as a "contact man": a liaison between the company, which sponsored numerous baseball games, the radio stations that broadcast them, and the various team owners. Slocum's duties also included improving relationships with the announcers who called the games, and even providing some training (as well as letting them know what the sponsor expected – which seemed to be a balancing act between being objective and factual about the play-by-play, but being enthusiastic about the sponsor's products).[24]

Slocum approached the Yankees management about getting on the air; surprisingly, he got a "yes." We may never know why: Perhaps it was because of his credibility as a longtime baseball writer, or his powers of persuasion. (The sponsors credited him with negotiating the deal, which put the games on WABC in New York.[25]) Then again, perhaps it was due to Yankees owner Jacob Ruppert having to miss attending the 1938 World Series due to a lingering illness, and relying on the radio networks to listen to the games.[26] But whatever the reason, by year's end, Ruppert announced that in 1939, Yankees games would be on the radio; he said this was his gift to people who were hospitalized, or who couldn't attend the games due to health problems. (However, the reporter covering the story noted that Ruppert wasn't being totally altruistic: The sponsors would be paying about $100,000 for the rights to broadcast the games.[27]) And the decision may also have been influenced by the early December 1938 announcement by Brooklyn Dodgers general manager Larry MacPhail that the Dodgers had agreed to broadcast their games in 1939.[28] MacPhail received about $75,000 from sponsors for the rights.[29]

WABC's lead announcer for the 1939 season was veteran broadcaster Arch McDonald, previously the voice of the Washington Senators. McDonald's duties included hosting daily sports reports, as well as play-by-play of both the Yankees and the Giants home games; his assistants on those broadcasts were a former newscaster named Garnett Marks, and an up-and-coming sportscaster named Mel Allen. Although some listeners found McDonald's style too "folksy," most fans seem to like him;[30] they especially liked his clever nicknames for some of the players – he called Joe DiMaggio the Yankee Clipper, and it stuck.[31] But at season's end, McDonald returned to the Washington Senators. His replacement was his former assistant, Mel Allen. A graduate of the University of Alabama, with a law degree, Allen fell in love with sportscasting; hired by CBS in 1937, he was trained by Ted Husing.[32] Allen was just 27 years old in 1940, making him one of the youngest major-league radio announcers.[33] His sidekick was Jay C. Flippen, a former comedian turned sportscaster, and his statistician was Jack Slocum (one of Bill Slocum's sons).

But in 1941 no agreement was reached, and while the Brooklyn Dodgers were on the radio (on WOR, with Red Barber doing the play-by-play, assisted by Al Helfer), the Yankees were not. Fortunately for their fans, the Yankees reached the World Series, which was broadcast via the Mutual Broadcasting System, on WOR. By April 1942, the Yankees games were back on the air, also on WOR; General Mills was the main sponsor again, with R.H. Macy as the cosponsor. Mel Allen returned to do the play-by-play, assisted by Cornelius "Connie" Desmond. Then, in 1943, the Yankees announced that no broadcasts of their games would be permitted, and the Giants did the same. This time, it was a dispute over fees: In 1942, sponsors had reportedly paid $75,000 to each team for the broadcasting rights.[34] In 1943, according to Yankees management, no sponsors came forward who were willing to pay that amount. Ed Barrow, president of the Yankees, and Giants executive Leo Bondy, were unwilling to broadcast anything for which there was

no sponsorship, and for which their clubs were not paid. As a result, the games remained off the air for the season.

Fortunately for the listeners, both the Yankees and the Giants obtained sponsors for the 1944 season for all home games; the broadcasts moved to station WINS, where Don Dunphy, best known for covering boxing, and Bill Slater, a former WOR staff announcer, did the play-by-play. Both got good reviews, but the next year, Dunphy was replaced by Al Helfer. Bill Slater stayed on, and the games remained on WINS. (If you are wondering about Mel Allen, he was serving in the Army for three years.)

When Allen returned from the service in 1946, he also returned to the broadcast booth, where he remained for the next 18 years – on WINS, then WMGM, and finally WCBS. During those years, he had numerous partners, including Russ Hodges, Curt Gowdy, Joe E. Brown, Red Barber, and former Yankees shortstop Phil "Scooter" Rizzuto, who became a broadcaster in 1957. (Almost immediately, he was identified with his catchphrase, "Holy Cow.")[35] Allen, too, had catchphrases – especially one that he popularized circa 1949, "How about that!" Like other broadcasters of the late '40s, Allen was not only asked to do radio play-by-play; he had to adapt to a new mass medium – television. During the 1947 World Series, when the games were televised for the first time, Allen teamed up with Red Barber, who was still announcing Dodgers baseball, to do the play-by-play on both radio and TV. Barber joined the Yankees broadcast team in 1954,[36] and the two veterans worked together for the next decade.

Allen was unexpectedly fired at the end of the 1964 season.[37] At first there was no official announcement, but when Phil Rizzuto suddenly took Allen's place on the TV-radio broadcasts of the 1964 World Series, reporters began asking questions. Red Barber was concerned too: he knew that if Allen was no longer the Voice of the Yankees, it would break his heart.[38] As it turned out, in late November, the Yankees finally announced that Allen's contract would not be renewed.[39] Several weeks later, Rizzuto was named the lead announcer for Yankee baseball; he was joined by a new member of the broadcast team, former St. Louis Cardinals catcher Joe Garagiola.[40] In addition, former Yankees second baseman Jerry Coleman, who had been added to the broadcast team in February 1963, remained in the booth, and so did Red Barber. But then, in September 1966, the popular Barber was suddenly fired, much to the consternation of many fans and baseball writers, who thought the Yankees management had made a terrible decision.[41] As for Garagiola, he stayed a Yankees broadcaster for only three seasons, before going on to a long career with NBC; Coleman, who spent a total of seven years calling Yankees games, left at the end of the 1969 season to join the California Angels broadcast team.

Rizzuto remained in the Yankees broadcast booth for four decades; he was heard on various New York radio stations (WHN, WMCA, WINS, and WABC), and seen on WPIX-TV (Channel 11). Two of his best-known broadcasting partners were Frank Messer (a former play-by-play announcer for the Baltimore Orioles)[42] and Bill White (a former major-league first baseman for the Giants, Cardinals, and Phillies; when he joined the Yankees broadcast team in early 1971, he was the only Black play-by-play announcer in the majors).[43] Not only did Rizzuto have a long broadcasting career, during which he called many key moments in Yankees history; he also became part of pop culture when his voice was heard on a classic 1977 album rock song by Meatloaf, "Paradise by the Dashboard Light."

In 1987 the Yankees finally brought in a new radio team: Hank Greenwald and Tommy Hutton. Greenwald (whose real name was Howard, but who changed it to Hank in honor of Hank Greenberg of the Detroit Tigers, a player he idolized while growing up in Detroit)[44] had previously been a play-by-play announcer with the San Francisco Giants, and Hutton, a former journeyman player who spent time with the Dodgers, Phillies, Blue Jays, and Expos, had worked for ESPN before doing play-by-play for the Expos. The two men were hired so that Rizzuto and White could focus exclusively on their work for WPIX-TV.

That paved the way for John Sterling, who previously did play-by-play basketball for the Atlanta Hawks and baseball for the Atlanta Braves. Another broadcaster who had a long career on Yankees broadcasts, he was hired for the 1989 season, after WABC – which had been broadcasting the games on radio since 1981 – did not renew the contracts of Greenwald and Hutton.[45] Sterling was born and raised in New York and was glad to be back home. He was expected to bring "an irreverent and colorful tone" to the broadcasts, as well as more enthusiasm (and by some accounts, more willingness to be friendly with the sponsors).[46] Over a career of more than three decades, Sterling became known for his remarkable work ethic: He broadcast 5,059 consecutive games, including the postseason, from September 1989 to July 2019.[47] And as of the 2022 season, Sterling was still on the air,

now in his 80s, with no known plans to retire. Among Sterling's memorable quirks was his call whenever the Yankees were victorious: an elongated "Theeeeeeeee Yankees win!!!"

Among Sterling's most popular sidekicks was Michael Kay. A former sportswriter who covered the Yankees for the *New York Post* and then the *New York Daily News*,[48] he teamed up with Sterling on WABC in 1992. After a decade on radio, Kay made the move to the television side in 2002, broadcasting the games for the Yankees Entertainment & Sports Network (YES). But he maintained ties with radio too, hosting a sports-talk program on 1050 ESPN; his radio show (and ESPN's entire programming lineup) later moved to FM, in April 2012.

And in a field dominated by men, the Yankees were among the first to hire a female sportscaster. Suzyn Waldman, who was with New York sports-talk radio station WFAN from its debut in 1987, distinguished herself as one of New York's most knowledgeable broadcasters, male or female. In 2005, she joined the Yankees broadcast team on WCBS Radio, which had been carrying the games since 2002. Waldman's hiring made her the major leagues' first full-time female color commentator.[49]

Today, the entire schedule of Yankees baseball is available – online, on TV, and on radio, a far cry from the days when fans were fortunate if they heard one game a year. The team has had a succession of well-respected radio announcers; many Yankee fans regard them as part of the family. As Bill Veeck pointed out more than 90 years ago, broadcasting the games hasn't hurt attendance: then, as now, fans appreciate being part of the action, whether in person or on their various devices.

NOTES

1   "74,200 See Yankees Open New Stadium; Ruth Hits Home Run," *New York Times*, April 19, 1923: 1.

2   "Baseball Writers Oppose Radio Use," *New York Times*, May 26, 1923: 11.

3   C.W. Horn, "Broadcasting the World Series," *Radio Age*, December 1922: 12.

4   Billy Kelly, "Before and After," *Buffalo Courier*, April 19, 1923: 11.

5   Zipp Newman, "Dusting 'Em Off," *Birmingham* (Alabama) *News*, May 14, 1943: 29.

6   Dave Anderson, "The End of the Latest Literary Lion," *Raleigh* (North Carolina) *News and Observer*, October 9, 1988: 20B.

7   James R. Walker, *Crack of the Bat: A History of Baseball on the Radio* (Lincoln: University of Nebraska Press, 2015), 29.

8   Raymond Francis Yates, "Reporting Baseball to Millions," *Wireless Age*, November 1923: 25, 27-28.

9   "WRC and the Times to Broadcast Game," *Washington Times*, April 14, 1925: 2.

10   While it took Bob Quinn until 1926 to permit even one Red Sox broadcast, as I wrote about for SABR, he gradually became a believer in having some of the games on the air; but my research has not found any quotes from 1926-1929 that explain what changed his mind. However, by the early 1930s, he was defending the broadcasts and praising Red Sox play-by-play announcer Fred Hoey. For example, in 1932, he said he believed that "the broadcasting of big league games helps the game and the clubs, and that it even stimulates the sale of the papers carrying the stories of the game." Burt Whitman, "Hoey's Baseball Broadcasts Not Definitely Lost to Fans; Up to Leagues, Says Quinn," *Boston Herald*, October 20, 1932: 30.

11   "Gus Rooney's Larynx Gets a Workout." *Boston Traveler*, April 14, 1926: 16.

12   "Broadcast Play By Play Yankees-Red Sox Game," *Brooklyn Eagle*, April 19, 1926: 4A.

13   "WNAC to Broadcast Red Sox Game Tuesday," *Boston Globe*, April 12, 1926: 16.

14   *Crack of the Bat: A History of Baseball on the Radio*, 52.

15   "Station WJZ Linked with Stations Which Will Radiate Play by Play Description of Today's Game, Beginning at 1:45 o'Clock," *New York Times*, October 3, 1926: XX15.

16   "Radio Program," *New York Daily News*, April 16, 1929: 30.

17   "World's Series Games to be Broadcast," *Montréal Gazette*, September 22, 1930: 24.

18   James F. Donahue, "More Ball Games to Go On Air This Year Than Ever Before," *Battle Creek* (Michigan) *Enquirer and Evening News*, March 23, 1930: 12.

19   World's Series Games to be Broadcast," *Montréal Gazette*, September 22, 1930: 24.

20   John B. Foster, "Rumor Formation of Third Major League," *Yonkers* (New York) *Herald*, December 7, 1931: 17.

21   James F. Donahue, "Most Major League Baseball Games Will Be Broadcast but Minor Managers Still Hesitate," *Miami* (Oklahoma) *News-Record*, March 28, 1930: 8.

22   "World Series Talk Fest," *New York Daily News*, September 27, 1932: 34.

23   James R. Walker, *Crack of the Bat: A History of Baseball on the Radio* (Lincoln: University of Nebraska Press, 2015), 86.

24   "Promotion Methods for Baseball Games Outlined at General Mills Gathering," *Broadcasting*, May 1, 1939: 36.

25   "Giants and Yanks Complete Arrangements for Broadcasting of Their Home Contests," *New York Times*, January 26, 1939: 29.

26   Tommy Holmes, "Cubs Bank on Bryant to Halt Yanks in Third," *Brooklyn Daily Eagle*, October 8, 1938: 1, 7.

27   "Ruppert Yields to Bring Cheer to Shut-Ins; Also $100,000," *Akron Beacon Journal*, December 23, 1938: 20.

28   "Dodger Baseball to be Broadcast," *New York Times*, December 7, 1938: 29.

29   "$75,000 Lures Dodgers to Radio, Giants and Yankees Due to Follow," *Boston Globe*, December 7, 1938: 20.

30   J. Anthony Lukas, "How Mel Allen Started a Lifelong Love Affair with Baseball," *New York Times*, September 12, 1971: SM 74.

31   Bob Considine, "On the Line," *Scranton Tribune*, July 1, 1939: 13.

32   Richard Sandomir, "Mel Allen Is Dead, Golden Voice of Yankees," *New York Times*, June 17, 1996: B9.

33   Jack House, "Alabama," *Birmingham News*, March 31, 1940: S5.

34   "Yanks, Giants Ban Action Broadcasts," *Broadcasting*, May 10, 1943: 45.

35   Harold A. Nichols, "All Star Grid Clash Due on Channel 10," *Rochester* (New York) *Democrat and Chronicle*, August 4, 1957: 5F.

36   Harold C. Burr, "Voice of Brooklyn Headed for Yanks," *Brooklyn Daily Eagle*, October 28, 1953: 19.

37   J. Anthony Lukas, "How Mel Allen Started a Lifelong Love Affair with Baseball," *New York Times*, September 12, 1971: SM 78.

38   Bob Edwards, *Fridays with Red – A Radio Friendship*, (New York: Simon & Schuster, 1993), 160-161.

39   Val Adams, "Yankees Schedule Omits Mel Allen," *New York Times*, November 25, 1964: L75.

40   "Joe Garagiola Replaces Mel Allen," *Ithaca* (New York) *Journal*, December 18, 1964: 17.

41   Doug Dederer, "Orioles Yes – Yankees No," *Orlando Evening Star*, October 6, 1966: 4A.

42   Kay Gardella, "Messer Yankee Voice," *New York Daily News*, January 12, 1968: 84.

43   Joe Trimble, "Bill White Joins Yank Telecast Team; First Negro," *New York Daily News*, February 10, 1971: C30.

44   Harvey Araton, "New Sounds in the Bronx," *New York Daily News*, February 5, 1987: 65.

45   Roger Fischer, "Sierens Won't Call Any NFL Games for NBC This Season," *Tampa Bay Times*, November 11, 1988: 4C.

46   Stan Isaacs, "New Voices in Town Shoot from the Lip," *Newsday* (Long Island, New York), April 2, 1989: B23.

47   "Broadcaster's Long Streak to End," *Tampa Bay Times*, July 3, 2019: C5.

48   Andrew Gross, "Two of a Kind: WABC's Sterling and Kay," *White Plains* (New York) *Journal News*, April 2, 2000: 10K.

49   Steve Zipay, "Listeners Need to Give Waldman Fair Chance," *Newsday*, March 1, 2005: A53.

BOB SHEPPARD: THE DIVINE VOICE
OF YANKEE STADIUM

By Scott Pitoniak

After completing the rough draft of his Hall of Fame acceptance speech during the summer of 1993, Reggie Jackson asked legendary New York Yankees public address announcer Bob Sheppard to critique it.

"Now, I want you to be honest with me," the verbose slugger known as Mr. October told the man he had dubbed "The Voice of God."[1]

Sheppard's first piece of advice was brutally honest. The longtime St. John's University speech professor suggested Jackson slice his 40-minute oratory in half.

"I reminded Reggie that brevity was the soul of wit," Sheppard recalled, enunciating his words in the same distinctive, eloquent manner he used to announce lineups at Yankee Stadium for 56 years. "Brevity, when it comes to public speaking, especially on a hot summer's day, also is a way of making friends."[2]

It can be argued that when it came to endearing oneself to audiences, few did it better than Sheppard, who preached and practiced what he called the three C's – "Be clear, correct, concise." Through the decades, the Queens, New York, native wound up working more than 4,500 Yankees games, as well as hundreds of New York Giants National Football League contests, at Yankee Stadium.

"He added to the aura of old Yankee Stadium; to the experience of being there," said longtime Yankees public relations director, historian, and author Marty Appel. "This was sacred baseball acreage, hallowed grounds, and Bob lent a divine voice."[3]

Over time, that dignified voice became as much a part of the House That Ruth Built as the scalloped copper frieze, the center-field monuments, and the scores of famous players whose names he announced.

It was a voice that Mickey Mantle, Derek Jeter, and numerous other ballplayers said sent shivers up their spines. A voice that from 1951 through 2007 greeted tens of millions of visitors with the words, "Good afternoon, ladies and gentlemen, and welcome to Yankee Stadium."

Even visiting players couldn't wait to hear him boom their names.

"You're not in the big leagues," said Boston Red Sox great Carl Yastrzemski, "until Bob Sheppard announces your name."[4]

Following the famed public-address announcer's death at age 99 in 2010, an Associated Press obituary noted that "Babe Ruth gave Yankee Stadium its nickname, but Sheppard gave the place its sound."[5]

On May 7, 2000 – in commemoration of his 50th year in the booth – the Yankees unveiled a plaque of him in Monument Park, just beyond the center-field wall. During pregame ceremonies that afternoon, New

From Joe DiMaggio to Derek Jeter, Bob Sheppard was the Yankees' main public address announcer from 1951 through 2007.

York City Mayor Rudy Giuliani proclaimed it Bob Sheppard Day in the Big Apple, and legendary CBS news anchor Walter Cronkite read the plaque's inscription, as past and present Yankee stars Yogi Berra, Phil Rizzuto, Mariano Rivera, Jeter, and Jackson looked on.[6] Roughly two months later, on July 23, Sheppard donated the microphone he had used for decades to the National Baseball Hall of Fame and Museum in Cooperstown, where it was put on display in a third-floor exhibit devoted to baseball parks.[7]

Sheppard's Yankee Stadium debut on April 17, 1951, coincided with Mantle's, and that was somewhat fitting because they shared the same October 20 birthday, though Sheppard was born in 1910 and Mantle 21 years later. That day's announcements featured nine future Hall of Famers: Joe DiMaggio, Johnny Mize, Casey Stengel, Rizzuto, Berra, and Mantle from the Yankees, and Ted Williams, Bobby Doerr, and Lou Boudreau from the Boston Red Sox. For the record, the first baseball name he announced at the Stadium was Red Sox leadoff hitter Dom DiMaggio.[8]

Sheppard's auspicious debut was a harbinger. Over the next 5½ decades, he introduced more than 70 Hall of Famers, and he had a voice in numerous historic games. All told, he was the public-address announcer for 22 American League pennant winners and 13 World Series championship teams. He worked a record 121 consecutive postseason games, and a total of 62 games in 22 different Fall Classics – two records that likely will never be broken.[9] Sheppard was on hand for six no-hitters at the Stadium, including one of his all-time favorite sports moments – Don Larsen's perfect game against the Brooklyn Dodgers in the 1956 World Series. He also did the announcing for David Wells' perfecto in 1998 and David Cone's 27-up, 27-down gem a year later.[10]

Sheppard manned the microphone for football's Giants for 18 years (1956-73) at the Stadium, and another 33 seasons after they left the Bronx. That means he was there for the Giants' 1956 NFL championship season as well as the 1958 overtime title contest between them and the Baltimore Colts – a game many pro football historians regard as the greatest ever played and a game that helped launch the NFL's popularity on television.[11]

Sheppard's work at North American Soccer League games involving the Pelé-led Cosmos, and football games between historically Black colleges Grambling and Morgan State, further cemented his reputation as the Voice of Yankee Stadium.

Although his memorable and often imitated intonations landed him recognition in both Cooperstown and Monument Park, he was prouder of the lesser-known but more influential work he did as a teacher at the high-school and college levels.

"I think teaching was more important in my life than public address because teaching had a greater impact on society," said Sheppard, who continued his work as a professor at St. John's into the 1990s. "I've heard from hundreds of students I taught. The number of ballplayers I've heard from you can count on one hand."[12]

Part of that was by design because he purposely avoided interacting with players.

"I'm not into hero worship," Sheppard said. "I usually keep my distance from players and managers, and that's as it should be. I have a job to do at the ballpark, and so do they."[13]

He may not have heard directly from many players through the years, but that doesn't mean he didn't make a lasting impact on them. Mantle told Sheppard he experienced goose bumps every time the announcer said his name. Sheppard, who delivered a stirring tribute at the ballpark the day Mantle died in 1995, told the Mick he had a similar reaction each time he introduced the Yankee slugger.[14]

In fact, of the thousands of names he announced through the decades, Mantle's was his favorite.

"It just rolled wonderfully off the tongue," Sheppard said. "There was, of course, the alliteration. But it also had to do with the emphasis on the first syllable of his last name. Mickey MAN-tle. So euphonious. What a name and what a ballplayer."[15]

Jeter may have paid Sheppard the greatest compliment of all. After illness, injury, and age forced Sheppard to the sidelines for good following the 2007 season, Jeter asked the announcer to record the Yankee shortstop's intro, which was played each time he came to bat at home games for the rest of his career.

"That's the only voice I had heard [at Yankee Stadium] growing up," Jeter said. "And that's the only voice I wanted to hear when I was announced at home games. He's as important as any player that's been here. He's part of the experience, you know. Part of the experience of Yankee Stadium is Bob Sheppard's voice."[16]

***

Though he was secretive about his age for most of his life, voter records showed that Robert Leo Sheppard was born in Richmond Hill, Queens, on

October 20, 1910. He developed a love of language at an early age, thanks to his parents.

"My father, Charles, and my mother, Eileen, each enjoyed poetry and music and public speaking," Sheppard told Maury Allen in *Baseball: The Lives Behind the Seams*. "They were very precise in how they spoke. They measured words, pronounced everything carefully and instilled a love of language in me by how they respected proper pronunciation."[17]

While attending St. John's Preparatory School in Queens, Sheppard had two Vincentian priests as teachers who, by example and counsel, steered him toward his future career as a teacher and announcer.

"One was Father McKellen, who was so precise in his speech that every word seemed to be a diamond," he said. "And grammatically he was without flaw. He taught English. ... Another priest taught religion. But he also preached on Sunday in my parish. And he was inspirational in language. From the emotional point of view, he made words seem colorful. So between the purist who taught English and the priest who taught religion, language appreciation in me grew and grew and grew. And I think it was, maybe in high school, that I dreamed of making speech my career ... along with sports."[18]

Long before he began announcing games, Sheppard enjoyed playing them. A left-handed-throwing first baseman and quarterback, he excelled at both positions in high school and earned an athletic scholarship to St. John's University, where he earned three varsity letters in baseball and four in football. Popular among his peers, Sheppard was elected president of his senior class.[19]

After graduating with a degree in English and speech, Sheppard played semipro football in the New York City area for $25 a game, but that was as far as his playing career went. His true passion was the spoken word, and at the urging of St. John's professor Walter Robinson – "a stickler for phonetic pronunciation" – he enrolled at Columbia University, where he earned a master's degree in speech education in 1933.[20]

Graduate degree in hand, he took an exam to become a speech teacher in New York City, landing a job at Grover Cleveland High School in the Ridgewood section of Queens.[21]

After World War II broke out, Sheppard joined the Navy as a gunnery officer aboard cargo ships in the Pacific theater and the Caribbean. Following his discharge, he became a teacher and chair of the speech department at John Adams, one of the finer high schools in the city, and stayed there for 25 years. During that time, he taught night courses at St. John's University and the Bankers' Institute of America.[22]

Sheppard also managed to find time to do the P.A. at Ebbets Field for Brooklyn Dodgers games in the old All-American Football Conference (AAFC) in 1946. When the Dodgers folded before the 1949 season, Sheppard was hired to do public address for New York Yankees football games at Yankee Stadium. (The Yankees also were members of the AAFC.)

Sheppard was so good at his job that officials from baseball's New York Yankees asked him to do their games as well, but he balked initially because early-season weekday games would interfere with his teaching. It wasn't until the Yankees allowed him to find an understudy to pinch-hit for him in the booth when there were scheduling conflicts that Sheppard agreed to become the baseball voice of Yankee Stadium, too.

"I never had a plan to make a career of it because you couldn't possibly make a living on $15 a game, which is what the Yankees were paying me – $15 a game and $17 for a doubleheader," he said. "I viewed it as something temporary, but that temporary job has wound up lasting half a century."[23]

For the longest time, Sheppard's duties were quite limited. He would announce the starting lineups and introduce the batter when he came to the plate for the first time. After that, there would be mostly silence, unless there was a pitching change or a pinch-hitter. To kill time, Sheppard would sit in his booth, reading books.

"It's hard to believe, in today's sports world, where P.A. announcers never seem to stop talking and screaming, but it wasn't until 1967 that the Yankees actually started having Bob introduce the batter each time he came to the plate, and do commercial announcements between innings," Appel said. "Ballparks, with the exception of the cheers and jeers of fans and organ music, once were much quieter places."[24]

Appel remembers Sheppard as "professorial and dignified, a true gentleman, who was a good listener." He also remembers him as a perfectionist, a stickler for correct pronunciations of names.

In addition to Mantle, he listed Shigetoshi Hasegawa, Salome Barojas, José Valdivielso, and Álvaro Espinoza among his favorite names to pronounce and announce. Sheppard expressed a special fondness for the natural resonance of Latino players' names.[25]

"Anglo-Saxon names are not very euphonious," he said. "What can I do with Steve Sax? What can I do with Mickey Klutts?"[26]

Sheppard always worried that he might trip over the announcement of former Washington Senator infielder Wayne Terwilliger's name. "I was concerned I would say 'Ter-wigg-ler,'" he said. "But I never did."[27]

One name he did mess up was that of Jorge Posada. The five-time Yankees All-Star made his major-league debut as a pinch-runner for Wade Boggs in Game Two of the 1995 American League Division Series. Sheppard wound up putting an "o" instead of an "a" at the end of Posada's name when he first announced it. Jeter picked up on the error, and started calling Posada "Sodo" – a nickname that stuck for the remainder of the catcher's career.[28]

Another rare and funny faux pas occurred in 1976 when Sheppard worked his first game at the then-new Giants Stadium and greeted spectators by saying, "Good afternoon, ladies and gentlemen, and welcome to Yankee Stadium."[29]

Early on, Sheppard developed a distinctive cadence that allowed his words to echo majestically throughout cavernous Yankee Stadium. His announcement of a player coming to bat followed a simple pattern. He would communicate the player's position, uniform number and name, then repeat the number. For example: "Now batting ... the shortstop ... number two ... Derek Jeter ... number two." He imbued each name and number with a gravitas more in keeping with a coronation than a ballpark outing. "Mr. Sheppard could read [rap star] Eminem lyrics and make them sound like the Magna Carta," Clyde Haberman wrote in a 2005 New York Times feature story.[30]

As sports evolved, and games became events, public-address announcers became more of the show, raising their voices in hopes of firing up the crowd. Sheppard deplored the showmanship, and remained true to his old school, understated approach right till his last game. As he once said: "A P.A. announcer is not a cheerleader, or a circus barker, or a hometown screecher. He's a reporter."[31]

Although few recognized Sheppard in person, his voice was unmistakable. Once, while ordering a scotch and soda at a bar, he watched heads turn his way. A devout Catholic, Sheppard served as a lector at the Church of St. Christopher near his home in Baldwin, Long Island, and often was greeted by parish newcomers who would tell him, "You sound like that announcer at Yankee Stadium." Sheppard would smile

mischievously and respond: "That's because I am that announcer."[32]

Besides reading scripture during Mass, Sheppard also worked with his parish priests on their sermons. "I electrified the seminary by saying seven minutes is long enough on a Sunday morning, but I don't think they listened to me," he told the Associated Press in 2006. "The best-known speech in American history is the Gettysburg Address, and it's about four minutes long. Isn't that something?"[33]

In addition to Larsen's perfect game and the Giants-Colts' NFL championship game, Sheppard's favorite Yankee Stadium moments included Roger Maris's record-breaking 61st home run in 1961, Chris Chambliss's walk-off homer against the Kansas City Royals in the final game of the 1976 American League Championship Series, and Jackson's three-homers-on-three-pitches explosion in Game Six of the 1977 World Series against the Los Angeles Dodgers.[34]

Chambliss's memorable blast was preceded by a stoppage in play because fans had thrown debris onto the field. Sheppard made an announcement telling the unruly spectators to refrain from such behavior. They stopped – and the game resumed. When Chambliss homered – ending the game and the 12-year Yankees World Series drought – thousands of spectators rushed onto the field. This time, Sheppard's microphone remained silent.

"The game was over, the Yankees had won, 10,000 people, as if they were shot out of a cannon, ran out onto the field, and I just folded my arms and let them do it," Sheppard recalled in a 2000 interview with USA Today. "I could never have stopped them. The Marines couldn't have stopped them. Nobody could have stopped them. It had to happen. I never saw anything like it before, and I've never seen anything like it since."[35]

Sheppard battled deteriorating health in his later years. In 2006 a hip injury forced him to miss his first home opener since his 1951 debut, and a bronchial infection the following year prevented him from working postseason games. Neither he nor anyone else knew it at the time, but a 10-2 Yankees win against Seattle on September 5, 2007, wound up being his final game, though Sheppard did record the starting lineups that were announced before the last game at the old stadium on September 21, 2008. His longtime understudy, Jim Hall, pinch-hit for him that season, and Paul Olden took over the duties when the team moved across the street to the new ballpark in 2009.[36]

Sheppard died on July 11, 2010 – three months shy of his 100th birthday and two days before the death of Yankees owner George Steinbrenner. Tributes poured in from far and wide. In a press release, Steinbrenner called him "a good friend and fine man whose voice set the gold standard for America's sports announcers. ... his death leaves a lasting silence."[37] New York Giants President John Mara called Sheppard "the most distinguished and dignified voice in all of professional sports."[38] Jeter noted that "players changed year in and year out, but he was the one constant. Every time you heard him say your name, you got chills."[39]

Sheppard was predeceased by his first wife, Margaret, who died of cancer in 1959. His survivors included his second wife, Mary, whom he met at his parish and married in 1961, and the four children he had with Margaret – sons Paul and Chris, and daughters Barbara and Mary.[40]

In memory of Sheppard, the Yankees wore an embroidered patch depicting a microphone, the Stadium scalloped frieze, and a baseball diamond on their sleeves for the remainder of the 2010 season. The day after his father's death, Paul Sheppard told the *New York Times*: "The Yankees and Bob Sheppard were a marriage made in heaven. I know St. Peter will now recruit him. If you're lucky enough to go to heaven, you'll be greeted by a voice, saying, 'Good afternoon, ladies and gentlemen. Welcome to heaven!'"[41]

Recordings of Sheppard's voice continue to be played before Yankee telecasts on the YES network, and often evoke nostalgic feelings among longtime fans.

"Any time you hear his voice it's like the key to a time machine and you're immediately transported back to the original Yankee Stadium," Appel said. "You feel the excitement you felt when you were a kid going through those turnstiles and hearing that unmistakable voice. It sounded like it was booming down from the clouds. Bob's impeccable intonations and that ballpark were synonymous. Reggie was right. It was like hearing the Voice of God."[42]

SOURCES

In addition to the sources cited in the Notes, the author consulted the following:

Appel, Marty. *Pinstripe Empire: The New York Yankees From Before the Babe to After the Boss*, (New York: Bloomsbury Publishing, 2020).

Additionally, the author used first-source material from a 25-minute in-person, interview he conducted with Bob Sheppard on July 7, 2007, and a 30-minute phone interview with Appel on October 7, 2022.

NOTES

1   Author interview with Reggie Jackson, July 7, 2007.

2   Scott Pitoniak, *Memories of Yankee Stadium* (Chicago: Triumph Books, 2008), 62.

3   Author interview with Marty Appel, October 7, 2022.

4   "Bob Sheppard Quotes," baseball-almanac.com, https://www.baseball-almanac.com/quotes/Bob-Sheppard-Quotes.shtml, accessed September 17, 2022.

5   "Bob Sheppard Obituary," Associated Press, https://obits.syracuse.com, July 11, 2010.

6   Bill Madden, "Bob Sheppard, New York Yankees Legend and Voice of the Bronx Bombers, Has Died at 99," *New York Daily News*, July 11, 2010.

7   *Memories of Yankee Stadium*, 65.

8   *Memories of Yankee Stadium*, 65.

9   *New York Yankees 2011 Media Guide.*

10   *Memories of Yankee Stadium*, 67.

11   *Memories of Yankee Stadium*, 65.

12   Author interview with Sheppard.

13   Author interview with Sheppard.

14   *Memories of Yankee Stadium*, 66.

15   Author interview with Sheppard.

16   Melissa Block, "Bob Sheppard Led Jeter to the Plate One Last Time," NPR. org, September 26, 2014. https://www.npr.org/2014/09/26/351811935/bob-sheppard-led-jeter-to-the-plate-one-last-time.

17   Richard Goldstein, "Bob Sheppard, Voice of the Yankees, Dies at 99," *New York Times*, July 11, 2010. https://www.proquest.com/usnews/docview/2218461499/39942373521140FDPQ/5?accountid=69.

18   Jerome Preisler, "An Interview with Bob Sheppard," YES Network, July 12, 2010. https://www.myyesnetwork.com/12493/blog/2010/07/11/an_interview_with_bob_sheppard:_pt._1.

19   Preisler.

20   Preisler.

21   Preisler.

22   Preisler.

23   Author interview with Sheppard.

24   Author interview with Appel.

25   Author interview with Sheppard.

26   "Bob Sheppard Quotes."

27   Author interview with Sheppard.

28   Greg Kristan, "Bob Sheppard: The Voice of the New York Yankees," *The Stadium Reviews*, https://thestadiumreviews.com/blogs/info/bob-sheppard/, May 27, 2020.

29   Kristan.

30   Clyde Haberman, "For the Yankees, as Constant as Pinstripes," *New York Times*, February 22, 2005. https://www.proquest.com/usnews/docview/2227729209/B3AD50F0925E4A29PQ/1?accountid=69.

31   "Bob Sheppard Quotes."

32   Author interview with Sheppard.

33   ESPN wire services, "Bob Sheppard, Longtime Yankee Stadium Announcer, dies at 99,", July 11, 2010. https://www.espn.com/new-york/mlb/news/story?id=5371001.

34   *Memories of Yankee Stadium*, 67.

35   *Memories of Yankee Stadium*, 67.

36   ESPN wire services, "Bob Sheppard, Longtime Yankee Stadium Announcer, Dies at 99."

37   "Bob Sheppard, Longtime Yankee Stadium Announcer, Dies at 99."

38   "Bob Sheppard, Longtime Yankee Stadium Announcer, Dies at 99."

39   "Bob Sheppard, Longtime Yankee Stadium Announcer, Dies at 99."

40   Goldstein, "Bob Sheppard, Voice of the Yankees, Dies at 99."

41   Goldstein.

42   Author interview with Appel.

MY SIX DECADES WITH THE YANKEES

By Tony Morante

As a New York Yankees employee from 1958 to 2018, I had the good fortune to witness or partake in the Stadium's illustrious history.

My dad, a Stadium usher, took me to my first game in 1949. The impression of walking out of the passageway in the upper deck behind home plate will last forever. As I was used to the small black and white TV at home, taking in the lush green manicured grass, the azure blue skies dressed in puffy white cumulus clouds, and the aromas from the Stadium vendors, the bombardment of my senses was pure fantasy.

At that time, ushers were allowed to take their youngsters to the game with no expense. The ushers had a shape-up seniority assignment, which took about an hour. While waiting for my dad to be assigned, I went to the right-field seating area. The gates were not open yet, allowing me to scramble for baseballs that landed in that area without much competition. At times, I would come home with two or three baseballs which I shared with my Little League teammates ... making me a popular kid!

My visits to the Stadium came to a screeching halt in 1958 when my dad informed me that if I wanted to continue to go to the games, I would now have to earn it as a part-time usher. So he flipped me an usher's mitt (used to clean off the seats), which I reluctantly took, beginning my 60 years of employment in Yankee Stadium while building its reputation as the mecca for outdoor events in our country. And, on December 28, 1958, I witnessed what many still consider the greatest football game ever played as the underdog New York Giants lost to the favored Baltimore Colts but in a very close contest.

In the following year, a new and exclusive section was added to the mezzanine section of the Stadium, extending from the press box in front of the box seats down the third-base line toward the left-field foul pole. This area, known as the Mezzanine Loge, was built at the behest of corporations such as Howard Johnson, Spencer Advertising, Mele Manufacturing, Hansen Real Estate, Bankers Trust Company, and WABC, to name a few. This secluded area is where I worked with my father from the late 1960s to 1973, when the pre-renovation Stadium was in its final year. I assisted the patrons of this section in procuring refreshments.

The 1950s were the greatest decade in the Yankees' history as they went to the World Series fall classic eight times and won six of those World Series. At the heart of the team's success was a strapping blond-haired and blue-eyed phenom from Oklahoma who possessed great power and speed to match – Mickey Mantle. By the end of the decade, Mickey's popularity had significantly grown. But, unfortunately, this became a problem.

As soon as the game ended, fans were permitted to exit by way of the field to the center-field area by the monuments. If the Yankees won, there was a mad rush by some fans to take advantage of this opportunity to approach Mickey Mantle. However, the fans became unruly from time to time, expressing their ardor for their hero, jostling Mickey. So Mickey asked for security to help escort him off the field. Six ushers immediately jumped the low fence at the game's end onto the field to meet The Mick by second base, forming a cordon around him to ensure his safe return to the dugout. The operation, called the "suicide squad,"

Tony Morante started the Yankee Stadium Tours Department in 1998.

usually went to the younger, faster ushers like me. Remembering when I was called on to guard my idol, Mickey Mantle, was one of my biggest thrills.

I joined the US Navy in 1962 for a four-year stint. While my ship was stationed in Charleston, South Carolina, in 1965, the Vatican announced that Pope Paul VI would come to Yankee Stadium. It was the first time a pope left the Vatican in Italy to visit the Western Hemisphere. Naturally, Yankee Stadium was the venue that he chose. The Stadium beckoned! So I hitchhiked my way up to New York to participate in this joyous celebration, which 90,000 people attended.

The Yankees stars who contributed to the great success the team enjoyed had passed their prime with a resounding thud as the team hit rock-bottom in 1966. But the memories of those championship seasons came back to life when June 8, 1969, was proclaimed Mickey Mantle Day. Players representing those great years with Mickey participated in paying homage to him. I was assigned to the area by third base in the loge level, where I witnessed the ceremonies.

Announcer Mel Allen, the Voice of the Yankees, introduced Mickey Mantle: "Ladies and gentlemen, a magnificent Yankee, the great number seven, Mickey Mantle." At this point, I stopped working as the sellout crowd gave Mantle a nine-minute standing ovation. By this time, tears streamed down my face. So it was with the men to my right and left. There could not have been a dry eye in the house as we remembered Mickey Mantle's thrills.

In 1973 I took an elective course at Fordham University while pursuing a degree at night involving walking tours of the Bronx. Although I was a ne'er-do-well in my early academic years, the Bronx tours that two historians took us on piqued my interest considerably. I befriended the Bronx historian and instructor, Dr. Gary Hermalyn. Over the next few years, we would have lunch at the Stadium from time to time and we would visit different parts of the ballpark, which led to his proposal for me to conduct a public walking tour. Little did I know at the time that this was a portent of bigger things to come. In due time, I became the Bronx County Historical Society VP. The BCHS was instrumental in helping to prepare the tour's route.

In January of that 1973 there was a changing of the guard. Mr. George M. Steinbrenner, a shipping magnate, became the principal owner and managing partner of the New York Yankees and held the position until his passing in 2010. With a consortium of 13 partners, he purchased the Yankees from CBS in January 1973 for $10 million. During his tenure, he brought seven World Series championships to New York and its fans.

With the passing of five decades of wear and tear, the Stadium was in dire need of refurbishment, which began immediately after the 1973 season ended. The projected cost of the refurbishment was $28 million, but when completed, the price tag had reached over $100 million. New York City Mayor John Lindsay was instrumental in keeping the Yankees franchise in New York. He did not wish to see them emulate the Yankees' former Stadium tenants, the NFL New York Giants, and move to the Meadowlands in New Jersey.

In May of 1973 I experienced a seismic shift in my employment as I shed my usher's uniform for business apparel as I took a position in the club's Group and Season Sales Department.

"Winning, after breathing, is the most important thing in life" was a quote that "The Boss" lived by to the nth degree. This attitude permeated the entire administration. He vowed to bring his mediocre team to a championship in three years, and true to his vow, watched the Yankees climb back to the top of the American League in their newly renovated ballpark in 1976.

Yankees President and General Manager Gabe Paul offered the 6,000 season-ticket holders an opportunity to obtain a seat from their complement of seats from the original Stadium. The Invirex Demolition Co. moved 6,000 seats to the players' parking lot across the street from the Stadium. I oversaw the seats' disbursement, which became a real "event" helping lead to a revival in the field of collectibles and memorabilia.

After 1976 with the advent of free agency and thanks to wise trades by sage GM Gabe Paul, the Yankees won back-to-back World Series championships in 1977 and 1978. Joyous celebrations were rampant in Yankeeland, capped off by ticker-tape parades up Broadway (the Canyon of Heroes) and World Series rings for the players.

Then in 1979, tragedy befell the Yankees. Their captain, catcher Thurman Munson, who was the first Yankee to be named captain since Lou Gehrig in 1939, perished in a plane crash in his new Cessna Citation jet plane while on a test run in Canton, Ohio, on August 2, 1979. Munson played for the Yankees in all his 11 seasons; he never visited the disabled list, and he was voted an All-Star in seven of those years. He won the Rookie of the Year Award in 1970, an MVP Award in 1976, and three Gold Glove Awards. Thurman's devotion to his family led him to seek a pilot's license so he could travel from New York to be with his family on his days off … against the best wishes of Mr. Steinbrenner. When they sat down to discuss Munson's 1979 contract, Mr. Steinbrenner had finally granted permission to Thurman to fly his airplane. After the fatal crash, Mr. Steinbrenner wanted a halt in play to remember the captain but Commissioner Bowie Kuhn issued an order not to miss a scheduled game. Nonetheless, defying the order, Mr. Steinbrenner took the entire Yankee squad to Ohio for the funeral service. He said they planned to be back in time for the game but if not, they would forfeit. I couldn't have been prouder of being a Yankee than at this time!

During the first couple of days of mourning, with emotions pretty much spent, we started to talk about the lighter side of Thurman's gruff exterior. I'll never forget a run-in I had with him in July of 1975, while I worked in the Group and Season Sales Department. We offered a program in which a community or organization that purchased 1,000 tickets to a game would be entitled to certain perks including 20 complimentary seats to the game, four VIP seats by the Yankees dugout, radio and TV promotions, and a ceremony by the Yankees dugout to present a plaque to the Yankee of their choice.

Pepsi-Cola of Bristol, Connecticut, was one such sponsor, purchasing tickets for a twin bill (a term we don't hear too often today) at Shea Stadium, the Yankees' home for the 1974 and 1975 seasons while Yankee Stadium was being refurbished. Two aces, Bill Lee of the Red Sox and Catfish Hunter of the Yankees, tossed up goose eggs through the first eight innings. The Red Sox broke the tie by pushing a run across in the top of the ninth inning. A plaque was to be presented to Munson by the Yankees dugout between games. However, when I went down to the dugout there was no Thurman. I went into the clubhouse by his locker … no Thurm. "Where's Thurm?" I shouted out. "He's in the bathroom" (language was a bit saltier), came the reply. As I entered the bathroom, I shouted, "Thurm, Thurm, it's Tony Morante!" His gruff reply from the stall was, "Whadda you want?" I answered, "We set up a presentation with your friend from Pepsi for a presentation that I told you about." He responded with, "Hell no, I ain't goin'!" Thurm had taken the bitter defeat hard and was in no mood to participate. Yankees sub Fred Stanley helped out by accepting the plaque.

Peace ended the decade of the 1970s as Pope John Paul II visited Yankee Stadium. Shortly after that, the Bronx Historical Society approached me to conduct a walking tour of the Stadium on Veterans Day. Bronx Borough President Stanley Simon led an entourage of 125 people, mostly from his office, to attend. The tour was a game-changer in my life. It led to my work with Yankee Stadium tours.

After touring VIPs at the Stadium for the next five years, we opened the historical tours to schoolchildren in 1985. They caught on immediately. The one-hour tour consisted of the press box, the field, Monument Park, the dugout, and, the clubhouse. The revenue from the Stadium tours benefited the Yankee Foundation, a nonprofit 501(c)(3) arm of the Yankees, which helped to bring educational and recreational programs to inner-city youths. In 1990 we opened the tours to the public. Also, in this year, I was honored to escort Nelson Mandela around Monument Park, which was one of my greatest thrills. In addition, at this time, we instituted the Yankee Caravan, bringing players to schools and hospitals to talk about life.

Around this time, after 14 seasons of mediocre play, the team began to reap the benefits of its farm system and returned to postseason play in 1995, at the precipice of a new dynasty. The Yankees went on to win four World Series in 1996, 1998, 1999, and 2000, and were proclaimed "The Team of the Century." Exciting celebrations followed the World Series victories, including ticker-tape parades from the Battery by floats up Broadway, the Canyon of Heroes, to City Hall for mayoral proclamations, and a great picnic to follow. Shortly after the 1996 World Series, I was called up to Mr. Steinbrenner's office, where I was presented with the 1996 World Series Championship ring in my name! What a great feeling it was for me!

In 1998 Mr. Steinbrenner permitted me to open a Yankee Stadium Tours Department. Tours began to grow rapidly at the start of the new century. A big push came in 2003 when the great Japanese ballplayer Hideki Matsui came to the Yankees. Since baseball was introduced to Japan in 1872, the game had become the national pastime in Japan. Matsui's arrival brought a tremendous infusion of Japanese tourists to Yankee Stadium during the period through 2009, when he left the Yankees. I conducted countless tours for enthusiastic Japanese tourists and the Japanese media. Hysterically, many tourists who had seen me on TV in Japan (something unbeknownst to me) asked me to take a picture with them. When I questioned the Japanese interpreter, Why all the fuss?" the reply was that the tourists recognized me from TV back home. I was honored! This period in time had a great influence on the globalization of our game.

In addition to the tours, we designed presentations on leadership in collaboration with middle-school teachers. Also, the Stadium Tours department presented a 45-minute PowerPoint educational program to the students on the Suite Level of the original Stadium. I also visited the middle schools with the program. In 2008, our last season in the Stadium, we opened special tours in conjunction with the Wounded Warrior Foundation and the Special Operations Warrior Foundation, including introductions to the ballplayers during batting practice. Over 150,000 people attended the Stadium Tours in our final season. Then, in 2009, the Yankees christened the new Yankee Stadium by winning the World Series, the same way that they christened the original stadium in 1923, replete with ceremonies and a ticker-tape parade up Broadway.

In July 2010, two Yankee icons passed away within three days of each other, Bob Sheppard, the Yankees public-address announcer for 57 years (1951-2007), and George Steinbrenner.

The erudite and dulcet tones of Shep's voice were given the sobriquet "The Voice of God" by Reggie Jackson. And Derek Jeter insisted on being introduced as he stepped into the batter's box by Shep's recording, "Now batting, number 2, Derek Jeeetah" until he retired.

Shep and I had a lot of fun in the press room before lunch or dinner. He had his own private table for four in the press room's corner where only invited guests were allowed to sit in his company. I was one of the guests from time to time. Being that he was a St. John's University professor and I, a Fordham University graduate, there was always live banter between us on who had the greatest sports teams. We enjoyed the laughter!

My relationship with "The Boss," Mr. Steinbrenner, was also unique. After giving me the opportunity to open the Yankee Stadium Tours Department, he said, "Tony, you don't have to report to anybody, just let me know how you're doing." So, year after year, as the tours were steadily improving, I sent favorable reports on their growth. The letters of acknowledgment that he sent to me are treasured.

Although Mr. Steinbrenner showed a lot of bluster, he was a humble man. One of his many quotes that stuck with me was, "If you do a good deed for someone and more than two people know about it, you and that person, then you are doing it for the wrong reason." Once, while leading a Stadium tour, I stopped the group by an exhibit of The Boss in the Yankees Museum and told of his benevolent side that maybe most did not see. Someone in the crowd shouted out how much gratitude he had for Mr. Steinbrenner after he helped his family out of dire straits. To my dismay, The Boss's daughter Jennifer was on the tour and reprimanded me as we left the museum for showing off the benevolence of her father.

In 2014 the National Assessment for Educational Progress stated that only 18 percent of our eighth-grade students were proficient in social studies. It was alarming to realize that 82 percent of our youngsters were at risk. So I designed a program that would help those struggling students understand American history through the eyes of baseball. In retirement, and not wanting to abandon the program, I wrote the book *BASEBALL The New York Game – How the National Pastime Paralleled U.S. History*, which was published in 2021.

Circuses, rodeos, Negro baseball, Women's Professional Baseball Exhibitions, three Papal masses, Jehovah's Witnesses assemblies, college and professional football, soccer, boxing, circuses, rodeos, and other interdenominational faith healings, besides 26 World Series championships, all passed through this structure that for 85 years[1] was one of our country's crown jewels, Yankee Stadium.

Thank you, my family, friends, and colleagues for helping me to wrap my life around our national pastime. You helped me achieve the distinction of being inducted into the 2022 Class of the New York State Baseball Hall of Fame.

NOTES

1   Although the Stadium was technically used for 84 seasons (1923-1973, 1976-2008), it is generally talked about in terms of its 85-year lifespan (1923-2008).

YANKEE STADIUM: THE HOUSE THAT RUTH (AND UNITAS) BUILT!

By Michael Gibbons

Director Emeritus, Historian, Babe Ruth Birthplace Museum

In my 40 years working at the Babe Ruth Birthplace Museum in Baltimore, my primary focus has been preserving and celebrating the life and legacy of George Herman "Babe" Ruth. But during my tenure, the museum also expanded its mission to chronicle the rich heritage of area sports, including serving as the official archives of the Baltimore Colts. Certainly Ruth, but also those Colts, have contributed to the unique history of Yankee Stadium.

What follows, then, is an offering of firsthand perspectives from the museum's archives that contribute to Ruth's profound impact on Yankee Stadium, plus reflections on the 1958 NFL title game, Colts vs. Giants, the "Greatest Game ever Played" in NFL history … and, perhaps in the history of Yankee Stadium as well.

* * *

Babe Ruth came to the Yankees in 1920, when his soaring popularity produced record numbers at the Polo Grounds turnstiles, overflow numbers that led to the warp-speed construction of Yankee Stadium, and its opening game on April 18, 1923. In a 1997 interview, Little Ray Kelly, an unlikely eyewitness, remembered that game … and that year, like yesterday.

Ray, you see, was Babe Ruth's official "mascot," a role he assumed starting in 1921 that carried through 11 seasons. Little Ray remembered playing catch with his dad along Riverside Drive as Ruth drove home after a game at the Polo Grounds. Out of habit, Babe stopped to watch the father and son's back-and-forth, and was so taken by the exchange that he invited them to be his guests at next day's game. In the clubhouse after the game, Ruth asked Ray's father if Little Ray could be his personal mascot, and thus began a chapter in the young boy's story that would generate profound, lasting memories.

Ray said the mascot idea was at first "just a PR thing" for the Babe, but that it quickly evolved into a "real game job" and a special relationship between the feisty youngster and his superstar sponsor. Ray did not travel with the Yankees, but had a steady presence for many of the Yankees' home games. In recalling that 1923 inaugural, Ray said Ruth not only jumped with joy after clouting the first home run ever in the House that Ruth Built, he also started the practice of consuming a game-day six-pack, "a couple of dogs at a time … up to six … plus soda-pop," which Ray would dutifully fetch.[1]

Ray also remembered that season's World Series, Yankees versus Giants, won by the Yankees four games to two. Ray recalled that the Babe cracked three homers, but that future Yankees manager Casey Stengel had the winning hits in both of the Giants' victories, which were at Yankee Stadium. His inside-the-park homer provided a one-run margin of victory in Game One, and his drive into the right-field bleachers gave John McGraw's team a 1-0 win in Game Three. Not to be outdone by Casey's bat, Ruth hit .368 with three homers and eight RBIs to lead the Pinstripers.[2]

* * *

Babe Ruth's 60th home run, launched September 30, 1927, is one of the most chronicled moments in Yankee Stadium history. But the museum's archives take us back to the day before, September 29, and home run number 59. To get there, let me propel you forward to May 1995, and the unveiling of the Babe Ruth statue at Oriole Park at Camden Yards, one of several special events the museum planned to commemorate Ruth's 100th birthday. A very prominent guest at the unveiling was Paul Hopkins, a former pitcher with the Washington Senators, who made his big-league debut at Yankee Stadium on – you guessed it – September 29, 1927.[3]

Paul told me he remembered warming in the fourth inning. "I was very excited, because I was making my first appearance, and it was at Yankee Stadium. When I came in to start the fifth, I walked through the outfield grass and took the mound. I didn't run." Hopkins' inaugural proved more than daunting, even for a rookie, as the Yankees loaded the bases with one out. Next up was Babe Ruth, who minced his way into the batter's box. Hopkins noted that veteran Washington catcher Muddy Ruel called for a sequence of curveballs, and when the count ran to 3-and-2, Ruel told the rookie to throw a "slow curve," which Hopkins did. Paul said the pitch was so slow that Ruth all but double-clutched, and then smacked the ball high and deep into the right-field stands. A grand slam! Welcome to the bigs, rookie!

After the game Hopkins grabbed a brand-new baseball and headed to the Yankees clubhouse. New York manager Miller Huggins stopped him short, but when Hopkins explained his mission, Huggins sent someone to get the ball signed. Ruth autographed the ball, dated it, and wrote "59th home run." And Paul Hopkins had the most significant memento of his major-league career. But when the Senators got back to Washington, the team doctor's 10-year-old son asked for the ball, and Paul gave it up. He said he had no idea what happened to the ball after that and could not imagine what the cash value might have been that day we talked at Camden Yards in 1995.

* * *

In 1946 Ruth was hired by General Motors to speak at area high schools. Future Baseball Hall of Fame broadcasting award winner Mel Allen, fresh off a stint in the Army, was hired by the Yankees to accompany Ruth, and to serve as emcee for the promotional visits. "Babe drove his Cadillac and did most of the talking," Allen recalled. "I listened." A year later, on April 27, 1947, Mel introduced the failing slugger on Babe Ruth Day at Yankee Stadium. Knowing that Ruth's throat was wracked with the cancer that would take his life a little more than a year later, Allen asked the Babe if he wanted to speak to the crowd. Ruth answered, "I must," and went on to deliver one of the most inspirational addresses in the history of our national pastime. "The only real game, I think, in the world, baseball," the Bambino whispered.[4]

Allen joked that the Yankees forgot to retire Babe's number 3 that day, and so brought him back the following April to officially retire his number as the team celebrated the 25th anniversary of Yankee Stadium, "The House that Ruth Built."

* * *

On August 16, 1948, Babe Ruth succumbed to cancer. His body lay in state at Yankee Stadium over the next two days, as more than 100,000 mourners paid a final tribute to their fallen hero. Among the throngs was Frankie Haggerty, a Danvers, Massachusetts, youngster who had written to Ruth when Brother Gilbert, Ruth's Xaverian mentor at St. Mary's Industrial School, passed away on October 19, 1947. Like most American kids, Frankie was aware of Babe's health struggles and asked if he could "stand in" for the Babe at Brother Gilbert's funeral. On October 21, Ruth telegrammed Frankie: "I will be most grateful to you – but will feel I am there through your gracious gesture to go in my place." Ruth arranged transportation for Frankie to and from the funeral at St. Peter's Church in Lowell, Massachusetts, on October 22. Frank Haggerty walked down the aisle and "did not cry." Local papers reported that Frank thus became one of the few people in history to pinch-hit for Babe Ruth.[5]

As Frankie Haggerty approached Ruth's casket at Yankee Stadium 10 months later, reporters asked the youngster to pose next to the man he stood for the previous autumn, and to show a little emotion. The photo in the next day's papers captured Frankie looking down on Ruth and wiping a tear from his eye. Years later, Haggerty moved to Baltimore and donated his Babe Ruth scrapbook, replete with original telegrams and news clippings, to the Babe Ruth Museum. He also shared that the famous wiping the tear photo … was staged.

* * *

On December 28, 1958, Yankee Stadium hosted what quickly became known as "The Greatest Game Ever Played," as the Baltimore Colts traveled to New York to challenge the Giants for the NFL championship. The game has withstood the test of time, mostly because of its trailblazing on-field exploits, with Colts quarterback John Unitas leading his team to a game-tying field goal in the final seconds of regulation (the genesis of the two-minute drill) and then detaching fullback Alan "The Horse" Ameche into the New York end zone for the winning score in pro football's first-ever sudden-death overtime. That game, with all the high drama of a *New York Times* best seller and played before a national television audience, put the NFL on the road to sports dominance. It's why Baltimoreans refer to Unitas as the "Babe Ruth" of the National Football League. His performance was so superior, so "Ruthian."

My perspective is more about what occurred behind the scenes than on the field. Here's some background: On November 10, 1928, Notre Dame was playing favored Army at Yankee Stadium. The teams played to a scoreless tie through the first half, and when the Fighting Irish gathered in the visiting locker room, coach Knute Rockne delivered his famous "Win one for the Gipper" speech, which inspired his chargers to a 12-6 win over the Black Knights in what turned out to be Rockne's worst season ever, with his team suffering through a 5-4 campaign.

Thirty years later, Colts coach Weeb Ewbank and his squad filled that same Yankee Stadium visitors locker room and, on the spur of the moment, Ewbank delivered a pregame talk that would have made Rockne proud. Of the 35 players suited for the game, he noted that 14 had been released outright by other teams, that seven were free agents, six came via trades, and one, Big Daddy Lipscomb, had been let go by the Rams and claimed off waivers for $100. He looked at John Unitas and said, "Pittsburgh didn't want you, but we picked you off the sandlots." To future Hall of Fame flanker Lenny Moore: "The idea was presented we might have a hard time getting you to practice."[6]

Coach Ewbank didn't mention every player, but they all got the message … that other teams didn't think too highly of them. Now they could show the football world what they were made of. Obviously, the speech worked.

Giants announcer Chris Schenkel and Baltimore's Chuck Thompson, the voice of the Colts until they left Baltimore for Indianapolis after the '83 season, had been assigned to broadcast the game for CBS Television. Because broadcasting NFL title games was a relatively new venture, there was nothing "routine" about the telecasting process. So, as Thompson recalled, he and Schenkel went to Commissioner Bert Bell's Manhattan office the day before the game to determine who would call play-by-play for each half. Bell flipped a coin, Schenkel won, and naturally chose the second half.[7]

When the game wound up in a tie at the end of regulation, Chuck naturally was in line to call the overtime period. Losing that coin toss would prove to be a career-altering luck of the draw! Thompson also recalled urging CBS to pull back on the closeups, especially after John Unitas dislocated a finger and trainer Charlie Winner pulled it straight. "Unitas," Thompson mused, "did not blink."

In 1994 we interviewed the Yankees' venerable public-address announcer, Bob Sheppard, who had been at the microphone to call the '58 thriller. Bob said he felt the Colts were the better team that day, and that the Giants were lucky to have kept the score so close. On the Colts' drive to tie the game at the end

of regulation, Sheppard recalled, "All I can remember saying was, 'Pass thrown by Unitas, complete to Berry,' over and over again."[8]

And finally, on that last drive in the fourth quarter, with Sheppard repeating, "Unitas to Berry," kicker Steve Myhra's field goal to send the game into overtime offers another off-the-field glimpse from that day. As the ball fluttered through the uprights, it headed in the direction of the Baltimore Colts Marching Band, seated just beyond the end zone. The ball was caught by honor guard member George Schaefer, who curled into a fetal position to protect himself and his newly found pigskin. New York fans piled on, attempting to usurp George's prize, and that prompted Colts band members to jump to the defense of their musical mate. New York police pounded their way in to disrupt the melee. Meanwhile, Schaefer, at the bottom of the scrum, rolled the ball to drummer Dan O'Toole, who punched a hole in his drumhead and put the ball inside. And that's how the Myhra ball made it successfully out of Yankee Stadium.[9] Years later, the museum displayed the ball … and the drum … as part of a 50th anniversary exhibit on the '58 championship game!

* * *

From George Ruth to John Unitas, Baltimore has served up two critical building blocks to the foundation of the original Yankee Stadium, the most historic sporting venue the world has ever known.

SOURCES

All interviews were conducted by the author. Thanks to producers Jackson Whitt and John Patti, who joined for the Mel Allen and Bob Sheppard interviews.

NOTES

1   Ray Kelly information from a September 1997 radio interview with Little Ray Kelly conducted by the author, WBAL Radio's Gerry Sandusky, and Doug Roberts. Babe Ruth Museum audio archives #128.

2   Ray Kelly interview.

3   Interview with Paul Hopkins, May 1995. Babe Ruth Museum audio archives #41.

4   Interview with Mel Allen, June 1994. Babe Ruth Museum audio archives #89.

5   Interview with Frankie Haggerty in 2001, and with additional material from Haggerty's scrapbook.

6   Reference to Weeb Ewbank's pregame talk is drawn from John F. Steadman, *Football's Miracle Men* (Cleveland: Pennington Press Inc., 1959), 169-171.

7   Chuck Thompson recollections from Babe Ruth Museum audio archive interview, 1997, #149B.

8   Bob Sheppard's recollections from Babe Ruth Museum audio archives interview, 1994, #003.

9   Story about Myhra ball and the Colts Marching Band from 2008 interview with Babe Ruth Museum senior staffer John Ziemann, president of Baltimore's Marching Ravens, formerly president of the Baltimore Colts Marching Band.

YANKEE STADIUM ON FILM

By Zac Petrillo

"Baseball stadiums are never only about baseball. Their utility is both more dynamic and more poetic."[1]

Some landmarks are so burned into our collective mind's eye that their image tells the story of their city, the people who live in it, and the joy shared by everyone who's experienced it. When actress and filmmaker Penny Marshall – an avid sports fan who grew up in the shadow of Yankee Stadium and made one of the great baseball movies, *A League of Their Own* – spoke of her youth, she said, "Yankee Stadium was the only thing we had in the Bronx. It was an institution."[2]

Marshall directed *Big* (1988), about a prepubescent kid who gets his wish to grow up and experience the excitement of New York City. To fully experience the city, she knew she needed to get her main character to Yankee Stadium. *Big*'s main character, Josh Baskin, played by Tom Hanks, enters the grandstand through an underexposed concrete tunnel. Marshall's camera inches toward the field to reveal what awaits them on the other side: the shimmering white façade and the glowing dot-matrix scoreboard. We don't see any more of what the characters see, but for anyone who's ever emerged from one of those tunnels, you don't need to see it to feel it: the expanse of green outfield grass, the crack of batting-practice line drives, and the golden, manicured infield dirt.

In an era of open concepts, those tunnels guiding our eyes to the grace of a field that always seems three times larger than our imagination are the pinnacle of baseball nostalgia. A moment shared by anybody who's ever entered a baseball stadium. Hanks' character in *Big* is an adult and a little boy at once. Through him, we can feel the awe of a child seeing Yankee Stadium's sprawling open space for the first time.

From almost the moment the original Yankee Stadium opened to the public in 1923, it appeared in motion pictures, both in baseball stories and not. In 1928, while the stadium was amid renovations, two of cinema's great comedy icons, Buster Keaton and Harold Lloyd, turned it into their muse.

When Keaton came upon an empty Yankee Stadium, he endeavored to improvise a scene for his film, *The Cameraman*. Keaton's character sneaks into the stadium and mimes a baseball game alone without bats, balls, or gloves. Using an empty stadium makes the impact of its presence even more powerful as it looms like the watchful Monument Valley landscapes of John Ford's westerns in the backdrop, painting a portrait of the intricacies that made the ballpark iconic in the ensuing decades.

The barren slope of outfield seats gives way to a diagonal wall, beyond which there are only a handful of buildings and the stadium's ongoing construction. *The Cameraman* was made before New York City development cascaded with housing projects and commercial real estate. Missing in the background is the well-known Gem Razor advertisement, which we can instead see as a more modest text along the outfield

The Detective *(1968), starring Frank Sinatra and Lee Remick, featured Yankee Stadium transformed into a football field.*

fence. Of course, there is also the famed frieze, which appears only fleetingly within the scene. In the few shots it does show, the lack of fans and the old, grainy film stock make the feat of architecture overwhelming and hint at why this bit of design became the most familiar part of the stadium's iconography.

The stadium plays an even more central role in Harold Lloyd's *Speedy* (directed by Ted Wilde). Early in the film, we learn that Lloyd's character, Harold 'Speedy' Swift, loses jobs as quickly as he gets them, partly because he insists on being near his beloved Yankee Stadium (referred to in the film's title cards as *the* Yankee Stadium). We get some brief gameplay shots from obscured angles within the stands, as if playing from a projector through Harold's mind. Later, Harold, now a cab driver one ticket away from going to jail, has a chance meeting with Babe Ruth, who needs a lift to get to the game as quickly as possible.

In a visually dazzling sequence, Harold narrowly evades other vehicles and pedestrians before pulling up to the stadium's front gate. Though Ruth comments, "If I ever want to commit suicide, I know who to call," he still invites his driver to watch the ballgame. In the stadium, we glimpse the box seats and some gameplay (taken from newsreel footage of Ruth smacking a home run). *Speedy* is Lloyd's love letter to the bustle of New York City and its burgeoning entertaining hotspots, such as Coney Island. Yankee Stadium's appearance as a vital part of the film speaks to its stature as essential to the city's rapid early-twentieth-century growth.

In 1942 two major Hollywood productions depicted Yankee Stadium, now 15 years older and more renowned thanks to its occupant's stature as the winningest ballclub of the 1920s and 1930s. They help paint the stadium's evolution and advancements in Hollywood technology. Most obviously, the two earlier pictures were without sync sound (filmed at the tail end of the silent era), while these newer films use dialogue as their primary mode of storytelling.

Woman of the Year, directed by George Cukor, is about two newspaper reporters who fall in love; one – played by Spencer Tracy – is a sportswriter, and the other – Katharine Hepburn – writes about culture and turns up her nose at low-hanging fruit like baseball. Tracy takes Hepburn to a Yankees game at the old stadium to show her the value of sports. It's the film's best scene. The press box is pretty clearly on a stage, while the angle on the field remains primarily from the third-base line behind home plate looking out at right field.

On the infield, the grass in front of second base takes on different shapes, occasionally well-manicured and in other instances displaying large chunks of browning grass or encroaching dirt patches. This makes it obvious that the actual stadium shots happened over multiple games. In the background, we get a distant glimpse of two monuments (Miller Huggins and Lou Gehrig), Jacob Ruppert's plaque on the center-field wall, and the flagpole in the field of play, behind which a sign warns that "persons throwing bottles or other missiles will be arrested and prosecuted." Outside the stadium, a water tower rests beyond left-center. Buildings have sprouted in the Bronx, including the one with a Marlin Blades advertisement that remained affixed across the top floor for the next decade.

The Pride of the Yankees, directed by Sam Wood, tells a very different kind of story, one that makes the stadium into the place where its hero, Lou Gehrig, becomes an icon. In actuality, Yankee Stadium rarely appears in the film.[3] Most scenes were staged 10 miles southwest of Hollywood, at Wrigley Field (home to the Hollywood Stars and Los Angeles Angels of the Pacific Coast League). Smartly, many games portray the Yankees on the road, as made clear by the away "New York" lettering across their jerseys. A few shots, however, were done at Yankee Stadium, including a shot of the exterior and another with in-game action in the outfield. Footage shot by a second unit at the real Yankee Stadium during the 1941 World Series is sporadically intercut with shots at Wrigley. During Gehrig's attempt to hit two home runs for Bill, the small boy who's sick with cancer, Gehrig's monument is vaguely visible in center field, despite being unveiled roughly a month after his death.[4]

In the film's most famous scene, Gary Cooper as Gehrig gives his "Luckiest Man" speech. As Richard Sandomir describes in his book on the making of the film, "The absence of a complete text, film, or audio copy means that it might have faded without the existence of *Pride*."[5] Although Sam Wood wanted the speech to look as though it was done inside of a real stadium, the primary shot, a low-angle to make Cooper look heroic with his teammates and throngs of fans hanging on his every word, was done on Samuel Goldwyn's sound stage. In post-production, the filmmakers superimposed this shot over the footage taken at Yankee Stadium during the World Series.[6]

A decade later, television was a ubiquitous form of entertainment in America. Yankee Stadium found itself as the backdrop for various shows such as *The*

Phil Silvers Show (1955-1959) and *Naked City* (1958-1963). In a 1961 episode of the latter entitled "A Hole in the City," we catch a sight of the Bronx neighborhood surrounding Yankee Stadium. Cops set up in front of Gate Six, preparing to apprehend a young criminal (played by Robert Duvall in an early guest role) who desperately hides away in his aunt's apartment, which directly overlooks the outfield. The stadium can be seen from unique vantage points throughout the episode, including when the climactic chase leads to the rooftop and provides a look at the frieze from the perspective of neighboring buildings.

At the movies, Yankee Stadium remained a fixture, making appearances in baseball stories such as *The Babe Ruth Story* (1948),[7] *It Happens Every Spring* (1949), and the critically maligned Doris Day and Ronald Reagan vehicle, *The Winning Team* (1952)[8] about Hall of Famer Grover Cleveland Alexander. Clarence Brown's 1951 version of *Angels in the Outfield* takes place primarily in Pittsburgh, prominently featuring Forbes Field, but a short moment at Yankee Stadium is notable for capturing Joe DiMaggio breaking his pregame warmup to directly address the camera. We get a view of the left-field bleachers in the background, with ads for Con Edison, Tydol, Philip Morris, and, most prominent of all, Manhattan Shirts.

The Stadium also showed up in two more comedies in the 1950s, *Trouble Along the Way* (1953) and the Martin & Lewis comedy/musical *Living it Up* (1954). In *Living It Up,* the stadium is grouped with iconic New York City landmarks when Jerry Lewis jumps onto a freight train in hopes of getting to New York for sites like "Broadway, Radio City, and the Yankee Stadium!" *Living It Up* was the first Hollywood film to shoot the stadium in color, revealing in just two angles the vibrant blue of each deck, the muted green of the seats, and the red, white, and blue bunting. *Living It Up* was also the first of several musicals and concerts to cement Yankee Stadium's status as an alluring place in which to perform.

In 1962 Doris Day starred in *That Touch of Mink,* which took her back to Yankee Stadium, this time arguing balls and strikes from inside the dugout with Roger Maris, Mickey Mantle, and Yogi Berra (each appearing as himself).[9] A year earlier, a bird's-eye shot of the stadium in the opening montage of *West Side Story* (1961) helped draw viewers into the geography and atmosphere of New York City (just as it did years later at the beginning of Woody Allen's *Manhattan* (1979)). *West Side Story's* choreographer, Bob Fosse – a Chicago native who made his breakthrough in 1955

by choreographing the baseball-themed Broadway hit *Damn Yankees* for the stage – must have found Yankee Stadium a compelling representation of New York because he set a pivotal scene in his directorial debut, *Sweet Charity* (1969), on the outfield grass.

In *Sweet Charity,* Shirley MacLaine plays a down-on-her-luck taxi dancer, beaten by false loves and an unforgiving city that she yearns to make her "personal property." When she meets the man who she believes will finally turn her luck, a sequence of shots begins tight on MacLaine's face then – as she declares, "Someone loves me!" – zooms out wide to reveal famous New York landmarks such as Times Square, the Plaza Hotel, the Metropolitan Opera House, and Yankee Stadium. Fosse films MacLaine from behind, the camera and actress gazing up at the grandiosity of the decks leading up to the frieze. Just like in Keaton's *The Cameraman,* the stadium is empty, only this time it's filmed in widescreen with vibrant color. Fans cheer over the soundtrack as if playing from the character's mind. The shot foreshadows more recent images of Mariano Rivera trotting in from the bullpen. The effect Fosse is aiming for, a woman finally confident enough to take this city by storm, is reminiscent of that of a famed closer about to take the mound and give his team the win.

Released a year before *Sweet Charity,* Gordon Douglas's subversive police procedural *The Detective* (1968), starring Frank Sinatra, contains a brief scene with Yankee Stadium that's notable for the game on the field being football rather than baseball. Set up for the New York Giants (who shared the stadium from 1956 to 1973), the end zones, adorned with "NY," stretch from the first-base dugout to the left-field wall, above which Sinatra and his girlfriend, Karen (played by Lee Remick), agree to marry. Nine years earlier, *FBI Story* (1959), starring Jimmy Stewart, also took place during a Giants game. Director Mervyn LeRoy staged an elaborate surveillance scene that moved from outside the stadium to the interior corridors and into the stands as fans watched football on the field.

Bang the Drum Slowly (1973)[10] mixed Yankee Stadium and Shea Stadium as the home for the fictional New York Mammoths. Sidney Lumet's *Serpico* (1973) filmed a key scene in a South Bronx park with the pre-renovation stadium lurking like an Old Hollywood matte painting in the background. The late '70s saw a dearth in films shot at Yankee Stadium, partly due to renovations keeping the stadium under construction from September 1973 through April 1976. The renovation turned the distinctive frieze into a façade behind the bleachers and removed the 119 classic columns within the stands.

The era is well-represented by ESPN's miniseries *The Bronx is Burning* (2007) which, as the title suggests, is as much a sociological study of a place and time as a baseball film. The stadium appears intercut with documentary-style stock footage of actual games and the uncanny lookalike cast acting in between. The effect is the feeling that we are watching nonfiction, centering Yankee Stadium as the heart in turmoil, reflecting the instability of late-70s New York as well as the Yankees. When the Yankees won the World Series in 1977, Yankee Stadium became a communal space injecting a town that endured financial crisis and the Son of Sam murders with hope in a time of lost optimism.

It's My Turn (1980) inserts Michael Douglas into an actual Old Timers Game that features Yankees legends Mickey Mantle, Roger Maris, and Whitey Ford and non-Yankees such as Bob Feller and Monte Irvin. At one point, Douglas appears to rob a nearly 50-year-old Mantle of an extra-base hit. In Bette Gordon's low-budget drama *Variety* (1983), an enigmatic man takes the main character on a date to his executive suite at Yankee Stadium. The filmmakers shot the scene off-the-cuff during the October 1, 1982, game between the Yankees and Red Sox. "We'd gotten permission to shoot in a private booth, claiming we were making a film about life in New York," Gordon said. "The game was in full swing, and all of a sudden, a manager burst in, screaming, 'Your lights are in the player's eyes.' He explained that unless we could film without the lights, we'd have to stop shooting."[11] Perhaps owing to the difficult conditions, in the finished film, shots of Ron Guidry pitching are edited against images of Steve Balboni batting as if they are facing each other. However, they were both Yankees.

Yankee Stadium returned to the movies in force in the late '80s and early '90s. It showed up briefly in baseball films like *Major League* (1989), *Mr. Baseball* (1992), *The Babe* (1992), *Little Big League* (1994), and *The Scout* (1994)[12] as well as the aforementioned *Big* and the action blockbuster, *Die Hard with a Vengeance* (1995).[13] *The Scout* turned the bright lights of Yankee Stadium into a performance anxiety trigger for two highly-touted pitching prospects, culminating in the titular scout talking "the best baseball player that ever lived" down from the stadium roof. Like Buster Keaton's film nearly 70 years earlier, *Die Hard with a Vengeance* depicted the stadium in its empty state. Zeus Carver (played by Samuel L. Jackson) arrives

to solve a riddle by the criminals leading him around the city looking for bombs. Unbeknownst to Carver, a sniper trains his crosshairs from beyond the drapes of the stadium executive suites. Groundskeepers work on the field in the background as an elevated train rushes past the slot behind the right-field bleachers, and we see the mid-'90s addition of "Welcome to Yankee Stadium" stenciled along the top of the visiting team dugout.

Perhaps the most famous contemporary appearance by the stadium came in *Seinfeld* (1989-1998). Beginning at the end of Season Five, George Costanza, the neurotic and perpetually unemployed friend of Jerry Seinfeld, lucks into a tumultuous job working for George Steinbrenner as the assistant traveling secretary of the Yankees. The Yankee Stadium shown in the series is covered in drab blues and concrete grays without any signage or unique iconography. The show's creators, Seinfeld and Larry David, turn Yankee Stadium into a reflection of the show's theme of being about nothing. Devoid of the mythical aura surrounding the stadium, it becomes a place where George comes to loathe working for the owner, which, in tandem with the drab depiction of the stadium, might presage criticisms leveled at the new Yankee Stadium for being a "soulless, corporate replica"[14] out of step with modern ballparks.

Billy Crystal's *61** (2001) did a fine job re-creating the old stadium by way of set dressing Tiger Stadium. A TV movie with a limited budget, *61** had the luxury of using an abandoned old ballpark since the Detroit Tigers had moved to Comerica Park in 2000 (the year the picture went into production). The film's production designer, Rusty Smith, went to painstaking lengths to dress Tiger Stadium's identifiable features with ones that matched Yankee Stadium in 1961. One such detail was painting all of the blue seats a color of green that matched Yankee Stadium exactly. Smith found the color match on an old stadium seat owned by Crystal.

Computer-generated imagery was still in its infancy in the early 2000s, but *61** used its limited budget to digitally enhance the location with an additional deck (Tiger Stadium had two tiers to Yankee Stadium's three) as well as the classic frieze. The overall effect is one of the truest representations of Yankee Stadium from the 1960s despite the filmmakers not recording even one frame in the actual space.

The film that most literally weaves the stadium throughout is *For Love of the Game* (1999). This baseball romance makes New York a critical part of its characters' psychology and, as such, centers Yankee Stadium as the pivot point for an aging Tigers pitcher trying to defy the odds one last time. New York is the place where he met the love of his life. The film contains late-'90s details, such as the sparse ads for brands like Kodak and *The Wiz* on the outfield fence along with the interlocking "NY" painted behind home plate. *For Love of the Game* understands that to tell a story about New York City within Yankee Stadium, the crowd must be a character, too. We get a view of stereotypical Yankees fans, passionate about the game and more than a little bit aggressive. Hecklers hiss and swear at the pitcher, who comments, "I always know when I'm in New York," and the announcer says, "Yankee Stadium is like a schoolyard, and [the umpire] is like a teacher who sees trouble." By the end of the film, the crowd, respecting the game, has come around to the opposing pitcher's achievement, giving him a round of applause. Nothing is more Yankee Stadium than that.

For the final feature shot at Yankee Stadium, filmmakers took us back to where we began: a comedy. In the Adam Sandler starrer, *Anger Management* (2003), the stadium stands as the location for the climactic scene where Sandler's character, believing his anger-management counselor intends to steal his girlfriend and propose to her on the stadium video screen, races onto the field and grabs the mic from Robert Merrill before the national anthem. Far from the high art of Keaton and Lloyd, the sentimental scene possesses madcap energy reminiscent of those earlier comedians. Granted free rein of Yankee Stadium over four nights, the filmmakers and hundreds of professional extras don't linger long on the stadium's architecture. However, the film secured the participation of people who were mainstays of the ballpark in Merrill (who began singing the national anthem for major events in 1969), Bob Sheppard (public-address announcer from 1951 to 2007), and former New York City Mayor Rudy Giuliani.

Over its 85 years, Yankee Stadium appeared in film and television dozens of times, sometimes as itself and sometimes with other stadiums standing in, dressed up with its iconic features. Sometimes the stadium was empty and sometimes it was filled with screaming fans. Sometimes the images were in black and white and sometimes in vibrant color. Each appearance tracks the evolution of not only the ballpark but time itself.

The common thread among each is that Yankee Stadium is a vital part of the fabric of New York City.

Each time the stadium showed up, the filmmakers, in their own way, tried to bottle that feeling that Penny Marshall portrayed in *Big* when her character moves into that magical space, with its looming façade and ghosts of memories past, beyond the tunnel.

NOTES

1   Dan Moore, The Baseball Stadium That 'Forever Changed' Professional Sports," *The Ringer*, August 4, 2022, https://www.theringer.com/mlb/2022/8/4/23288546/camden-yards-30th-anniversary-baltimore-influence (last accessed August 8, 2022).

2   Penny Marshall, "The Tie That Binds a Girl to Her Borough," *New York Times*, September 20, 2008.

3   Two TV movies about Lou Gehrig – an episode of CBS's *Climax!* called "The Lou Gehrig Story" (1956) and NBC's "A Love Affair: The Eleanor and Lou Gehrig Story" (1978) – also featured Yankee Stadium.

4   Richard Sandomir, *The Pride of the Yankees: Lou Gehrig, Gary Cooper, and the Making of a Classic* (e-book edition), (New York: Hachette Books, 2017), 131.

5   Sandomir, 210.

6   Sandomir, 218.

7   *The Babe Ruth Story* contains some wonderful shots in and around Yankee Stadium, including a shot from beyond the elevated train looking in at the stadium, a shot inside the press box with Mel Allen, and one featuring William Bendix as Babe Ruth rounding first base with a Ballantine Beer ad in the background, despite the Yankees' partnership with the beer brand beginning after Ruth's career ended.

8   See, e.g., Bosley Crowther, "'The Winning Team,' Story About Grover Cleveland Alexander, Arrives at the Mayfair," *New York Times*, June 21, 1952: 15. In Crowther's review, he sarcastically mocks the film's blatant inaccuracies: "But this only goes to show you how misleading the records can be, since this picture version is presented by the Warners (who are honorable men) as 'true.' Certainly Ted Sherdeman, Seeleg Lester and Merwin Gerard wouldn't have written the script this way if there were even the slightest question of the facts as presented on the screen." Not mentioned, and perhaps most egregious, is the final out of the 1926 World Series. Famously, Babe Ruth was caught stealing to end the Series. In the film, Alexander records a strikeout to end the game.

9   American League umpire Art Passarella also makes a cameo as the person on other end of Day's complaints.

10 The opening scene where the main characters jog around the edge of the field (from which the film's famous poster art is taken) was shot at Yankee Stadium. In the background, there are minor details from just before the stadium's renovation, such as the dark blue padding at the base of the perimeter, the blue seats, and the tunnels that lead into the stands.

11 Bette Gordon, "Voyeurism and Half-Lit Streets: Bette Gordon on Variety," *Talkhouse*, https://www.talkhouse.com/voyeurism-and-half-lit-streets-bette-gordon-on-variety/ (last accessed August 13, 2022)

12 *The Scout* contains notable cameos, including George Steinbrenner, John Sterling, Bobby Murcer, Keith Hernandez, and Bret Saberhagen.

13 In a bit of trivia with a Yankee Stadium link, 1968's *The Detective* was adapted from the book of the same name by Roderick Thorp. Thorp's sequel, *Nothing Lasts Forever*, was adapted into *Die Hard*. Making *The Detective* something of a prequel to the much later action hit.

14 Andrew Joseph, "All 30 MLB stadiums, ranked: 2022 edition," *USA Today*, https://ftw.usatoday.com/lists/best-mlb-stadiums-ranked-2022-edition-baseball-ballparks (last accessed August 8, 2022).

SILENT ICONS: BUSTER KEATON, HAROLD LLOYD, AND YANKEE STADIUM

By David Krell

1928 was a phenomenal year for the New York Yankees.

Babe Ruth led both leagues in slugging percentage, home runs, walks, and runs scored as the Yankees marched toward sweeping the St. Louis Cardinals in the World Series and winning their second consecutive title. He also graced the silver screen in *Speedy*, one of two silent movies featuring Yankee Stadium.

Harold Lloyd plays the title character, a taxi driver who spots Ruth signing autographs at an orphanage. Ruth asks Speedy to drive him to the game; it's an excruciating trek full of near-crashes with other cars. Yankee Stadium appears as Speedy drives over the Macombs Dam Bridge in a nicely framed shot with the ballpark in the background toward the right part of the screen.

Lou Gehrig appears briefly in the background of a conversation between Ruth and Speedy at the Stadium. The Sultan of Swat asks Speedy if he'd like to see the game, which presents an opportunity to show the field. But the shots are limited to a few moments from newsreel footage; Ruth swings for a strike and then hits a home run. Another player is shown hitting a foul ball.

Ruth was not a stranger to films, having starred in *Headin' Home* and *Babe Comes Home*.

Whether his presence added to *Speedy's* box-office success is not known, because Lloyd's fame was at its height already. But it did offer a valuable piece of verisimilitude, particularly in the establishing shot from the bridge. The audience sees what drivers and passengers see – the Stadium appearing in the distance and getting increasingly imposing as one gets nearer.

It's one of several New York City locations that Lloyd uses throughout the film; a series of scenes for Speedy's date with Jane Dillon at Coney Island showcases the area's iconic attractions in black-and-white glory.

As Ruth biographer Jane Leavy points out, Lloyd knew Ruth's business manager, Christy Walsh, which explains how the bespectacled silent film star was able to procure the appearance of one of the biggest celebrities in 1920s sports. Ruth's fee: $5,750.[1]

Speedy was filmed in the summer and fall of 1927 as Ruth astounded baseball fans by breaking his own home-run record, finishing the season with 60 round-trippers. In one scene, Lloyd holds a copy of the *New York Times* from August 7. A scoreboard in the window of a sporting-goods store indicates the lineups for a Yankees-White Sox game.

Indeed, the Yankees hosted a two-game series against the Chicago ballclub on August 6-7. The scoreboard indicates Herb Pennock pitching against Ted Blankenship in either the fourth or fifth inning of a game that the Yankees lead 3-1. But the game never happened with the lineups depicted; Blankenship and Pennock did not oppose each other in a game during the 1927 season.

Blankenship pitched on August 7 in a 4-3 loss to the Yankees. Urban Shocker was the starting pitcher for the home squad; he went five innings and was credited with the victory. Wilcy Moore pitched the remaining four innings.

Speedy was a home run for theaters. The Tampa Theater made almost 50 percent of its average weekly gross during the first day that the film – Lloyd's last in the silent era – was on the marquee. In St. Louis, it took the Ambassador Theater two days to exceed the 50 percent number. The Indiana Theater in Indianapolis tallied 65 percent in the first two days.[2]

Baseball was just one sport to which Lloyd was devoted. "He loved baseball," says his granddaughter, Suzanne Lloyd. "He used to take me to the Dodger games. He had a handball court up at Greenacres, his estate in Beverly Hills. That's how he got his hands strong enough after the accident. He loved to golf and run. *Speedy* was shot in New York because he wanted it to be totally authentic. His films stand up because they're true to life. You can relate to them."[3]

Ebbets Field or the Polo Grounds could have been used by Lloyd. But 1927 was far from auspicious for Brooklyn – the Dodgers/Robins finished in sixth place with a 65-88 record. The Giants were in third place, only two games behind the pennant-winning Pittsburgh Pirates. With five players hitting above .300 that season – Bill Terry, Rogers Hornsby, Travis Jackson, Freddie Lindstrom, Edd Roush – Lloyd had his choice of top batters. Any player from that quintet would have been known to baseball fans.

But the South Bronx ballpark, then in its fifth season, was a gargantuan edifice famous even to people who didn't know how many balls equal a walk or what position Lazzeri played for the Yankees. Ruth's fame ran parallel to the Stadium in the way that sports icons are simply known by the public at large because they transcend their given sport. His success was a huge draw at the Stadium, leading it to be nicknamed The House That Ruth Built.

Yankee Stadium's depiction in *Speedy* does not, in any way, match the majesty in *The Cameraman*, which premiered in September 1928.

The Stadium gave an immediate sense of grandeur with its frieze, size, and mystique. Ebbets Field had charm, contained in a Flatbush city block. You could see Babe Ruth smile if he hit a home run at Yankee Stadium, but you could see Dazzy Vance sweat at Ebbets Field. That's how close the fans were to the action.

The Polo Grounds had size, but its architecture was unappealing – a bland, horseshoe shape making the fences at the ends of left and right fields less than 300 feet from home plate.

Buster Keaton, a prominent baseball fan in show-business circles, plays the title role – a struggling MGM newsreel cameraman also named Buster – in *The Cameraman*, which premiered in September 1928. While it's visually appealing and an example of Keaton's filmmaking brilliance, the Yankee Stadium scene is not necessary to the plot revolving around a rival cameraman taking credit for Buster's amazing footage of a Tong War in Chinatown and dating his crush, Sally. In the end, Buster is rightfully credited. Sally winds up with him as the rival is shown to be a cad who also took credit for saving Sally from drowning when it was, in fact, Buster.

At the beginning of the ballpark sequence, Keaton runs across the expanse of the outfield with his camera and tripod, hoping to set them up and capture game footage that his bosses can use for newsreels. Taken from the vantage point of the left-field stands, it's a beautiful shot encompassing the ballpark's massive size framed by the famous frieze.

A cardigan-wearing gentleman, presumably a groundskeeper, delivers unfortunate news to Buster – the Yankees are in St. Louis. The timeline tracks with the film's release. A Yankees-Browns series took place at the beginning of August, in the middle of an exhausting 21-game road trip to Boston, Detroit, Cleveland, St. Louis, Chicago, and Boston again. The Yankees lost two of the three games in St. Louis; they returned to the Bronx with a 10-11 record in the rival cities.

With the gentleman gone, Buster heads to the Yankee Stadium pitching mound and mimes a bases-loaded scenario of trying to pick off a runner at third base; checking the runners at first and second; and directing his right fielder to move toward the foul line. Buster then acts out a double play: fielding a groundball and tossing to the infielder covering second base, presumably the shortstop, then covering home plate, where he jumps to snare a high throw from the third baseman and tag out the remaining baserunner.

Buster continues his imaginary game on offense with an inside-the-park home run, beating the throw – from either an outfielder or the cutoff man – with a headfirst slide into home plate. It's filmed in one fluid motion, a wide shot keeping Buster in the center of the frame from a point of view behind the left-field foul line and near home plate. The 32-year-old filmmaker sprints around the bases in a 17-second dash. It's a remarkable feat.

Most prominent in the background of Buster's run to glory are the advertisement for Gem Razor Blades with the slogan "Never Miss a Whisker" stretching on the outfield wall from right field to center field, and a corresponding men's grooming advertisement for Ever-Ready Shaving Brushes. The scene ends with the cardigan-wearing man emerging and chasing Buster off the field with a scowl.

Because it's filmed at ground level, the audience gets a better understanding of the Stadium's magnificence than they do from the newsreel films shot with cameras in the stands. The scene lasts about 3½ minutes, with Buster's home run taking up almost a third of that time.

The Yankee Stadium scene in *The Cameraman* offers a terrific visual chronicle of the celebrated ballpark that housed the iconic 1920s teams anchored by Babe Ruth, Lou Gehrig, Tony Lazzeri, Waite Hoyt et al. It's even more impressive in its emptiness; one gets a true, almost eerie, sense of quietude.

Keaton biographer Dana Stevens, author of *Camera Man: Buster Keaton, the Dawn of Cinema, and the Invention of the Twentieth Century*, believes that the scene exemplifies Keaton's innovation and appeal. "It brings together some of his best skills as a performer and director," offered Stevens. "It's entirely improvised, wordless, shot from a distance in long takes, and shows us not only the mechanics of a ballgame but the psychology of the various players and their relationship to each other – a tour de force of pantomime.[4]

"The falling house in *Steamboat Bill* is a breathtaking stunt, but this is a more powerful character moment, and also, because it was improvised on the spot when Keaton and his crew learned that Yankee Stadium was free, is a better glimpse into his working methods than that stunt, which required a specially built set and weeks of preparation. What makes the baseball scene so magical is that it required nothing other than Keaton's body, a camera and Yankee Stadium."[5]

Martin Dickstein of the *Brooklyn Daily Eagle* highlighted Keaton's pantomime in his contemporary review of the film: "It is undoubtedly one of the funniest things the screen has brought forth this season."[6]

Film exhibitors embraced Keaton's work, as well. J.M. Reynolds of the Opera House in Elwood, Nebraska, said, "I think I have played every Buster Keaton picture that he has made, and I class this one as one of the best."[7] William Martin of the New Patriot Theatre in Patriot, Indiana, praised, "This is a fine picture with Buster doing his best work that we have seen. Pleased all that saw this."[8]

In Pella, Iowa, E.P. Hosack revealed the impact at the Strand Theater: "Buster takes well [here] but I did not know it was so strong – did not put out any extra advertising. If you are strong on Buster, bill it heavy, tie your lobby doors back and start the [show]. Had more laughs in general on this show than I have had for some time – comedy all the way through. Not silly but clever."[9]

Inclusions in *The Cameraman* and *Speedy* during the Yankees' prominence in the late 1920s helped begin a long, prosperous, and fascinating journey for Yankee Stadium as a facility of cultural importance in baseball and beyond.

NOTES

1 Jane Leavy, *The Big Fella: Babe Ruth and the World He Created* (New York: HarperCollins, 2018), 104-105.

2 "Records Go Flooey!" *Variety*, April 11, 1928: 21.

3 Suzanne Lloyd, telephone interview with David Krell, July 24, 2022. During a photo shoot in 1919, Harold Lloyd severely damaged his right hand when he lit a cigarette with a prop bomb that was actually explosive. He lost a thumb and a finger, which necessitated wearing a special glove in his movies. "Harold Clayton Lloyd (1893-1971)," https://haroldlloyd.com/harold-clayton-lloyd/ (last accessed July 29, 2022).

4 Dana Stevens, email to David Krell, September 30, 2022.

5 Stevens email. In *Steamboat Bill*, an entire side of a house drops intact to the ground. Keaton's character escapes harm by standing squarely and unknowingly in a space where an empty window frame will fall around him.

6 Martin Dickstein, "The Cinema Circuit," *Brooklyn Daily Eagle*, September 18, 1928: 14A.

7 "What the Picture Did for Me – Verdicts on Films in Language of Exhibitor: Metro-Goldwyn-Mayer, *The Cameraman*," *Exhibitors Herald-World*, February 23, 1929: 57.

8 "What the Picture Did for Me," *Exhibitors Herald-World*, April 13, 1929: 60.

9 "What the Picture Did for Me," *Exhibitors Herald-World*, January 19, 1929: 62.

THE HOUSE THAT ORATORY BUILT

Great Speeches at Yankee Stadium

By David H. Lippman

All baseball fans are familiar, if not from the movie, then from the grainy newsreel footage, with Lou Gehrig's legendary speech at Yankee Stadium home plate on July 4, 1939.

Yet that was not the first nor the last time a speech would have a dramatic impact at The House that Ruth Built. Baseball, football, and faith have all been occasions for legendary rhetoric at Yankee Stadium.

The first such speech was made on November 10, 1928, and did not involve baseball. The orator was Notre Dame's legendary head football coach Knute Rockne, during halftime with a game against West Point. The game was scoreless, and the Fighting Irish were seen as underdogs. Nearly 85,000 people packed Yankee Stadium to see the football rivalry between the two teams play out.

In the locker room, Rockne reminded his players of the late Notre Dame star George Gipp. In four seasons with the Fighting Irish, Gipp rushed for 2,341 yards, passed for more than 1,750 yards, and died at the age of 25 of pneumonia.

Now, to inspire his men to victory, Rockne told his players: "The last thing (Gipp) said to me was: 'Rock, sometime when the team is up against it and the breaks are beating the boys, tell them to go out there with all they got and win just one for the Gipper.'"[1]

Notre Dame stormed out and beat Army, 12-6. Both Gipp's career and Rockne's speech were immortalized on celluloid in the 1940 movie *Knute Rockne-All American*, with Pat O'Brien in the title role, and Ronald Reagan as the Gipper.

Ironically, historians say it's unlikely Gipp made such a request – as some say Rockne wasn't in the hospital when he died.

There is far less controversy about the next major speech at Yankee Stadium. "Baseball's Gettysburg Address" is how many people have referred to Lou Gehrig's tear-filled farewell to the sport between games of a doubleheader on July 4, 1939.

The ceremony is one of the best-known events in baseball history, with Gehrig receiving gifts from his teammates, other teams, and reporters who covered the Yankees. Modest to the end, shoulders limp, showing his sunken chest, Gehrig gazed down at the trophies while the fans shouted, "We want Lou."[2]

Gehrig's speech was poorly recorded by newsreel cameras and was spontaneous. In his thick Manhattan accent, Gehrig opened with the words, "For the past two weeks you've been reading about a bad break.[3] Today, I consider myself the luckiest man on the face of the earth." After honoring his teammates, opponents, manager, general manager, fans, wife, and even his in-laws, he finished: "So I close in saying that I might have been given a bad break, but I've got an awful lot to live for."[4]

The producer of *The Pride of the Yankees,* Sam Goldwyn, had little interest in shooting a baseball film until he saw the newsreel of the speech, and broke into tears. That got the movie rolling.[5]

Gary Cooper, who played Gehrig, rendered a shorter version of the speech for the movie cameras. However, when he went to the South Pacific during World War II to entertain the troops, they asked for the speech at his first appearance in New Guinea's jungles.

Cooper did not remember the speech's precise words. To his credit, Cooper asked for a few minutes to prepare, turned the stage over to his colleague Jack Benny, and wrote down the words in pouring rain. "They were a silent bunch that listened to me," he said later. "They were the words of a brave American who had only a short time to live, and they mean something to those kids in the Pacific."[6]

Yankee Stadium's next great address was delivered by Gehrig's great teammate, Babe Ruth, on April 27, 1947. Suffering from the malignant tumor in his neck that would kill him in 1948 at the early age of 53, Ruth had lost weight; his hair had turned gray, and his voice hoarse.

Commissioner A.B. "Happy" Chandler decreed that April 27 would be Babe Ruth Day throughout the majors and every other organized league in the United States.

The Yankees faced the Washington Senators at home that day, under mid-60s temperatures; 58,339 fans jammed the House That Ruth Built to say farewell to its "builder," who arrived in his usual camel-hair jacket.

In a 10-minute ceremony, the Ford Motor Co. presented the slugger with a $5,000 Lincoln, the Yankees gave him a check to pay for his treatments, and baseball itself announced it would create a foundation to promote youth programs.[7]

Six speakers preceded the Sultan of Swat. Cardinal Francis Spellman gave an invocation, praising Ruth as "a manly leader of youth in America." Chandler was booed for suspending Dodgers manager Leo Durocher that year for consorting with gamblers ... but drew some cheers when he ended with "the spirit of Babe Ruth ... will be with us as we build a new generation capable of protecting our own heritage as a free people."[8]

To introduce the Bambino, Legion ballplayer Larry Cutler, speaking for the youth of America, said, "From all of us kids, Babe, it's swell to have you back." Cutler went on to play ball for City College of New York, and spent time in the White Sox and Pirates organizations.[9]

Two friends, former teammates Wally Pipp and Joe Dugan, helped Ruth shuffle to the microphone. The crowd greeted him "with such thunder from their throats as the home run king had never heard in his moments of greater glory."[10]

In a hoarse voice, Ruth told the crowd, ad-libbing all the way, "You know how bad my voice sounds – well, it feels just as bad. You know this baseball game of ours comes up from the youth. That means the boys. And after you're a boy and grow up and know how to play ball, then you come to the boys you see representing themselves today in your national pastime. The only real game, I think, in the world, baseball. As a rule, some people think that if you give them a football, or a baseball, or something like that, naturally they're athletes right away. But you can't do that in baseball.

"You've gotta start from way down the bottom, when you're six or seven years of age. You can't wait until you're 15 or 16. You gotta let it grow up with you. And if you're successful, and you try hard enough, you're bound to come out on top, just like those boys

have come to the top now. There's been so many lovely things said about me, and I'm glad that I've had the opportunity to thank everybody. Thank you."[11]

Ruth then hobbled to a front-row box seat, to watch a tight pitchers' duel between the Nats' Sid Hudson and the Bombers' Spud Chandler. The Senators won, 1-0, on a single by Hudson, a bunt, and a single by Buddy Lewis.

Ruth made one more appearance at Yankee Stadium, a year later, on June 13, 1948, a grim, cloudy day, to celebrate the stadium's 25th anniversary. Old teammates, some in uniform, joined him. The visiting team was the Cleveland Indians.

Mel Allen introduced the old-timers, some in uniform, who included Pipp, Waite Hoyt, and Dugan. A bugler played "Taps" to honor Yankee stars who had passed on. Ruth stood at home plate, facing the cavernous stadium and World Champion banners hanging from the legendary façade, supported by a bat provided by Indians first baseman Eddie Robinson. The bat in turn belonged to their pitching titan Bob Feller, who was warming up in the bullpen to start the day's game. Dugan and Pipp again helped their dying leader to home plate.

Barely able to speak, Ruth said, "I am proud I hit the first home run here in 1923. It was marvelous to see 13 or 14 players who were my teammates going back 25 years. I'm telling you it makes me proud and happy to be here."[12]

The original plan called for the old-timers to face each other in a two-inning exhibition, with Ruth managing one side. However, he was too exhausted to do it, and left the ballpark for the last time before it took place, losing one last chance to manage a team, even if it was a collection of old-timers.

Ceremonies done, Feller faced New York native Eddie Lopat. The future Hall of Famer got a quick 1-0 lead, but the Yankees won, 5-3.

However, after the ceremonies, Ruth sipped a beer with Dugan in the empty clubhouse and said to his old teammate, "Joe, I'm gone. I'm done, Joe."[13]

The fact that October 1, 1949, was the last scheduled day of an American League pennant race between the Yankees and the Red Sox that came down to the wire was a major reason 69,551 people jammed Yankee Stadium. However, the Yankees were also honoring Joe DiMaggio, whose incredible return from a heel injury that July had vaulted the team back into contention and just one game behind the visiting Red Sox.

However, before the game, DiMaggio, determined to play despite a fever of 102 from pneumonia, stood through the ceremonies of Joe DiMaggio Day, receiving two cars, a boat, and other gifts, with his brother, Red Sox star center fielder Dom DiMaggio, beside him.

In his remarks, the Yankee Clipper paid tribute to his old skipper, Joe McCarthy, now managing the Red Sox, his teammates, his friends, the fans, and New York. He finished with words that the Yankees would post in their dugout tunnel and the 2009 stadium a memorable elegy that summed up his feelings about the Pinstripes: "I want to thank the Good Lord for making me a Yankee."[14]

Yankee Stadium hosted another major address on October 4, 1965. The Bombers had failed to get to the World Series for the first time in five years, but the consolation prize was a Papal Mass celebrated by Pope Paul VI, the first such celebrated in the entire Western Hemisphere.

A crowd of 80,000 jammed Yankee Stadium to greet the Pope, who ceremoniously accepted a pair of blue jeans as a sign of his commitment to youth. He also blessed a stone from St. Peter's Basilica in Rome, to be placed in the foundation of a seminary being built in the New York Archdiocese.

Thousands of extra seats were installed to accommodate the crowd, who heard a homily calling for world peace between nations and peoples. The pope greeted all New Yorkers, saying, "We feel, too, that the entire American people are here present, with its noblest and most characteristic traits."[15]

On June 8, 1969, the Yankees honored another legend – a man baseball broadcaster Bob Costas simply described as "Our Guy" in his eulogy in 1995.[16] Some 60,096 fans filled up Yankee Stadium that day to join in the festivities to retire Mickey Mantle's number 7.

Yankee public-relations head Bob Fishel choreographed the event superbly, bringing in major figures from Mantle's life, including his mother, Lovell Mantle; former general manager George Weiss; Mantle's minor-league manager Harry Craft; and the scout who signed him, Tom Greenwade. Casey Stengel, still boycotting the Yankees since his 1960 firing, did not appear, and when the master of ceremonies, broadcaster Frank Messer, mentioned Roger Maris's name, the crowd booed. Mel Allen, who had introduced Gehrig, Ruth, and Joe DiMaggio on their "Days," did the same for Mantle.

DiMaggio and Mantle presented each other with plaques to be hung on the center-field wall.

After that, Messer turned the home-plate microphone over to Mantle, whose words reminded older fans of another Yankee star who was remembered for his tenacity in the face of injuries: "When I walked onto the field 18 years ago, I guess I felt the same as I do now. I can't describe it. I just want to say that playing 18 years in Yankee Stadium for you folks is the best thing that could happen to a ballplayer. Now having my number join 3, 4, and 5 kind of tops everything. I never knew how a man who was going to die could say he was the luckiest man in the world. But now I can understand."[17]

Mantle drew a 10-minute ovation from fans who remembered the significance of Lou Gehrig, and that the Mick, at the time of his retirement, held the record for most games played as a Yankee.

Mantle was then driven around the warning track by groundskeeper Danny Colletti in a golf cart with Yankee pinstripes on its sides, and license plates that read "MM-7." A visibly moved Mantle struggled to hold back tears.

Yankee Stadium's next farewell address was another ceremony to retire a uniform number, but under far less nostalgic terms.

The team's captain and leader, Thurman Munson, died in an air crash while trying to land his plane in Summit County, Ohio, on August 2, 1979, an offday for the team. He was 32. He left behind a wife, Diane, and three children, all aged less than 10.

The next day a stunned and devastated Yankees team had to take the home field to face the Baltimore Orioles in a steady drizzle. With Munson's face appearing on the center-field Diamond Vision screen, all the Yankees except the catcher at their positions, Cardinal Terence Cooke delivered a prayer for the lost captain.

"We pray for Your son and our brother, Thurman Munson," Cooke intoned, as a paid attendance of 51,151 cried, including Reggie Jackson, Munson's sometime nemesis, who visibly sobbed into his mitt in right field. Metropolitan Opera star and Yankee fan Robert Merrill sang "America the Beautiful," followed by a moment of silence, and then an eight-minute standing ovation for Munson's career. After the moving ceremonies, the two teams went through the motions of playing a game, with the Orioles winning, 1-0.[18]

The next major address came that same year, for another career ending. This one was expected and announced, and the honoree was present to accept the cheers. Yankees pitching ace Catfish Hunter, worn down by a bad arm and diabetes, had promised his family that he would retire at the end of the 1979, and September 16 was Catfish Hunter Day at the Stadium.

On the field, joined by his wife, Helen, and two children, Hunter said, "There's three men who should have been here today. One's my pa."

That drew cheers.

"One's the scout who signed me," he continued, referring to Clyde Kluttz, Charlie Finley's master of talent. More applause.

Hunter then paused, and said, "The third one is Thurman Munson." The fans leapt to their feet in what Catfish described in his autobiography as a "a wild riotous ovation. They wouldn't stop. 50,000 people stood on their feet, stomping, whistling. Not so much for me – more for my father, for Clyde, and for Thurman. Cheering, I guess, for what friends mean in all our lives."

Then Catfish offered his last words as a Yankee: "Thank you, God, for giving me strength and making me a ballplayer."[19]

Three weeks later, the Cathedral of Baseball became a cathedral again, welcoming the charismatic Pope John Paul II for a Papal Mass on October 2. The first non-Italian to lead the Church in more than 450 years, Karol Wojtyla had started his life in the World War II Polish Underground, battling Nazi occupiers.

Now 80,000 people came to hear his homily in a festive environment, which included Mayor Edward I. Koch.

The pope arrived in an open car, greeting attendees warmly. Once behind the microphone, the pontiff gave a sterner message, lashing out against the West's rampant consumerism, warning against "the temptation to make money the principal means and indeed the very measure of human advancement," adding that it was "a joyless and exhausting way of life."[20]

Another devout, if raucous, Catholic, Billy Martin, made his memorable speech on August 19, 1986, when his number 1 was retired in a grand ceremony. It included a collection of gifts, his entire family in attendance, and the unveiling of a plaque in Monument Park to honor Billy, his lifelong dream.

Dressed in a light beige suit with boutonniere, "Casey's Boy" told the audience, "The fans always lifted me up no matter the circumstances. If I ran faster and hit the ball farther, it was because you gave me the strength. I know you were always rooting me on. I wanted to make you proud and I hope I did. I may not have been the best Yankee to put on the pinstripes, but I am the proudest."[21] Those words were engraved on his tombstone after his death three years later.

Another powerful voice for humanity spoke at Yankee Stadium on June 21, 1990, when 71-year-old Nelson Mandela, freshly released from South Africa's prisons as apartheid ended, visited New York in a whirlwind tour that included the usual ticker-tape parade up the "Canyon of Heroes."

A fundraising concert was held that evening at the Stadium, with 55,000 in attendance. The climax came when Mayor David Dinkins presented Mandela with a Yankees jacket and hat, the African leader donned them, and addressed the audience, saying, "Now you know who I am. I am a Yankee."[22] A moved Yankees owner George M. Steinbrenner promptly wrote a check to cover the costs of Mandela's entire visit to New York.

September 27, 1998, saw an embarrassing moment for the Yankees when, realizing that the Yankee Clipper was dying, they hurriedly slapped together Joe DiMaggio Day,[23] on the final day of the season. It should have gone better. … The present team was setting records, the weather was perfect, and in a blue suit, the "Greatest Living Ballplayer" was driven around the warning track in a vintage 1956 Thunderbird. The highlight saw DiMaggio's old teammate Phil Rizzuto presenting the honoree with replacement World Series rings for those that had he had lost in a robbery. The lowlights included misspelling DiMaggio's name on the Instant Replay screen, shots of Marilyn Monroe in the highlight reel, and when the ailing Hall of Famer tried to climb up the Yankee dugout steps, he nearly tottered and collapsed.[24]

During the presentations, DiMaggio twice tapped at the microphone to see if it would transmit his prepared speech, but it didn't work. Visibly fuming, after being given his rings, he strode back to the Yankee dugout for the last time. Nor did he ever wear the rings – he was hospitalized a few days later with terminal cancer.[25]

Hordes of speakers and singers took the stage at Yankee Stadium on September 25, 2001, in the wake of the ghastly 9/11 attacks on the World Trade Center and the Pentagon in the "Prayer for America" multidenominational service. Television host Oprah Winfrey served as mistress of ceremonies, introducing Edward Cardinal Egan, Archbishop of New York, and Fire Department Chaplain Rabbi Joseph Potasnik to give the invocations. They were followed by four more rabbis; singer Placido Domingo to sing "Ave Maria"; and Mayor Rudy Giuliani, who discussed the attacks, New York's strength, and those lost.

Alternating with political leaders, series of speakers read prayers from many faiths: Christian, Sikh, Islam, the Armenian Church in America, and the Greek Orthodox Church. Governor George Pataki and former President Bill Clinton paid tribute to the first responders and the fallen. In his benediction, New York Police Chaplain Izak-El M. Pasha said, "We Muslims, Americans, stand today with a heavy weight on our shoulder – that those who would dare do such a dastardly act claim our faith. They are no believers in God at all."[26]

The year 2008 saw the final major speeches at the Stadium, the first on April 20, when the last of a trifecta of popes delivered a homily and mass there. Some 57,100 attendees greeted Pope Benedict XVI by chanting in unison, "Be-ne-dict, Be-ne-dict," and "Viva Papa!"

The Pope told the audience, "Our celebration today is a sign of impressive growth which God has given to the Catholic Church in your country in the past 200 years. From a small flock like that described in the first reading, the Church in America has been built up in fidelity to the twin commandments of love of God and love of neighbor. The Catholic Church has contributed significantly to the growth of American society as a whole." Noting the joy and hope he had seen in youth in his visit to New York, he urged attendees to give them "all the prayer and support you can give them."

After the homily and mass, 500 priests offered Communion to tens of thousands of attendees.

The very last speech at Yankee Stadium was another impromptu address, and came from another Yankee captain who defined excellence in his play and character. Unlike Lou Gehrig, Derek Jeter was able to end his career and the life of Yankee Stadium on his own terms.

On September 21, 2008, the final home game at the old Stadium, behind Andy Pettitte and Mariano Rivera, the Yankees defeated the Baltimore Orioles, 7-3. With two out in the top of the ninth, Yankees manager Joe Girardi pulled Jeter out of the game, so that the captain could hear one last personal round of applause before the game ended. As he left, Jeter realized that he would be called upon to bid farewell to the House that Ruth Built on behalf of the current tenants. "Two outs in the ninth, I better think of something," he told reporters later, when asked how he came up with the speech.[27]

After the final out, the Yankees assembled in front of the pitcher's mound. Someone handed Jeter a working microphone. With Jorge Posada at his left and Rivera at his right, Jeter began his impromptu speech.

"For all of us out here, it's a huge honor to put this uniform on and come out every day to play. And every member of this organization, past and present, has been calling this place home for 85 years. It's a lot of tradition, a lot of history, and a lot of memories. Now the great thing about memories is you're able to pass it along from generation to generation. And although things are gonna change next year, we're gonna move across the street, there are a few things with the Yankees that never change. That's pride, tradition, and most of all, we have the greatest fans in the world. And we're relying on you to take the memories from this stadium, add them to the new memories to come at the new Yankee Stadium, and continue to pass them from generation to generation. So on behalf of the entire organization, we just want to take this moment to salute you, the greatest fans in the world."[28]

With that, Jeter doffed his cap, his teammates followed, and he led them on a lap around the field.

NOTES

1   Mark Vancil and Alfred Sanastiere III, *Yankee Stadium, the Official Retrospective* (New York: Pocket Books, 2009), 90.

2   *Yankee Stadium, the Official Retrospective*, 82.

3   On newsreel footage of the speech, Gehrig seems to be saying "brag."

4   Jonathan Eig, *Luckiest Man, The Life and Death of Lou Gehrig* (New York: Simon & Schuster, 2005), 317.

5   Richard Sandomir, *Pride of the Yankees* (New York: Hachette Books, 2017), 42.

6   Sandomir, 236-237.

7   Hy Turkin, "Ruth Whispers His Gratitude to Cheering Fans," *New York Daily News*, April 28, 1947, which also provides other quotes that follow.

8   Leigh Montville, *The Big Bam: The Life and Times of Babe Ruth* (New York: Anchor, 2007), 359.

9   Montville, 359.

10   Turkin.

11   Montville, 359.

12   Montville, 364.

13   Bob Klapisch, *New York Yankees Official 2008 Yearbook*, 238.

14   Marty Appel, *Pinstripe Empire* (New York: Bloomsbury, 2012), 279. The Yankees beat the Red Sox that day, 5-4, creating a tie for first place, and necessitating the deciding game the following day. The Yankees won that one, too, and faced the Dodgers in the 1949 World Series.

15   Edward Cardinal Egan, "10 Monumental Moments," *New York Yankees Official 2008 Yearbook*, 281.

16   Tony Castro, Mickey *Mantle: America's Prodigal Son* (Dulles, Virginia: Brassey's, 2002), 303.

17   Castro, 224.

18   Bobby Murcer with Glen Waggoner, *Yankee for Life* (New York: Harper, 2008), 124.

19   Catfish Hunter and Armen Keteyian, *Catfish* (New York: McGraw-Hill, 1988), 206-207.

20   Klapisch, 280.

21   Bill Pennington, *Billy Martin, Baseball's Flawed Genius* (Boston: Houghton Mifflin Harcourt, 2015), 439.

22   Ryan Cortes, The Undefeated, June 22, 2016, https://andscape.com/features/rememberwhensdays-nelson-mandela-visits-yankee-stadium/. Accessed October 27, 2022.

23   Richard Ben Cramer, *Joe DiMaggio: The Hero's Life* (New York: Simon & Schuster, 2000), 497. Cramer writes: "You could count on one hand the people in the stadium who knew enough to see how quickly this had been thrown together – and how it failed to live up to the standard. … Those three words on the scoreboard: no capitalization for the letter "M" in DiMaggio … The film clips on the big TV: there was the newsreel footage from the day Joe got put out of Marilyn's house on North Palm Drive … and that bent old man, who looked frail and ill, as the T-Bird drew to a stop at the Yankee dugout. Joe could barely get out of the car – and almost killed himself when he stumbled on the dugout steps." While the Cramer book was an extremely hostile biography of DiMaggio, it won the Pulitzer Prize for Biography, which gives this author a sense of inconsistency to puzzle out. My belief is that the top Yankees management, knowing that DiMaggio was dying, wanted to honor him while he still lived, doing so on the last day of the season when they could control pregame events (as opposed to postseason events), and had very little time to plan the event.

24   Ben Cramer, 498.

25   Ben Cramer, 498; https://www.youtube.com/watch?v=_SFkWNPRv5k.

26   The Paley Center for Media Summary of the service. The service also included musical performances by the Boys Chorus of Harlem singing a medley of hymns and spirituals, Lee Greenwood singing "God Bless the USA," Bette Midler singing "Wind Beneath My Wings," and Marc Anthony singing "America the Beautiful." https://www.paleycenter.org/collection/item/?item=T:67939.

27   Danny Peary, *Baseball Immortal: Derek Jeter, A Career in Quotes* (Salem, Massachusetts: Page Street Publishing, 2015), 276.

28   Peary, 277.

A NUMBER 7 SPECIAL — FOUR STADIUM CELEBRATIONS OF MICKEY MANTLE

By Scott Pitoniak

Mickey Mantle stepped up to the microphone not far from where he had stepped up to the plate for 18 seasons, but it was no use. The 60,096 adoring spectators who had gathered at Yankee Stadium to celebrate his jersey retirement on June 8, 1969, were not going to let him speak until they had their say. For nearly 10 minutes, they were in full throat, cheering the legendary Yankees slugger who had retired before the start of spring training three months earlier.[1]

"It was a love-fest," recalled longtime Yankees public-relations director, historian, and author Marty Appel. "There wasn't a great deal of excitement about that year's team. Attendance was way down. But that day there was plenty of buzz with the biggest crowd of the season on hand. And it was all because of the affection the fans had for Mickey."[2]

The Yankees pulled out all the stops for the 40-minute ceremony, which took place between games of a doubleheader with the Chicago White Sox. Joe DiMaggio, Mantle's pinstriped predecessor in center field, presented him with a plaque to be hung on the outfield wall. Whitey Ford, the legendary Yankees pitcher, handed his former teammate a flannel uniform with the navy blue number 7 on the back.[3]

Mickey Mantle's wife, Merlyn, and eldest son Mickey, Jr. attended the first Mickey Mantle Day on September 18, 1965.

Banners from each of Mantle's 12 American League pennant-winning teams were spread on the outfield grass. Standing next to each banner was a former Mantle teammate representing a specific championship club: Eddie Lopat (1951), Gene Woodling (1952), Joe Collins (1953), Phil Rizzuto (1955), Jerry Coleman (1956), Gil McDougald (1957), Ford (1958), Bobby Richardson (1960), Elston Howard (1961), Tom Tresh (1962), Joe Pepitone (1963), and Mel Stottlemyre (1964).[4]

Also on the field were Tom Greenwade, the scout who signed Mantle, as well as Mickey's minor-league managers, Harry Craft and George Selkirk.[5]

Each fan received a special souvenir foldout that included a color photo of Mantle by *Sport* magazine photographer Ozzie Sweet. Mayor John Lindsay issued a proclamation declaring Mickey Mantle Day in New York City.[6]

Frank Messer, one of the Yankees' radio and television announcers, served as the master of ceremonies. Mel Allen, the longtime Voice of the Yankees, was brought back to introduce Mantle, calling him from the dugout with the words, "The great number 7, the magnificent Yankee, Mickey Mantle."[7]

Appel, who was a Yankees PR assistant at the time, remembered the ground shaking from the ovation as Allen completed his intro.

"It would have registered on a Richter scale," Appel joked. "We thought the cheering would never end. A few times, Mickey motioned to quiet the crowd, but each time he raised his arms, the fans roared even louder."[8]

After the ovation finally began to peter out, Mantle addressed the throng.

"When I walked into this stadium 18 years ago, I felt much the same way I do right now," he began. "I don't have words to describe how I felt then or how I feel now, but I'll tell you one thing: Baseball was real good to me, and playing 18 years in Yankee Stadium is the best thing that could ever happen to a ballplayer."

"And now," he continued, after still more applause, "to think the Yankees are retiring my number seven with numbers three [Babe Ruth], four [Lou Gehrig] and five [DiMaggio] tops off everything I could ever have wished for."

"I often wondered how a man who knew he was going to die could stand here and say he was the luckiest man in the world, but now I think I know how Lou Gehrig felt. ... It's been a great honor. I'll never forget it. God bless you all and thank you very much."[9]

Mantle then boarded a pinstripe-painted golf cart, and groundskeeper Danny Colletti drove him around the entire length of the warning track. Off to the side, Bob Fishel, the Yankees PR director, who had planned the entire ceremony, couldn't help but smile.[10]

"It was beautifully choreographed by Bob," Appel said. "Everything was just perfect. The great Yankees who had been invited back. The pennants spread out in the outfield for all to see. Mel Allen's intro. The ride around the park, which was an idea Fishel got from the St. Louis Cardinals when they honored Stan Musial a few years earlier. And I thought Mickey really rose to the occasion with his speech – when he finally got a chance to deliver it."[11]

This was not the first time the Yankees honored Mantle with a special day. Nor would it be the last. In fact, there were three other Mantle Days at the original Stadium. The first occurred on September 18, 1965, and coincided with his 2,000th game as a Yankee. Mantle was suffering through his worst season, and that, along with his mounting injuries, increased concerns that he might soon retire, prompting the team to hastily throw together a day in his honor.[12]

It wasn't the production that his jersey retirement day was. Then-Mayor Robert Wagner issued a Mickey Mantle Day proclamation, and at Mantle's request, proceeds from that day's game were donated to Hodgkin's disease research in memory of his father and several other relatives who had died from the disease. Yankee broadcaster Red Barber emceed the ceremony, which included DiMaggio and US Senator Robert F. Kennedy. Mantle told reporters he was more nervous than he had been on his wedding day. After thanking the Yankees, his family and his fans, Mantle told the crowd of 51,664, "I just wish I had 15 more years with you."[13]

Mantle was in the lineup that day, and when he came up in the bottom of the first, Detroit Tigers pitcher Joe Sparma walked from the mound to the batter's box to shake his hand.[14]

"I'd never seen anything like that before or since," Appel said. "I think it spoke to the admiration players throughout baseball had for Mickey. It wasn't just teammates, but opponents, too. They respected that Mickey always played the game hard, even while being in so much pain. And he was a guy who never tried to show up his opponent. He played the game right."[15]

Mantle lined out to deep left field during that at-bat and went 0-for-3 with a walk. He played three more seasons after that one. On August 4, 1968, the

Yankees held Mickey Mantle Banner Appreciation Day at the Bronx ballpark. Hundreds of young fans made up signs and paraded past a beaming Mantle, who stood near the top step of the Yankees dugout. Only 20,704 fans showed up for the game, a 5-3 loss to the Baltimore Orioles.[16]

The fourth and final game honoring Mantle at the old Stadium occurred on August 25, 1996, roughly a year after the Hall of Famer's death. On that day, in front of 50,808 fans, the Yankees unveiled a granite monument and plaque in in memory of Mantle in Monument Park, just beyond the left-center-field wall. Mantle became just the fourth person to wear a Yankees uniform honored with a monument, joining manager Miller Huggins, Ruth and Gehrig. Ford did the unveiling honors. A special commemorative baseball was used during that day's game against Oakland. It featured Mantle's signature and his number 7 and had blue stitching.[17]

"This is a great day for us – and a sad one, too," said David Mantle, one of the slugger's three surviving sons at the time.[18]

SOURCES

In addition to the sources cited in the Notes, the author consulted the following:

Pitoniak, Scott. *Memories of Yankee Stadium* (Chicago: Triumph Books, 2008).

Additionally, the author used firsthand source material from a 30-minute phone interview with Appel on October 7, 2022.

The author also referred to audio from a 33⅓ RPM record, "A Day to Remember: June 8, 1969," produced by CBS Records, a division of Columbia Broadcasting System, Inc. (New York). It was a recording of that year's Mickey Mantle Day ceremonies and was given to fans attending Old-Timers Day at Yankee Stadium on August 9, 1969.

NOTES

1   "A Day to Remember: June 8, 1969," CBS Records, a division of Columbia Broadcasting System, Inc. (New York), 2014.

2   Author interview with Marty Appel, October 7, 2022.

3   "A Day to Remember."

4   George Vecsey, "61,157 Hearts Here Throb for Mantle as No. 7 Joins 3, 4 and 5 in Retirement," *New York Times,* June 9, 1969. https://www.nytimes.com/1969/06/09/archives/61157-hearts-here-throb-for-mantle-as-no-7-joins-3-4-and-5-in.html.

5   Vecsey.

6   "Yanks to Retire No. 7 and Honor Mantle Here Today," *New York Times,* June 8, 1969. https://timesmachine.nytimes.com/timesmachine/1969/06/08/284717872.html?pageNumber=317.

7   "A Day to Remember."

8   Author interview with Appel.

9   "A Day to Remember."

10 Author interview with Appel.

11 Author interview with Appel.

12 Author interview with Appel.

13 Arthur Daley, "Sports of the Times: The Nervous Hero," *New York Times,* September 18, 1965. https://www.nytimes.com/1965/09/18/archives/sports-of-the-times-the-nervous-hero.html.

14 Marty Appel, *Pinstripe Empire: The New York Yankees From Before the Babe to After the Boss* (New York: Bloomsbury Publishing, 2020), 362.

15 Author interview with Appel.

16 Steve Contursi, "The Day Mickey Mantle Came to Life for a New York Yankee Fan," EliteSportNY.com, December 17, 2017. https://elitesportsny.com/2017/12/17/mickey-mantle-life-new-york-yankees-fan/.

17 Ira Berkow, "A Final Sweet Ovation for Mantle," *New York Times,* August 26, 1996. https://www.nytimes.com/1996/08/26/sports/a-final-sweet-ovation-for-mantle.html.

18 Berkow.

THE RENOVATION OF '76

By Jim Griffin

In the spring of 1976, the Yankees celebrated a grand reopening of Yankee Stadium.[1] It was the culmination of a 2½-year renovation project intended to modernize the House That Ruth Built and its surrounding areas in the Bronx. But the seeds for a Yankee Stadium facelift were sown about two decades earlier and were cultivated by a series of events that drastically altered New York City's relationships with its professional sports teams.

Brooklyn Dodgers owner Walter O'Malley had a valuable asset in a team that was a perennial World Series contender in the 1950s. Yet the Dodgers' ballpark, Ebbets Field, stood in an inconvenient location and was falling into disrepair. In order to realize the full potential of his franchise, O'Malley looked to buy up land in a more accessible part of Brooklyn and build a new ballpark there. He just needed Robert Moses to use his political power as New York City parks commissioner to sell him land at the intersection of Atlantic and Flatbush Avenues and he would fully fund the cost of construction.

Moses denied O'Malley's plan and instead offered only to use city funds to build a ballpark on city-owned land in Queens.[2] O'Malley had no desire to pay rent for his team's home field. Meanwhile, Los Angeles city officials got the attention of O'Malley by offering him exactly what he wanted, albeit 3,000 miles away. After the 1957 season, he accepted the offer and decided to do the unthinkable: move the Dodgers out of Brooklyn. He also persuaded the New

The 1976 renovation removed the columns that obstructed views on the lower decks and the seats in center field that obstructed batters, but it also relegated the recognizable frieze to above the outfield wall.

York Giants – in a similar situation with their home field sitting in the outdated, run-down Polo Grounds – to join him in bolting New York City for California.[3] The Yankees had the Big Apple to themselves starting in 1958.

By 1962, the expansion New York Mets were poised to fill the massive void left by the Dodgers and Giants. They did so with the promise of a new city-owned stadium in Flushing, Queens – the same one that Robert Moses would have built for Walter O'Malley – set to open in 1964. Dubbed Shea Stadium, this multipurpose concrete monstrosity was one of a trend of similar "cookie cutter" stadiums that were built in major cities across the United States during the 1960s and '70s. Public officials jumped at the chance to use tax money to fund these stadiums as tangible evidence that they were improving their cities and creating jobs.[4] Through complex accounting, team owners also found that leasing a stadium after letting taxpayers pay for it was quite lucrative.

In the early 1970s, the almost 50-year-old Yankee Stadium was approaching the run-down state that Ebbets Field was in 20 years earlier. Despite its rich history of being the home to championship baseball, it became rapidly outdated with so many new ballparks being built elsewhere. It didn't help that the team was descending into mediocrity. In 1971 the New York football Giants, who were tenants in Yankee Stadium, then dropped another bombshell on the city. They were moving across the Hudson River after striking a deal to get a new stadium built in New Jersey.[5] New York City officials went into full-blown panic mode. To keep the Yankees in New York, something had to be done about Yankee Stadium, and fast.

***

The Giants' announcement accelerated a conversation between Mayor John Lindsay and Michael Burke, president of the Yankees, that had started a year earlier. Observing that the state of Yankee Stadium would soon be at a tipping point, in August of 1970 Lindsay asked Burke to identify the most important factors in keeping the Yankees in New York. Burke wasted no time issuing Lindsay a letter detailing his thoughts.[6]

Unsurprisingly, the letter centered on the future of Yankee Stadium, or lack thereof. If Lindsay was offering, Burke wanted one of three things from him. They were, in order of preference, a new domed multipurpose stadium, a new open-air multipurpose stadium, or a major renovation of Yankee Stadium.[7] Lindsay was offering, and by early 1971 he hatched a plan based on

what New York City had done for the Mets a decade earlier.

The $24 million price tag of Shea Stadium seemed like a number that Lindsay could get approved by city officials for the new Yankee project. However, in 1971 that number fell well short of what it would take to build a new stadium. So the only option was to use the $24 million to purchase Yankee Stadium and the land it sat on, lease it back to the Yankees, and foot the bill for a renovation that the club would oversee. Burke was satisfied, but very little action was taken until the football Giants shocked New York. By early 1972, the city began its acquisition of Yankee Stadium, and Operation Keep the Yankees in New York was in full effect.[8]

A year later, the renovation deal could have been in jeopardy when CBS sold the Yankees to a group of investors led by George Steinbrenner. Michael Burke was a minority partner in the group and was retained as CEO of the club. Three months later, Steinbrenner disagreed with Burke's general approach to the business of baseball and brought in Gabe Paul and Lee MacPhail to run the day-to-day operations, rendering Burke obsolete. Whether their differences in opinion included the stadium renovation was unclear, but a press conference in May 1973 quelled any fears. Steinbrenner was on board with the renovation plan, and the Yankees would stay in New York under a 30-year lease with the city.[9]

***

After falling short of the playoffs for eight straight seasons, the 1973 Yankees seemed destined to make Yankee Stadium's swan song a triumphant one. For all of July, they sat in first place of the American League East Division, but that proved to be fool's gold. Their record for August and September was 14 games under .500, and they finished the year in fourth place, 17 games behind the Baltimore Orioles. This diminuendo to finish the season set the stage for an underwhelming finale at the original stadium on September 30.

In front of a half-capacity crowd of just over 32,000, the Yankees put on a performance that was a microcosm of their season. After seven innings they held a 4-2 lead over the Detroit Tigers, then squandered it by surrendering six runs in the top of the eighth and took an 8-5 loss. In a scene that would look surreal today, after the final out, fans either ripped seats out of the stadium's concrete with tools they brought to the game or ran onto the field to grab their own personal handful of dirt or grass as a souvenir.[10]

A ceremony hosted by Mayor Lindsay was held at the stadium the following morning. Amid the amateur demolition work done by fans the night before, the mayor presented first base to Eleanor Gehrig, Lou's widow, and home plate to Claire Ruth, Babe's widow.[11] Shortly after the ceremony, professional demolition began and Yankee Stadium as it was known for nearly 50 years would be no longer.

During the makeover the Yankees needed a temporary home, and with New York City as their new landlord, they were allowed to share space with the Mets in a suddenly very crowded Shea Stadium. In 1975 Shea was home to the Yankees and Mets for baseball, and that fall hosted both the Giants and Jets for football. By the spring of 1976, the Shea Stadium grounds crew got a much-deserved break as the Yankee Stadium renovation was complete.

***

The renovation plan wasn't limited to Yankee Stadium itself. New parking lots were added in the surrounding neighborhood to make travel more convenient for the growing suburban fan base. Walkways from the subway station to the ballpark were given a makeover, including the newly crowned Hall of Fame Plaza, which featured a 138-foot-tall smokestack. The outside of the smokestack was designed to resemble a giant baseball bat, complete with a "Louisville Slugger" logo and tape around the handle. Theoretically, this served as a great landmark for a pregame rendezvous with friends. In reality, the sea of fans surrounding the bat made it a great place to get lost at.

The outer walls of the renovated stadium looked largely untouched apart from a good cleaning and some fresh paint. Three modern-style escalator towers were installed next to the walls behind left field, right field, and home plate to allow for more efficient entrance and exit. The block lettering signifying "YANKEE STADIUM" on the back of the upper deck was given neon lighting that glowed at night. On the other side of those letters, the awning that once covered most of the upper-deck seating was removed to accommodate the largest structural change of the renovation.

In the original design, over 100 pillars stood in the grandstand to support the upper deck. While fans appreciated the deck above not falling on top of them, these pillars obstructed the view from many seats. This was fixed by using a cantilever system that removed the pillars, added 10 rows of seating to the upper deck, gave it a steeper slope, and pushed it back to sit on new supports behind the grandstand.[12] Additional seats

at the back of the grandstand that were obstructed by the decks above were removed to make way for an expanded concourse. Thanks to modern technology, there wasn't a bad seat in the house anymore. The seats themselves also changed, as the old green wooden ones were replaced with a wider blue plastic model, which reduced the seating capacity from 65,010 to 54,028.[13] The Yankees were willing to bet that more comfortable seats would increase their average per-game attendance from the 12,000-to-15,000 range they saw in the early 1970s, even if it meant slightly smaller sellout crowds.

A new lighting system was installed at the top of the upper deck: a thin row of bulbs that spanned the entire structure. This made the lighting more uniform on the field below, but also had the effect of removing a trademark feature of Yankee Stadium. The copper frieze that had adorned the top of the upper deck turned a sea green color over the years due to oxidation and was eventually painted white for the last few years before the renovation. Its removal represented the largest visual departure from the iconic look of the original stadium.

The bottom of the revamped upper deck was given a smooth finish to serve as a ceiling to fans sitting in the decks below, none more important than those fortunate enough to occupy one of 16 new luxury boxes in the mezzanine level. In addition to a few rows of seating, these came with a lounge area featuring couches, a TV, and a fully stocked refrigerator.

For fans who still wanted to sit in the cheap seats, there was a new experience for them as well.

The vast sea of bleachers that spanned the entire outfield was trimmed down significantly from 11,000 seats to just 2,500. This made room for expanded bullpens in left-center field. Wedged in between the bullpens was a fan-accessible park built to house the growing number of monuments and plaques by the flagpole that once stood in play in center field. Monument Park was easily the best feature of the new-look Yankee Stadium.

In three sections of the center-field bleachers, the benches were removed and the entirety of the sections were painted jet black. Otherwise, they were left untouched, even the entrance/exit ramps. This eerie remnant of the original stadium, endearingly known as the black seats, served as the batter's eye post-renovation. The distance to the seats from home plate became a standard unit of measurement for monster home runs hit to dead center field – the most famous being Reggie Jackson's third home run in Game Six of the 1977 World Series.[14]

Behind the bleachers, a massive new scoreboard was installed. At 24 feet high, it spanned 565 feet and was broken up into seven sections. Three of the sections were intended to enhance the game experience for fans. An electronic version of a traditional scoreboard tracked the score by inning. A second electronic board was used for messaging and game information. There was also a video board which allowed fans to see replays of close calls on the field, much to the dismay of the umpiring crew. The other four sections, of course, were for advertisements. Trimming the top of the new scoreboard was a replica of the copper frieze that once graced the upper deck. This version was a fraction of the size, cast in concrete and painted white. It seemed out of place in center field, but it was a nice gesture nonetheless.

On the field of play, the most notable difference was a blue wall, uniformly nine feet in height, which replaced the green wall that sloped downward near the foul lines. The outfield dimensions changed significantly. While it didn't take on the symmetrical dimensions that were in vogue at the time, it became a far tamer version of the extreme original configuration. Home plate originally stood less than 300 feet from each foul pole, but now was 312 feet from the left-field pole, and 310 feet from right field. The infamous "Death Valley" in left-center field was brought in from 457 feet to a still formidable 430 feet, while right-center was pulled in from 407 feet to 385 feet. The most significant change was the distance to dead center, which shrank from 461 feet to 417 feet from home plate.[15] Over the years, the Yankees continued to normalize the dimensions, but they always kept the same basic shape that favored left-handed hitters.

After a flirtation with installing artificial turf to make the stadium more conducive to football, thankfully natural grass was planted on the resurfaced field.[16] However, it was a different kind of green that became most concerning in New York as the renovation work progressed.

From late 1973 until the finishing touches were complete in 1976, city officials reported the rising cost of the project in small increments. The total cost came in at over $100 million, or more than four times the original $24 million cost estimate. To make matters worse, it was reported in 1976 that those in charge of the project had calculated the cost at over $80 million before it even started. They just neglected to tell the

board making the decision to approve it and the taxpayers who would ultimately pay for it.[17]

The final slap in the face came in December 1975 when city officials decided to abandon a neighborhood improvement plan that was originally part of the renovation project. As costs ballooned, they decided to draw the line at the one aspect of the project that would directly benefit Bronx residents. At least a portion of the $2 million that was earmarked to improve local businesses was instead used for some of the finishing touches within the stadium, including the luxury boxes.[18] Under this shroud of controversy, a rejuvenated Yankee Stadium was ready to be revealed to the public.

***

Controversy be damned; George Steinbrenner was ready to throw his first extravagant party as owner of the Yankees. Opening Day at the new-look stadium took place on April 15, 1976, and in front of a packed house, he trotted out a roster of New York sports dignitaries for a pregame ceremony. Joe DiMaggio, Yogi Berra, Mickey Mantle, and Elston Howard got rousing ovations from the crowd. Don Larsen, who in 1956 pitched the only perfect game in World Series history, was invited to bring a bit of luck to the new grounds. Bob Shawkey, who started the first game at the original Stadium in 1923, was in attendance with a host of players from that team and threw out the ceremonial first pitch.

The guest list wasn't limited to former Yankee players. Frank Gifford and Kyle Rote, who each scored in the Giants' NFL Championship Game victory over the Chicago Bears at Yankee Stadium in 1956, were showered with applause. Joe Louis waved to the crowd, no doubt reliving his monumental knockout of Max Schmeling at the Stadium in 1938. Broadcaster Mel Allen made a triumphant return to the Bronx. More than a decade after being unceremoniously fired by the Yankees, he again became a play-by-play announcer for the team in 1976. Even Toots Shor, proprietor of the eponymous restaurant that served as the stomping grounds for Mickey Mantle, Whitey Ford, and many other sports stars of the 1950s, was brought in for the festivities.[19]

Once the pomp and circumstance concluded, the current Yankees did have a game to play. The Minnesota Twins did their best to play spoiler, tagging Yankees starter Rudy May for three runs in the first inning. In the bottom of the fourth, Oscar Gamble's triple sparked a rally that gave the Yankees a lead they did not relinquish, much to the fans' delight. Every move manager Billy Martin made in the 11-4 victory was the right one, and thankfully for the Yankees that would continue. The inaugural season of the new Yankee Stadium serendipitously coincided with a resurgent team that won its first pennant since 1964. They were an eclectic bunch, most of them far from angels, but they were also damn good baseball players led by the wildest of the bunch in Martin. The renovated stadium would serve as the grand stage for one of the most entertaining runs in Yankee history.

***

The legacy of post-renovation Yankee Stadium is a complicated one. While it was basically impossible to justify the ever-increasing cost of the project as it happened, it looked even worse as economic conditions in New York City reached rock bottom in the late 1970s. Money that was spent on constructing luxury boxes and giant scoreboards could have saved the city from bankruptcy. Instead, the income from these features bolstered George Steinbrenner's bottom line. A lot of New Yorkers understandably have never forgiven the Yankees for that.

Taking finance and politics out of it, the renovation itself was a compromise in style. It attempted to be on the cutting edge of modern technology and keep up with the multipurpose stadiums of the era while retaining the charm and character of the old Stadium. However, it fell short on both accounts. The Stadium was rarely used for football after the renovation and even for baseball it looked like a watered-down replica of the original. The cement frieze in center field paled in comparison to its predecessor. The more conservative field dimensions made balls hit to the gap less exciting, and the shade of royal blue used throughout was not "Yankee" blue no matter what they called it.

Despite these shortcomings, the renovated Yankee Stadium did take on a legacy all its own. As the home for three straight pennant winners and two World Series champions in its first three years, it became synonymous with a return to glory for the Yankees. This winning legacy would reemerge 20 years later when Derek Jeter served as the face of four championship teams from 1996 through 2000. When the House That Ruth Built closed for good in 2008 in favor of a brand-new stadium on the other side of 161st Street, the memories that stood out most were of these championship teams. During those magical Octobers, rowdy fans packed the upper deck, which seemed to hang right over the field, and made Yankee Stadium a crucible for the opposition. Loud, raucous playoff baseball in the post-renovation ballpark was the ultimate Yankees fan experience, and something that's sorely missed in the new building across the street.

SOURCES

In addition to the sources cited in the Notes, the auhor consulted a number of articles including the following:

Chass, Murray. "Yankee Stadium: Modern Comforts and Hairdryers," *New York Times*, March 7, 1976. https://www.nytimes.com/1976/03/07/archives/yankee-stadium-modern-comforts-and-hairdryers-yankee-stadium-modern.html.

Cosell, Howard. "1976-Howard Cosell Feature on Yankee Stadium Re-Opening," YouTube video, 7:46. Posted by user "epaddon," October 25, 2019. https://www.youtube.com/watch?v=Y2L0MAAZEGA.

Harvin, Al. "Fans Call Stadium 'Beautiful' But Have Doubts About Cost," *New York Times*, April 16, 1976. https://www.nytimes.com/1976/04/16/archives/fans-call-stadium-beautiful-but-have-doubts-about-cost.html.

McCarron, Anthony. "The First Goodbye: Old Yankee Stadium Said Farewell in 1973," *New York Daily News*, September 20, 2008. https://www.nydailynews.com/sports/baseball/yankees/goodbye-old-yankee-stadium-farewell-1973-article-1.323687.

Ranzal, Edward. "City to Buy Yankee Stadium in Move to Keep 2 Teams," *New York Times*, March 3, 1971. https://www.nytimes.com/1971/03/03/archives/city-to-buy-yankee-stadium-in-move-to-keep-2-teams-city-to-buy.html.

"Yankee Stadium: 1974 75 Renovation of the Original," YouTube video, 0:47. Posted by user "Zickcermacity," February 29, 2016. https://www.youtube.com/watch?v=beAFgRgys94.

NOTES

1   Murray Chass, "Yankees Defeat Twins, 11 to 4, Using Two Big Innings to Erase 4-0 Deficit," *New York Times*, April 16, 1976. https://www.nytimes.com/1976/04/16/archives/yankees-defeat-twins-11-to-4-using-two-big-innings-to-erase-40.html.

2   Neil J. Sullivan, *The Diamond in the Bronx* (New York: Oxford University Press, 2008), 115.

3   "Sport: Walter in Wonderland," *Time*, April 28, 1958. https://content.time.com/time/subscriber/article/0,33009,868429-5,00.html. Accessed December 1, 2022.

4   Neil J. Sullivan, 138-140.

5   Ronald Sullivan, "Football Giants to Leave City for Jersey After 1974 Season," *New York Times*, August 27, 1971. https://www.nytimes.com/1971/08/27/archives/football-giants-to-leave-city-for-jersey-after-1974-season-a.html.

6   Neil J. Sullivan, 118.

7   Neil J. Sullivan, 117.

8   Leonard Koppett, "Yanks Hope to Open '75 In House the City Rebuilt," *New York Times*, January 29, 1972. https://www.nytimes.com/1972/01/29/archives/yanks-hope-to-open-75-in-house-the-city-rebuilt.html.

9   Murray Chass, "Burke's Eclipse With Yankees Explained," *New York Times*, May 14, 1973. https://www.nytimes.com/1973/05/14/archives/burkes-eclipse-with-yankees-explained-series-of-meetings-burke.html.

10   Marty Appel, Introduction to *Greatness In Waiting: Yankee Stadium Renovation 1973-1976*, appelpr.com. Accessed October 1, 2022. http://www.appelpr.com/?page_id=72.

11   Appel.

12   Allen M. Siegal. "Stadium Repairs Touch All Bases," *New York Times*, August 29, 1974. https://www.nytimes.com/1974/08/29/archives/stadium-repairs-touch-all-bases.html.

13   https://web.archive.org/web/20020201224929/http://www.ballparks.com/ baseball/american/yankee.htm.

14   Scott Ferkovich, "October 18, 1977: Reggie Becomes 'Mr. October' with 3 Home Runs in World Series," SABR Games Project, https://sabr.org/ gamesproj/game/october-18-1977-reggie-becomes-mr-october-with-3-home-runs-in-world-series/.

15   http://www.andrewclem.com/Baseball/YankeeStadium.html.

16   Siegal.

17   John L. Hess, "Memo Indicates City Obscured Stadium's High Cost," *New York Times*, February 3, 1976. https://www.nytimes.com/1976/02/03/archives/ memo-indicates-city-obscured-stadiums-high-cost.html.

18   Martin Waldron, "Yanks Get Windfall as City Shifts Plans," *New York Times*, December 1, 1975. https://www.nytimes.com/1975/12/01/archives/yanks-get-windfall-as-city-shifts-plans.html.

19   "Bob Sheppard 1976 – Yankee Stadium Re-Opening, 4/15/1976, Pt. 1," YouTube video, 13:46. https://www.youtube.com/watch?v=_nyrCeSe0YA; "Bob Sheppard 1976 – Yankee Stadium Re-Opening, 4/15/1976, Pt. 2," YouTube video, 13:40. Both posted by user "YanksAtShea," October 25, 2010. https://www.youtube.com/watch?v=hXjtU-uVLj4. "Bob Sheppard 1976 – Yankee Stadium Re-Opening, 4/15/1976, Pt. 3," YouTube video, 6:20. Posted by user "YanksAtShea," October 24, 2010. https://www.youtube.com/ watch?v=If7eTZUbkpQ.

OF MONUMENTS AND MEN:
THE STORY OF MONUMENT PARK

By Daniel R. Epstein

Here's a thought exercise: Get a piece of paper and a pen or pencil. Write down the names of as many of the most important individuals in Yankees history as you can think of in two minutes. They can be players, managers, owners, team employees, broadcasters, or anyone else you feel plays a significant role in Yankee lore. No cheating, though! You have to think of the names off the top of your head.

Ready? Begin!

…

Almost done?

…

Okay, pencils down!

Look over your list. Undoubtedly, it includes the names Ruth, DiMaggio, and Jeter. You probably wrote down Steinbrenner and Stengel as well, but how far down is Miller Huggins' name? Is he below Bernie Williams or John Sterling? Did you neglect to mention him at all? You're forgiven if you succumbed to recency bias, but Huggins' Yankee legacy is more than simply being the guy who substituted Lou Gehrig for Wally Pipp.

***

Miller Huggins was listed at 5-feet-6, 140 pounds, but both of those figures were likely inflated. Some sources believe he was closer to 5-1, 125 pounds. After graduating from the University of Cincinnati and playing three years for the minor-league St. Paul Saints, he joined the Cincinnati Reds in 1904 as a 26-year-old rookie second baseman. Being smaller and less athletically gifted than most other players, he strived to eke out every possible advantage he could – learning to switch-hit and taking as many free passes as possible. Over a 13-year playing career for the Reds and Cardinals, Huggins led the National League in walks four times and on-base percentage once. He was unafraid to push against the rules of baseball – written or unwritten – to get an edge, mastering the hidden-ball trick and (illegally) storing baseballs in a freezer to deaden them.

His scrappy cunning, relentless desire to win, and unwillingness to take flak from players much larger than himself made Huggins an ideal managerial candidate. He took the helm of the Cardinals as their player-manager in 1913 and remained their skipper for five up-and-down seasons. After a difference of opinion with ownership, he allowed his contract to expire and signed on as the Yankees manager in 1918.

Since their inception 15 years earlier, the Highlanders/Yankees franchise had experienced hardly any success and never reached the World Series. From 1912 to 1917, they went 397-519. It would be easy to portray Huggins' arrival two years before Babe Ruth's as fortuitous timing, but after a respectable 60-63 finish in his first season, he led the club to an 80-59 record in 1919, finishing a close third place in the American League and 13 games better than Ruth's Red Sox.

As much as Ruth revolutionized the game, much of the Yankees' incomparable success in the 1920s was attributed to Huggins. Those were the days when the manager was the judge and jury of his players, ruling as an unassailable monarch in the clubhouse. He was as respected, beloved, and feared as his legendary players and viewed as just as responsible for the team's accomplishments. Those included six pennants and three championships from 1921 through 1928.

During the 1929 season, a red blemish appeared under his left eye. He steadfastly refused to see a doctor – after all, the club was in a pennant race – until mid-September, when the bacterial skin infection had spread throughout his body, sapping his strength completely. By the time he checked into a hospital, it was too late, and he died a few days later, on September 25 at age 51.

It is impossible to overstate the emotional devastation caused by Huggins' death. All major-league games were canceled on September 27 for his funeral. The 1929 Yankees roster featured seven future Hall of Famers (nine if you include Huggins himself and his managerial protégé Leo Durocher), yet they limped to a distant second-place finish 18 games behind the Athletics.

The respect, love, and admiration for Huggins mixed with the shock and anguish of his untimely passing did not abate over the following years, even as Ruth continued to clobber the American League and Gehrig established his legacy of everyday excellence. On May 30, 1932, the Yankees held a ceremony at Yankee Stadium to honor their beloved deceased manager. In front of 42,990 witnesses, the monument was unveiled in the deepest part of left-center field, roughly 460 feet from home plate.

It was the first in what has become known as Monument Park.

***

It was somewhat common at the time for statues or objects to be erected in the field of play. The New York Giants built a monument to infielder Eddie Grant in center field at the Polo Grounds after he died in World War I. Fenway Park's center-field flagpole stood on the field until 1970 and Tiger Stadium's flagpole remained in center field until the ballpark was replaced after the 1999 season. Yankee Stadium's own flagpole was in play, too, just behind Huggins' monument.

The modern practice of retiring numbers was impossible, because players didn't begin wearing uniform numbers until 1929. Originally, they noted where a player usually batted in the lineup, and they weren't always stable. For example, Tony Lazzeri started with number 6, then switched to 5, then 23, then 7, and finally back to number 6 over the course of his Yankee career. Due to their impermanence, early jersey numbers usually didn't carry the weight of a player's legacy as they would later on.

Of course, there are exceptions for exceptional players. Lou Gehrig wore only number 4 until ALS forced him to retire during the 1939 season. The club held Lou Gehrig Day on July 4 of that year, during which he delivered his famous "Luckiest Man" speech at the Stadium. A less memorable speaker at the ceremony was general manager Ed Barrow, who made history with an innovation of his own. He announced that Gehrig's number 4 would never be worn again by another Yankee, thereby making it the first retired

Courtesy of Wikimedia Commons.

The renovation of Yankee Stadium created Monument Park as a permanent home to monuments to Lou Gehrig, Miller Huggins, and Babe Ruth, as well as plaques to general manager Ed Barrow and others that previously sat in fair territory.

number in baseball history. (To be fair, it's an idea that Barrow borrowed from hockey, where the Toronto Maple Leafs had retired number 6 for Ace Bailey in 1934.)

Gehrig's ceremonial uniform number originally was not publicly displayed. The team framed a cloth swatch of his jersey with the inscription "Lou Gehrig Number Retired July 4, 1939" embroidered in cursive under the familiar number 4. This hung in the Yankees clubhouse, where it would be joined later by numbers 3, 5, 7, and others until the 1970s Yankee Stadium renovations. On July 6, 1941, just over two years after his historic number retirement and 34 days after his tragic death, the Yankees dedicated a second monument directly to the left of Huggins'.

Just as Ruth, Gehrig, and Huggins were responsible for the ascendance of the first Yankee dynasty, the three legends shared a fate of untimely demise due to illness. Ruth was diagnosed with throat cancer in 1946 and his health declined rapidly over the next two years. He made his final appearance at Yankee Stadium on July 13, 1948, keeping himself upright by leaning on a baseball bat so that the team could retire his number 3. He died two months later at age 53. On Opening Day the following season, the team dedicated the ballpark's third monument, just to the right of Ruth's former manager.

To say the three grave-like markers remain untouched until the early 1970s wouldn't be entirely accurate. After all, they *were* in the field of play. There's a famous video highlight of young Bobby Murcer jumping between Huggins' and Ruth's monuments to chase down a ball in the gap on June 24, 1970. Red Sox outfielder Dom DiMaggio (Joe's brother) maintained a healthy fear of them when he patrolled center field. "It was scary. Very scary. Oh yeah. It was a good way to eliminate yourself," he recounted in 2008.

Comically and somewhat irreverently, former Red Sox outfielder Jimmy Piersall once engaged Ruth in a conversation during a pitching change. "(The Yankees) were pounding us. We used a lot of relief pitchers, so I sat up on the monuments. I sat on Babe and I said to Babe, 'You wouldn't play in these games, Babe. These are terrible games.'"

By the time Yankee Stadium approached its 50th birthday, the ballpark was no longer in great condition. Rice University had owned the stadium since 1962 and failed to adequately maintain it. In 1972 New York City used eminent domain to buy the park just a few months before George Steinbrenner and a group of partners purchased the franchise itself in January 1973.

Not long thereafter, the city approved a $24 million stadium renovation that forced the Yankees to play in Shea Stadium for the 1974 and 1975 seasons.

It's an understatement to say that Steinbrenner had a flair for dramatizing – and monetizing – Yankee legacy. Rather than leaving the three monuments as a curiosity in the field of play and the retired numbers hanging inaccessibly in the clubhouse, he pushed the fences in to make room for a memorial area beyond the outfield wall and between the bullpens. Even though this outdoor museum would not become accessible to fans until 1985, it was named Monument Park.

On top of that, the Stadium had amassed an assortment of commemorative plaques over the years which were mounted on the center-field wall for players including Yogi Berra, Bill Dickey, Joe DiMaggio, and Mickey Mantle as well as managers Joe McCarthy and Casey Stengel, owner Jacob Ruppert, GM Ed Barrow, and Pope Paul VI. All of these were displayed in Monument Park as well.

No organization celebrates its heroes quite like the Yankees, who have now (through the 2022 season) retired 24 numbers for 26 players and managers. Joe DiMaggio's number 5 joined numbers 3 and 4 in 1952 as the only three numbers removed from circulation for the next 17 years. A retired-number boom kicked off a few years before the 1970s renovations with Mickey Mantle's number 7 in 1969. This was followed by four more in the 1970s, five in the 1980s, three in the 1990s (including Jackie Robinson's number 42, which was retired by all 30 major-league teams), and eight since 2000. Each retired number was displayed on the back wall of Monument Park with a plaque commemorating the individual's accomplishments. Additional plaques have joined the collection for a handful of players whose uniform numbers aren't retired as well as ones honoring visitors to Yankee Stadium like Popes John Paul II and Benedict XVI and Nelson Mandela, and to commemorate the Stonewall Inn Uprising.

As Monument Park swelled with retired numbers and plaques, the honor of a monument was reserved just for the greatest of Yankee legends, and only after their passing. In 1995 Mickey Mantle's plaque was moved from the wall to its own red granite monument to match those of Huggins, Gehrig, and Ruth. In 1999 Joe DiMaggio's followed suit. On September 11, 2002, a special monument was dedicated to the victims of the September 11 terrorist attacks the year before, situated off to the side of Monument Park away from the player monuments.

Throughout the 1970s renovations and subsequent changes to the ballpark, the monuments themselves never moved, but when the Yankees relocated to a new ballpark across the street in 2009, Monument Park came with them. Instead of being located beyond the deep left-center field fence, it now resides in straight-away center beneath the batter's eye. In September 2010, two months after Steinbrenner's death, his family dedicated a seventh monument. The enormous monument to The Boss is 35 square feet – nearly triple the size of the others.

Yankee Stadium opens to ticket-holders 90 minutes before the scheduled first pitch on every game day. Monument Park opens at the same time and closes 45 minutes before the game begins. Even as nearly everything else at Yankee Stadium has a sponsorship or requires a separate expenditure, Monument Park remains free to enter with the purchase of a ticket to the ballgame.

***

Among the most universal human experiences is loss. When someone dies unexpectedly, they never truly leave us. We carry them and feel the weight of their absence for the rest of our lives – but only for the rest of *our* lives. When we pass on, our memories of loved ones go with us. The next generation is left with the stories we tell them.

When the Yankees built an everlasting monument to Miller Huggins in 1932, it was a comforting tribute for the bereaved – even three years after losing someone we remain bereaved – but in equal measure, it was built for our own generations 90 years later. It's a testament to the enormous legacy of a man so admired and missed that our fore parents could not allow him to become merely a historical footnote. His monument and each monument and plaque that followed is a lesson, a story, and a demand that we *remember*. A person is more than a won-lost record; we are each the amalgamation of our experiences and the emotions and actions we inspire in others.

A 56-game hitting streak matters not just because of statistical record-keeping. It's about the stories it collects along the way. The legacy of playing 2,130 consecutive games isn't tarnished whatsoever just because it's no longer the major-league record. The inspiration and reverence, the close calls and famous quotes, the glory and anguish – all of these are what our elders passed on to us. They're right there beyond the center-field fence waiting for us to discover and remember. They're a command from our parents and grandparents to say to our children, "Do you see the one over there that says 'Derek Sanderson Jeter?' Let me tell you a story …"

SOURCES

https://sabr.org/bioproj/person/miller-huggins/

https://www.mlb.com/news/history-of-monument-park-c263612104

https://goldinauctions.com/Lou_Gehrig_s_Retired__Number_4___That_Hung_in_Yank-LOT41271.aspx

https://thisdayinbaseball.com/1949-the-new-york-yankees-unveil-a-granite-monument-to-babe-ruth-monument-park-located-in-the-deep-center-field-region-of-yankee-stadium-also-includes-monu/

https://www.nydailynews.com/sports/baseball/yankees/yankee-stadium-monument-park-stories-place-legends-article-1.296782

http://bronxpinstripes.com/yankees-history/yankees-retired-numbers-uniforms/

https://www.yankeenumbers.com/retired.asp

ELEVEN MASTERPIECES:
YANKEE STADIUM'S NO-HITTERS

By Larry DeFillipo

The number 11 has a prominent place in human history, both real and imagined. The First World War ended on the 11th hour of the 11th day of the 11th month of 1918. Apollo 11 was the first manned spacecraft to land on the moon. And in the popular Netflix series *Stranger Things*, the fate of 1980s humanity rests on the supernatural powers of a teenage girl named Eleven.

Eleven is also the number of no-hitters fashioned on the hallowed ground of the original Yankee Stadium. Five before the mid-1970s renovation and six after. Eight were crafted by the Yankees and three by their opponents. All were shutouts, completed in regulation (nine innings).

Only Fenway Park and Dodger Stadium have witnessed more no-hitters than the original Yankee Stadium, with 14 and 13 respectively.[1] Fifteen years and six World Series championships accumulated between Yankee Stadium's opening and its first no-hitter, in 1938.[2] The end of the millennium and a pair of World Series victories passed between Yankee Stadium's last no-hitter, in 1999, and its closing.

The eight Yankee pitchers who threw Yankee Stadium no-hitters include:

- One World Series hero pushing the envelope on limited rest (Monte Pearson).

- Another nursing a balky elbow (Allie Reynolds).

- A selfish playboy who found World Series perfection (Don Larsen).

- A young southpaw upset by an All-Star snub (Dave Righetti).

- A one-of-a-kind inspiration branded an under-achiever (Jim Abbott).

- A fallen prodigy who honored his gravely ill father by playing (Doc Gooden).

- Two well-traveled Davids, one who followed in the footsteps of a pair of free-spirited legends (David Wells), and another who shared the spotlight with a long-absent giant (David Cone).

Opposing pitchers who no-hit the Yankees at the original Yankee Stadium include a fireballing icon unhappy with premature news of his decline (Bob Feller), a hard-luck pitcher helped by a diligent official scorer (Virgil Trucks), and five Houston Astros relievers who combined to bring a nascent no-hitter to fruition after the starter (Roy Oswalt) went off with a nagging injury.

No pitcher contributed to more than one no-hitter at Yankee Stadium but two catchers have caught a pair of them. Yogi Berra was behind the plate for Reynolds' and Larsen's, and Joe Girardi caught Gooden's and

Pitcher	Date	Year	Team	Opponent	Score	Comment
Monte Pearson	August 27	1938	NYY	CLE	13-0	
Bob Feller	April 30	1946	CLE	NYY	1-0	
Allie Reynolds	September 28	1951	NYY	BOS	8-0	
Virgil Trucks	August 25	1952	DET	NYY	1-0	
Don Larsen	October 8	1956	NYY	BRO	2-0	Perfect game – WS
Dave Righetti	July 4	1983	NYY	BOS	4-0	
Jim Abbott	September 4	1993	NYY	CLE	4-0	
Dwight Gooden	May 14	1996	NYY	SEA	2-0	
David Wells	May 17	1998	NYY	MIN	4-0	Perfect game
David Cone	July 18	1999	NYY	MON	6-0	Perfect game
Oswalt et. al.	June 11	2003	HOU	NYY	8-0	Combined–six pitchers

Pitcher	Year	Team	Opponent	Yankee Hall Of Famers In Lineup	Opponent Hall Of Famers In Lineup
Monte Pearson	1938	NYY	CLE	DiMaggio, Gehrig, Gordon	Averill
Bob Feller	1946	CLE	NYY	Dickey, DiMaggio, Gordon, Rizzuto	Boudreau, Feller, Lemon
Allie Reynolds	1951	NYY	BOS	Berra, DiMaggio, Rizzuto	Boudreau, T. Williams
Virgil Trucks	1952	DET	NYY	Berra, Mantle, Mize, Rizzuto	**None**
Don Larsen	1956	NYY	BRO	Berra, Mantle	Campanella, Hodges, Reese, Robinson, Snider
Dave Righetti	1983	NYY	BOS	Winfield	Boggs, Rice
Jim Abbott	1993	NYY	CLE	Boggs	Thome
Dwight Gooden	1996	NYY	SEA	Boggs, Jeter	Griffey, Martinez
David Wells	1998	NYY	MIN	Jeter	Molitor
David Cone	1999	NYY	MON	Jeter	V. Guerrero
Oswalt et al	2003	HOU	NYY	Jeter	Bagwell, Biggio

Cone's. Hall of Fame catcher Bill Dickey never caught one, but his little used backup, Joe Glenn, did, calling signs for Pearson's no-hitter on a day that Dickey had off.

Every team that played in a Yankee Stadium no-hitter, except for the 1952 Tigers, had at least one future Hall of Famer in its lineup. One of them, Derek Jeter, along with Paul O'Neill, are the only players to appear in four Yankee Stadium no-hitters. Jeter and O'Neill are joined by Bernie Williams as the only players in the winning lineup for three of them. Phil Rizzuto is the only player to appear in the losing lineup for more than one.

Yankee Stadium no-hitter lineups have also included some surprises. Long-time Oakland A's shortstop Bert Campaneris played in Abbott's as a Yankee third baseman,[3] and Mr. Red Sox, Johnny Pesky, played shortstop for the Detroit Tigers in Trucks'. An influential left-handed hitting Yankee named Babe also saw action in Trucks' no-hitter but it was Loren Babe, an early mentor to Hall of Fame manager Tony LaRussa, not Babe Ruth.[4]

No ballplayer has made his major-league debut in a Yankee Stadium no-hitter. Hall of Fame pitcher Bob Lemon played his sixth game as a Cleveland Indians *outfielder* in Feller's no-hitter, two weeks *before* making his major-league mound debut. A 21-year-old Manny Ramirez, well before *being Manny*, saw his third major-league game turn into Righetti's no-hitter.

Red Sox catcher Aaron Robinson is the only player to have played his last game in a Yankee Stadium no-hitter.[5] Robinson's final at-bat, during Reynolds' no-hitter, produced a deep fly ball that "caused the most alarm" to fans rooting for that no-hitter, according to the *New York Daily News*.[6] Umpire Babe Pinelli, behind the plate for Don Larsen's perfect game, retired immediately after the 1956 World Series, telling

reporters "Why go on? I won't see a better pitched game."[7]

GAME SUMMARIES

A brief synopsis of each no-hitter follows, including the circumstances, and in some cases emotions, leading up to the game. Detailed descriptions of these games can be found in the pages of this publication or online in the SABR Research Collection, within the Games Project no-hitter archive at https://sabr.org/gamesproj/category/milestones/no-hitters/.

#1 — August 27, 1938. Monte Pearson downs former mates on two days' rest in first Yankee Stadium no-hitter

New York Yankees 13, Cleveland Indians 0

Pitching line: 9 IP, 0 H, 0 R, 7K, 2 BB, 29 BF, UNK pitches

Frequent rain during the 1938 season forced the Yankees to play 10 doubleheaders between August 12 and August 27, the last five on consecutive days. In the final game of that twin bill gantlet, Monte Pearson, a surprise winner over Carl Hubbell in Game Four of the 1936 World Series, no-hit the Cleveland Indians on two days' rest.[8] Winner of his last nine decisions, Pearson had last been defeated by those same Indians, nine weeks earlier. Perfect for the first three innings, Pearson walked two batters to start the fourth, then retired the final 18 he faced. Two home runs each by Tommy Henrich and rookie Joe Gordon paced a Yankees offense that gave Pearson a 13-run cushion for the final two innings. Bruce Campbell, whose three-run home run sealed Pearson's last loss, lined out to left fielder George Selkirk for the final out of the game.

#2 — April 30, 1946. Bob Feller proves critics wrong, gets second career no-hitter

Cleveland Indians 1, New York Yankees 0

Pitching line: 9 IP, 0 H, 0 R, 11K, 5 BB, 32 BF, 133 pitches[9]

The day after the Japanese attacked Pearl Harbor, Cleveland Indians ace Bob Feller joined the US Navy for a tour of duty that lasted until August 1945. When Feller lost two of his first three starts in 1946, a newswire story suggested he was in decline.[10] Feller disagreed. "It maddened me as nothing ever written about me had before." "I … promised myself that the Yankees would get everything I could throw when I met them [on April 30]."[11] On that day, Feller navigated around five walks and two Cleveland fielding errors for the first Yankee Stadium no-hitter by a visiting pitcher.[12] The game was scoreless until Indians catcher Frankie Hayes hit a one-out home run in the top of the ninth. On the final play of the game, second baseman Ray Mack stumbled to his knees before gathering the ball and throwing to first for the out.[13] Two days later, the *Cleveland Plain Dealer*, the newspaper that first claimed Feller had declined, ran an editorial apologizing for its "unsound judgment in the Feller-is-slipping incident."[14]

#3 — September 28, 1951: Allie Reynolds overcomes balky elbow to become the first AL pitcher to hurl two no-hitters in a season

New York Yankees 8, Boston Red Sox 0

Pitching line: 9 IP, 0 H, 0 R, 9K, 4 BB, 30 BF, 119 pitches[15]

Recurring elbow problems kept Allie Reynolds, winner of Game Two in the 1950 World Series, from pitching in a single spring-training game in 1951, and at times limited him to bullpen duty throughout the season. But in July 1951, Reynolds no-hit his former teammates, the Cleveland Indians, 1-0 at Cleveland Stadium. Two months later, Reynolds no-hit the Boston Red Sox at Yankee Stadium in the second game of a doubleheader to become the first American League pitcher to throw a pair of no-hitters in the same season.[16] The 8-0 win also clinched for the Yankees at least a tie for the AL pennant. Reynolds walked four and struck out nine, his second highest strikeout total for the season. With two out in the ninth, Ted Williams lofted a foul pop behind home plate that catcher Yogi Berra muffed. On the next pitch, Williams popped another pitch foul that Berra caught in front of the Yankee dugout. Asked afterward, Reynolds said "My arm never hurt for a minute."[17]

#4 — August 25, 1952: Virgil Trucks tosses his second no-hitter of the season, thanks to a diligent official scorer

Detroit Tigers 1, New York Yankees 0

Pitching line: 9 IP, 0 H, 0 R, 8K, 1 BB, 30 BF, UNK pitches

Virgil Trucks had thrown a two-hitter, a one-hit shutout, and a no-hitter (the last two against the Washington Senators) and carried an ERA 0.12 below league average, but when he stepped onto the field at Yankee Stadium on August 25, 1952, his record for the Detroit Tigers was a dismal 4-15. In the bottom of the third inning, Tigers shortstop Johnny Pesky bobbled a Phil Rizzuto grounder that official scorer (and *New York Times* sportswriter) John Drebinger first ruled an error, then changed to a hit.[18] Unsure about his decision, Drebinger called the dugout and spoke to Pesky, who said he should've caught the ball.[19] Moments before the Tigers rallied in the seventh to take a 1-0 lead, Drebinger reversed himself again and declared the play an error.[20] One out after the Rizzuto play, Trucks had walked Mickey Mantle, but he didn't allow another Yankee to reach base. He retired Hank Bauer for the game's final out on a "sizzling one-hopper" that almost knocked down Detroit second baseman Al Federoff.[21]

#5 — October 8, 1956: An imperfect Don Larsen is perfect in Game Five of the 1956 World Series

New York Yankees 2, Brooklyn Dodgers 0

Pitching line: 9 IP, 0 H, 0 R, 7K, 0 BB, 27 BF

When Don Larsen walked into the Yankees locker room before Game Five of the 1956 World Series against the Brooklyn Dodgers, he found a warm-up ball in his locker, signifying that manager Casey Stengel had picked him to start the game. Also in his locker was a court order directing Larsen, the Yankees and Commissioner Ford Frick to show cause why his upcoming World Series share should not be held to cover unpaid child support.[22] A notorious playboy,[23] Larsen had secretly wed a Baltimore woman pregnant with his child two years earlier, then abandoned them so that he could continue "a life of free and easy existence."[24] Betrayed by his own wildness in frittering away a six-run Game Two lead, Larsen was flawless in Game Five. He went to a three-ball count on only one batter and struck out seven. A two-out solo home run in the fourth inning by Mickey Mantle gave Larsen the only run he'd need, and Mantle's backhanded stab of Gil Hodges' drive to left-center field an inning later proved the defensive play of the game. Larsen recorded the game's final out by striking out pinch-hitter Dale Mitchell with a high fastball that Mitchell tried to check his swing on, but couldn't. Shortly after his perfect game, Larsen settled his delinquent child-support issue out of court.[25]

#6 — July 4, 1983: Dave Righetti rebounds from All-Star snub to no-hit the Red Sox on Independence Day

New York Yankees 4, Boston Red Sox 0

Pitching line: 9 IP, 0 H, 0 R, 9K, 4 BB, 29 BF, 132 pitches[26]

When southpaw Dave Righetti was left off the initial American League roster for the 1983 All-Star Game, he was disappointed. When Righetti was passed over to replace an ailing Ron Guidry on the All-Star roster because his July 4 fill-in start for Guidry would leave him only one day's rest before the All-Star Game, he got mad.[27] Righetti channeled his anger against the Boston Red Sox that day for the first Yankee Stadium no-hitter since Don Larsen's perfect game in the 1956 World Series. He collected nine strikeouts while walking four, including giving two free passes to Jim Rice, who'd clubbed four home runs in his last three games. Wade Boggs, on the way to his first of five AL batting crowns, swung at and missed a Righetti slider to end the game. Afterward Righetti portrayed his performance as a gift for his mother, whose birthday coincided with the coming All-Star Game. "I won't be there, but this is a much better present anyway."[28]

#7 — September 4, 1993: Jim Abbott bounces back to no-hit the Indians

New York Yankees 4, Cleveland Indians 0

Pitching line: 9 IP, 0 H, 0 R, 3K, 5 BB, 30 BF, 119 pitches, 9 swinging strikes, 1 line drive

In December 1992, the Yankees acquired pitcher Jim Abbott, a former Sullivan Award winner, Olympic champion, and top-three finisher for the 1991 American League Cy Young Award. Born without a right hand, Abbott had taught himself how to pitch and play his position as well as anyone. In mid-August 1993, Abbott's middling record for a Yankee team unable to break away from the pack in the AL East prompted Yankees beat writer Jack Curry to call him an underachiever.[29] Pummeled soon after in Cleveland (allowing seven earned runs and 10 hits over 3⅔ innings), Abbott responded in his next start by no-hitting the Indians at Yankee Stadium. Abbott's gem started off inauspiciously, as his first pitch sailed wide of catcher Matt Nokes. He walked five batters and struck out only three. The Yankees gave Abbott a 3-0 lead in the third inning, on a little league home run by Dion James that began with a single through Cleveland pitcher Bob Milacki's legs and ended with throwing errors by center fielder Kenny Lofton and third baseman Jim Thome. Lofton proved a villain leading off the ninth, when he tried to bunt for a hit. After the ball rolled foul, Abbott retired the side in order.

#8 — May 14, 1996: Doc Gooden honors his father by playing and no-hitting the Mariners

New York Yankees 2, Seattle Mariners 0

Pitching line: 9 IP, 0 H, 0 R, 5K, 6 BB, 33 BF, 134 pitches, 10 swinging strikes, 3 line drives

Days before Doc Gooden's May 14, 1996, Yankee Stadium start against the Seattle Mariners, he learned that his father, Dan, would be having open-heart surgery for complications associated with diabetes, gout, and kidney failure. Gooden had manager Joe Torre's blessing to miss his start, but realized that his father would want him to "take the baseball and pitch."[30] Gooden, a Rookie of the Year and Cy Young Award winner released before his 30th birthday by a New York Mets franchise no longer willing to tolerate his struggles with drug addiction, followed his heart to no-hit a talent-laden Seattle Mariners lineup. Yankees center fielder Gerald Williams made the play of the day in the first inning, backhanding a tracer hit by 20-year-old Alex Rodriguez[31] in the top of his glove raised high. "Like he was scooping ice cream out of the sky."[32] Gooden walked six batters in the game, and saw a hard-hit grounder that ricocheted off Martinez's chest in the sixth ruled an error. With the tying run on second base, Gooden retired Paul Sorrento for the final out of the game on a popup to Derek Jeter. Doc made it to Tampa the next morning, just as Dan's successful surgery began.

#9 — May 17, 1998: David Wells becomes the second pitcher from Point Loma High to pitch a perfect game at Yankee Stadium

New York Yankees 4, Minnesota Twins 0

Pitching line: 9 IP, 0 H, 0 R, 11K, 0 BB, 27 BF, 120 pitches, 14 swinging strikes, 0 line drives

On May 16, 1998, the cast and crew of *Saturday Night Live*, along with invited guests that included New York Yankees pitcher David Wells, attended a season-ending wrap party. At 5 o'clock the next morning, a "drunk, exhausted, reeking [and] reeling" Wells dropped into his bed at home, "a comatose heap."[33] Later that day, he threw the 15th perfect game in major-league history and the first by a Yankee since Don Larsen's in the 1956 World Series. Wells, like Larsen a graduate of Point Loma High School in San Diego, had rooted for the Yankees since childhood, and idolized Babe Ruth — so much so that during a Yankee Stadium game in June 1997 he wore a Ruth game-worn hat, earning himself a $2,500 fine.[34] Wells spent 15 seasons with four different organizations before becoming a Yankee after the 1996 season. He fanned 11 and thoroughly dominated an underwhelming Minnesota Twins lineup that included future Hall of Famer Paul Molitor, hampered by a left shoulder injury,[35] and a cleanup hitter (Marty Cordova) who had no home runs in 100 plate appearances. Bernie Williams led the Yankees offense, scoring in the second inning after a leadoff double, hitting a solo home run in the fourth, and doubling in the seventh to start a two-run rally that closed out the Yankees scoring. After recording the final out, Wells rode off the diamond on the shoulders of his teammates, waving his regulation Yankees hat.

#10 — July 18, 1999: David Cone is perfect on Yogi Berra Day

New York Yankees 6, Montreal Expos 0

Pitching line: 9 IP, 0 H, 0 R, 10K, 0 BB, 27 BF, 88 pitches, 18 swinging strikes, 0 line drives

In February 1985 George Steinbrenner declared Yankee manager Yogi Berra's job secure,[36] then fired him 16 games into the season. Outraged, Yogi vowed to "never return to Yankee Stadium as long as The Boss is in charge."[37] Thirteen years later, a dying Joe DiMaggio pushed Steinbrenner to reconcile with Berra.[38] To honor Berra's legacy, the Yankees scheduled Yogi Berra Day for July 18, 1999.[39] Don Larsen threw out a ceremonial first pitch before that afternoon's contest with the Montreal Expos, then gave way to Yankees starter David Cone. Wearing his age (36) on his back and the Yankee Clipper's uniform number (5) on his sleeve, Cone threw the third perfect game in Yankee history. He struck out 10 and never once went to three balls against an inexperienced and inexpensive Montreal lineup,[40] none of whom had ever faced him in a regular-season game. The defensive play of the game happened in the top of the first, as Yankees right fielder Paul O'Neill robbed Terry Jones of a hit with a sliding catch.[41] The Yankees gave Cone a five-run lead in the second inning, highlighted by two-run home runs by Ricky Ledee and Derek Jeter, who hit his into Monument Park.[42] Cone threw only 88 pitches, the fewest in a perfect game since 1908.[43]

#11 — June 11, 2003: Five Astros relievers hold the Yankees hitless after an early injury to starter Roy Oswalt

Houston Astros 3, New York Yankees 0

Pitching line: 9 IP, 0 H, 0 R, 13K, 3 BB, 33 BF, 151 pitches, 21 swinging strikes, 2 line drives

As Roy Oswalt approached second base on May 15 with his first extra-base hit of the 2003 season, he stumbled, landing him on the disabled list with a strained right groin for the third time in his career.[44] His third start after coming off the DL ended with the Astros throwing a combined no-hitter over the Yankees on June 11, 2003 at Yankee Stadium. Oswalt's first inning was perfect, but he reinjured his groin two pitches into the second. Five Astros relievers — Flushing, New York, native Peter Munro, 2001 draft pick Kirk Saarloos, rookie Brad Lidge, set-up man Octavio Dotel, and closer Billy Wagner — allowed six Yankees batters to reach base, none via base hit. The last Yankee to reach base got there on a third-strike wild pitch by Dotel in an inning in which he struck out four batters swinging.[45] The Astros offense scored early and often, leading 4-0 after three innings and 8-0 by the ninth. After the game, George Steinbrenner told reporters he felt Houston tried to humiliate the Yankees by using so many pitchers to protect a large lead. "I was just trying to win the game," said Astros manager Jimy Williams in response.[46]

COMPARING YANKEE STADIUM NO-HITTERS

Each Yankee Stadium no-hitter was one-of-a-kind as compared with the other 10. As the number 11 comes from the Old English word *endleofan*, which means "ten and one left over,"[47] it's appropriate that one game stands above the rest: Don Larsen's perfect game, fashioned during a World Series. David Cone's perfect game was breathtaking for being completed with the fewest pitches of any Yankee Stadium no-hitter (88). David Wells pitched his perfect game in front of the largest crowd of any regular season no-hitter at Yankee Stadium (49,820).

Dwight Gooden allowed the most walks (6), against a lineup with more 150 OPS+ batters than any other (3). Monte Pearson enjoyed the largest cushion, a 13-run lead during the last two innings of his no-hitter. Jim Abbott pulled off the greatest turnaround, having allowed seven earned runs in his previous start, more than any other Yankee Stadium no-hit author had. Bob Feller and Virgil Trucks pitched in the tightest contests, winning their no-hitters 1-0, with Feller pitching the most innings without a lead (8), and Trucks retiring the most consecutive batters to finish a nonperfect-game no-hitter (20).[48]

Allie Reynolds' no-hitter was the only one to clinch a piece of a pennant. Dave Righetti's was the only one to end with that season's batting champ at the plate (Wade Boggs). The no-hitter thrown by Roy Oswalt et al. took the most time (2 hours 52 minutes), included the most strikeouts (13) and needed more pitchers than any other in major-league history (6).[49]

The question remains: How do the Yankee Stadium no-hitters stack up against one another? For the six no-hitters thrown before 1988, official pitching statistics for games are limited to the number of batters faced, innings pitched, strikeouts, and walks (classic metrics). Starting in 1988, official statistics also included the number of pitches thrown, number and percent that were strikes, how many of those were swinging vs. contacted vs. called, number of groundouts vs. fly outs and how many line drives were hit. All of the no-hitters in the original Yankee Stadium came before the current Statcast era, in which the type, spin rate, and movement of every pitch are tracked, the velocity, direction, and angle of ascent of every struck ball are recorded, and the expected outcome of every ball struck fair (hit or out) is calculated from a probabilistic analysis that relies on thousands of previous outcomes.[50]

We can compare original Yankee Stadium no-hitters against one another by using classic pitching metrics plus a few advanced metrics developed in the last few decades that can be applied retroactively.

COMPOSITE BATTING AVERAGE COMPARISON

Gary Belleville, in SABR's Spring 2021 *Baseball Research Journal*, attempted to answer the question of who threw the greatest regular-season no-hitter in the modern era. To do so he used the composite batting average of the lineup that was no-hit to quantify a sort of improbability for each no-hitter.[51] For every no-hitter from 1901 through 2021, Belleville calculated a composite batting average (cBA) for the lineup that was no-hit, using each batter's year-end batting average, neutralizing it for that team's home ballpark effects, weighting it based on the number of at-bats in the game by each batter, and adjusting it by one-year park factors for hits associated with the ballpark where the no-hitter took place. The higher the cBA, the more improbable the no-hitter and, by Belleville's rationale, the greater the feat.

Using Belleville's cBA values for each of the original Yankee Stadium no-hitters, Doc Gooden's no-hitter against the 1996 Seattle Mariners comes out on top, followed by Monte Pearson's.

Gooden's no-hitter was ranked ninth all-time by Belleville among nine-inning nonperfect no-hitters between 1901 and 2021. No other original Yankee Stadium no-hitter falls in his top 50.

				cBA	GS
Doc Gooden	NYY	1996	Seattle Mariners	.27853	86
Monte Pearson	NYY	1938	Cleveland Indians	.2581	92
Virgil Trucks	DET	1952	New York Yankees	.25688	94
Roy Oswalt, et al	HOU	2003	New York Yankees	.25682	55
Dave Righetti	NYY	1983	Boston Red Sox	.25299	92
Jim Abbott	NYY	1993	Cleveland Indians	.24635	85
Don Larsen	NYY	1956	Brooklyn Dodgers	.24265	94
David Wells	NYY	1998	Minnesota Twins	.24061	98
David Cone	NYY	1999	Montreal Expos	.23996	97
Bob Feller	CLE	1946	New York Yankees	.23164	93
Allie Reynolds	NYY	1951	Boston Red Sox	.21804	92

YANKEE STADIUM 1923-2008

None of the three Yankee perfect games cracked Belleville's list of the top 10 perfect games, but they do fall together in chronological order, occupying 12th, 13th, and 14th place. Comparing perfect games on the basis of the defeated team's composite on-base percentage rather than cBA might produce a different ranking, an analysis left to a future publication.

Tabulated alongside cBA in the table here are Game Score (GS) values, as listed by Baseball-Reference.com. Devised by Bill James in the 1980s, GS credits starting pitchers for innings pitched and strikeouts, and subtracts for hits, walks, and runs allowed. While useful in comparing typical starts, it's of lesser value in comparing complete-game no-hitters to one another: Score differences become simply differences in net strikeouts minus walks. Thus, Larsen's seven-strikeout perfect game carries an identical score to Trucks' eight-strikeout, one walk not-quite-perfect game. More significantly, unlike Belleville's cBA metric, GS doesn't take into account the strength of an opposing team's lineup or the contribution of relief pitchers.

ALMOST

Fifteen no-hitters were broken up in the ninth inning at the original Yankee Stadium. Seven Yankee pitchers (six starters and one reliever replacing a future Hall of Famer) lost Yankee Stadium no-hitters in the ninth, as did eight opposing pitchers. Only one, Billy Rohr of the 1967 Boston Red Sox, came within a single out of making the Yankee Stadium no-hitter list a dozen strong.

Horace Clarke, whose average-ness is often cited as emblematic of the Yankees' late-1960s descent into mediocrity, broke up three potential Yankee Stadium no-hitters in the ninth inning over a four-week span in the middle of the 1970 season. That feat has earned Clarke a place in Yankee Stadium no-hitter lore, alongside Monte Pearson and those who followed him.

ACKNOWLEDGMENTS

The author is grateful for help from Gary Belleville in guiding him to his cBA calculations for modern-era no-hitters.

SOURCES

In addition to the sources cited in the Notes, the author utilized game summaries published in the *New York Times*, *New York Daily News,* and hometown newspapers of the opposing teams, including the *Cleveland Plain Dealer*, *Detroit Free Press,* and *Houston Chronicle*. The list of no-hitters broken up at Yankee Stadium in the ninth inning was based upon Stew Thornley's *Lost in the Ninth* monographs posted at milkeespress.com/lostninth.html. The author also utilized player and game details from Baseball-Reference.com, retrosheet.com, stathead.com, baseball-almanac.com, and baseballsavant.mlb.com, as well as ballpark history information from seamheads.com/ballparks.

Date	Pitcher, team	Opponent	GS differences	# out	first hit/batter
May 30, 1934	Earl Whitehill, WSH	NY Yankees	1-0	1 out	1B – Ben Chapman
August 8, 1953	Bob Kuzava, NYY	Chi. White Sox	3-0	1 out	2B – Bob Boyd
May 12, 1956	Don Ferrarese, BAL	NY Yankees	1-0	0 out	1B – Andy Carey
July 4, 1959 (2)	Bob Turley, NYY	Wash. Senators	7-0	0 out	1B – Julio Becquer
July 17, 1959	Ralph Terry, NYY	Chi. White Sox	0-2	0 out	1B – Jim McAnany
May 22, 1962	Jim Coates, NYY*	LA Angels	2-1 (12)	1 out	1B – Buck Rodgers
August 27, 1963 (1)	Jim Bouton, NYY	Bos. Red Sox	5-0	0 out	1B – Russ Nixon
April 14, 1967	Billy Rohr, BOS	NY Yankees	3-0	2 out	1B – Elston Howard
June 4, 1970	Jim Rooker, KCR	NY Yankees	1-2 (12)	0 out	1B – Horace Clarke
June 19, 1970	Sonny Siebert, BOS	NY Yankees	7-4	0 out	1B – Horace Clarke
July 2, 1970	Joe Niekro, DET	NY Yankees	5-0	1 out	1B – Horace Clarke
May 2, 1976	Rudy May, NYY	KC Royals	1-2 (11)	0 out	2B – Amos Otis
July 23, 1976	Doyle Alexander, NYY	Bos. Red Sox	9-1	0 out	1B – Rick Burleson
September 12, 1981	Bob Ojeda, BOS	NY Yankees	2-1	0 out	2B – Rick Cerone
September 28, 2006	Daniel Cabrera, BAL	NY Yankees	7-1	1 out	1B - Robinson Cano

*Whitey Ford started and pitched seven innings, relieved by Jim Coates in the eighth.

^Numbers in parentheses are the length of extra-inning games

NOTES

1. Ring Central Coliseum in Oakland, California, formerly known as Oakland-Alameda County Coliseum, has also hosted 11 no-hitters in its 55 years as home to the Oakland Athletics.

2. At that time, only four major-league ballparks had gone longer without a no-hitter; Pittsburgh's Forbes Field (29 years), Cleveland's League Park IV (21 years), Washington's Griffith Stadium (20 years), and Pittsburgh's Exposition Park III (17 years). Not a single no-hitter was ever thrown at Forbes Field in its 62 years as home to the Pittsburgh Pirates.

3. It was the last of 11 no-hitters in which Campaneris appeared, the most of any ballplayer between 1956 and 2008. "No-Hitter Involvement Since 1956," July 30, 2008, Recondite Baseball website, http://reconditebaseball.blogspot.com/2008/07/no-hitter-involvement-since-1956.html, accessed September 25, 2022.

4. La Russa credits Loren Babe with teaching him much about managing when La Russa was a minor-league player-coach under Babe in the mid-1970s. "I was a player/coach for a great man named Loren Babe, and it was just like an awakening. He showed me things about managing — and I thought I was a player who paid attention over the years. I had no clue at all what was involved with managing." Trucks' no-hitter came in Babe's sixth major league game. Tony La Russa page, Baseball Hall of Fame website, https://baseballhall.org/hall-of-famers/larussa-tony, accessed September 26, 2022.

5. Brooklyn's Jackie Robinson and Dale Mitchell retired after the 1956 World Series, but did play in the Series after Larsen's perfect game.

6. Joe Trimble, "Reynolds, Vic Triumph, 8-0, 11-3," *New York Daily News*, September 29, 1951: 28, 31.

7. Larry Gerlach, Babe Pinelli SABR biography, https://sabr.org/bioproj/person/babe-pinelli/#_edn3.

8. Pearson had thrown a nine-inning complete game in his last start. He last had two days off between starts two years earlier, but it had been five years since he did so coming off a nine-inning start.

9. Pitch count as reported in the *Cleveland Plain Dealer*. Associated Press, "133 Feller Pitches Brings No-Hitter," *Cleveland Plain Dealer*, May 1, 1946: 19.

10. "Feller Slipping?," *Hazelton* (Pennsylvania) *Plain Speaker*, April 27, 1946: 10.

11. Bob Feller, *Bob Feller's Strikeout Story* (New York: Grosset & Dunlap, 1947), 226.

12. Floyd Clifford "Bill" Bevens, who took the loss in this game, came within one out of his own no-hitter in Game Four of the 1947 World Series.

13. Mack also earned an assist on the last play of Feller's Opening Day no-hitter in 1940, making a sparkling play to knock down a line drive hit by White Sox right fielder Taft Wright. Joseph Wancho, Ray Mack SABR biography, https://sabr.org/bioproj/person/Ray-Mack/.

14. "We Apologize," *Cleveland Plain Dealer*, May 2, 1946: 10.

15. Pitch count as reported in Gregory H. Wolf, "September 28, 1951: Allie Reynolds throws his second no-hitter of the season," https://sabr.org/gamesproj/game/september-28-1951-allie-reynolds-throws-his-second-no-hitter-of-the-season/.

16. Reynolds' feat had been matched to that point only by Johnny Vander Meer of the 1938 Cincinnati Reds.

17. Shortly after the World Series, Reynolds announced that he would not undergo surgery to remove bone chips from his right elbow. "I was pitching so well down the stretch that I don't think it necessary to have an operation." There's no record of Reynolds ever having surgery on that elbow over the rest of his playing career. "Reynolds Delays Operation on Arm," *New York Times*, October 17, 1951: S39.

18. Drebinger later said he'd changed his initial decision to a hit "upon the insistence of several colleagues." John Drebinger, "Detroit Star Wins at Stadium, 1 to 0," *New York Times*, August 26, 1952: 16.

19. Drebinger, "Detroit Star Wins at Stadium, 1 to 0."

20. Drebinger reportedly directed that his revised decision be announced over the public-address system during the top of the seventh inning. Since the Tigers were rallying at that time, the announcement was held off until they were done batting. "Trucks Wins 2nd No-Hitter of Year, 1-0," *Detroit Free Press*, August 26, 1952: 19.

21. "Detroit Star Wins at Stadium, 1 to 0."

22. "Larsen's Wife Petitions Court to Withhold His Series Share," *New York Times*, October 9, 1956: 55.

23. Larsen was characterized in newspapers as "more concerned for good times than good games," and *San Diego Union* sports editor Jack Murphy called Larsen a "pitcher previously known for living as though every day were New Year's Eve." Teammate Mickey Mantle described Larsen as "easily the greatest drinker I've known and I've known some pretty good ones in my time." Lew Paper, *Perfect: Don Larsen's Miraculous World Series Game and The Men Who Made It Happen* (New York: New American Library, 2009), 12; Kirk Kenney, January 1, 2020, "Don Larsen, Who Pitched Perfect Game for Yankees in '56 World Series, Dies at 90," *San Diego Union-Tribune* website, https://www.sandiegouniontribune.com/sports/mlb/story/2020-01-01/don-larsen-perfect-game-yankees-1956-world-series-point-loma-high-dies-at-90, accessed September 22, 2022.

24. *Perfect: Don Larsen's Miraculous World Series Game*, 17.

25. Mrs. Larsen continued to seek whatever portion of his estimated $5,400 to $8,100 World Series share the courts would allow but that proceeding was quietly removed from the Bronx Supreme Court calendar a week later. "Only One Cloud Over Larsen's Day; Touch on 2d Don Too," *New York Daily News*, October 9, 1956: 3, 4; Dick Young, "Herman Perfect Man; He Didn't Give a Sign," *New York Daily News*, October 9, 1956: 51; "Court Cleans Larsen's Slate," *New York Daily News*, October 16, 1956: 41.

26. Pitch count reported in Murray Chass, "Righetti Pitches First Yankee No-Hitter Since 1956," *New York Times*, July 5, 1983: B9-B10.

27. An assistant to MacPhail labeled Righetti a "worthy replacement" but made clear he wouldn't be Guidry's replacement since he was on course to have only one day's rest before the All-Star Game. When Tippy Martinez was announced as Guidry's replacement, Righetti was flabbergasted. "I wanted to replace Ron Guidry, because I thought I deserved it off my pitching. I wasn't picked, and that's the way it goes. I tried to use the anger (I had) against the Red Sox," Righetti later explained. "Guidry Lost to All-Stars," *New York Times*, July 2, 1983: 27; Eric Compton, "Hot Righetti Was Driven by AL Snub," *New York Daily News*, July 5, 1983: 68.

28. Compton, "Hot Righetti Was Driven by AL Snub."

29. Jack Curry, "A Pennant Tries to Grow in the Bronx," *New York Times*, August 20, 1993: B9.

30. Dwight Gooden and Ellis Henican, *Doc: A Memoir* (New York: Houghton Mifflin Harcourt, 2013), 153.

31. The press would begin calling Rodriguez "A-Rod" the very next week. The nickname was taken from the shortened version of his name that Rodriguez wrote on his Mariners equipment bag. "A-Rod lifs [*sic*] M's to 7-3 win," *Longview* (Washington) *News*, May 20, 1996: 23; Alan Cohen, Alex Rodriguez SABR biography, https://sabr.org/bioproj/person/alex-rodriguez/#_edn10.

32. *Doc: A Memoir*, 155.

33. David Wells with Chris Kreski, *Perfect I'm Not* (New York: Harper Collins, 2003), 274.

34 Wells, who paid $35,000 for the hat, had asked manager Joe Torre for permission to wear the hat before the game, but was turned down. As of February 2022, the hat, which Wells put up for auction in 2012, was worth over $537,000. Mike Thomas, "What Happened to the $35K Yankees Hat David Wells Wore for 1 Inning?" February 25, 2022, Sportscasting website, https://www.sportscasting.com/what-happened-to-the-35k-yankees-hat-david-wells-wore-for-1-inning/, accessed August 27, 2022.

35 Yankees MSG network TV broadcast of May 17, 1998 game, https://www.youtube.com/watch?v=gfREpwb6mPM, accessed September 1, 2022.

36 Bill Madden, "Steinbrenner Says Yogi's Job Is Safe for the 1985 Season," *New York Daily News*, February 21, 1985: 64.

37 David Goldiner, "Burying the Bitterness," *New York Daily News*, January 6, 1999: 3.

38 Bill Gallo, Owen Moritz, and Bill Hutchinson, "Yogi, Boss Lovefest Prompted by Joe D." *New York Daily News*, January 7, 1999: 5.

39 When Yankees manager Joe Torre heard that Yogi's day would fall on Joe's 59th birthday, he jokingly told Berra "Screw your day, that's my birthday." Ralph Vacchiano, "Even on Joe's Birthday, Yogi Takes Cake," *New York Daily News*, July 18, 1999: 58.

40 The Expos team payroll was described as $10 million ($75 million less than the free-spending Yankees), during the Fox TV broadcast of the game. Fox TV Broadcast of July 18, 1999 game, https://www.youtube.com/watch?v=wwod7qO4y4o, accessed September 3, 2022.

41 After the play, broadcaster Tim McCarver remarked, "A right-handed thrower doesn't get to that ball." Fox TV Broadcast of July 18, 1999 game.

42 Fox TV Broadcast of July 18, 1999 game.

43 Addie Joss of the Cleveland Naps needed only 74 pitches in his October 2, 1908, perfect game against the Chicago White Sox.

44 Jose De Jesus Ortiz, "Oswalt Hopes Shot Keeps Him off DL," *Houston Chronicle*, June 13, 2003: 10.

45 Dotel was the first Astros pitcher to strike out four batters in an inning since NL Cy Young Award winner Mike Scott did it in 1986. The last pitcher to fan four in one inning at Yankee Stadium was Chuck Finley of the Anaheim Angels on May 12, 1999.

46 Tyler Kepner, "Steinbrenner Saves Barbs for Opposing Manager," *New York Times*, June 13, 2003: D5.

47 "the number eleven," Britannica website, https://www.britannica.com/science/the-number-eleven , accessed September 25, 2022.

48 In his next start against the Yankees, on September 17 at Detroit's Briggs Stadium, Trucks allowed eight runs, seven earned, in 3⅓ innings. Since 1876, only three pitchers have allowed more runs to a team they'd no-hit when next they started against them. Trucks remains the only pitcher to throw two no-hitters in a season in which he had a losing record. Larry DeFillipo, Adonis Terry SABR biography, https://sabr.org/bioproj/person/adonis-terry/, endnote 32.

49 It was also the only Yankee Stadium no-hitter in which the visiting team had a better record coming into the game than did the Yankees.

50 The combined no-hitter thrown by three Houston hurlers against the Yankees on June 25, 2022, the first no-hitter at the new Yankee Stadium, would be a candidate for comparison to contemporary no-hitters using Statcast data.

51 Gary Belleville, "Who Threw the Greatest Regular-Season No-Hitter since 1901?" *Baseball Research Journal*, Spring 2021, https://sabr.org/journal/article/who-threw-the-greatest-regular-season-no-hitter-since-1901/.

THE MOST EXCLUSIVE CLUB ON EARTH: WOMEN WHO HAVE UMPIRED AT YANKEE STADIUM

by Perry Barber

On Sunday, September 9, 1973, Ronnie Bromm became the lone member of the most exclusive club on the planet: Women Who Have Umpired at Yankee Stadium. She held that title all by herself for a long time, and until she called an exhibition game there as part of a Yankees Old Timers vs. author George Plimpton's All-Stars contest, in the entire history of the half-century-old ballpark, no woman had ever umpired a game on that hallowed ground. Ronnie Bromm was the first, and for more than a decade afterward, the only.[1]

She was a housewife living in the Bronx with her daughter and husband, who had been her softball coach during her playing days, when she sweet-talked her way into the Stadium on a spur-of-the-moment impulse that had been 30 years in the making and dreaming and regretting. She found herself sitting behind home plate amid a group of men, women, and children who'd been selected from applications they'd mailed in, all of them there to try out for Plimpton's team of regular people pitted against a Yankees lineup featuring some of the greatest stars of recent decades, including Mickey Mantle, Joe Garagiola, Elston Howard, Moose Skowron, and Whitey Ford. Basically, it was an early iteration of Fantasy Camp, an absolute dream assignment for a woman who had given up all hope that her cruelly dashed childhood aspirations of playing for Joe McCarthy's Yankees would ever be given a second chance at coming true. Remarkably, after putting on a display of her catching talents for an hour while Plimpton and newly anointed Yankees PR director Marty Appel watched and assessed the varying degrees of skill among the 30 or so contestants, she was asked to umpire instead of catch, a role she happily embraced since she and her husband had been calling youth baseball games for the Bronx-Manhattan Sports Officials Association for the past 15 years — another extremely rare accomplishment for a housewife and mother in the 1960s and '70s. When Appel

and Plimpton asked her to umpire at the plate for the three-inning exhibition scheduled before the Brewers-Yankees game the next day, Ronnie's decades-long dream deferred became her new reality.

She wrote a brief account of that memorable experience, from which I've extracted most of the biographical information about her included in this story, and she also authored a book titled *There's No Pink in Baseball: A Memoir For Every Girl Told "Girls Can't Do That."*[2] Beyond her athletic exploits as a star softball player and then an umpire, Ronnie also added "actor" to her résumé after her triumph at the Stadium, and as far as I've been able to determine, lived in or near the Bronx all her life right up until the end, which arrived only this past April of 2022 when she died at age 93.

I think about Ronnie Bromm often, and wonder how a woman could have done what she did, something so unique, even epic in an obscure footnote-to-history kind of way, yet she never made a big deal out of it, didn't capitalize on it for any financial gain until very late in her life; *There's No Pink In Baseball* wasn't published until 2019, when she was 90 years old. I wish now more than anything that I'd met her before she died, as once I learned about her via an article in the *Newark Star-Ledger* of October 2004, I became mildly obsessed with getting to know as much about her as I could – for a very specific reason.[3]

Remember I said Ronnie Bromm was the first and only woman to umpire a game at Yankee Stadium? She retained that distinction for 12 years until another woman was tapped to umpire a 1985 high school intra-city championship there. Neither woman knew of the other back then, but I wish with all my heart they had, because *I* was that umpire: the second, one of only two, and now, sadly, the last woman to call a game at old Yankee Stadium. It was only my fifth season umpiring baseball, and my résumé at the time, as the result of having to beg for assignments from skeptical assignors, was what could charitably be described as "unimpressive" and "full of holes."

A *Daily News* article about the event identifies me as the plate umpire for the first of two games.[4] Some angel of a supervisor somewhere believed in me enough to entrust that daunting task to me, a green, 30-something former debutante and *Jeopardy!* champion who had just completed her fourth trip through the Wendelstedt Umpire School in Florida without ranking high enough in her class to secure a job as a professional umpire. Like Ronnie's, my dreams of big-league glory had been dashed, but the broken shards of my longing somehow became a mystical trail of bread crumbs leading me to 161st Street and River Avenue in the Bronx. I don't remember many details about that day or the game itself, but I do recall marveling at the sight of mushrooms peeking out among the blades of emerald green outfield grass, and afterward making my way to Monument Park with my friend Dan Berliner, where we cheerfully desecrated the memorial plaques by climbing all over them as if they were the Alice in Wonderland statue in Central Park instead of dignified

tributes to some of the greatest baseball players ever to wear the uniform. It was a heady experience for a young umpire, and just as Ronnie did, I'll cherish the memory of all of it until the last inning is played and I'm finally called safe at home, maybe by her or a mildly miffed Miller Huggins.

SOURCES

In addition to the sources cited in the Notes, please see Veronica Bromm obituary page: https://www.tributearchive.com/obituaries/24592114/veronica-elizabeth-bromm/wall

Special thanks to former Yankees P.R. director Marty Appel and to Tara Krieger.

NOTES

1   Ronnie Bromm's memories of the day are available at "The Lady Ump," *Ronnie's Memoirs* https://sites.google.com/site/ronniebromm/ladyump. Accessed December 2, 2022.

2   The book was published independently in November 2019. It is available from online book retailers.

3   Jennifer Golson, "Her Big Day in the Bronx," *Newark Star Ledger*, October 18, 2004: 15, 20.

4   Bill Travers, "Suburbia blanks city ballplayers, 13-0," *Daily News* (New York) July 25, 1985: W10. The event was the *Daily News'* Metropolitan High School Classic.

Courtesy of Perry Barber

Perry Barber was just the second woman to umpire at Yankee Stadium, in 1985.

REVISITING YANKEE STADIUM,
"THE HOUSE THAT REGGIE BUILT":
PLAYER AND STAFF REFLECTIONS
FROM THE 1970S AND 1980S

By Scott Melesky

Five former Yankees players and staff shared their thoughts on working in the renovated Yankee Stadium. I chose them because of the wide-ranging and different perspectives they had working and playing in the Stadium during their careers in baseball. Some of these players and staff were on teams that won the World Series and others were on last-place teams. Their careers varied from several years to just a few months in Yankee Stadium.

The makeup of the interviewees includes authors, superstars, and everyday players. I wanted to give the readers a reflection of how Yankee Stadium is special from an insider's point of view. The interviewees are Marty Appel, public-relations director of the New York Yankees from 1973 to 1977; Dom Scala, who was the Yankees bullpen catcher from 1978 to 1986; Billy Sample, an eight-year veteran outfielder who played for the Yankees in 1985; Steve Sax, a 13-year veteran second baseman who played for the Yankees from 1989 to 1991; and Kevin Mmahat, who pitched for New York in 1989.

Marty Appel was born and raised in Brooklyn, New York. He began working full-time for the Yankees in 1969, when he was hired by public-relations director Bob Fishel at the age of 19 to handle future Hall of Famer Mickey Mantle's fan mail. In 1970 Appel began working as an assistant public-relations director under Fishel. Three years later, new Yankees owner George Steinbrenner named Appel, at the age of 23, the youngest public-relations director in professional sports. Appel remained with the Yankees until 1977.[1]

Dom Scala became the Yankees bullpen catcher in 1978 after infielder Mickey Klutts broke his thumb warming up a pitcher before a game. The injury to Klutts infuriated Steinbrenner, who wanted to hire a full-time bullpen catcher. Scala got the job after working successfully with pitcher Dick Tidrow under the

guidance of Yankees bullpen coach Elston Howard.[2] Scala received the nickname of Disco from teammate Paul Blair for his likeness to John Travolta's Tony Manero character in the 1977 movie *Saturday Night Fever*. Scala's Yankees teammates were shocked that he talked like Manero and would disco dance in the players lounge before games with Mickey Rivers and Thurman Munson.[3] After completing his tenure with the Yankees in 1986, Scala was an advance scout for the Pittsburgh Pirates from 1987 to 1990 and coached at Adelphi University from 2004 to 2021.[4]

Billy Sample was a legendary college baseball player at James Madison University, his career batting average of .388 setting a school record. In 1976, as a junior, Sample batted .421 with 27 stolen bases and led his team to the NCAA Division II Tournament.[5] That June, he was drafted by the Texas Rangers. Sample played outfield for the Rangers, Yankees, and Atlanta Braves from 1978 to 1986. In 1985 Sample played 59 games for the Yankees and hit .288 with one home run and 15 RBIs. After retiring from baseball, Sample worked as a broadcaster and commentator. He is also a prolific writer: He has contributed to *Sports Illustrated*, the *New York Times*, and *USA Today Baseball Weekly*; self-published a book on Amazon; and produced the screenplay for the 2013 movie *Reunion 108*.[6]

Steve Sax is a former second baseman and played in the majors from 1981 to 1994. He was a five-time All-Star and won the 1982 NL Rookie of the Year and the Silver Slugger Award in 1986. Sax also played on the 1981 and 1988 World Series champion Los Angeles Dodgers teams. In his three years with the Yankees, from 1989 to 1991, Sax compiled a .294 batting average with 19 home runs and 161 RBIs. In 1989 Sax set the Yankees team record for most singles in a season with 171.[7]

YANKEE STADIUM 1923-2008

Kevin Mmahat pitched at Tulane University from 1983 to 1986 and in the minor leagues from 1987 in 1992, where he had a 35-26 record with a 3.50 ERA. On July 5, 1991, Mmahat threw a no-hitter for the Yankees' Triple-A Affiliate Columbus Clippers in a 6-0 win over the Louisville Redbirds in an International League game. In his time in the major leagues, he had four appearances with the Yankees in relief work in 1989.[8]

Melesky: Thank you everyone for your help and time. I very much appreciate it, and I greatly appreciate the recollections that you are sharing with us.

Steve, before you played for the Yankees, you were a Dodger for seven years. Were there any similarities or differences? How did Yankee Stadium and the atmosphere compare to Dodger Stadium?

Sax: One big difference that I remember between the two stadiums is the proximity to the field. In New York, the fans are very close to the field. Also, the fans in New York are more opinionated but also more knowledgeable and intense about the game. Dodger Stadium's atmosphere is also very loyal, very involved but also will leave at the bottom of the seventh inning of the game ... whereas New York was usually full for batting practice and rarely anyone left until the game was complete.

Melesky: Did you feel the tradition of past players playing at Yankee Stadium?

Sax: Oh yes, it was very highlighted at Yankee Stadium and even somewhat mystical. To know that Babe Ruth played there was almost surreal. Yankee Stadium was one of a kind and I was

honored to be part of that tradition during my tenure with the Yankees. As a history buff, I never took that for granted ever and felt the nostalgia and honor each time I set foot in the Stadium.

Scala: I absolutely felt the ghost of past players from the Babe Ruth and Lou Gehrig era. We also had some of the all-time greats come to Old Timers Day each year. Joe DiMaggio, Whitey Ford, Mickey Mantle, Yogi Berra, Johnny Mize, Bobby Richardson, Don Larsen. It was hard not to feel honored to be in the pinstripes. The old Yankee Stadium had the feel of no other stadium. The history and championships made you feel special and knowing all the greats that graced the locker room, dugout and field made you

feel ten feet tall. I wouldn't be the baseball lifer I am today if I wasn't a Yankee.

Mmahat: As far as the stadium, "Wow!" is what I have been telling family and friends for years. Deion [Sanders] and I got called up the same day. The limo driver dropped us off outside the stadium in left field. Good thing Deion was with me because the grounds crew recognized him and not me. [The Yankees grounds crew] let us in and showed us to the locker room. But first we had to walk past Monument Park. I was numb. When we actually started walking on the warning track to the first-base dugout, I was very emotional, all I could think of was the [Adidas TV commercial that ran in June 1989]. It mentioned "the smell of the fresh cut grass of Yankee Stadium."[9] My dad grew up in New Orleans and was a huge fan of the New York Yankees. When I finally got to start a game in the stadium, I was overwhelmed with the history.

Appel: The original Stadium was most magnificent of that generation of ballparks. Baseball's marketing was basically "play good, open the gates, people will come," then gift days were added in the 1960s. The second stadium did away with the pillars, added escalators and an entertaining scoreboard and people realized it was better than the original. Over time, people grew nostalgic for the first one, and when Yankee Stadium I closed in 2008, people were saying that they preferred the original one. The current one has even more creature comforts and you can still see the game from the concession stands, which are varied. It has the Yankee Museum which is free to fans and wonderfully curated. I like that fans can circle the park, discover the bleachers, party there. The original two stadiums kept the fans locked out [or in] the bleachers.

Melesky: How was the Yankee Stadium field in terms of hitting and fielding?

Sax: Yankee Stadium was well known for the "slope" from the infield to the outfield, so the batters were hitting somewhat "downhill." The character and structure while beautiful and nostalgic was not as polished as Dodger Stadium, which is impeccably groomed and pristine.

Sample: [Yankee Stadium] had corners in left field where the ball can roll in the corners forever. [It] can give the ball in the corner the "hockey rink" effect. Hal McRae hit a curving drive into the corner. I knew I had to get there in a hurry because if I can't beat the ball to the sidewall, then I'll never be able to keep McRae to a double. Well, I got to the sidewall and threw my body up against the padding to keep the ball from kicking out of the zone. It looked a bit awkward, but I did what I had to do.

Scala: It was a huge ballpark to hit homers in except to right field. Left-handed pitching always had the advantage in Yankee Stadium. The Yankee batters from 1978 to '86 were line-drive hitters and drove the ball in the gaps to score many runs.

Melesky: Is there a memorable game that stood out for you when you played and worked there?

Appel: Mickey Mantle Day was a perfect tribute as I have ever seen, before or since. It was odd that there were no presents, it was just Mick surrounded by his life story, and then the golf cart ride around the field. Beautiful. The most memorable game that I saw was Chris Chambliss's walk-off home run to beat Kansas City (7-6).

Scala: [In 1984], Dave Winfield and Don Mattingly both were exceptional hitters with power [and battled each other all season for the American League batting title]. Dave Winfield had such a quick bat, was athletic, fast, and a fantastic outfielder. They were raking that year. As you know the batting title race went to the last day. Both were class guys and rooted for each other. I remember Winny saying on the last day … "May the best man win this thing."

Mmahat: In my first game on the mound at Yankee Stadium, I was in relief against Milwaukee. In the bottom of the sixth inning, their pitcher threw at Luis Polonia. The benches emptied. In the top of the seventh, I knew I had to earn the respect of my teammates. I did not intentionally throw at batter Charlie O'Brien. I just wanted to come up and then it just so happened the ball wound up hitting him and he charged the mound. I was able to hold my own in

the brawl. That night, we flew out and my teammates were extremely proud of my efforts and treated me with respect the rest of the season. It's unfortunate that injuries plagued the remaining three years of my career, and I was not able to get off the disabled list to pitch again in New York. My cup of coffee tasted delicious even though it was a small cup.

Sax: Yes, there were several. I remember one of my first games at Yankee Stadium. We were playing the Twins the second week of the season and it was freezing cold which I do not like at all. It was a rough adjustment for me in 1989 and especially that game since I really do not like cold weather at all and especially not to play in cold weather. The press gave me a pass in the beginning as I was new in the American League, but I definitely had to earn their confidence. I hit a bloop hit that day into center field and from that moment on, the press and the New York fans warmed up to me and those years in New York were some of the best years ever for me. The fans in New York held you accountable and I loved the banners [and] support from the fans.

Sax: There was another memory that really stands out that is hard to forget. We had a day game scheduled to start at noon and we had a rain delay until 8:00 at night. Some fans stayed around during the rain delay and at around 3:00, a fan had fallen from the upper level and in the fall impaled himself on the fence below where he perished. The police came into the clubhouse as the players were just hanging out waiting for the rain to pass and asked us if we wanted to see a "dead body" so some of us went out to see it and as we arrived there was someone in the Bronx who was stealing the shoes off the impaled body. Only in New York.

Melesky: Thank you everyone for sharing your insights and stories about your time at Yankee Stadium. It is a very special place that has benefited from all your contributions to it.

NOTES

1   Irvin Cohen, "Chat with PR Maven Marty Appel," *Jewish Press,* July 7, 2010: 1-4.

2   Ray Negron, "Disco Era Begins at Yankee Stadium," *New York Sports Day*, November 18, 2019: 1-2.

3   Negron, 1-2.

4   Negron, 3-4.

5   2013 Hall of Fame Roster – 1988-Billy Sample, JMU Hall of Fame, https://jmusports.com/sports/hall-of-fame/roster/billy-sample/2201, Accessed September 5, 2022.

6   Billy Sample, *A Year in Pinstripes ... And then Some* (CreateSpace Independent Publishing Platform, 2016), 116.

7   Alan Cohen, "Steve Sax," SABR BioProject, https://sabr.org/bioproj/person/Steve-Sax/.

8   Kevin Mmahat statistics, BaseballAlmanac.com, https://www.baseball-almanac.com/players/player.php?p=mmahake01.

9   Adidas, *Fresh Cut Grass,* June 1989. https://www.youtube.com/watch?v=8GBD3T5P7mc. Accessed September 6, 2022.

9/11 AND YANKEE STADIUM

By Bill Nowlin

At Yankee Stadium over the weekend of September 7-9, 2001, the Yankees had swept the visiting Boston Red Sox. Boston was in second place, but then a full 13 games behind the Yankees. The two teams were set to play a fourth game on the evening of the 10th, but it was rained out. Boston was then to go to Tampa Bay, and the Yankees were to host the Chicago White Sox.[1]

At 8:46 on Tuesday morning, September 11, American Airlines Flight 11 crashed into the North Tower of the World Trade Center in New York City. All 87 passengers and crew aboard were killed instantly, as were the hijacker and an unknowable number of people inside the building. Less than 20 minutes later, at 9:03 A.M., another group of terrorists aboard

United Airlines Flight 175, with 65 innocents on board, piloted that plane into the South Tower. At 9:59, the South Tower collapsed and at 10:28 the North Tower collapsed as well. Some in the World Trade Center had been able to escape, evacuating before the collapse, but the death toll was large.

Two other planes were hijacked. One deliberately crashed into the Pentagon outside Washington at 9:37 A.M. A fourth plane, thought to have been one targeting the White House or the US Capitol, saw passengers rise up and fight with the terrorists; the plane crashed in a field in Somerset County, Pennsylvania.

In all, the four suicide missions claimed nearly 3,000 lives. Across the country, no one knew how

The pregame ceremonies before Game 3 of the 2001 World Series included a giant American flag in center field and President George W. Bush throwing out the first pitch.

many other airplanes there might be, or what else terrorists might have planned. Anyone who lived through that time can remember the shock and uncertainty.

Police nationwide swung into action. All regular commercial air traffic was halted, an embargo that lasted for days. Potential targets were identified, and actions were taken to try to guard against other unpredictable possibilities.

YANKEE STADIUM

Police shut down the grounds around Yankee Stadium and also scoured the nearby Macombs Dam Bridge for possible bombs. As Yankees GM Brian Cashman drove into the city from Westchester, he "saw the devastation from a distance" and got on the phone trying to make sure that all the players were accounted for. Some of them – the *New York Times* mentioned Roger Clemens and Chuck Knoblauch – lived in apartments unspecifically described as "some distance from the World Trade Center area."[2] Tino Martinez could see the smoking Towers from his window.[3]

Red Sox CEO John Harrington had been on his way to an owners' meeting in Milwaukee but his flight was diverted.[4]

Cashman acknowledged concern that Yankee Stadium itself could be a terrorist target because it was such a symbol. "I've always worried about it," he said.[5] The Stadium had been described that day as "perhaps the building that most symbolizes American sports. ... It was evacuated within 90 minutes of the first attacks on the World Trade Center." Yankees spokesman Rick Cerrone said after leaving his office, "The ballpark is ringed with police."[6]

Yankee Stadium was indeed perhaps the preeminent structure identified with American sports. It had hosted other moments related to tragedy. Pro Football Hall of Famer Larry Wilson recalled that nearly 50 years earlier, after President John F. Kennedy was assassinated in November 1963, his St. Louis Cardinals NFL team had played a game in New York. "When they announced the national anthem, the entire crowd, every person in Yankee Stadium for a sellout, rose and sang the anthem together."[7]

On September 12 the Stadium was closed. At least a couple of pitchers turned up, but were unable to gain entry.[8] Arthur Richman, a senior adviser and consultant to the Yankees, was seen leaving the empty Stadium, closed for business as were most enterprises in the area. He had been the only one there. There had been a few others for a while, but a bomb threat resulted

in their all being sent home. "I've been coming here since 1928," he said, "I can never remember being the only one in Yankee Stadium."[9]

All play was suspended, as was true throughout the sports world and much of American society. A couple of days later, on September 13, it was announced that baseball games would be called off for the week but resume on Monday, September 19. Commissioner Bud Selig and others wrestled with the decision, "weighing baseball's role as the national pastime against the need to maintain proper decorum in the face of one of the country's greatest tragedies."[10]

Two employees in the Yankees' ticket office had lost sons in the attack.[11]

BASEBALL ACTIVITIES RESUME

The Yankees had a workout at the Stadium on Saturday the 15th, getting in some throwing, fielding, and batting. But Ground Zero was very much still on their minds. "Players stood in small groups and when they talked, they spoke little of baseball."[12] Each flagpole that typically bore a banner for each team in the American League was graced by an American flag, at half-staff. Despite President Bush's call for citizens to try to resume their lives and show that America would not be cowed, Yankees third baseman Scott Brosius said it was perhaps too soon, but later said the workout was almost "therapeutic," adding, "Maybe for three hours a day we can take minds off realities."[13] After the workout, three vans of Yankees went to Manhattan to visit rescue workers at the 23rd Street Armory and St. Vincent's Hospital. Derek Jeter said, "It was good to see the people, the volunteers and the firemen and the police. They were asking for autographs and you felt like you should be asking for their autographs."[14]

The team went on the road – to Chicago and then Baltimore. It was an emotional first game in Chicago, with the team wearing New York City Fire Department and Police Department hats in pregame ceremonies. Several of the Yankees were said to have wept, and manager Joe Torre had to go back to his office to compose himself. Bernie Williams said he had never heard White Sox fans root for the Yankees before.[15]

Their first game back at Yankee Stadium was on September 25, hosting Tampa Bay.

The Mets had returned to play in New York first, at Shea Stadium hosting the Atlanta Braves on September 21. Every member of the team donated his pay for the day to a charity benefiting the families of the first responders who had lost their lives.[16] There were, of course, much tighter security measures for fans and others attending the game.

MEMORIAL SERVICE AT YANKEE STADIUM

The Yankees held a memorial service at Yankee Stadium on Sunday the 23rd. An estimated 20,000 attended the city-sponsored program, "A Prayer for America." The program, lasting for more than five hours, featured James Earl Jones and Oprah Winfrey as co-hosts. Religious leaders, the mayor, the governor of New York, both of New York's US senators, and former President Bill Clinton also attended.[17]

One essayist suggested that while "a common enemy brings people together … as does grief," there was something inherently fitting about Yankee Stadium as the venue for such a service. It brought together representatives of all faiths, including Islam. It "wasn't about God, nor was it about religion. It was about the kind of place – unique on earth, unique in history – in which such a thing is possible. And there was no mistaking what place it was, with the Bud Light and Utz potato chip and Adidas signs clearly visible behind the prelates and patriarchs."[18]

THE FIRST GAME BACK

For the Yankees' first game back in New York, there was very tight security, even including bomb-sniffing dogs in the Yankees clubhouse.[19] In pregame ceremonies on the 25th, public-address announcer Bob Sheppard disclosed that the club would erect a special memorial in the Stadium's Monument Park. Saxophonist Branford Marsalis played "Taps," and the Boys Choir of Harlem sang "We Shall Overcome," which prompted cheers during the verse "We are not afraid." Michael Bolton followed with "Lean on Me," and Ronan Tynan's voice resonated with "God Bless America" with a giant American flag as a backdrop. The national anthem was sung by Max Von Essen, the son of the New York City fire commissioner, as Challenger the bald eagle was brought to the pitcher's mound. Four emergency workers threw out the ceremonial first pitch.

The Yankees had clinched at least a tie for the division title the day before. They won the division championship on the 25th, but there was no spraying of champagne.[20] Celebrations were muted. "I guess it's kind of strange," said Roger Clemens. "To be honest with you, I was just proud to be a part of this game."[21]

Some fans made it a point to visit the Stadium. Laura Prichard, described as a lifelong Yankees fan,

lived two hours away and hadn't been to a game all year, but she made sure to come, saying, "It'll show to Americans that we can come out to a gathering like this and not be afraid." Manhattan public school teacher Richard Cirino said, "A lot of people like to go to church to feel together with the city, with different people. I get that same feeling here at Yankee Stadium, and I expect that feeling today."[22]

The Yankees lost that night, but won five of the eight games on the homestand (two losses, one tie), then wrapped up the season in Tampa Bay.[23]

THE 2001 POSTSEASON

This was a team coming off back-to-back-to-back World Series championships and aiming for a fourth. In the Division Series they prevailed against Oakland in five games, after losing the first two games at home and coming to the brink of elimination.[24] They took the best-of-seven American League Championship Series in five games over a Seattle team that had finished the season with a major-league record-tying 116 victories.[25]

At the final ALCS game, on October 22, in which the Yankees pounded the Mariners, 12-3, fans in attendance understood the gravity of what was happening as the team inched closer to the pennant. They began chanting "over-rated" at their impressive opponents in the late innings, and "No Game 6!" in response to Mariners manager Lou Piniella's guarantee that the game would go back to Seattle.[26]

Piniella managed to take the loss in stride. "This city has suffered a lot and tonight they let out a lot of emotions," he said. "And I felt good for them in that way."[27]

After the Yankees celebrated their 38th pennant with another muted clubhouse champagne toast, fans welcomed the diversion of the team's seemingly unbelievable run so far. Hundreds waited for hours outside the Stadium that night into the next morning for World Series tickets to go on sale, including Mike Burke, a carpenter working at Ground Zero.

"We are here to support the Yankees. They are going to win the World Series again," he said optimistically. "And we're going to rebuild New York again."[28]

"We need to be distracted from issues like anthrax and war," added Gilda Carle, a psychology professor at Mercy College.

And Mayor Rudolph Giuliani, who seemed never to miss an important game from his box at the Stadium, agreed. "It does so much for the civic pride of New

York," he said. "But in addition to that, it puts so much focus and attention on New York and gets people to start thinking about other things."[29]

Though much of America was always primed and predisposed to root for "any team that plays the Yankees," this year was different. Many fans across the country were rooting for the Yankees, in a certain sense of solidarity with the city.[30]

From the heart of the Red Sox/Yankees rivalry, on the day before the World Series began, the *Boston Globe* published an editorial, "New Best Friends." It started:

Go New York!

The cheer arises from an untapped well deep within the psyche of Red Sox Nation. The voice sounds strange but feels exactly right. The World Series begins tonight and the Yankees must win their fourth-in-a-row enchilada grande.

Were this a normal year, they would have to lose, and swiftly, as Boston hissed every run scored against the Diamondbacks … [but f]eeling good for the Yankees and for New York is feeling good for our country and ourselves.[31]

THE 2001 WORLD SERIES AT YANKEE STADIUM

The 2001 World Series was against the Arizona Diamondbacks. The first two games were on the road, in Phoenix, and Arizona won easily, 9-1 and 4-0. On the eve of Game Three, the first game at the Stadium, October 30, *Boston Globe* columnist Dan Shaughnessy wrote, "In the aftermath of Sept. 11, the Yankee Stadium experience has been louder and more raucous than ever. …" He noted that "each game has been preceded by an American bald eagle landing on the mound at the conclusion of the anthem."[32]

After arriving at the Stadium, Arizona Diamondbacks first baseman Mark Grace said, "I think this will be the safest place in America. I think a lesson we learned after the 11th was, not only for myself but all of us, we are not going to live our lives in fear, no way."[33]

President George W. Bush threw out the ceremonial first pitch before Game Three. Other than Jimmy Carter in 1979, Bush was the first president to throw a first pitch at a World Series game since Dwight Eisenhower had at Ebbets Field in 1956. There was exceptionally tight security with even one of the umpires a Secret Service agent in disguise, during the pregame.[34]

Bush discussed the moment afterward: "I had never had such an adrenaline rush as when I finally made it to the mound. I was saying to the crowd, 'I'm with you, the country's with you.'… And I wound up and fired the pitch. I've been to conventions and rallies and speeches: I've never felt anything so powerful and emotions so strong, and the collective will of the crowd so evident."[35]

After losing the first two games at Bank One Ballpark in Arizona, the Yankees rebounded by winning all three games at Yankee Stadium. A dominant performance from Clemens in Game Three (one run, three hits, nine strikeouts in seven innings) and two perfect innings from closer Mariano Rivera put away Game Three. Then Games Four and Five were won in extra innings – with the tying run in each coming on a two-run homer with two outs in the ninth off Diamondbacks closer Byung-Hyun Kim.

Tino Martinez hit the game-tying blast over the center-field wall in Game Four. Then, at the stroke of midnight in the bottom of the 10th, Yankee Stadium became the first ballpark to host November baseball, and Derek Jeter became "Mr. November" (per a sign held up by a fan) when he swatted the game-winner to right.

Not 24 hours later, lightning seemed to strike twice, this time off the bat of Scott Brosius. Game Five went 12 innings, with Alfonso Soriano's walk-off single scoring Chuck Knoblauch.[36]

The Yankees left New York one win away from a fourth straight championship.

Back home in Phoenix, however, the Diamondbacks scored early and often in Game Six, winning 15-2, and ultimately won the 2001 World Series by overcoming a 2-1 Yankees lead in the bottom of the ninth inning in the final Game Seven, taking the game 3-2.

It had been an important World Series in many regards, helping to some degree in healing after the death and destruction that had been visited on the country on September 11.

ACKNOWLEDGMENTS

Thanks to Tara Krieger for her assistance in preparing this article.

NOTES

1   The White Sox had arrived in New York around 2: 00 A.M. on the 11th and learned of the attacks upon waking at their Midtown hotel. See Paul Sullivan, "White Sox Find Themselves Close to Action," *Chicago Tribune*, September 12, 2001. The Red Sox flew to Tampa on Monday night.

2   Buster Olney, "Cashman Accounts for Players as Stadium Is Evacuated," *New York Times*, September 12, 2001: C18.

3   Nathan Maciborski, "Yankees Magazine: Never Forgotten," MLB.com, September 10, 2019, https://www.mlb.com/news/bernie-williams-9-11-experience.

4   Jeff Horrigan, "Tragedies Hit Hard for Fossum, Sox," *Boston Herald*, September 12, 2022.

5   He added, "They've always taken the steps necessary to protect it the best they can, but I just see what took place today. Sometimes the best steps still can't prevent things from happening." Bryan Heyman, "'No Place for Sport,'" *White Plains* (New York) *Journal-News,* September 12, 2001: C1.

6   "No Events Today; Events Postponed," *Newport News* (Virginia) *Daily News,* September 12, 2001: B3. Wire service reports said that two National Hockey league scouts had been among the passengers killed on United 175.

7   Wilson added, "I got chills then, and I got chills now thinking about it." Will McDonough, "Vivid Memories of Playing Through Pain in '63," *Boston Globe*, September 16, 2001: C1.

8   Orlando Hernandez and Jay Witasick were both mentioned. George A. King III, "Yank Minds Not on Playing," *New York Post*, September 13, 2001.

9   Rafael Hermoso, "Empty Yankee Stadium Is Filled with Eerie Sounds of Silence," *New York Times*, September 13, 2001: C14. Richman lived in Greenwich Village and said that from his window, he personally had seen the plane slam into the South Tower.

10   Dave Sheinin, "Baseball to Resume Monday," *Washington Post*, September 14, 2001: D6.

11   Ben Walker, "Baseball Leads Sports World in Return to Action," *Quincy* (Massachusetts) *Patriot Ledger,* September 17, 2001: 19. The grieving Yankees employees were vice president of ticket operations Frank Swaine and Hank Grazioso, who worked in advance ticket sales. Swaine's son, John, and Grazioso's boys, Tim and John, were all employed at Cantor Fitzgerald, on the 104th floor of the North Tower.

12   Buster Olney, "Yankees Are Back, Even if They're Not," *New York Times*, September 17, 2001: C18.

13   Joel Sherman, "Yankees Begin Long and Emotional Road Back," *New York Post*, September 16, 2001.

14   George A. King III, "Yankee Hearts Feel the Pain," *New York Post*, September 17, 2001.

15   Buster Olney, "Triumph and Cheers Greet Yanks in Return," *New York Times*, September 19, 2001: D1.

16   Tyler Kepner, "Emotional Return Home for the Mets," *New York Times*, September 21, 2001: D1. George Vecsey wrote an article on the same page of the *Times* headlined "New York's Ballparks Have Served the Nation Before."

17   Robert D. McFadden, "The Service: In a Stadium of Heroes, Prayers for the Fallen, and Solace for Those Left Behind," *New York Times*, September 24, 2001: A1.

18   Peter Freundlich, "Getting It Together," *Washington Post*, October 7, 2001: B1.

19   Dave Sheinin, "Yankees Return to City," *Washington Post*, September 26, 2001: D7.

20   They had actually lost the game, 4-0, but the Red Sox had lost their game and so the Yankees had clinched.

21   Buster Olney, "Sense of Loss Mars Yanks' Division Championship," *New York Times*, September 26, 2001: D9. Clemens also passed Bert Blyleven that night with his 3,702nd career strikeout, for what was then the third-most all-time.

22   Edward Wong, "Runs, Hits and Healing at Stadium," *New York Times*, September 26, 2011: D11.

23   The tie game with Baltimore was called, 1-1, after 15 innings due to rain and was the last road game of Cal Ripken's 21-year career.

24   The tide turned against the Athletics in Game Three at the Oakland Coliseum, in which the Yankees won a 1-0 thriller, a lead preserved when shortstop Derek Jeter's improbable "flip" from behind home plate to catcher Jorge Posada prevented Jeremy Giambi from scoring the tying run.

25   Seattle's 116 regular-season wins tied them with the 1906 Chicago Cubs for the most ever. It also broke the American League record of 114 set by the 1998 Yankees.

26   George A. King III, "Yanks Put Another Flag in Their Bag: Crush M's to Bring 38th Pennant to Bx.," *New York Post*, October 23, 2001, https://nypost.com/2001/10/23/yanks-put-another-flag-in-their-bag-crush-ms-to-bring-38th-pennant-to-bx/.

27   Opinion, "The Likeable Yankees," *New York Times*, October 24, 2001: A20.

28   Mark Stamey, "Thanks, Yanks! – Team Brings Smiles to Grieving City," *New York Post*, October 24, 2001, https://nypost.com/2001/10/24/thanks-yanks-team-brings-smiles-to-grieving-city/.

29   Stamey.

30   Firefighters in Phoenix watching the World Series, for instance, showed some support for the Yankees because of their ties to New York. Alan Feuer, "In City Primed to Hate Yankees, the Ground Zero Workers Demur," *New York Times*, October 28, 2001: A1. All the Yankees love drove Nicholas Dawidoff to pen an op-ed for the *New York Times*, "It's Still OK to Root Against the Yankees," October 20, 2001: A23.

31   "New Best Friends," *Boston Globe*, October 27, 2001: A14.

32   Dan Shaughnessy, "Yankees Fans Are Loud, Proud," *Boston Globe*, October 30, 2001: D1.

33   Gordon Edes, "A Secure Feeling at the Ballpark," *Boston Globe*, October 31, 2001: F5.

34   Bill Nowlin, "U.S. Secret Service Agent Puts His Life on the Line Posing as a Major-League Umpire," in Larry R. Gerlach and Bill Nowlin, *The SABR Book of Umpires and Umpiring* (Phoenix: SABR, 2017), 425-6.

35   Mike Bertha, "Today in Postseason History: President Bush's Iconic First Pitch at Game 3 of the '01 World Series," MLB.com, October 30, 2015. https://www.mlb.com/cut4/president-bush-throws-first-pitch-at-yankee-stadium/c-155935460.

36   Game Five of the 2001 World Series also was the last game right fielder Paul O'Neill played at Yankee Stadium. The fan favorite had hinted at retirement, and the Bleacher Creatures gave him a standing ovation before the game, chanting his name periodically throughout. Jack Curry, "On Baseball: An Emotional End for All the O'Neills," *New York Times*, November 2, 2001: S8.

CREATING A LOGO FOR THE
STADIUM'S FINAL SEASON

By Todd Radom

Over the course of my career, I have created opening and/or closing ballpark logos for numerous major-league clubs, including the Cardinals, Reds, Twins, Mets, Rangers, Braves, and others. I grew up about 10 miles north of Yankee Stadium and attended hundreds of games there, so the opportunity to create the official logo for the final season of the old ballpark was a job that I took on with knowledge and enthusiasm (even though I am a Red Sox fan, which is another story for another day).

From a visual perspective, the Yankees have a brand personality like no other franchise – austere, rooted in tradition, and devoid of excessive color and detail. Commemorating the Stadium in logo form necessitated a devolved approach and clear, direct messaging.

The club and Major League Baseball provided me with concise direction on what they wanted to be depicted. We focused on the original 1923 exterior, embracing the Gate 4 entrance. It was especially important to get the YANKEE STADIUM lettering just right. An authentic representation of the four-foot-high copper letters delivers the bulk of the information here, accompanied by a simple "1923-2008." We explored a range of retaining shapes and colors, ultimately

The logo for Yankee Stadium's final season appeared as a patch on the left sleeve of the team's uniform.

opting to bathe the façade in a romantic golden light. I couldn't help but remember my first encounter with the place, when it was a stark, bright white.

Closing logo in hand, mission accomplished, I soon moved on to the official logo for the inaugural season of the new Yankee Stadium.

RUNNING AND JUMPING AT YANKEE STADIUM, 1923 TO 1938

By Jack Pfeifer

Yankee Stadium was built for baseball, but it turned out to be an exceedingly versatile structure. Football was played there. Championship boxing, concerts, religious revivals. Popes visited. And, it turns out, track meets, beginning the year it opened, in 1923. A dozen meets were held at Yankee Stadium over the next 11 years, the last on Columbus Day 1934, a day on which the police were called to break up a riot.[1] There were also a few exhibition footraces, ending in 1938 (by 1942 the track was gone) as well as motorcycle racing, a rodeo, and a marathon, all 26 miles 385 yards of it.

The starting line was in the left-field corner. From there came a 120-yard, five-lane straightaway, between the third-base line and the stands, the finish line near home plate.[2] Was there room? Until 1937, home plate to dead left-center was 490 feet![3] It was a 400-yard cinder track, 20 feet wide, along the perimeter of the outfield. There was a sharp turn to the left just past home plate. The track was 40 yards less than regulation, so for longer races, the starting line was adjusted. Instead of a mile relay, at times that race was 4x400 (yards, not meters).

The full track during the early years of Yankee Stadium was a precursor to the "warning track" that is now a ballpark standard.

YANKEE STADIUM 1923-2008

The track wasn't *added* to the stadium. It was built that way. It was there on Opening Day, April 18, 1923, and three weeks later the first track meet – between two Bronx high-school teams – took place.[4]

Sometimes track meets and ballgames were held on the same day. In 1925 a track meet was held in the evening, after a doubleheader, under the lights, two decades before the Yankees played a night game at home.

Some meets were fundraisers. In the Olympic years – 1924, 1928, and 1932 – track meets previewed that year's Olympic Games, giving New Yorkers a chance to see America's Olympians in person.

The 1934 event drew some 25,000 fans, making it the best-attended one-day track meet in the city's history to this day.[5] That was one of the reasons to hold track meets in the stadium. There were other track venues in the city, but none with 60,000 seats.

There have been a few other American stadiums that accommodated baseball, football, and track and field – most famously the Los Angeles Memorial Coliseum, which also opened in the spring of 1923. The Coliseum hosted the 1932 Olympic Games, was home to USC and UCLA football, and, when they moved west, the Dodgers. But Yankee Stadium may have been unique as a building built for baseball that handled so many other activities.

When Triborough Stadium opened on Randalls Island in 1936, the city finally had its own signature outdoor track facility. On that stadium's Opening Day, Jesse Owens ran, qualifying for the Berlin Olympics.

MAY 7, 1923: MORRIS VS. EVANDER CHILDS

With 10,000 people – many of them students at the two schools – in the stands, Evander Childs beat Bronx rival Morris High 9-3 in a baseball game, immediately followed by a dual track meet, won by Morris, 32-30. The first-base stands were taken up by Evander students wearing their orange and black, while the third-base side was Morris maroon, including the school band. The events were the 100, 220, 440, 880, mile, and a relay.[6]

MAY 20, 1923: DAILY NEWS MARATHON

With some 30,000 people in the stands, a men's marathon was held, sponsored by the *New York Daily News*. The starting gun was fired by the Wild Bull of the Pampas, the Argentinean heavyweight Luis Firpo, who had championship fights in Ebbets Field, the Polo Grounds, and Yankee Stadium.[7]

The race was almost 116 times around the 400-yard circuit and was won by a 28-year-old toolmaker from Stamford, Connecticut, Albert "Whitey" Michelson. He ran the distance in 2:48:23⅘ and thus was credited with a world record for a marathon run on a track, rather than on the roads. (The previous best had been indoors, at Madison Square Garden, in 1909.)

As the race neared its conclusion, thousands of overly enthusiastic spectators poured out of the stands, flooding the track. The 13 finishers – 31 started – had to fight their way to the finish line.

Two years later, Michelson set the world record for the regulation marathon, running 2:29:01 in Port Chester, New York,[8] and he made the 1928 and 1932 US Olympic teams.

Unless you count a long doubleheader, it was also Yankee Stadium's final marathon.

MAY 30, 1923: FORDHAM UNIVERSITY GAMES

With 4,000 fans in attendance, the feature race was the mile, where the veteran Joie Ray was taking a shot at the world's record of 4:12.6, set in 1915 by American Norm Taber.[9] The athletes used the baseball clubhouses to change; Ray stored his clothes in The Babe's locker.

Thanks to a 25-yard handicap advantage, the first finisher was a runner from Columbia, Walter Higgins, who came across in 4:15⅗, half a second ahead of Ray.

SEPTEMBER 8, 1923: WILCO PRE-OLYMPIC GAMES

With the Yankees leading the American League by 13 games, a meet intended as a preview of the Paris Olympics – scheduled for the summer of 1924 – was held on a cool, wet, windy Saturday afternoon.[10]

In addition to running events, four field events were contested – the broad jump, high jump, pole vault, and shot put – scattered throughout the stadium.

The Yankees were on their way back from a road trip, comfortably in first place, headed to a rematch with the rival Giants in the World Series, sore from being swept the previous fall (there was one tie) when all five games had been played at the Polo Grounds, across the Harlem River in Manhattan. There were individual contests dominating the Yankees' headlines that month as well. Sam Jones was coming off a no-hitter – he was scheduled to pitch again on Monday against the A's – and Babe Ruth was battling Harry Heilmann of the Tigers for the batting crown, Tris Speaker of Cleveland for the RBI crown, and Cy Williams of the Phillies for the major-league lead in home runs. All three would come down to the final days of the season.

The track meet was held in a drizzle. The event, sponsored by the Wilco Athletic Association, drew a respectable crowd of 8,000. A portion of the gate receipts were to be donated to the Red Cross relief fund for survivors of the Great Kanto earthquake that had devastated Japan a week earlier.

For those fans who hoped to see stars of those coming Olympics, they got their money's worth. Most fans sat on the third-base side, along the straightaway.

Five American men who were to win Gold Medals in Paris – the Olympics of *Chariots of Fire* fame – competed that day. (There was also a women's relay race.) There was an international flavor to the meet, as Finland's Willie Ritola, who resided and trained in the New York area, won the 5,000. Ritola eventually won three lifetime Olympic Gold Medals, including a victory over his legendary countryman Paavo Nurmi in 1928.

The other gold medalists competing that afternoon were DeHart Hubbard in the broad jump; Harold Osborn, double Olympic champion in the high jump and decathlon; Alan Helffrich, anchor of the winning 4x400 for the Americans; and two members of the winning 4x100 team, Lou Clarke and Loren Murchison.

The big race of the day was the men's mile, where Joie Ray ran 4:14⅘.

The ballfield was then quickly reassembled overnight for baseball. The Yankees had been on the road (or the rails) – a 6-3 win over the A's in Shibe Park on Wednesday, September 5; a 10-4 defeat of the Yankees farm team in York, Pennsylvania, in which even the big man, Ruth, played, hitting two home runs; then south to the nation's capital, where they were shut out by the Senators, 4-0.

As Sunday the 9th dawned, The Babe was two behind Williams in home runs, with 33, and one point behind Heilmann in batting average, at .393. The Yankees swept the Red Sox that day, 6-2 and 4-0. Ruth hit number 34, an inside-the-parker, and the two games were played in a *combined* 3 hours and 30 minutes.

The next day, Jones pitched six more no-hit innings, extending his streak to a record 15 consecutive no-hit innings, and for the second day in a row, Ruth homered – again inside the park.

Ruth finished the 1923 campaign with 41 homers, 130 RBIs, and a .393 batting average but did not win the Triple Crown. He tied with Speaker – player-manager that year for the Indians – in RBIs, equaled

Williams, the NL leader, for HRs, but lost the AL batting crown to Heilmann, who hit .403.

In the World Series, in spite of two game-winning home runs by the Giants' Casey Stengel, the Yankees prevailed, four games to two, their first championship.

JUNE 7, 1924: EASTERN OLYMPIC TRIALS SECTIONAL TRYOUT

With the final selection meet for the 1924 Olympic team one week away in Boston, there was an excellent turnout of Olympic hopefuls. In the stands, the biggest noise came from the right-field bleachers, where an enthusiastic crowd of students from Stuyvesant High School in Manhattan came to cheer for a fellow student, Frank Hussey, that year's city schoolboy sprint champ. Grantland Rice covered the meet for the *New York Herald Tribune*.[11]

Running against veterans, Hussey did not disappoint, finishing a close third behind two future Olympians, Jackson Scholz and J. Alfred LeConey. Scholz won the Olympic 200-meter Gold Medal that summer in Paris, defeating the legendary Brit Eric Liddell, while Hussey qualified for the US relay pool and led off the American 4x100 team that won the Olympic championship and broke the world record.[12]

Some of the event winners that day included Sabin Carr, a 19-year-old prep-school student who later became the first man to pole vault 14 feet;[13] 45-year-old Pat McDonald, the 1912 Olympic champion in the shot put who directed traffic in Times Square as a New York City cop, and Leroy Brown, a Dartmouth grad, who had some good tries at 6-7¾ in the high jump, just shy of the world record.[14]

MAY 26, 1925: FINNISH-AMERICAN A.C. MEET

Yankee Stadium was a busy place on Tuesday, May 26. Thousands of baseball fans showed up early to watch Ruth – who had yet to play a game that season – take batting practice. He was released from St. Vincent's Hospital that day after a seven-week stay during which he lost 30 pounds and showed he might be able to play baseball again.[15] At 1:30, the Yankees and Red Sox began a doubleheader, each winning a game, The Babe a spectator. The ballclubs needed to get off the field, because there was a track meet at the Stadium, that night!

It would be years before the Yanks, or any other major-league team, played night baseball – the first night game at the Stadium was in May 1946 – but Yankee Stadium was outfitted for an evening track meet. It began at 7:45 P.M. and lasted until 10, with some 20,000 in attendance.[16] Floodlights that had been set up in 1924 for a rodeo were used to illuminate the track. Night events began there with boxing, using a lighted ring, in 1923.

The big draw was the Flying Finn, Paavo Nurmi, who was wrapping up a monthslong tour of the United States. He took on and defeated all comers, at all distances, rushing by overnight train from city to city, in a lucrative grand tour, but on this night, he ended the stay in defeat, losing the 880 to New Yorker Alan Helffrich, a star runner in his own right, who ran 1:56⅘ for the win.

Miller Huggins' Yankees, meanwhile, had a disastrous season, finishing next to last. Ruth played 98 games and hit .290 with 25 homers, the last time he would fail to win the home-run crown until 1932.

SEPTEMBER 14, 1925: KNIGHTS OF COLUMBUS MEET

Some 5,000 people attended on a Monday afternoon. The Yankees were in Philadelphia playing the A's.

The feature race, the 880, was won by Pincus Sober, captain of the City College of New York team, who defeated a powerhouse field of Philip Edwards of New York University, George Marsters of Georgetown, and the Olympian Alan Helffrich in 1:57⅖.[17] Sober went on to a lifetime in the sport in New York, as an administrator and meet announcer.

JULY 7, 1926: ST. JOHN THE DIVINE BENEFIT

A meet was held to benefit restoration work on the Cathedral of St. John the Divine, in Upper Manhattan.[18] The feature event was the shot put, with competition held with 8-pound, 12-pound and 16-pound implements. John Kuck, a student at Kansas State, won all three – 68-75/8, 57-9¼, and 48-3½. World records were claimed for the smaller weights. Two years later, Kuck became Olympic champion and set the world record.[19]

It was an international show, including wins by Pierre Lewden of France in the high jump, Ove Anderson of Finland in the 3,000, and Sweden's Sten Petterson, a three-time Olympian, in both hurdles.

After the disastrous 1925 season, the Yankees turned the corner, winning the AL in '26 but losing to the Cardinals in seven games in the Series. Ruth returned to form – 47 home runs and 153 RBIs but was again denied the Triple Crown when he lost the batting title to the Tigers' Heinie Manush .372 to .378.

JUNE 16, 1928: EASTERN SECTIONAL OLYMPIC TRYOUTS

The final US Olympic Trials were three weeks away, in Boston. For some competitors, this was a final tune-up; for others, a hope that they had a shot at the team. Commuter trains stopped at the Stadium. The fare was 5 cents.

Four events were held elsewhere a day later. "One reason the steeplechase has been transferred to Travers Island," the *New York Times* slyly wrote, "along with the hammer, discus and javelin, is that the Yankee ball club objected to having a big hole dug in the outfield to provide a pond for the water jump."[20]

A number of athletes who would make the 1928 team competed that day, including Boston's Lloyd Hahn, fifth in the Olympic 800; Leo Lermond, fourth in the Olympic 5-K; New Jerseyan John Gibson, 400 hurdles; and Penn State's Alfred Bates, bronze in the broad jump.[21]

Paying little heed to the Olympics in Amsterdam the Yankees and their stars – Ruth hitting third and Lou Gehrig fourth – were on a tear, sweeping the 1927 Series from the Pirates and 1928 from the Cardinals.

JUNE 17, 1929: WINGATE FUND BENEFIT

On a steamy summer night in front of 5,000 spectators, Lermond came close to the world and American records in the mile, running 4:13.0. He was paced by Brooklyn's Gus Moore, who ran 440-yard splits of 61-2:09-3:11 before finishing a close second in 4:15, the fastest mile of his career.[22]

JUNE 11, 1932: SENIOR MEETS

The local AAU Association meet, a major annual event on the New York City track calendar, was held at Yankee Stadium for the only time in its long and storied history, with 4,000 in attendance.[23]

Some historic meet records were broken, including Pete Bowen running 48.4 to break Maxey Long's 1897 record in the 440, and Otto Rosner running 1:54.4 to break Mel Sheppard's 880 record from 1911. Both Long and Sheppard had been Olympic champions in their day. In the triple jump, Sol Furth, a graduate of NYU and New Utrecht High School in Brooklyn, jumped 48-3 to break Platt Adams's 1914 record.

In baseball, the A's dominated the game in 1929-30-31, winning two World Series, but Joe McCarthy's Yankees ballclub won 107 in 1932 and swept the Cubs in the Series.

SEPTEMBER 10, 1932: VICTORY TRACK & FIELD GAMES, SPONSORED BY THE WETHERED J. BOYD COUNCIL OF THE KNIGHTS OF COLUMBUS

A month after the LA Olympics had ended on the West Coast, New York fans got the chance to see some of the stars of those Games in person.

Philip Edwards, a 1930 NYU graduate, and Alex Wilson, who between them won five medals in LA for Canada, ran individual and relay races. Edwards won the mile while he and Wilson teamed up to run an odd relay distance, 4x400 yards – because the track at the Stadium was 400 yards. The Canadian squad won in 3:01.7. Another unusual relay, the 4x800 yards, was won by the German AC, in 7:04.7.[24]

Wilson was upset in the 400-yard dash by Milton Sandler, a graduate of Townsend Harris High School in Queens and NYU, in 45.5 seconds. Sandler went on to dental school and served in the Pacific in World War II.

Edwards went on to medical school at McGill University in Montreal, specializing in tropical diseases. He won a Gold Medal for his native British Guiana in the Commonwealth Games in 1934 and made three more finals at the Berlin Olympics in 1936.

Ralph Metcalfe, double LA sprint medalist, won the 100 meters (10.6) and 150 yards (14.5), and New Yorker George Spitz took the high jump (6-4). The shot put was won by the Olympic champion, Leo Sexton (52-5½), a Georgetown graduate.

The Yankees were in Detroit, where they swept a doubleheader from the Tigers, to increase their lead in the American League to 13 games, on their way to the World Series victory over the Cubs, their first in four years. An aging Babe Ruth missed the games in Detroit because of an attack of appendicitis.[25] For the first time in seven seasons, he failed to win the home-run title, despite hitting 41. He did however hit two homers in Game Three against the Cubs, including the famous "called shot" off Charlie Root.

OCTOBER 12, 1934: AMERICAN-ITALIAN UNIVERSITY GAMES

Before a raucous Columbus Day crowd of 25,000, the United States beat an excellent Italian team, 8-5.[26] But it was action outside the Stadium that got the headlines.

The biggest race of the day was the 1,500, where the reigning Olympic champion, Luigi Beccali, defeated the American Joe McCluskey by 30 yards. McCluskey came back to win the 3-K.

By 1934, Benito Mussolini had been in control of Italy for a decade, and Adolf Hitler was taking over Germany. In New York these developments produced an outcry as some 3,000 anti-Fascists surrounded the Stadium in protest. While inside Yankee Stadium some fans wore the notorious "black shirts," outside signs read, "Down with Fascism!" Eventually, the police were called and three people were arrested for civil disorder.[27]

The Yankees did not make the Series that year, bested by the Tigers in the AL after finishing second to the Senators the year before. With the arrival of a young Joe DiMaggio, New York returned to dominance, winning every Series from 1936 to '39. And by then, another world war was on the horizon.

EXHIBITION EVENTS: JULY 5, 1930

With the Yankees on the road in Washington, several footraces were held during the intermission of a Negro Leagues doubleheader between the Lincoln Giants and the Baltimore Black Sox. The activities, before 15,000 fans, were a benefit for the Brotherhood of Sleeping Car Porters. Philip Edwards ran the 880 and NYU teammate Sol Furth the 100.[28]

SEPTEMBER 7, 1937, AND SEPTEMBER 7, 1938: PARADE OF STARS

Parade of Stars fundraisers were staged at the Stadium by the Police Athletic League, broadcast by WOR Radio and attended by 35,000 to 40,000 people, many of them children from local hospitals, orphanages, and children's homes.

In addition to some track races, in 1937 there was a scrimmage between the Fordham University and Brooklyn Dodgers football teams, while Yankees stars including Lou Gehrig and Joe DiMaggio took batting practice. Baseball, football, running – a busy day at the ballyard.[29] As part of the activity in 1938, New York City's finest had a tug of war.[30] This is believed to have been the final time the Yankee Stadium track was used for competitive races.

When the track was pulled out, it was replaced by grass that went all the way to the outfield wall. The "warning track," now standard in ballparks, became mandatory in parks in 1950, especially as a result of collisions the Dodgers' Pete Reiser had with the left-field wall in Ebbets Field.[31]

ACKNOWLEDGMENTS

The author is indebted to Brian Richards and his former assistant, Danny Cohen, of the Yankees; Cassidy Lent and Jim Gates (retired) of the Hall of Fame; Bob McGee, author of *Ebbets Field: The Greatest Ballpark Ever*; and SABR colleague David S. Johnson, of Philadelphia, for their invaluable research assistance.

NOTES

1 Correspondence with Brian J. Richards, museum curator, New York Yankees, and Danny Cohen, November 1, 2022.

2 Jack Masters, "Joie Ray Will Try for Record at Yankee Park," *New York Tribune*, May 14, 1923: 14.

3 Philip J. Lowry, *Green Cathedrals: The Ultimate Celebration of all Major League and Negro League Ballparks,* fifth edition (Phoenix: Society for American Baseball Research, Inc., 2019), 213.

4 A photo of the Stadium before it opened, showing the track, is available at this link: https://www.gettyimages.com/detail/news-photo/general-view-of-yankee-stadium-the-new-ballpark-for-the-new-news-photo/73495008. Accessed November 21, 2022.

5 George Currie, "Joe McCluskey Wins Race He Wanted to Pass Up after Bowing to Beccali," *Brooklyn Daily Eagle*, October 13, 1934: 8.

6 "Evander Nine Wins Before 10,000 Fans," *New York Times*, May 8, 1923: 15.

7 Jack Masters, "Albert Michelson, Stamford Runner, Shatters World's Record in Winning Marathon Race," *New York Tribune*, May 21, 1923: 16.

8 Richard Hymans and Imre Matrahazi, *Progression of IAAF World Records* (Monaco: IAAF, 2015), 370.

9 "Higgins Beats Ray in Handicap Race," *New York Times*, May 31, 1923: 19.

10 "Ray Runs Fast Mile in Meet at Stadium," *New York Times*, September 8, 1923: 124.

11 Grantland Rice, "Scholz Flashes to Victory over Leconey and Hussey at Stadium," *New York Tribune*, June 8, 1924: C1.

12 Hymans and Matrahazi, 164.

13 Hymans and Matrahazi, 164.

14 Rice, C4.

15 "Ruth Is Discharged from the Hospital," *New York Times*, May 27, 1925: 19.

16 Richards Vidmer, "Nurmi Beaten by Helffrich Before 20,000 in Farewell Race," *New York Times*, May 27, 1925: 18.

17 James P. Dawson "Michelson Takes 15-Mile Title Run," *New York Times*, September 15, 1925: 21.

18 "Kuck Smashes Two World's Shot-Put Records in Meet at the Yankee Stadium," *New York Times*, July 8, 1926: 23.

19 Hymans and Matrahazi, 184.

20 John Kieran, "Sports of The Times," *New York Times*, June 16, 1928: 22.

21 "Hahn and Gibson Set Track Marks," *New York Times*, June 17, 1928: 139.

22 Arthur J. Daley, "Mile Run in 4:13 by Lermond in Wingate Fund Meet at Yankee Stadium," *New York Times*, June 18, 1929: 42.

23 Arthur J. Daley, "New York A.C. Team Wins Track Title," *New York Times*, June 12, 1932: 105.

24 Arthur J. Daley, "Meet Honors Won by Canadian Stars," *New York Times*, September 11, 1932: S1.

25 "Ruth Much Better, Escapes Operation," *New York Times*, September 11, 1932: B7.

26 Louis Effrat, "Beccali Captures 1,500 by 30 Yards," *New York Times*, October 13, 1934: 17.

27 "Cracked Skulls Are Remembrances of Columbus Day," *Brooklyn Daily Eagle*, October 13, 1934: 21. An 11-minute film clip from Fox Movietone News resides in the University of South Carolina film archive and is viewable at this link: https://digital.tcl.sc.edu/digital/collection/MVTN/id/1422/rec/13.

28 "Lincoln Giants Split with Baltimore Team," *New York Times*, July 6, 1930: 117.

29 "Children Dazzled by Stars' Parade," *New York Times*, September 8, 1937: 25.

30 "40,000 Youths See Police Sports Fete," *New York Times*, September 8, 1938: 25.

31 Peter Morris, *A Game of Inches: The Story Behind the Innovations That Shaped Baseball* (Chicago: Ivan R. Dee, 2010), 388.

RODEOS AND CIRCUSES AT YANKEE STADIUM

By Sharon Hamilton

The same year in which the House That Ruth Built began to house baseball games, it also hosted events of a very different sort. That summer, workers laid down 100,000 square feet of mats made from coconut coir to save "Babe Ruth's front yard" from possible damage during the first rodeo held at Yankee Stadium, which ran from August 15 to August 26, 1923. This protection proved necessary in more ways than imagined. The planned entertainments for Yankee Stadium that summer included a Tex Austin Rodeo that spun wildly out of control: on the event's opening day, a cowgirl was trampled by a wild horse; a rider was thrown by an angry steer and seriously injured; and spectators in lower left-field seating had to scramble for cover while cowboys "raced over seats" to secure the angry animal.[1] The unconscious rider was taken to a hospital with a suspected skull fracture, but without the protective mats in place the immediate outcome could have been much worse.[2]

Over its history the original Yankee Stadium witnessed numerous non-baseball events, including rodeos and circuses.[3] Such events could occupy the space for an extended time; for example, an advertisement for the Tex Austin Rodeo that managed to go so disastrously wrong on its first day said it would occupy Yankee Stadium for 11 days.[4] These miscellaneous events proved reliably popular, attracting large crowds, and thus contributed to some of the ballpark's largest yearly attendance records.

For example, a nine-day rodeo held from May 30 to June 7, 1947, attracted 27,000 spectators to its first performance in Yankee Stadium.[5] This show – which was billed as a "Rodeo and Thrill Circus" – promised its audiences not only "bronc riding" and "bull-dogging" cowboys and cowgirls but also "dare-devil stunts by motion-picture stunt men" who would crash motorcycles through "flaming barriers."[6] Events like these contributed to Yankee Stadium's record-setting

Bonnie McCarroll riding Morning Glory, Tex Austin's Rodeo, Yankee Stadium.

attendance that year, although baseball still brought in the most attendees. An article at year's end observed that even without "the benefit of any championship boxing matches and the Army-Notre Dame game," people had gone to Yankee Stadium "in greater numbers than ever before," with an attendance record of 3,415,957. The largest part of that number came from fans going to Yankees games along with other baseball events, including Negro Leagues matches. The rest of the total came from attendance at such entertainments as football, soccer, and rodeo.[7]

Circuses also numbered among the ballpark's other sources of funding from miscellaneous events. These performances could be quite the spectacle. Reading about them in retrospect feels somewhat surreal – like something in a dream. An article promoting the Cole Brothers Circus that ran at Yankee Stadium for five days from June 21 to 25, 1950, said the event would feature "personnel of 1,080" along with "500 horses," as well as elephants, camels, zebras, llamas, and an assortment of "jungle beasts."[8] The act also promised that the Wallenda aerialist family would defy death in a "seven-human pyramid 120 feet above the ground."[9]

A review of the show, once it opened, reported that it had left "12,000 patrons, mostly small fry, hoarse from shouting and whistling." The three-hour show, for which three rings had been placed on the "lush green infield," included a bravura moment from a wire-walker. Witnesses recalled that she climbed to the top of a "116-foot sway pole in short centerfield." Lights focused on her as she tilted the top section of the pole at "precarious angles" before planting her foot in a loop and sliding upside down along a "sharply angled rope from centerfield to home plate."[10]

Holding circuses and rodeos at Yankee Stadium brought in more attendees, and therefore more revenue, but also served as source of tension. In October 1923, just a few months after the first rodeo had been held in the stadium, a headline in the *New York Times* proclaimed, "Johnson Puts Ban on Bouts in Park," with the subheading, "Rodeos Also Frowned On." American League President Ban Johnson expressed his opinion that baseball and prizefighting "do not go together." He explained that the league was "opposed to the association of the two sports" and had "taken a stand against the use of its parks for prize fights." He also said he was against holding rodeo contests "such as were held in the Yankee Stadium recently" on the basis that "it was impossible to keep the fields in good condition if such contests were permitted."[11]

In 1947 Joe DiMaggio expressed similar concerns directly to Larry Sunbrock, promoter of the "World's Greatest Rodeo and Thrill Circus," just before their early-summer show in Yankee Stadium. DiMaggio pleaded with Sunbrock not to "ruin our ball park." DiMaggio's worries were understandable. The Yankees were on their way to being World Series winners, and DiMaggio the season's most valuable player. A sportswriter expressed understanding of DiMaggio's position, observing: "This is a common first reaction of ball players and fans" when a rodeo moves into a baseball arena; "They can vision pennants skipping out of the window as a ground ball skids off a hoof-print left by a Brahma bull."[12]

The controversial nature of holding rodeos and circuses in a major-league ballpark may have contributed to the relatively small number of such events that appear to have taken place within the confines of the original Yankee Stadium. More often such events took place at Madison Square Garden or on grounds near the Stadium.[13] When such entertainments took place in the ballpark itself, it appears this was sometimes motivated by extenuating circumstances, for example repairs taking place to Madison Square Garden in 1923.[14]

While the hosting of such events as rodeos and circuses in a ballpark generated understandable concern from ballplayers, there is ultimately something symbolically appropriate about the fact that such awe-inspiring events as rodeos and circuses took place at Yankee Stadium. The articles proclaiming these events promised wondrous acts: prodigious feats of strength and courage in staying on angry steers, and human pyramids towering skyward. There is a similarity in that to baseball, a sport in which a defensive maneuver – one involving a particularly impressive act of concentration and athleticism – is referred to as a "circus catch."

This sports idiom perfectly captures such seemingly impossible plays as that, in 2015, of Blue Jays outfielder Kevin Pillar appearing to fly up a left-field wall to catch a baseball torpedoing over its top. Professional baseball, like a circus or a rodeo, is at base a form of entertainment involving an exchange of money for amusement. But it too can seemingly transcend this reality. At their best, each of these forms of human diversion possesses within it an extraordinary ability. These are amusements capable of metamorphosing before our eyes into the actuality of what the carnival barkers promise: spectacles worthy of our astonishment.

NOTES

1 "Cowboy Badly Hurt, Thrown by a Steer," *New York Times*, August 16, 1923: 10.

2 The injured cowboy, Buford (or Beauford) B. Polk (born 1885), survived this rodeo incident and made it to 1958 when, on March 22, he died in Payson, Arizona; see "Arizona, Mesa LDS Family History Center, Obituary Index, 1959-2014," FamilySearch database, Beauford Brown B.b. Polk, 1958.

3 For example, a detailed breakdown of attendance at Yankee Stadium for 1947 included the following baseball events: Yankees home games, the World Series, Yankees vs. Giants, as well as "Negro baseball," amateur baseball, other exhibitions, and tickets allotted for the Yankee Juniors organization. (The Yankee Juniors provided free tickets to teenagers to "combat juvenile delinquency." See "Yanks Give Free Tickets," *New York Times*, May 1, 1947: 30 and "Hardy Adult Fans Jam Stadium, but Many 'Free' Seats Go Begging," *New York Times*, December 15, 1947: 37.) Nonbaseball events that year included football, rodeo, and exhibition soccer. A note in the article mentions that there had been three boxing matches among miscellaneous events at the Stadium in 1946 but none in 1947. See "Crowds in 1947 Set Mark for Stadium," *New York Times*, December 28, 1947: 97. An article on attendance in 1948 at Yankee Stadium listed similar baseball and nonbaseball events as in 1947, noting that in 1948 the Stadium hosted football games of various sorts, along with boxing, rodeo, soccer games, and rallies. See John Drebinger, "Yanks Surpassed 2-Million Mark in Attendance Third Year in a Row," *New York Times*, December 30, 1948: 25.

4 "Cowboys Invade Stadium," *New York Times*, August 15, 1923: 17.

5 "Rodeo Opens 9-Day Run," *New York Times*, May 31, 1947: 17.

6 "Stadium Rodeo Nears," *New York Times*, May 29, 1947: 17.

7 "Crowds in 1947 Set Mark for Stadium," *New York Times*, December 28, 1947: 97. An article a year later broke down the attendance by category.

John Drebinger, "Yanks Surpassed 2-Million Mark in Attendance Third Year in Row."

8 "Circus Here June 21 at Yankee Stadium," *New York Times*, June 6, 1950: 31. A photograph in the *New York Times* shows the elephants of the Cole Brothers Circus lined up in front of Yankee Stadium. See "A New Herd Marches on the Yankee Stadium," *New York Times*, June 20, 1950: 22.

9 "Circus Here June 21 at Yankee Stadium."

10 "Cole Circus Opens at Yankee Stadium," *New York Times*, June 23, 1950: 36.

11 "Johnson Puts Ban on Bouts in Park," *New York Times*, October 20, 1923: 13. Although Johnson was opposed to prizefighting in Yankee Stadium, that does not appear to have stopped it from happening. Notable championship bouts took place in the original Yankee Stadium regularly during its history, including throughout the 1920s. See "Other Events at the Original Yankee Stadium," *2022 Yankees Media Guide*: 405.

12 "Conservative AP Recognizes Importance of Big Sid, Gives Him Feature Writeup," *Knoxville Journal*, June 5, 1947: 16. Big Sid was a bull in the "World's Greatest Rodeo and Thrill Circus." According to this article, other ballparks that hosted this same rodeo and circus included Braves Field in Boston, Briggs Stadium in Detroit, Wrigley Field in Chicago, and Crosley Field in Cincinnati. With respect to the controversies surrounding possible damage to the field, the event organizer Larry Sunbrock claimed "not a single ground ball" had "ever gone astray" because of his show.

13 For example, the "Miller Brothers' 101 Ranch Wild West Show" took place for 15 days on the grounds north of Yankee Stadium. See "Rodeo Halts Traffic," *New York Times*, July 22, 1928: 34.

14 The article "Late Bob Crosby, Rodeo Star," *Lubbock* (Texas) *Avalanche-Journal*, December 28, 1970: 6 says "the world's top rodeo" took place in Yankee Stadium in 1923, because Madison Square Garden was under repair.

GRUNTS, GROANS AND THEATER

Wrestling at Yankee Stadium

By Luis Blandon

Sir Ray Davies of The Kinks wrote and sang in "Over the Edge": "Everybody is a victim of society, Comedy, tragedy, vaudeville, variety, Pantomime players in the grand tradition, Forced into roles that leave them totally driven."[1] The melodic lyric unknowingly described the phenomenon of professional wrestling in the United States.

On the amateur level, wrestling is a sport. On the professional level, it is vaudeville theater. The ring is the stage. The wrestlers are the pantomime. The audience are active participants. It is elaborate and bombastic with thrills and comedy. This is the heartbeat of pro wrestling. A fight for glory, realistic violence, and manufactured championships. It tells a story. It is an escape from reality.

In the first half of the twentieth century, wrestling's popularity in the United States was just below that of baseball, horse racing, and boxing. In New York City, matches were held at each iteration of Madison Square Garden, the Seventy-First Regiment Armory, Bronx Coliseum, St. Nicholas Rink, the Broadway Arena, the Coney Island Velodrome, Queensboro Stadium, and sometimes, perhaps reluctantly in a handful of instances, Yankee Stadium in the Bronx.

The original Yankee Stadium evolved into baseball's hallowed grounds from the moment it opened in 1923. Iconically known as "The House That Ruth Built" and as the birthplace of Yankees' winning history, "The Cathedral of Baseball" hosted an abundance of sporting and nonsporting events during its existence on East 161st Street and River Avenue in the Bronx.

Professional wrestling has a hold on a segment of the American sports-watching population and the heartbeat of the sport has been in New York City with Madison Square Garden serving as its mecca. Since 1879, professional wrestling has been on the Garden's calendar, evolving into a profitable attraction for the promoters and for the arena's owners. Though the Garden was anointed "wrestling's holy grounds," the five boroughs of New York had several venues where wrestling matches were held.[2] Syndicates or cartels controlled professional wrestling by territory, dictating who won or lost, who was a champion, and who was a good or bad guy. Battle plans and strategy were prepared and acted out and championship bouts were critical to the sport and for the profits for all involved. It was an act, as noted by the *New York Times* in 1934: "The wrestling fans of New York and

The match between Antonino Rocca and Don Eagle, postponed to July 12 due to rain, received poor reviews for its length and lack of an interesting story line.

vicinity are accustomed to airplane spins, grind and lofty tumbling, butting, gouging and common assault and battery in the good-natured guise of wrestling, all in a spirit of fun."[3]

When Yankee Stadium open its doors in 1923, it was apparent that it would compete with the Polo Grounds for non-baseball events. It was expected that "there probably will be frequent boxing bouts and wrestling bouts" at Yankee Stadium.[4] Instead, wrestling evolved as a minor bit player.

Wrestling matches were performed in Yankee Stadium in 1931, 1933, and 1935. From 1936 until 1950, no matches were held there. The following are stories of four cards, the charity that benefited from the matches, and the story of an Italian heavyweight boxer, nicknamed the Ambling Alp, who boxed and wrestled on the hallowed infield.

CARD #1: THE FREE MILK FUND FOR BABIES

Millicent Hearst was the wife of publisher William Randolph Hearst. Married on April 28, 1905, and having raised five sons, they separated in 1933.[5] An active philanthropist in New York focused on poverty and children, Millicent Hearst founded the Free Milk Fund for Babies, Inc. in 1921.[6] The fund provided daily milk to children of families in need. For decades, the Free Milk Fund was the beneficiary of donations from charitable contributions collected from the percentage of tickets sold at events throughout the city such as movie premieres, Broadway openings, Metropolitan Opera festivities, fashion shows, and boxing and wrestling matches.[7] By 1950, the Fund had distributed "9,252,453 quarts of milk free."[8]

The Free Milk Fund shared in the proceeds of the wrestling cards held at Yankee Stadium. One of these first occurred in a 10-match card on June 29, 1931. Promoter Jack Curley expected "the event to surpass anything ever attempted in wrestling."[9] With Mayor Jimmy Walker in attendance, "a throng of 30,000" arrived to see the festivities.[10] The card featured the Golden Greek, Jim Londos, retaining his heavyweight title "in a grueling struggle" that kept the crowd "on edge for the entire duration of the thrilling match," pinning Ray Steele in a double armlock and half-nelson in 1:09:34.[11] "Standing groggily with his hand on the top strand of the ring rope," Londos took in the adulation of the fans.[12] With receipts totaling $63,000 ($1,238,338.01 in 2022 dollars), the Free Milk Fund "profited handsomely from the battle."[13] The 11:00 P.M. curfew was extended by the head of the New York State Athletic Commissioner, Brigadier General

John J. Phelan, so the championship match could be held.

CARD #2: A SOGGY MESS

On June 12, 1933, the Free Milk Fund shared in the profits from the eight-match card that featured Jim Browning keeping his heavyweight title, defeating Jumping Jack Savoldi, the former Notre Dame grid-iron star. The event drew 6,000 spectators who braved a wet, dreary evening with rain a constant presence. When the wrestlers were introduced, "rain descended and the few spectators who occupied ringside seats rushed for the grandstand."[14] The two men "pulled, tugged and battered each other until 11 o'clock[,]" when the curfew halted the grappling.[15] The match was awarded to Browning by decision in 1:18:05. The afternoon rains quelled the expected high attendance and gate.

CARD #3: CHAMP DEFENDS TITLE

In the 1930s, wrestling was controlled by the "Trust." It was a cartel or syndicate of promoters who determined what happened in wrestling, whom to put their financial resources behind, and who would be the champion. The Trust determined in 1935 that Irishman Danno O'Mahony was to be the champion instead of Jim Londos.[16] According to wrestling historian Tim Hornaker, Londos received $50,000 ($1,040,036 in 2022 dollars) for losing the title to O'Mahony on June 27, 1935 in Boston.[17]

The July 8, 1935, six-match wrestling card was the last one held at Yankee Stadium until 1950. Jack Curley predicted a crowd of 20,000 and a profitable gate because "interest in the bout was widespread."[18] The featured match was heavyweight title match between O'Mahony and Chief Little Wolf of Trinidad, Colorado (his real name was Ventura Tenario).

The year 1935 saw O'Mahony as "arguably the most famous Irish sports star in the world."[19] His rise was rapid from a private in the Irish Free State Army at the end of 1934 to coming to United States on a leave of absence and being encouraged to wrestle by his manager, Jack McGrath. O'Mahony was known for the "Irish Whip," which saw him lift his opponent over his shoulder and throwing him onto the mat. Wolf used his "Indian Death Lock," a leg hold, to defeat his foes. In press accounts of the era, racism and stereotypes were in the forefront. The *New York Daily News* said "[L]ogic dictates that Danno will down the Chief because con-census [*sic*] figures show that there are more brogues than war-whoops in our fair city."[20] The ring was built upon home plate. A crowd of 40,000 was expected. The Milk Fund "will slice 10 per cent. of the gate receipts."[21]

Little Wolf was born in Hoehne, Colorado, second of four children of Porfirio (Joseph) Tenario, "half Navajo-half Spanish," and his wife, Maria Soleila "Mary" Tenario, "a full-blooded Navajo Indian."[22] He was known for his compassion for children, performing Navajo dances in children's hospitals. With his success in the ring, Wolf acquired "a 500-acre ranch near Trinidad, Colorado, where he raised cattle and horses and grew sugar beets."[23] He later became a wrestling icon in Australia.

Far from the promised near-sellout, 12,000 spectators walked through the turnstiles to see O'Mahony's first title defense. The wrestlers were introduced in costumes befitting a vaudeville-era production. O'Mahony was clad in a green dressing gown alluding to a golfer that "made you ache for a putter and ball."[24] Wolf wore a blanket adorned with images of Native Americans and culture that "looked as if someone had taken a snapshot of the inside of an Indian trading post."[25] Likely part of the script, before the match Wolf primped and bellowed in the ring, "Whooooooo" at the seated patrons.[26] Wolf dominated the match until the act's climax, when O'Mahony pinned him to the mat after several forearms to Wolf's face that bloodied his nose. Defending his "title," O'Mahony won the match via a pinfall, after 28 minutes and 23 seconds.[27]

Both men had tragic outcomes later in life. In 1958 in Melbourne, Australia, Chief Little Wolf suffered a series of devastating strokes "that badly affected one side of his body and face" and left him wheelchair-bound for the rest of his life.[28] Highly respected in Australia, he lived at the Mount Royal Special Hospital for the Aged from 1961 to 1980, then returned to the United States, where he died on November 13, 1984, in Seattle.

After his tenure as champion was deemed to end, O'Mahony wrestled in the United States through 1948. He was considered a popular ethnic draw for promoters. He served in the US Army during World War II and was later employed as a publican in Santa Monica, California.[29] He returned home to Ireland in 1950. On November 3, 1950, O'Mahony suffered fatal injuries in a crash involving his parked truck in Port Laighaise.[30] He was 38. A bronze statue of O'Mahony welcomes all to his home village of Ballydehob.[31]

"THE AMBLING ALP"

About two weeks earlier, on June 25, 1935, at Yankee Stadium, the 21-year boxer Joe Louis, known as the Brown Bomber, knocked out a slow ex-heavyweight champion of the world, the 6-foot-5.75-inch, 265-pound Primo Carnera, known as the Ambling Alp, in the sixth round of a scheduled 15-round bout.[32] The Free Milk Fund shared in the gate profits of $375,000 ($8,124,306.57 in 2022 dollars). Carnera returned to fight at Yankee Stadium 15 years later, this time as a professional wrestler.

From Sequals in northern Italy, Carnera was previously a circus strongman who became a mediocre boxer rumored to be under the influence of the mob. He later became an actor and wrestler.[33] Budd Schulberg's novel *The Harder They Fall* has been called a thinly disguised portrayal of Carnera's life.[34] After the Louis loss, Carnera fought sporadically.[35]

Carnera lived with his family in Sequals during World War II and was used as a reluctant propaganda tool by Benito Mussolini. In 1941 during the British North African campaign against Italy, Mussolini dictated that a boxing match occur between Carnera and a captured hulking black South African Army POW, Kay Masaki, to demonstrate the superiority of the White race over Blacks in a propaganda film. Carnera was "the victim of the most ignominious defeat in his ponderous career."[36] Though he had never boxed and after being knocked to the canvas by Carnera at the start of the fight, Masaki was not the easy foil for the Italians, knocking Carnera out in the first round by delivering "a fearful haymaker under the Italian's jaw. Carnera fell in a heap. The cameras ceased grinding."[37] At the war's conclusion, broke and needing to take care of his family, he turned to professional wrestling as an avenue to make money. He became a popular attraction and a financial success at the box office in the American grunt-and-groan world into the 1960s. Carnera is the only man in history to be both boxing's world heavyweight champion and professional wrestling's world champion.[38] Carnera was one of a handful who both wrestled and boxed at Yankee Stadium.

CARD #4: WRESTLING RETURNS

Like few events in human history, television changed the way Americans existed. TV and wrestling were natural partners. In 1949 wrestling aired three times a week on New York City television. And there was a demand for more. Promoter Billy Johnson pushed to have a wrestling show at Yankee Stadium, negotiating an event for the summer of 1950. He envisioned a gate of more than $250,000 with a top ticket price of $5. ($3,078,921.16 and $61.58 in 2022 dollars). He dreamed of a future $1 million gate at the Stadium ($12,315,684.65 in 2022 dollars).[39]

After an absence of 15 years, "grapplers performed in the House that Ruth Built" in an all-star wrestling card on Wednesday, July 12, 1950.[40] Postponed from July 10 due to rain, the eight bouts featured Italian-born Argentine Antonino Rocca vs. 23-year-old Canadian Mohawk Indian Don Eagle "in a finish combat."[41] Rocca was the top attraction in professional wrestling, "who been driving wrestling fans wild on television."[42] Known as Mr. Perpetual Motion and wrestling with his trademark bare feet, Rocca was a popular icon for Italians and Latinos in New York City and other major Eastern cities.

"The main event was the dullest, aside from being the longest," observed the New York Times.[43] Rocca and Eagle demonstrated little comedy, a poor storyline, no suspense, and no thrills. In the undercard matches, "the crowd was treated to an overabundance of [comedy and slugging] … when laughs were the proverbial dime a dozen."[44] As Rocca and Eagle tugged and groaned attempting dropkicks, holds and slaps, the state's "11 o'clock curfew dictated a halt" with both men still standing at the end.[45] The match ended in a draw after 55 minutes and 5 seconds.[46]

Carnera was featured in a preliminary match against Emil Duskek of Omaha, Nebraska. Carnera had been on the road traveling from "New York to Caracas Venezuela, and back then to Nome, Alaska, in pursuit of bucks, pesos, etc."[47] Past his glory years, Carnera was said to have been making "a comfortable living in this sport."[48] He pinned Dusek in a "hold described as a leg grapevine and body press" at the 15:27 mark for a victory.[49] To the eyes of the paying fans, other than Rocca and perhaps Eagle, "the wrestlers were overaged, overfed and, as a result, decidedly overweight."[50] Nonetheless, "[I]t was fun … and no one complained."[51]

Local and national press accounts considered that the matches were not up to expected standards. But for the Free Milk Fund, "there were 11,328 men and women who could find no humor in an infant's need for milk and a portion of $33,746.90 ($415,616.18 in 2022 dollars) they paid to watch the show will go to the fund."[52]

The hyped financial windfall and huge crowd never manifested. The poor turnout, hindered by the postponement, was challenged by the middleweight boxing championship bout between champion Jake LaMotta and Italian contender Tiberio Mitri at Madison Square Garden. LaMotta "laughed off the first defense hoodoo last night to conquer the previously unbeaten" Mitri in a unanimous decision.[53] With 16,369 providing receipts of $99,841 ($1,229,610.27 in 2022 dollars), boxing at a smaller venue outperformed wrestling in New York City that evening.

Carnera became a US citizen in 1953. His life in wrestling was better than the life he experienced as a boxer. Carnera wrestled into the early 1960s. He found a third chapter in his life as an actor in bit roles in Hollywood.[54] A heavy drinker and his health weakened by diabetes and liver cirrhosis, he died at the age of 60 in his home village of Sequals, on June 28, 1967.

WRESTLING TODAY

Wrestling never became an enduring attraction at the original Yankee Stadium. The new Yankee Stadium is not even a minor player in professional wrestling in New York City. Instead, World Wrestling Entertainment hosts events at the Madison Square Garden, Barclay Center, the Meadowlands Sports Complex, and Prudential Center, among others.

Wrestling is now a billion-dollar industry with productions held in major cities and available to all by pay per view, streaming, or cable television. Gimmick or concept matches have spawned well-known actors and celebrities. It is still an act with good and evil characters and a show now with a wider reach. But as it was nearly 100 years ago, it is still just theater.

NOTES

1 Raymond Douglas Davis, "Over the Edge," performed and recorded by The Kinks, produced by Raymond Douglas Davies, Phobia (compact disc), Columbia Records, 1993: Track 9.

2 Jamie Greer, "Wrestling Meccas: Madison Square Garden, New York City," Last Word on Pro Wrestling, May 27, 2020. https://lastwordonsports.com/prowrestling/2020/05/27/wrestling-meccas-madison-square-garden-new-york-city, accessed September 20, 2022. The phrase "wrestling's holy grounds" has historically been used to describe the impact Madison Square Garden had on the growth and popularity of professional wrestling in the United States. See: Graham Cawthorn, Holy Ground: 50 Years of WWE at Madison Square Garden (The History of Professional Wrestling) (Scotts Valley, California: CreateSpace Independent Publishing Platform, 2014) and Kevin Sullivan, "Madison Square Garden Really is the Mecca of Wrestling Arenas," yesnetwork.com, July 12, 2014. See https://web.archive.org/web/20181215065850/http://web.yesnetwork.com/news/article.jsp?ymd=20150602&content_id=128106928&fext=.jsp&vkey=news_milb, accessed November 30, 2022.

3 John Kieran, "Sports of the Times: Wrestling, Southern Style," New York Times, March 27, 1934: 26.

4 W.O. McGeehan, "Boxing at Polo Grounds Opens Promoters' Battle," New York Herald, August 4, 1923: 10.

5   Millicent Hearst survived her separated husband, who died on August 14, 1951. She died on December 5, 1974.

6   "Millicent Hearst (1882-1974)," Hearst Castle, https://hearstcastle.org/history-behind-hearst-castle/historic-people/profiles/millicent-hearst/. When the Free Milk Fund was founded, federal government antipoverty and nutrition programs were not available for those in need of such assistance.

7   For example, the Fund was the targeted charity designated by a special performance at the Metropolitan Opera of Strauss's *Salome* and Puccini's *Gianni Schicchi*, on January 10, 1952. See "'Met' to Aid Free Milk Fund," *New York Times*, December 6, 1951: 42. For more, see "Exhibition: A Pictorial Review, Greater New York's Silver Jubilee, May 26-June 23, 1923, William Randolph Hearst Archive, http://www.liucedarswampcollection.org/betahearst/education.php, accessed August 16, 2022.

8   "Opera on Friday to Aid Milk Fund," *New York Times,* January 31, 1950: 17.

9   "Londos and Steele Wrestle Tomorrow," *New York Times*, June 28, 1931: S11.

10   Arthur J. Daley, "30,000 See Londos Retain Mat Crown," *New York Times*, June 30, 1931: 28.

11   Daley.

12   Daley.

13   Daley. In several instances, the conversion rates are taken from CPI Inflation Calculator, US Bureau of Labor Statistics. At https://www.bls.gov/data/inflation_calculator.htm.

14   Joseph C. Nichols, "Browning Retains World's Title," *New York Times*, June 13, 1933: 24.

15   Nichols.

16   The American press frequently misspelled his name as "O'Mahoney."

17   Tim Hornaker, "New York City Wrestling Today," www.legacyofwrestling.com. On June 27, 1935, at Boston's Fenway Park, O'Mahony "defeated" Londos to win the New York State Athletic Commission World Heavyweight Championship, which was also recognized by the National Wrestling Association.

18   Joseph C. Nichols, "O'Mahoney to Risk Heavyweight Mat Title Against Little Wolf at Stadium Tonight," *New York Times*, July 8, 1935: 19.

19   Joe O'Shea, "Danno – Champion of the World," *Southern Star* (West Cork, Ireland), November 8, 2016. See https://www.southernstar.ie/sport/danno-champion-of-the-world-4129576, accessed October 12, 2022.

20   Kevin Jones, "Danno Rassles Chief in 1st Title Defense," *New York Daily News,* July 7, 1935: 70.

21   Kevin Jones, "Danno vs. Chief Is Expected to Draw 40,000," *New York Daily News*, July 8,1935: 8.

22   Barry York, "Tenario, Ventura (Chief Little Wolf) (1911-1984)," *Australian Dictionary of Biography*, National Centre of Biography, Australian National University, https://adb.anu.edu.au/biography/tenario-ventura-chief-little-wolf-15813/text27012, published in 2012, accessed online October 7, 2022.

23   York.

24   Henry McLemore, United Press, "'Strictly Dishonorable' Is Mac's Title for Mat Face," *The Times* (Munster, Indiana), July 9, 1935: 24.

25   McLemore.

26   Kevin Jones, "O'Mahoney Pins Indian in 28:23," *New York Daily News*, July 9, 1935: 47.

27   Joseph C. Nichols, "Crowd of 12,000 See O'Mahoney Retain Wrestling Championship at the Stadium," *New York Times*, July 9, 1935: 26.

28   York, "Tenario, Ventura (Chief Little Wolf) (1911-1984)."

29   Jack McCarron, "Ballydehob's Danno O'Mahony Was the 'the First True Ethnic Super-Draw' in Professional Wrestling," *Southern Star* (West Cork, Ireland), April 7, 2020. https://www.southernstar.ie/sport/ballydehobs-danno-omahony-was-the-the-first-true-ethnic-super-draw-in-professional-wrestling-4203430, accessed October 10, 2022. O'Mahony managed a pub/bar.

30   "O'Mahoney Dies in Crash: Wrestled Here Many Times," *Washington Evening Star,* November 4, 1950: A-10; Associated Press, "Danno O'Mahoney Dies," *New York Times*, November 4, 1950: 20.

31   McCarron.

32   James P. Dawson, "Louis Knocks Out Carnera in Sixth; 60,000 See Fight," *New York Times*, June 26, 1935: 1. Carnera was the world heavyweight boxing champion from June 29, 1933, to June 14, 1934. He won the championship by knocking out Jack Sharkey in the sixth round of the 15-round title match. He lost the title to Max Baer via a technical knockout in the 11th round of a scheduled 15-round title match.

33   Carnera had a small noncredited part in *On The Waterfront* (1954) that starred Marlon Brando.

34   The novel is the story of an Argentine peasant and circus performer, Toro Molina, who becomes a boxer managed by an unscrupulous fight promoter and his press agent. Molina cannot box. He is subsequently betrayed by all.

35   In 1938 the diabetic Carnera had a kidney removed, which forced him into semi-retirement. See Joseph S. Page, *Primo Carnera: The Life and Career of the Heavyweight Boxing Champion* (Jefferson, North Carolina: McFarland & Company, 2010), 179.

36   "Sport: Carnera v. Masaki," *Time*, August 28, 1944, https://content.time.com/time/magazine/article/0,9171,885648,00.html, accessed October 26, 2022.

37   "Sport: Carnera v. Masaki."

38   For more on Carnera's life and career as a boxer and wrestler, see Jack Sher, "The Strange Case of Carnera," *Sport*, February 1948.

39   Lawton Carver, International News Service, "Mat Gate Is New Dream," *Stockton* (California) *Evening and Sunday Record*, March 8, 1950: 45.

40   "11,328 See Wrestling Return to Stadium," *New York Times*, July 13, 1950: 32.

41   "Wrestling at Yankee Stadium," *Morning Call,* (Paterson, New Jersey), June 27, 1950: 14.

42   "Rocca Breaks Crowd Mark," *Journal Herald,* (Dayton, Ohio), July 13, 1950: 9. Rocca's birth name was Antonino Biasetton.

43   "11,328 See Wrestling Return to Stadium."

44   "11,328 See Wrestling Return to Stadium."

45   "11,328 See Wrestling Return to Stadium."

46   "11,328 See Wrestling Return to Stadium."

47   Hugh Fullerton, "Newcomers in All-Star Polls," *The Record*, (Hackensack,New Jersey), June 30, 1950: 18.

48   "11,328 See Wrestling Return to Stadium."

49   "11,328 See Wrestling Return to Stadium"

50   "11,328 See Wrestling Return to Stadium."

51   "11,328 See Wrestling Return to Stadium."

52   "11,328 See Wrestling Return to Stadium."

53   Associated Press, "LaMotta Trims Italian Easily," *Newsday* (Suffolk Edition) (Melville, New York), July 13, 1950: 53.

54   For a list of credited Carnera acting roles, see https://www.imdb.com/name/nm0138712/.

BOXING AT THE BIG BALLPARK
IN THE BRONX

By John J. Burbridge, Jr.

Certain sporting events have the ability to gain the attention of an entire nation. The World Series, Super Bowl, and World Cup are such examples. Some heavyweight boxing matches can also create such interest. Two such fights in the 1930s between Joe Louis and Max Schmeling at Yankee Stadium became instant classics as they had the attention of most of the world, especially Louis's America and Schmeling's Germany. The following article will explore the role Yankee Stadium played in boxing history with particular emphasis on the two Louis-Schmeling fights.

In the early twentieth century, baseball was America's sport. Its popularity was enhanced by the emergence of Babe Ruth, the Sultan of Swat. His ability to hit home runs, 59 in 1921 and 60 in 1927, changed the game and made The Babe a national hero. This 1920s also saw the advent of radio. Listening to baseball games created new fans throughout America.

Another sport that grew in popularity in the 1920s was boxing. Once again, the surge in interest was fueled by a charismatic figure, Jack Dempsey, the Manassa Mauler. Dempsey became heavyweight champion in 1919 with his vicious knockout of Jess Willard in Toledo, Ohio. With Dempsey's arrival on the scene, boxing promoters began looking for large venues to stage fights.

To illustrate, boxing promoter Tex Rickard realized his upcoming match between Dempsey and Georges Carpentier, a handsome and popular Frenchman, would attract a huge crowd. Since it proved difficult to stage

Yankee Stadium hosted its first boxing match on May 12, 1923.

the fight in New York City, Rickard decided to build a stadium in Jersey City at Boyle's Thirty Acres.[1] This wooden stadium, built in several months, could accommodate over 90,000 fans. Before a packed house on July 2, 1921, Dempsey knocked out Carpentier in the fourth round. This was the first boxing match that generated gate receipts of over $1 million.[2] It clearly demonstrated the need for large stadiums to house boxing matches.

In 1920 the New York Giants informed the ownership of the New York Yankees that they would not renew the lease allowing the Yankees to play at the Polo Grounds, home of the Giants, after the 1920 season.[3] The Yankees had been playing at the Polo Grounds since 1913. With Sunday baseball now allowed in New York City, the Giants no longer wanted to share lucrative weekend dates with the upstart Yankees.[4] The Giants did soften their eviction stance but raised the rent by a significant amount.[5] Given such actions by the Giants, the Yankees owners decided they needed their own ballpark. They acquired property across the Harlem River in the Bronx and built Yankee Stadium. It opened for the 1923 baseball season.

On May 12 of that year, The Stadium held its first boxing matches. Headlining the fight card were separate matches featuring former heavyweight champion Jess Willard and heavyweight contender Luis Angel Firpo. Willard won on a technical knockout while Firpo won via knockout before 63,000 fans.[6] This large crowd for nontitle fights clearly illustrated that Yankee Stadium could house major boxing matches.

Dempsey went on to lose his heavyweight title by decision to Gene Tunney in 1926. While Dempsey considered retiring, he returned to the ring in 1927 for his only appearance at Yankee Stadium. He knocked out Bob Sharkey in the seventh round before 80,000 fans. Dempsey went on to fight Tunney once again in 1928, losing by decision.

In 1936 and 1938, the two most memorable fights at Yankee Stadium were held. They featured Max Schmeling from Germany and Joe Louis. Schmeling had been the heavyweight champion when his foe, Jack Sharkey, was disqualified for a low blow in the seventh round in a 1930 fight. Sharkey later regained the title by beating Schmeling via a split decision. Joe Louis had won his first 24 fights, most by knockout. By fighting and defeating Schmeling, he would be in line for a title fight against James J. Braddock, the recently crowned heavyweight champion. Schmeling was also hopeful of a title fight if he defeated Louis.

The first fight between the two was scheduled for June 19, 1936.

The rise of Adolf Hitler and Nazism in Germany contributed significantly to the atmosphere surrounding these two fights, especially the second. The so-called Nuremberg Laws supposedly purifying the Aryan race had been passed in 1935.[7] Schmeling was considered a representative of that society and the Aryan race although not a member of the Nazi Party. Louis, being an African American, was viewed as inferior in Nazi Germany and by some people in the United States.

It was fairly obvious Louis did not consider Schmeling a serious challenger prior to the first fight. Training in Lakewood, New Jersey, he was seen often on the golf course instead of sparring. He also appeared to be very active sexually.[8] Louis may have been influenced by the fact that Max Baer had knocked out Schmeling, and Louis did the same to Baer.

While Louis may have considered Schmeling lightly, Schmeling prepared very seriously for the match. In December 1935 he attended the fight between Louis and Paulino Uzcudun. After that fight, Schmeling proclaimed that he "saw something."[9] Had Schmeling unearthed a flaw in Louis's approach? While a 10-to-1 underdog, Schmeling felt he would win the fight.

That flaw became apparent before a sellout crowd at Yankee Stadium. For the first three rounds, Louis punished Schmeling with left jabs, but Max was still confident. In the fourth round Schmeling exploited the weakness. Louis, after jabbing with his left hand, would drop that hand, exposing him to a right cross from Schmeling. Schmeling was able to knock Louis down in that round. As the round ended, Louis was obviously dazed.

While the fourth round went to Schmeling, the fifth round was the beginning of the end. At the end of the round, Schmeling once again hit Louis with a right cross. Nat Fleischer, the famous boxing writer, proclaimed, "That punch was the turning point of the fight. … [S]o powerful was that punch that it made Louis's legs take on a rubber appearance and befuddled Joe's brains that he never came out of the stupor."[10] Some felt that Schmeling took advantage of Louis dropping his fists thinking the round was over. From that point on, Schmeling took complete control of the fight, eventually knocking out Louis in the 12th round.

Schmeling was a national hero. On his return to Germany, he dined with Joseph Goebbels, the Nazi propaganda minister. Goebbels proclaimed the victory as an example of the superiority of the Aryan race. On the day after dining with Goebbels, Schmeling, along with his wife, mother, and Adolf Hitler, watched a film of the fight while eating cake.[11]

While Schmeling felt he was next in line to fight Braddock, that match never materialized. Between 1936 and 1938, the persecution of the Jews and others in Germany became widely known, creating significant resistance to scheduling a Schmeling title fight. Braddock's camp also decided that by fighting Louis they would experience a greater financial reward.

Louis knocked out Braddock in the eighth round to become the heavyweight champion. After his victory, Louis stated he wouldn't feel like a heavyweight champion until he defeated Schmeling. The stage was set for the second fight between Louis and Schmeling, which would once again be held at Yankee Stadium, on June 22, 1938.

The escalating international tension provided an electric backdrop for this second match. Austria had been annexed in March 1938. It was becoming obvious that Hitler had further territorial desires. While the resistance to Germany in America had grown, pro-German groups like the German American Bund were being heard in the United States, adding to the tense environment.

As they prepared for this second fight, both Louis and Schmeling were aware of this new dynamic. While Schmeling had received the support of many White Americans in 1936, given that Louis was African American, he was now surprised at their hostility. Reflecting on this, Louis commented that White Americans, "even while some of them were lynching black people in the South – were depending on me to K.O. Germany."[12] Two days before the fight, Schmeling received the following message from Hitler: "To the coming World's Champion, Max Schmeling. Wishing you every success."[13] Louis summed it up best by stating, "The whole world was looking to this fight. …"[14]

Before the fight, Schmeling admitted being nervous in his Yankee Stadium dressing room. Louis exercised for 30 minutes instead of his normal 10 and told his handlers he was going all out for three rounds. With the preliminaries and introductions concluded, the fight was ready to begin.

Early in the first round, Louis hit Schmeling with a barrage of punches that dazed the German boxer, forcing him to grab onto the ropes. Louis then unleashed a vicious right hand that caught Schmeling in the midsection, probably his left kidney. He then proceeded to knock Schmeling down twice. On both occasions Schmeling quickly got to his feet to endure more punishment. With a third knockdown, Schmeling's handlers jumped into the ring, forcing the referee to stop the fight. Louis's strategy of going all out early paid big dividends.[15] A column by sportswriter Grantland Rice summed it up with this succinct headline: "Louis Retains Title, Winning in First Round."[16] In a postfight interview, Schmeling said he could not recover after the punch to the kidney.[17] He was taken to a hospital, where he was kept for 10 days.

Harlem celebrated. A "Louis for President" sign was seen in an exuberant crowd on 129th Street.[18] While Black America and those protesting the Nazi regime were overjoyed, Germany had seen a member of their Aryan race destroyed by the supposedly lowly Negro. On Schmeling's return to Germany, there was no hero's welcome.

The 1940s saw other major fights at Yankee Stadium. In 1941 Joe Louis had a title defense against Billy Conn, the light heavyweight champion, at the Polo Grounds. For 12 rounds, Conn outboxed Louis and appeared on the verge of victory. But in the 13th round, Conn got careless and Louis knocked him out. A rematch was held at Yankee Stadium after World War II. Both fighters showed their rust from the war years, but Louis prevailed, knocking out Conn in the eighth round before 45,266 fans. This was the first heavyweight title fight to be televised.

In 1947 Louis was outclassed in a title fight with Jersey Joe Walcott at Madison Square Garden in New York City. Though Louis thought he had lost the fight, he was given the victory via a split decision. Six months later, Louis fought Walcott at Yankee Stadium and knocked out Jersey Joe in the 11th round. In 1949 Louis announced his retirement but did return to fight Ezzard Charles at Yankee Stadium on September 27, 1950. Charles was recognized as the National Boxing Association heavyweight champion. Before 22,357 fans, Charles won a unanimous decision easily outpointing Louis.

While the fights that have been discussed were at the heavyweight level, bouts at other weights attracted significant interest. Middleweights Tony Zale and Rocky Graziano staged three thrilling fights in the late 1940s. The first of these was held at Yankee Stadium on September 27, 1946. Graziano seemed on the verge of victory, but Zale knocked him out in the sixth round to retain his title.

A series of four fights in the late 1940s and early 1950s between featherweights Willie Pep and Sandy

Saddler excited boxing fans. The third of these was held at Yankee Stadium. Pep was unable to come out for the seventh round, and the title went to Saddler.

Another fighter who was unable to continue in a title fight was Sugar Ray Robinson. Sugar Ray, who fought mainly as a welterweight and middleweight, has been considered by many to be the greatest fighter at any weight. On June 25, 1952, he fought Joey Maxim for the light heavyweight crown at Yankee Stadium. On an extremely hot night, Robinson was unable to come out for the 14th round due to heat exhaustion, letting Maxim keep his title. Robinson also lost a fight at Yankee Stadium with Carmen Basilio.

Yankee Stadium was also the scene of three Rocky Marciano title fights during the 1950s. The first two were against former heavyweight champion Ezzard Charles. Before 47,585 fans on June 17, 1954, Marciano won a close decision. Given the closeness of the fight, Rocky gave Charles a rematch three months later, also at Yankee Stadium. This fight ended with Marciano knocking Charles out in the eighth round. Marciano then defended his title on September 21, 1955, again at Yankee Stadium, against light heavyweight champion Archie Moore. Marciano knocked out Moore in the ninth round before 61,574. Marciano retired after this fight.

As television entered more homes in the 1950s, it had a major effect on boxing attendance. In the New York City region, you could watch boxing on television on Monday, Wednesday, and Friday nights. While major heavyweight fights still drew large crowds, small fight clubs suffered. However, options to show major matches on television grew, and its impact would be felt.

After Marciano vacated his title, Floyd Patterson became the heavyweight champion. On June 26, 1959, Ingemar Johansson, a Swede, won the title at Yankee Stadium with a technical knockout in the third round after Patterson was knocked down seven times during the round. The attendance was a disappointing 18,215 fans. However, the fight was widely shown on closed-circuit TV, and brought in additional revenue of over $1 million.[19] The impact of such an option meant large venues like Yankee Stadium were no longer needed to attract large gate receipts.

The 1960s saw Muhammad Ali burst on the scene, winning the title when Sonny Liston did not answer the bell for the seventh round. Ali was later stripped of his title when he was convicted of draft evasion. He claimed he was a conscientious objector, and his conviction was overturned by the United States Supreme Court. After three fights with Joe Frazier, Ali defeated heavyweight champion George Foreman via a decision in the "Rumble in the Jungle" fight in Zaire.

The recently renovated Yankee Stadium saw its last heavyweight title fight with Ali fighting Ken Norton on September 28, 1976. Before Ali won the title against Foreman, he had split two fights with Norton. In this third fight, Ali won a contested decision with many writers thinking Norton won. Bob Arum, the promoter, stated that while over 30,000 tickets were sold in advance, the real attendance was only about 19,000.[20] New York City was in the midst of a police strike, which held the crowd down and limited the number of walkups to an estimated 10.[21] This was the last fight to be held at the original Yankee Stadium.

On June 5, 2010, boxing was back, but at the new Yankee Stadium, opened in 2009. Bob Arum promoted a boxing card featuring Miguel Cotto fighting Yuri Foreman for the World Boxing Association super-welterweight title. Before over 20,000 fans, Cotto stopped Foreman in the ninth round to win the title. Since then, no boxing matches have been held at Yankee Stadium.

Since its opening in 1923, the original Yankee Stadium was the scene for 30 championship fights. Of those 30, it was the heavyweight contests that attracted the most fans and excitement. The two Joe Louis-Max Schmeling matches, even though the first was not for the championship, are unforgettable. The second has become known as the fight of the century. These were not just fights between two boxers, but contests between an American Negro and a member of Aryan Germany. As such, they became politically significant, given what was happening on the world stage in the 1930s. These two fights and the role Yankee Stadium played will always be remembered.

NOTES

1 Dempsey-Carpentier Fight, https://njcu.libguides/dempsey, March 18, 2022.

2 Dempsey-Carpentier Fight.

3 Lyle Spatz and Steven Steinberg, *1921 The Yankees, The Giants, and The Battle for Baseball Supremacy in New York* (Lincoln: University of Nebraska Press, 2010), 34.

4 Spatz and Steinberg, 33.

5 Spatz and Steinberg, 34.

6 Dan Steinberg, "The Best Boxers, the Grandest Stage," *Wall Street Journal*, May 27, 2010. https://www.wsj.com/articles/SB100014240527487042260045752 62652086100516.

7 Holocaust Encyclopedia, *United States Holocaust Memorial Museum*, https://encyclopedia.ushmm.org/content/en/article/the-nuremberg-race-laws

8 Lewis A. Ehrenberg, *The Greatest Fight of Our Generation, Joe Louis versus Max Schmeling* (New York: Oxford University Press, 2005), 89.

9 Ehrenberg, 88.

10   Ehrenberg, 90.

11   David Margolick, *Beyond Glory: Joe Louis vs. Max Schmeling and a World on the Brink* (New York: Alfred A. Knopf, 2005), 182.

12   Ehrenberg, 138.

13   Ehrenberg, 141.

14   Ehrenberg, 138.

15   Jesse A. Linthicum, "Louis Follows Orders to Letter to Retain Title in One Round," *Baltimore Sun,* June 23, 1938: 10.

16   Grantland Rice, "Louis Retains Title, Winning in First Round," *Baltimore Sun,* June 23, 1938: 1.

17   "Punch to Body Won, Says Joe," *Baltimore Sun*, June 23, 1938: 10.

18   "Harlem Booms Joe Louis for U.S. President," *Baltimore Afro-American,* July 2, 1938: 15.

19   Bert Randolph Sugar, "Greatest Knockouts: Patterson vs. Johansson," September 26, 2006. https://www.espn.com/sports/boxing/news/story?id=2606226.

20   Bernard Fernandez, "Muhammad Ali-Ken Norton 3: Chaos at Yankee Stadium 45 Years Later," https://www.ringtv.com/627543-muhammad-ali-ken-norton-3-chaos-at-yankee-stadium-45-years-later/.

21   Michael Woods, "The Real Action Was Outside The Stadium," March 28, 2010. https://www.espn.in/news/story?id=5230628. Accessed October 18, 2022.

SOCCER AT YANKEE STADIUM

By Stephen R. Keeney

Yankee Stadium had a long history hosting soccer, both exhibition matches and as a home field. The exhibition games often featured teams reflecting New York City's historical immigrant communities. The first friendly at The Stadium featured Celtic, a beacon for the Irish community. Since the 1930s, several matches have featured teams of Jewish heritage. In the 1960s, Italian teams drew the biggest crowds, often playing against the legendary Pelé. While Yankee Stadium was not the city's only host for such exhibitions, it was arguably the most prestigious.

The first soccer match at Yankee Stadium was an exhibition between Celtic (Glasgow, Scotland) and a local team known as the New York Yankees, on June 28, 1931.[1] Celtic won 4-1, avenging a 4-3 loss to the Yankees in Boston earlier on Celtic's dozen-plus-game preseason tour of several North American cities.[2] The match drew 10,000 spectators.[3] Two previous matches on Celtic's national tour, at New York's Polo Grounds, drew crowds of 30,000[4] and 20,000.[5] Both teams were reigning champions. Celtic won the 1931 Scottish Cup.[6] The Yankees won the 1931 US Challenge Cup[7] as the Fall River (Massachusetts) Marksmen before moving.[8]

Over the next decade, many exhibitions at Yankee Stadium featured teams of ethnic or national identity, especially Jewish identity. In September 1934 a team of local Jewish All-Stars beat a team of local Irish All-Stars, 3-0. The match drew 3,000 fans with the proceeds going to building funds for the Hope of Israel Centre and the Catholic Boys Club of New York.[9] In September 1936, Israeli club Maccabi Tel-Aviv (called the "Maccabees" by the *New York Times*) played an exhibition match at Yankee Stadium against a New York State All-Stars team. The Maccabees won, 6-0, before 30,000 spectators,[10] after an exhibition match between the Furriers Union and the International Ladies' Garment Workers' Union.[11] The Maccabees match was part of a world tour to persuade the International Olympic Committee to recognize an independent team from Palestine – then a British colony encompassing modern Israel and Palestine – to be included in the 1940 Olympics.[12] Those Olympics were originally award to Tokyo, who withdrew as host under pressure from the Japanese government, in part due to Japan's need of resources to conduct its wars of conquest in China.[13] The games were transferred to Helsinki, Finland, before being canceled due to the onset of World War II.[14] The Maccabees returned for another exhibition on November 8, 1936, which they lost 4-1 to a team of American Soccer League All-Stars.[15] A similar bid to join FIFA,[16] global soccer's governing body, was complicated because the organization was almost exclusively Jewish,[17] which contradicted FIFA's rule requiring national associations to represent the whole population of the territory they represented.[18]

In May 1947, Hapoel, from soon-to-be-Israel, began a goodwill tour of America with a game at Yankee Stadium. The mayor of New York, delegates from the United Nations, and other dignitaries were slated to attend.[19] While the organizers allegedly sold 60,000 tickets, the *Times* later reported that only 36,115 had attended an unnamed soccer exhibition in 1947.[20] Another source listed the attendance at 43,117, making it the most-attended soccer game ever at old Yankee Stadium.[21] This trend would continue. On April 29, 1956, the Israeli Olympic Team[22] earned a 2-1 victory at the end of what the *New York Times* described as an "Arms for Israel" event attended by local and national politicians, including then-US Senator John F. Kennedy.[23] That October, Israel, aided by France and England, invaded Egypt after Egypt nationalized the Suez Canal in July. The Israeli National Team returned to Yankee Stadium, where it defeated an American Soccer League All-Star Team, 3-1, on October 15, 1967 – just months after the Six Day War between Israel and several Arab nations.[24]

Yankee Stadium hosted exhibitions for international teams and world-class clubs from Europe and South America. On June 15, 1952, 24,582 fans saw Tottenham defeat Manchester United, 7-1.[25] The two teams were in top form, with each team topping the other for first and second place in the English Football League[26] the prior two seasons, and playing each other in exhibitions earlier in that tour.[27] That match was preceded by a warm-up match – the final of the Lewis Cup – in which the Philadelphia Nationals beat the New York Americans, 2-1.[28]

The 1950s brought bigger and bigger soccer teams to Yankee Stadium. For five weeks in October-November 1952, The Stadium hosted a weekly double-header of matches in the eight-team American Soccer League.[29] On June 8, 1953, Yankee Stadium hosted a friendly between the United States and England. England won 6-3 in a rematch of one of the most famous upsets in World Cup history – the United States' 1-0 victory over England at the 1950 World Cup in Brazil.[30] Also in June 1953, Liverpool finished an exhibition tour against the Swiss team BSC Young Boys at Yankee Stadium.[31]

The 1960s saw even more illustrious teams from around the world play at Yankee Stadium, especially Italian teams, often in matches featuring the legendary Pelé. Arguably the greatest player ever, Pelé visited Yankee Stadium several times with his Brazilian club, Santos. After his side won the first of his three World Cups with Brazil in 1958, the Brazilian government declared Pelé a national treasure to prevent Santos from selling his contract rights to European clubs.[32]

On September 5, 1966, Santos played the Italian powerhouse Inter Milan at Yankee Stadium.[33] Santos had just won the Cup of Champions exhibition tournament[34] on its American tour, and the two teams together had won the last four Intercontinental Cups: Santos in 1962 and 1963, and Inter in 1964 and 1965.[35] Over 41,500 spectators – "the majority loudly pro-Italian" – saw Pelé score in Santos's 4-1 win.[36] The crowd was termed the largest for a soccer match in the United States in 40 years.[37] The teams met again the following summer, with Inter winning 1-0 before over 37,000 fans on August 26, 1967.[38] The match had been stopped for over 10 minutes when an on-field scuffle brought fans out of their seats and onto the field in defense of the Italian club.[39]

In 1968 Santos defeated the Italian club Napoli,[40] 4-2, at Yankee Stadium, with Pelé scoring before the crowd of 43,702.[41] A few weeks later, Santos lost to the New York Generals, 5-3.[42] Later that year, almost 37,000 fans turned out to see two of the world's best individual players when Pelé's Santos faced Eusebio's Benfica (Lisbon, Portugal). The game ended in a 3-3 draw, with Eusebio scoring for Benfica.[43] Real Madrid, the most successful club in European club competition, also appeared at Yankee Stadium that summer, defeating the New York Generals 4-1 on August 21.[44]

In 1969 several of Italy's top clubs played exhibition matches at Yankee Stadium. On May 30, Barcelona defeated Juventus (Turin), 3-2.[45] On July 27 Inter Milan defeated Sparta Prague on penalties after a 2-2 draw in regular time.[46] That same day, AC Milan defeated the Greek club Panathinaikos 4-0.[47] Two days later, AC Milan and Inter Milan played each other at Yankee Stadium, with AC Milan winning 6-4.[48] Years later, continuing the Italian tradition, the Italian National Team played a friendly against England on May 28, 1976, as part of the USA Bicentennial Cup,[49] a tournament eventually won by Brazil.[50]

In 1967 two different soccer teams called Yankee Stadium home. The New York Skyliners played in the United Soccer Association, finishing fifth out of six teams in the Eastern Division over the 12-game season. The USA was officially sanctioned as the top American league by FIFA.[51]

The New York Generals played in the National Professional Soccer League in 1967, finishing third out of five teams in the Eastern division in a 32-game season. The NPSL faced a minor scandal when a referee claimed that CBS employees secretly told referees to call imaginary fouls[52] at certain intervals so the network could squeeze in commercials without fans missing any of the game.[53]

In 1968 the two leagues merged into the North American Soccer League, which operated until 1984. The Generals continued to play home games at Yankee Stadium in 1968, which was their last season. They finished third in the Eastern Conference's Atlantic Division, missing the playoffs.[54]

The most successful soccer team to call the old Yankee Stadium home was the New York Cosmos. The Cosmos played in the North American Soccer League from 1971 until the league folded in 1984. But they played at Yankee Stadium for only the 1971 and 1976 seasons. The league had been reduced from 17 teams in four divisions in 1968 to eight teams in two divisions by 1971. That year, the Cosmos finished second in the Northern Division, losing the first two of the best-of-three semifinal series to the Atlanta Chiefs. The Cosmos' Bermudan forward Randy Horton was named Rookie of the Year, finishing second in the league in goals.[55] After drawing small crowds, the Cosmos moved to Hofstra Stadium (at Hofstra University in Uniondale, New York, on Long Island)[56] and then Downing Stadium (Randall's Island, New York City).[57] During the 1975 season, the Cosmos finally succeeded in bringing Pelé out of retirement. His arrival sparked a massive increase in attendance, and the Cosmos turned away would-be spectators because of the lower capacity of Downing Stadium.[58]

To handle bigger crowds, the Cosmos moved back to Yankee Stadium for the 1976 season. By then the league had increased to 20 teams in four divisions. The Cosmos finished second in the Eastern Division, making the playoffs, losing in the division final to the Tampa Bay Rowdies. Predictably, Pelé won league MVP.[59] The next season, the Cosmos permanently moved to the larger Giants Stadium in East Rutherford, New Jersey. The Cosmos were consistently successful throughout their existence. They reached the playoffs in all but three seasons (1974, 1975, and 1984), and won five NASL Championships (1972, 1977, 1978, 1980, and 1982).[60]

The Cosmos were the last soccer team to call the old Yankee Stadium home. But the new Yankee Stadium is home to New York City FC of Major League Soccer. NYCFC is owned by the City Football Group, a conglomerate of soccer teams from all over the world,[61] which in turn is owned primarily by the royal family of Abu Dhabi.[62] Yankees Global Enterprises, which owns the New York Yankees, owns 20 percent of NYCFC.[63] Since joining MLS in 2015, NYCFC has made the playoffs every season except for 2015, winning the MLS Championship in 2021.[64]

From the early days of exhibition matches to becoming the home field for the greatest player ever, the old Yankee Stadium hosted some of the greatest teams and players in soccer history. Hundreds of thousands of fans watched champions from around the world play in The House that Ruth Built. Yankee Stadium has been a palace of champions, both on the diamond and on the pitch.

NOTES

1   Jack Bell, "Yankee Stadium, Like Its Predecessor, Is a Home to Soccer," *New York Times*, July 21, 2012, https://www.nytimes.com/2012/07/22/sports/soccer/yankee-stadium-as-its-predecessor-did-opens-its-doors-to-soccer.html. Most of the exhibitions in this article were part of a national or continental tour by the foreign team played during the offseason, similar to barnstorming or traveling offseason trips played by baseball teams.

2   "Glasgow Celtics Conquer Yankees," *New York Times*, June 29, 1931.

3   "Glasgow Celtics Conquer Yankees."

4   May 24: Celtic (3) vs. (2) New York (Soccer) Giants; *see* "Soccer Giants Lose to the Celtics," *New York Times*, May 25, 1931.

5   June 14: Celtic (1) vs. (1) Hakoah; *see* "Hakoah and Glasgow Celtics Play 1-1 Tie Before 20,000 at the Polo Grounds," *New York Times*, June 14, 1931.

6   "Soccer Giants Lose to the Celtics."

7   Precursor to the US Open Cup. (See Note 8.) In soccer, most countries have at least one tournament (usually with at least some knockout component) that runs concurrent with but separate from the league season. Imagine MLB having the regular season and at the same time having a full-league

playoff, with each competition having its own distinct winner. In 1931 the US Challenge Cup was played in January-March before the regular season began. In Europe, soccer seasons usually run fall-spring, meaning the 1931 champion was the champion of the 1930-1931 season.

8   "Past Open Cup Winners," USSoccer.com, https://www.ussoccer.com/us-open-cup-preview/past-open-cup-winners.

9   "Jewish Team Downs Irish at Soccer, 3-0," *New York Times*, September 17, 1934.

10 "Maccabees Score, 6-0, Before 30,000," *New York Times*, September 28, 1936.

11 "Maccabees Play All-Stars Today," *New York Times*, September 27, 1936.

12 "Palestine Making Progress in Sport," *New York Times*, September 20, 1936.

13 "Japanese Shamed by Loss of Games," *New York Times*, July 15, 1938.

14 "Finnish Officials Cancel Olympics," *New York Times*, April 24, 1940.

15 *2022 New York Yankees Official Media Guide and Record Book*, 405; accessible at https://pressbox.athletics.com/Publications/MLB%20Media%20Guides/2022%20New%20York%20Yankees%20Media%20Guide.pdf.

16 The Fédération Internationale de Football Association (International Federation of Association Football).

17 In fact, several *New York Times* articles refer to the team as the "Jewish" team.

18 See Tamir Sorek, "Palestinian Nationalism Has Left the Field: A Shortened History of Arab Soccer in Israel," *International Journal of Middle Eastern Studies*, 35 (2003): 417-437.

19 "60,000 to Watch Stadium Contest," *New York Times*, May 4, 1947.

20 "Crowds in 1947 Set Mark for Stadium," *New York Times*, December 28, 1947.

21 Clemente Lisi, "European Soccer at Yankee Stadium," USSoccerPlayers.com, July 23, 2012, https://ussoccerplayers.com/2012/07/european-soccer-at-yankee-stadium.html.

22 Israel was later eliminated in Olympic Qualifying by the Soviet Union, which ended up winning the Gold Medal. "Russia Beats Israel, 2-1," *New York Times*, August 1, 1956; "Olympic Football Tournament Melbourne 1956," FIFA.com, https://www.fifa.com/tournaments/mens/mensolympic/melbourne1956.

23 "Arms for Israel Urged at Rally," *New York Times*, April 30, 1956; Gordon S. White Jr., "Israel Olympic Team Beats American Soccer League Stars at the Stadium," *New York Times*, April 30, 1956.

24 *2022 New York Yankees Official Media Guide and Record Book*, 405.

25 Michael Strauss, "Tottenham Routs Manchester Before 24,582 Fans at Yankee Stadium," *New York Times*, June 16, 1952.

26 The First Division of the English Football League was the top league in England at the time, but it became the Championship (the second-highest tier) after the creation of the English Premier League, the current top tier in English soccer.

27 "Top British Teams Clash Here Today," *New York Times*, June 15, 1952.

28 Strauss, "Tottenham Routs Manchester."

29 "Soccer Contract Signed," *New York Times*, August 3, 1952; "Soccer Twin Bill at Stadium Today," *New York Times*, October 12, 1952.

30 Travis Clark, "Tame Those Lions: Here's How the USA Have Fared vs. England at All Levels," MLSSoccer.com, October 19, 2017, https://www.mlssoccer.com/news/tame-those-lions-heres-how-usa-have-fared-vs-england-all-levels.

31 "Liverpool to Face Swiss Team Today," *New York Times*, June 14, 1953.

32 "Pelé," Britannica.com, https://www.britannica.com/biography/Pele-Brazilian-athlete.

33 "Inter Milan and Santos to Play on Yankee Stadium Bill Today," *New York Times*, September 5, 1966.

34 Held at Downing Stadium in New York City, a public stadium owned by the city, which also hosted many famous soccer clubs for exhibitions on their American tours.

35 The Intercontinental Cup was a two-legged championship between the champions of CONMEBOL (South America) and UEFA (Europe), which was later expanded to other federations. It was also the precursor to today's FIFA Club World Cup.

36 Gerald Eskenazi, "41,598 See Santos Win in Soccer, 4-1," *New York Times*, September 6, 1966.

37 "41,598 See Santos Win in Soccer, 4-1."

38 Gerald Eskenazi, "37,063 See Inter Defeat Santos, 1-0," *New York Times*, August 27, 1967.

39 "37,063 See Inter Defeat Santos, 1-0."

40 Future home of fellow "greatest ever" candidate Diego Maradona.

41 Michael Strauss, "43,702 Watch Santos Turn Back Napoli, 4-2, in Soccer at Yankee Stadium," *New York Times*, June 22, 1968.

42 *2022 New York Yankees Official Media Guide and Record Book*, 405.

43 Gerald Eskenazi, "36,904 See Late Rally by Santos Tie Benfica, 3-3; Generals Triumph 4-1," *New York Times*, September 2, 1968.

44 *2022 New York Yankees Official Media Guide and Record Book*, 405.

45 Michael Strauss, "Barcelona Defeats Juventus Here, 3-2," *New York Times*, May 31, 1969.

46 *2022 New York Yankees Official Media Guide and Record Book*, 405.

47 *2022 New York Yankees Official Media Guide and Record Book*, 405.

48 *2022 New York Yankees Official Media Guide and Record Book*, 405.

49 *2022 New York Yankees Official Media Guide and Record Book*, 405.

50 Alex Yannis, "Brazilians Take Soccer Cup," *New York Times*, June 1, 1976.

51 K. Michael Gaschnitz, *Statistical Encyclopedia of North American Professional Sports: All Major League Teams and Major Non-Team Events Year by Year, 1876 through 2006*, 2d. Ed. (Jefferson, North Carolina: McFarland and Company, Inc., 2008), 480-481.

52 See, "Foul: Letter to the Editor," *New York Times*, March 31, 1968.

53 Gaschnitz, 482-483.

54 Gaschnitz, 498-499, 1508.

55 Gaschnitz, 543-544, 1507.

56 Gaschnitz, 1972, 1973.

57 Gaschnitz, 1974, 1975.

58 Gavin Newsham, "When Pele and Cosmos Were Kings," TheGuardian.com, June 10, 2005, https://www.theguardian.com/football/2005/jun/10/sport.comment.

59 Gaschnitz, 634-636, 1507.

60 Gaschnitz, 1507.

61 "Our Clubs," CityFootballGroup.com, https://www.cityfootballgroup.com/our-clubs/, last accessed September 9, 2022. The company's flagship club is Manchester City, who have won four of the last five Premier League titles in England (2017/18, 2018/19, 2020/21, and 2021/22). "Seasons," PremierLeague.com, https://www.premierleague.com/history/season-reviews, last accessed September 9, 2022.

62 "Ownership," CityFootballGroup.com, https://www.cityfootballgroup.com/our-business/ownership/, last accessed September 9, 2022.

63 Mike Ozanian, "New York Yankees Hold Substantial Rights in $66 Billion Disney-Fox Deal," Forbes.com, December 15, 2017, https://www.forbes.com/sites/mikeozanian/2017/12/15/new-york-yankees-hold-substantial-rights-in-66-billion-disney-fox-deal/?sh=5ffa23474a34.

64 "MLS 2022 Fact and Record Book," Major League Soccer, available at https://mlssoccer.app.box.com/s/qw8arv6wycfn127r8p847chr6185n2ed, last accessed September 9, 2022.

A BRIEF REVIEW OF FOOTBALL
AT OLD YANKEE STADIUM

By Bryan Dietzler

Old Yankee Stadium played host to several athletic contests over its 85 years in existence. Even though the Stadium was built for baseball, it did host well over 100 football games over its long and storied history. The first football game played there took place on October 20, 1923. That game was between the University of Pittsburgh and Syracuse University. Syracuse's Orange was victorious, notching a 3-0 victory over Pop Warner's Panthers in front of a crowd of 25,000.[1] The lone score came on a third-quarter 25-yard field goal.[2]

After that debut, old Yankee Stadium played host to 185 college football games.

PROFESSIONAL FOOTBALL

Professional football teams started to play in old Yankee Stadium, as well. The first recorded exhibition game saw the football team of the US Army's Third Corps Area rout the Toronto Argonauts 55-7 on November 3, 1923. Neither team had an affiliation with any professional football league at that time. There were three touchdowns in the first 10 minutes of play.[3] The star of the game was Vic Noyes, former Navy quarterback, who had joined the Army team in what was "practically an all West Point line-up supported by a number of former college stars."[4]

The first professional football team in a league to play at old Yankee Stadium was a squad in the American Football League formed by Chicago Bears star Harold "Red" Grange. He named his team the New York Yankees. The league more than anything was a way for Grange to propel his career even further and earn him more fame and fortune.

Opening the season, the football Yankees had their first game in old Yankee Stadium on a rainy Sunday, October 24, 1926. The Yankees took on the Los Angeles Wildcats in front of a crowd of 18,521 undeterred by the weather, and barely squeaked by, winning, 6-0.

The new American Football League was intended to challenge the growing National Football League, but it never quite got off the ground. It existed for just one year before it folded. The New York Yankees football team continued for two more seasons in the NFL before fading into memory.

One of the most important games in the history of the Stadium, and perhaps in fact for the city of New York, happened on December 16, 1928, when the City Championship, which was for bragging rights, took place. The game pitted the NFL New York Yankees football team against the New York Giants. The game was scoreless at halftime. The Giants put up six points in the third quarter, and the Yankees barely beat the Giants, 7-6, when the first play of the fourth period saw a 20-yard touchdown pass and a placement kick that broke the tie. The game drew 15,000 spectators.[5]

According to the *New World Encyclopedia*, the famous fan cheer, "Dee-FENSE!" was first used at the Stadium.[6] The football Giants played there from 1956 to 1973. Their first game was against the Pittsburgh Steelers on October 21, 1956. In their first season playing at the Stadium, they won the NFL championship, defeating the Chicago Bears, 47-7.

During their time there, the Giants played in three playoff games in Yankee Stadium – in 1956, 1958, and 1962.[7] Perhaps the most famous of them all was the Giants-Baltimore Colts NFL championship game in 1958, dubbed "The Greatest Game Ever Played." It was the first sudden-death overtime game in National Football League history. The Colts won, 23-17. In that game, the score went back and forth before the game ended up in overtime. The Colts, under the leadership of quarterback Johnny Unitas, led the team on a 14-play, 80-yard drive capped off by a touchdown scored by Alan Ameche.[8]

Another standout was the 1962 NFL Championship game between the Green Bay Packers and the Giants on December 30, 1962. What was significant about this game was the temperature: 20 degrees when the game began and, by the time it ended, a mere 14 degrees. What made it even worse were the 25 to 30 mph winds, with gusts of 45 miles per hour.[9] Red Smith wrote, "Polar gales clawed topsoil off the barren playground and whipped it in tan whirlwinds about the great concrete chasm of Yankee Stadium. ... It was a scene of wild desolation."[10] The game still drew 64,892.

The *Chicago Tribune* reported that the US flag on the center-field flagpole was shredded.[11] Playing football in those conditions had to have been tough.

Vince Lombardi's Packers ended up beating Y.A. Tittle and the Giants, 16-7, to win the NFL title for the second year in a row. Three field goals kicked by Jerry Kramer made the difference in the game.

With Yankee Stadium in need of refurbishing by the early 1970s, the Giants opted not to renew their lease and instead build a stadium of their own in New Jersey. They played their final home game at Yankee Stadium on September 23, 1973, after which it underwent a two-year renovation.

The last professional football game played in old Yankee Stadium took place on August 28, 1976, the year the Stadium reopened after the renovation. The New York Jets faced the Washington Redskins in an exhibition game, losing 38-7, and the original Yankee Stadium never again saw a professional football game.

COLLEGE FOOTBALL

College football teams played many more games in the Stadium than the pro leagues did. The winningest college football team in The Stadium was the New York University Violets, with a record of 70 wins, 40 losses, and 5 ties. The team that struggled the most was Army: 15 wins, 21 losses, and 5 ties.[12]

One of the most famous college football games played at Yankee Stadium was Army-Notre Dame on November 10, 1928. This game was famous for the speech given by Notre Dame head coach Knute Rockne to his team at halftime, when the game was a scoreless tie. The speech included the famous phrase, "Win one for the Gipper," a reference to the late Notre Dame All-American George Gipp. Inspired by their coach, the Irish went on to win the game, 12-6, after falling behind 6-0 to start the second half.[13]

Another Army-Notre Dame classic was played on November 9, 1946. Both teams came into the games undefeated. Army and Notre Dame were ranked numbers one and two in the nation. Army had won the national championship the previous two seasons. The game was a defensive gem, ending in a scoreless tie.[14]

MILITARY CONTESTS

Armed forces teams played at Yankee Stadium from time to time. The Navy's Atlantic Fleet Championship took place on December 9, 1923, when elevens from the USS Wright and the USS Wyoming battled to a 6-6 tie in front of a crowd of 8,000. The Army team played there often and others to use the field included the Quantico Marines and the Third Army Corps.

ATTENDANCE

Attendance at the games varied greatly. Crowds of 85,000 witnessed the "Gipper" game in 1928, as well as Notre Dame-Army on November 30, 1929, a 7-0 Notre Dame victory.

Other games were sparsely attended, including a 6-0 affair on December 1, 1923, when just 5,000 people watched Georgetown beat Fordham.

One game that overshadowed them all in terms of crowds: Stanford vs. Army on December 1, 1928, with a reported attendance of 88,000. Stanford won, 26-0.

OTHER CONTESTS

Starting in 1971, the Stadium played host from time to time to the Whitney M. Young Jr. Memorial Football Classic. The foes were historically black colleges. The games were played at Shea Stadium while Yankee Stadium underwent renovations.

The last football game in old Yankee Stadium was the Young Urban League Classic on September 12, 1987, when Central State University of Ohio defeat Grambling State, 37-21.

When the new Yankee Stadium opened in 2009, it was announced that football would again be played there.[15] In the first football game in the new ballpark on November 20, 2010, Notre Dame beat Army 27-3.

SOURCES

For a listing of college and amateur football games played at Yankee Stadium, see Football Games at Yankee Stadium, http://www.luckyshow.org/football/ys.htm. Retrieved September 27, 2022.

ACKNOWLEDGMENT

The author would like to give special thanks to Brian J. Richards, senior museum curator for the New York Yankees, whose information was valuable in writing this article.

NOTES

1   For an overview of football at Yankee Stadium, see "Yankee Stadium Football History: New York Yankees," MLB.com, https://www.mlb.com/yankees/tickets/events/football/yankee-stadium-history. Accessed September 26, 2022

2   "Syracuse Stops the Panthers by Placement Kick," *Brooklyn Daily Eagle*, October 2, 1923: 2D.

3   "Third Corps Team Crushes Argonauts," *New York Times*, November 4, 1923: S3.

4   "Third Army Corps Eleven Finds Canadians Easy," *Brooklyn Standard Union*, November 4, 1923: 18. The Argonauts' lone touchdown came in the second quarter "when the Soldiers were represented by their entire second team." "3rd Corps Finds Easy Rivals in Canadians," *Washington Evening Star,* November 4, 1923: S3.

5   "Pro Yankees Win; Annex City Title," *New York Times*, December 17, 1928: 35.

6   New World Encyclopedia.com, Yankee Stadium. https://www.newworldencyclopedia.org/entry/Yankee_Stadium#Professional_football. Accessed December 9, 2022.

7   Stadiums of Pro Football, Yankee Stadium. https://www.stadiumsofprofootball.com/stadiums/yankee-stadium/.

8   "Colts Win NFL Title in Greatest Game Ever Played," History.com. https://www.history.com/this-day-in-history/nfl-greatest-games-colts-giants-1958. Retrieved December 10, 2022.

9   Michael Jackson, "Classic NFL Games, 1962 Championship." thegamebeforethemoney.com, January 15, 2015. https://www.thegamebeforethemoney.com/62nflc1/. Retrieved December 10, 2022.

10   Red Smith, "Yankee Stadium Like Valley Forge," *Boston Globe*, December 31, 1962: 13.

11   "Packers Keep Title; Beat Giants, 16-7," *Chicago Tribune*, December 31, 1967: B1.

12   See the listing at http://www.luckyshow.org/football/ys.

13   Richards Vidmer, "Notre Dame Wins One for the Gipper," *New York Times*, November 10, 1928. http://archive.nytimes.com/www.nytimes.com/packages/html/sports/year_in_sports/11.10.html?scp=7&sq=whistle&st=cse. Accessed December 13, 2022. This appears to be a reconstructed article of some sort, dated on the day of the game rather than as it appeared in the newspaper. Vidmer's actual game story ran the day after the game: "Notre Dame Beats Army Eleven, 12-6; as 85,000 Look On," *New York Times*, November 11, 1928: Sports 1. There was no mention of the speech in his article.

14   Ralph D. Russo, "1946 Army-Notre Dame, Game of the Century," *San Diego Union Tribune*, November 18, 2010. https://www.sandiegouniontribune.com/sdut-1946-army-notre-dame-game-of-century-2010nov18-story.html. Retrieved December 8, 2022.

15   [15] Ken Belson, "Yankees Announce the Return of Football to the Stadium," *New York Times*, July 21, 2009: B15.

ARMY SINKS NAVY WITH LATE SCORE
IN FIRST FOOTBALL MEETING
AT YANKEE STADIUM

December 13, 1930: Army 6, Navy 0, at Yankee Stadium

by Mike Huber

On a sunny day in the middle of December 1930, the House That Ruth Built was converted into a football stadium. Yankee Stadium hosted America's Rivalry – Army vs. Navy – in a postseason football game "on the turf hallowed by Babe Ruth and Lou Gehrig."[1]

This was nothing new. The first football game played at Yankee Stadium took place on October 20, 1923, as Syracuse defeated Pittsburgh, 3-0, before an estimated crowd of 25,000.[2] Less than a week before, in baseball, the Yankees had beaten the New York Giants to win the 1923 World Series in six games. Ruth smashed three home runs, batted .368 and posted a 1.556 OPS as the Yankees captured their very first World Series crown. In the days afterward, the diamond was transformed into a gridiron.

Army's football team also played at Yankee Stadium. On October 17, 1925, Army battled the University of Notre Dame in the Bronx before 80,000 fans. The two teams had started an annual rivalry in 1913, played at West Point. However, West Point's Michie Stadium (capacity 38,000) could not hold the ever-larger crowds anticipated for this game, so in 1923 Army played Notre Dame at Ebbets Field in Brooklyn. The 1924 contest was held at the Polo Grounds; then, from 1925 until 1946 (except for 1930, when Notre Dame was the home team and the game was played in Chicago's Soldier Field),[3] Army battled the Fighting Irish in the Bronx at Yankee Stadium. However, it was not until 1930 that Army met its rival Navy at Yankee Stadium.

Army and Navy first met on the gridiron on November 29, 1890, playing on The Plain, the parade field at West Point.[4] The tradition continued, off-and-on, through 1927. Then, on January 8, 1928, it was revealed that the superintendents of both academies (Rear Admiral Louis M. Nulton of Annapolis and Major General Edwin B. Winans of West Point) had met in Washington on January 7. The two schools were unable to reach an agreement pertaining to the three-year eligibility rule for their players and "mutually agreed that the Army-Navy game for 1928 [would] not be played."[5] The impasse was not prevented the next year, either, so the heretofore annual rivalry was canceled again in 1929.

So Army and Navy did not have each other marked on their schedules when the 1930 football season began. Economic struggles facing the country forced a change, however. America was in the Great Depression, with millions of people out of work. Thus, the two teams forgot their differences, so that "the hungry might be fed, the homeless sheltered!"[6] Proceeds from an exhibition game were to benefit the Salvation Army, "for the relief of the unemployed."[7] A capacity crowd (reported at 70,000) welcomed the rivalry's return on December 13, 1930. This was the first time the two teams had played each other at Yankee Stadium,[8] and "there were no vacant patches visible anywhere in the towering steel stands or the broad reaches of the open bleachers."[9]

Army sported a record of 8-1-1. Under their first-year head coach, Major Ralph Sasse, the Cadets had shut out their previous opponents six times, and in their one defeat (November 29 to Notre Dame), they had fallen 7-6.[10] In those 10 games, Army had outscored its opponents by a total of 262 to 22.[11]

Navy had not beaten Army since 1921.[12] Now, in their fifth season under head coach Bill Ingram, the Annapolis Eleven had won six of its 10 regular-season games, four by shutout. This game against Army was to be a defensive battle; scoring would be difficult and both sides knew it.

To start the pageantry, 1,200 cadets from West Point marched onto the field, "rolling steadily through the portal and spreading over the field to stand finally a motionless picture of military precision."[13] Then came the 2,000 midshipmen, who filled the entire field. The weather was "glorious."[14] The *New York Times* reported, "The trumpets and the flourish of military swank, the bands and the hoarse, never-ending shouting of the corps of cadets from West Point and the regiment of midshipmen from Annapolis completed the picture."[15]

Approximately one hour before kickoff, "hostilities commenced"[16] as the mascots, Army's mule and Navy's goat, were brought onto the field. Suddenly, the mule lifted a front foot and brought it down onto the goat's head, causing the Navy mascot, although unharmed, to "beat a hasty retreat."[17]

The team captains, Bob Bowstrom for Navy and Charles Humber[18] for Army, met at midfield for the coin toss. Navy won[19] and elected to defend the north goal. Army received the kickoff.

As anticipated, much of the game was played in a scoreless tie. West Point's Thomas Kilday caught the opening kick at Army's 7-yard line and raced 23 yards before being tackled. The offense drove down the field, ultimately reaching Navy's 20-yard line before yielding the ball. Navy's first possession started in disaster. The snap was sent skidding 19 yards behind the quarterback, where "the frantic [Lou] Kirn clutched it and fell on it one yard from his own goal."[20] For the rest of the first quarter, the two teams "see-sawed up and down the field in fitful spurts as if regulated by invisible green and red traffic lights."[21] Army gained yardage but could not push the ball over the goal line. The first quarter ended with Army in possession at midfield again, but neither team had scored.

In the second period, "the elevens waged a punting duel."[22] Navy could not move the ball. Each time Navy attempted a long pass, the ball was "slapped down by alert Army secondaries."[23] Army established one promising drive, but it ended in an interception. The ball had been in Navy's territory for much of the first half, which ended in a scoreless tie. Navy had not yet made a first down.

The third quarter was no different. Army made a few first downs, but the third period ended still in a tie. The good news for Navy was that it was able to keep Army off the scoreboard. With eight minutes left to play in the game, however, Army quarterback Wendell Bowman took the snap and "thrust the ball into the belly of Cadet Ray Stecker,"[24] who "faked giving it to another Army back,"[25] then burst through

the right side of Navy's defensive line "to the distant goal where a late afternoon sun slanted through the stands of the Yankee stadium."[26] Touchdown, Army! Charles Broshous attempted a drop-kick for the extra point, but he missed. West Point led, 6-0.

Navy had a chance to win the game on its final possession. Army's Bowman fumbled a punt on his own 37-yard line, and Navy recovered. The offense drove 12 yards, but was stopped on downs. Army took over and advanced to the Navy 7-yard line as time ran out. Army had won its 16th game in this rivalry.

The Cadets finished with 238 yards of total offense, compared with 86 for the Midshipmen.[27] Army had gained 182 yards with 12 first downs on the ground, compared with Navy's 63 yards and three first downs. The game produced 25 total punts, seven fumbles (each team lost only one fumble to the other side), and 110 penalty yards. Yet the game was a success; "No game of football has ever yet been played with teams so ready, down to the last man, to give everything."[28] That spirit has come to describe many of the contests in this storied rivalry.

Afterward Coach Sasse praised his team, saying, "For absolute unselfishness of spirit I have never seen a bunch like this one. It has been an inspiration to work with them."[29] Sasse further praised the opponent, saying that Navy "was a fine team and gave us the opposition we looked for."[30]

Likewise, Coach Ingram commended his Navy players: "I'm delighted with the fight the boys showed. It was fight, fight, fight from the start and the Navy can feel proud of the game our boys put up. We were overpowered by a bigger and stronger team. But they can't say heads down to me."[31]

The game was a financial success. Ticket sales exceeded $600,000, which "would go to the Salvation Army fund for the unemployed, most of it to be used to relieve conditions in the city."[32] In addition, an autographed football was auctioned off, bought by the Salvation Army's Commander Evangeline Booth, for $5,000.[33]

The famed and fierce football rivalry continued in 1931, played once again at Yankee Stadium. In an action-packed 60 minutes, Army won, 17-7. Since 1930, the two teams have competed on the fields of friendly strife annually, just not again at Yankee Stadium.

SOURCES

In addition to the sources mentioned in the Notes, much of the play-by-play was taken from the following sources:

Danzig, Allison. "Army-Navy Contest Described in Detail," *New York Times*, December 14, 1930: S3.

Powers Jimmy. "Army Gets Navy Goat, 6-0," *New York Daily News*, December 14, 1930: 86, 88.

Lewis, Perry. "Hazleton Lad Runs 57 Yards to Score as 70,000 Look On," *Philadelphia Inquirer*, December 14, 1930: 41, 42.

Amazingly, audio-video footage of the event (from MyFootage.com), including the touchdown score, can be found online at https://www.youtube.com/watch?v=zlKe-TemjOXM. Accessed July 2022. The television was invented in 1927, so this is a major achievement in the early days of TV broadcast.

NOTES

1 Perry Lewis, "Hazleton Lad Runs 57 Yards to Score as 70,000 Look On," *Philadelphia Inquirer*, December 14, 1930: 41, 42.

2 "Football Games at Yankee Stadium," found online at http://www.luckyshow.org/football/ys.htm. Accessed July 2022. A total of eight football games were played at Yankee Stadium in 1923, including the Navy's Atlantic Fleet Championship, when on December 9 the USS Wright team played to a 6-6 tie against the USS Wyoming squad. For the next several years, New York University played its home football games in the Stadium. In addition, the New York Yankees football team (also known as the Grangers) began playing at Yankee Stadium in 1926. The NFL's New York Giants played all of their home games at the Stadium from 1956 to 1973.

3 Instead of playing Notre Dame at Yankee Stadium in 1930, Army hosted Illinois on November 8, defeating the Fighting Illini 13-0, before an estimated 74,000 fans.

4 The Midshipmen prevailed, 24-0, and one of America's most traditional football rivalries had begun. The next three years saw the venue alternating between The Plain and Navy's Thompson Stadium in Annapolis. See "Army-Navy Game Scores," found online at the Naval History and Heritage Command website, history.navy.mil/browse-by-topic/heritage/customs-and-traditionso/navy-athletics/army-navy-football-game.html. Accessed July 2022. Navy won three of those first four encounters. No games were played between 1894 and 1898, and when the rivalry resumed, the two teams agreed to play in Philadelphia, which is roughly equidistant from the two academies. In 1909 Army suddenly canceled the rest of its season after Cadet Eugene Byrne, a left tackle, died in a game against Harvard on October 30. An Associated Press story told readers, "The army is accustomed to death, but not in this deplorable form, and this tragedy of the gridiron has brought such poignant grief to officers and cadets alike that the end of football at West Point and Annapolis is predicted by many." No games were played in 1917 or 1918, due to World War I, but the series resumed again in 1919. See Deb Kiner, "110 Years Ago, the Army-Navy Football Game Was Canceled After the Death of a Cadet," found online at the Penn Live website, www.pennlive.com/sports/2019/12/110-years-ago-the-army-navy-football-game-was-canceled-after-the-death-of-a-cadet.html. Accessed July 2022.

5 "Officials Cancel Army-Navy Game."

6 Lewis.

7 "Notables Present at Service Game," *New York Times*, December 14, 1930: S1.

8 The football teams of Army and Navy had competed at a stadium in New York City before, on several occasions. The two squads played each other at the Polo Grounds nine times, between 1913 and 1927. Army had won five of those contests; Navy had won three times, and there was one tie.

9 Robert F. Kelley, "70,000 Watch Army Beat Navy, 6 to 0: Gate Over $600,000," *New York Times*, December 14, 1930: S1.

10 1930 was the final season that legendary coach Knute Rockne coached at Notre Dame, leading them to an undefeated national championship. (Rockne was killed in a plane crash on March 31, 1931.)

11 "1930 Army Black Knights Roster," found online at www.sports-reference.com/cfb/schools/army/1930-roster.html. Accessed July 2022. The 22 points allowed ranked third-fewest out of 106 college teams across the country. The 24.4 points scored per game was 15th-best in the country.

12 In the six games played from 1922 to 1927, Army had won four times; there were two ties. Coming into this game, Army held the series advantage with 15 wins against 12 losses (there had been three tie games as well).

13 Kelley.

14 Kelley.

15 Kelley.

16 Arthur J. Daley, "Navy Wig-Wag Talk Keeps Crowd Happy," *New York Times*, December 14, 1930: S3.

17 Daley.

18 Team captain Humber played as a left guard for Army. In 1930 Humber received second-team All-America honors from the International News Service. See James L. Kilgallen, "All-American Team Selected," *Chester* (Pennsylvania) *Times*, December 1, 1930: 15.

19 According to Perry Lewis of the *Philadelphia Inquirer*, Navy had not lost a coin toss all season.

20 Jimmy Powers, "Army Gets Navy Goat, 6-0," *New York Daily News*, December 14, 1930: 86, 88.

21 Powers.

22 Allison Danzig, "Army-Navy Contest Described in Detail," *New York Times*, December 14, 1930: S3.

23 Powers.

24 Powers.

25 Kelley.

26 Powers.

27 Associated Press, "Statistics Reveal Why Cadets Won," *San Bernardino County* (California) *Sun*, December 14, 1930: 24.

28 Kelley.

29 "Major Sasse Pays Tribute to Cadets," *New York Times*, December 14, 1930: S3.

30 "Major Sasse Pays Tribute to Cadets."

31 "Navy Coach Proud of Middies' Battle," *New York Times*, December 14, 1930: S2.

32 Kelley.

33 "Army Eleven Defeats Navy, 6-0, Before 70,000; Jobless Fund Gets $600,000 From Stadium Game," *New York Times*, December 14, 1930: 1.

OUT OF THE HOUSE THAT RUTH BUILT EMERGES THE MODERN NFL

December 28, 1958: Baltimore Colts 23, New York Giants 17, at Yankee Stadium

By Bill Pruden

As the crowd of 64,185 streamed into Yankee Stadium for the 2:00 kickoff on the afternoon of December 28, 1958, they were treated to comparatively balmy weather with the temperature at 47 with clear skies.[1] Conditions seemed ideal for the National Football League championship matchup pitting the Western Division champion Baltimore Colts, an offensive powerhouse led by quarterback John Unitas and wide receiver Raymond Berry, against the Eastern Division champ New York Giants who boasted the league's

Courtesy of the Babe Ruth Museum.

The first of back-to-back NFL Championships for Baltimore Colts coach Weeb Ewbank (center, suit) and players (left to right) Raymond Berry, Lenny Moore, and John Unitas came at Yankee Stadium in 1958.

most feared defense, headed by middle linebacker Sam Huff.[2]

Though built for baseball, the Stadium had been hosting football games since 1923.[3] In 1956, after the football Giants abandoned the Polo Grounds, Yankee Stadium became their home field and it was the Eastern Division's champion's turn to host. The Giants christened their new home in spectacular fashion, routing the Chicago Bears 47-7 to win the NFL crown.[4]

For all the anticipation, the Giants-Colts game began as a comedy of errors, with the first quarter featuring three turnovers, a total doubled by halftime.[5] Indeed, Baltimore's first drive ended with Huff forcing a fumble while sacking Unitas, only to have the Colts return the favor a play later. Battling back and forth, the Colts threatened after a 60-yard completion from Unitas to Lenny Moore took them to the Giants' 26, but the drive came up empty when Huff blocked Colts kicker Steve Myhra's field-goal attempt.[6]

The Giants mounted a drive late in the first quarter but had to settle for Pat Summerall's 36-yard field goal after a wide-open Alex Webster slipped trying to corral a pass from quarterback Charlie Conerly. Two fumbles by Giants running back Frank Gifford were turned into touchdowns by the Colts. The first was on a 2-yard run by Alan Ameche, and the other was on a 15-yard touchdown pass from Unitas to Berry, the culmination of a 15-play, 86-yard drive. The half ended with the Colts ahead 14-3.[7]

The quality of play improved significantly in the second half. After forcing the Giants to punt, the Colts started a drive from their own 41 and quickly marched down the field. Midway through the third quarter, they had first and goal on the Giants' 4-yard line. With the game seemingly hanging in the balance – years later Gifford recalled, "We had to hold them. We didn't have the offense to recover from a 21-3 deficit." – the Giants defense went to work.[8]

After Giants defensive back Emlen Tunnell came seemingly out of nowhere to stop an Ameche sweep, a sneak by Unitas and another try by Ameche left the Colts still short of the goal line. On fourth and goal, Unitas called a trick play, an option pass. But when Ameche misunderstood the call and simply tried the sweep, he was wrapped up short of the goal line, while tight end Jim Mutscheller stood alone waiting for the pass that never came.[9] The Giants defense had turned the tide.

With the momentum suddenly shifted, the Giants offense took a turn. With a third and 2 from their own 13, Conerly threw a pass to flanker Kyle Rote, who caught it in stride at the 35 and kept going. But as Rote was being dragged down on the Colts 45, he fumbled, only to have the trailing Webster pick up the bouncing ball and take it all the way to the 1-yard line, where he was forced out of bounds. The 86-yard play left the Giants poised to score their first touchdown – which they did two plays later with Mel Triplett scoring on a 1-yard run. Summerall's extra point cut the Colts' lead to 14-10.[10]

After a Colts three and out, the Giants opened the fourth quarter with Conerly hitting wide receiver Bob Schnelker on a 46-yard bomb that took the Giants to the Colts' 15. That was followed by a pass to Gifford for a touchdown and the lead, 17-14. Pandemonium reigned.[11]

Behind for the first time since the first quarter, the Colts offense got to work, but the Giants defense held firm, stalling two short drives. Frustrated and still trailing, the Colts got the ball on their own 14-yard line with 1 minute and 56 seconds remaining.[12]

Now under the lights, with dropping temperature having left some spots on the field frozen, Unitas started with two incomplete passes, but on third down he connected with Moore for 11 yards and a first down. Although Unitas missed L.G. Dupre on his next attempt, he then proceeded to hit Berry on three consecutive passes – a 25-yarder to midfield, a 15-yarder that took them to the Giants 35, and a 22-yarder to the left sideline that gave the Colts first down on the Giants' 13.[13] The sequence became embedded in Colts lore. Defensive back Milt David recalled, "All the preparation I'd seen Johnny put in – now it was coming to fruition."[14] Strong safety Andy Nelson said simply, "That was the best pitch and catch I'd ever seen."[15] With seven seconds left, Myhra's 19-yard field goal tied the game, 17-17.

After Don Maynard returned the ensuing kickoff to the 18, the Giants had time for only a single play before time ran out, the struggle ending in an unsatisfying tie – or so many of the players already heading to the locker room thought.[16] But in fact, Commissioner Bert Bell had previously declared that if the championship game was tied at the end of regulation play, the teams would play a sudden-death overtime to determine the league champion.[17] The tired players regrouped for the coin flip to determine which team got the ball to start the overtime period.

Unitas, standing in for Colts captain Gino Marchetti, who had broken his ankle in the fourth quarter, called tails. When it landed heads, the home crowd roared.[18]

After the kickoff for the unprecedented overtime resulted in a touchback, the Giants took possession on their own 20-yard line.[19] The Colts defense held for a three and out, before Don Chandler's 62-yard punt and Carl Taseff's 1-yard return left the Colts to start on their own 20.[20]

Masterfully mixing his plays – an 11-yard run by Dupre, an incomplete pass attempt to Moore, a short gain by Dupre, and then an 8-yard pass to Ameche for the first down – Unitas put on a clinic, keeping the Giants constantly off-balance. Even when stopped, the Colts seemed in control. Years later a still frustrated Sam Huff recalled, "John had me psyched ... I thought he could read my mind … because it seemed like the son of a bitch knew every defense I was in."[21]

After a sack left the Colts on their own 37, Unitas hit Berry along the left sideline for 21. That was followed by a trap by Ameche up the middle that victimized Huff. After Dupre was held to no gain, Unitas again hit Berry, this time for 12, taking the Colts to the Giants' 8 and a first down.[22] Seeking to regroup, the Giants called time out. Then all at once, television sets across the land lost their picture. NBC had lost its cable connection.[23]

NBC technicians were able to fix the problem, and as their pictures returned, viewers saw the Colts lining up on the Giants' 8. A plunge by Ameche netted 2 yards.[24] Then Unitas surprised everyone by throwing a sideline pass to Mutscheller, who caught the ball on the 1 but slipped on the now frozen field, falling out of bounds before he could reach the end zone.[25] From there, on third and goal, with 6:45 left in the first overtime period, Ameche plunged over the goal line for the game-winning touchdown.[26]

The Baltimore Colts were the NFL champions. Bedlam ensued. Fans charged onto the field tearing up chunks of the sod for souvenirs while battles over the pulled-down goal posts raged.[27] An ecstatic Commissioner Bell spoke for many when he told *New York Times* reporter Louis Effrat that it was "the greatest game I have ever seen."[28]

So it was that in Yankee Stadium, the "house that [Baltimore native Babe] Ruth built," his hometown Colts had emerged triumphant, in the process jump-starting the elevation of the NFL into the front ranks of professional sports while making Johnny Unitas the first superstar quarterback of the modern era.

NOTES

1 Mark Bowden, *The Best Game Ever: Giants vs. Colt, 1958, and the Birth of the Modern NFL* (New York: Grove Press, 2008), 191-192.

2 Bowden, 14-15.

3 "Football Games at Yankee Stadium," http://www.luckyshow.org/football/ys.htm.

4 Lou Sahadi, *One Saturday in December: The 1958 NFL Championship Game and How It Changed Professional Football* (Guilford, Connecticut: Lyons Press, 2008), 81.

5 Sahadi, 198-201.

6 Bowden, 152-154.

7 Bowden, 156-161.

8 Frank Gifford with Peter Richmond, *The Glory Game: How the 1958 NFL Championship Game Changed Football Forever* (New York: HarperCollins, 2008), 177.

9 Sahadi, 170; Bowden, 8-10.

10 Sahadi, 171; Bowden, 16-18.

11 Sahadi, 172.

12 Louis Effrat, "Colts Beat Giants, Win in Overtime," *New York Times*, December 29, 1958.

13 Sahadi, 205; Bowden, 183-185.

14 Gifford, 209.

15 Gifford, 209.

16 Bowden, 191-192.

17 Bowden, 193.

18 Bowden, 194; John F. Steadman, *The Greatest Football Game Ever Played: When the Baltimore Colts and the New York Giants Faced Sudden Death* (Baltimore: Press Box Publishers, Inc., 1988), 41.

19 Bowden, 195, Sahadi, 201.

20 Bowden, 197; Sahadi, 206.

21 Bowden, 202.

22 Bowden, 198-203.

23 Bowden, 203.

24 Brian Cronin, "Sports Legend Revealed: Did NBC Send an Employee on the Field to Delay an NFL Title Game?" *Los Angeles Times*, July 28, 2010; Bowden, 206-207.

25 Bowden, 206-207.

26 Sahadi, 206.

27 Steadman, 44.

28 Bowden, 208.

VINCE LOMBARDI TRIUMPHS IN HIS HOMETOWN: THE 1962 NFL TITLE GAME

December 30, 1962: Green Bay Packers 16, New York Giants 7, at Yankee Stadium

By Dan Neumann

Even most casual sports fans are aware of the 1967 NFL title game, commonly referred to as the Ice Bowl. Played in subzero temperatures at Lambeau Field on New Year's Eve of 1967, and won by the Green Bay Packers, this game cemented the legacy of Vince Lombardi and gave the Packers their third consecutive NFL championship. Lesser known, but equally important, is the NFL title game of 1962, played in similar conditions at Yankee Stadium and just as important to the Lombardi legacy.

Professional football's New York Giants had moved from the Polo Grounds to Yankee Stadium in 1956, and immediately began dominating the NFL's Eastern Conference. The team won the NFL title over the Chicago Bears in 1956 before losing to the Baltimore Colts in the 1958 and 1959 games. Winning brought increased esteem for both the team and its players, with Giants stars like Frank Gifford, Sam Huff, and Charlie Conerly rivaling the Yankees' Mickey Mantle, Whitey Ford, and Yogi Berra in popularity. After a third-place finish in 1960, the Giants returned to the title game in 1961, where they were blown out by the Green Bay Packers at New City Stadium (later renamed Lambeau Field), 37-0.

Much of the media attention prior to the game focused on Lombardi. The week of the game, he had graced the cover of *Time* magazine, under a cover line reading, "The Sport of the 60's."[1] Lombardi's New York roots, and five years as a Giants assistant coach, added another wrinkle to the storyline. In fact, Lombardi had seriously considered returning to as head coach before the 1961 season, before opting to remain in Green Bay.[2] Nonetheless, the specter of Yankee Stadium and New York hung over the Packers and the title game. Before leaving Green Bay that week, Lombardi had installed a sign above the Packers locker room: "HOME OF THE GREEN

BAY PACKERS. THE YANKEES OF FOOTBALL."[3] Pro Football Hall of Famer Jerry Kramer, who played guard and kicked field goals for the Packers in the game, said years later that "Yankee Stadium was hallowed ground, and it was an awesome experience to walk into the stands."[4]

Despite the blowout of a year before, the two teams entered the game as virtual equals, and with the two best regular-season records in the NFL. The Packers were playing in their third straight NFL title game, having lost to the Eagles in 1960. The Giants, meanwhile, were making their fifth appearance in seven years. Giants quarterback Y.A. Tittle had split MVP honors for 1962 with Packers fullback Jim Taylor.[5] The Giants were eager to avenge their loss from a year before. "It won't be enough just to win this game," said defensive end Andy Robustelli. "We have to destroy the Packers and Lombardi. It's the only way we can atone for what happened to us last year."[6] The Giants were cheered on by 64,892 fans at Yankee Stadium, although a citywide newspaper strike prevented fans from reading about the game, and NFL TV blackout rules kept most local residents from watching it.[7]

The game-time temperature on December 30, 1962, was 20 degrees. It dipped to single digits in the second half.[8] Winds gusted over 40 MPH and created what Jerry Kramer later called "real Green Bay weather."[9] These conditions represented a clear advantage to the Packers, as Tittle and the Giants' pass-oriented offense were rendered largely ineffective by the heavy winds. "The ball was like a diving duck," Tittle said after the game. "I threw one pass, and it almost came back to me. The short ones worked, but the long ball broke up. We needed the long one."[10] Tittle ended up with 18 completions in 41 pass attempts, with one interception and no touchdown passes, mediocre numbers even for

1962. In fact, the Giants' only scoring of the day came on a blocked punt by defensive back Erich Barnes.

The Packers were led on this day by a trio of future Hall of Famers. Fullback Jim Taylor led the team in rushing with 85 yards on 31 carries and scored the team's only touchdown on a 7-yard run in the second quarter. Taylor battled throughout the day with another Hall of Famer, Giants middle linebacker Sam Huff. Both men enjoyed reputations as hardened, smash-mouth players. In 1960 Huff had been the subject of a CBS News special, *The Violent World of Sam Huff* (hosted by Walter Cronkite). Taylor, for his part, was perhaps the most hated of Packer players and had been booed the loudest by Yankee Stadium fans during pre-game introductions.[11] Early in the game, after a particularly rough tackle by Huff on the icy surface, Taylor returned to the huddle coughing blood.[12] According to one postgame account, "Taylor looked gaunt. He had lost ten pounds. It would not be known until weeks later that he had hepatitis. He bit his tongue and was spitting blood throughout the game, and his gashed elbow had to be stitched up at halftime."[13] Huff expressed admiration for his rival after the game: "Taylor isn't human. No human being could have taken the punishment he got today … but he kept bouncing up, snarling at us, and asking for more."[14]

Equally tough, and equally important to the Green Bay victory, was Jerry Kramer, Taylor's longtime roommate on the Packers. An All-Pro guard in 1962, Kramer with his blocking helped power the Green Bay rushing attack throughout the game. More importantly, he kicked three field goals and an extra point in the game, having taken over placekicking duties from an injured Paul Hornung. The victory was particularly sweet for Kramer, who had missed the 1961 title game with a broken leg.

Kramer was voted the game ball by his teammates for his performance in the game but missed out on the brand-new Corvette awarded by *Sport* magazine to the most outstanding player in the championship game.[15] That honor belonged to linebacker Ray Nitschke, the anchor of the Packers defense. Nitschke recovered two fumbles in the game and in the first quarter deflected a Tittle pass that was intercepted by Green Bay line-backer Dan Currie. This thwarted the most serious Giants scoring threat of the afternoon. Later that evening, Nitschke celebrated the victory with an appearance on the popular game show *What's My Line?*[16] Several legendary baseball players had appeared on the show throughout the 1950s, beginning with Phil Rizzuto on the very first episode,[17] but Nitschke was

the first NFL player. This could only bolster the claim made by *Time* (in the Lombardi cover issue) that the NFL was the "Sport of the 60's."

The Packers' 16-7 victory represented a turning point for the Giants, the Packers, and the future of the NFL. The game was the first filmed by Blair Motion Pictures, a Philadelphia-area company. Owned and operated by Ed Sabol and his son Steve, Blair soon rebranded itself as NFL Films, a company that "would be responsible for creating the films and television shows that shaped the new mythology of profession-al football for the rest of the century," according to Lombardi biographer David Maraniss.[18]

With several of their key players over the age of 30, the Giants were nearing the end of their golden age. They returned to the title game a year later, losing to the Chicago Bears at Wrigley Field. The subsequent two decades brought ownership turmoil, coach fir-ings, and a seemingly endless string of losing seasons. They did not return to the postseason until 1981. By that time, the Giants had left New York City almost a decade earlier and now resided in the New Jersey Meadowlands. Yankee Stadium never again hosted an NFL title game.

For the Packers, 1963 was a particularly trying season for Lombardi and the team, punctuated by the suspension for gambling of his favorite player, Paul Hornung. The coach was also deeply impacted by the assassination of President John F. Kennedy, with whom Lombardi had developed a friendship. The team did not return to the NFL title game until 1965, embarking on a three-year run that culminated with victories in the first two Super Bowls.

In his best-selling biography of Lombardi, Maraniss writes of the aftermath of the 1962 title game: "They were headed home to Green Bay, Lombardi and his family and his Packers, champions once more, best ever, and none of them knew at that moment how much could be lost so soon, a President and a Golden Boy (Hornung) and even a way of life."[19] Lombardi himself was less poetic, referring to the game simply as "football as it should be played."[20] Either way, the 1962 NFL title game remains a singular moment in the history of both Yankee Stadium and the NFL.

NOTES

1   Jack Cavanaugh, *Giants Among Men: How Robustelli, Huff, Gifford, and the Giants Made New York a Football Town and Changed the NFL* (New York: Random House, 2008), 250.

2   David Maraniss, *When Pride Still Mattered: A Life of Vince Lombardi* (New York: Simon & Schuster, 1999), 266-268.

3   Maraniss, 328.

4   Bob Berghaus, *The First America's Team: The 1962 Green Bay Packers* (Cincinnati: Clerisy Press, 2011), 12.

5   Taylor had been elected MVP by the Associated Press and Newspaper Enterprise Association, while Tittle had been chosen by the United Press International and *The Sporting News*.

6   Edward Gruver, *Nitschke* (Lanham Maryland: Taylor, 2002), 88.

7   Gerald Eskenazi, *There Were Giants in Those Days* (New York: Grosset & Dunlap, 1976), 197.

8   Keith Dunnavant, *Bart Starr: America's Quarterback and the Rise of the National Football League* (New York: Thomas Dunne Books, 2011), 140.

9   Jerry Kramer, *Farewell to Football* (New York: World Publishing Company, 1969), 160.

10   Berghaus, 16.

11   Bud Lea, *Magnificent Seven: The Championship Games That Build the Lombardi Dynasty* (Chicago: Triumph Books, 2002), 33.

12   Lea, 41.

13   Lea, 41.

14   Lea, 45.

15   Kramer, 162.

16   Gruver, 140.

17   Rob Edelman, "What's My Line and Baseball?," *Baseball Research Journal*, Vol. 43. No. 2. Fall 2014: 36-41.

18   Maraniss, 330.

19   Maraniss, 334.

20   Berghaus, 20.

CONCERTS AT YANKEE STADIUM

By Bob Webster

During the late 1960s and the '70s, stadium concerts became quite popular. Bands could play for much larger crowds and make lots more money. New York City and its surrounding area had a few stadiums for the bands to choose from.

Yankee Stadium, Shea Stadium, Downing Stadium, Roosevelt Stadium, Forest Hills Tennis Stadium, the Singer Bowl at the World's Fair site, and Central Park were all used for outdoor concerts. When Giants Stadium opened in 1976, it became the venue of choice, since it was used only for NFL football games and had plenty of nights available during the summer.

With all of the choices, it would be interesting to find out how a band or their promoter chose a venue. Scheduling would be an easy problem to identify. Ticket prices would probably be the same regardless of venue, so perhaps the cost of renting a facility would be the deciding factor. The surface and condition of the field could be a determining factor. Natural grass could be damaged easier than artificial turf. It could also be prestige. Before stadium concerts became popular, Madison Square Garden seemed to be the popular place to play a concert.[1] It could also have been that the Yankees' owner, George Steinbrenner, didn't want to risk any damage to the playing field. He did have a concern when Nelson Mandela was going to have a rally followed by Billy Joel concerts the next two nights in 1990.[2]

Yankee Stadium did have its share of concerts over the years; here are some of the highlights.

THURSDAY, AUGUST 2, 1928: POLYPHONIC SYMPHONY ORCHESTRA

The New York Polyphonic Symphony Orchestra made its inaugural appearance at Yankee Stadium. The Polyphonic Symphony was formed after the New York Symphony was discontinued. This event was held in an attempt to institute summer music festivals in New York similar to those held in Europe each year featuring music of Wagner, Mozart, and others.

The Polyphonic Symphony Orchestra was organized by Alexis Kudisch, former conductor of the Vienna Volksoper. For the performance of this Wagner program, five American soloists joined the orchestra: Julia Peters, Rita Raymond, Anita Tully, Evelyn Brandt, and Bennett Challis.

Michael Feveisky conducted the program that featured selections from "Tannhäuser," "Lohengrin," "Tristan und Isolde," "Rienzi," "The Flying Dutchman," and "Die Meistersinger."[3]

FRIDAY, JUNE 10, 1966: "SOUNDBLAST '66" RAY CHARLES, THE BEACH BOYS, THE BYRDS, STEVIE WONDER, AND THE McCOYS

"Soundblast '66" was the brainchild of three young men who rented Yankee Stadium with hopes of filling the ballpark with rock 'n' roll fans. One review called it a "pop happening masquerading as a concert."[4] The festivities began an hour and 15 minutes late with 66 go-go girls on bicycles. They screamed and waved streamers as if they were cheerleaders. The Cowsills were first to perform, followed by The McCoys, but with the crowd that did not come close to filling the 65,000 seats, the sound seemed to echo off the wooden seats and created feedback.

The stage was set up on the pitcher's mound, with no seating on the field, so the nearest fans were quite a distance from the stage. The Marvelettes, The Byrds, and Jerry Butler closed the first half and it became apparent that each group was going to sing only three or four songs.

After the intermission, many fans had already left because of the chilly weather. The tempo changed, the go-go girls were gone, and it was time for some soul music. Little Stevie Wonder opened the second half, followed by Ray Charles singing a medley of old favorites.[5] The Beach Boys then arrived via an armored vehicle that entered the playing field through the bullpen.

SATURDAY, JUNE 22, 1968: JAMES BROWN NATIONAL SOUL FESTIVAL

James Brown performed at Yankee Stadium in front of 40,000 fans just after he returned from a goodwill tour to visit American military bases in Japan, Korea, Okinawa, and Vietnam.

The set list included "Licking Stick," "I Got the Feelin'," "If I Ruled the World," "Knock on Wood," "Funky Broadway," "Kansas City," and "It May Be the Last Time."[6]

SATURDAY, JUNE 21, 1969: ISLEY BROTHERS

The "Soul Brothers Summer Music Festival" turned out to be a live concert, a recording studio, and a movie location all in one night.

An album, *Live at Yankee Stadium*, was recorded that night and released on the Isley Brothers T-Neck label. The Isley Brothers performed on the recording, but it was mainly a showcase of other recording artists signed to their label along with Buddah Records. Appearing at the concert and captured on the live recording were Judy White, the Sweet Cherries, the Edwin Hawkins Singers, and the Five Stairsteps. With the exception of the Edwin Hawkins Singers, they all performed songs that were written and produced for them by the Isleys. The Isleys performed "It's Your Thing," "I Turned You On," and the 1959 hit "Shout."

The concert was filmed and funded by the Isleys. The film *It's Your Thing* was released in Chicago, New York, and Los Angeles on August 12, 1970. It presented highlights of the Yankee Stadium concert.[7]

Others appearing that night included Patty Austin, the Chambers Brothers, Jackie "Moms" Mabley, the Clara Ward Singers, the Young Gents, the Brooklyn Bridge, the Winstons, and Ike and Tina Turner.[8]

FRIDAY AND SATURDAY, JULY 7 AND 8, 1972: NEWPORT JAZZ FESTIVAL NEW YORK

The Newport Jazz Festival moved to New York for the 1972 season, holding events from July 1 to July 9. Venues included six days of concerts in Carnegie Hall, six days of concerts in Philharmonic Hall, and two outdoor concerts at Yankee Stadium.

The festival was moved out of Newport because of an incident in 1971. During the second night of the scheduled four-night festival, young people broke through a chain-link fence and onto the Festival Field. Newport City Manager B. Cowles Mallory ordered the festival closed on the recommendation of the Police Chief Frank H. Walsh.[9]

Friday's scheduled performers at Yankee Stadium included B.B. King, Clark Terry, Illinois Jacquet, Jimmy Smith, Joe Newman, Kenny Burrell, Nina Simone, Ray Charles, Roy Haynes, Zoot Sims, and the Dave Brubeck Quartet.

Saturday's program included Herbie Mann, Les McCann, Lou Rawls, and Roberta Flack.[10]

A six-record set, *Newport in New York '72*, was released in 1972 and included clips from all of the shows.[11] *Newport in New York '72: The Jam Sessions, Volumes 1 & 2* was released in April, 1973.[12]

A number of other albums from the festival were also released.

FRIDAY, AUGUST 24, 1973: FANIA ALL-STARS

This Latin American concert took place shortly before Yankee Stadium was due to go through a renovation, but the demolition stage almost started that night.

A small record label from Spanish Harlem, Fania Records, assembled some of its best artists and called them the Fania All-Stars. The musicians had played together twice previously, in 1968 and in 1971. The events were very popular with the Latin American community.

Producer Jerry Masucci wanted to have the group perform at Yankee Stadium so badly that he invested lots of money in order to do so. Since the season still had a month to go, he had to put down a deposit of $25,000 against any possible damage to the playing field.

At the time, most of the Latino population of New York City was Puerto Rican. Besides the Fania All-Stars, the lineup for the concert included three popular Latin bands as the opening acts: Tapica 73 with Adalberto Santiago, El Gran Combo with Andy Monta Mongo Santamaria.

Then the Fania All-Stars took the stage. The crowd got so excited by a conga duel between Mongo Santamaria and Ray Barretto that they stormed the field. The band members, frightened, locked themselves in the trailers behind the stage. Other musicians ran to the dugout and locked themselves in the clubhouses. The concert was never completed.

The field was repaired just before the Yankees returned from their road trip.

Needless to say, Masucci did not get his deposit back.[13]

Using concert footage, *Live at Yankee Stadium, Volumes 1 & 2* was released in 1975.[14] It was reissued by Fania Records in 2019.[15] *Mongo Santamaria Live at Yankee Stadium* was released in 1974.[16]

SUNDAY, JUNE 26, 1988: THE BEACH BOYS

The Yankees staged a promotion that hadn't been seen at Yankee Stadium in almost 20 years. After a game against the Cleveland Indians (the Yankees lost, 4-3), the 53,037 fans in attendance were treated to a Beach Boys concert on this cloudy, 73-degree Sunday afternoon.[17] The set list consisted of 25 of their most popular songs followed by an encore session that included "Wipeout," "Barbara Ann," and "Fun, Fun, Fun."[18]

Yankees rookie pitcher Al Leiter was one of the first Yankees dressed and out of the clubhouse to see the Beach Boys. "I like them. … Everybody likes the Beach Boys. They're a legend," Leiter said.[19]

TUESDAY, JULY 4, 1989: THE BEACH BOYS

After the Yankees edged out the Detroit Tigers, 1-0, a DJ from a local radio station took the field with about 40 dancers to entertain the crowd as the stage was being moved into position in the outfield beyond second base.

The Beach Boys then took the stage and sang more than 40 songs. Actor John Stamos sat in on drums, and former Dodgers and current Yankees second baseman Steve Sax joined in on guitar for a couple of songs.

After the concert ended and the sun set, fireworks began. In all, it was a nine-hour day at Yankee Stadium.[20]

SUNDAY, AUGUST 27, 1989: THE CHARLIE DANIELS BAND

The Charlie Daniels Band played after the Yankees' 8-5 loss to the Orioles. With the Yankees having a down year, many of the 43,799 fans in attendance chanted, "George Must Go" during the game.[21]

Billy Martin, who was fired by the Yankees during the 1988 season, had a PR relationship with the Charlie Daniels Band and planned to introduce the band for the concert but decided not to.[22] According to the band's Facebook page, Mickey Mantle introduced the band.[23]

FRIDAY AND SATURDAY, JUNE 22 AND 23, 1990: BILLY JOEL

How could an event take place at Yankee Stadium without a controversy involving George Steinbrenner?

This time he had a legitimate concern. With a Nelson Mandela rally on June 21 followed by two nights of Billy Joel concerts, Steinbrenner was worried about the grass at Yankee Stadium being damaged after being covered for three days. Steinbrenner held up the sale of tickets to the Mandela rally for two days until he was satisfied that the city would pay for damages to the field up to and including replacing the turf at a maximum cost of $50,000. Steinbrenner really wanted the Mandela rally to take place, and through negotiations, the city agreed to remove the tarp every night, and Billy Joel said he was willing to help pay for any damage to the turf.[24]

The concerts were a big hit. Billy Joel always liked Yankee Stadium, its architecture and history.[25]

There were some comments about Joel's just playing nonstop music without much interaction with the crowd. From past experience in large stadiums, Joel has said, "You can't make 'stadium-sized gestures,' there is no such thing, but you have to keep your banter to a minimum, because few people can understand when you talk."[26]

As with any other superstar, the sold-out crowd loved the concerts.

A DVD called *Billy Joel Live at Yankee Stadium* was released on November 4, 2022.[27] The film was also shown at AMC and Fandango movie theaters across the country in October 2022.[28]

SATURDAY AND SUNDAY, AUGUST 29 AND 30, 1992: U2/PRIMUS/THE DISPOSABLE HEROES OF HIPROPRISY

Two Yankee Stadium dates were part of U2's worldwide Zoo TV Tour in support of their 1991 album *Achtung Baby*. The band played a 19-song set list, then encored with five songs, finishing with *Can't Help Falling in Love*.[29]

Primus and The Disposable Heroes of Hiproprisy opened up for U2.[30]

FRIDAY AND SATURDAY, JUNE 10 AND 11, 1994: PINK FLOYD

Pink Floyd really put on a show to remember. Playing mostly outdoor stadiums those days, Pink Floyd knew that they look like tiny specks on the stage, so they relied on big screens, lights, and polytechnics. Knowing this, they designed their shows to the person in the top row, farthest away from the stage.[31] Reviews from patrons said the new music that was performed in the first half of the show was not as exciting as their music from years gone by. But the second half of the show, with earlier music from when Roger Waters was with the band, was described as marvelous. Even for the people who sat far away, the lights, flying animals, and movie bits on the big screens were said to be fantastic. But Jim Farber's review in the *New York Daily News* was negative.[32]

ADDITIONAL APPEARANCES BY RECORDING ARTISTS:

SUNDAY, APRIL 25, 1999: PAUL SIMON – JOE DIMAGGIO DAY AT YANKEE STADIUM

A tribute to Joe DiMaggio, who died on March 8, 1999, was held at Yankee Stadium on April 25.

Paul Simon, a lifelong Yankees fan, sang "Mrs. Robinson." The crowd applauded when he got to the lines, "Where have you gone, Joe DiMaggio, our nation turns its lonely eyes to you" and "What's that you say, Mrs. Robinson, Joltin' Joe has left and gone away."[33]

MONDAY, JULY 14, 2008: 3 DOORS DOWN AT THE MLB HOME RUN DERBY

3 Doors Down performed their hits "Kryptonite" and "It's Not My Time" before the 2008 Home Run Derby at Yankee Stadium as part of the All-Star Week festivities.[34]

NOTES

1. "History of Madison Square Garden," Retrieved from https://www.msg.com/madison-square-garden/history, Accessed on November 13, 2022. All internet sourcing is from November 2022.

2. Adam Nagourney, "Grass Grows as Tickets Sit," *New York Daily News*, June 15, 1990: 2.

3. "Wagner Festival in New York," *Macon* (Georgia) *News*, August 14, 1928: 12. Retrieved from: https://www.newspapers.com/image/823546409/?terms=%22polyphonic%20symphony%22&match.

4. Richard Goldstein, "Pop Eye: Soundblast '66," *Village Voice*, June 16, 1966. Retrieved from https://www.villagevoice.com/2009/12/10/a-yankee-stadium-concert-and-a-new-face-at-the-voice/.

5. "Soundblast '66," retrieved from https://www.bapresley.com/silverthreads/history/soundblast/index.html.

6. "James Brown Setlist at Yankee Stadium in the Bronx, United States on 22 June 1968," Retrieved from: https://guestpectacular.com/artists/james-brown/events/1968-06-22/united-states/the-bronx/yankee-stadium-xbzlz; "Campbell's Corner," *Dayton Daily News*, June 22, 1968: 30.

7. "It's Your Thing." Retrieved from https://www.imdb.com/title/tt0196649/.

8. "Isley Bros. Show Lists Film Dates," *Billboard*, August 15, 1970: 24. Retrieved from https://worldradiohistory.com/Archive-All-Music/Billboard/70s/1970/Billboard%201970-08-15.pdf.

9. Louis Calta, "'72 Newport Jazz Festival Is Moving to New York," *New York Times*, January 5, 1972: 42. Retrieved from https://www.nytimes.com/1972/01/05/archives/-72-newport-jazz-festival-is-moving-to-new-york.html.

10. Retrieved from https://www.setlist.fm/festival/1972/newport-jazz-festival-new-york-1972-3d715af.html.

11. Retrieved from https://www.jazzmessengers.com/en/65578/various-artists/newport-in-new-york-1972.

12. Retrieved from https://www.allmusic.com/album/newport-in-new-york-72-the-jam-sessions-vols-1-2-mw0000881569.

13. Will Gonz"Yankee Stadium Fielded a Memorable Night of Music in 1973," ESPN.com, September 18, 2008. Retrieved from https://www.espn.com/espn/hispanicheritage2008/news/story?id=3596100.

14. Will González.

15. https://www.discogs.com/release/14305347-Fania-All-Stars-Live-At-Yankee-Stadium-Vol1-Vol2-.

16. https://music.apple.com/ve/album/live-at-yankee-stadium/1464276360?l=en.

17. https://www.baseball-reference.com/boxes/NYA/NYA198806260.shtml.

18. https://members.tripod.com/~fun_fun_fun/6-26-88.html.

19. "'Boy' at Heart," *New York Daily News*, June 27, 1988: 51.

20. Backstage Bruce, "NY Yankees, the Beach Boys, and Fireworks." *NY Music Scene,* July 4, 1989. Retrieved from https://nycmusicscene.blogspot.com/2017/06/ny-yankees-beach-boys-fireworks.html.

21. Phil Pepe, "Bronx Cheer: Ban Boss, Fans Serenade George as Yanks Fall 13½ back," *New York Daily News*, August 28, 1989: 145.

22. "All Dent's Asking For Is a Chance," *New York Daily News*, August 28, 1989: 145.

23. Retrieved from https://www.facebook.com/charliedanielsband/photos/a.10150185195103287/10152849217628287/?type=3.

24. Adam Nagourney, "Grass Grows as Tickets Sit," *New York Daily News*, June 15, 1990: 2.

25. Wayne Robins, "Next Batter: Billy Joel," *Newsday* (Long Island, New York), June 22, 1990: 173. Retrieved from https://www.newspapers.com/image/711624645/?terms=%22billy%20joel%22&match=1.

26. Wayne Robins, "Next Batter: Billy Joel."

27. https://www.billyjoel.com/music/live-at-yankee-stadium/.

28. https://www.amctheatres.com/movies/billy-joel-live-at-yankee-stadium-70869; https://www.fandango.com/billy-joel-live-at-yankee-stadium-228690/movie-overview.

29. https://www.u2gigs.com/show653.html.

30. https://www.concertarchives.org/venues/yankee-stadium?page=2#concert-table.

31. Email correspondence on November 3, 2022, with John Bennett, a big Pink Floyd fan who was at the concerts.

32. Jim Farber, "Pink Floyd Can't Hack It at Yankee Stadium," *New York Daily News*, June 13, 1994: 652. Retrieved from https://www.newspapers.com/image/472943384/?terms=%22Pink%20Floyd%22&match=1.

33. Brian Lewis, "DiMaggio Ceremony Special," *New York Post*, April 26, 1999. Retrieved from https://nypost.com/1999/04/26/dimaggio-ceremony-special/.

34. Pollstar staff, "3 Doors Down Meets the Boys of Summer," Pollstar.com, July 10, 2008. Retrieved from https://news.pollstar.com/2008/07/10/3-doors-down-meets-the-boys-of-summer/.

BAD MOON RISING OVER THE BRONX AND OTHER UNUSUAL EVENTS AT YANKEE STADIUM

By Ken Carrano

The history of Yankee Stadium would be incomplete without mentioning some of the unusual events held there. Yes, baseball is King in the House that Ruth Built, but many other events besides baseball were held there, including football games, boxing and wrestling matches, political speeches, papal masses, and soccer games. One of the more unusual events that took place in the Stadium was a visit by the Rev. Sun Myung Moon at the time of the United States Bicentennial.

Born in what is now North Korea, Moon founded the Holy Spirit Association for the Unification of World Christianity in 1954.[1] After moving to the United States in 1971, Moon gained notoriety by supporting President Richard Nixon during the Watergate scandal, and for performing "mass weddings," often involving couples who were meeting for the first time.[2] Followers of Moon were referred to as Moonies, often thought to be a cult, alienating children from their parents.

Moon had held a rally at Madison Square Garden in New York City in September 1974, drawing thousands more than could be seated in the 20,000-seat arena.[3] Hopes were high that Yankee Stadium would be filled to overflowing with Moon's devotees for a rally called the "God Bless America Festival" to be held on June 1, 1976. However, on the day of the event, many seats remained empty, with attendance estimates ranging from 25,000 to 40,000. A downpour about two hours before the start time of the rally was thought to have held down attendance.

Those in the Stadium were witness to a brass band, an orchestra, two groups of singers, and a Korean folk ballet.[4] They also witnessed youths in attendance throwing programs and decorations from the upper deck, running through the corridors, and lighting firecrackers and at least one smoke bomb.[5] To get into the Stadium, attendees also had to make it past many

Yankee Stadium prepares to host its first Papal visit in 1965.

protesters who denounced Moon as "among other things, a fascist dictator, a false Christian and a deluder of American youth."[6] "It's a religious smorgasbord," exclaimed a bystander.[7] Yellow-robed Hare Krishnas chanted, peddled their books and sought contributions. Hundreds of Christians passed out tracts and preached and warned that Moon was a "false prophet" and the "devil himself."[8] Police reported seven arrests in and around the Stadium, including a robbery, an assault, and two charges of possession of a gun.[9]

Moon's experience at Yankee Stadium did not spoil him on New York. In 1982 he held a "mass wedding" at Madison Square Garden with over 2,000 couples participating. That same year, he was convicted of filing false income-tax returns and conspiracy and spent 13 months at the Federal Correctional Institution in Danbury, Connecticut. Moon died in 2012.

Moon's event at Yankee Stadium may have been among the strangest, but it was certainly not the only unusual thing that happened at the ballpark in the Bronx. Here are a few other events that may be surprising:

JULY 24, 1923 – BENNY LEONARD DEFEATED LEW TENDLER IN FRONT OF 58,522

Yankee Stadium still had that new-stadium smell when lightweights Benny Leonard and Lew Tendler clashed on the afternoon of July 24, 1923, in the first championship boxing match held there. Leonard retained his lightweight title easily, though the fight went the full 15 rounds. The gate receipts of $452,648 for the match were reported as the second largest in history.[10]

AUGUST 2, 1950 – 72,674 ATTEND THE INTERNATIONAL CONVENTION OF JEHOVAH'S WITNESSES

The international convention of Jehovah's Witnesses was held in New York City in late July and early August of 1950. The attendees were so numerous that a trailer city had to be set up in New Jersey to help accommodate the throng.[11] The Yankee Stadium portion of the convention was an all-day affair, with foreign-language sessions held in the morning and general sessions in the afternoon and evening, with reports offered from representatives of various countries.[12]

The leader of the organization, Brother Nathan H. Knorr gave a fiery speech, in which he warned that Armageddon might come before the next conventions of the Witnesses could be held.[13] In addition, after three years of research, the Jehovah's Witnesses organization released a new translation of the New Testament at the convention. The group expected to sell one million copies of the new translation during the first year – 100,000 copies were sold at the Stadium that day.[14]

APRIL 29, 1956 – "AMERICA SALUTES ISRAEL" RALLY AT YANKEE STADIUM

A crowd of 42,455 gathered at Yankee Stadium at this celebration as Israel marked its eighth anniversary as a nation. The speakers, including Senator John F. Kennedy of Massachusetts, argued that since Arab nations were receiving weapons from Communist countries, it was necessary to restore the balance of arms by supplying Israel.[15]

JULY 20, 1957 – REV. BILLY GRAHAM'S APPEARANCE DRAWS 100,000

An additional 10,000 were turned away from the event, at which the Rev. Dr. Billy Graham called upon sinners to repent. Among the throng was Vice President Richard M. Nixon. When introducing Graham, Nixon joked that even the Yankees couldn't draw the crowd that the Rev. Graham did.[16] The 100,000 (estimated by Stadium manager James K. Thompson) eclipsed the earlier record attendance at Yankee Stadium of 88,150 for the Joe Louis-Max Baer heavyweight championship fight in 1935. Graham's appearance at Yankee Stadium was part of a 60-evening crusade throughout New York City, primarily at Madison Square Garden, that drew 1,102,600.[17]

SEPTEMBER 7, 1957 – CARDINAL FRANCIS SPELLMAN CELEBRATES HIS 25TH YEAR AS BISHOP OF NEW YORK

The event was thought to be the largest gathering of Roman Catholic hierarchy ever to attend a liturgical function in New York. It included five cardinals (including Spellman), 18 archbishops, 83 bishops, and two abbots. The Stadium was converted into an outdoor cathedral with a specially constructed sanctuary 48 feet high and 180 feet long, running from foul line to foul line. Some 50,000 gathered for the service.[18]

OCTOBER 4, 1965 – POPE PAUL VI VISITS THE UNITED NATIONS AND YANKEE STADIUM

In what would be the first of three papal visits to Yankee Stadium, Pope Paul VI had three things to tell American Catholics during his sermon at Yankee Stadium: "First of all, you must love peace. Second thought: You must serve the cause of peace. Third thought: Peace must be based on moral and religious principles."[19] The Pope also addressed the United Nations, asking for the elimination of offensive weapons.

OCTOBER 2, 1979 – POPE JOHN PAUL II HOLDS MASS AT YANKEE STADIUM FOR 80,000

The end of the first day of a two-day visit to New York City found Pope John at Yankee Stadium, where he reminded the parishioners that the poor were "your brothers and sisters. You must never be content to leave them just the crumbs from the feast."[20] The assembled crown listened so intently that subway trains could be heard in the background as the pontiff spoke.

JUNE 21 AND 22, 1990 – NELSON MANDELA & BILLY JOEL APPEAR ON CONSECUTIVE DAYS

On February 11, 1990, Nelson Mandela was released from Victor Verster Prison in South Africa. Just over four months later, Mandela visited New York

City to campaign against the South African policy of apartheid. The trip included church services, a visit to Harlem, and a rally at Yankee Stadium. During the rally, New York Mayor David Dinkins placed a Yankees jacket on Mandela's shoulders, and a Yankees cap on his head. Mandela smiled and declared, "You now know who I am. I am a Yankee."[21] Preparations for the event had been full of uncertainty, but a crowd of 80,000 (estimates ranged from 55,000 to an impossible 200,000) came to support Mandela and the African National Congress. "The man is a holy man," said Larry Minor of the Bronx.[22]

The next evening, 60,000 came to see Billy Joel perform at the Stadium. "You hate to say Yankee Stadium had a better week when its team was out of town," David Hinckley of the *New York Daily News* reported, "but not much the Yankees have tried so far this year has come close to the triumph Billy Joel registered Friday night before some 60,000 happy rock-n-roll fans."[23]

SEPTEMBER 23, 2001 – A MULTI-FAITH PRAYER FOR AMERICA

A service in honor of the missing and dead from the September 11, 2001, attacks on the United States was held at Yankee Stadium. Organizers had hoped for a larger attendance, but 20,000 attended the five-hour ceremony that featured celebrities and religious leaders from nearly every faith. Actor James Earl Jones opened the ceremony by stating, "Our nation is united as never before. We are united not only in our grief, but in our resolve to build a better world. At this service, we seek to summon what Abraham Lincoln called 'the better angels of our nature.'" Later in the service, New York Mayor Rudolph Giuliani inspired the crowd, stating, "Our skyline will rise again. In the words of President Bush, 'We will rebuild New York City.' To those who say our city will never be the same, I say you are right. It will be better."[24]

MARCH 10, 2006 – WEDDING BELLS

Ed Lucas was a huge baseball fan who lost his sight after being hit in the face with a line drive in 1951, playing ball after celebrating Bobby Thomson's "Shot Heard Round the World."[25] This accident did not diminish Lucas's love of the game. His mother took him to a clothing store to meet Phil Rizzuto, and the two struck up a friendship that lasted until Rizzuto's death.

Lucas eventually became a reporter, doing most of his work at Yankee Stadium.[26]

Many things had happened over the years at home plate at Yankee Stadium, but a wedding was not one of them. This changed on March 10, 2006, when Lucas asked to hold his wedding there. Weddings had been held at the Stadium previously, but never at home plate. Yankees owner George Steinbrenner not only approved the request but paid for a dinner reception for 350 guests.[27] Rizzuto had introduced Lucas to his wife, Allison Pfeifle, a lifelong baseball fan who had also lost her sight and was Rizzuto's florist.[28]

APRIL 20, 2008 – "THANKS A MILLION, HOLY FATHER"

The final papal visit occurred during the final days of Yankee Stadium. Pope Benedict had become the first pope to visit an American synagogue and had also visited Ground Zero and met with 9/11 survivors before the Mass. Speaking before the pope addressed the crowd, Cardinal Edward Egan, Archbishop of New York, exclaimed "Thanks a million, Holy Father" for his visit.[29] "I've never seen Yankee Stadium look more beautiful, and I have season tickets," exclaimed Philip Giordano of Greenwich, Connecticut.[30]

MAY 14, 2008 – GRADUATION

New York University usually held its annual graduation ceremonies at Washington Square Park in New York. That site was undergoing renovations, so NYU turned to another location – Yankee Stadium. Honorary-degree recipients included constitutional scholar Laurence Tribe and actor Michael J. Fox. Michael Strahan, a former defensive end for the New York Giants and television personality, received NYU's Lewis Rudin Award for Exemplary Service to New York City.[31]

The ceremony was highlighted not by speeches, but by the efforts of graduate Will Lopez. Wearing only his graduation gown, boxer shorts, socks and shoes, Lopez hopped the fence behind first base, ran across the infield to tag third, and was headed for home when tackled by security guards.

"He's going to always be remembered as the guy who ran around the bases and got tackled, which is pretty cool," said Alex Gavlin, a NYU medical student. When asked if he regretted the incident, Lopez replied, "Are you kidding me? It was the best moment of my life."[32]

SOURCES

In addition to the sources listed in the Notes, the author accessed mlb.com, Retrosheet.org, and Baseball-Reference.com, and Scott Pitoniak, *Memories of Yankee Stadium* (Chicago: Triumph Books, 2008). All weblinks accessed November 23, 2022.

NOTES

1 Emma Brown, "Sun Myung Moon Dies at 92," *Washington Post,* September 2, 2012. The entity Moon founded is commonly known as the Unification Church.

2 https://www.insider.com/who-are-the-moonies-and-what-is-the-unification-church-2022-7.

3 Eleanor Blue, "Moon Sect Invites Parents to Rally," *New York Times,* May 31, 1976: 5.

4 Eleanor Blue, "Moon Rally Draws 25,000, Half of Stadium Capacity," *New York Times,* June 2, 1976: 28.

5 "Moon Rally."

6 "Moon Rally."

7 Marjorie Hyer, "Rev. Moon Festival Eclipsed," *Washington Post,* June 2, 1976: A7.

8 "Rev. Moon Festival Eclipsed."

9 Lindsay Miller, "Moon's Night – A Deluge of Rain, Rowdies and Rhetoric," *New York Post,* June 2, 1976.

10 "Rickard Seeking to Match Leonard," *New York Times,* July 25, 1923: 20; Harry Newman, "Leonard Wins From Tendler," *New York Daily News,* July 25, 1923.

11 See "International Assemblies (1946-1950)," Watchtower Online Library, https://wol.jw.org/en/wol/d/r1/lp-e/1956123.

12 "International Assemblies (1946-1950)."

13 "Witnesses Pack Yankee Stadium, Largest Crowd," *New York Amsterdam News,* August 12, 1950: 13.

14 "A New Translation of the New Testament," *New York Times,* August 3, 1950: 19.

15 "Arms Urged for Israel," *New York Times,* April 30, 1956: 2.

16 Danny Lewis, "The Time Billy Graham Packed Madison Square Garden and Yankee Stadium to the Brim," WNYC.org, February 21, 2018. https://www.wnyc.org/story/time-billy-graham-packed-madison-square-garden-and-yankee-stadium-brim/.

17 George Dugan, "100,000 Fill Yankee Stadium to Hear Graham," *New York Times,* July 21, 1957: 1.

18 Russell Porter, "50,000 at Yankee Stadium Honor Spellman on His 25th Year as Bishop," *New York Times,* September 8, 1957: 1.

19 "90,000 at Stadium Attend Papal Mass and Hear a Homily," *New York Times,* October 5, 1965: 2

20 Francis X. Clines, "Closes First of 2 Days at a Mass for 80,000 in Yankee Stadium," *New York Times,* October 3, 1979: 2.

21 John Kifner, "The Mandela Visit; Mandela Takes His Message to Rally in Yankee Stadium," *New York Times,* June 22, 1990: 1.

22 Mitchel Powell, "Yankee Stadium Erupts in Ecstasy," *Newsday* (Long Island, New York), June 22, 1990: 3.

23 David Hinckley, "Billy I: The Kid Scores Big," *New York Daily News,* June 25, 1990: 27.

24 Robert D. McFadden, "A Nation Challenged: The Service," *New York Times,* September 24, 2001: B7.

25 Richard Sandomir, "Ed Lucas, Blind Baseball Chronicler, Is Dead at 82," *New York Times,* November 16, 2021.

26 Sandomir.

27 Sandomir.

28 Osborn, "Today Marks Ten Years Since Ed Lucas Was Married at Home Plate in Yankee Stadium," pinstripealley.com, March 10, 2016. https://www.pinstripealley.com/2016/3/10/11185848/yankees-marriage-ed-lucas-yankee-stadium-mantle-rizzuto.

29 Larry McShane, Melissa Grace, Stephanie Gaskell and Corky Siemaszko, "Thanks a Million, Holy Father," *New York Daily News,* April 21, 2008: 1.

30 McShane.

31 NYU news release, "NYU to Hold 2008 Commencement in Yankee Stadium," NYU.edu, May 6, 2008. https://www.nyu.edu/about/news-publications/news/2008/may/nyu_to_hold_2008_commencement.html.

32 Rick Shapiro, "NYU Grad: No MSG," *New York Daily News,* May 16, 2008: 12.

SELECTED GAMES

BABE RUTH HOMERS IN YANKEE STADIUM'S GRAND OPENING, HINTING AT FRANCHISE'S DYNASTIC FUTURE

April 18, 1923:
New York Yankees 4, Boston Red Sox 1,
at Yankee Stadium

By Frederick C. Bush

In 1913 the New York Highlanders were renamed the Yankees and moved from Hilltop Park into the Polo Grounds, the home field of the National League's New York Giants. Two years later, the franchise was under the new co-ownership of Jacob Ruppert and Tillinghast L'Hommedieu Huston, who initiated the team's transformation into an American League powerhouse by purchasing Babe Ruth from the Boston Red Sox in December 1919. The Big Bam's prodigious home-run output eventually resulted in the tenant Yankees outdrawing the landlord Giants in their own home park.

As a result, John McGraw, the Giants' manager, minority owner, and noted hater of the American League, could no longer abide the Yankees. It was not enough for him that he had led the Giants to consecutive World Series triumphs over his despised rivals in 1921 and 1922, including holding the vaunted Sultan of Swat to a .188 batting average with no home runs in a four-game sweep in the latter Series. He wanted the Yankees gone and persuaded majority owner Horace Stoneham to banish them in the hope that the team would falter and fold. When McGraw found out that the Yankees' new stadium would be built in the Bronx, right across the Harlem River from the Polo Grounds, he gleefully crowed, "They are going up to Goatville. And before long they will be lost sight of. A New York team should be based on Manhattan Island."[1]

Although McGraw was an innovator who had a long, successful career in baseball, his assessment of the Yankees' new home and the team's future could not have been more in error. The $2.5 million structure

was situated on a 10-acre plot, and it took 500 workmen 11 months to complete "the first ballpark to be referred to as a stadium" just in time for opening day of the 1923 season.[2] In light of its size and price tag, the *New York Times* rhapsodized:

> Down on the Potomac, close by the National Capitol, they are thinking about erecting an impressive monument to the national game of baseball. But in the busy borough of the Bronx … the real monument to baseball will be unveiled this afternoon — the new Yankee Stadium … comprising in its broad reaches of concrete and steel the last word in baseball arenas.[3]

Little Ray Kelly became Babe Ruth's "mascot" at age 3 and was seen around the Stadium often throughout the 1920s, including on Opening Day 1923.

Everyone who was someone, along with a host of anyones — more than 25,000 of whom were unable to gain admission to the sold-out stadium — wanted to be part of the grand opening on April 18, 1923. The Yankees gave the official attendance that day as 74,200, but later amended that number to 62,200.[4] The list of dignitaries present included Baseball Commissioner Kenesaw Mountain Landis, New York Governor Al Smith, and New York City Mayor John Hylan.

John Philip Sousa directed the Seventh Regiment Band as it marched to the center-field flagpole, where New York manager Miller Huggins and Boston skipper Frank Chance raised the American flag and the Yankees' 1922 pennant as the band played "The Star-Spangled Banner." After Governor Smith threw the ceremonial first ball to Yankees catcher Wally Schang, it was time to play ball. New York hurler Bob Shawkey threw the first pitch in Yankee Stadium history, a ball high and inside, to Schang with Chick Fewster at bat for Boston.

Another notable moment took place in the top of the second inning, when Red Sox first baseman George Burns got the first hit in stadium history. Burns then attempted to garner the first stolen base of the day, but he was gunned down at second base by Schang. Second baseman Aaron Ward made the first base hit for the home team when he singled in the third. After the game Burns received a box of cigars and Ward received 50 "ropes" [cigars] for their landmark hits.[5]

Ruth, whose popularity had made this new stadium both possible and necessary, naturally provided the day's biggest thrill as the Yankees scored all four of their runs in the third inning. Shawkey and Whitey Witt had reached base on consecutive singles, and Joe Dugan followed with a base hit of his own to drive in the first run. The next batter to step to the plate, with runners at first and third, was The Bambino.

Ruth was seeking redemption after a miserable 1922 season in which he had batted .315 with 35 homers after hitting .378 and clouting 59 round-trippers in 1921; there was also the cloud of that .188 World Series performance hanging over his head. Ruth knew "[t]he talk was that he was boozing it up a lot and couldn't be managed, and maybe he was through."[6] He had spent the offseason walking the straight and narrow and working his way back into playing shape. In spite of his efforts, he had not performed well in spring-training exhibition games, and he told his teammates, as they left the clubhouse on Opening Day, "I'd give a year off my life to hit one today."[7]

Ruth now had his second opportunity of the day to deliver the desired blow. He fouled off Red Sox pitcher Howard Ehmke's first pitch, took a ball, hit another pitch foul, and watched ball two go by. Then Ehmke left a letter-high curveball over the plate that Ruth ripped several rows up into the bleachers for a three-run blast that gave the Yankees a 4-0 lead. As he crossed home plate, Ruth "lifted his Kelley and smiled from ear to ear as he faced the multitude and made those graceful bows rehearsed so many times in his great season of 1921."[8]

Ever the showman, and often a bit of a huckster, Ruth afterward asserted that his blast had been forecast earlier in the week. He claimed that Hendrik Willem van Loon, author of *The Story of Mankind*, had given him a silver dollar for good luck and had promised him, "You'll get a homer in the third inning with two on base."[9] The fact that the certainty expressed in this story did not exactly jibe with Ruth's willingness to sacrifice a year of his life for an Opening Day homer did not faze The Big Bam.

Ruth's clout was the climax of the game, though the Yankees did threaten to score again in the fourth inning. Bob Meusel led off the frame with a double, but Ehmke fielded Schang's bunt and nailed Meusel at third base. After Ward struck out, Everett Scott, playing in his 987th consecutive game, delivered a double of his own.[10] Schang tried to score from first base but was gunned down at home on a nice play from right fielder Shano Collins to first baseman Burns, who fired the relay throw to catcher Al DeVormer.

The Red Sox scored their lone run in the top of the seventh inning when Shawkey walked Burns and Norm McMillan drove him in with a triple. It was the only hiccup of the afternoon for Shawkey, who pitched a complete-game three-hitter to earn the first win in Yankee Stadium history.

The final noteworthy event occurred in the ninth inning, with Burns batting for Boston, when fans from the bleachers scaled the outfield wall and surrounded Ruth in right field. Home-plate umpire Tom Connolly stopped the game but soon realized "the futility of trying to clear the outskirts. Accordingly, Ruth had plenty of comrades in right when the game closed."[11]

The Yankees emerged victorious in their 1923 debut, and everyone seemed certain that Ruth was back on track. However, the *New York Times* summarized the importance of the day by stating, "But the game, after all, was only an incident of a busy afternoon. The stadium was the thing. For the Yankee owners it was the realization of a dream long cherished. For the fans it was something which they had never seen before in baseball."[12] Perhaps to the chagrin of McGraw and Stoneham, the *Times* added, "The Yankees' new home, besides being beautiful and majestic, is practical. It was emptied yesterday of its 74,000 in quicker time than the Polo Grounds ever was."[13]

After slugging his Opening Day home run, Ruth had referred to his offseason training regimen and abstinence from his vices, saying, "I guess there must be something in that old gag about virtue being its own reward."[14] By the end of the 1923 season, the tenants of the new "beautiful, majestic, and practical" baseball cathedral called Yankee Stadium would be World Series champions for the first time after defeating the denizens of their previous home, McGraw's Giants, in six games. Ruth batted .393 and led the league with 41 homers in the regular season. He redeemed himself in the World Series as well by battering Giants pitching for a .368 average and three home runs. It was indeed quite a reward.

SOURCES

In addition to the sources cited in the Notes, the author consulted Baseball-Reference.com and Retrosheet.org.

https://www.baseball-reference.com/boxes/NYA/NYA192304180.shtml

https://www.retrosheet.org/boxesetc/1923/B04180NYA1923.htm

NOTES

1   Harvey Frommer, "Remembering the First Game at Yankee Stadium April 18, 1923," travel-watch.com/remembering1stgameatyankeestad1.htm, accessed May 18, 2018.

2   Frommer.

3   "Yanks' New Stadium to Be Opened Today: Record Crowd Expected to Witness Dedication of $2,500,000 Baseball Arena," *New York Times*, April 18, 1923: 17.

4   Robert Weintraub, *The House That Ruth Built: A New Stadium, the First Yankees Championship, and the Redemption of 1923* (New York: Little, Brown and Company, 2011), 17-18. According to Weintraub, a boxing match was held at Yankee Stadium in May for which 10,000 extra seats were placed on the field. The total number of tickets printed for the match was 70,000, which indicated that the current capacity for baseball games was approximately 60,000. Yankees business manager Ed Barrow then admitted that he had added standing-room fans to his original estimate and amended his Opening Day figure to 62,200. Weintraub writes that even this figure is "probably still exaggerated, but [it was] nevertheless by far the largest crowd in the sport's history."

5   Ed Cunningham, "Echoes from That Babe Ruth Swat," *Boston Herald*, April 19, 1923: 14.

6   John Durant, "April 1923: First Day at Yankee Stadium," si.com/vault/1963/04/22/602983/april-1923-first-day-at-yankee-stadium, accessed May 18, 2018.

7   Weintraub, 27.

8   "The Paying Colonels Draw Dividend When King George Whacks," *Boston Herald*, April 19, 1923: 14.

9   "Ruth Says Van Loon Predicted Home Run," *Springfield* (Massachusetts) *Republican*, April 19, 1923: 6.

10   Everett Scott played in a major-league record 1,307 consecutive games between June 20, 1916, and May 5, 1925. His record would eventually be broken by another Yankees player, a rookie who had debuted in 1923 but had played in only 13 games and had been left off the team's playoff roster. Lou Gehrig would eventually shatter Scott's record by playing in 2,130 consecutive games.

11   Cunningham, "Echoes from That Babe Ruth Swat."

12   "74,200 See Yankees Open New Stadium; Ruth Hits Home Run," *New York Times*, April 19, 1923: 1.

13   "74,200 See Yankees Open New Stadium," 15.

14   "Ruth Says Van Loon Predicted Home Run."

AN EPIC WEDDING ANNIVERSARY

October 14, 1923:
New York Yankees 8, New York Giants 1,
at Yankee Stadium
Game Five of the 1923 World Series

By Kirk C. Jenkins

In the early afternoon of Sunday, October 14, 1923, two old friends, Alice Wray Bush and Marie Aubrey Schang, found their way to their box seats in the six-month-old Yankee Stadium.[1] The women had known each other for a decade as their husbands played together, first in Philadelphia, then in Boston, and most recently in New York. It was a big day. It was both women's wedding anniversary: the Bushes' ninth, the Schangs' eighth. And they were there to watch their husbands, the starting battery for the New York Yankees in the pivotal Game Five of the World Series.[2]

The Yankees had lost the 1921 and 1922 Series to the New York Giants, but this year things might be different. The Series was knotted at two games each, with the visiting team having won each of the first four contests. In the Yankees' clubhouse, a player asked the starting pitcher, Bullet Joe Bush, what he wanted for his anniversary. "Give me 10 runs, boys, and I don't want anything else," Bush answered.[3]

The day had dawned cold and misty, but undeterred, 3,000 fans had already lined up near Yankee Stadium by dawn. A reporter counted license plates

Fans line up for bleacher seats during the 1923 World Series.

from 10 states among the fans waiting in their cars, and there were hundreds of bonfires. The ticket booths opened at 10:00 A.M. The bleachers were sold out by 11:30, and general-admission seats were all gone 90 minutes later.[4] Scalpers were doing a brisk business, with $3.30 bleacher seats going for $10. By game time, the going rate had risen to $15.[5] In the end, Yankees owner Jacob Ruppert estimated that 50,000 fans were turned away.[6]

Giants manager John McGraw was showing the strain. He had settled on Mule Watson as his Game Five starter, but Watson became ill in the hours before the game, so McGraw had to go with Jack Bentley.[7] McGraw never missed a chance to try to throw Yankees slugger Babe Ruth off his game, so just before the game began, he picked a fight with the umpires, arguing that Ruth was stepping out of the box after each pitch and should be called out. When the umpires declined to act, McGraw did the next best thing and retired to the clubhouse to bellow at his ballplayers.[8]

Giants shortstop Dave Bancroft led off the game a few minutes after 2:00. He was out on a two-strike roller to second baseman Aaron Ward. After Heinie Groh flied out to Babe Ruth, second baseman Frankie Frisch was out on a groundball to Aaron Ward.[9] In the bottom of the first, Yankees third baseman Joe Dugan – whose parents and uncle had unexpectedly arrived from their home in New Haven before the game without tickets and were ushered into box seats by Yankees general manager Ed Barrow – got the team started with a sharp single to right.[10] After Babe Ruth drew a full-count walk, Bob Meusel slammed a triple to left, scoring Dugan and Ruth.[11] The next day, a *New York Times* reporter wrote, "Bullets may travel faster than that ball, but it is doubtful."[12] Ross Youngs made a great one-handed catch on the right-field terrace on Wally Pipp's fly, but Meusel trotted in after the catch, scoring the Yankees' third run.[13]

The Giants broke through in the top of the second. With one out, Yankees outfielder Bob Meusel's older brother Emil "Irish" Meusel pounded a long triple to left. Giants center fielder Casey Stengel hit a roller to first baseman Pipp. Pipp tried to make a quick flip to first for the out, but Bush was a bit slow covering the bag. Although the Yankees got the out at first, Meusel scored on Bush's mental mistake.[14]

The Yankees blew the game open in the bottom of the second. After one out, Bush got things started by lining a single to center. After center fielder Whitey Witt drew a walk, Dugan crushed a liner to right-center. Stengel tried for a diving catch, but the ball

bounced over his glove, and with Ross Youngs trying for the catch too, the ball rolled to the wall. By the time the Giants got the ball back to the infield, Dugan had a stand-up three-run inside-the-park homer.[15]

After first baseman George Kelly misplayed Babe Ruth's bouncing ball for an error, Giants manager McGraw removed Bentley in favor of pitcher Jack Scott. As McGraw trudged slowly to the mound, a Yankees fan shouted, "Start them two at a time – that way we won't have to wait for the change later!"[16]

Bob Meusel greeted Scott with a line-drive single to right, as Ruth came around to third. Pipp sent a bouncing grounder to Frankie Frisch, and when Frisch tried to cut off the run, Ruth executed a magnificent hook slide to evade the tag and score the Yankees' seventh run.[17] "No toe dancer could have come in with such grace," Grantland Rice wrote.[18]

The Yankees added an eighth run in the bottom of the fourth when Dugan led off with his third hit of the day, and after Ruth singled him to right, Bob Meusel drove in the run on his third hit. After Pipp drew a four-pitch walk, McGraw yanked Scott, bringing in Virgil Barnes.[19] But "by that time, the Yanks were so far ahead they were planning on their fishing and hunting trips when the series would be all over," according to the *New York Daily News*.[20] A half-inning later, the Yankees mounted another minor threat when Dugan bagged his fourth hit of the day, with a single to right that sent Whitey Witt to second.[21]

The Giants threatened for only the second time in the top of the seventh. With one out, Irish Meusel sliced a liner past Yankees second baseman Ward for his third base hit of the day. The Yankees got Stengel on a fly ball, but then George Kelly drew a four-pitch walk. Bush managed to ring up Giants catcher Hank Gowdy on a groundball, which Ward tossed to shortstop Everett Scott for the force out.[22]

After the Giants went out in order in the top of the eighth, with Bush striking out two, the crowd began to file out. Leading off, Ruth got the closest thing he had all day to a homer, crushing a long fly ball to center that Stengel caught at the fence. After the Giants finally got Bob Meusel out, on a bouncer to their latest pitcher, Claude Jonnard, Pipp ended the eighth by striking out.[23]

Given that Bush held a commanding lead and had thrown only 101 pitches through the first eight innings, Yankees manager Miller Huggins sent him back to the mound in the ninth to wrap things up. He did so easily, getting Frisch on a bouncer to Dugan and Youngs on a fly ball to Witt. The final hitter was Irish Meusel, the only Giant to get a hit off Bush that day. Bush finally coaxed Meusel into hitting a bouncing ball to Ward to end the game.[24] Grantland Rice summarized Bush's dominating performance: "Against this display of stuff any belated hope of a Giant rally went glimmering where the woodbine twineth and the Wangdoodle mourns its requiem."[25]

The day was not just a masterful performance but redemption for Yankee pitcher Bush, who had lost the deciding game of the 1922 World Series and the first game of the 1923 Series. In addition to Irish Meusel's three hits, Bush struck out three and walked only two. For the day he threw only 107 pitches – 24 called strikes, 10 fouls, 14 infield outs, and 10 outfield outs against 46 balls.[26] "His work was away above the expert stuff," one reporter wrote the next day. "It was the kind that is gained only by years and years of experience and study and effect."[27]

The Yankees were "happy as kids" in the clubhouse after the game. Outside, the "two happiest people in all New York" waited, "nervous, modest and almost speechless with joy" after a day "rooting and praying together in the grandstand" – Mrs. Bush and Mrs. Schang.[28] The next morning, Babe Ruth predicted that the Yankees would end the Series with a win in Game Six.[29] But Giants manager McGraw was putting a brave face on things: "I have just as much confidence as when we started. We feel able to do it. ... You can bet there will be a seventh game. Arthur Nehf will see to that."[30] In the end, Ruth was right: Back at the Polo Grounds for Game Six, the Yankees wrapped up the Series, 6-4, their first Series championship.

SOURCES

In addition to the sources cited in the Notes, the author consulted Baseball-Reference.com and Retrosheet.org.

https://www.baseball-reference.com/boxes/NYA/NYA192310140.shtml

https://www.retrosheet.org/boxesetc/1923/B10140NYA1923.htm

NOTES

1. Babe Ruth, "Wives Boost for Joe and Wally," *Tacoma* (Washington) *Daily Ledger*, October 15, 1923: 13.

2. Ruth, "Wives Boost for Joe and Wally"; James Crusinberry, "Battery's Wedding Day Celebrated in Style," *New York Daily News*, October 15, 1923: 2.

3. "Yankees Rout Giants; Win Fifth Game, 8-1; 50,000 Fail to Get In," *New York Times*, October 15, 1923: 12; "Joe Bush Is Hero of Yankee Players," *New York Times*, October 15, 1923: 11.

4. "Fans Gather Early at Stadium's Gates," *New York Times*, October 15, 1923: 11; Robert Weintraub, *The House That Ruth Built* (Boston: Little, Brown & Company, 2011), 342.

5. "Fans Gather Early at Stadium's Gates."

6. "Yankees Rout Giants; Win Fifth Game, 8-1," 1.

7. Weintraub, 344.

8. Weintraub, 344.

9. "Terrific Attack Again Carries Yanks to Victory," *Hutchinson* (Kansas) *News*, October 15, 1923: 11.

10. "Pa, Ma and Uncle Make It Dugan Day," *New York Times*, October 15, 1923: 11; Grantland Rice, "Brains at Discount Before Yanks' Drive," *Boston Globe*, October 15, 1923: 9; "Yanks Have Giants Backed to the Wall," *New York Times*, October 15, 1923: 11.

11. "Yankees Rout Giants; Win Fifth Game, 8-1."

12. "Yankees Rout Giants; Win Fifth Game, 8-1."

13. Rice, "Brains at Discount"; "Yankees Rout Giants; Win Fifth Game, 8-1"; "Yanks Have Giants Backed to the Wall."

14. "Play by Play Story of Yankees' Easy Victory," *Boston Globe*, October 15, 1923: 9; James Crusinberry, "Dugan and R. Meusel Lead Heavy Attack," *New York Daily News*, October 15, 1923: 22.

15. Rice, "Brains at Discount." Rice also wrote, "The baffled Casey decided to respond with a shoestring catch, but his judgment of the distance cracked under the strain. He couldn't quite reach the ball, which bounded on beyond and then began rolling like a half-topped mashie shot pointed in the general direction of a flock of bunkers. ... Casey whirled and began to chase it with the alacrity of a stocky poodle pursuing a meat wagon, but he never could catch up." Grantland Rice, "Irish Meusel Only Player to Hit Yankee Sharpshooter," *Bridgeport* (Connecticut) *Telegram*, October 15, 1923: 14; "Yankees Rout Giants; Win Fifth Game, 8-1."

16. Rice, "Brains at Discount"; "Yankees Rout Giants; Win Fifth Game, 8-1"; Weintraub, 345.

17. Rice, "Brains at Discount"; "Yankees Rout Giants; Win Fifth Game, 8-1."

18. Rice, "Brains at Discount"; Rice, "Irish Meusel Only Player to Hit Yankee Sharpshooter."

19. Rice, "Brains at Discount."

20. Crusinberry, "Dugan and R. Meusel Lead Heavy Attack."

21. Rice, "Brains at Discount"; "Terrific Attack Again Carries Yanks to Victory."

22. "Terrific Attack Again Carries Yanks to Victory."

23. Rice, "Brains at Discount"; "Yankees Rout Giants; Win Fifth Game, 8-1."

24. "Terrific Attack Again Carries Yanks to Victory"; "Bush Pitched 107 Balls," *New York Times*, October 15, 1923: 11.

25. "Rice, "Brains at Discount."

26. "Bush Pitched 107 Balls."

27. James Crusinberry, "Bush's Pitching Places Hugmen One Game From World Title," *New York Daily News*, October 15, 1923: 2.

28. "Wives Boost for Joe and Wally."

29. Babe Ruth, "Yankees Are Happy as Kids – Ruth," *Tacoma Daily Ledger*, October 15, 1923: 13. It's unclear whether the ghostwriter for this article was Westbrook Pegler, Ford Frick, or another ghostwriter employed by Ruth's agent, Christy Walsh.

30. John McGraw, "Better Baseball Beat Us," *Tacoma Daily Ledger*, October 15, 1923: 13; Weintraub, 346. McGraw's column was likely written by either Christy Walsh or one of his assistants.

"MURDERERS' ROW" KICKS OFF NEW PENNANT CHASE AMID OVERFLOWING CROWDS

April 12, 1927:
New York Yankees 8, Philadelphia Athletics 3
at Yankee Stadium

By Tara Krieger

For the first of its eventual 110 wins, the 1927 Yankees team braved overflowing crowds, raised its 1926 pennant, and saw the Bambino whiff twice before being removed for a pinch-hitter in an 8-3 Opening Day victory against the favored Philadelphia Athletics.

"The weather was lovely, the peanuts and hot dogs were unusually tasty," wrote James Harrison of the *New York Times*.[1]

The headlines heralded the attendance – around a quarter-million fans swarmed the seven American and National League parks hosting Opening Day 1927.[2] Baseball was as popular as ever in the Roaring Twenties, as the reported 230,000-plus rivaled a similar mark in 1925, when eight games were played.[3]

And the biggest draw of all was at Yankee Stadium, still shiny and new at just four years old, where 72,000 faithful packed through the gates to get a glimpse of the reigning American League champions. Word had it that another 25,000 were turned away.

The *New York Times* broke that down: 62,000 paid customers, 9,000 invited guests, and 1,000 "other deadheads."[4] Joe Vila in *The Sporting News* was more skeptical about the Yankees' reports, estimating 65,000. "Some of the newspapers went crazy and announced that the total count was 72,000, or 9,000 more than the capacity crowds that saw two of the World's Series games in the Stadium last Fall. It was ridiculous bunk, of course, but it served to convince the skeptics who had been knocking the game all Winter, that the grand old pastime still is very much alive."[5]

Vila also highlighted that the crowds may have turned out to see the Athletics' most recent acquisitions, a pair of 40-year-olds who would be early inductees into the then-hypothetical Baseball Hall of Fame: batting king Ty Cobb and fan favorite Eddie Collins, back for a second stint. Dodgers star Zack Wheat, nearly 39, was another Athletics pickup that winter, in what would be his final season.

Having Babe Ruth play for the home team didn't exactly drive people away, either.

Despite the Yankees being the AL champions, most sportswriters had picked the Athletics to win it all in 1927.[6] Beyond Cobb, Collins, and Wheat, Philadelphia was cultivating young stars like catcher Mickey Cochrane, outfielder Al Simmons, and the starting pitcher of the day, Robert "Lefty" Grove.[7]

Grove, 27, had led the league in earned-run average (2.51) and strikeouts (194) in 1926, his second season in the majors.[8] Opposing him was Brooklyn native Waite Hoyt, a mere five months older but with nearly a decade of big-league experience. The 1927 season proved to be Hoyt's breakout year, as he led the league with 22 wins. Although he had pitched consistently in six prior seasons with the Yankees, he was often overshadowed by more famous teammates, including stars Herb Pennock and Urban Shocker.

The Yankees lineup had proven power in veterans Ruth and Bob Meusel, not to mention emerging second- and third-year starters Tony Lazzeri, Lou Gehrig, and Earle Combs. But some writers thought their pitching would be their Achilles' heel.[9]

Although the Yankees did not usually broadcast their home games (believing it would hurt in-person attendance), that particular day they arranged for famed radio voice Graham McNamee to call play-by-play on

YANKEE STADIUM 1923-2008

WEAF and WJZ. The microphones went live on the only 1927 regular-season game to grace the airwaves at Yankee Stadium at 2:45 P.M.[10]

The traffic, however, had started before noon. Subways, taxicabs, and buses packed with people all made their way to the Bronx. Police lined River Avenue and the entrances as gatekeepers to those without tickets ($1.10 for the grandstand, 50¢ for bleachers).[11]

"No question it was the greatest crowd that ever saw a baseball game," said general manager Ed Barrow, who estimated the crowd at 70,000. "We had to be careful about overloading the runways to comply with fire and police rules or we could have sold more tickets."[12]

Shortly before game time (3:30), the Yankees "Mite Manager" Miller Huggins shook hands with the Athletics skipper, the "Tall Tactician" Connie Mack, as the Seventh Regiment Band blared. Pete Vischer of the *New York World* describe the photo-op between the 5-foot-6 Huggins and the 6-foot-1 Mack as "Mutt and Jeff."[13] Ruth and Cobb were also photographed together.

The festivities began. The marching band led the two teams onto the field, trailed by a "mysterious left-handed gentleman in a brown coat and hat" pushing a four-foot baseball.[14] As the notes of the "Star-Spangled Banner" played on, the home team raised the American flag, and then their 1926 American League pennant, twice the size. Around 3:25, Mayor Jimmy Walker threw the ceremonial first pitch from owner Jacob Ruppert's box.[15]

As the umpires, led by Billy Evans, conferred at the pitchers' mound, a man with a megaphone announced the game's batteries – Hoyt and catcher Johnny Grabowski, and Grove and Cochrane. Play ball.

Although Grove and Hoyt allowed just three hits between them by the middle of the fifth, the game itself turned out less exciting. All of the Yankees' scoring came on a pair of four-spots in the fifth and sixth innings – the first demonstration of the "five o'clock lightning" that would come to define that season.[16]

In the bottom of the fifth, Earle Combs hit a bases-loaded double to score two. Lou Gehrig drove in the other two (the first of his record 173 RBIs that year)[17] on a double to right. (Both of those runs – scored by

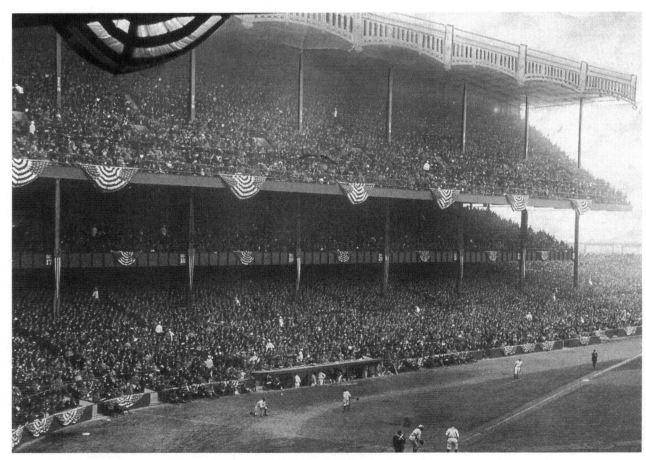

S4BR/The Rucker Archive.

The Yankees' win on Opening Day 1927 was the first in a season that culminated in their fourth World Series, shown here.

Hoyt, who had reached on a sacrifice and an error by first baseman Dud Branom, and Combs – were unearned.)

The Athletics came back with two in the top of the sixth. The speedy Cobb, who'd reached on a bunt single and slid safely under third baseman Joe Dugan's glove on a short base hit by Sammy Hale, scored on Branom's groundout. Cochrane followed with a single to score Hale.

The Yankees tacked on insurance in the bottom of the inning, on Grabowski's RBI single. Combs reached on an error by shortstop Joe Boley (his second) to score Grabowski (unearned), then Mark Koenig tripled to score Combs (also unearned).

Ruth was scheduled to be the next batter. Grove had sent him down swinging twice with a weak popup to second sandwiched in between. In all three at-bats there was a runner on third (or in the case of the second strikeout, second base, too). Now, with Koenig 90 feet away, he was nowhere to be found. Ruth said he felt dizzy.[18] Huggins claimed the Babe had a "bilious attack" – perhaps something he ate. But Fred Lieb in the *New York Post* suspected Ruth may have just been frustrated by "Grove's left-handed speed ball."[19]

Instead, up came Ben Paschal, who made history as one of only a handful of men to pinch-hit for The Babe. The Yankees' fourth outfielder, whose chances to do more of distinction were blocked by his inability to crack the Ruth-Combs-Meusel juggernaut, he swatted a single to drive in Koenig (unearned). Paschal finished the game in right.

The Athletics added a run in the eighth on a double by Al Simmons and Hale's RBI single – Hale was thrown out trying to stretch it into a double.

Hoyt went the distance, allowing three earned runs on nine hits (eight singles, one double), fanning three, and walking three.

Grove, burned by five Athletics errors, was tagged with all eight runs – only three were earned – in six innings, striking out six. Jack Quinn relieved him for the final two scoreless frames.

Dugan went 3-for-4 (all singles) and Gehrig and Combs each had two RBIs. Al Simmons had the Athletics' lone extra-base hit, the eighth-inning double.

Beyond making headlines for leaving the game, Ruth also made news during his first at-bat when a fan, not wearing the fashionable hat most men wore at the time, ran onto the field with a silver punchbowl, trailed by a chorus of boos. As The Babe stared confusedly, Mayor Walker jumped over the rail, took off his hat,

and shook Ruth's hand, as though handing him the trophy. The hatless man disappeared.[20] Ruth then proceeded with the first of his three disappointing at-bats.

"But we call your attention to one thing," wrote Walter Trumbull in the *New York Evening Post* the next day. "There will be a lot of other games this season and the fact that the Babe didn't sock one yesterday is not the slightest indication that he will not wallop one today."[21]

The 1927 Yankees, known to history as Murderers' Row, won six of their first seven games to start the season (with the outlier a tie halted by darkness[22]) and set the American League record in wins, at 110-44.[23] They finished 19 games ahead of second-place Philadelphia and swept the Pittsburgh Pirates for their second World Series championship.

Ruth, who returned the next game, led the league with 89 strikeouts. He also hit 60 home runs.

NOTES

1   James R. Harrison, "72,000 Pack Park, Set Crowd Record, as Yanks Triumph," *New York Times*, April 13, 1927: 20.

2   Although there were 16 major-league teams at the time, the scheduled game that day at Sportsman's Park, where the St. Louis Browns were due to host the Detroit Tigers, was rained out.

3   The Associated Press on April 13 reported attendance at just above 230,000. The *Buffalo Evening News* on the same date stated 234,000. The *New York Times* said 241,000. Standing-room and "comp" tickets could vary attendance numbers, so figures then were estimates that fluctuated from source to source. Some sources say the Yankees hosted as few as 60,000 fans, and some said it was more than 73,000. Baseball-reference puts the overall major-league total at more than 254,000: Yankee Stadium (New York) 72,000; Wrigley Field (Chicago) 45,000; Redland Field (Cincinnati) 37,758; Baker Bowl (Philadelphia) 30,000; Griffith Stadium (Washington) 30,000; Dunn Field (Cleveland) 25,000; Braves Field (Boston) 15,000.

4   Harrison.

5   Joe Vila, "Huggins' Fast-Breaking Yankees Show Old Traits in Early Games," *The Sporting News*, April 21, 1927: 1.

6   Gary Sarnoff, *The First Yankees Dynasty* (Jefferson, North Carolina: McFarland, 2014), 130. Fred Lieb of the *New York Post* said the Yankees' pitching strength was "doubtful" as excerpted in G.H. Fleming, *Murderers' Row: The 1927 New York Yankees* (New York: William Morrow & Company, Inc., 1985), 80. The *New York Telegram* said they'd be "astonished" if the Athletics "don't breeze in" and gave the Athletics 9-to-5 odds, the Yankees 3-to-1; excerpted in Fleming, 84, 86. Walter Trumbull of the *New York Post*, Joe Vila of the *New York Sun*, Grantland Rice of the *New York Herald-Tribune*, and Monitor of the *New York World* all picked the Athletics to finish first, all excerpted in Fleming, 87-88.

7   Also on the bench that day was 19-year-old Jimmie Foxx, whose major-league career at that point consisted of just 36 games. He made his season debut on April 15.

8   Grove also led in strikeouts during his rookie campaign, the first of six straight seasons he captured that title, through 1931. As for ERA, just one other AL pitcher, Cleveland's George Uhle (2.83), had finished with an ERA below 3.00 in 1926.

9   In addition to Lieb's doubts (quoted in Fleming, 84), Bill Corum of the *New York Evening Journal* said that Pennock was the Yankees' only "reliable"

pitcher: "'Dutch' Reuther is an uncertain quantity. Waite Hoyt pitches in streaks. Bob Shawkey is old. Walter Beall is wild." Fleming, 83.

10   Among those tuning in was Johnny Sylvester, the sick boy for whom Babe Ruth hit three home runs in the 1926 World Series. Young Johnny had been invited to the game, but his parents nixed it, worried he would not be strong enough to go. "Johnny Sylvester Wont [sic] See Yankees Play; Babe Ruth's 11-Year-Old Friend Not So Well," New York Times, April 12, 1927: 1; "Babe Ruth's Protege Fails to See Game; School Wins Over Baseball, but Radio and Phone Call From His Idol Help Johnny Sylvester," New York Times, April 13, 1927: 27.

11   Joe Vila in The Sporting News reported that the opening four-game series with the Athletics netted $120,000, of which Philadelphia took $30,000.

12   Pete Vischer, New York World, April 13, 1927, excerpted in Fleming, 90.

13   Vischer in Fleming, 91.

14   Vischer in Fleming, 91.

15   James Harrison of the New York Times said that the pitch was thrown to Yankees backup catcher Johnny Grabowski. Peter Vischer of the New York World said that Yankees mascot Eddie Bennett caught it, noting that Walker "did it like a veteran, repeating the performance twice to make sure that every photographer had a record of the event." Fleming, 91.

16   The game time was 2 hours, 5 minutes. As it started at 3:30 – as most weekday games did those days – the sixth inning would likely have come right around 5 o'clock.

17   Gehrig's 173 RBIs stood as a major-league record for three years, when the Cubs' Hack Wilson drove in 191 in 1930. Gehrig raised the American League record to 185 in 1931.

18   Harrison.

19   Fred Lieb, New York Post, quoted in Fleming, 94. His colleague Walter Trumbull felt similarly. See "Babe Didn't Hit, Time Taking Toll, Lefty Grove's Support," New York Evening Post, April 13, 1927. Paul Gallico of the Daily News thought perhaps Ruth was out of shape as "something seemed to quiver and shake as the Babe jogged in from the outfield." Fleming, 94.

20   Vischer in Fleming, 92. The Associated Press said the presentation "jinxed" Ruth. See Associated Press, "Yankees Capture First Game of Season Over Athletics," Rochester Democrat and Chronicle, April 13, 1927. Both the AP and James Harrison of the New York Times claimed Walker made the presentation himself, with no mention of the suspicious man. The odd timing of the event – in the middle of play – would be the strongest evidence that Vischer's account was more accurate about it being an impromptu decision on the part of Walker.

21   Walter Trumbull, "Babe Didn't Hit, Time Taking Toll, Lefty Grove's Support."

22   The third of the opening four-game series against the Athletics ended in a 9-9 tie after 10 innings due to darkness. The Yankees took games two and four, 10-4 and 6-3 respectively.

23   That record has since been surpassed by the 1954 Cleveland Indians (111-43), the 1998 Yankees (114-48), and the 2001 Seattle Mariners (116-46). However, the 1927 Yankees still have the highest winning percentage of any AL team that won the World Series (.714).

DEATH AT THE STADIUM

May 19, 1929:
New York Yankees 3, Boston Red Sox 0,
at Yankee Stadium

By Craig Garretson

It began with a clap of thunder and a sudden deluge of rain, and ended with Babe Ruth cradling a dying teenager in his arms. In between were 4⅔ innings of baseball rendered meaningless by what is still the worst tragedy in the history of Yankee Stadium.

It was May 19, 1929. The Yankees, after three straight American League pennants and back-to-back World Series sweeps had started the season just as strong, winning 13 of their first 17 games. But a four-game losing streak had dropped them a game and a half behind the hard-charging Philadelphia Athletics.

During this third weekend in May, the Yankees were looking to make hay as they had a five-game home series against the lowly Boston Red Sox, who had finished last or next to last every year since 1922. They did so again in 1929 (and in 1930).

The first game, played Friday, May 17, was a heartbreaker as the Yankees lost 5-3 in 12 innings despite three-hit days from Earle Combs and Tony Lazzeri. The Yankees bounced back on Saturday, sweeping both ends of a doubleheader behind Herb Pennock and George Pipgras, setting the stage for Sunday's scheduled doubleheader.

About 50,000 fans were there as the first game began in sunshine, with about 9,000 having paid their 50 cents to sit in the uncovered right-field bleachers – known as "Ruthville" because of its proximity to Ruth's usual right-field position at Yankee Stadium, as well as where many of his home runs landed.[1]

On the mound for the Yankees was Fred "Lefty" Heimach, a 28-year-old World War I veteran, who after pitching seven years with the A's and Red Sox had been acquired by the Yankees from the St. Paul Saints the previous August. The New Jersey-born twirler was 2-1 with a 2.32 ERA in two starts and three relief appearances when he took the mound that afternoon.

The Red Sox countered with 23-year-old Jack Russell, who despite his youth was in his fourth major-league season. Entering the game, he was 2-3 with a 4.08 ERA in six starts.

Heimach set down the Red Sox in order in the top of the first. In the bottom of the frame, Russell walked Earle Combs, who advanced on Mark Koenig's groundout to second. An excited chatter filled the

PE- 1

TWO KILLED, 62 HURT IN YANKEE STADIUM AS RAIN STAMPEDES BASEBALL CROWD; VICTIMS ARE CRUSHED AT BLEACHER EXIT

PILE UP AT FOOT OF STAIRS

Hunter College Girl and Man Are Trampled to Death.

TANGLED MASS OF BODIES

---

300 Policemen Speed to Scene and Physicians Fight Way Into Struggling Crush.

MANY BOYS AMONG INJURED

Panic Occurs in 'Ruthville' Part of Stands—Most Fans Are Unaware of Accident.

Stadium as Babe Ruth strode to the plate. The buzz grew louder when Russell whirled and threw to second, only to have shortstop Hal Rhyne mishandle the pickoff attempt, allowing Combs to reach third.

Ruth then grounded out to second baseman Bill Regan, and Combs scampered home for the first run of the game.

Boston's miscues continued: Lou Gehrig reached on an error by first baseman Phil Todt, and Bob Meusel on an error by third baseman Bobby Reeves. Tony Lazzeri then walked to load the bases, but Lyn Lary hit a fly ball to center that Jack Rothrock got under and, to Russell's relief, caught.

Another perfect inning for Heimach in the top of the second, and Russell allowed just a walk in a scoreless bottom half.

In the third, the Red Sox had their first baserunner of the day when Regan beat out a grounder to Lary at shortstop, but catcher Bill Dickey threw him out as he attempted to steal. Heimach got the next two outs to end the inning.

In the home half of the inning, The Babe gave the fans in Ruthville what they'd came to see: He crushed a home run to deep right field. Lou Gehrig followed that up with an inside-the-park home run to make the score 3-0. Russell then retired Meusel, Lazzeri, and Lary to escape further trouble.

In the fourth, Heimach again had a perfect inning, and Russell had one of his own. But it was during the inning that the first signs of trouble appeared. What had been sunny skies when the game began had become overcast, and a drizzle began to fall after the bottom of the inning.

Some spectators in Ruthville began to make for the exit,[2] but many stayed behind and braved the rain because Ruth was due up second in the bottom of the fifth. Others left the bleachers but stood near the exit, lingering so they could see the action.[3]

Koenig was retired, then Ruth grounded out. As Gehrig came up to the plate, there was a rumble of thunder, and then the deluge began.

The following day's *New York Herald-Tribune*[4] reported that 5,000 fans were still crowded into the bleachers when the skies opened; the Associated Press estimated 6,000,[5] and other newspapers estimated that there were even more. But all sources agreed that the thunder and heavy downpour incited a stampede toward the exits. (The *Brooklyn Daily Times* added that in the confusion, some fans believed the bleachers in the six-year-old stadium would collapse.[6])

Witnesses told reporters that two of the three exits initially were closed, forcing everyone toward the same exit – one that required descending 14 wooden stairs into a narrow corridor that took fans through a gate and into the street.[7]

The first to leave were still descending those 14 steps when those caught in the rain surged ahead. The people on the stairs tumbled forward into the corridor below and were trampled by the surging crowd.

The New York Times reported, "In an instant, the area at the foot of the stairs, a space about ten feet wide, was a screaming struggling mass of people. Men, women, and children – a preponderance of children – were jammed together in a pile so tightly that they could not breathe, let alone work their way out without assistance. The weight of those on top bore down on those beneath, crushing them before anything could be done, while others continued to fall over them and trample them under foot."[8]

Meanwhile, the game had been halted due to the rain, and fans in the grandstand were leaving their seats in an orderly fashion.[9] The Yankees, watching the rain from the dugout, were unaware of what was happening under the bleachers until Elias Gottlieb, a probationary police officer, ran onto the field carrying a 14-year-old boy who had been trampled.[10]

"Babe Ruth ran from the Yankees' dugout and asked what the trouble was," the *New York Herald Tribune* reported. "He then shouted for a physician. Dr. Edward S. Cowles, the well known neurologist and psychiatrist, of 591 Park Avenue, ran from the stands and took the boy into the club's dressing room. Then Ruth called for other physicians, and a half dozen of them made their way to the scene of the catastrophe."[11]

Dozens were injured and taken to the clubhouse, where the summoned physicians attempted to treat them, but the clubhouse did not have enough medical supplies to treat the number of wounded nor the severity of the injuries. The *Herald Tribune* reported that nearly 100 were injured – so many that, when ambulances proved insufficient, two buses were called in to take them to hospitals – and 18 remained hospitalized overnight.[12] Ruth and his wife, Claire, visited 16 boys still at Lincoln Hospital when rain canceled a doubleheader scheduled for Tuesday.[13]

Two did not recover from their injuries and died at the ballpark: 60-year-old Joseph Carter, a truck driver, and Eleanor Price, a 17-year-old Hunter College student. It is believed they were the first two game-related deaths since the Stadium opened in 1923.[14]

"Miss Price, who had taken her young brother to the game as a Sunday afternoon treat, died in the arms of 'Babe' Ruth, the idol of the fans, who responded coolly to the first cries for help and remained at emergency work until the end," the *Brooklyn Daily Times* reported.[15]

As for the game, it was rained out – with the top of the fifth played and New York in the lead, it was an official game, and a 3-0 win for the Yankees. The second game of the doubleheader was canceled. The Yankees lost seven of their next 11 games; by June 1 they were eight games out, and the A's cruised to an easy pennant.

Fans sued the Yankees, saying the game should have been called when rain began to fall in the fourth inning, before thunder panicked the crowd. Others blamed two exits they said remained closed, forcing the crowd into one. A lawsuit was finally settled in 1932 for $45,000 – nearly $1 million in 2020s-era dollars – with the money to be divided among the victims based upon the severity of their injuries.[16]

SOURCES

In addition to the sources cited in the Notes, the author consulted Baseball-Reference.com and Retrosheet.org.

https://www.baseball-reference.com/boxes/NYA/NYA192905190.shtml

https://www.retrosheet.org/boxesetc/1929/B05190NYA1929.htm

NOTES

1   Testimony of Joseph Syrop. Supreme Court – Appellate Division – First Department, 1932: 33. https://www.google.com/books/edition/Supreme_Court_Appellate_Division_First_D/ijbzfyrHmToC?hl=en&gbpv=1&pg=PA97

2   "Rain followed the spectacular play of the two long-distance hitters, and the fans started huddling and trying to protect their thousands of new straw hats from the drizzle," *Boston Globe*, May 20, 1929: 8. New straw hats getting ruined by rain was a concern at the time. A police officer who was at the Stadium that day was asked about new straw hats in the court case cited in note 1. "Q: Did you notice anything on that day with regard to whether the people in the bleachers were wearing straw hats at the time? A: I believe it was the first straw hat Sunday, that is, that day, when everybody started to wear straw hats. Q: Were there a number that had new straw hats on? A. It must have been, because we had 50 or 60 in the station house that night that we picked up underneath the bleachers."

3   Robert M. Gorman and David Weeks, *Death at the Ballpark* (Jefferson, North Carolina: McFarland, 2015), 205.

4   Dean A. Sullivan, *Middle Innings* (Lincoln: University of Nebraska Press, 2001), 135-137, quoting the *New York Herald Tribune* of May 20, 1929.

5   Associated Press, "Two Killed At Yankee Stadium in Fans' Rush to Escape Rain; Victims Pile Up in Passageway," *Cincinnati Enquirer*, May 20, 1929: 1.

6   "Stadium Victims Blame Officials for 2 Fatalities," Brooklyn Daily Times, May 20, 1929: 1-2. The newspaper reported that the panic began with "the scream of a woman accompanied by the thunder clap and the downpour that made many believe the bleacher stands were about to crumble."

7   Gorman and Weeks, *Death at the Ballpark*, 205.

8   "Two Killed, 62 Hurt in Yankee Stadium as Rain Stampedes Baseball Crowd; Victims are Crushed at Bleacher Exit," *New York Times*, May 20, 1929: 1.

9   *Boston Globe*, May 20, 1929: 8.

10 Brooklyn Daily Times, May 20, 1929: 1-2.

11 Sullivan, 136.

12 Sullivan, 135.

13 Associated Press, "'The Babe' Visits 16 Injured Fans," Wilkes-Barre Times Leader, May 21, 1929: 1. The AP reported that Claire Ruth fainted when she saw the bruised and battered face of one of the victims, and had to be revived with smelling salts.

14 Email interview with Robert M. Gorman, October 17, 2022.

15 *Brooklyn Daily Times*, May 20, 1929: 1.

16 "A multi-party $960,000 negligence lawsuit involving the families of the deceased and 32 of the injured was instituted against the Yankees. A jury verdict in February 1932 found the club 'guilty of negligence, but the plaintiffs guilty of 'contributory negligence.' An appellate court set aside the 'contributory negligence' finding, stating that 'under the law the plaintiffs could not be held partly responsible, because in a heavy rainstorm it was their natural instinct to seek shelter and they could not be held for the resultant stampede.' Later that summer a new trial was ordered to address this issue. At the beginning of this second trial on December 15, 1932, the Yankees settled the claims for $45,000, the money to be divided according to 'the severity of the injuries and the sums spent for medical treatment.'" *Death at the Ballpark*, 205.

SATCHEL PAIGE AND SLIM JONES THROW HEAD-TO-HEAD PITCHING GEMS AT YANKEE STADIUM

September 9, 1934:
Pittsburgh Crawfords 1, Philadelphia Stars 1, at Yankee Stadium

By James Overmyer

Of the more than 200 Negro League games played at Yankee Stadium in the 1930s and '40s, one of the most memorable was a pitching duel between Satchel Paige and Stewart "Slim" Jones in September 1934 that ended not with a victory, but in a 1-1 tie. Black baseball's fans could have been excused for thinking this was a matchup that would continue to thrill them for many seasons. But Fate – not the low-grade sort that influences bad-hop grounders and fly balls lost in the sun, but the kind that actually affects men's lives – stepped in to ensure that this exciting face-off wouldn't be repeated in future years.

Black major-league teams first played at Yankee Stadium in 1930. After two years of no action in the depths of the Depression, Negro League ball returned in 1934, courtesy of William A. "Gus" Greenlee, owner of the Negro National League's Pittsburgh Crawfords and president of the Negro National League. A natural entrepreneur, Greenlee took responsibility for obtaining the Stadium for Black games when the New York Yankees were on the road.

The four-team doubleheader set up for Sunday, September 9, 1934, was a fundraiser for Harlem's Colonel Charles Young American Legion Post. The Chicago American Giants beat the New York Black Yankees, 4-3, in the first game. Greenlee's Crawfords, for whom Paige pitched, and the Philadelphia Stars, Jones's team, would match up in the second game.

The most-quoted attendance estimate in the newspapers covering the doubleheader was 30,000 fans. This was far better than the numbers that same afternoon for the National League's Brooklyn Dodgers at Ebbets Field (12,000) and New York Giants across the

East River at the Polo Grounds (20,000). Such was the drawing power of the already-famous Paige.

His opponent, Slim Jones, a left-hander who at 6-feet-6 and 185 pounds lived up to his nickname, was at age 21 only in his third professional season. But he, like the 28-year-old Paige, already was a star.

Paige, reliably stellar (when not suffering from arm trouble), had a great season in 1934, with a 13-3 won-lost record and a 1.54 ERA. Jones, however, surpassed him – and everyone else. He logged a 20-4 record (in only 22 starts and eight relief appearances), with a 1.24 ERA. Jones's Society for American Baseball Research biographer, Frederick C. Bush, declared that "his 1934 campaign still stands as one of the greatest seasons by any pitcher in any league and era."[1]

The Crawfords and Stars were among the class of the Negro National League in 1934. Philadelphia, with a .684 won-lost percentage, won the league championship. The Crawfords had a .635 winning percentage, the second best in the league. The lineups at Yankee Stadium listed seven future members of the Hall of Fame – Paige, center fielder James "Cool Papa" Bell, first baseman (and manager) Oscar Charleston, catcher Josh Gibson and third baseman Judy Johnson for Pittsburgh, and first baseman Jud Wilson and catcher Raleigh "Biz" Mackey for Philadelphia.

But, even with all those feared bats in the lineups, this was a pitchers' game. Slim dominated the first two-thirds of the contest before fading just a little toward the end. Satchel was in and out of jams until the late innings, but it was noted that he "always seemed to have something in reserve for the pinches."[2] Satch, in fact, got into hot water in the bottom of the first when he walked the Stars' leadoff hitter, shortstop Jake Stephens, who immediately went to third on a hit-and-run single by third baseman Dewey Creacy, and scored one out later on Wilson's groundout.

Meanwhile, for 6⅔ innings Jones was untouchable, with a perfect game until Charleston singled in the seventh. In the third and fourth innings, he struck out four Crawfords in a row, including Bell, Charleston, and Gibson.

Pittsburgh finally reached Jones for its sole run in the top of the eighth, aided by Jones's mental miscue. Judy Johnson opened the inning with a double, which sportswriters implied could have been held to a single if right fielder Jake Dunn had pounced on it a little more quickly.[3]

The *New York Daily News*'s Edgar T. Rouzeau wrote that Slim then "grew nervous," and when second baseman Chester Williams laid down an easy-to-field bunt, he automatically chose to throw him out at first, ignoring a chance to hold Johnson at second or catch him going to third. Jones then walked pinch-hitter Clarence "Spoony" Palm and gave up a single to shortstop Leroy Morney to let in Pittsburgh's run.[4]

The game was tied after 8½ innings, but it was getting dark. The announced starting time for the first game was 1:30 P.M., and there had been four hours of actual baseball played, plus time between the two games. Sunset that day was at 7:17 P.M., and Black sportscaster Jocko Maxwell, who was there, reported that "the shades of night were falling fast."[5]

But the game wasn't over, and the Stars nearly won it, except for Paige again rising to the occasion. With one out in the bottom of the ninth, Jud Wilson hit a sharp grounder back to the box that bounded off Satchel's leg and toward Williams at second. Williams's desperation throw to first was too late to nip Wilson, and it was wild and carried to the grandstand. The 38-year-old Wilson was no speedster, but he was extremely competitive, and he made it to third.

Biz Mackey was the next hitter, and Paige walked him after going to a full count. Philadelphia manager Webster McDonald then ran out a trio of left-handed pinch-hitters, including himself, to try to get the platoon advantage in the gathering dusk that must have favored a pitcher like Paige. Satchel intentionally walked the first one, Mickey Casey, to set up a force at any base. The move worked. McDonald went down on called strikes, and Ameal Brooks swung heartily at Paige's offerings but didn't hit any of them. Then the umpires called the game for darkness.

Brooks's strikeout was Paige's 12th. He walked three batters and gave up six hits. Jones struck out nine, gave up three hits, and walked one. Maxwell, in a year-end article for the *Age*, picked the game as his biggest sports thrill of the year. Veteran sportswriter W. Rollo Wilson of the *Pittsburgh Courier* wrote in 1943 that the game was his biggest thrill, period.[6]

Right after the game, popular music lyricist Andy Razaf, a devout baseball fan, penned a poem "To Judge Landis," arguing that the doubleheader showed what White baseball was missing. The final stanza read:

"It's time you and your crowd woke up. In this new and enlightened age. Oh, by the way, your 'Schoolboy Rowe' should see these pitchers, Jones and Page [*sic*]."[7]

Paige and Jones had a rematch at Yankee Stadium on September 30. Again, both pitchers starred, although this time the Crawfords won, 3-1. The two hurlers had opposed each other twice in May, games that the Stars had won. They had appeared as teammates on August 26 for the East All Stars at the annual Negro Leagues East-West Game. Jones pitched three shutout innings as the East starter, and Paige got the win with four shutout frames at the end of the contest when the East scored the game's only run in the eighth. So as the 1934 season came to an end, the chances of many more exciting Paige-Jones matchups in future seasons seemed bright.

But while Satchel pitched for decades longer and became more and more famous, 1934 was Slim Jones's last good season. He started off well in 1935, but developed trouble with his left shoulder, as well as with Stars owner Edward Bolden, who became concerned that Jones was abusing alcohol to deal with the arm pain.[8] When the season was over, Slim had compiled a subpar 4-5 won-lost record and a worse 5.88 ERA. After that his days as a Negro League starter were basically over. He hung with the Stars through 1938, but McDonald and his successor as manager, Jud Wilson, were mostly inclined to use him in relief, or as an occasional first baseman and outfielder.

In the fall of 1938, back in his hometown of Baltimore, Slim became gravely ill. He died in Bay View Hospital on November 19, at only 25 years of age. Bush, his biographer, cut through a lot of incorrect information about Jones's death, and concluded from his research that Slim's kidneys had failed. Jones was gone, but not forgotten by his opponent of that 1934 faceoff at Yankee Stadium. Paige told an interviewer 42 years later that Slim was one of the three best pitchers he had ever seen, along with Bob Feller and Dizzy Dean.[9]

SOURCES

Negro League player statistics were not always reliably and completely compiled at the time the games were actually played. But efforts have been made in recent years to use box scores and game stories to retroactively compile annual stats. The team won-lost records and pitching statistics cited here are from the Seamheads. com Negro Leagues Database, as of December 2021. The database is considered the most complete of the efforts to re-create Negro League statistics, but it is an ongoing project, and the numbers cited here may change in the future.

The author also relied on information from Baseball-Reference.com and Retrosheet.org.

NOTES

1   Frederick C. Bush, "Slim Jones," SABR Baseball Biography Project, https://sabr.org/bioproj/person/slim-jones/.

2   Bessye J. Bearden, "Giants, Trent Win All-Star Ball Game," *Chicago Defender*, September 15, 1934: A5.

3   Edgar T. Rouzeau, "Chi Giants Top Black Yanks, 4-3; Crawfords, Stars Tie, 1-1," *New York Daily News*, September 10, 1934: 171; Bearden, "Giants, Trent Win All-Star Ball Game."

4   Rouzeau.

5   Display advertisement for "The Stars of Colored Baseball in a Four (4) Team Double Header," *New York Amsterdam News*, September 1, 1934: 10; "Daily Almanac," *New York Daily News*, September 9, 1934: 2; Jocko Maxwell, "Sports Biggest Thrill in 1934," *New York Age*, December 29, 1934: 7.

6   Maxwell, "Sports Biggest Thrill in 1934"; W. Rollo Wilson, "My Greatest Thrill!: Sportswriter Gets Biggest Thrill from 1-1 Game," *Pittsburgh Courier*, July 3, 1943: 19.

7   Andy Razaf, "To Judge Landis," *New York Amsterdam News*, September 15, 1934: 10.

8   Courtney Michelle Smith, *Ed Bolden and Black Baseball in Philadelphia*, (Jefferson, North Carolina: McFarland & Co., 2017), 107.

9   Bush, "Slim Jones."

NEXT IN THE LINE: THE FIRST GAME OF JOE DIMAGGIO'S CAREER

May 3, 1936:
New York Yankees 14, St. Louis Browns 5,
at Yankee Stadium

By Kevin Larkin

Earle Combs began a string of Hall of Fame players who were starting center fielders for the Yankees. After Combs, who played from 1924 to 1935, was Joe DiMaggio, who played from 1936 to 1951, and after DiMaggio was Mickey Mantle, who played in center field from 1952 until 1966.[1] Combs became the regular center fielder in 1925. Dixie Walker started 59 games in center field in 1933. In late July of 1934 Combs suffered a fractured skull when he crashed into the outfield fence in St. Louis chasing a fly ball. He was out for the rest of the season, and Ben Chapman took over the position. After a two-month hospital stay, Combs came back in 1935 and played in a total of 89 games.

Chapman played center field in 138 games in 1935 and began play as the Yankees' center fielder in 1936 before being traded to the Washington Senators for Jake Powell on June 14. He had caught a cold earlier and never was right after that.[2]

DiMaggio started his first game in left field with Chapman in center field. After also spending time in both right field and center field in 1936, DiMaggio became the Yankees' center fielder in 1937.

Joe DiMaggio was born Giuseppe Paolo DiMaggio on November 25, 1914, in Martinez, California, to Giuseppe and Rosalia (Mercurio) DiMaggio. The elder DiMaggio was a fisherman and young Joe was the eighth of nine children, one of five sons. Joe and brothers Vince and Dominic played major-league baseball; the other two brothers became fishermen like their father.

Vince DiMaggio persuaded the San Francisco Seals to give his younger brother a chance, and in 1932 the Seals signed Joe to a contract as a shortstop, a position he played in the final three games of the 1932 season. Joe played for the Seals from 1933 to 1935. In 1934 he batted .341 but a knee injury made most major-league teams a bit leery of signing him. The Yankees ended up buying his contract with the proviso that he play with the Seals in 1935 to prove that he was healthy.[3] "The $75,000 rookie had been on the bench with a burned foot since the season began. He made his first start in left field[4] for the Yankees."[5]

DiMaggio had burned his foot in a diathermy machine during spring training.[6] He was such a shy individual that he did not ask anyone why his foot was getting so hot, and when he finally took his foot out of the machine, it was red, blistered, and too sore for him to play. It took two weeks for his foot to heal.[7]

Despite his misadventure with the diathermy machine, DiMaggio proved himself to his coaches and teammates during spring training. Dan Daniel, the baseball writer for the *New York World Telegram & Sun*, wrote, "Here is the replacement for Babe Ruth" after the 21-year-old smashed line drives over the fences of the Florida ballparks.[8]

DiMaggio's major-league debut came on May 3, 1936, in a game at Yankee Stadium against the St. Louis Browns. New York had last made the World Series in 1932. Babe Ruth and Earle Combs had retired, but it was still a potent Yankees lineup that contained future Hall of Famers Lou Gehrig, Bill Dickey, Tony Lazzeri, and Lefty Gomez as well as manager Joe McCarthy.

The Browns had not finished in the first division since 1929, when they were in fourth place, 26 games behind the Philadelphia Athletics. Their starting pitcher on May 3 was Jack Knott. Gomez started for the Yankees.

The Browns got to Gomez for three runs in the first inning on an error by third baseman Red Rolfe, singles by Jim Bottomley and Beau Bell, and a double by Harland Clift. DiMaggio's first at-bat in the major leagues came in the first inning and his fielder's choice scored Frankie Crosetti, who had tripled. DiMaggio and Red Rolfe came around to score on a double by Ben Chapman, and Lazzeri's fly ball scored Gehrig with a run that gave the Yankees a 4-3 lead.

DiMaggio's next at-bat came in the second inning and he got his first major-league hit, off Earl Caldwell, who had replaced Knott in the first inning. After Rolfe singled, DiMaggio's single sent him to second base. A single by Gehrig, a fly ball by Dickey, and a triple by Chapman added three runs to the Yankees total and gave them a lead of 7-3.

Gomez gave up a leadoff home run to Ray Pepper in the third inning to make the score 7-4. Neither the Yankees in the third nor the Browns in the fourth scored. DiMaggio came to bat in the fourth inning and struck out.[9] Later in the inning, a single by Gehrig and a walk to Dickey was followed by Chapman's triple, which added two more runs to the Yankees' total, giving them a 9-4 lead.

Leadoff doubles by Lyn Lary and the pesky Pepper made the score 9-5 in the top of the fifth inning. DiMaggio's next at-bat came in the bottom of the sixth, and his second major-league hit was a triple. It scored Rolfe, who had led off with a double. Gehrig followed with a single to score DiMaggio and after an out by Dickey, Chapman's single sent Gehrig to second base. George Selkirk singled to score Gehrig with Myril Hoag (who ran for Chapman) advancing to third base. A fly out by Lazzeri scored Hoag and the Yankees' lead was now 13-5.

DiMaggio led off the seventh inning with a popup to second base. Then Gehrig singled, Dickey worked a walk, and Hoag was hit by a pitch to load the bases. Browns pitcher Elon Hogsett uncorked a wild pitch that allowed Gehrig to score. The Browns got out of the jam on a groundout and fly out and trailed 14-5.

St. Louis did not score in its half of the eighth. With two outs in the bottom of the inning, DiMaggio came up for the sixth time in the game. He responded with a single, but the Yankees did not score. Neither did the Browns in their half of the ninth inning and the Yankees came away with the 14-5 win.

Gehrig led the Yankees' offense with four hits in five at-bats, two RBIs, and five runs scored. Ben Chapman was 4-for-4 with two triples, a double, and five RBIs. DiMaggio was 3-for-6, two singles and a triple. He scored three runs and drove in one.

The Yankees finished the year with a record of 102 wins, 51 losses, and 2 ties, giving them the American League pennant by 19½ games over the Detroit Tigers. New York then defeated the New York Giants in six games in the World Series, the first of four consecutive Series championships. DiMaggio played in 138 games in 1936, hitting for a .323 average; his 15 triples tied for the league lead with teammate Rolfe and Cleveland's Earl Averill. He also made the first of his 13 appearances in an All-Star Game.

SOURCES

In addition to the game story and box-score sources cited in the Notes, the author consulted the Baseball-Reference.com and Retrosheet.org websites.

https://www.baseball-reference.com/boxes/NYA/NYA193605030.shtml

https://www.retrosheet.org/boxesetc/1936/B05030NYA1936.html

NOTES

1   DiMaggio was absent from 1943 through 1945, when he was in the US Army. (Johnny Lindell got most of the starts in center field in those seasons.) Mantle played right field in 1951 and took over for DiMaggio in center field in 1952. In his last two seasons (1967-68), he played first base.

2   Bill Nowlin, "Ben Chapman," SABR Biography Project, sabr.org, accessed October 13, 2022.

3   Lawrence Baldassaro, "Joe DiMaggio," SABR Biography Project, sabr.org, accessed July 25, 2022.

4   DiMaggio played 64 games in left field, 54 in center field, and 20 in right field in 1936 before taking over as the full-time center fielder in 1937. https://www.baseball-reference.com/players/d/dimagjo01.shtml, https://www.retrosheet.org/boxesetc/D/Pdimaj101.htm.

5   Don Hallman, "3 Hits for 'DiMag' as Yanks Win, 14-5," New York Daily News, May 4, 1936: 42.

6   Diathermy is the use of electrical current to cut or coagulate tissue during surgery. https://teachmesurgery.com/skills/surgical-equipment/diathermy/. Accessed October 13, 2022.

7   Bart Barnes, "Joltin' Joe Has Gone Away," Washington Post, March 8, 1999: A1.

8   Barnes.

9   DiMaggio struck out 39 times in 1936, the highest season total of his career, during which he struck out only 369 times in 6,821 at-bats.

MONTE PEARSON TOSSES YANKEE STADIUM'S FIRST NO-HITTER

August 27, 1938:
New York Yankees 13, Cleveland Indians 0
(second game of doubleheader),
at Yankee Stadium

By Tara Krieger

Between April 1923 and August 1938, there were 13 no-hitters in the major leagues. None were at Yankee Stadium.

Although the Yankees had their share of Hall of Famers on the mound, Yankee Stadium was known as a hitters' park, with pinstriped sluggers taking the home-run crown in 12 of the park's first 15 years of existence.[1] So it seemed almost on-brand that the first no-hitter in the House That Ruth Built took a decade and a half to happen.[2]

And it came as the exclamation point on a particularly auspicious stretch of play for both the Yankees and the pitcher who threw it, Monte Pearson.

The 1938 Yankees, despite a 12-game lead en route to their third straight championship season, were exhausted. When Pearson took the mound for the second game of a Saturday twin bill, the team was playing its 10th game in five days – the string of doubleheaders resulting from four days of rain the third week of July.[3]

After an erratic first two months (3-5, 4.66 ERA), Pearson had won nine straight decisions since June 26 – but he still was walking more (89) than he was striking out (73), and the doubleheaders forced him to pitch on short rest. He threw a complete game on August 24.

That Saturday, August 27, he was facing his former mates, the team that had brought him to the majors, the Cleveland Indians, who were a distant third place in the American League. As a rookie in 1933,[4] Pearson had led the AL with a 2.33 ERA. In 1934, he'd won 18 games. The Yankees had traded for him after an underwhelming 1935 season – and he flourished, going 19-7 in 1936, and 9-3 in an injury-plagued 1937. Now,

a week from his 30th birthday, the Fresno, California, right-hander stood 12-5 with a 3.99 ERA.

The Yankees had won an 8-7 thriller in the opener on Joe DiMaggio's walk-off two-run triple, his record-tying third three-bagger of the game. The Indians had scored four in the top of the ninth to lead by two, but the Yankees had plated three in the bottom off Johnny Allen, who had been traded for Pearson three years earlier.[5]

Pearson's opponent in the nightcap, decidedly mediocre rookie Johnny Humphries, would lead the league in appearances that year, with 45, but was making just his fifth major-league start.

He didn't take long to get into trouble, no thanks to two groundball errors by shortstop Lyn Lary (another Yankees castoff). After Pearson retired the side on three straight groundouts, the Yankees sent eight men to the plate and scored five runs, only two which were earned, but all of which were off the long ball. Tommy Henrich's homer to deep right drove in Frank Crosetti (reached on a walk) and Red Rolfe (E-6), and Joe Gordon went deep to left to drive in DiMaggio (E-6).

Another two Yankees runs came in the third, on George Selkirk's RBI single and Joe Glenn's fly ball. Pearson had a 7-0 lead before he allowed a baserunner.

Back-to-back walks to lead off the fourth were all that stood between Pearson and perfection. But with Lary on second and Bruce Campbell on first, Pearson caught Jeff Heath looking. He then induced Earl Averill to ground out to the right side of the infield (advancing the runners), and struck out Hal Trosky.

Humphries was done after allowing another three runs in the fourth inning (Selkirk's RBI single,

Gordon's two-run triple). The devastation: 10 runs (seven earned), nine hits, three walks, three strikeouts.

The Yankees tacked on three more off reliever Denny Galehouse when Gordon and Henrich each homered a second time – Gordon's a two-run shot to left in the sixth, Henrich's a solo shot to right in the seventh.

Pearson was perfect for the next five innings.

"Monte pitched with the flawless precision of an intricate piece of mechanism," wrote John Drebinger in the *New York Times*. And, "with the Indians going down like reeds before a high gale," the crowd of 40,959 "began to sit up and take notice."[6]

"Control did it," Pearson said after the game. "I could put the ball wherever I wanted it. I lost La[r]y and Campbell to the fifth [sic] because I was too confident. Until the seventh my mind wasn't set on

shooting for a no-hitter but when I got that far I began to think about it."[7]

Pearson had come close before.[8] With Cleveland on August 29, 1933, he lost a no-hitter against Washington in the ninth, allowing two runs on two hits. On May 10, 1937, with the Yankees, he allowed a single in the first inning, then held Chicago hitless for the next eight.[9]

So, after six innings, "I said to myself, 'Gosh, will I be lucky enough to pull it off?'"[10]

Pearson's superstitious teammates, on the other hand, including manager Joe McCarthy,[11] gave him the cold shoulder.

"I'd sit in my seat all by myself," Pearson said. "The rest of the fellows wouldn't look at me. They talked about everything else, everything under the sun except a no-hitter. Then when we had to take the field, Joe McCarthy would say to me: 'Go get 'em, boy.'

Courtesy of the National Baseball Hall of Fame.

During his no-hitter, Monte Pearson allowed only five outs to leave the infield.

"And I went out to get 'em. Believe me, beginning with the seventh I really began to powder that ball through. I was more excited than any other time since I've been in baseball."[12]

After a groundout to start the seventh, Indians manager Ossie Vitt tried a pinch-hitter. He subbed Roy Weatherly for Averill; pop fly to second. Trosky then fouled out to catcher Glenn. The eighth inning rolled along similarly – grounder, fly ball, pop to short.

"For every fast ball I threw I retaliated with a curve," Pearson said. "I was faster Saturday than at any time during the past three years. I felt as though I could have pitched another nine innings. And between you and me the roar of the crowd the last two innings inspired me to that no-hitter. I felt as though I was in a world series game."[13]

With Galehouse leading off the ninth, Vitt sent up another pinch-hitter, Julius "Moose" Solters. Pearson got him on three pitches. Then, a second pinch-hitter, for Lary, in Frankie Pytlak, who had caught Pearson in Cleveland.

"He's a dangerous little hitter – Frankie," Pearson said. "And I thought to myself: 'Is this guy going to be cute and lay down a bunt?' When I pitched to him I determined to make a dash over to the third base side to field any possible bunt. But he hit to Gordon. Joe made a dandy play."[14] Gordon scooped up a slow roller and fired to first baseman Lou Gehrig, just beating Pytlak to the bag.

With the Indians' final hope in Campbell approaching the plate, DiMaggio kept fans in suspense by running in for a better pair of sunglasses. "He was the only player now on the field playing with the glaring light right in his eyes," noted Drebinger.[15]

"Only one more to go," Pearson narrated. "I thought to myself is this going to be like that Washington game. Campbell hit to left and I went: 'Oh-oh, will Selkirk catch the ball?' Selkirk did and I was in. All of a sudden I went limp and the crowd was all over me."[16]

Indeed, after Selkirk caught the line drive, Drebinger wrote, "[T]he fans cut loose with an ear-splitting roar. They almost mobbed Monte before he had a chance to struggle to the dugout."[17]

Pearson had pitched to two batters over the minimum, striking out seven. Of the 20 balls put into play, 15 never left the infield.

Henrich and Gordon were the hitting stars, driving in 10 of the Yankees' 13 runs. Each had a pair of homers within their three hits; Gordon also had a triple and six RBIs, and Henrich drove in four.

Every Yankees position player drove in or scored at least one run. Gehrig (three runs scored), Selkirk (two RBIs, one run), and Rolfe (two runs) each had two hits. The only player who did not contribute to the Yankees' offense was Pearson, who went 0-for-3.

Pearson's no-hitter was the last of 10 straight "W" decisions for Pearson that year,[18] and his only shutout. He finished 16-7 with a 3.97 ERA and 17 complete games. Two weeks later, his wife would give birth to their second child.

"Pearson's no-hitter against the Indians was typical of the way the Yanks have of coming up with something downright shattering and applying it to the subject at the psychologically correct moment," wrote Bob Considine of the International News Service. "Assuming that the Indians had a measure of fight left in them when they came to the stadium last Thursday, it was utterly gone when they left Saturday evening.[19]

The Yankees won five in the six-game series and sent Cleveland away 16 games back. They clinched the pennant on September 18.

The next no-hitter at Yankee Stadium came in 1946 from a visiting opponent – Bob Feller of the Cleveland Indians.

SOURCES

In addition to the Sources cited in the Notes, the author consulted Baseball-Reference.com and Retrosheet.org.

https://www.baseball-reference.com/boxes/NYA/NYA193808272.shtml

https://www.retrosheet.org/boxesetc/1938/B08272NYA1938.htm

NOTES

1 The only years a Yankee did not hold the AL home-run title between 1923 and 1937 were in 1932 and 1933, when it went to the A's Jimmie Foxx, and in 1935, when Foxx tied with the Tigers' Hank Greenberg. Babe Ruth finished second in '32 and '33, and Lou Gehrig was the runner-up in '35.

2 The Yankees had two previous no-hitters, but they were both on the road: George Mogridge on April 24, 1917, at Fenway Park, and Sad Sam Jones on September 4, 1923 at Shibe Park.

3 The Yankees played 23 games – including 10 doubleheaders—between August 12 and August 27.

4 Pearson actually was brought up in 1932, but pitched a total of eight innings in eight appearances out of the Indians' bullpen. Meaning in 1933 he was still technically a rookie.

5 The Yankees also got Steve Sundra in the Allen-for-Pearson trade.

6 John Drebinger, "No-hit, No-run Game Hurled by Pearson as Yanks Win Two," *New York Times*, August 28, 1938: S1. The AL had not seen a no-hitter in more than a year, the most recent being the White Sox' Bill Dietrich on June 1, 1937. The National League had seen two no-hitters in 1938 – Johnny Vander Meer's pair earlier in the season.

7 Bill McCullough, "Classy Triumvirate: Work of Pearson, DiMaggio, and Henrich Featured Yankee Conquests During Past Week," *Brooklyn Daily Eagle*, August 29, 1938: 12.

8   Dick Walsh noted that Pearson had pitched "some no-hitters" in his semipro days in Oakland, California, but never professionally. "Dick Walsh's Comment: It Must Have Been Case of 'Try Again' When Pearson Hurled No-Hitter," *Albany Times-Union,* September 6, 1938: 13.

9   Pearson helped himself at the plate that day, as well, with three hits and two RBIs.

10   Max Case (International News Service), "Pearson Felt No-Hitter in 6th," *Washington Times,* August 29, 1938: 17.

11   "I tried to make conversation with McCarthy but he didn't give me a tumble. It's a bad omen when you tell a pitcher he hasn't allowed a hit," Pearson said. McCullough.

12   Case.

13   McCullough. Pearson dominated in October, with a 4-0 record and a 1.01 ERA in 35⅔ innings. The comment foreshadowed his fourth and final World Series appearance in Game Two of the 1939 fall classic, when he pitched 7⅓ no-hit innings against Cincinnati, also at Yankee Stadium.

14   Case.

15   Drebinger.

16   Case.

17   Drebinger.

18   In his next start, on September 1, 1938, Pearson allowed six runs on 10 hits in a 6-3 loss to Detroit.

19   Bob Considine, "On the Line," *Albany Times-Union,* August 29, 1938.

YANKEES DOMINATE, BUT AN INDIAN SAVES THE DAY IN FIRST BRONX ALL-STAR GAME

July 11, 1939:
American League 3, National League 1,
at Yankee Stadium

By Vince Guerrieri

Yankee Stadium was the natural choice to hold the All-Star Game in 1939. The game originated in Chicago in 1933, as an activity adjacent to the city's Century of Progress World's Fair. Six years later, New York was home to another World's Fair, touting "The World of Tomorrow." Companies like Westinghouse and National Cash Register showed off their newest, state-of-the-art products, and industrial engineer Norman Bel Geddes touted his Futurama, a city from the far-off future in 1960, a world where elevated highways and transcontinental flights were not just possible but part of everyday life.[1] Even baseball got into the act, with an Academy of Sport at the fair. In anticipation of the fair, Uniforms for New York

In 1939, Yankee Stadium hosted the seventh All-Star Game between the American and National Leagues.

City's three teams, the Brooklyn Dodgers, New York Giants, and New York Yankees, included a minimalist patch with the Fair's logo of the Trylon and Perisphere buildings in 1938.[2]

Because of the opportunity to showcase the city, Yankee Stadium was picked to host the 1939 midseason classic, just five years after the Polo Grounds hosted the second All-Star Game, in 1934.[3] It was the second newest venue in baseball (only the Indians' part-time home, Cleveland Stadium, had been built more recently, opening in 1931), but it was the culmination of an early ballpark-building boom, as steel and concrete edifices supplanted rickety wood structures.

As the most ostentatious new ballpark in America's biggest city, Yankee Stadium almost immediately became the center of the sports universe. It hosted prizefights. It hosted football games. And because its opening came not long after the debut of Babe Ruth as a Yankee – and the same year another Yankee legend, Lou Gehrig, made his major-league debut – it became home to a lot of championship teams. The Yankees won their first World Series in 1923, the year the stadium opened, and six more before the 1939 season, including the previous three.

By then, the tradition was in place that the managers of the previous year's World Series teams would manage the All-Star squads. The Cubs' Gabby Hartnett led the National League squad, but because it was the "centennial" year for baseball,[4] Athletics manager Connie Mack, an inductee into the National Baseball Hall of Fame that had opened earlier that summer in Cooperstown, New York, was chosen as the American League manager.[5] Ultimately, Mack begged off due to health issues, and the job fell back to Joe McCarthy, who'd managed each of the previous three All-Star squads.[6]

Ticket prices were the same for the All-Star Game as for any other Yankees game,[7] which seemed appropriate; in many ways, it was a Yankees home game. McCarthy managed, and his coaching staff included Art Fletcher, who served as assistant to McCarthy as well as his predecessor, Miller Huggins. And no fewer than nine Yankees were named to the American League team, which made sense, given that the team was out to so far a lead that New York oddsmaker Jack Doyle had considered it a foregone conclusion that they'd win the pennant, offering odds only on who would finish second.[8]

Gehrig was one of the Yankees named to the American League team (he'd been named to the previous six as well), but he would not be playing. In fact,

his retirement was announced the month before, and just a week before the All-Star Game, he was honored between games of an Independence Day doubleheader at the Stadium, telling fans, "Today, I consider myself the luckiest man on the face of the earth."

Gehrig delivered the American League lineup card to the umpires and received the loudest cheers of the day. It was one of his final appearances in a Yankees uniform, and his ailment was noticeable. "Gehrig walks with a distinct limp," said *Cleveland Plain Dealer* sports editor Gordon Cobbledick. "It is not the limp of an injured athlete. It is the halting, jerky limp of a cripple."[9]

The only non-Yankees in the starting lineup were the Tigers' Hank Greenberg, replacing Gehrig at first base, and Red Sox shortstop Joe Cronin and right fielder Doc Cramer. Red Rolfe started at third base, Joe DiMaggio was in center field, George Selkirk was in left field, Joe Gordon was at second, and Red Ruffing was pitching to Bill Dickey.[10]

Scoring started in the top of the third. Pirates shortstop Arky Vaughan led off the inning and singled for the National Leaguers. Paul Derringer hit two foul balls in an effort to sacrifice and advance Vaughan, but struck out swinging. Stan Hack hit a bloop that fell in in shallow left field to advance Vaughan to second. Lonny Frey then hammered a double over first base into right field, scoring Vaughan. Ival Goodman was intentionally walked to load the bases. Frank McCormick struck out on three pitches, and Ernie Lombardi flied out to end the threat.

In the bottom of the fourth, Derringer had been relieved by Cubs pitcher Bill Lee.[11] With two on and two out, Selkirk hit a ball to right field. Goodman laid out but couldn't make the catch, and Dickey scored to even up the game. The next batter, Gordon, hit a line drive to Vaughan, which he muffed, allowing Greenberg to score. Tommy Bridges struck out looking to end the inning. In the bottom of the fifth, the American League added an insurance run when DiMaggio hit a towering home run to left field with two outs.

The American Leaguers found themselves in a bind in the sixth inning. McCormick led off the frame with a groundout to Gordon. Lombardi singled to left-center on the very next pitch. Joe Medwick hit a roller to Cronin, who was too eager to turn a double play on the slow-footed Lombardi. Cronin booted the ball, leaving Medwick and Lombardi on first and second. Mel Ott hit a single that was batted down just past the infield dirt by Gordon, keeping a run from scoring.

In the Yankee Stadium bullpen, Bob Feller was warming up. He was planning to relieve Bridges in the seventh, but McCarthy called him in earlier. Not yet 21, the Indians pitcher had already shown himself to be one of the supreme hurlers of the day. Indeed, this was already his second All-Star Game appearance. And he was going to bring the heat.

"The best thing I could do was come overhand and throw him a fastball, which I did," Feller recalled in a 2008 interview.[12] And Vaughan hit it right to Gordon, who shoveled it to Cronin for the force at second. Cronin then fired to Greenberg for the double play to get out of the jam.

Feller dominated the rest of the way, earning the save. The first batter of the seventh inning, Babe Phelps, who pinch-hit for Lee, took a pitch – and demanded to see the ball, believing it was doctored![13] Vaughan had one more chance at Feller, in the ninth inning with Ott on first, but he popped out to DiMaggio.

"It is no trick whatever to pick out the All-Star goat," Tommy Holmes wrote in the next day's *Brooklyn Eagle*. It was Arky Vaughan. "This was the first time the Pittsburgh shortstop ever saw the Yankee Stadium. He'll see it in a hundred nightmares from now on."[14]

Feller struck out pinch-hitter Johnny Mize with a curveball that "looked like an aspirin tablet that rolled off a table,"[15] and with a full count, struck out Hack looking to end the game.[16]

"Nice work all around, fellers," McCarthy said after the game. "It was a good ball game. We got our share of the breaks and capitalized on them."[17]

SOURCES

In addition to the sources cited in the Notes, the author consulted Baseball-Reference.com and Retrosheet.org for pertinent information, including box scores.

https://www.baseball-reference.com/allstar/1939-allstar-game.shtml

https://www.retrosheet.org/boxesetc/1939/B07110ALS1939.htm

NOTES

1   Bel Geddes later designed a state-of-the-art domed ballpark in Brooklyn for the Dodgers. Obviously, it was never built.

2   "Baseball Clubs to Advertise Fair," *Brooklyn Daily Eagle*, April 4, 1938: 14.

3   Frederick G. Lieb, "Victory Gives American League Five-to-Two Edge Over National in 'Dream Game' Competition," *The Sporting News*, July 13, 1939: 5.

4   The 1939 season was celebrated as baseball's centennial year, with all players wearing a patch on their uniform commemorating it. It was based on the finding – later disproven – that Abner Doubleday invented the game on the fields of Cooperstown a century earlier. Further reading: John Thorn, "Baseball in 25 Objects: The 1939 Sleeve Patch," https://ourgame.mlblogs.com/the-1939-centennial-sleeve-patch-e3d8ca0f4e65.

5   "Mack Made Manager for All-Star Game," *New York Times*, June 2, 1939: 37.

6   McCarthy and the Yankees had won the previous three World Series, and McCarthy filled in as manager in place of the Tigers' Mickey Cochrane in 1936. "McCarthy to Lead All-Star Team; Mack, Ill, Gives Up Job," *New York Times*, July 2, 1939: S1.

7    $2.20 for box seats; $1.65, reserved grandstand; $1.10, unreserved grandstand; and bleacher seats were 55 cents.

8   "American All-Stars Favored at 9 to 20," *New York Times*, July 7, 1939: 21.

9   Gordon Cobbledick, "Plain Dealing," *Cleveland Plain Dealer*, July 12, 1939: 15. Cobbledick described Gehrig's ailment as "a form of chronic infantile paralysis."

10   By comparison, the Reds, leading the National League race at the time, started five players, pitcher Paul Derringer, second baseman Lonny Frey, first baseman Frank McCormick, catcher Ernie Lombardi, and right fielder Ival Goodman. John Drebinger, "Six Yanks to Start for Favored American Leaguers Today," *New York Times*, July 11, 1939: 12.

11   Rules of the day limited pitchers to three innings in the All-Star Game; similarly, in the top of the inning, the Tigers' Tommy Bridges had come on to pitch. "Mack Made Manager for All-Star Game."

12   Jack Curry, "Going Back, Back, Back to '39 All-Star Game at the Stadium," *New York Times*, June 23, 2008: D1. At the time, Feller and Frey were the only players still living from the game.

13   Tommy Holmes, "NL Beaten but Not Disgraced as Arky Vaughan Sprouts Horns," *Brooklyn Eagle*, July 12, 1939: 14.

14   "NL Beaten but Not Disgraced as Arky Vaughan Sprouts Horns."

15   "NL Beaten but Not Disgraced as Arky Vaughan Sprouts Horns."

16   Technically, Feller had violated the rules by pitching more than three innings, but accountability on this issue varies. In his autobiography, Feller notes that National Leaguers "cried foul" and in the 2008 *Times* story, said Hartnett protested but was told to return to the dugout. But the *Times* game story from the next day says no protest was lodged, noting that "[t]he National Leaguers always had insisted they could pin Feller's ears back any time they met."

17   Associated Press, "Harridge Helps in Pummeling of Hero Bob Feller," *Cleveland Plain Dealer*, July 12, 1939: 15.

HOT STREAKS: JOE DIMAGGIO, THE YANKEES, AND THE WEATHER

July 2, 1941:
New York Yankees 8, Boston Red Sox 4,
at Yankee Stadium

By Jeff Allan Howard

Beginning with a base hit on May 15, 1941, Joe DiMaggio just kept hitting, game after game. Nobody noticed it much at first, but like a boulder that starts out slowly and picks up speed rolling down a hill, the story eventually took hold and the streak captivated a country during the summer of 1941.

On June 17 DiMaggio set a Yankees record by hitting in his 30th game in a row.[1] The 41-game hit streak set by George Sisler in 1922 was generally considered the modern-day standard.

The Yankees outfielder cast the illusion of indifference until acknowledging in an interview after the June 26, 1941 game against the St. Louis Browns when he extended the streak to 38 games, "As long as I've gone this far, I might as well try to keep it rolling. At the start I didn't think much about it … but naturally I'd like to get the record since I'm this close."[2]

From sea to shining sea; from Toots Shor's Restaurant in Manhattan to DiMaggio's Grotto Restaurant at Fisherman's Wharf in San Francisco, and all the way in between, the pursuit of the hitting streak became a national phenomenon and was a common conversation starter on the streets. People avidly tuned on their radios, looking for updates as regularly scheduled broadcasts were interrupted on game days when news of another Joe DiMaggio hit came through.

Through June 28 he had hit in 40 games in a row, with a doubleheader on tap in Washington the next day. A double in the first game one broke Ty Cobb's mark of 40 games. A single in the nightcap broke Sisler's 41-game mark.[3]

While such things were not tracked with modern-day scrutiny at the time, it had come to light that Willie Keeler hit in 44 consecutive games in the 1890s.[4]

Having set a new modern record with 42, DiMaggio said, "I'm glad the strain is over. Now I'm going after that forty-four-game mark and I'll keep on swinging and hitting as long as I can."[5]

In a July 1 doubleheader against the Boston Red Sox at Yankee Stadium, he got two hits in the first game and, even though the second game was called

Courtesy of the National Baseball Hall of Fame.

Joe DiMaggio's smile in breaking a near half-century-old record obscures that he did it in 98-degree heat.

after five innings, he had another hit, tying Keeler's record.

On Wednesday, July 2, braving 98-degree temperatures, Boston and New York played again.[6]

The heat was so intense that the scheduled Red Sox starter, the 41-year-old Lefty Grove, was a scratch, passing the baton to 31-year-old rookie right-handed knuckleballer Dick Newsome, who was given the task of facing the streaking DiMaggio.[7]

Lefty Gomez, DiMaggio's best friend on the team and his roommate on the road, was the Yankees' starting pitcher when the home team took the field. Joe's younger brother, Dominic DiMaggio, led off the game with a fly ball to left field. Gomez struck out Lou Finney for the second out. Ted Williams singled to right field, and Joe Cronin drew a walk, but Stan Spence flied out to DiMaggio in center field to end the inning.

DiMaggio was the cleanup hitter in the Yankees lineup and was afforded a first-inning at-bat when the number-two hitter, Red Rolfe, drew a walk. DiMaggio ended the inning as he lined out to right fielder Spence.

After Gomez set the Red Sox down without a run in the top of the second inning, Charlie Keller led off the bottom of the second inning with a home run to right field to give the Yankees a 1-0 lead. Newsome gave up a two-out double to Phil Rizzuto but got three ground-outs to escape the inning without further damage.

The Red Sox failed to score again in the top half of the third inning. In the home half, back-to-back singles by Rolfe and Tommy Henrich with one out put runners on the corners and brought DiMaggio to the plate for his second swing at history. John Drebinger of the *New York Times* described what happened next: "A snappy pick-up and throw by third-baseman Jim Tabor on a difficult bounding ball checked DiMaggio again. ..."[8] The stroke, though, was enough to drive in Rolfe from third base to give DiMaggio an RBI and the Yankees a 2-0 lead.

Nine consecutive outs followed, six by ground-outs signaling perhaps that the heat was beginning to fatigue both teams. (Gomez had changed his sweat-soaked flannel jersey after the third inning.[9])

In the Yankees fifth, first baseman Johnny Sturm, in his only major-league season, led off with a walk and stole second base. Rolfe doubled to right to drive in Sturm. Henrich lined out to Finney at first base, and that brought DiMaggio to the plate for his third at-bat.

Newsome, the visiting pitcher, could do no right. The fans booed at ball one and ball two, which were wide of the plate. Then, according to Associated Press writer Judson Bailey, DiMaggio "clouted a high foul into the third tier of Yankee Stadium and finally blasted a mighty fly into the lower stands in left field."[10] Red Sox left fielder Williams simply turned and looked as the blast went over his head.[11]

The blow sent Newsome to the showers, relieved by right-hander Jack Wilson to put out the fire. He didn't, and the Red Sox defense didn't help much either, as the first batter he faced, Keller, reached first base on an error by Red Sox player-manager Joe Cronin. Bill Dickey walked, and Joe Gordon reached on a fielder's choice to load the bases. After Phil Rizzuto popped out to the catcher, Gomez helped his own cause with a single up the middle, scoring Keller and Dickey and moving Gordon to third base. Gordon then scored the sixth run of the inning on a passed ball by catcher Frankie Pytlak. Wilson struck out Sturm, and the inning ended with the Yankees ahead 8-0.

The Red Sox grabbed three runs back in the top of the sixth, and Gomez, perhaps fatigued by the heat and maybe even the energy expended running the bases with his RBI singl5 e, left the contest when four of the first five batters reached base in the inning. Yankees manager Joe McCarthy summoned Johnny Murphy, the team's 1941 bullpen ace, to secure the victory. He did, with a 3⅔-inning, one-hit relief job. The Yankees won 8-4.

Many fans filtered out of the Stadium early to escape the heat before the victory was confirmed, having seen what they came for, DiMaggio's record-setting hit. Several stayed the distance and swarmed the field to celebrate when the game ended.[12]

Press photos from the time document DiMaggio on the field after the game amid a montage of baseball bats arranged to portray the number 45. Another showed DiMaggio celebrating with teammates in the locker room. Yet another portrayed his starlet wife, Dorothy, standing and cheering vigorously in the stands amid a throng of spectators after his home run in the fifth inning.

DiMaggio went on to hit in 11 more games through July 16 to make the number 56 an icon in baseball annals.[13] The Yankees went on to win the American League pennant with 101 victories and beat their rival Brooklyn Dodgers in the World Series, four games to one.

SOURCES

For game play-by-play details and box score information, the author referenced:

https://www.baseball-reference.com/boxes/NYA/NYA194107020.shtml

https://www.retrosheet.org/boxesetc/1941/B07020NYA1941.htm

The author revisited the following books that covered the streak and in particular this game:

Auker, Elden, with Tom Keegan. *Sleeper Cars and Flannel Uniforms: A Lifetime of Memories from Striking Out the Babe to Teeing It Up with the President* (Chicago: Triumph Books 2001).

Kennedy, Kostya. *56: Joe DiMaggio and the Last Magic Number in Sports* (New York: Sports Illustrated Books Time Home Entertainment, 2011).

Vaccaro, Mike. *1941 – The Greatest Year In Sports: Two Baseball Legends, Two Boxing Champs, and the Unstoppable Thoroughbred Who Made History in the Shadow of War* (New York: Doubleday 2007).

These videos provided further background on the 56-game hitting streak and contained footage of this game:

MLB Network. *56: The Streak* (2016).

HBO Sports. *Where Have You Gone Joe DiMaggio?* (1998).

PBS Special. *Joe DiMaggio – The Hero's Life* (2000).

NOTES

1   Roger Peckinpaugh had hit in 29 consecutive games in 1919, and Earle Combs tied that in 1931.

2   Associated Press, "DiMaggio Taking Interest in Hit Streak. Finally Decides He'd Like to Break Sisler's Streak," *Meriden Record* (Meriden, Connecticut), June 27, 1941: 12.

3   Dan Daniel, "19-Year-Old Record of Sisler Falls Before Relentless Drive of Yankees' Great Outfielder," *The Sporting News*, July 3, 1941: 18. Someone even pilfered DiMaggio's bat between games, but that didn't hinder his setting the record.

4   Keeler's streak was described by sportswriter Bob Considine as "an ancient and slightly questionable mark set in 1897." "Italian Star Runs Streak to 44 games: New York Defeats Bosox, 7-2," *Washington Post*, July 2, 1941: 2.

5   James Dawson, "Yankees Conquer Senators, 9-4, 7-5: DiMaggio Getting Hit in Each Game," *New York Times*, June 30, 1941: 20. The strain was not over for Dan Daniel, the official scorer for the game, who wrote, "This streak is of his is wearing me down. It's tougher on me than it is on DiMaggio." Dan Daniel. "Trials of an Official Scorer," *The Sporting News,* July 17, 1941: 4.

6   The Yankees as a team were on fire, too, in the middle of a 14-game winning streak and having just set a team home-run streak of 25 straight games that was ended in the June 29 doubleheader in Washington.

7   He won 19 games in 1941, seven more wins than anyone else on the second-place Red Sox. He was the league's best rookie pitcher." Bill Nowlin, "Dick Newsome," SABR BioProject, https://sabr.org/bioproj/person/dick-newsome/."

8   John Drebinger, "DiMaggio Sets Hitting Record as Yankees Win; Dodgers Triumph/Home Run in Fifth Tops Keeler Mark," *New York Times*, July 3, 1941: 22.

9   "Joe DiMaggio's Streak, Game 45: DiMaggio Stands Alone in Baseball history," joedimaggio.com; https://bleacherreport.com/articles/757234-joe-dimaggios-streak-game-45-dimaggio-stands-alone-in-baseball-history, BleacherReport.com, July 4, 2011.

10   Judson Bailey (Associated Press), "DiMaggio's Home Run Tops Keeler. Yankee Outfielder Continues Sensational Hitting Streak," *Ottawa Evening Citizen*, July 3, 1941: 14.

11   The celebration at home plate was chronicled by an Associated Press photo and included DiMaggio; Rolfe, the runner he drove in; Frankie Pytlak, the Red Sox catcher; and the Yankees batboy. Tim Sullivan, "DiMaggio Hits in 45th Straight Game; Sets Record," *Chicago Tribune*, July 3, 1941: 19.

12   Drebinger. One bold fan even clipped the Yankee Clipper's cap as he ran in from center field but was thwarted in his escape by "the Stadium's vigilant secondary defense of special guards."

13   During the streak DiMaggio batted .408, hit 15 home runs, and drove in 55 runs. "Perhaps even more unbelievably, he struck out a mere five times over that stretch." MLB.com, https://www.mlb.com/news/joe-dimaggio-56-game-hitting-streak.

BOB FELLER NO-HITS THE
NEW YORK YANKEES, 1-0

April 30, 1946:
Cleveland Indians 1, New York Yankees 0,
at Yankee Stadium

By Lyle Spatz

Cleveland's Bob Feller had been baseball's best pitcher in the years leading up to World War II. When war came, he was among the first to enlist, causing him to miss the 1942, 1943, and 1944 seasons, and most of the 1945 season. He made a dramatic return on August 24, 1945, against Detroit's Hal Newhouser, who had already won 20 games that season. Newhouser, who had won the American League's Most Valuable Player Award in 1944 and again in 1945, had replaced Feller as the game's best pitcher. In a dramatic matchup that drew more than 46,000 fans to Cleveland Stadium, the Indians, behind Feller's four-hitter, won, 4-2. Feller finished the season with a 5-3 record and a 2.50 earned-run average.

Much was expected of Feller when the 1946 season opened, the first since 1941 with the United States at peace. He did not disappoint. On Opening Day he defeated Chicago, 1-0, at Comiskey Park. He allowed three hits, three more than he allowed the White Sox in the same park on Opening Day 1940.[1] He lost his next two starts, to Detroit and Chicago, in games in which the Indians scored just two runs in each. Feller had demonstrated that he had not lost his fastball by striking out 28 batters in the three games. Manager Lou Boudreau, scoffing at rumors that his ace had lost his prewar brilliance, declared: "All I can say to that is just come out and watch him pitch. In the three games he's worked we've given him exactly five runs. The only time he won he had to pitch a shutout."[2]

Nevertheless, Feller was under scrutiny when he faced the Yankees at Yankee Stadium on April 30. He had won a game against New York the previous September, defeating Spud Chandler. But that was the wartime Yankees. The 1946 Yankees had started 9-4, and they had Joe DiMaggio in center field, not

Russ Derry, along with fellow future Hall of Famers shortstop Phil Rizzuto, second baseman Joe Gordon, and catcher Bill Dickey. The Indians also had three future Hall of Famers in their lineup: Feller, shortstop Boudreau, and center fielder Bob Lemon.[3] The game drew a crowd of 38,112 on a mild, partly cloudy afternoon.

The 27-year-old Feller started wildly, walking a batter in each of the first four innings and another to start the sixth. But overall, he and his opponent, 29-year-old Bill Bevens, 13-9 in 1945, staged a magnificent pitching duel. Through eight innings neither pitcher had allowed a run; but more riveting was the crowd's awareness of the Yankees' failure to get a hit. "Why I've never seen a no-hit game and I don't expect to see one today," said Red Patterson, the Yankees' director of public relations.[4] The Yankees had not been no-hit since Ray Caldwell, also of Cleveland, threw one against them in the first game of a doubleheader at the Polo Grounds on September 10, 1919.

Feller retired the side in order in the seventh, and got the first two batters in the eighth, including a strikeout of Bevens, his 11th and final strikeout of the game. In retrospect it seems odd that Yankees manager Joe McCarthy did not pinch-hit for pitcher Bevens in this situation. Next up was Rizzuto, who hit a high pop foul near third base. It was a routine play, but the usually sure-handed Indians third baseman Ken Keltner dropped it. Rizzuto had another chance, but Feller retired him on a groundball to Boudreau to end the inning.

The Indians broke the scoreless deadlock when with one out in the ninth, Feller's batterymate, Frankie Hayes, homered into the left-field seats. The Cleveland right-hander was three outs away from his second no-hitter, but they would not be easy. He would have to get by George Stirnweiss, the defending AL batting champion, clutch-hitting Tommy Henrich, and the great DiMaggio.

Stirnweiss led off the home ninth by pushing a bunt up the first-base line, that Les Fleming had trouble coming up with, allowing Stirnweiss to reach base. With Henrich at bat, it was announced over the loudspeaker that Fleming had been charged with an error on Stirnweiss's bunt. A loud roar went up from the crowd, indicating that the fans were rooting for Feller to get his no-hitter. This was the first time such an announcement of a scorer's ruling had been made at Yankee Stadium.

Henrich sacrificed Stirnweiss to second, and the confrontation between Feller and DiMaggio began. The two all-time greats, who came into the league 10 years earlier, had not faced each other in a league game since 1941.

"I threw DiMaggio my best fast ball on a 3-and-2 count, and he hit a grounder to Boudreau's left," Feller told author Bill Gilbert in a memoir. "Lou threw him out at first as Stirnweiss moved to third."[5]

One out to go, but the batter was the always dangerous Charlie Keller. "You're a long way from a no-hitter even when you have two men out in the ninth," Feller said after the game. "But when I got through the seventh, I began to hope – and I could see that the other fellows were hoping with me."[6]

On a 1-and-2 pitch, Feller's 133rd of the game, Keller hit a groundball to second baseman Ray Mack. Mack fumbled the ball momentarily as the crowd held its breath, but he recovered in time to throw Keller out.[7] Feller had his no-hitter. The crowd stood and cheered, and hundreds of fans surrounded him as he struggled to get to the dugout.

"I had more stuff today than when I pitched that other no-hitter against the White Sox on Opening Day in 1940," he said later in the dressing room.[8]

Feller also credited the defensive plays turned in by Boudreau and Mack. "You made it possible, Lou," he said. "They were great plays out there and I'm sure grateful."[9]

"It was a Frank Merriwell game," remarked Joe McCarthy. "I never saw anything like it."[10]

"Anybody who had the stuff Feller had today," chimed in DiMaggio, "deserved a no-hitter. We didn't hit the ball solid all day."[11]

Feller led the league with 26 wins in 1946, the fourth of his six 20-win seasons. He also led in games, games started, complete games, shutouts, innings pitched, walks, and strikeouts. Five years later, on July 1, 1951, he would throw a third no-hitter, defeating Detroit, 2–1.

SOURCES

In addition to the sources cited in the Notes, the author consulted Baseball-Reference.com and Retrosheet.org.

https://www.baseball-reference.com/boxes/NYA/NYA194604300.shtml

https://www.retrosheet.org/boxesetc/1946/B04300NYA1946.htm

NOTES

1   Feller no-hit the White Sox on April 16, 1940.

2   "Feller Faces Yanks Today in Big Test," *Akron Beacon Journal*, April 30, 1946: 26.

3   During the season the Indians would convert Lemon from an outfielder to a pitcher, where he would compile a Hall of Fame career.

4   Ted Meier, "Feller's No-Hit Story Has Punch, No Wallop," *Dayton* (Ohio) *Daily News*, May 1, 1946: 18.

5   Bob Feller with Bill Gilbert, *Now Pitching Bob Feller* (New York: HarperPerennial, 1990), 131.

6   J.G. Taylor Spink, "Looping the Loops," *The Sporting News*, May 9, 1946: 2.

7   Mack had also made the last play in Feller's 1940 no-hitter, throwing out another left-handed-hitting outfielder, Taft Wright.

8   Meier.

9   Joe Trimble, "Feller's Second No-Hitter Blanks Yanks, 1-0," *New York Daily News*, May 1, 1946: 59.

10   Meier.

11   Meier.

THE NEW YORK YANKEES HAVE TROUBLE HITTING DUTCH LEONARD'S KNUCKLEBALL IN THE FIRST NIGHT GAME AT YANKEE STADIUM

May 28, 1946:
Washington Senators 2, New York Yankees 1,
at Yankee Stadium

By Aaron Tallent

Jackie Robinson once said that Emil John "Dutch" Leonard's knuckleball "comes up, makes a face at you, then runs away."[1] On May 28, 1946, the New York Yankees had trouble with the Washington Senators knuckler's elusive pitch in a 2-1 loss. Leonard may have had a little help that night, though, because the Bronx Bombers were playing their first night game in Yankee Stadium. With this game, the Yankees became one of the last American or National League teams to play at home under the lights.[2]

Yankee Stadium had hosted night events in the past with perhaps the most famous being the heavyweight title fight between Joe Louis and Max Schmeling in 1938. For that bout, all of the lights inside Yankee Stadium were turned off except for floodlights next to the boxing ring, so the only light in the Stadium other than the fight were lit cigarettes.[3]

When it came to other sports, Yankees President Ed Barrow did not believe in night baseball and refused to permit it at the Stadium, saying, "Baseball was made to be played in God's sunshine and I won't have any of it at Yankees Stadium."[4] In addition, War Production Board restrictions on resource allocation prohibited stadiums from starting projects with materials that could be used in the World War II effort.[5] Illuminating Yankee Stadium for baseball required a change in ownership and an end to World War II.

In January 1945 a three-person syndicate of Dan Topping, Del Webb, and Larry MacPhail bought the Yankees from the heirs of the late owner Jacob Ruppert.[6] MacPhail was the pioneer of night baseball.

As general manager of the Cincinnati Reds, he pushed for lights to be installed at Cincinnati's Crosley Field, leading to the first night game in major-league history on May 24, 1935, when the Reds beat the Philadelphia Phillies, 2-1. MacPhail then went to the Brooklyn Dodgers, who erected lights at Ebbets Field in 1938. By 1945 the Yankees were one of only five teams whose ballparks did not have lights.[7]

With the $3 million purchase ($49.5 million in 2022 dollars), MacPhail made it clear that the new ownership was not going to shake up the franchise. It would keep Barrow (in a symbolic position) and manager Joe McCarthy, who had won seven World Series with the Yankees. "You don't spend half a lifetime looking for a guy like McCarthy and then let him go," MacPhail said when the purchase was announced.[8]

One change MacPhail did say would be coming was night baseball to Yankee Stadium once the franchise was in a position to install lights.[9] On September 2, 1945, Japan formally surrendered, ending World War II. The next month, MacPhail assistant Tom Gallery indicated that lights would be installed at Yankee Stadium for the next season, saying, "We've been up there all week with the General Electric people, the man who built the stadium, and representatives of the light company. It should all be on paper in written form within the next week to 10 days."[10]

On October 30 MacPhail announced that construction of the $250,000 ($4.1 million in 2022) lighting system that would be the best in baseball would begin on January 1.[11] The 2.1-million-watt illumination system included 1,409 floodlights of 1,500 watts each across six towers connected by 15 miles of wiring and 30,000 feet of steel electrical conduits. The lights featured enhancements that GE had developed during World War II.

The 348-ton steel towers were placed so that the illumination would be evenly spread around the field. With the previous lighting systems for other stadiums, the infield was often brighter than the outfield. Overall, the lights were the equivalent of five full moons and if used for other purposes, could light US Highway 1 from Washington, DC, to New York City.

The lights were not the only upgrade to Yankee Stadium. An additional $350,000 was being spent to build 15,000 box seats, two concession rooms, a new clubhouse for the Yankees, and additional spaces for stadium staff.[12]

In February, MacPhail announced that 14 night games would be played at Yankee Stadium during the 1946 season. The first was scheduled for May 27 against the Washington Senators.[13]

By the time the game rolled around, it would have been understandable if the Yankees were distracted going into it. First, McCarthy had gone to his farm in East Amherst, New York, after illness brought on by bouts with alcoholism, and had resigned on May 24. Catcher Bill Dickey was named player-manager.[14] The team was six games behind the Boston Red Sox for first place in the American League and was in danger of being overtaken the visiting Senators, who had won 12 of their last 14 games. To make matters worse, a steady, all-day rain on May 27 had forced the game to be postponed until the next night.[15]

On May 28, a crowd of 49,917 came to Yankee Stadium, fewer than expected because of cold weather and the threat of rain.[16] Pitcher Clarence "Cuddles" Marshall and the Yankees held the Senators scoreless in the top of the first inning, and then Leonard took the mound.

Knuckleball pitchers had been giving major-league batters fits since Toad Ramsey deployed the pitch with the Louisville Colonels in the 1890s,[17] and Leonard was no different. He was 4-0 and had beaten New York earlier in the season. However, McCarthy had indicated a lack of respect for him by once saying he had no interest in signing him because "[h]e keeps us on top. We can beat him every time and if we don't whip him, he'll beat himself on a passed ball with those knucklers."

In the first inning, it looked as though McCarthy's statement might be prophetic. Third baseman Snuffy Stirnweiss doubled and took third on a groundout. Joe DiMaggio brought him home with a single for a 1-0 Yankees lead. Nick Etten singled but Leonard retired the side, and allowed only three more hits, two walks, and no runs in the final eight innings. The Senators tied the game in the second inning when Marshall walked first baseman Mickey Vernon, who had a 22-game hit streak coming in, and Jeff Heath sent him home with a double to center field. In the fourth inning, Leonard hit a single to center field and shortstop Cecil Travis scored to give New York a 2-1 lead, one which held for the rest of the game.

Leonard pitched a complete game, which he capped in the ninth by getting pinch-hitter Bill Drescher to ground into a force out at second base for the win. For the Senators, the only sour note was that Vernon's 22-game hitting streak came to an end.

The win pulled the Senators to within a half-game of the Yankees,[13] but neither team was able to keep up with Boston. The Red Sox finished 104-50 while New York was 17 games behind them, and the Senators were 28 games out of first place.

The big winner in New York in 1946 was night baseball. The Yankees set a major-league record for attendance with 2,265,512. The largest crowd for a night game was 71,551 for a game on August 28 that Cleveland Indians pitcher Bob Feller started after throwing a no-hitter against the Yankees earlier that season, the second of his career.[18] To put this into perspective, the attendance for Feller's no-hitter on the afternoon of April 30, 1946, was 38,112.

The first World Series night game was not played until 1971, so Yankee Stadium did not host one until New York returned to the fall classic in 1976. However, the financial success playing under the lights during the 1946 season brought night baseball to the Bronx for good.

SOURCES

In addition to the sources cited in the Notes, the author consulted Baseball-Almanac.com, Baseball-Reference.com, and USInflationCalculator.com.

https://www.baseball-reference.com/boxes/NYA/NYA194605280.shtml

https://www.retrosheet.org/boxesetc/1946/B05280NYA1946.htm

NOTES

1   Stan Baumgartner, "Jackie Asks for Fans' Advice on '48 Pay, Gets '$20,000' Reply," *The Sporting News*, November 12, 1947: 11.

2   Jack Hand (Associated Press), "Yankee Stadium to Have Lights, Night Baseball," *Salt Lake Telegram*, October 20, 1945: 6.

3   Francis E. Stan, "Win, Lose or Draw," *Washington Evening Star*, June 22, 1938: A14.

4   United Press, "MacPhail Hopes to Get Giant Okay to Use Polo Grounds," *Passaic* (New Jersey) *Herald News,* May 3, 1945: 25.

5   "MacPhail Hopes to Get Giant Okay to Use Polo Grounds."

6   Jack Smith and Dick Young, "MacPhail, Topping, Webb Buy Yanks," *New York Daily News*, January 27, 1945: C16.

7   Oscar Eddleton, "Under the Lights," SABR Business of Baseball Committee, sabr.org. Retrieved October 29, 2022. http://research.sabr.org/journals/under-the-lights.

8   Leo M. Peterson (United Press), "See Sale of Yankees as Hopeful Sign for Baseball This Year," *Olean* (New York) *Times Herald,* January 27, 1945: 6.

9   Peterson.

10 Associated Press, "Yankee Stadium to Have Lights in '46," *Marysville* (California) *Appeal-Democrat,* October 20, 1945: 8.

11 "Joe McCarthy Set to Guide Yankees," *Edmonton Journal*, November 1, 1945: 6.

12 "Yankees to Have Best Illuminated Park," *Cincinnati Enquirer*, January 16, 1946: 21.

13 International News Service, "Yankee Stadium Lights Will Flash on May 27," *Fort Worth Star-Telegram*, February 14, 1946: 11.

14 "McCarthy Resigns Yankee Job; Dickey Named Manager," *Buffalo Evening News*, May 25, 1946: 5; Mike Vaccaro, *Emperors and Idiots: The Hundred-Year Rivalry Between the Yankees and Red Sox, from the Very Beginning to the End of the Curse* (New York: Doubleday, 2005), 250-251.

15 Associated Press, "Yanks First Night Tilt Postponed by Rain," *Montgomery* (Alabama) *Advertiser*. May 28, 1946: 3.

16 Burton Hawkins, "Leonard's Convincing Work Booms," *Washington Evening Star*. May 29, 1946: 14.

17 Ben McGrath, "Project Knuckleball," *New Yorker*, May 17, 2004, newyorker.com. Retrieved October 29, 2022. https://www.newyorker.com/magazine/2004/05/17/project-knuckleball.

18 Associated Press, "Year's Yankee Stadium Sports Draw 3,302,535," *Chicago Tribune*. November 30, 1946: 19. Yankee Stadium capacity at the time is listed as 70,000. See Philip J. Lowry, ed., *Green Cathedrals*, fifth edition, (Phoenix: Society for American Baseball Research, 2019), 214.

YANKEES COME OUT ON TOP IN WINNER-TAKE-ALL CONTEST

October 2, 1949:
New York Yankees 5, Boston Red Sox 3,
at Yankee Stadium

By Mike Whiteman

At the end of the 1948 season, the New York Yankees fired their manager, Bucky Harris. The team had just completed what was for them a subpar year, finishing in third place behind the Boston Red Sox and Cleveland Indians. Harris was not without credentials, having guided the Yankees to the 1947 World Series championship, his second ring as a manager. A look at the 1948 team revealed a veteran squad, with five primary position-player starters 30 years old and over, as were two of the top three winning pitchers.

An influx of youth and energy was in order, but general manager George Weiss hired a 58-year old former National League manager with a lifetime losing record to replace Harris. Casey Stengel had managed in the major leagues for almost nine seasons with an undistinguished 581-742 record – his best finish a 77-75 showing and a fifth-place finish with the Boston Bees in 1938. He was not yet Casey Stengel, Hall of Fame manager. He was an old, undistinguished skipper, widely considered a clown for his antics as a player and a gift for the gab in his managerial career.

The baseball world howled, with predictions of doomsday for the New Yorkers. In *Baseball Digest,* Chicago sportswriter John Carmichael predicted another third-place finish for Stengel's crew.[1] This forecast was charitable in comparison to that of *The Sporting News*, which anticipated the team finishing in fourth place.[2]

Clearly, Stengel had something to prove.

Casey was a prodigy of John McGraw, but his reverence and lessons learned hadn't provided the results he craved. Behind the "Stengelese" – the goofiness – there was a fierce competitor.

The image of Stengel and the notoriously corporate Yankees didn't seem to align. Stengel himself in his initial press conference seemed to recognize this, stating, "This is a 5 million dollar business. They don't hand out jobs like this because you're a friend."[3]

Stengel and Weiss oversaw an overhauling of the roster, with all but one position during the season primarily manned by someone different than in the 94-win 1948 version. Injuries were a big part of the equation: Due to aches and pains the heart of the batting order – Tommy Henrich, Joe DiMaggio, and Yogi Berra – was in the same lineup only 17 games all year. *The Sporting News* chronicled at least 71 injuries suffered by Yankee players.[4] No doubt the most devastating was the bad heel that sidelined center fielder Joe DiMaggio all season until June 28.

Despite the uphill climb, Stengel deftly steered the Yanks to a 41-24 start prior to DiMaggio's return. The team held first place from Opening Day through September 26, when it was passed in the standings by the Red Sox, who were managed by longtime Yankees skipper Joe McCarthy and had come back from a 12-game deficit on July 4. Over the week after September 26, the teams stayed within a game of each other, setting up the final two-game confrontation of October 1 and 2 at Yankee Stadium. Boston came into the set leading by a game and needing only one win to clinch the American League pennant. They seemed on their way to the flag on October 1, when they jumped out to an early 4-0 lead. An improbable Yankees comeback ended up taking that first game, moving the teams into a tie for the final contest.

On the morning of October 2, 1949, the Yankees and Red Sox had identical 96-57 records. This day's game would decide who represented the American League in the World Series against either the St. Louis Cardinals or Brooklyn Dodgers, who were separated by just one game in the race for the National League flag. It was a baseball fan's dream; both pennant races were coming down to the last day of the season, only the second time in baseball history (after 1908) that this had happened.[5]

For the biggest game of his managerial career, Stengel handed the ball to ace right-hander Vic Raschi, who came into the contest with a 20-10 record and a 3.35 ERA. Boston sent out Ellis Kinder, a previously undistinguished 34-year-old right-hander finishing up the season of his life, 23-5 and 3.45. Kinder had been 4-0 against the Yankees in 1949.

Against the backdrop of a jam-packed crowd of 68,055 in Yankee Stadium, the hometown team jumped onto the scoreboard right away. Phil Rizzuto led off the bottom of the first with a triple down the left-field line and was driven in on Henrich's ground-out to second.

Raschi and Kinder then settled into a classic pitchers' duel, both hurlers putting zeros on the scoreboard for the next six innings. In the top of the eighth, Kinder's spot in the batting order came up, but with his team behind, Boston manager McCarthy went to the bench in search of a spark. He sent up Tom Wright, fresh off a .368 season in Triple-A Louisville, to hit for his pitcher. Wright came through, drawing a walk, but was wiped out when Dom DiMaggio grounded into a double play.

In the bottom of the frame, McCarthy sent to the mound his other ace pitcher, Mel Parnell, the 25-game-winning All-Star left-hander who later finished fourth in the American League MVP voting. Henrich greeted Parnell with a solo home run and Berra singled. McCarthy didn't waste any time, going again to the bullpen, this time for Tex Hughson, an ace of the 1946 pennant-winning Red Sox. Hughson induced a double-play grounder by Joe DiMaggio, and the threat seemed to be over. Alas, things were just beginning, as two singles and a walk brought Jerry Coleman to the plate with the bases loaded. The Yankees second sacker, who later went on to finish third in Rookie of the Year balloting, lifted a short fly to right field which barely escaped the grasp of the diving right-fielder Al Zarilla.[6] The bases cleared, and though Coleman was thrown out going for a triple, the Yankees suddenly had a 5-0 lead and with the dominant Raschi going for the shutout. Things looked good for the hometown team. It wouldn't be easy, though, as the Red Sox had their heavy hitters due up.

Raschi retired Johnny Pesky on a fly ball to center field, then walked Ted Williams and allowed him to advance to second on a wild pitch. Vern Stephens singled him to third. Bobby Doerr's triple past Joe DiMaggio cut the lead to 5-2, and the game was starting to get more interesting. At this point, DiMaggio took himself out, exhausted. Cliff Mapes slid from right field to center.

Al Zarilla then flied out to Mapes in shallow center, with Doerr holding third. Billy Goodman singled him in, and it was 5-3, with the tying run coming to the plate in catcher Birdie Tebbetts. Henrich and Berra walked toward the mound to give Raschi some encouragement. Raschi, an intense, angry man while on the mound, would have none of that.

"Give me the goddamn ball and get the hell out of here."[7]

Both players immediately returned to their positions. Raschi induced Tebbetts to foul out to Henrich. The Yankees were the 1949 American League champions.

Boston fans, who had endured a final-game defeat in 1948, were devastated and questioned the removal of Kinder, though many pundits, including Harold Kaese of the *Boston Globe,* gave McCarthy the benefit of the doubt: "To leave Kinder in was playing for what? For a 1-0 defeat.[8]

For Ted Williams, the loss was doubly frustrating, as on top of the pennant race disappointment, his hitless performance allowed Detroit's George Kell to overtake him for the AL batting crown by the slimmest of margins – .3429 to .3427.

Word came afterward of Brooklyn's win over Philadelphia to sew up the NL flag. For the eighth time – the third with the Dodgers –the Yankees would engage in a Subway Series.

Stengel was humble in victory: "I didn't catch a fly ball, make a base hit, or strike out a guy all season. So why should I take any credit."[9] To his players went the ultimate praise: "I want to thank all these players for giving me the greatest thrill of my life."[10]

SOURCES

In addition to the sources cited in the Notes, the author consulted Baseball-Reference.com and Retrosheet.org.

https://www.baseball-reference.com/boxes/NYA/NYA194910020.shtml

https://www.retrosheet.org/boxesetc/1949/B10020NYA1949.htm

NOTES

1   In the April 1949 Issue of *Baseball Digest*, Carmichael wrote, "This Yankee team may be on the verge of bending, if not entirely breaking, under the slender thread of too little in the way of top-flight players." 5-6.

2   "Pennants Expected to Fly from New Poles," *The Sporting News*, April 20, 1949: 3.

3   Robert Creamer, *Stengel, His Life and Times* (New York: Fireside, 1984), 212.

4   "Chart on Yankee Hospital List," *The Sporting News*, October 12, 1949: 10.

5   On the final days of their season in 1908, the Chicago Cubs beat the New York Giants for the National League pennant. Two days earlier, the Detroit Tigers beat the Chicago White Sox for the AL pennant. The Cubs won the World Series in five games.

6   "Yanks Whip Red Sox in Season Finale to Win Sixteenth American League Pennant," *The New York Times, October 3, 1949:21.*

7   Peter Golenbock, *Dynasty: The New York Yankees 1949-64* (New York: Berkley, 2000), 42.

8   Harold Kaese, "McCarthy's Lifting of Kinder in 8th Called Good Baseball," *Boston Globe*, October 3, 1949: 18.

9   "Stengel an Elder Statesman Now," *Baseball Digest*, November 1949: 19.

10   Creamer, *Stengel, His Life and Times,* 233.

MARTIN'S RECORD-SETTING HIT LEADS YANKEES TO FIFTH CONSECUTIVE WORLD CHAMPIONSHIP

October 5, 1953:
New York Yankees 4, Brooklyn Dodgers 3,
at Yankee Stadium
Game Six of the 1953 World Series

By Brian M. Frank

The New York Yankees entered Game Six of the 1953 World Series against the Brooklyn Dodgers looking to secure a record fifth consecutive World Series title. The Yankees had taken control of the Series by beating Brooklyn 11-7 in Game Five at Ebbets Field to take a three-games-to-two lead.

Billy Martin had been the star of the fall classic. The feisty second baseman entered Game Six hitting

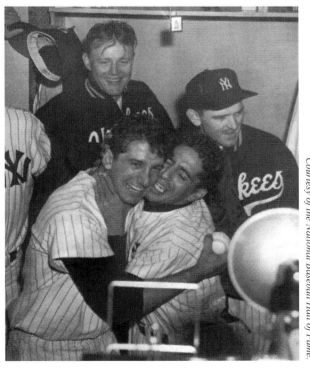

World Series star Billy Martin is embraced by Phil Rizzuto and celebrated by an amused Ralph Houk.

.526 with four extra-base hits in the Series. Game Six would only add to his October legacy.

The Yankees sent Whitey Ford to the mound. Ford had gone 18-6 with a 3.00 ERA during the regular season, but had a disastrous Game Four start just two days earlier, when he lasted only one inning and allowed three earned runs.

Brooklyn countered with Carl Erskine, who'd gone 20-6 with a 3.54 ERA during the regular season and was coming off a masterful performance in Game Three, when he allowed two runs in a complete-game win and struck out a World Series-record 14 batters. However, Erskine was taking the mound on only two days' rest.[1]

After Freddy Parent, shortstop for the 1903 Boston Red Sox, threw out the first pitch to celebrate the 50th anniversary of the first World Series, the two teams took the field at Yankee Stadium in front of 62,370 fans on a chilly, overcast day.

The Yankees wasted no time getting to Erskine. Gene Woodling drew a walk to lead off New York's half of the first. After Joe Collins struck out, Hank Bauer singled to left. Yogi Berra then brought home the first run of the contest on a liner to right field, "the ball skipping and bouncing along before being deflected into the stands by (Carl) Furillo's mitt for a ground-rule double as Woodling scored," wrote Joe Trimble of the *New York Daily News*.[2]

Mickey Mantle was intentionally walked to load the bases for the red-hot Martin, who hit a one-bounce liner to the right of second baseman Jim Gilliam.

Gilliam managed to knock it down, but failed to make a play as the ball dribbled away from him. All the runners were safe, as Bauer raced home.

Aware that Martin was approaching the record for hits in a single World Series, those in attendance did not take kindly when Gilliam was charged with an error, rather than Martin being awarded a hit. When an "E" was put on the scoreboard, "there was a roar of disapproval from the crowd and virtually every player on the Yankees bench stood and waved derisively at the press box."[3]

"I've fielded others like that – and I've missed 'em too," Gilliam said of the misplay. "But I expected to get the ball. It was a low liner that came on a short hop. It hit my glove but it didn't stick."[4]

The Yankees continued to put pressure on Erskine in the second inning. Phil Rizzuto and Ford each singled to put runners at the corners with no outs. Woodling hit a sacrifice fly to deep left field to bring Rizzuto home for the Yankees' third run. Collins hit a tapper up the third-base line that Erskine fielded, but he threw over Gil Hodges' head at first, allowing Ford to go to third and Collins to second. Bauer was then walked to load the bases.

Berra stepped to the plate with a chance to break the game wide open. He hit a fly to deep center field that Duke Snider caught, and "the blow was so deep that Duke conceded the run, throwing to second to keep Bauer at first."[5] But as Gilliam caught the ball, "he heard Campy (catcher Roy Campanella) screaming for a throw."[6] Gilliam fired home to Campanella who applied the tag on Ford for an inning-ending double play.

Ford later explained why he didn't score on what looked like an easy sacrifice fly.

"I was unable to see Duke Snider complete the catch and left early," he said of the mishap. "(Third base coach) Frankie Crosetti told me to return and tag up. I did and was an easy out at the plate."[7]

Erskine left the game after the fourth inning, having allowed three runs on six hits and three walks. He was replaced by rookie Bob Milliken, who tossed two shutout innings.

The only run Ford allowed came in the sixth inning. Jackie Robinson doubled to left field with one out. He stole third without drawing a throw and came home when Campanella hit a slow groundball to short.

After the seventh inning, "in a move as startling as any in his brilliant managerial career," Casey Stengel removed Ford and replaced him with Allie Reynolds.[8] "A murmur of disapproval from the crowd" met the pitching change.[9] Ford seemed to have been rolling, allowing only one run on six hits and a walk, while striking out seven.

"Whitey pitched well," Stengel said, "but that Bobby Morgan's fly at the end of the seventh was hit real hard. I didn't want to take any chances against those good hitters the Dodgers would have coming up in the eighth. I figured Reynolds with a two-run lead would hold it for two innings."[10]

"I felt bad when Casey took me out," Ford said. "Then I thought, 'Well, he hasn't been wrong in five years.'"[11]

Reynolds had strained a muscle in his back while starting the Series opener. He'd returned to the mound to record the final two outs of Game Five. As he walked to the mound to try to secure the Yankees' fifth consecutive championship, the stadium lights turned on. It was only slightly after 3 P.M., "but the raw, cold, overcast weather made it seem like nightfall."[12]

Reynolds surrendered a harmless single to Robinson in the eighth inning. In the ninth, Snider worked a one-out walk to bring Furillo to the plate as the game's tying run. Furillo drilled a two-run home run to right field, as "the stadium roared in the wildest moment of the Series, the lights went on again in Brooklyn and Dodgers bench-warmers streamed out to shake the hand of the man who had brought them from the jaws of death."[13]

Furillo's game-tying home run was the 17th homer hit by the two teams in the Series, breaking the record set by the same two teams a year earlier.

Reynolds rebounded after Furillo's big blast to strike out Billy Cox and Clem Labine and send the game to the bottom of the ninth tied, 3-3.[14]

Labine, who'd entered the game in the seventh inning, took the mound for the Dodgers in the ninth. He walked Bauer to start the inning, but was able to get Berra to line out to right field for the first out. Mantle then hit what Trimble called "a sleazy little roller to the third base side of the mound" that went for an infield hit.[15]

That brought Martin, who'd already doubled in the fifth inning for his 11th hit of the Series, to the plate with runners at first and second. The Series star hit the second pitch he saw back through the box and into center field. Bauer "stormed home from second, as Snider forlornly trotted in and fielded the ball."[16]

"When I was up there, I don't know exactly what I was thinking, except that I just wanted to get that run home," an exuberant Martin said.

The victory gave the Yankees their 16th World Series championship and record-setting fifth in a row. Many Yankees players believed the team was only getting started.

"I don't see why this ball club shouldn't keep winning pennants indefinitely," Rizzuto said. "After all, we're loaded with young players. I'm the only old guy on the club."[17] (Rizzuto was 35.)

But this Series was all about Martin's performance. His 12 hits tied Buck Herzog (1912), Shoeless Joe Jackson (1919), Pepper Martin (1931), and Sam Rice (1925) for the most hits in a World Series. Many of his teammates felt he should have had one more hit and broken the record – if the groundball to Gilliam in the first inning had been scored a hit rather than an error.

"I never saw such lousy scoring," Yankees coach Bill Dickey complained. "A hit if I ever saw one. What have you got to do to get one these days? Hit one into the seats? It's a shame to take that one away from him."[18]

Martin, who batted .257 during the season, finished the series 12-for-24 with two home runs, two triples, one double, one walk, five runs scored, and eight RBIs.

Rizzuto, who'd just finished playing in his eighth fall classic, proclaimed that Martin "played the greatest Series I ever saw."[19]

"We got beat by a .250 hitter," Dodgers manager Chuck Dressen complained. "That little stinker is the best damned ballplayer they got."[20]

"He'd run through a buzz saw to beat you," Dressen added.[21]

"Biggest moment of my life," an elated Martin said of his Series-winning hit. "I was damn glad to get that 12th hit. The hell with the 13th. We won, didn't we? That's all that counts."[22]

SOURCES

In addition to the sources cited in the Notes, the author consulted Baseball-Reference.org and Retrosheet.org.

https://www.baseball-reference.com/boxes/NYA/NYA195310050.shtml

https://www.retrosheet.org/boxesetc/1953/B10050NYA1953.htm

NOTES

1. Erskine struggled in the opening game of the Series, also played at Yankee Stadium, when he allowed four earned runs and lasted only one inning.

2. Joe Trimble, "Yankees Win 5th Series in a Row," *New York Daily News*, October 6, 1953: 62.

3. Trimble, 62.

4. Roscoe McGowen, "Vanquished Praise Martin of Victors," *New York Times*, October 6, 1953: 36.

5. Trimble, 62.

6. Trimble, 62.

7. Louis Effrat, "Hurling Strength Needed, Pilot Says," *New York Times*, October 6, 1953: 35.

8. John Drebinger, "Yankees Capture 5th Series in a Row, a Record; Martin's Hit in 9th Beats Dodgers, 4 to 3," *New York Times*, October 6, 1953: 35.

9. Trimble, 60.

10. Effrat.

11. Red Smith, "Martin Hits in 9th, New York Wins Yanks 5th Series in Row," *New York Herald Tribune*, October 6, 1953: 26.

12. Trimble, 60.

13. Trimble, 62.

14. Despite allowing Furillo's two-run home run in the game's final frame, Reynolds recorded the win, giving him seven career World Series wins, tying Red Ruffing for most all time.

15. Trimble, 62.

16. Trimble, 62.

17. Dave Anderson, "Giants Lost Out on Martin in Cash-and-Carry Trade," *Brooklyn Daily Eagle*, October 6, 1953: 15.

18. Dana Mozley, "Martin Wuz Robbed, Yell Yanks," *New York Daily News*, October 6, 1953: 61.

19. Anderson, 15.

20. Dick Young, "Like Being Hit by Son Moans Chuck," *New York Daily News*, October 6, 1953: 61.

21. Young.

22. Mozley.

MANTLE SLAMS THREE HRS AGAINST TIGERS, INCLUDING FIRST CAREER SWITCH-HITTING PAIR

May 13, 1955:
New York Yankees 5, Detroit Tigers 2, at Yankee Stadium

By Richard Cuicchi

Only 22 years old at the start of his fifth major-league season in 1955, Mickey Mantle was on a clear path to stardom. He had become the New Yankees' new wonder-boy, providing a seamless transition from legendary Joe DiMaggio in center field. Since his second season in 1952, Mantle had battled right knee and left leg problems, requiring knee surgery at the end of 1953. Another surgery to remove a cyst on his knee in February 1954 caused him to miss nine games early in the season. Having recovered by the 1955 season, the switch-hitting Mantle raised his game another level. His three home-run clouts against the Detroit Tigers on May 13, including a rare occurrence of homers hit from both sides of the plate, were indicative of how much he would spur the team's success.

The Yankees' string of five straight American League pennants had been interrupted in 1954 by the Cleveland Indians, so they were anxious to return to their seemingly perennial position atop the league. However, the Indians and Chicago White Sox turned out to be formidable opponents, and the three teams held either the first, second, and third spots in the league for practically the entire season.

Coming into the contest on May 13, Casey Stengel's Yankees and Bucky Harris's Tigers were tied for third place, 3½ games behind the Indians. The Yankees were playing their third game of a scheduled 16-game homestand, having lost to the Indians in the first two games.

The Friday afternoon game was played before only 7,177 spectators. The Yankees' Whitey Ford and the Tigers' Steve Gromek started the game as mound opponents.

Batting left-handed, the muscular Mantle began his home-run onslaught in the first inning. After Andy Carey got on base with a bunt single, Mantle hit a line drive that cleared the bleacher wall above the auxiliary scoreboard near the Yankees bullpen. It was the first of three massive blasts that the *New York Times* reported

In his career, Mickey Mantle homered from both sides of the plate in 10 games.

"end to end would have measured in the neighborhood of 1,300 feet."[1]

Ford was efficient in this first three innings, yielding only a walk that was erased by a double play.

In the third inning, Mantle was again involved in the scoring. Hank Bauer singled and advanced to second on Carey's sacrifice. Mantle's single scored Bauer for the Yankees' third run.

Ford was aided by another double play in the fourth inning and didn't give up his first hit until Ray Boone singled in the fifth inning.

In the bottom of the fifth inning, Mantle got the best of Gromek again with a towering home run into the seats by the 407-foot sign in right-center field. With no one on base, the Yankees lead went to 4-0.

Ford retired the side in order in the sixth, and then gave up the Tigers' only runs the next inning on Boone's two-run homer. Ford left the game after the seventh because of a blister on his middle finger.

Leading off the bottom of the eighth, Mantle batted right-handed against lefty relief pitcher Bob Miller and smashed his longest home run of the day for a 5-2 final score. It followed the same course as his first home run, except it was higher and farther. In the process, he became the first Yankee and only the fourth American League player to homer from both sides of the plate in a game. The *New York Times* speculated that Mantle was the first in American League history, a belief that was later promulgated in numerous publications. In fact, Philadelphia's Wally Schang was the first in either league to accomplish the feat, on September 8, 1916.[2] It was Mantle's only three-homer game.

The Sporting News reported that Mantle said he had used two borrowed bats in his homer spree. One had been discarded by Enos Slaughter when he was sold to Kansas City earlier in the week. The other bat was borrowed from teammate Bill Skowron.[3]

Mantle went on to homer from both sides in a game 10 times during his 18-year career. Mark Teixeira and Nick Swisher are tied for the record for most occurrences (14), while Carlos Beltran (12) is also ahead of Mantle. Mantle became the model for modern power-hitting switch-hitters. He hit 536 career home runs and is followed by prolific switch-hitters Eddie Murray (504), Chipper Jones (468), Beltran (435), and Teixeira (409).

In picking up his fourth win of the season, Ford gave up three hits and two walks while striking out three in seven innings. He wound up tied for the American League lead in victories (18). Tom Morgan, who had emerged as a reliable Yankees reliever, finished the game with two hitless innings. Gromek took only his second loss of the season against five victories. Boone collected 20 homers for the season and with 116 RBIs tied with Jackie Jensen for the lead in the American League.

The Yankees proceeded to win 12 of the 16 home games to take first place by 2½ games over Cleveland by May 26. They were led during that stretch by Mantle's hitting, which included a slash line of .462/.592/1.000, 14 extra-base hits among his total of 24, and 19 RBIs.

Mantle had changed his batting stance at the start of the 1955 season, to cut down on his strikeouts, after leading the league with 107 in 1954. His new approach was to crowd the plate more and be more selective with pitches.[4] His numbers by the end of May indicated that the change was working.

He finished the season leading the league in on-base percentage, slugging average, OPS, triples (tied with Andy Carey), home runs, and walks. His accomplishments that season set the stage for one of the best single-season batting performances the following year, when he won the Triple Crown and the MVP Award.

The Yankees recaptured the American League pennant in 1955, capitalizing on an eight-game winning streak between September 13 and 21. After securing first place by two percentage points on September 16, they never relinquished the lead, finishing three games ahead of the Indians and five games ahead of the White Sox.

The Yankees lost the World Series in seven games to the Brooklyn Dodgers, who finally achieved a championship after losing five in as many attempts against the Yankees, dating back to 1941. The Dodgers got a huge break in the '55 Series when Mantle was limited to 10 plate appearances in three games because of a leg injury.

Mantle continued with the Yankees until his retirement in 1968, although his performance declined significantly after the 1964 season. Various injuries curtailed his playing time, but he remained one of the most popular players in the game. The three-time MVP was elected to the Baseball Hall of Fame in his first year of eligibility, 1974, with one of his many hallmarks being his prodigious switch-hitting.

SOURCES

In addition to the sources cited in the Notes, the author consulted:

Middlesworth, Hal. "Mantle Puts Slug on Tigers, 5-2," *Detroit Free Press*, May 14, 1955: 13.

Leavy, Jane. *The Last Boy: Mickey Mantle and the End of America's Childhood.* (New York: HarperCollins, 2010).

NOTES

1   Joseph Sheehan, "Yanks Best Tigers on Mantle's 3 Homers," *New York Times*, May 14, 1955: 14.

2   Baseball Almanac, baseball-almanac.com/feats/feats20.shtml. (Accessed May 5, 2020).

3   "Mantle Borrows, Two Bats and Belts Three Homers," *The Sporting News*, May 25, 1955: 21.

4   Al Silverman, *Mickey Mantle: Mister Yankee* (New York: G.P. Putnam's Sons, 1963), 131.

MICKEY DIS-MANTLES THE WHITE SOX WITH CYCLE AND EXPLOSIVE HOME RUN

July 23, 1957:
New York Yankees 10, Chicago White Sox 6,
at Yankee Stadium

by Mike Huber

Switch-hitter Mickey Mantle banged out a single, double, triple, and home run, accomplishing the 12th cycle in New York Yankees history. His home run almost escaped Yankee Stadium and caused a tremendous roar by the crowd, but his triple with the bases loaded in the seventh inning was the decisive blow, leading the Yankees to a 10-6 victory over the Chicago White Sox.

The Yankees were red-hot, winners of 19 of their previous 24 games entering this contest (with one win against the White Sox). Over the same stretch, Chicago had gone 14-10, depositing them in second place, 4½ games behind New York. The Yankees sent Don Larsen against Chicago's Bob Keegan. Both pitchers had winning records (5-2 for Larsen, 6-3 for Keegan), but Larsen, who pitched a perfect game in the previous year's World Series, had been wild in his last outing, against Detroit, walking seven batters in less than six innings.

This was a seesaw contest. In the bottom of the first Mantle lifted a soft fly ball to center which Larry Doby lost in the twilight. The ball landed a few inches from Doby's feet, and by then Mantle was cruising into second base with a fluke double. Harry Simpson followed with a home run to right-center, his eighth of the season.

With two outs in the bottom of the third inning, Mantle "lashed into a 3-1 pitch with the full force of his explosive power."[1] The ball landed in the next-to-last row of the center-field bleachers, just to the right of the scoreboard. According to the *New York Times*, "a hasty check of blueprints by Jim Thompson, the Stadium superintendent, indicated that Mantle's drive had landed about 465 feet from home plate,"[2] making the mammoth homer "a conversational item for the 42,422 fans at the Stadium."[3] Mantle himself claimed that the solo shot "was one of the hardest balls I've hit left-handed."[4] The headline in the next day's *New York Herald Tribune* read, "His Homer Almost Out of Stadium."[5] The Yankees now had a 3-0 lead.

Larsen had a no-hitter going through 4⅓ innings, but he was again having difficulty with his control. After allowing six walks and two hits, Larsen left the game in the fifth with the Yankees leading, 3-1. Manager Casey Stengel brought in Tommy Byrne, who got Earl Torgeson to hit into a force out, but it also produced a second run charged to Larsen. New York added a solo run in the fifth. But in the sixth inning, Chicago sent 10 batters to the plate, capitalizing on the continued wildness of the Yankees' pitchers. With two outs Byrne walked Les Moss, Sammy Esposito, and pinch-hitter Walt Dropo to load the bases. Stengel called to the bullpen for Art Ditmar with Ron Northey batting, and Ditmar completed a walk to Northey, driving in a run. (The walk was charged to Byrne, giving him four consecutive walks.[6]) Ditmar then served up singles to both Nellie Fox and Torgeson before walking Minnie Minoso. The rally ended when Doby forced out Minoso for the last out in the inning (Doby was 0-for-2 in the frame), but Chicago had captured the lead, 6-4.

The Yankees did not score in their half of the sixth, although Mantle, batting right-handed against new pitcher Paul LaPalme, did lead off with a single to center, his third hit of the game. He moved to second on a single by Simpson and stole third. However, the Yankees did not capitalize. Yogi Berra popped out to the White Sox third baseman Esposito in foul territory, and, with Dixie Howell now pitching, Mantle was doubled off the bag by a line drive off the bat of Hank

Bauer right at Esposito. An inning later, it was New York's turn to score big; they put five runners across the plate on only three hits. Elston Howard led off with a triple off Howell and scored on a wild pitch. After Howell walked Coleman, left-hander Jack Harshman came on in relief as the fourth White Sox hurler of the game. The next three New York batters reached on two walks and a bunt single, which tied the game. Mantle stepped to the plate with the bases loaded. On the first pitch he saw, Mantle, batting right-handed, hit a "vicious liner"[7] into the left-field corner that eluded Minoso's grasp. The ball rattled around the outfield, and "Mantle legged his way to third."[8] The bases-clearing triple unknotted the tie game, and the Yankees led, 9-6.

Two singles around a sacrifice bunt led to another New York tally in the eighth, and Mantle came to the plate with Tony Kubek at second and Gil McDougald at first. This time he grounded out to the second baseman for the Yankees' third out. The final score was New York 10, Chicago 6.

Ditmar was awarded his seventh win of the season and the victory improved New York's record to 60-30; Chicago dropped to 54-35. Harshman took the loss. The Yankees had 15 hits in the game. The White Sox managed only six safeties, all singles, but the 13 walks issued by New York's pitching staff kept the game close. Byrne had pitched 1⅓ innings for the Yankees, allowing four earned runs on no hits, but he did allow the four consecutive walks.[9] The White Sox left 10 men on base.

Mantle became the first switch-hitter to hit for the cycle. His four runs batted in proved to be the margin of victory over the White Sox. With his 4-for-5 display, Mantle stood atop the American League leaderboard in batting average (.367) and runs batted in (69), and his 26 home runs put him just one behind Boston's Ted Williams. Mantle's OPS shot up to 1.236. The reigning American League Most Valuable Player convinced voters that he should (and did) win a second MVP Award. According to the *Chicago Tribune*, Mantle's

triple "climaxed one of the greatest games in the Oklahoman's career."[10]

This was the second and last cycle of the 1957 season. Lee Walls, left fielder for the Chicago Cubs, accomplished the rare feat on July 2, 1957, against the Cincinnati Redlegs. The next cycle would come two years later when Cincinnati's Frank Robinson achieved it on May 2, 1959.

SOURCES

In addition to the sources mentioned in the Notes, the author consulted base-ball-reference.com, mlb.com, retrosheet.org, and:

Ray, James Lincoln. "Mickey Mantle," sabr.org/bioproj/person/61e4590a.

NOTES

1   Joseph M. Sheehan, "Mantle Is Star of 10-6 Triumph," *New York Times*, July 24, 1957: 17.

2   Sheehan.

3   Sheehan.

4   Andrew Mearns, "This Day in Yankees History: Mickey Mantle Cycles, Destroys a Baseball – July 23, 1957," online at *pinstripealley.com/2012/7/24/ 3177129/this-day-in-yankees-history-mickey-mantle-cycle-july-23-1957*. NOTE: On May 22, 1963, batting left-handed, Mantle hit a ball that clipped the upper façade of the right-field stands, 108 feet above the level of the playing field, making it the closest that a ball has come to leaving Yankee Stadium. Mantle told reporters after that game, "It was the hardest ball I ever hit, but though I knew it would be well up there I didn't think it would go out of the park." See Michael Huber, "Mick Has (Almost) Left the Building," *Chance*, Volume 23, Number 4, December 2010.

5   Cecilia Tan, "With Fireworks, Too," in *The 50 Greatest Yankee Games*, (Hoboken, New Jersey: J. Wiley & Sons, 2005), 97.

6   Unfortunately, the pitch count is not available from *baseball-reference.com*, and the newspaper accounts do not show it.

7   Sheehan.

8   Tan, 98.

9   The record for most consecutive walks in a game is seven, accomplished twice: by the Chicago White Sox, in an August 28, 1909, game against the Washington Senators (Game 1 of a doubleheader – no box score available), and by the Pittsburgh Pirates' Jim Bibby (4) and Jim Winn (3), in a May 25, 1983, game against the Atlanta Braves (see retrosheet.org/boxesetc/1983/ B05250ATL1983.htm).

10   Edward Prell, "Sox Waste Rally; Bow to Yanks, 10-6," *Chicago Tribune*, July 24, 1957: Sports 1.

ROGER MARIS CLUBS NUMBER 60

September 26, 1961:
New York Yankees 3, Baltimore Orioles 2,
at Yankee Stadium

By Paul Semendinger

Sometimes it's the statistics few know that tell the story. Or at least part of the story. If nothing else, they tell a story.

After Babe Ruth hit his 60th home run in 1927, the legend of that epic blast grew and grew. A number of great sluggers, including Jimmie Foxx and Hank Greenberg, challenged Ruth's record, but they all fell short. Year after year, and then decade after decade, Ruth's 60th home run grew in legend and stature. Some felt it was baseball's greatest record – one that could never be broken. And in the archival footage that the fans have always seen of that blast, along with Ruth's swing, there was a stadium packed with adoring and excited fans.

But the movie reels didn't tell the true story. Those reels must have been spliced and added to with footage from other games. For the biggest statistic, the one very few people know regarding Ruth's 60th, is the following: 8,000. Longtime Yankees clubhouse man Pete Sheehy claimed there were fewer than 2,000 fans in attendance when Ruth hit his blast.[1]

8,000. That's how many people were in attendance at Yankee Stadium on September 30, 1927, when Ruth hit his legendary 60th home run. It was a great moment, but it was not a moment that drew fans to the Bronx to see the famous slugger. No, not at all. When Ruth hit his blast, Yankee Stadium was all but empty.

Thirty-four years later, on September 26, 1961, Roger Maris clubbed a pitch from Baltimore's Jack Fisher into the right-field seats at Yankee Stadium to tie the Babe. While anticipation of his blast didn't fill the Stadium, more than 19,000 came to see if Maris could actually do it. It was Maris's quest that brought more people to the ballpark than Ruth's gargantuan legend.

The night of September 26, 1961, was a beautiful one for baseball. At the game's 8:00 P.M. start, the weather was 68 degrees. There was, and had been, no precipitation. The setting was perfect.

The mighty Yankees (105-52) were playing the somewhat surprisingly competitive Baltimore Orioles (92-66). By this time the Yankees had eliminated the rest of the league and were on their way to the World Series, but first they had the schedule to play out and, of course, there was Roger Maris's chase of the Babe.

Jack Fisher took the mound for the Orioles against the Yankees' Bud Daley. On this day, both hurlers pitched well.

Baltimore scored first. After both teams went quietly in the first inning, the Orioles put together a rally in the second inning to plate two runs. Earl Robinson singled, Dave Philley walked, and Ron Hansen singled to load the bases with one out. After Jack Fisher struck out (on a fouled-off bunt attempt with two strikes), future Hall of Famer Brooks Robinson drove home Robinson and Philley to give Baltimore a 2-0 lead.

An inning later, in the bottom of the third inning, Roger Maris dug in against Jack Fisher. On this day,

Catcher Gus Triandos called the pitch that Roger Maris sent into the right-field stands in the third inning.

Maris was the Yankees' number-three batter, just in front of Mickey Mantle in the batting order. In his first plate appearance, Mantle walked, and was removed for pinch-runner Hector Lopez. Mantle had been battling flu systems for many days and needed the rest.[2]

Maris had singled in front of Mantle in the first inning. Now, this at-bat in the third inning was his second chance on this day for number 60. Maris's last home run, #59, came on September 20, also against the Orioles, but down in Baltimore.

In this third inning, Maris came to bat with two outs. On the fifth pitch of the at-bat, with a 2-and-2 count, Maris connected, and it was clear almost right from the start that he had hit number 60.[3] The ball careened off the right-field stands – it may have hit stairs, or a railing, or even a seat – and bounded back onto the field. Baltimore right fielder Earl Robinson retrieved it and tossed it to the umpire to be given to Maris. But as players did back in those times, Maris simply put his head down and circled the bases. He returned to the dugout tied, at last, with the mighty Bambino. After the game, Maris, gripping the baseball in his hand, said, "I wanted that homer badly. I'd like one more, too."[4]

When one listens to the play-by-play, the difference between how players and fans respond to big events stands in mighty contrast to what transpires today.[5] Sportscaster Mel Allen first let the moment speak for itself. All one hears as Maris circles the bases is the crowd cheering. The moment needed no other explanation. As Maris approached home plate, Allen said, "How about that! A standing ovation! A standing ovation for Roger Maris, who got number 60."[6] In the dugout Maris received congratulations from his teammates and manager Ralph Houk. Maris sat down, but in a moment that was unique at this time, the crowd wanted more. Moments passed. Mel Allen described the scene: "And they are calling him out of the dugout. This is most unusual. They are calling him out of the dugout." Reluctantly, after about 20 seconds, Maris obliged the fans' wishes. He popped out, waved his cap, and returned to his seat.

Maris's blast made the score 2-1, but it was only the third inning, and there was more baseball to be played. There was no other fanfare. No politicians or former baseball greats came on to the field. To paraphrase from "Casey at the Bat," in his own way, "Maris calmed the rising tumult and he bid the game go on." And on the game progressed.

For the next few innings, both teams went quietly. In the Yankees' fifth, Maris, in his first attempt to eclipse Babe Ruth by hitting number 61, flied out to right field. In the sixth inning the Yankees mounted a scoring rally. Hector Lopez and Yogi Berra led off with walks. Elston Howard hit a long fly that allowed Lopez to advance to third, and Johnny Blanchard singled Lopez home to tie the game at 2-2.

An inning later, with one out, Billy Gardner and Tom Tresh both singled. Maris again flied out to right field but center fielder Jackie Brandt miscued on Lopez's fly ball and Gardner scored with the Yankees' third run. That was all they needed. And it was all they'd get.

In the end, the Yankees got their 106th win of the season, 3-2. Bud Daley, who had been removed for Rollie Sheldon after six innings of work, did not figure in the decision. Sheldon worked the final three innings, retiring all nine batters he faced, including striking out the last four, to earn the win, his 10th of the year. For the Orioles, Jack Fisher went the distance and took the loss. His record fell to 10-13.

After the game, Fisher seemed more frustrated by the loss than by being the pitcher who surrendered a famous home run. "I'm out there to win," he said. "I don't care who hits home runs as long as I win."[7]

But the big story was Roger Maris, who finally took his seat next to Babe Ruth.

Understated, as was his style, in the immediacy of it all, Maris simply said, "This was easily the greatest thrill of my life."[8] Later he added, "As I trotted around the bases, I was in a fog. I couldn't believe what happened. Had I really hit 60 home runs? Had I tied Babe Ruth for the highest total ever hit in a season?"[9]

At that time, and for decades after, these two Yankees sluggers were the only players in baseball history to reach the magical number of 60, a mark that wouldn't be reached again until 1998, when it was surpassed by Mark McGwire and Sammy Sosa.

AUTHOR'S NOTE

At the time, much was made about the fact that the 1961 season was 162 games rather than the 154-game seasons played in Babe Ruth's day. The story of the so-called asterisk attached to Maris's home run record is common in baseball lore. A writer for *Newsday*, Stan Isaacs, decades before the birth of sabermetrics, went to great lengths to break down Maris's accomplishment as compared to Ruth's: He wrote: The records will show that – all times at bat included – Maris hit No. 60 on his 684th trip to the plate. Ruth in his 687th. On the other hand, Maris' 60th came in his 579th at-bat (excluding walks, etc.) while Ruth did it in official at-bat No. 537. It was Maris' 158th game, Ruth's 153th.[10]

Joe Trimble of the New York Daily News reported, "As it hit, Maris happily flung his bat away and began a jog around the bases in the majestic tread of the Babe. The 19,401 spectators were on their feet, screaming with delight-even the little lady who broke into tears as the ball soared to glory. That was Mrs. Claire Ruth, the Babe's widow."[11]

Maris met Mrs. Ruth after the game. She said, "I know if the Babe were here, he would have wanted to congratulate you."[12]

Of further note, Roger Maris's children were on hand to watch as Aaron Judge tied and surpassed their father's American League record in 2022.

SOURCES

In addition to the sources cited in the Notes, the author consulted the Baseball-Reference.com website for pertinent material and also viewed the game footage on YouTube.

https://www.baseball-reference.com/boxes/NYA/NYA196109260.shtml

NOTES

1   Stan Isaacs, "Rog and Babe Stand Alone," *Newsday* (Long Island, New York), September 27, 1961: 119.

2   Associated Press, "Mantle Ill, Maris Rests—Yanks Lose," *Hartford Courant*, September 28, 1961: 43.

3   Joe Trimble, "Maris Blasts No. 60 to Tie Ruth's High," *New York Daily News,* September 27, 1961: 62.

4   Trimble.

5   In today's game, when records are achieved, the game often comes to a halt. There is much more pomp and circumstance. For Maris in 1961, his celebration was a trip around the bases and a return to the dugout.

6   Youtube: https://www.youtube.com/watch?v=cCZPGUzxNls. Accessed November 2, 2022.

7   "Pardon Jack Fisher for Not Celebrating," *Newsday,* September 27, 1961: 119. Fisher just the year before had surrendered a home run to Ted Williams in Williams's final at-bat.

8   John Drebinger, "Maris Hits No. 60 as Yankees Win," *New York Times*, September 27, 1961: 45.

9   Maury Allen, *Roger Maris: A Man for All Seasons* (New York: Donald J. Fine, Inc., 1986), 158.

10   Isaacs, "Rog and Babe Stand Alone."

11   Trimble.

12   Phil Pepe, *1961: The Inside Story of the Maris-Mantle Home Run Chase* (Chicago: Triumph Books, 2011), 218.

TRESH'S HEROIC HOMER MOVES
YANKEES ONE GAME CLOSER

October 10, 1962:
New York Yankees 5, San Francisco Giants 3,
at Yankee Stadium
Game Five of the 1962 World Series

By Bill Johnson

Between its opening in April 1923 and its final game in September 2008, Yankee Stadium hosted 161 postseason games. That stadium's legacy is larger, perhaps, than even our collective memory of it, a true baseball cathedral that hosted so many of the sport's immortal players and moments that it is inextricably meshed with the lore of the game. The fans sat much closer to the field than in the current iteration, but the outfield farthest outfield fences were originally 490 feet from home plate. When paired with a 295-foot right-field line, the facility was unique to baseball. So many of those contests at that stadium now fill baseball's collective lore: part myth, part memory, and part fact, those unforgettable events are tiny tiles in the mosaic of the game's history. One of the most notable games occurred on October 10, 1962. It was Game Five of a World Series against the San Francisco Giants, and the 5-3 New York victory put the Yankees up 3 games to 2 to send the Series back to California for what would prove to be a compelling seven-game championship for the Yankees.

To that point, the first pitch of Game Five, the Series had been a see-saw battle between the longtime rivals. Whitey Ford and the Yankees won Game One by a 6-2 score, but San Francisco's Jack Sanford shut out Ralph Terry and New York, 2-0, in the second game.[1] The Yankees took a 2-games-to-1 Series lead with a tight 3-2 Game Three win, but again the Giants roared back to tie the Series at two games each with Chuck Hiller's grand slam pacing a 7-3 win in Game Four.[2] In a plot twist found only in baseball, the Giants' winning pitcher in Game Four was none other than Don Larsen, who tossed one-third of an inning and thus became the

pitcher of record for the day.[3] This was the same Don Larsen who had tossed the only perfect game in World Series history for the Yankees in 1956. Game Five, it turned out, ratcheted up the drama a few more clicks,

Giants right fielder Matty Alou lunged over the wall at Tom Tresh's homer, but he never had a chance.

248

ultimately ending on a dramatic eighth-inning home run by young outfielder Tom Tresh.[4]

The game actually began later than originally planned because of a one-day rain postponement. The scheduling problem caused a bit of trouble for the visiting Giants. They "checked out of their hotel and their bags were at the airport," according to *The Sporting News*.[5] The team had ultimately found lodging, but scheduled starting pitcher Jack Sanford was not pleased. Not only did key Yankees Bill Stafford and Bill Skowron enjoy an extra, free day to heal various dings, but ace Whitey Ford picked up an extra day of rest as well, all while the emotional Sanford had to temper his competitive juices for another day.

The next day, October 10, turned out to be a beautiful early autumn day. The game-time weather was clear, the temperature a brisk 65° F. The outfield was reportedly still a bit slick from the previous day's rain, but *The Sporting News* reported that the infield was "in splendid shape."[6] The first pitch was finally thrown on Wednesday afternoon, in front of 63,165 spectators, a ball from Ralph Terry to Giants second baseman Chuck Hiller. After Hiller walked, Terry struck out Jim Davenport and Matty Alou before ending the inning on Willie Mays' lineout to left field.

Tony Kubek led off the Yankees attack with a single to right-center field. Second baseman Bobby Richardson hit a sure-thing double-play grounder to Hiller at second base, but Hiller misplayed the ball and Richardson was safe on the error. Tom Tresh then smote a liner up the middle, but it somehow found Sanford's glove. *The Sporting News* characterized the play: "Apparently unaware for the moment that he had it, Sanford looked down to find it – and that cost him what could have been triple play."[7] Mickey Mantle hit a grounder between first and second, with first baseman Willie McCovey deflecting the ball toward Hiller as he attempted to field it. Even after 10 years in the majors, Mantle was still quick enough to beat the toss to Sanford, covering first. Mantle then proceeded to steal second base as well, before Roger Maris flied out to end the rally.

Both teams went down one-two-three in the second. Chuck Hiller's double drove in shortstop Jose Pagan for the first run of the game in the third, but the Yankees knotted the score in the bottom of the fourth. Tresh hit a popup to shortstop Jose Pagan, but the ball bounced out of Pagan's normally reliable glove. Mantle walked, and Tresh took third when Maris's grounder forced Mantle at second. Catcher Elston

Howard struck out, but Sanford's wild pitch allowed Tresh to score.

Pagan atoned for his earlier miscue with a home run on a 1-and-0 count to lead off the fifth, but a Sanford offering that catcher Tom Haller couldn't handle, scored as a passed ball, once again tied the score, 2-2, in the bottom of the sixth. Haller retrieved the ball and rifled it to Sanford, covering home, but plate umpire Al Barlick called Richardson safe. The seventh inning passed, like the entire game to that point, in relative quiet, a figurative calm before the eighth-inning storm. Through seven innings, a Yankees lineup that featured Mantle and Maris, the M-and-M boys of the preceding season's home-run race to the record, had been able to score only two runs, on a passed ball and a wild pitch.

Terry mowed down the Giants in the top of the eighth inning: Jim Davenport struck out, Matty Alou flied out to left, and Mays grounded out to third to end the frame. Both teams had squandered earlier scoring opportunities. While Sanford had wriggled out of several potential threats earlier, continuing to put Yankees on base was bound to cause trouble for the visitors. After the game there was some murmuring that manager Alvin Dark had intended to relieve Sanford. According to one national writer, "Sanford was doing a good bit of talking (to the manager), Dark kept looking at the bull pen and once appeared to almost raise his hand as if to call in a reliever."[8] The manager stuck with his starter, a pitcher with a 24-7 record that season and certainly one of the stars of the talented pitching staff.

Opening the bottom of the eighth, Terry struck out, but then Tony Kubek lined a single to right field. Bobby Richardson pushed Kubek to second with another single, this time to left, which brought Tresh to the plate. According to *The Sporting News*, Tresh "blistered" Sanford's third pitch over the right-field fence, at the 344-foot marker, for a three-run homer. That blow pushed the score to a 5-2 Yankee advantage.[9] Tresh later told reporters that "I was choked up on the bat, just trying for a base hit, especially with [Sanford] pitching." He continued, saying, "But he threw me a fast ball right down the pipe. I was sure surprised to see it, because I hadn't seen anything like that off him in two games. … It was the biggest hit of my life."[10]

After the bases cleared, Dark brought in Stu Miller to relieve Sanford, and Miller coerced a weak grounder to second base by Mantle. Maris walked, but the inning ended on Elston Howard's fly ball to center field.

Willie McCovey led off the Giants' ninth, their last shot, with a single, but Felipe Alou struck out for the first out. Haller smacked a double to center field to drive in McCovey, but Pagan grounded out and pinch-hitter Ed Bailey lined out to right to end the threat and the game.

For the game, Ralph Terry threw 120 pitches in going the distance for New York. At the time, according to *The Sporting News*, that was considered "about par for a nine inning effort."[11] On the San Francisco side, Jack Sanford pitched into the eighth, throwing 129 pitches, but still absorbed the loss. In all, the game lasted 2 hours and 42 minutes.

With the 5-3 win, the Yankees took a 3-games-to-2 lead and headed to San Francisco needing only one win to take the Series. The Giants prevailed in Game Six, 5-2, but Sanford and Terry matched up again in Game Seven, a 1-0 win for Terry, who threw a four-hitter.[12] It was the 20th championship in the storied history of the franchise.

SOURCES

In addition to the sources cited in the Notes, the author consulted Baseball-Reference.com and Retrosheet.org.

https://www.baseball-reference.com/boxes/NYA/NYA196210100.shtml

https://www.retrosheet.org/boxesetc/1962/B10100NYA1962.htm

NOTES

1   Associated Press, "Dark Shakes Up 'Shook-Up' Giants," *Elmira* (New York) *Star-Gazette,* October 5, 1962: 14.

2   Jack Hand (Associated Press), "Giants Even Series on Hiller Grand Slam," *Rochester Democrat and Chronicle,* October 9, 1962: 34.

3   Associated Press, "He's Hit So Few – Hiller Wasn't Sure It Was Homer," *Syracuse Post-Standard,* October 9, 1962: 13.

4   Tresh, the son of former major-league catcher Mike Tresh (White Sox and Indians between 1938-1949), had made his major-league debut in September 1961 at age 22.

5   "Rain Drops," *The Sporting News,* October 20, 1962: 23.

6   "Yanks Ride to 5-3 Victory on Tresh's Three-Run HR," *The Sporting News,* October 27, 1962: 25.

7   "Yanks Ride to 5-3 Victory on Tresh's Three-Run HR."

8   "Did Sanford Outtalk Dark?" *The Sporting News,* October 27, 1962: 25.

9   "Yanks Ride to 5-3 Victory on Tresh's Three-Run HR."

10 Associated Press, "Tresh Hero of Yankees' 3rd Series Win," *Paterson* (New Jersey) *News,* October 11, 1962: 41.

11 "Skowron Whiffs Three Times," *The Sporting News,* October 27, 1962: 25.

12 The lone run of the game scored when, with the bases loaded and nobody out, Tony Kubek grounded into a 6-4-3 double play.

YANKEES PITCHER MEL STOTTLEMYRE HITS INSIDE-THE-PARK GRAND SLAM

July 20, 1965:
New York Yankees 6, Boston Red Sox 3, at Yankee Stadium

By Bruce Harris

Thirteen years before Yankee Stadium opened, Pittsburgh Pirates pitcher Deacon Phillippe hit a second inning inside-the-park grand slam in Forbes Field during a 14-1 rout of the Brooklyn Superbas.[1] Phillippe remained the only pitcher to achieve the feat until 55 years later, when right-hander Mel Stottlemyre lined Bill Monbouquette's first pitch between Red Sox left fielder Carl Yastrzemski and center fielder Jim Gosger during a Tuesday afternoon game at Yankee Stadium.[2]

By the third week of July 1965, it must have been painfully obvious to the Yankees faithful that their beloved perennial-winner Bronx Bombers were no longer invincible. Fresh off a seven-game World Series loss to the St. Louis Cardinals in 1964, Johnny Keane (the 1964 Cardinals manager) had replaced Yogi Berra as Yankees manager. Coming into the July 20 contest, the Yankees had a record of 44-48, and were mired in sixth place, 13½ games behind the Minnesota Twins. The Red Sox, having beaten the Yankees 3-1 behind Jim Lonborg in the first game of a two-game series, were worse. Their 33-54 record found them in ninth place, 22 games behind the league-leading Twins. Boston had not had a winning season since 1958.

Monbouquette got the start for the Red Sox. The veteran right-hander came into the game with a 7-10 record. In 1963 he was a 20-game winner. He had a 16-12 lifetime record against the Yankees, and a 1.40 ERA against them in 1965.[3] The Yankees starter was 23-year-old Stottlemyre, sporting a 9-5 record. He had five consecutive wins over Boston. In his first season in New York, the year before, Stottlemyre appeared in 13 games and finished with a 9-3 record and a 2.06 ERA. He worked in three games of the 1964 World Series against the Cardinals, winning one

and losing one. Now he was on the way to a terrific season. Despite a mediocre Yankees team that finished in sixth place (77-85), Stottlemyre compiled a 20-9 record with a 2.63 ERA. His 18 complete games led the American League.

The game began with a bang. Leadoff hitter Gosger hit Stottlemyre's fifth pitch for a home run into the third row of the right-field grandstand. New York took the lead in the bottom of the fourth inning. Bobby Richardson opened the frame with an infield single. Tony Kubek, attempting to sacrifice Richardson to second, failed twice, then lined a pitch that curled around the right-field foul pole into the lower deck for a two-run home run.

The historic fifth inning began with the Yankees ahead, 2-1. Joe Pepitone walked. Clete Boyer bunted and beat the throw from first baseman Lee Thomas to second baseman Felix Mantilla covering first. Roger Repoz, battling a 0-for-23 slump, walked to load the bases. That brought up Stottlemyre. Although not a great hitter (lifetime .160 average with 7 home runs in 11 seasons), he had connected for a home run on June 5 off Gary Peters of the White Sox. And in a September 26, 1964, game against the Washington Senators, Stottlemyre went 5-for-5. The three Red Sox outfielders – Gosger, Yastrzemski, and Tony Conigliaro – moved in about five yards. Stottlemyre recalled, "I guess they thought I was going to bunt to squeeze in a run. Anyway, he threw me a high fastball."[4] Stottlemyre drilled Monbouquette's first pitch between Yastrzemski and Gosger. The ball rolled toward the 475-foot mark on the bleacher wall in left-center field, in what Mickey Mantle had called "death valley." Yastrzemski retrieved it and fired to cutoff man Rico Petrocelli. The Red Sox shortstop's throw home was "strong and about five feet up the first base line."[5] The ball skipped past catcher Bob Tillman and Stottlemyre was safe. "The play would have been close if the catcher got the ball," manager Keane said.[6]

The outcome surprised Stottlemyre. "I thought [third base coach Frank Crosetti] was going to stop me, but I was running as fast as I could and kept going."[7] The exertion worried Keane. "We were very much concerned about that," he said after the game.[8]

Stottlemyre gave up a single and a walk in the top of the sixth inning, but escaped without allowing a run. He stranded two runners in the seventh, and ran into trouble in the eighth inning. Frank Malzone opened the inning with a single. Yastrzemski followed with a base hit, sending Malzone to third. Mantilla hit a groundball to Kubek that appeared to be a certain double play, but five-time Gold Glover Richardson dropped the ball at second base. Malzone scored, and the Red Sox had runners on first and second with no out. Mantilla was forced out at second base on Thomas's groundball. Yastrzemski advanced to third on the play and scored on Conigliaro's sacrifice fly. Stottlemyre retired Tillman to end the inning. The score stood at 6-3.

The Red Sox went down in order in the ninth inning. Gosger, who led off the game with a home run, made the final out. Boston outhit New York, 10-7, but the game and the day belonged to the Yankees and to Stottlemyre. Improving his record to 10–5, Stottlemyre went the distance, giving up three runs (two earned), walking one, and fanning five. The grand slam was his only hit of the day. He struck out against Monbouquette in the third inning and again against reliever Bob Duliba in the seventh.

Stottlemyre was a five-time All-Star. During an 11-year career, all with the Yankees, he finished with a 164-139 won-lost record and a 2.97 ERA. He struck out 1,257 in 2,661⅓ innings pitched. With his inside-the-park grand slam, Stottlemyre joined an exclusive, heady list of hitters, including Hall of Famers Ty Cobb, Honus Wagner, Lou Gehrig, Zack Wheat, Rabbit Maranville, Rogers Hornsby, Roberto Clemente, Tony Gwynn, and Willie Mays.[9] Given today's DH, it is likely the 24,594 Yankee Stadium fans saw the last inside-the-park grand slam hit by a pitcher.[10]

SOURCES

In addition to the sources cited in the Notes, the author consulted Baseball-Reference.com and Retrosheet.org for pertinent information, including the box score and play-by-play.

https://www.baseball-reference.com/boxes/NYA/NYA196507200.shtml

https://www.retrosheet.org/boxesetc/1965/B07200NYA1965.htm

NOTES

1   The Phillippe grand slam was hit on July 22, 1910.

2   Although not inside-the-park, Yankees pitchers Red Ruffing (Yankee Stadium, April 14, 1933), Spud Chandler (Comiskey Park, July 26, 1940), and Don Larsen (Yankee Stadium, April 22, 1956) hit grand slams before Stottlemyre's blast.

3   On May 31, 1967, the Yankees signed Monbouquette as a free agent.

4   Joe Durso, "Stottlemyre's Grand Slam for Yanks Beats Red Sox, 6-3," *New York Times*, July 21, 1965: 27.

5   Joe Trimble, "Stott's Inside Grand Slam in 5th Batters Bosox, 6-3," *New York Daily News*, July 21, 1965: 80, 85.

6   Trimble, 80.

7   "Stottlemyre Socks Himself into Yanks' Slugging Book," *The Sporting News*, July 31, 1965: 30.

8   Durso, 27.

9   For a comprehensive list compiled in 2002, see: https://www.baseball-fever.com/forum/baseball-almanac-baseball-fever-website/baseball-fever-exclusives/175-inside-the-park-grand-slams. See also Derek Bain, "Fun Facts About Inside-the-Park Home Runs," June 8, 2016. Among other facts, his listing includes inside-the-park grand slams between 1950 – 2015: https://seamheads.com/blog/2016/06/08/fun-facts-about-inside-the-park-home-runs/.

10   The *New York Daily News* reported the attendance at 14,745.

SMALLEST ATTENDANCE AT YANKEE STADIUM: 413

September 22, 1966:
Chicago White Sox 4, New York Yankees 1, at Yankee Stadium

By Mitchell Manoff

The 1966 New York Yankees were two seasons removed from a seven-game World Series loss to a powerful St. Louis Cardinals team in 1964. The 1965 season saw the Yankees collapse into sixth place in the American League, their worst finish since 1925. As the 1966 season began, the team's future looked slightly brighter. In its preseason review, Sports Illustrated wrote, "The Yankees have more question marks than a true-false quiz. There should be enough positive answers to get them back to the first division, but not enough for first place."[1]

The 1966 team boasted three recent MVPs: Mickey Mantle, Roger Maris, and Elston Howard, plus a former Cy Young Award winner, Whitey Ford. The lineup also included Joe Pepitone, Bobby Richardson, Clete Boyer, Tom Tresh, Jim Bouton, and Mel Stottlemyre, all important contributors to the 1964 pennant winner. Rounding out the roster were promising newcomers including pitchers Fritz Peterson and Dooley Womack, and hard-hitting position players Roy White and Bobby Murcer.

So how did this epic decline from "first to worst'" occur? Age and injuries had something to do with it.

Although the Yankees were made up of only three players older than 35 – Howard and Whitey Ford at 37 and Hector Lopez at 36 – their age was reflected in their ability to stay healthy. Mantle was a banged-up medical miracle at 34, but still effective, though he was limited to 108 games that season, none after September 18. Also on the roster, injured and without effective replacements, were Jim Bouton, Roger Maris, Ford, and new shortstop Ruben Amaro. Amaro's replacement at short, the rookie Bobby Murcer, who would go on to a successful career in center field, slumped

in a few appearances and was sent to the minors until September.

The Yankees players also did not get along with the old-school style of their manager in 1965 and the start of 1966, Johnny Keane. He was fired on May 6. Ralph Houk, the manager of the pennant-winning 1961-63 clubs who became GM before 1964, moved from the front office back to the dugout. However, that didn't help the Yankees' fortunes.

Over two years starting in 1964, CBS purchased the Yankees from Dan Topping and Del Webb. On September 20, 1966, Michael Burke took over as the Yankees' president and CEO.

Both the Yankees and the fourth-place White Sox had been mathematically eliminated when they faced each other on September 22, 1966. The game was preceded by four days of 30-year record-breaking rain in New York City. As a result, no games were played from September 19 through September 21. This game itself was in doubt as there was a fine mist just prior to the start with a prediction of heavier rain. Even Yankees play-by-play announcer Red Barber, believed the game would be called as he drove to the park, but it wasn't.

As the game commenced, the Yankees languished in last place, 28 games behind the league-leading Baltimore Orioles. As a result of the Yankees' poor performance, attendance continued to decline as the season progressed. Three of the five prior games and their next two final games of the season had attendance under 10,000. The average attendance was 13,715 per game for 1966. With no pennant implications, wet weather, plus the lack of publicity after several cancellations provided a recipe for poor attendance for a daytime midweek game, and just 413 fans showed up.

Despite having no pennant implications, the game itself did have the potential for some exciting moments. The starting pitchers were Joe Horlen for the White Sox and Stan Bahnsen for the Yankees. Bahnsen, a 1965 draft pick and September call-up, had a complete-game victory in his first major-league start, on September 15. Horlen was known as "Hard Luck" for both low ERAs and low run support – in 1966, he finished second in ERA (2.43), but went 10-13.

The few fans who were there also welcomed a visiting former Yankee hero, Chicago first baseman Moose Skowron.

The game was a scoreless pitchers' duel for the first four innings. Bahnsen retired the first 13 batters through the top of the fifth until Duane Josephson, the second batter in the fifth inning, singled and scored on a two-out double to left by Jerry Adair. In the sixth inning, Don Buford doubled and was driven home by a single to center by Tommy Agee. In the ninth, Agee hit an inside-the-park home run, followed by Tom McCraw's home run to right to build the White Sox lead to four runs. McCraw replaced Skowron at first base, batting fourth, in the bottom of the sixth inning. Horlen continued to blank the Yankees through seven innings, allowing just seven hits, when he was relieved by Hoyt Wilhelm.

Wilhelm rode his knuckleball to dazzle hitters for a 21-year Hall of Fame career. He set the Yankees down in the eighth inning. The bottom of the ninth provided some excitement as Josephson, the White Sox catcher, had a difficult time with Wilhelm's dancing knuckleball. The Yankees provided their only real rally in that inning, which started when Billy Bryan singled. Boyer popped out but Hector Lopez got a pinch-hit single. After Horace Clarke fouled out for the second out, Bobby Murcer singled to drive in Bryan. That was all of the offense the Yankees could muster when Joe Pepitone struck out on three pitches to end the game.[2]

The game provided other off-the-field drama. Red Barber, the longtime Yankees announcer, refused Yankees management's instructions to not broadcast the virtually empty stands, which stood to embarrass the team. But Barber mentioned it on the air, believing that the lack of fans in the stands "is the story, not the game."[3] This was the last straw between Barber, whose relationship with the Yankees broadcast team over the years had grown frosty, and the new Yankees management led by Mike Burke. Burke fired Barber at a breakfast meeting four days later, on September 26.

Barber, 58 when he was fired, never announced full time for another team. It was a loss to the industry as Barber was instrumental in the development of many great announcers, most prominently Vin Scully.[4]

The September 22 attendance figure of 413 was a record low for Yankee Stadium. What is astonishing is that consistently, from 1925 to 1965, the Yankees had been first or second in American League attendance. At the close of the 1966 season, the Yankees' cumulative attendance was 1,124,648, dropping the team to fifth place out of 10 teams. From that season the attendance continued to slip, falling to under 1 million by 1972 largely due to the consistently disappointing performance by the team.

The CBS entertainment conglomerate continued to own the Yankees until January of 1973, when it sold the team to a consortium led by George Steinbrenner for $8.7 million. It remains one of the few times that a major-league team was sold at a loss. The Yankees returned to the World Series in 1976 and saw their highest attendance (2,012,434) since 1950. From 2005 until the Stadium closed until 2008, attendance averaged over 4 million. As of April 2022, Sportico valued the Yankees at an estimated $7 billion with an average game attendance of 38,648, back to being number one in the American League.[5]

SOURCES

In addition to the sources cited in the Notes, the author accessed Baseball Reference.com, Retrosheet.org, SABR.org, and the following:

Kelley, CJ. "In Their Ruin: The 1966 New York Yankees," in How They Play, May 16, 2022. https://howtheyplay.com/team-sports/In-Their-Ruin-The-1966-Yankees.

Featherston, Al. "The Demise of the Yankees 1964-1966," in www.diamondsin-thedusk.com.

NOTES

1   "Things are Looking Up for the Americans," *Sports Illustrated,* April 18, 1966: 89. https://vault.si.com/vault/1966/04/18/43179#&gid=ci0258bed330102 78a&pid=43179---095---image.

2   Mark Strauss, "White Sox Defeat New York, 4-1: Smallest Crowd of the Season," *New York Times,* September 23, 1966: S27.

3   David Halberstam, "Red Barber and the Empty Yankee Stadium – September 22, 1996," AwfulAnnouncing.com, September 22, 2016. https://awfulannouncing.com/2016/red-barber-and-the-empty-yankee-stadium-september-22-1966.html. Accessed June 18, 2022.

4   Judith R. Hiltner and James R. Walker, *Red Barber: The Life and Legacy of a Broadcasting Legend* (Lincoln: University of Nebraska Press, 2022), 330-335.

5   Team Valuations, https://www.sportico.com/valuations/teams/2022/yankees-red-sox-dodgers-mlb-valuations-1234671197/. Accessed April 14, 2022

MURCER HITS FOUR HOME RUNS IN A DOUBLEHEADER. AND MUCH MORE

June 24, 1970:
Cleveland Indians 7, New York Yankees 2;
New York Yankees 5, Cleveland Indians 4,
at Yankee Stadium

By Lewis (Lew) Insler

The morning after the Yankees hosted the Indians in a doubleheader on June 24, 1970, the *Cleveland Plain Dealer* wrote, "Yankee Stadium was filled with trouble makers yesterday, but the biggest one, as far as the Indians were concerned, was New York center fielder Bobby Murcer."[1]

Murcer led off the bottom of the ninth inning of the first game with a home run to right field, his 10th of the season and first in four straight at-bats for the day.[2] It was one of the many unusual events that happened on that wild day in the Bronx.

Bobby Murcer's four home runs came in five plate appearances, with a walk in between.

Courtesy of Lew Insler.

Sam McDowell won the first game of the twin bill for his 10th win of the season in a complete-game five-hitter with Murcer's solo shot making it a 7-2 final.

In the first of many occurrences that made this a special day, 6-foot-6 Yankees reliever Steve Hamilton came on in relief in the top of the ninth and unleashed his "folly floater[3]" against Tony Horton. The Indians first baseman had stroked a single off the pitch earlier in the season. After Horton fouled the first one back, Hamilton told Horton it was coming again, and Yankees catcher Thurman Munson caught the second foul pop after a long run behind the plate. Horton took it in good humor, crawling into the dugout after throwing his bat and batting helmet into the air.[4] Later, he said, "I felt like crawling in a hole."[5] Some feel that was an early sign of Horton's psychological problems, as he left the team two months later to seek treatment, and never played again.[6]

After retiring Ted Uhlaender with conventional pitches, Hamilton threw two more folly floaters to rookie Roy Foster. With two strikes Hamilton then threw the even rarer "hesitation hummer." a pitch that started with the classic slow delivery of the folly floater but then was hummed in as a fastball.[7] Munson caught the foul tip for the third strike "and Foster blew his stack as Ham walked off the mound to the thunderous applause of the crowd."[8]

The fireworks continued in the second game, literally and figuratively. Again batting second in the order, Murcer started the game as he ended game one, with another homer to right field, off Indians starter Mike Paul to give the Yankees a 1-0 lead in the bottom of the first. Horton led off the fourth for the Indians with a monstrous shot off Yankee starter Stan Bahnsen that wound up behind the center-field monuments for a triple that could have easily been an inside-the-park home run, as Murcer had to run between two of the monuments to retrieve the ball while Horton made a wide turn around third.[9] Horton scored on a sacrifice fly by Uhlaender, putting the Indians ahead 2-1. Murcer said, "[A]ll I was worried about was getting it over Babe's head and hitting the cutoff man," referring to the Babe Ruth monument, behind which he found the ball.[10]

Murcer walked in the fourth but got no farther than third as Gene Michael popped out to third baseman Graig Nettles to end the inning with the bases loaded. Cleveland's Vada Pinson, playing left field, singled to right in the fifth and went to second on catcher Ray Fosse's groundball to shortstop. He was tagged out at home for the third out by Bahnsen while trying to score from second on a wild pitch.

Pinson came in hard. After tagging Pinson out, Bahnsen slammed the ball down. It bounced and hit Pinson, who angrily challenged Bahnsen. The Yankees pitcher reminded Pinson he'd have to bat against him again. The two tangled briefly at home plate as Pinson landed a solid punch on Bahnsen's jaw, leading to his ejection while Bahnsen remained in the game. This led to Tribe manager Alvin Dark playing the game under protest, a futile effort that was later dismissed. As players from both teams milled around after the fight, a cherry bomb was tossed on the field from the upper deck.

The crowd was riled up and, with Yankees third baseman Jerry Kenney at the plate, another cherry bomb thrown from the upper deck exploded at the feet of catcher Fosse, burning his right foot. Fosse stayed in the game after receiving first aid. According to *Newsday,* many people pointed out the perpetrator[11] and Louis Espada, a 24-year-old Manhattanite, was arrested to the cheers of the crowd and was later held on $1,500 bail.[12]

When order was restored, Kenney led off the bottom of the fifth with a ground-rule double. With two out, Murcer launched his second homer of the game and third of the day deep into right field, putting the Yankees up 3-2. Starter Mike Paul got the final out but was replaced at the start of the sixth inning by Phil Hennigan. After walking Munson, Hennigan got out of the inning when right fielder Ron Woods struck out and Munson was thrown out trying to steal second.

Fred Lasher replaced Hennigan for the seventh and struck out the side. With Fosse on first after a single in the Indians eighth, Nettles put the Indians ahead 4-3 with a homer. That set the scene for Murcer, up second in the bottom half of the inning. With one out he hit a homer in his fourth consecutive at-bat, and third of the game, this one off Lasher, to tie the game, 4-4. The homer came on a 3-and-2 count in an at-bat in which Murcer fouled off seven pitches, three after the count reached 3-and-2, and including a few into the stands that were just a few feet foul. As he crossed the plate, Murcer tipped his hat to the crowd. He said later he appreciated their ovation, that "you know they're pulling for you as much as you are for yourself."[13]

Roy White followed Murcer's homer with a double and scored the go-ahead run on Danny Cater's single to center. Dean Chance replaced Lasher and got the final two outs in the eighth when Cater was caught stealing and Munson struck out. Lindy McDaniel recorded his seventh save of the season with a one-two-three top of the ninth.

Reports of the games pointed out how special the day had been. *Newsday*'s Joe Donnelly closed his column saying, "Finally the crowd, too, went home. They had been given a lot to remember."[14] In the *New York Post*, Maury Allen said tongue in cheek, "[T]hose routine Wednesday afternoon doubleheaders with the Indians just wouldn't be the same without (Murcer)."[15]

Manager Ralph Houk rewarded Murcer's accomplishments with the number-three spot in the batting order the next night. After walking in his first at-bat, Murcer was unable to make history, popping out to second on a checked swing with the count 2-and-2 and two men on against Cleveland rookie Steve Dunning, who had been the club's first-round draft pick out of Stanford three weeks before. The Yankees won that one 3-1 with Roy White garnering all three RBIs, giving Fritz Peterson his 10th win.[16]

Murcer ended the doubleheader with 13 homers and finished his second full season for the Yankees with 23 homers and 78 runs batted in. In the course of his 18 years in the majors, 13 of which were in two stints with the Yankees, Murcer hit 252 home runs. The 31,295 fans at Yankee Stadium on this day in 1970 saw four of them. And a whole lot more.

SOURCES

In addition to the sources cited in the Notes, the author consulted Baseball-Reference.com and Retrosheet.org.

https://www.baseball-reference.com/boxes/NYA/NYA197006242.shtml

https://www.retrosheet.org/boxesetc/1970/B06242NYA1970.htm

NOTES

1   Russell Schneider, "Murcer Hits Four as Indians Split," *Cleveland Plain Dealer,* June 25, 1970: 1F.

2   Since walks do not count as at-bats, Murcer is considered to have homered in four consecutive at-bats.

3   Hamilton played for the Minneapolis Lakers in the 1959 finals against the Celtics, one of just two players to be in the World Series and the NBA Finals. According to Leonard Koppett, "[t]he Folly Floater is the direct descendant of Rip Sewell's Ephus Pitch of the 1940's and Satchel Paige's celebrated Hesitation Pitch. Out of a jerky, delayed wind-up, Hamilton's delivery makes a high, slow parabola and drops through the strike zone;" Leonard Koppett, "Hamilton's Pet Pitch - The Folly Floater," *The Sporting News*, September 6, 1969: 6. Hamilton is also remembered for once swallowing his chewing tobacco and getting sick while on the mound for the Yanks.

4   One can find the video and Phil Rizzuto's call at https://www.youtube.com/watch?v=WFvp7kMraAw, last accessed October 4, 2022.

5   Russell Schneider, "Batting Around," *Cleveland Plain Dealer*, June 25, 1970: 2F.

6   Chris Jaffe, "15,000 Days Since Murcer's Biggest Day and Tony Horton's Declining Mental Health," *Hardball Times,* July 19, 2011, https://tht. fangraphs.com/tht-live/15000-days-since-murcers-biggest-day-and-tony-hortons-declining-mental-heal/.

7   Paul Dickson, *The Dickson Baseball Dictionary*, Third Edition (New York: W.W. Norton, 2009), 407-08.

8   "Murcer Hits 4 as Yankees Split," *New York Daily News,* June 25, 1970: 122.

9   Recollection of author, who was at the game, confirmed by YouTube video of the event at https://www.pinstripealley.com/2017/3/16/14954770/my-favorite-yankee-stadium-memory. Last accessed October 4, 2022.

10   Larry Merchant, "Summer Festival," *New York Post,* June 25, 1970.

11   Joe Donnelly, "Bronx Bomber Faces 2 Years, 7 Months," *Newsday* (Suffolk edition), June 25, 1970: 49.

12   "Cherry Bomb Tosser Held in $1500 Bail," *New York Daily News,* June 26, 1970: 86.

13   "Murcer Hits Four as Indians Split"; Pete Alfano, "Murcer's Day of Greatness: 4 HR's," *Newsday,* June 25, 1970: 50.

14   Joe Donnelly, "Floaters, HR's, Fights – The Stadium Had It All," *Newsday,* June 25, 1970: 48.

15   Maury Allen, "Murcer Hits Glory Road," *New York Post,* June 25, 1970.

16   Leonard Koppett, "Peterson Allows Indians 9 Singles," *New York Times,* June 26, 1970: 49.

AFTER TWO YEARS, THE YANKEES RETURN TO THE BRONX

April 15, 1976:
New York Yankees 11, Minnesota Twins 4, at Yankee Stadium

By Rich D'Ambrosio

After the 1973 season, Yankee Stadium underwent a $100 million renovation, forcing the Yankees to share Shea Stadium with the New York Mets in 1974 and 1975. Finally, on the unseasonably warm afternoon of April 15, 1976, the Yankees returned to the Bronx and their remodeled stadium, as a spirited crowd of 52,613 (the largest Opening Day crowd at Yankee Stadium since 1946) welcomed them home. Owner George Steinbrenner said, "I'm excited for the kids. They've been on a two-year trip. It will be good for them to be home."[1]

The "new" Yankee Stadium retained the same shape as the original, but there were noticeable differences. The famous friezes that draped the upper deck were removed, and the steel girders that obstructed the view of many fans disappeared. There was also a new $2 million scoreboard with concrete replicas of the friezes above it. While there were some minor problems that day, such as the scoreboard malfunctioning and the Yankees reaching an agreement with the ticket takers just 10 minutes before the gates opened, everyone agreed that the Stadium retained its classic charm while offering fans all of the modern conveniences.

The pregame program, emceed beautifully by Bob Sheppard, was an ode to the history of Yankee Stadium. Yankee heroes Joe DiMaggio, Mickey Mantle, Whitey Ford, Don Larsen, and Yogi Berra, as well as pro and college football stars who played at the Stadium were honored. The wives of Babe Ruth and Lou Gehrig were also present. Bob Shawkey, who was the starting pitcher in the first game ever in the Stadium, threw out the ceremonial first pitch while Whitey Witt, the Yankees' leadoff hitter in 1923, stood at the plate. Robert Merrill sang the National Anthem, former Yankee Bobby Richardson delivered the invocation, and Cardinal Terence Cooke gave a blessing.

The Yankees came into their home opener with a 3-1 record after a season-opening road trip on which they split a two-game series in Milwaukee and took two in Baltimore. The starting pitcher for the Yankees in the home opener was Rudy May, who had won 14 games in 1975. The opponents were the Minnesota Twins, who had lost three of their first five games. Dave Goltz, the starter for the Twins, was also coming off a 14-win season.

In the first inning May walked the Twins' leadoff hitter, Jerry Terrell, and Dan Ford followed with a 430-foot home run to left-center. Yankees left fielder Roy White said, "It wouldn't have gone out in the old park but it would have been awful close. I didn't think anyone would be hitting one that far this soon."[2] After Rod Carew grounded out, May hit the next batter, Larry Hisle, who stole second, went to third on an error by second baseman Willie Randolph, and scored on a sacrifice fly by Craig Kusick, giving the Twins a 3-0 lead. Yankees manager Billy Martin commented after the game that "Rudy was on edge. He was rushing himself, and when he does that, he loses his control."[3]

During the Yankees' half of the first inning someone released a little pig near the first-base boxes. On the one side of the pig was the word "Go." On the other was "Yogi." Berra denied any knowledge of its origin, but said, "I'd like to have it, though, to barbecue."[4]

Minnesota increased its lead to 4-0 in the third inning. With one out, Carew walked, stole second, went to third on a throwing error by catcher Thurman Munson, and scored on Steve Braun's groundout. Dick

Tidrow relived May and averted further damage. The Yankees got on the board in the bottom of the inning. Jim Mason doubled, took third on Mickey Rivers' single, and scored on White's force-play grounder.

The Yankees' bats came alive in the fourth inning. With one out, Graig Nettles walked and scored on a triple by Oscar Gamble. (The malfunctioning scoreboard had his batting average at .999.[5]) Randolph singled to drive in Gamble and make the score 4-2. Twins manager Gene Mauch brought in left-hander Vic Albury to face Lou Piniella, who was pinch-hitting for designated hitter Rich Coggins. Randolph stole second and scored on Piniella's single. Otto Velez pinch-hit for Mason. Albury uncorked a wild pitch, sending Piniella to second. Velez singled to drive in Piniella and the Yankees led, 5-4.

Meanwhile Tidrow kept the Twins off the scoreboard. Pitching for five innings, he allowed four hits and struck out four. The Twins mounted a threat with one out in the eighth inning, when Hisle and Steve Braun singled with one out. Sparky Lyle relieved Tidrow and quickly got two outs.

The Yankees put the game away in the bottom of the eighth inning, scoring six runs on five hits, the biggest being Gamble's double. He would finish the day with three hits – a single, double, and triple. Gamble downplayed his performance, saying, "I still don't feel like I'm hitting the ball that good."[6] Lyle pitched a scoreless ninth and the Yankees christened the new Stadium with an impressive 11-4 win. "That's twice we came back," said Piniella. "We were down 6-0 to Milwaukee and won, and today we did it again. It's a new park, a full house, and a come-from-behind win. What could be better."[7]

Randolph, who went 2-for-4 in his first game at Yankee Stadium, remarked, "I came here when I was a kid, but I was never a Yankee fan. It seemed like they were always winning and the Mets were always losing. I rooted for the Mets, and went to Shea much more than I came here. It's great knowing I was a part of an Opening Day here, however. I always wanted to be a big-league ballplayer, and while I was sitting on the bench before the game, I realized I was part of it all now."[8]

Chris Chambliss commented, "It's certainly a different feeling here than at Shea. At Shea, it seemed people were against us, and every time we looked into the stands, there was a fight going on. Now, at least for today, it helped having all those people pulling for you."[9] Even Mauch commented, "Years ago, you were astounded by the tradition and immensity of Yankee Stadium. Now it is astounding in its beauty. It's right there with Dodger Stadium as the most beautiful park in baseball."[10]

Buoyed by their return to the Bronx, the Yankees went 45-35 at home in 1976 and coasted to the American League East title. They defeated the Kansas City Royals for the American League pennant, but were swept by the Cincinnati Reds in the World Series.

SOURCES

In addition to the sources cited in the Notes, the author used the Baseball-Reference.com and Retrosheet.org websites for pertinent material.

https://www.baseball-reference.com/boxes/NYA/NYA197604150.shtml

https://www.retrosheet.org/boxesetc/1976/B04150NYA1976.htm

NOTES

1   Phil Pepe, "Yankees Dedicate New Stadium With Old-Style Bombs," *The Sporting News*, May 1, 1976: 8.

2   Joe Donnelly, "The Housewarming's a Winner," *Newsday* (Long Island, New York), April 16, 1976: 118.

3   Al Mari, "Yankee Power Right at Home," *Journal-News* (Rockland County, New York), April 16, 1976: 108.

4   Dick Young, "Pig in Poke," *New York Daily News*, April 16, 1976: 79.

5   Phil Pepe, "Yankee Bats Boom in Stadium Return," *New York Daily News*, April 16, 1976: 79.

6   Phil Pepe, "Yankee Bats Boom in Stadium Return," 72.

7   Mari, "Yankee Power Right at Home."

8   Mari.

9   Mari.

10 Donnelly, "The Housewarming's a Winner."

CHRIS CHAMBLISS'S HOME RUN DELIVERS PENNANT TO THE BRONX

October 14, 1976:
New York Yankees 7, Kansas City Royals 6
at Yankee Stadium
Game Five of the 1976 American League Championship Series

By Joseph Wancho

It had been 12 years since the Yankees participated in the postseason. In 1964 they lost a thrilling seven-game World Series to the St. Louis Cardinals. Up to then they had won the American League pennant in 14 of 16 seasons beginning in 1949. Love the Yankees or hate them, it is unquestionably one of the greatest runs of success in the history of any professional sport.

Not many non-Yankees fans felt bad for the team when it hit rock bottom in 1966, finishing last in the 10-team AL standings. After their appearance in the 1964 World Series, the Yankees did not challenge for the flag, and were still stagnant when each league was divided into two divisions in 1969.

Baltimore was king of the hill in the AL East Division as the Yankees floundered. The Orioles won five of six division titles from 1969 to 1974, and in that last season the Yankees began to make their come-back. New York finished in second place, two games behind Baltimore.

Baltimore thumped the Yankees during the 1976 regular season. But New York posted a winning record in each month of the season. When July ended, the Yankees had a double-digit lead (10½ games) over Baltimore that they never relinquished on their way to winning the division.

Kansas City won in the West Division, putting an end to the dominance of the Oakland Athletics, who had won five straight division titles beginning in 1971 and World Series championships each season from 1972 to 1974.

Atg that time the ALCS was played in a best-of-five-games format. The Royals and Yankees each won a game on the road and the series was tied at two wins apiece with the deciding game set for October 14 at Yankee Stadium. Perhaps it was appropriate that a game with so much riding on it was being played in the Bronx. The Yankees had played their home games at Shea Stadium in Queens the previous two seasons as Yankee Stadium underwent a facelift.

The weather was clear and chilly, with the temperature in the low 40s. Still, 56,821 spectators braved the cold.

The pitching matchup was the Royals' Dennis Leonard (17-10) vs. the Yankees' Ed Figueroa. (19-10). Each had led his team in wins, but it was a safe

Chris Chambliss's walk-off homer sent the Yankees to their first World Series in 12 years.

assumption that for the pitching staffs, it would be all hands on deck in a winner-take-all game.

In the top of the first inning, George Brett stroked a two-out double to right field and came home on John Mayberry's home run. The Royals' 2-0 lead was short-lived. For the Yankees, Mickey Rivers led off with a triple to left-center and came home on a single by Roy White. White stole second base and went to third on a single to left by Thurman Munson, who took second base on the throw to third.

Royals manager Whitey Herzog went to the bullpen, bringing in left-hander Paul Splittorff. The left-handed-swinging Chris Chambliss tied the score with a sacrifice fly to left field.

Just as quickly as the Yankees had tied the game, the Royals untied it in the top of the second inning. Cookie Rojas singled to center field with one out and stole second. Freddie Patek struck out, but Buck Martinez singled to right field, scoring Rojas and giving the Royals a 3-2 lead.

As if the two clubs were playing a game of "Anything You Can Do I Can Do Better," the Yankees reached Splittorff for two runs in the bottom of the third. Their first three batters reached base: Rivers singled to center, White walked, and Munson hit an RBI single to center. White went to third and scored on Chambliss's force-play grounder to second. That made it 4-3, Yankees.

Marty Pattin relieved Splittorff with two outs in the fourth and Andy Hassler replaced Pattin in the fifth. In the sixth the Yankees added to their lead. Rivers led off with a bunt single and took second on a sacrifice by White. Munson singled to right field to plate Rivers, but the Yankees catcher was thrown out trying to get to second. With two down, Chambliss singled to center field and stole second, then scored when Brett threw away Carlos May's grounder.

The Yankees led 6-3 going into the top of the eighth inning. With the pennant within the New Yorkers' grasp, their fans were ecstatic. Figueroa was still on the mound; he had blanked Kansas City since the second inning. But when Al Cowens singled to left field to open the eighth, Yankees manager Billy Martin brought in left-hander Grant Jackson. Herzog was pushing buttons in the opposing dugout, and called on right-handed-batting Jim Wohlford to pinch-hit for Tom Poquette. The move worked; Wohlford singled to center. Brett stepped up and smashed a pitch by Jackson over the fence, tying the game, 6-6.

Dick Tidrow came on to pitch for the Yankees in the top of the ninth. With two down, the Royals got a single from Martinez and a walk to Cowens. Wohlford slapped a slow grounder to Graig Nettles at third base. Nettles threw to second and umpire Joe Brinkman called Cowens out. TV replays clearly showed that it was a blown call. The Royals would have had the bases loaded and Brett coming to the plate had the correct call been made. Herzog, who did not argue the call, disagreed with Brinkman. But Herzog knew arguing the call would fall on deaf ears, and also did not want to take the chance of getting pelted with the various projectiles that were flying out of the stands.

As the bottom of the ninth began, Chris Chambliss was first up against Royals reliever Mark Littell, who had pitched a clean eighth. As Chambliss waited for Littell to finish his warm-ups, Yankees' public-address announcer Bob Sheppard cautioned the crowd against throwing debris onto the field. The game had already been stopped several times for bottles, firecrackers, beer cans, and rolls of toilet paper thrown from the stands.

Chambliss stood by the bat rack, annoyed by the delay. Littell was annoyed, too. With an 8-4 record, 16 saves, and a 2.08 ERA, the 23-year-old possessed a live fastball and a wicked slider. The delay prevented Littell from staying loose and interfered with his rhythm.

Finally, at 11:43 P.M., Chambliss stepped into the box and home-plate umpire Art Frantz yelled, "Play ball!" Chambliss was 10-for-20 with 7 RBIs in the series so far. He narrowed his eyes, looking for a fastball from Littell.

Littell indeed threw a high, inside fastball. Chambliss reared back, stepped into the pitch, and smashed it over the right-field wall. Chambliss stood momentarily at home plate, watching the ball fly through the autumn air, not sure if it would leave the ballpark. "It felt good," he said. "I thought it had a chance."[1] Meanwhile fans poured onto the field.

As Chambliss rounded first base, fans ripped second base from the ground. Chambliss touched the base with his right hand and continued to run through the maze of humanity. He fell in the basepath, accidentally knocking a rampaging fan over, then he tagged third and headed home. When fans tried to grab his helmet, Chambliss tucked it under his arm, like a football.

Like a fullback looking for a small hole at the line of scrimmage, Chambliss was spun completely around in a circle and powered his way through the throng.

He was then escorted to the Yankees clubhouse by two policemen.

"I had gone to home plate to congratulate him," said Yankees coach Dick Howser. "I saw him rounding first, then I lost him. I caught him again between second and third, but he disappeared. I figured eventually he'd make his way around if he followed the green outline."[2]

"Home plate was completely covered with people," said Chambliss. "I wasn't sure if I tagged it or not. I came in the clubhouse and all the players were talking about whether I got it. I wasn't sure, so I went back out."[3] Graig Nettles urged Chambliss to return to home plate to make it official. "I wanted to make sure there was no way we were going to lose it," Nettles said.[4]

Dressed in a police raincoat to avoid further harassment from the scores of fans still milling around on the field, Chambliss jogged out to home plate, found it had been dug up and removed, replaced by a hole. He touched the hole with umpire Frantz still on the scene, and returned to the champagne party.

In a most historic and memorable fashion, Chris Chambliss delivered the first American League pennant to New York in the renovated Yankee Stadium, and the first one for the team since 1964, ending the 12-year drought. It was a dramatic victory for the Yankees, won by a player who prided himself on steady professionalism, not drama.

SOURCES

The author accessed Baseball-Reference.com for box scores/play-by-play and other data, and also used Retrosheet.org. https://www.baseball-reference.com/boxes/NYA/NYA197610140.shtml

https://www.retrosheet.org/boxesetc/1976/B10140NYA1976.htm

NOTES

1   Phil Pepe, "Yanks Chambliss Makes the Right Connection," *The Sporting News*, October 30, 1976: 12.

2   Gerald Eskenazi, "As Chambliss Rounded First, Bedlam Broke Out at Stadium," *New York Times*, October 15, 1976: A19.

3   Murray Chass, "Yanks Win Pennant on Chambliss' Leadoff Homer in Ninth, 7-6," *New York Times,* October 15, 1976: A19.

4   Chass.

HAT TRICK? YANKEES' UNCONVENTIONAL LINEUP SPURS WIN OVER BLUE JAYS

April 20, 1977:
New York Yankees 7, Toronto Blue Jays 5,
at Yankee Stadium

By John Fredland

After bolstering their pennant-winning roster with high-profile free agents Reggie Jackson and Don Gullett, the New York Yankees skidded into last place in the American League East two weeks into the 1977 season. Manager Billy Martin responded with a revamped batting order, purportedly drawn from a hat, on April 20 against the Toronto Blue Jays at Yankee

Billy Martin's seemingly random lineup that had No. 8 hitter Willie Randolph leading off and leadoff hitter Mickey Rivers batting fifth also somehow left Reggie Jackson batting third and Bucky Dent batting ninth.

Stadium. The new lineup produced New York's most robust offensive performance to date in a 7-5 win over the Blue Jays, beginning the Yankees' climb toward a World Series title and catalyzing second baseman Willie Randolph's emergence as a top-of-the-lineup hitter.

The 1976 Yankees, in Martin's first full season at the helm, won the franchise's first pennant in 12 seasons before falling to the Cincinnati Reds in the World Series. During the 1976-77 offseason – baseball's first under a collective bargaining agreement formalizing free agency – New York added two of the market's biggest names: right fielder Jackson, who had spent 1976 with the Baltimore Orioles after establishing himself as a superstar with the Oakland A's; and lefty starter Gullett, Cincinnati's winning pitcher in Game One of the 1976 World Series, one of 10 postseason starts before his 26th birthday.[1]

But the Yankees opened 1977 by winning just two of their first 10 games. After New York mustered only one win in six games against the Milwaukee Brewers, who had finished last in the AL East in 1976,[2] the expansion Blue Jays won the first two games of their first-ever visit to the Bronx.[3] Losers of five in a row, scoring fewer than three runs per game, the Yankees were already 5½ games back in the division.

Various measures – authoritarian, superstitious, and tactical – were employed to jump-start the Yankees. Owner George Steinbrenner called for a voluntary workout on an offday, then a team meeting before the second Toronto loss.[4] Martin shaved off his mustache for better luck.[5] A mild lineup makeover for April 13's 5-3 win over the Kansas City Royals, New York's biggest offensive outburst in its first 10 games, had catcher Thurman Munson – the regular number-three hitter – batting second; Jackson shifted from fifth to third; and left fielder Roy White, generally in the second slot, at sixth.[6]

Still, the Yankees' slide persisted. "Everything has gone awry," observed *Newsday*. "Nobody is hitting. … The defense is suddenly shabby. A pack of writers wait every day in the [locker room]. The headlines the next morning scream at them."[7]

After the second loss to the Blue Jays on April 19, Martin announced that the Yankees would deploy a radically revamped batting order for the next day's game.[8] Newspapers reported that Martin – aided by Jackson and venerable clubhouse man Pete Sheehy – had picked the lineup "out of a hat" as the 8-3 defeat ran its course.[9]

But Martin's lineup card for Wednesday afternoon's game was not completely unfamiliar. As they had a week earlier in Kansas City, Munson and Jackson batted second and third, and White was sixth. With right-hander Steve Hargan pitching for Toronto, designated hitter Carlos May, a lefty who had hit fifth through seventh in earlier games against righties, was seventh.

Shortstop Bucky Dent, acquired from the Chicago White Sox two days before Opening Day,[10] batted ninth, just as he had for New York's first 10 games.

Other Yankees had more unusual roles. Leading off was the 22-year-old Randolph, New York's regular eighth hitter but an AL All-Star in 1976, his first full major-league season.[11] Veteran center fielder Mickey Rivers, the usual leadoff man, shifted to fifth for the first time in his career.

Graig Nettles, the AL's leading home-run hitter in 1976, was at cleanup instead of his customary sixth or seventh. Eighth was Chris Chambliss, generally fourth or fifth but batting nearly 100 points below his career .283 average.[12]

Before the Yankees could test out their new order, Toronto went ahead against Gullett, seeking his first win of 1977 after two losses to Milwaukee. A single by former Yankee Otto Vélez – who had four hits and four RBIs in the series' first two games – drove in Hector Torres, and Bob Bailor scored on Doug Ault's groundout for a 2-0 Blue Jays' lead.

Toronto had selected Hargan, a 34-year-old veteran of 205 starts with the Cleveland Indians and Texas Rangers, in the expansion draft. Against the Yankees, he struggled with control, and New York's reordered lineup capitalized immediately.[13]

Randolph started the first with a walk, then took third when Munson – who had observed in 1976 that

"[o]n most other clubs [Randolph] would be batting leadoff"[14] – sliced a double down the right-field line, his first hit in 15 at-bats. Jackson's single to center scored both runners, tying the game.

Jackson stole second without a throw, as catcher Alan Ashby failed to handle Hargan's forkball. A walk to Nettles put runners on first and second with none out. Rivers sacrificed, and the Blue Jays walked White intentionally to load the bases.

One out later, Chambliss singled home Nettles to put the Yankees in front, 3-2. All nine Yankees batted in the first, and it was just New York's fourth multi-run inning of the season.[15]

When the Yankees came up in the second, Randolph led off again. He drove Hargan's full-count pitch deep to the opposite field and into the bleachers behind the 385-foot sign in right for his second career homer.[16]

May greeted Randolph in the dugout, the *Yonkers Herald Stateman* reported, "waving a towel at him and giving him the royalty treatment."[17] For the second time in two innings, the Yankees' new batting order had made a difference.

"I had a full count on [Randolph] and just wanted to throw a strike," Hargan said. "I didn't want to walk him with Munson, Jackson, and Nettles coming."[18]

"It'll probably be my one [home run] for the year," Randolph said.[19]

New York kept on rolling, as Munson singled and Jackson walked. Toronto manager Roy Hartsfield replaced Hargan with Jerry Johnson.

After Nettles' fly ball to right moved Munson to third, spotty Toronto defense let in another run. Ault bobbled Rivers' grounder to first, tried to tag the speedy Rivers, and missed him. Everyone was safe, and Munson scored for a 5-2 lead.

Toronto scored in the third when Ault's single drove in Torres. But the Yankees clustered singles and productive outs in the fourth and fifth innings against Johnson to build a cushion. Jackson and Nettles started the fourth with singles, and Rivers' sacrifice fly drove in Jackson. Dent and Randolph singled to put runners at the corners in the fifth; when Toronto settled for a force at second on Munson's grounder, New York's advantage was 7-3.

In five innings, Martin's "hat" lineup had generated seven runs on 10 hits. It was more runs than in any previous game in 1977, and more hits than in all but one game. The first four batters – Randolph, Munson, Jackson, and Nettles – had reached base 10 times in 15 plate appearances, scored six runs, and driven in four.[20]

Gullett had found his groove in the meantime, holding the Blue Jays hitless from the fourth inning through the seventh.

"I started to get better location on my pitches in the middle innings," he said. "My mechanics got better, and I was able to move the ball around."[21]

Dave McKay's two-run double in the eighth brought Toronto within 7-5, but Martin called on Sparky Lyle for the final five outs of New York's slide-snapping win.

"Same lineup tomorrow," Martin said afterward. "What the heck, I can't go against the hat, can I?"[22]

"If [Martin] keeps me leadoff, I'll be a happy man," Randolph added.[23]

A day later, the Randolph-Munson-Jackson-Nettles-Rivers-White-May-Chambliss-Dent parade racked up 13 more hits in an 8-6 win over Toronto, as Chambliss broke out for a homer and five RBIs.[24] With some adjustments – swapping May and White's lineup positions, then substituting Jim Wynn against a lefty – Martin stuck with the "hat" order for six games.

The Yankees won all six, averaging more than eight runs per game.[25] It began a surge of 14 wins in 16 games that boosted New York to first in the division.[26] As 1977 progressed, six of the Yankees' nine starters on April 20 started at least 14 games in their "hat-selected" slots,[27] and New York won its first World Series since 1962.

No Yankee returned to his "hat" spot more often than Randolph, who hit leadoff in 37 of the next 38 games and 68 times overall in 1977. Whether Randolph's April 20 assignment came from a random draw, or whether it reflected Martin recognizing a young player's potential in a new role – accompanied by a pressure-deflecting cover story about a hat[28] – it was a watershed in his career.

Randolph had batted eighth in more than 80 percent of his starts before the "hat" game.[29] Going forward, he became a table-setter, hitting first or second over 80 percent of the time and batting leadoff most often.[30] Randolph finished in the AL's Top 10 in steals four times and walks eight times and retired in 1992 with a career .373 on-base percentage.

ACKNOWLEDGMENTS

SABR member Gary Belleville provided helpful research assistance with Canadian newspaper coverage of this game.

SOURCES

In addition to the sources cited in the Notes below, the author consulted Baseball-Reference.com and Retrosheet.org for pertinent information, including the box score and play-by-play. He also reviewed game coverage in the *Globe and Mail, Newsday, New York Daily News,* and *Toronto Star* newspapers and SABR Baseball BioProject biographies of several individuals involved in this game, especially Charles F. Faber's Don Gullett biography and Nancy Snell Griffith's Willie Randolph biography.

https://www.baseball-reference.com/boxes/NYA/NYA197704200.shtml

https://www.retrosheet.org/boxesetc/1977/B04200NYA1977.htm

NOTES

1   Red Foley, "Yankees Land Gullett – Go for Grich: 6-Year Contract Is Worth $1.7M to Cincy Free Agent," *New York Daily News,* November 19, 1976: 86; Dick Young, "Jax Agrees to Take Yanks' $2M," *New York Daily News,* November 28, 1976: 132.

2   Bill Verigan, "Brewers Sweep Yanks into Cellar," *New York Daily News,* April 18, 1977: 50.

3   Red Foley, "Yanks Fall Again; Cat Lost 21 Days," *New York Daily News,* April 19, 1977: 50; Red Foley, "Slumping Yanks Bow to Jays, 8-3," *New York Daily News,* April 20, 1977: C22.

4   Bill Pennington, *Billy Martin: Baseball's Flawed Genius* (Boston: Mariner, 2016), 247-257. Joe Gergen, "This Club Is Going to Win. An Acorn Doesn't Make a Fall," *Newsday* (Long Island, New York), April 20, 1977: 115.

5   Foley, "Yanks Fall Again; Cat Lost 21 Days"; Red Foley, "Slumping Yanks Bow to Jays, 8-3."

6   Steve Jacobson, "3 Little Bombers Power the Yankees," *Newsday,* April 14, 1977: 182.

7   Dan Lauck, "Words Fail Yankees After 8th Loss," *Newsday,* April 20, 1977: 116.

8   Al Mari, "Martin Unveils Hat Trick," *Yonkers* (New York) *Herald Statesman,* April 20, 1977: 39.

9   Mari, "Martin Unveils Hat Trick"; Associated Press, "Martin Takes 'Em from a Hat," *Ithaca* (New York) *Journal,* April 20, 1977: 17.

10   The Yankees had traded outfielder Oscar Gamble, two minor-league pitchers, and cash to the White Sox for Dent on April 5. Bill Nack, "One Minute You're There and the Next You're Not," *Newsday,* April 7, 1977: 119.

11   Randolph had batted eighth in the Yankees' first nine games of 1977 before hitting seventh on April 19.

12   After starting the season with one hit in his first 17 at-bats, Chambliss was batting .189 through the Yankees' first nine games, and Martin benched him on April 19.

13   The *Daily News* noted that Hargan "was behind virtually every batter." Red Foley, "Yankees Pull One out of Hat, 7-5: Top Jays to End 5-Slide," *New York Daily News,* April 21, 1977: 96.

14   Joe Donnelly, "How the Yankees Raised the Flag," *Newsday,* September 27, 1976: 70.

15   In 93 innings at bat before this game, the Yankees had only one three-run inning (April 15 in Milwaukee) and two two-run innings (April 11 in Kansas City and April 16 in Milwaukee).

16   The home run came in Randolph's 611th career plate appearance. He had also homered off Baltimore's Jim Palmer on April 13, 1976.

17   Al Mari, "Yanks New Hat Fits Perfectly," *Yonkers Herald Statesman,* April 21, 1977: 36.

18   Neil Campbell, "Lyle Snuffs out Jays' Rally as Yankees End Losing Streak," *Globe and Mail* (Toronto), April 21, 1977: 48.

19   Red Foley, "Yankees Pull One out of Hat, 7-5."

20 At that point, Hartsfield summoned 26-year-old left-hander Mike Willis to appear in his second big-league game. Willis contained the Yankees for three innings, allowing four hits but keeping them scoreless.

21 Foley, "Yankees Pull One out of Hat, 7-5." Gullett finished April with a 1-2 record and 7.13 ERA. For the rest of the season, he won 13 of 15 decisions and posted a 2.95 ERA. A series of injuries, culminating in rotator cuff surgery in September 1978, ended his major-league career at the age of 27.

22 Foley, "Yankees Pull One out of Hat, 7-5."

23 Jim Smith, "Yankees Find Solution for a Day: Out-of-the-Hat Batting Order Produces 14 Hits and 7 Runs," *Newsday,* April 21, 1977: 192.

24 Phil Pepe, "Chambliss' 5 RBI Spark Yanks, 8-6," *New York Daily News*, April 22, 1977: 72.

25 Phil Pepe, "Yank Streak at 6; Reggie Raps HR," *New York Daily News*, April 26, 1977: 48.

26 Bill Verigan, "Yankees Rock Dock, Thump A's, 10-5," *New York Daily News*, May 9, 1977: 40.

27 Randolph batted leadoff 68 times, Munson was second 14 times, Jackson third 21 times, Nettles cleanup seven times, Rivers fifth seven times, White sixth 28 times, May seventh 16 times, Chambliss eighth six times, and Dent ninth 149 times.

28 The *Yonkers Herald Statesman* offered a note of skepticism on the alleged selection of the Yankees' April 20 lineup. "The Yanks swear the lineup came from a hat, but it is an amazing coincidence that little Willie [Randolph] has been dying to lead off, and big Reggie [Jackson] itching to hit third." Mari, "Yanks New Hat Fits Perfectly." On two other occasions during his managing career, Martin claimed to have selected lineups from a hat: on August 13, 1972, when he managed the Detroit Tigers, and June 23, 1982, with the Oakland A's. In contrast to the persistence of many elements of the 1977 "hat" lineup, Martin's 1972 lineup included three players batting in positions for the only time all season and another player who hit in that spot in just one other game. The 1982 lineup had five "one-time" players. Jim Hawkins, "Still Falling … Tigers in 3rd Place," *Detroit Free Press*, August 14, 1972: 1D; Kit Stier, "No Runs in Martin's Hat," *Oakland Tribune*, June 24, 1982: F-1.

29 Prior to this game, Randolph had started in 145 major-league games and batted eighth 117 times.

30 From April 20, 1977 through the end of his career, Randolph started 1,967 games. He batted leadoff in 859 of those games and second in 743.

SUTTON PLACE: DODGER DON DOMINATES AL IN YANKEE STADIUM DEBUT

July 19, 1977:
National League 7, American League 5,
at Yankee Stadium

By Andrew Milner

The New York City hosting the 1977 All-Star Game had drastically changed in the 13 years since the Mets hosted the 1964 Midsummer Classic. In the summer of '77, Big Apple residents lived in fear of the "Son of Sam" serial killer stalking the outer boroughs, and on July 13, the entire city was plunged into a blackout – interrupting the sixth inning of a Mets-Cubs game at Shea Stadium – and unprecedented looting resulting in a $300 million loss. To top it off, New York was sweltering in 102-degree heat on the afternoon of July 19, a record high for the date.[1]

The American League entered the contest having lost 13 of the last 14 All-Star Games. Junior circuit manager Billy Martin, who had played in the 1956 All-Star Game for the Yankees, saw two of his potential starting pitchers for the game unavailable because of injuries. Mark Fidrych, the Tigers' rookie sensation of 1976 who had won six straight games in June 1977, was sidelined with tendinitis in his right shoulder. Frank Tanana of the Angels, sporting a 12-6 record at the

break with a 2.15 ERA, suffered an inflamed tendon in his left elbow. Martin added Tanana's teammate Nolan Ryan to the AL staff, but Ryan – disappointed at not already being selected despite 13 wins, 16 complete games, and an otherworldly 234 strikeouts by July 16 – announced that he would be spending the break lying on the beach in Laguna instead: "If I can't go on my own merits, I'm not going."[2] Martin thus had only four starting pitchers and four relievers to work with, and gave the starting nod to Baltimore's Jim Palmer. "I know I have a great defense behind me," Palmer said before the game. "And like the rest of the guys here, I'd like to see the American League win for a change."[3]

National League manager Sparky Anderson of the Reds passed up an opportunity to select Tom Seaver, traded from the Mets to Cincinnati five weeks earlier, as his starting pitcher, making a more ecumenical choice by picking Don Sutton of the Dodgers, Cincinnati's rival in the National League West

Five Yankees players (Willie Randolph, Reggie Jackson, Thurman Munson, Graig Nettles, Sparky Lyle) made the AL roster of the first All-Star Game to be played at the renovated Yankee Stadium.

Division. Sutton, long suspected of scuffing the base-ball, dryly told reporters before the game, "I got a note from Sparky asking me what grain of sandpaper I wanted, and what size carpenter's apron I wanted to wear."[4]

As the thermometer cooled to a more reasonable 87 degrees by game time, the 56,683 in attendance at the renovated Yankee Stadium settled in. One of the evening's highlights came during the player introductions, when ex-Met Seaver received a standing ovation from the fans in his return to New York. Seaver waved to the crowd with his right hand while placing his left hand over his heart. Dick Young, Seaver's tabloid archnemesis, deadpanned, "It really touched me right there."[5]

Honoring the 30th anniversary of Jackie Robinson's joining the Brooklyn Dodgers, his widow, Rachel, threw out the ceremonial first pitch. In attendance were several of Jackie's Brooklyn teammates, including Joe Black, Pee Wee Reese, and Roy Campanella.

Palmer started the 1977 game having not allowed a run in eight innings of All-Star competition. His scoreless streak ended after six pitches, when leadoff batter Joe Morgan of the Reds deposited a 3-and-2 slider into the right-field stands. The NBC cameras caught right fielder Reggie Jackson, in his first season with the Yankees, burying his face into the padded right-field fence in frustration as the ball landed.[6] "Palmer had problems with his location tonight," Morgan said after the game. "He had good stuff, but he couldn't find the plate. That was his trouble."[7] Morgan's blow was only the third leadoff home run in All-Star Game history, and the first since Willie Mays' homer in 1965.

After striking out Dodger Steve Garvey, Palmer gave up a single to left to Dave Parker of the Pirates. Cincinnati's George Foster stepped up to the plate; of Foster's 29 home runs and 90 RBIs at the break, NBC's Joe Garagiola marveled, "He could go home right now and get himself a $100,000 raise."[8] Foster then drove in Parker with a double to left field, Parker beating the Red Sox relay of Carl Yastrzemski to Rick Burleson to catcher Carlton Fisk. Foster advanced to third on Palmer's wild pitch. The Phillies' Greg Luzinski then connected on a 3-and-2 slider for a two-run home run to right field, in almost the same location as Morgan's blast. Luzinski told reporters afterward, "It was a big thrill for me to be able to hit a home run in my first time at bat in this stadium. To be in Yankee Stadium, with all you hear about it, was like being in a World Series for me."[9] A calmer Palmer then fanned

Ron Cey of the Dodgers and the Reds' Johnny Bench to (after a fashion) strike out the side.

After a scoreless second, Palmer began the third by surrendering another home run, this one to Garvey for a 5-0 National League lead. Phil Pepe wrote that "Garvey ... cut Yankee Stadium's so-called Death Valley down to size, hitting one over the fence in left, midway between the 387 and 430 signs." Martin then replaced Palmer with Cleveland's Jim Kern, who stanched any further bleeding that inning with two strikeouts and a groundout.

Sutton had little difficulty dispatching the American League's top hitter, Rod Carew, whose .394 average was the talk of the sports world, inducing a comebacker to the mound in the first inning. Carew connected on a fly to deep center in the third before Foster made a leaping catch at the wall, the eventual 1977 National League Most Valuable Player soundly putting out the season's eventual American League MVP. In his first-ever appearance at Yankee Stadium, Sutton was in command during his three innings of work, striking out four and allowing one walk and giving up only one hit, a second-inning single by new Yankee Jackson.

In the fourth, Anderson replaced Sutton with Gary Lavelle of the Giants, who allowed one hit and struck out two over the next two innings. In the sixth, Seaver finally came to the mound to the second enormous ovation of the night. Staked to a five-run lead, Seaver gave up a leadoff single to Carew before getting the Yankees' Willie Randolph and the Royals' George Brett to ground out. Boston's Fred Lynn then lofted a foul popup to the third-base side, which caused Seaver's new teammate Pete Rose to fall down in a vain attempt to catch. A reprieved Lynn then walked, and Richie Zisk of the White Sox dampened Seaver's homecoming with a two-run double to right-center. The score was now 5-2.

Seaver suffered another spell of bad luck in the seventh; Minnesota's Butch Wynegar singled to right and advanced to second when Cardinals shortstop Garry Templeton booted the Yankees' Graig Nettles's one-out grounder. After Boston's George Scott flied to center, New York's Willie Randolph drove in Wynegar with a single to center to bring the tying run to the plate. Pinch-hitter Ron Fairly, at 39 the expansion Blue Jays' lone representative (he had also played for Montreal in the 1973 game), almost became a hero with a fly to deep right that went just foul. Then he struck out.

The National League added two insurance runs in the eighth. Templeton doubled to left off the Yankees'

Sparky Lyle, who then hit Chicago's Jerry Morales (then hitting .331) in the leg with a pitch. Both runners advanced on a wild pitch before scoring on Padre Dave Winfield's single to left.

In the bottom of the ninth, Pirates reliever Goose Gossage – who would call Yankee Stadium home a season later – gave up a leadoff walk to the Rangers' Bert Campaneris. After Nettles struck out, George Scott crushed a home run to right-center field that brought the American League within two runs again. Gossage closed out the 7-5 NL victory by inducing future teammates Randolph and Thurman Munson to ground out and strike out, respectively.

Sutton was named the game's MVP for his solid start. Having grown up a Yankee fan in Florida,[10] Sutton was indifferent to the evening's weather. "The way I felt tonight, I didn't know if it was raining, snowing, sleeting; if I was on the desert, in the mountains or at the ocean," adding, "The way I feel about pitching in this stadium for the first time, I really expected to around and see Kubek, Richardson, and Mantle playing behind me. The only other thing that could have happened was if Mantle made a catch behind the monuments to win the game."[11]

SOURCES

In addition to the sources cited in the Notes, the author consulted Baseball-Reference.com and Retrosheet.org.

https://www.baseball-reference.com/allstar/1977-allstar-game.shtml

https://www.retrosheet.org/boxesetc/1977/YAS_1977.htm

NOTES

1   Paul Meskil, "Ol' Sol Is a Real Sun of a Gun!" *New York Daily News,* July 20, 1977: 3.

2   Associated Press, "Nolan Ryan to Skip All-Star Game," *White Plains* (New York) *Journal News,* July 15, 1977: 29.

3   Dan Shaughnessy, "N.L. Confident, A.L. Present For 48th All-Star Classic," *Baltimore Evening Sun,* July 19, 1977: 23.

4   Stan Hochman, "Yankee Stadium Is Just Dreamy for Sutton," *Philadelphia Daily News,* July 19, 1977: 67.

5   Dick Young, "Young Ideas," *The Sporting News,* August 6, 1977: 14.

6   NBC-TV telecast of the 1977 All-Star Game, YouTube: https://tinyurl.com/2k5t963y. Accessed October 16, 2022.

7   Associated Press, "NL's Domination Isn't a Mystery to Morgan," *Santa Cruz* (California) *Sentinel,* July 20, 1977: 14.

8   NBC-TV telecast.

9   Allen Lewis, "NL Turns Back AL Again, 7-5," *Philadelphia Inquirer,* July 20, 1977: C1.

10 SABR BioProject Don Sutton biography: https://sabr.org/bioproj/person/don-sutton/.

11 Bob Verdi, "Same Old Song: NL All-Stars Triumph," *Chicago Tribune,* July 20, 1977: Sports, 3. Sutton would pitch again at Yankee Stadium for the Dodgers in the 1977 and 1978 World Series with an 0-1 record and a 5.40 earned-run average – and in six subsequent regular-season starts at the Stadium while pitching in the American League, Sutton went 0-4 with an 8.78 ERA.

YANKEES LEAVE DODGERS BLUE IN
WORLD SERIES GAME ONE

October 11, 1977:
New York Yankees 4, Los Angeles Dodgers 3 (12 innings),
at Yankee Stadium
Game One of 1977 World Series

By Ed Gruver

Yankees President Gabe Paul told reporters on November 18, 1976, that the Bronx Bombers considered newly signed southpaw ace Don Gullett "a modern Whitey Ford."[1]

At the time of his free-agent signing, Gullett's .684 winning percentage led all active major-league pitchers who had 100 or more decisions. Ford, like Gullett a left-handed hurler, owned a .690 winning percentage with the Yankees from 1950 to 1967.[2]

Paul's comparison proved prescient. Nearly 11 months later, on October 11, 1977, Gullett joined Ford and new teammate and former Oakland A's star Ken Holtzman as the most recent pitchers who were Game One starters in at least three consecutive World Series. Just as Ford did decades earlier, Gullett stood on the Yankee Stadium mound, wearing pinstripes and facing a formidable Dodgers squad.

Gullett split his prior two World Series openers, falling in Fenway Park to the Boston Red Sox in 1975 before rebounding in Riverfront Stadium in 1976 against the Yankees. Taking the view that if you can't beat 'em, buy 'em, Yankees owner George Steinbrenner III signed Gullett away from the Reds.[3]

Gullett was familiar with the Dodgers, having pitched against them since joining the Reds as a 19-year-old rookie in 1970. He was also familiar with his mound opponent, Dodgers ace right-hander Don Sutton. They dueled through the years in games that proved pivotal in deciding the National League Western Division champion.

While Gullett went 14-4 with a 3.58 ERA and a league-leading .778 winning percentage, Sutton was 14-8 in '77 with a 3.18 ERA and a .636 percentage. In their League Championship Series, the two Dons went

a combined 1-1. Gullett lost to Kansas City, 7-2, in Game One in an afternoon game at Yankee Stadium on October 5; Sutton shut down the Philadelphia Phillies, 7-1, that night in Dodger Stadium.

Sutton was no stranger to Yankee Stadium. The previous July 19 he started there for the NL All-Stars and was named Most Valuable Player in a 7-5 victory. He might have been more familiar with Yankee Stadium had his fate taken a different turn. Sutton, in fact, might have been starting for the Yankees and Gullett for the Dodgers.

When the 19-year-old Sutton was offered only a $2,000 signing bonus by the Yankees, he accepted the Dodgers' offer of $15,000.[4] Sutton signed with Dodgers scout Leon Hamilton on September 11, 1964.[5]

In 1976 Los Angeles was one of the clubs seeking to sign Gullett before the free agent agreed to terms with the Yankees.[6]

Because Gullett had left his ALCS Game One start after just two innings because of a sore shoulder, he was a surprise choice for the World Series opener. The 26-year-old tried to calm the fears of Yankee fans by stating that his use of heat treatment and 1- and 2-pound weights in the interim keyed his rapid recovery.[7]

To the 56,668 in attendance on a cool night – the game-time temperature in the Bronx stood at 59 degrees Fahrenheit – Gullett didn't appear to be in prime condition when Davey Lopes led off with a walk and Bill Russell roped a run-scoring triple to left-center field. Reggie Smith followed with a walk on a 3-and-1 pitch, prompting Yankees manager Billy Martin to get right-handed reliever Dick Tidrow throwing in the bullpen. Ron Cey, perhaps bolstered by the black magic of a witch's brew he acknowledged taking to deal with a batting slump, bombed a 410-foot sacrifice fly to Lou Piniella in left-center field to score Russell for a 2-0 lead.[8]

Next up was Steve Garvey, who banged 33 home runs and drove in 115 runs in the regular season. With the Dodgers threatening a big inning, Gullett called for catcher and team captain Thurman Munson to head to the hill. "If we get this fellow," Gullett told Munson, "somebody's in trouble."[9]

In immediate trouble was Smith, who was trapped off first base and run down. Garvey worked the Dodgers' third walk of the inning, but Gullett got Dusty Baker to ground to Graig Nettles at third base for the final out.

"Gullett was all psyched up for the game," Munson told reporters. "He was hyper, he was overthrowing. As soon as he settled down, he was all right."[10]

The Yankees halved their deficit in their first at-bat. Sutton retired jackrabbits Mickey Rivers and Willie Randolph on groundouts. Munson stroked a single to left field, Reggie Jackson singled to center, and Chris Chambliss singled to right for New York's first run.

Gullett and Sutton settled in and did not allow further scoring for the next four innings. Los Angeles rallied in the top of the sixth, Garvey reaching on a one-out bunt single along the third-base line. Baker flied out to Rivers in short center field, but Glenn Burke lined a two-out single to the gap in right-center. Seeking to score from first base, Garvey stormed home as third-base coach Preston Gomez gave the former Michigan State football player the green light. Rivers' throw bounced before reaching Munson, who grabbed the ball on the first-base side and lunged to his left to tag the sliding Garvey.

Plate umpire Nestor Chylak, peering through the dust and dirt kicked up by the collision, called Garvey out, raising a storm of protest by the Dodgers. Steve Yeager saw the play from the on-deck circle and said Chylak was screened and could not see that Garvey was safe. Dodgers skipper Tommy Lasorda agreed. Garvey told reporters Munson "tagged me somewhere from the calf up, which meant my foot had to be across the plate."[11]

In the bottom of the sixth, Randolph, who hit just four homers in the regular season, pulled a Sutton pitch into the left-field seats, tying the game, 2-2. In the eighth inning, Sutton surrendered a leadoff walk to Randolph, who raced home when Munson picked on a first pitch and drilled a line-drive double down the left-field line. Down 3-2, Lasorda replaced Sutton with reliever Lance Rautzhan. The Dodgers escaped further damage, then tied the game in the ninth.

Gullett gave up a leadoff single to Championship Series MVP Baker, then retired pinch-hitter Manny Mota on a short fly ball to right field. A walk to Yeager brought on ace reliever Sparky Lyle to face pinch-hitter Lee Lacy. Lyle had 26 saves in the regular season and would be named the American League's Cy Young Award winner. He had also won the final two playoff games in Kansas City. Lyle, however, yielded a single to left by Lacy that scored Baker with the tying run.

Lyle ended the threat by getting Lopes to fly out and Russell to line out. Mike Garman, the fourth Los Angeles pitcher, set down the Yankees to force the second extra-innings World Series game in three years.[12]

The Dodgers and Yankees dueled deep into the New York night. In the bottom of the 12th, the Yankees faced the fifth Dodgers pitcher of the game, right-hander Rick Rhoden. Randolph led off with another big hit, a double down the left-field line. Munson was intentionally walked, and Paul Blair, a veteran of the Baltimore Orioles' World Series squads between 1966 and 1971 whom Martin had inserted in the ninth as a defensive replacement for Jackson in right field, approached the plate. Ordered to move Randolph to third to give sluggers Chambliss and Nettles the opportunity to plate the winning run, Blair twice attempted to bunt.

A conference with third-base coach and future Yankees manager Dick Howser ensued, and Blair followed by redirecting a Rhoden fastball past Russell at shortstop. Baker tried to barehand the ball in left field but failed to grip it and Randolph ran home with the winning run. The 4-3 victory was the Yankees' first in a World Series game since Game Six in 1964, ending a run of five straight losses. It also snapped a streak of four consecutive home defeats in World Series play, the Yankees not having won in the Bronx since a ninth-inning homer by Mickey Mantle beat the St. Louis Cardinals in Game Three of the 1964 fall classic.

Blair told reporters the game-winning single ranked among his more memorable postseason memories, including another one against the Dodgers, in 1966 against Claude Osteen that gave the Orioles a 1-0 win.[13]

Gullet worked 8⅓ innings and allowed three runs, all earned, on five hits. He struck out six and walked six. Lyle got the win, working 3⅔ innings and surrendering just one hit while striking out two. The victory was Lyle's third straight in the 1977 postseason.

YANKEE STADIUM 1923-2008

SOURCES

Along with the sources cited in the Notes, the author consulted Baseball-Reference.com and Retrosheet.org for additional information on players and teams.

https://www.baseball-reference.com/boxes/NYA/NYA197710110.shtml

https://www.retrosheet.org/boxesetc/1977/B10110NYA1977.htm

NOTES

1 Associated Press and United Press International Wire Services, "Yankees Snare a 'New Ford': Don Gullett," *St. Petersburg Times*, November 19, 1976: 1C.

2 "Yankees Snare a 'New Ford.'"

3 Murray Chass, "Yankees Sign Gullett to 6-Year Pact Worth a Reported $2 Million," *New York Times*, November 19, 1976: 25.

4 Lowell Reidenbaugh, "Yanks' Extra-Innings Heroics Subdue Dodgers," *The Sporting News*, October 29, 1977: 5.

5 Ronnie Joyce, "Former Aggie Sutton Signs Dodger Contract," *Pensacola News-Journal*, September 13, 1964: 37.

6 Murray Chass, "Yankees Sign Gullett to 6-Year Pact Worth a Reported $2 Million," *New York Times*, November 19, 1976: 25.

7 Reidenbaugh 5.

8 John Holway, "Those Witches' Brews Could Be Good For You," *The Sporting News*, October 29, 1977: 16.

9 Reidenbaugh.

10 Reidenbaugh.

11 Reidenbaugh.

12 In the 1975 World Series, Carlton Fisk's dramatic 12-inning home run gave the Boston Red Sox a sixth-game victory over the Cincinnati Reds.

13 Reidenbaugh.

REGGIE BECOMES "MR. OCTOBER" WITH THREE HOME RUNS IN ONE WORLD SERIES GAME

October 18, 1977:
New York Yankees 8, Los Angeles Dodgers 4,
at Yankee Stadium
Game Six of the 1977 World Series

By Scott Ferkovich

Joe DiMaggio was scheduled to throw out the ceremonial first pitch prior to Game Six of the 1977 World Series between the New York Yankees and the Los Angeles Dodgers. In the Yankees dressing room before the game, DiMaggio grabbed a stool and sat next to New York's star right fielder Reggie Jackson. A high-priced free agent, Jackson had endured a rough (albeit productive) first season in The Bronx, battling his teammates, the press, his manager Billy Martin, and his boss, George Steinbrenner. DiMaggio and Jackson chatted for a while. DiMaggio had been the Oakland A's hitting coach back in 1968, when a young Jackson was in his first full season in the big leagues. Now, DiMaggio was telling Jackson that he thought

Only Babe Ruth had hit three homers in a World Series Game before Reggie Jackson did it in Game Six.

he was a great ballplayer. It was the confidence boost that Jackson needed and thrived on. At this point in the Series he was hitting .353 with two home runs. The second one had come in his last at-bat in Game Five, at Dodger Stadium, a titanic shot off Don Sutton. Johnny Oates, the Dodger catcher, called it, "the single hardest-hit ball I ever saw."[1]

After the talk with DiMaggio, Jackson headed out to the field for batting practice, where he put on a show of awesome power. As Jackson drove ball after ball into the seats, the Yankee Stadium crowd began chanting, "Reg-gie, Reg-gie, Reg-gie!" (Decades later, Jackson estimated that during batting practice that night he "probably took 50 swings and had to hit 35 balls in the stands, all within about a 50-feet radius in right field."[2] Baseball writer Roger Kahn, who witnessed the carnage, puts the ratio at 40/20.) "Hey," teammate Willie Randolph shouted, "would you maybe save a little of that for the game?" Reggie nodded and noted, "I'm feeling good. I mean I'm feeling great."[3]

The Yankees led the Dodgers three games to two, so they could put the Series on ice with a victory this night. To the mound the Yankees sent Mike Torrez, the winner in Game Three. The Dodgers countered with Burt Hooton, whose fine performance helped Los Angeles take Game Two.

On the cool, clear night, 56,407 fans jammed The House That Ruth Built.

The Dodgers scored two quick runs in the first. In the second, New York's Chris Chambliss smacked

273

a home run to score Jackson (who had reached on a four-pitch walk) tying up the ball game at 2-2. Reggie Smith homered in the third to put Los Angeles up by a run.

Following a Thurman Munson single in the fourth, Jackson came up for his first official at-bat of the game. On the first offering from Hooton, he blasted a high, arching drive into the lower deck in right, giving the Yankees the lead they would never relinquish. "Hooton tried to come in with a fastball," Jackson said, "As soon as I hit it, I knew it was gone."[4] Reggie was expecting Hooton's heater – he had checked with the Yankees' top scout, Gene Michael, prior to the game. Michael had flatly stated, "Hooton's gonna pitch you a fastball in."[5]

It was Reggie's second consecutive home run in two official at-bats, going back to the one he'd hit in the previous game at Dodger Stadium. That made two swings, two home runs. But Reggie's rendezvous with history was only beginning.

His home run had sent Hooton to the showers. Dodgers manager Tommy Lasorda brought in Elias Sosa to pitch. Jackson came up again in the fifth. Facing Sosa with Willie Randolph on first, Reggie figured Sosa would also come inside with a fastball. He did. Reggie again swung at the first pitch, hammering a line shot into the first row in the lower deck in right field. "I hit it good but I was hoping that the ball would stay up. I hit it like a 3-iron and hoped it would hang on."[6] In the dugout after the home run, an exuberant Jackson waved to the television cameras, flashed two fingers, and mouthed, "Hi Mom! Two!" with a wide grin. "I was still in batting practice," Reggie said after the game. "That's how I felt."[7]

Randolph recalled years later, "Once he hit the second home run, I knew he was going to hit another one, because he was in such a good groove."[8] With his two home runs, he had knocked Hooton and Sosa out of the game. The score was now 7-3, and for all intents and purposes the Dodgers were finished.

Jackson led off the bottom of the eighth, facing knuckleballer Charlie Hough. The Yankee Stadium crowd was anticipating another home run, but Hough had other plans. Hough apparently thought he might get him out, but catcher Steve Yeager lamented, "It was a knuckler, a perfect pitch for him to hit."[9] Jackson slammed Hough's first pitch high and deep and over the center-field wall. Jackson stood at home plate for several seconds, admiring the titanic moonshot. "I hit knuckleball pitchers very well and I couldn't believe

they had brought in Charlie Hough. He threw me a Hit-Me knuckleball and I dropped a bomb...."[10]

Howard Cosell, part of the ABC-TV broadcasting crew, was in awe: "What??!!" he shouted, as the ball left the yard. Then, as Jackson rounded the bases: "Ooohh, what a blow! What a way to top it off! Forget about who the most valuable player is in the World Series! How this man has responded to pressure! Oh, what a beam on his face! How can you blame him? He's answered the whole world!" As Jackson's teammates mobbed him in the dugout, Cosell continued: "What are they all thinking now? After all the furor, after all the hassling, it came down to this!"[11]

Red Smith, writing in the *New York Times*, was a little more poetic: "This one didn't take the shortest distance between two points. Straight out from the plate the ball streaked, not toward the neighborly stands in right but on a soaring arc toward the unoccupied bleachers in dead center, where the seats are blacked out to give batters a background. Up the white speck climbed, dwindling, diminishing, until it settled at last halfway up those empty stands, probably 450 feet away."[12]

As Reggie rounded the bases, he "felt like I was running on clouds. Certainly, it was one of my greatest moments."[13] The only comparison, he wrote later, was being inducted into the Hall of Fame in 1993.

Jackson headed for the Yankee dugout, where all of his teammates – with whom he had a difficult relationship – reached out to shake his hand and hug him. Jackson looked over at the dugout camera, held up three fingers, and said, "That's three, Mom!"[14]

As chants of "Reg-gie, Reg-gie, Reg-gie" rolled through the stadium, the man himself emerged from the dugout again to doff his helmet and salute the crowd.

"That was a helluva pitch," Lasorda admitted. "When I seen him hit that pitch that far I seen the greatest performance I ever seen in a World Series."[15] Who could argue with Lasorda? In two World Series games, Jackson had hit four consecutive home runs, on four swings, against four different pitchers. His three shots in Game Six had all come on the first pitch of the at-bat. At the time, only Babe Ruth had ever hit three home runs in a World Series game, having done the deed twice, in 1926 and 1928 (As of this writing, the feat has since been equaled by Albert Pujols in 2011 and Pablo Sandoval in 2012.). Jackson's five home runs in a single Series are still a record (Chase Utley also hit five in the six-game 2009 World Series).

Torrez caught the final out of the contest, a popup of an attempted bunt by pinch-hitter Lee Lacy. Yankees fans stormed the field, overwhelming police officers. Jackson shoved his glasses in his pocket, took off his helmet and tucked it under his arm like a football, and started weaving through the crowd like the fullback he had been at Arizona State University. Without glasses, he had poor depth perception, and knocked over a fan in his drive to the dugout.[16]

The final was Yankees 8, Dodgers 4. For the first time since 1962, the New York Yankees were the champions of baseball. And Reggie Jackson had led them there in a World Series display for the ages.[17]

Red Smith wrote: "In his last times at bat, this Hamlet in double-knits scored seven runs, made six hits and five home runs and batted in six runs for a batting average of .667 compiled by day and by night on two sea-coasts 3,000 miles and three time zones apart. Shakespeare wouldn't attempt a curtain scene like that if he was plastered."[18]

SOURCES

In addition to the sources cited in the Notes, the author consulted Baseball-almanac.com and Baseball-reference.com.

https://www.baseball-reference.com/boxes/NYA/NYA197710180.shtml

https://www.retrosheet.org/boxesetc/1977/B10180NYA1977.htm

NOTES

1   Roger Kahn, *October Men* (New York: Harcourt, 2004), 165.

2   SiriusXM, "Reggie Jackson Remember His 3-Homer Game in '77 World Series," YouTube video, 3:30. http://www.youtube.com/watch?v=upyOTrEtDOk. Accessed January 29, 2014.

3   Kahn, 167.

4   George A. King III, "The Homers That Made Reggie 'Mr. October' – The Jackson 3," NYPost.com, http://nypost.com/2004/11/19/the-homers-that-made-reggie-mr-october-the-jackson-3/, accessed January 29, 2014.

5   Reggie Jackson with Kevin Baker, *Becoming Mr. October* (New York: Doubleday, 2013), 178-179.

6   King.

7   Kahn, 168.

8   ARCHSENTINEL1, "NEW YORK YANKEE GREAT MR. REGGIE JACKSON HITS 3 (4) HOME RUNS 1977 WORLD SERIES 11-22-12," YouTube video, 3:32. http://www.youtube.com/watch?v=IoQBkBJkiGw. Accessed January 29, 2014. Removed from YouTube.

9   Lowell Reidenbaugh, "Reggie Reigns Supreme, And So Do Yankees," *The Sporting News*, November 5, 1977: 7.

10   King.

11   MLB. YouTube video. https://www.youtube.com/watch?v=LZNTzxVNv24

12   Quoted in Cecilia Tan, *The 50 Greatest Yankee Games* (Hoboken, New Jersey, John Wiley & Sons, 2005), 143.

13   *Becoming Mr. October*, 182.

14   *Becoming Mr. October*, 183.

15   Kahn, 168.

16   Jackson's frantic run to safety can be seen on a video posted to YouTube by MLB. https://www.youtube.com/watch?v=dnLR9Ln4hqo

17   It should be noted for the record that on Opening Day 1978 at Yankee Stadium (in the sixth game of the young season, New York having started on the road), Jackson hit a home run with two men on in the first inning, against Wilbur Wood of the Chicago White Sox, on a 2-0 pitch. That made for an astonishing four consecutive home runs at Yankee Stadium, on four swings.

18   Tan, 145.

HOW SWEET IT IS!
THE REGGIE BAR MAKES ITS DEBUT

April 13, 1978:
New York Yankees 4, Chicago White Sox 2,
at Yankee Stadium

By Rich D'Ambrosio

While playing for the Oakland A's in 1976, Reggie Jackson once commented that if he played in New York, they would name a candy bar after him.[1] Jackson must have been prescient because that is exactly what happened, and that confectionery treat would make a big contribution to the dramatic lore of Yankee Stadium.

A free agent after the 1976 season, Jackson signed a five-year, $2.96 million contract with the Yankees and proved he was well worth the investment, hitting .286 with 32 home runs (which led the American League) and 110 RBIs. In the World Series against the Dodgers, Jackson hit five homers, four of which came on consecutive swings (one in Game Five at Dodger Stadium and three in Game Six at Yankee Stadium) as the Yankees won their first World Series championship in 15 years. After the Series, the Reggie Bar was born.

Only one player in baseball history to that point had his name on candy bar – Babe Ruth. The Curtiss Candy Company brought out the Baby Ruth bar in 1921. So that it would not have to pay royalties to the Babe, it asserted that the bar was named after nineteenth-century President Grover Cleveland's daughter Ruth.

The same Curtiss Candy Company (at this point owned by Standard Brands) produced the Reggie Bar in 1978. The Reggie Bar was actually a large patty filled with peanuts and caramel and covered in chocolate. What made the candy extra-special was the attractive orange wrapper with Jackson's image and the large REGGIE label. The candy was advertised heavily in television ads that featured Jackson himself saying, "Reggie, you taste pretty good."[2]

After a disappointing road trip to Texas and Milwaukee to open the 1978 season (losing four of five games), the Yankees returned home on Thursday afternoon, April 13, to face the Chicago White Sox before a crowd of 44,667 (all of whom were handed a Reggie Bar upon entering). Before the game, Yankee heroes Mickey Mantle and Roger Maris raised the 1977 World Series Championship flag. It was Maris's first appearance at the Stadium since he was traded in 1966.

Ron Guidry was the starting pitcher for the Yankees. It was his second start of the season after pitching seven innings on Opening Day in Texas. Starting for the White Sox was veteran Wilbur Wood, who had lost his first outing, against Boston, four days earlier despite pitching a complete game. The Red Sox were off to a fast start, having won four of their first five games.

The Yankees scored three runs in the first inning. Willie Randolph led off with a walk and Mickey Rivers

Courtesy of the National Baseball Hall of Fame.

Many Reggie Bars handed out to fans ended up on the field as the guy in the picture homered in his first at-bat.

singled. Thurman Munson struck out and Jackson came to the plate. With the count 3-and-1, Jackson hit a long homer to right field, giving the Yankees a 3-1 lead. The fans went wild. "Like biblical manna, (Reggie) candy bars rained from the heavens at Yankee Stadium," declared a sportswriter,[3] referring to the fact that more than 500 fans threw the candy onto the field to show their appreciation for Jackson, who had just homered in his fourth straight plate appearance (and fourth consecutive swing) at The Stadium. It was the perfect marketing ploy for the Reggie Bar. The game was delayed five minutes as the grounds crew and 20 youngsters from the left-field stands scooped up the candy bars.

Despite the fans' good intentions. PA announcer Bob Sheppard told the crowd, "The Yankees can understand your enthusiasm in the last half-inning. However, we ask you once again, in the name of good sportsmanship, to refrain from throwing anything on the field. Thank you."[4] The White Sox scored two runs in the second when Eric Soderholm doubled and Wayne Nordhagen, Don Kessinger and Junior Moore singled, making the score 3-2.

Wood settled down and his knuckleball baffled the Yankees, who managed just four singles from the third inning to the eighth. The Yankees got another run in the eighth on a sacrifice fly by Bucky Dent, making the score 4-2. In the meantime, Guidry went the distance for the Yankees, allowing 10 hits while striking out four to earn the first win of what would turn out to be a spectacular 1978 season for the left-hander.

After the game Jackson said he thought the fans didn't like the Reggie Bar. White Sox manager Bob Lemon grumbled, "Must be some great candy bar if they throw it instead of eating it. They ought to advertise it as the candy bar built for throwing."[5] Yankees manager Billy Martin had a different take: "Naw, they were throwing sweets. It shows you we have sweet fans. Wait until the next time we have a full house. I'm going to collect them all by myself and open a candy store. And I'll sell them for a nickel less with a label on them that says, 'These candy bars were thrown once.'"[6]

Jackson focused more on the significance of the day for the Yankees and himself: "It's fun now. You're damn right it's fun. We're back home, we're on the right track. And it's better to be 2-4 than 1-5. Today was special for me. You see the championship flag, Mantle and Maris, everything. Roger told me several times they ran him out of town. They almost did that to me last year. I never want to go through another year like last year. Right now, mentally, I'm happy."[7]

The Reggie Bar was popular and reportedly made $11 million in the New York area alone in 1978, due in part to the success of the Yankees. Despite its popularity, the Reggie Bar had a short life. It was pulled off the market in 1981 during a dispute with the Securities and Exchange Commission. In the late 1990s Clark Candies briefly reissued the bar, but it disappeared shortly afterward.

SOURCES

In addition to the sources cited in the Notes, the author used the following websites:

https://classicnewyorkhistory.com/history-of-the-baby-ruth-bar-and-reggie-bar/

https://www.retrosheet.org/boxesetc/1978/B04130NYA1978.htm

NOTES

1   "Reggie Jackson quotes," baseballalmanac.com. https://www.baseball-almanac.com/quotes/quojackr.shtml, accessed September 20, 2022.

2   "Reggie Candy Bar 1978 Commercial," YouTube.com., https://www.youtube.com/watch?v=lLO62LkosDI, accessed July 25, 2022.

3   Dick Young, "Bars Are Hurled Down Upon Reggie," *New York Daily News*, April 14, 1978: C26.

4   Reggie Jackson Recalls Yankees Fans Throwing Reggie! Bars on Field at 1978 Yankee Stadium Opener, YouTube.com, https://www.youtube.com/watch?v=LYV4sziN2Vk, accessed July 25, 2022.

5   Steve Jacobson, "Yanks' Opening-Day Production," *Newsday* (Long Island, New York), April 14, 1978: 138.

6   Al Mari, "A Real Sweet Home Opener," *Yonkers* (New York) *Herald Statesman,* April 14, 1978: 23.

7   Al Mari, "Reggie Basks in the Limelight," *Yonkers Herald Statesman*, April 14, 1978: 23.

YANKEES OUTSLUG ROYALS IN ALCS GAME THREE

October 6, 1978:
New York Yankees 6, Kansas City Royals 5,
at Yankee Stadium

By Ed Gruver

American League umpire **Ron Luciano** relished pulse-quickening pitcher-batter confrontations. It was when working behind home plate in those moments that Luciano wished he didn't have to call balls and strikes, preferring instead to savor the situation.[1]

The beginning of Game Three of the 1978 American League Championship Series in Yankee Stadium provided such a confrontation between two future Hall of Famers. **George Brett** was leading off for the Western Division champion Kansas City Royals. Jim "Catfish" Hunter was on the mound for the Eastern Division champs, the New York Yankees. An audience of 55,445 was filling up the big ballpark in the Bronx for the 3:35 P.M. start.

Brett, in the Royals' powder-blue road uniform, settled into the batter's box. Luciano knew the routine of Kansas City's left-handed hitter. Brett would take "three or four easy practice swings, then stiffen his shoulders, cock his bat and glare out at the pitcher."[2]

Luciano considered Hunter the finest control pitcher he'd ever seen: "He was so good he could pick the sprinkles off an ice cream cone from the pitcher's mound."[3]

Luciano had been a big-league umpire since 1970 and had worked many of Hunter's games when Catfish wore the gaudy green, gold, and white of the Oakland A's dynasty and then the classic pinstripes of the Yankees after becoming baseball's first free agent on December 31, 1975.[4]

Luciano was aware that Hunter would throw his first pitch over the outside black edge of the plate. If Luciano called it a strike, the Cat would aim his next offering another inch outside. "If he got that one," Luciano said, "he'd go out another five-eighths of an inch, always moving just a hair further outside."[5]

Luciano thought Hunter tended at times to get lazy with his fastball and give up home runs. But not just ordinary home runs. "Majestic home runs," said Luciano. "Mammoth shots. Launchings that would have made a space-director happy."[6]

Three pitches into the game, Brett launched a deep drive into right field. On the Yankees' television station, WPIX Channel 11, announcer and former Yankees great **Phil Rizzuto** knew the ball was gone. "It is way in the upper deck!"[7]

Of the 16 homers Hunter surrendered during the 1978 regular season, 10 had come in the first two innings.

Hunter's pitch was in the middle of the plate. Baltimore Orioles ace **Jim Palmer** provided the color analysis on ABC-TV and said that if Catfish didn't locate the ball where he wanted to, he would not win.

Thurman Munson's eighth-inning home run proved the game winner.

"He doesn't throw like he used to," Palmer said of the 32-year-old Hunter. "Not many people do when you've thrown 3,300 innings like he has."[8]

Hunter started the 1978 season with a sore right shoulder and was on the disabled list twice. He helped fuel the Yankees' stirring comeback by winning nine of his 11 decisions. He pitched poorly in the regular-season finale against Cleveland but had worked on three days' rest rather than his customary four. Still, Hunter was a proven big-game player, having earned eight postseason victories.

"A money pitcher," said Palmer. "Couldn't think of a better pitcher to have out there if you needed to win a big game."[9]

New York needed to win this big game, the best-of-five series being tied 1-1. Hunter escaped further damage in the first inning and longtime teammate Reggie Jackson tied the game when he led off the bottom of the second with a home run off Paul Splittorff. The Royals' southpaw had pitched well against the Yankees in past playoffs, going a combined 2-0 in the 1976 and 1977 ALCS. He was 0-2 against New York in the '78 regular season, but he was a 19-game winner who had won eight of his last 12 decisions entering the postseason.

Palmer informed viewers that Splittorf changed speeds on his pitches and had a good fastball, curve, and slider. Splittorf's 3-and-1 delivery found the middle of the plate, however, and Jackson ripped a high drive into the right-field seats. On WPIX, Rizzuto issued his patented "Holy Cow!" and called Jackson "unbelievable" in the month of October.[10]

The Royals regained the lead in the top of the third, Brett scraping the sky with his second solo homer, a 400-foot-plus blast to right-center field. The Yankees tied it again in the next inning, Jackson scoring Thurman Munson from second base with a single to center field. An error on Lou Piniella's single sent Jackson home with New York's first lead at 3-2. Piniella sought to score on a fly to left by Graig Nettles but was ruled out at home plate on a controversial call by Luciano. Piniella put forth a passionate argument, which didn't surprise Luciano.

"Piniella," he said, "only argues on days ending in 'y.'"[11]

When the Yankees took the field in the next inning, Luciano said, Munson told him, "You really screwed up that time. … Don't worry. I'll get you off the hook."[12]

The Royals tied it again in the fifth, Brett leading off with his third homer of the game to right field,

equaling the LCS record set by Pittsburgh first baseman Bob Robertson against San Francisco in Game Two of the 1971 NLCS. Hunter said later that while Brett's feat was noteworthy, it typified his style of pitching: "three dingers with nobody on base, no other runs."[13]

Reggie Jackson agreed. "Cat will do that. He'll give up homers with no one on."[14]

Watching from the Yankees dugout, southpaw ace Ron Guidry knew age and injuries had robbed Hunter of some of the velocity on his pitches. Still, Guidry marveled at the Cat's guile and grit.

"There was a time nobody could match his pitching arsenal," Guidry said. "Even in his later years, with diminishing stuff, he could get guys out because he was so dang smart on the mound and knew how to work hitters. Pitchers like me could learn a lot just by watching him pitch."[15]

Kansas City manager Whitey Herzog agreed and considered Hunter a mound master in the mold of Yankees great Whitey Ford.[16]

Jackson's sacrifice fly to center field in the sixth scored Roy White to reclaim the lead. Guidry believed Game Three had become a battle between two greats – Brett and Jackson. Each time Brett gave KC the lead in odd-numbered innings, Jackson retaliated in even-numbered innings.[17]

Hunter left after six innings owning a 4-3 lead and was replaced by reliever Rich "Goose" Gossage. KC came back in the eighth to tie the game for the fourth time. Amos Otis led off with a double and scored on a single to left by Darrell Porter. The Royals retook the lead when a single by Clint Hurdle sent Porter to third and Al Cowens scored him on a groundout.

Back came the Yankees in the bottom of the inning, White lining a one-out single to center. The right-handed-hitting Munson had doubled and singled in his two previous at-bats against Splittorf, so Herzog summoned righty reliever Doug Bird.

Injuries limited Munson's power production in 1978; he hit just six homers in the regular season. But he was the Yankees' first captain since Lou Gehrig for a reason, and Guidry felt the reason was that Munson was a man who led by example: "He led by playing damn near every game even when he was aching. He led by demanding excellence not just from himself but from the 24 other guys in the clubhouse."[18]

Leading by example, Munson muscled a high, 2-and-0 fastball over the left-center-field wall and into Monument Park to put New York back in front, 6-5.

Varying estimates put Munson's homer at 410 to 440 feet. "Crushed it," Keith Jackson said on ABC-TV.[19]

Reggie Jackson called it "the *shot* that decided the ball game." When Munson crossed home plate he growled at Luciano, "Pulled your ass out of the fire."[20]

Luciano recalled Munson grinning and issuing a sarcastic "You're welcome." Luciano responded by telling Thurman, "Lucky shot."[21]

It was Munson's first homer in 52 games, and the roar of the crowd caused Yankees broadcaster Bill White to exclaim, "Thurm Munson coming through in the clutch!"[22]

Guidry agreed: "In big spots, [Munson] did what winners do, and what no creaky knees could stop him from doing."[23]

"Last year I came in and struck him out," said Bird. "Things didn't work out so well this time."[24]

Herzog lamented the Royals' having to relive their recent past of playoff failures against the Yankees. "What it came down to was the same old thing – we couldn't get their big hitters out when we had to with the game on the line."[25]

Gossage retired the Royals in order in the ninth inning, the Goose's fiery fastballs providing the final flourish in a classic contest.

SOURCES

Along with sources cited in the Notes, Baseball-Reference.com, and Retrosheet.org were consulted by the author for additional information on players and teams.

https://www.baseball-reference.com/boxes/NYA/NYA197810060.shtml

https://www.retrosheet.org/boxesetc/1978/B10060NYA1978.htm

NOTES

1   Ron Luciano and David Fisher, *The Umpire Strikes Back* (New York: Bantam Books, New York, 1982), 132.

2   Luciano, 225.

3   Luciano, 114.

4   Baseballhall.org.

5   Luciano, 114.

6   Luciano, 114.

7   WPIX television broadcast, October 6, 1978.

8   ABC television broadcast, October 6, 1978.

9   ABC television broadcast, October 6, 1978.

10   WPIX television broadcast, October 6, 1978.

11   Luciano, *The Umpire Strikes Back*, 134.

12   Luciano, 103

13   Jim "Catfish" Hunter and Armen Keteyian, *My Life in Baseball* (New York: McGraw Hill Book Company, 1988), 194.

14   Reggie Jackson with Bill Libby, *Reggie* (Chicago: Playboy Press, 1975), 208.

15   Ron Guidry with Andrew Beaton, *Gator: My Life in Pinstripes* (New York: Crown Archetype, 2018), 110.

16   Guidry, 110.

17   Guidry, 120.

18   Guidry, 120.

19   ABC television broadcast, October 6, 1978.

20   Reggie Jackson and Kevin Baker, *Becoming Mr. October* (New York: Doubleday, 2013), 277.

21   Luciano, 104.

22   WPIX television broadcast, October 6, 1978.

23   Guidry, 120.

24   Mike DeArmond, "Brett: We're Not Out of It Yet," *Kansas City Times*, October 7, 1978: 1D.

25   Del Black, "Yankees Force Royals to Relive Past," *Kansas City Times*," October 7, 1978: 1D.

YANKEES TIE WORLD SERIES WITH ONE EXTRA-BASE HIT AND ONE EXCESSIVE HIP

October 14, 1978:
New York Yankees 4, Los Angeles Dodgers 3 (10 innings), at Yankee Stadium
Game Four of the 1978 World Series

By Gordon Gattie

Heavy clouds hung over Yankee Stadium before Game Four of the 1978 World Series. The Los Angeles Dodgers led the New York Yankees two games to one in the best-of-seven series. Although Graig Nettles' defensive heroics from the previous night lightened New Yorkers' moods,[1] the afternoon's forecast for occasional showers and the tarp covering the infield dampened their spirits.

The Dodgers won the first two games in Los Angeles. Dusty Baker's second-inning solo homer and Davey Lopes's two round-trippers enabled the Dodgers to build an early 7-0 lead and cruise to an 11-5 Game One win.[2] Ron Cey's sixth-inning three-run homer gave the Dodgers a lead they didn't relinquish during their 4-3 victory in Game Two.[3] The Series shifted to New York for the next three games, with Ron Guidry's complete-game eight-hitter and Nettles' spectacular defense sparking New York to win Game Three, 5-1.

The American League champion Yankees had returned to the World Series by defeating the Kansas City Royals three games to one in the AL Championship Series. All-Star catcher Thurman Munson directed the Yankees pitching staff, which posted an AL-low 3.18 team ERA and featured a historic season by Cy Young Award winner Guidry (25-3, 1.74 ERA, 248 strikeouts), 20-game winner Ed Figueroa, and AL saves leader Goose Gossage. First baseman Chris Chambliss, second baseman Willie Randolph, shortstop Bucky Dent, and third baseman Nettles composed the infield. Leadoff hitter Mickey Rivers and superstar Reggie Jackson paced the outfield. The Yankees overcame a 14-game deficit and manager Billy Martin's midseason resignation,[4] then won a dramatic one-game tiebreaker against the Boston Red Sox to reach the postseason.[5]

The National League champion Dodgers returned to the World Series by defeating the Philadelphia Phillies three games to one in the NL Championship Series. They were eager to atone for the previous season's World Series loss to the Yankees. The established Dodgers infield consisted of perennial All-Star corner infielders first baseman Steve Garvey and third baseman Cey, with second baseman Lopes and shortstop Bill Russell hitting first and second in the batting order. Slugging outfielder Reggie Smith led the offense with 29 home runs and a .942 OPS. The pitching staff, which led all major-league staffs with a 3.12 team ERA, included Burt Hooton, who finished second in the NL Cy Young Award voting, future Hall of Famer Don Sutton, and closer Terry Forster. Second-year manager Tommy Lasorda piloted the Dodgers.

Figueroa celebrated his 30th birthday by starting for New York in Game Four. The right-hander amassed a 20-9 record with a 2.99 ERA over 253 innings during the regular season, but struggled during the postseason. In the ALCS, Figueroa was pulled in the second inning of New York's lone loss. During the World Series opener, he allowed three earned runs over 1⅔ innings and was charged with the loss. During a pregame interview, Yankees manager Bob Lemon defended his decision to start Figueroa in spite of his postseason struggles, commenting, "Well, he's one of my best pitchers. We wouldn't be here unless Ed won 20 ballgames. I think anybody can have an offday with their control, and that's been his only problem."[6]

Tommy John started for Los Angeles. The 35-year-old left-hander was 17-10 with a 3.30 ERA over 213 innings during the regular season. He fired a four-hit shutout during the NLCS Game Two and won the World Series opener, allowing three runs on eight hits in 7⅔ innings. He was three years removed from the revolutionary arm surgery that now bears his name. John's pitching repertoire included a sinking fastball, a curveball, and a cut fastball.[7]

Encountering a muddy infield and soft outfield, neither team took hitting or fielding practice. As the clouds dissipated, the 56,445 attendees applauded each team's rosters and Eleanor Gehrig's ceremonial first pitch.

Lopes, who homered off Figueroa during Game One, worked a full count before flying out to start the game. Russell beat out a bunt on his first pitch. Smith walked. Garvey lined out to right fielder Lou Piniella. Without breaking his stride, Piniella threw to Chambliss at first base, but couldn't double off Smith. Chambliss fired to second base after a short hesitation, doubling off Russell, who had already rounded third base, to end the inning.

Paul Blair led off for New York. With an 0-and-2 count, Blair's tapper down the third-base line allowed him to reach first. He advanced to second on Roy White's groundout. Munson, nursing a sore shoulder, singled to right. Smith cleanly fielded Munson's grounder and immediately threw a single-bounce strike to Steve Yeager at home plate, who firmly planted his left foot, blocked the plate, and tagged out Blair. Jackson grounded out to complete a scoreless but eventful first inning.

Figueroa's control problems surfaced during the second inning. Cey singled on a 3-and-1 pitch and Rick Monday earned a one-out walk on four pitches. Figueroa escaped unharmed as Bill North flied out and Yeager popped out. In the Yankee half, John induced three consecutive groundouts.

Nettles made another outstanding defensive play when he backhanded Lopes's line drive to open the third, preventing a potential extra-base hit. During the Yankees' half, Dent singled with one out. With Blair up, the expected showers arrived. After a 40-minute rain delay, the game resumed with Blair facing John. Blair popped out. White flied out.

Figueroa's control problems resurfaced. North grounded out on a high fastball to start the fifth inning. Yeager doubled on a 2-and-0 pitch. Lopes walked on five pitches. Russell clobbered a long fly ball down the left-field line that drifted foul, then struck out

swinging. Smith blasted a 1-and-0 offering into the right-field bleachers for a three-run home run. After five innings, Los Angeles led, 3-0.

Starting the sixth inning, right-handed sinkerballer Dick Tidrow relieved Figueroa and allowed a harmless single. John experienced his first trouble during the bottom half. White's one-out single dribbled just beyond Russell's glove. Munson walked on a full count. The crowd came alive as Jackson, representing the tying run, walked to home plate. His single to right, which narrowly missed Munson in the basepath, scored White with New York's first run.

With one out and runners on first and second, Piniella lined to short. Russell, anticipating a potential double play, knocked the ball down, scooped it, and stepped on second base to force out Jackson. But Russell's throw to first base plunked Jackson's hip and caromed past Garvey at first base.[8] During the ensuing confusion, Munson scored. Lasorda vigorously argued the call for several minutes, claiming Jackson intentionally interfered with the throw by standing in the basepath and using his hip to deflect the relay. Russell, charged with a throwing error, claimed Jackson's actions were intentional: "Reggie saw the ball coming. He moved right into it. That's interference."[9] Jackson countered, "[W]hen it hit Russell's glove, my instinct was to go back to first. Then he dropped it, and I didn't know where to go. I just froze."[10] When the dust cleared, Jackson's interference was ruled unintentional.[11] The Dodgers led, 3-2, with two outs and Piniella on first. But Nettles grounded out.

Tidrow retired six of the next seven batters while John in the seventh induced three consecutive groundouts for the second time.

Blair singled to start the eighth. Left-hander Forster relieved John.[12] The switch-hitting White sacrificed Blair to second. Munson fouled off the first two pitches, then doubled down the left-field line – New York's only extra-base hit – scoring Blair with the tying run as the enthusiastic crowd cheered. Jackson was hit by a pitch. Rookie sensation Bob Welch relieved Forster. Piniella popped out to Garvey in short right field, though Garvey and Lopes nearly collided. Nettles struck out.

Entering the ninth, Gossage relived Tidrow. Monday walked but didn't advance. During the bottom half, Welch set down the Yankees on two strikeouts and a fly out. The teams headed into extra innings.

During the 10th, the Dodgers were retired on 10 pitches as Russell flied out and Smith and Garvey struck out swinging. During the Yankees' half, leadoff man Mickey Rivers fouled out, then Welch walked White on a full count. Munson popped out to shortstop. Jackson, whose celebrated strikeout against Welch ended Game Two,[13] singled just beyond Lopes's outstretched glove, moving White into scoring position.

With the crowd chanting "Luuuuu," Piniella swung and missed at Welch's first pitch. On the next pitch, Piniella connected with a high outside fastball. His single into center field plated White with the winning run.[14] Euphoric Yankee fans continued yelling "Luuuuu" as the team celebrated. Piniella had disregarded Jackson's advice about facing Welch: "He was telling me to lay off the high ball – which I never do – and I'm glad I didn't."[15] In his autobiography, Piniella fondly recalled his historic hit, saying, "Winning a World Series game with a hit in the tenth inning is about as exciting a moment as I can remember."[16]

The World Series was tied at two games apiece. Gossage earned the win with two scoreless innings while Welch suffered the loss.

The Yankees routed the Dodgers 12-2 in Game Five, then clinched their 22nd World Series championship with a 7-2 Game Six victory. Bucky Dent won World Series MVP honors by hitting .417 with 7 RBIs.

ACKNOWLEDGMENTS

The author thanks Tara Krieger and Bill Nowlin for their feedback, Carl Riechers for his fact checking, Len Levin for his editing, and Lisa Gattie for her meaningful input.

SOURCES

Besides the sources cited in the Notes, the author consulted Baseball-Reference.com, Retrosheet.org, TheBaseballCube.com, and the following:

https://www.baseball-reference.com/boxes/NYA/NYA197810140.shtml.

https://www.retrosheet.org/boxesetc/1978/B10140NYA1978.htm.

Lyle, Sparky, and Peter Golenbock. *The Bronx Zoo* (New York: Crown Publishers, 1979).

MLB Film Room. *Piniella's game-winning single*. https://www.mlb.com/video/piniella-s-game-winning-single-c28159909. Accessed October 2, 2022.

MLB Film Room. *Reggie's hip deflects throw*. https://www.mlb.com/video/reggie-s-hip-deflects-throw-c28130223. Accessed October 1, 2022.

Munson, Thurman, and Martin Appel. *Thurman Munson* (New York: Coward, McCann & Geoghegan, Inc., 1979).

NOTES

1   Joe Donnelly, "Yanks' Stopper – Nettles," *Newsday* (Long Island, New York), October 14, 1978: 6.

2   Ross Newhan, "Dodgers Bomb the Bombers With 15 Hits," *Los Angeles Times*, October 11, 1978: Part III, 1.

3   Ross Newhan, "Cey Magnifique and So Is Welch," *Los Angeles Times*, October 12, 1978: Part III, 1.

4   Jack Lang, "Martin Exits in Tears: Don't Want to Hurt Team," *New York Daily News*, July 25, 1978: 100.

5   Jerome Holtzman, "Yankees Lucky … No One to Bat for Bucky," *Binghamton* (New York) *Press and Sun-Bulletin*, October 3, 1978: 1C.

6   1978 World Series, Game Four (Dodgers-Yankees) (NBC-Pt.1), https://www.youtube.com/watch?v=SeXfHi6VVx4. Accessed October 1, 2022.

7   Bill James and Rob Neyer, *The Neyer/James Guide to Pitchers: An Historical Compendium of Pitching, Pitchers, and Pitches* (New York: Fireside Books, 2004), 256.

8   Scott Ostler, "Dodgers Claim 'Dirty Pool,' 'Illegal Tactics," *Los Angeles Times*, October 15, 1978: Part III, 1.

9   Associated Press, "It's 2-2, Thanks to Piniella," *Binghamton Press and Sun-Bulletin*, October 15, 1978: 1B.

10   Greg Boeck, "Yankees Survive Dogfight; Dodgers Howl," *Rochester* (New York) *Democrat and Chronicle*, October 15, 1978: 6D.

11   Larry Felser, "Yankees Win, 4-3, on Piniella's Hit," *Buffalo News*, October 15, 1978: B1. During the sixth inning's play involving Jackson and the potential interference call, if first-base umpire Frank Pulli ruled Jackson's interference intentional, Piniella would have been ruled out and the inning over without the Yankees scoring their second run.

12   Tommy John pitched his last game for Dodgers that evening, joining the Yankees as a free agent in November.

13   Ross Newhan, "Yanks Get Even on Old Hip-and-Run Play," *Los Angeles Times*, October 15, 1978: Part III, 1.

14   Piniella hadn't faced Welch prior to this plate appearance. Piniella turned to Jackson for advice; one piece was comparing Welch with Jim Palmer (Felser, "Yankees Win, 4-3, on Piniella's Hit"). The second piece was not swinging at high fastballs. The latter tidbit Piniella ignored. (Mike Shalin, "Lou Turns Deaf Ear To Jackson's Advice," *Buffalo News*, October 15, 1978: B1.)

15   "Lou Turns Deaf Ear to Jackson's Advice."

16   Lou Piniella and Maury Allen, *Sweet Lou* (New York: G.P. Putnam's Sons, 1986), 206.

MATTINGLY OVERTAKES TEAMMATE WINFIELD FOR BATTING AVERAGE TITLE ON SEASON'S LAST DAY

September 30, 1984:
New York Yankees 9, Detroit Tigers 2,
at Yankee Stadium

By Richard Cuicchi

New York Yankees owner George Steinbrenner became the champion of player free agency and trade transactions, routinely looking past his top prospects to build out his roster. His 1984 team was built around free-agent acquisitions Dave Winfield, Don Baylor, Steve Kemp, and Phil Niekro, as well as Ken Griffey, Omar Moreno, Toby Harrah, and Butch Wynegar, who had been acquired through trades. Although the Yankees' highly prized prospect Don Mattingly was on the rise, no one expected him to have the type of campaign he would turn in during his first full season with the Yankees. He became involved in a fierce battle for the league batting average title with the veteran Winfield that wasn't settled until the last day of the season.

Mattingly had become one of the Yankees' most promising rookies since Bobby Murcer, Thurman Munson, and Roy White in the late 1960s. Since other recent prospects Willie McGee, Otis Nixon, and Fred McGriff had already been traded, Mattingly represented the Yankees' best hopes from within their farm system to help the team return to prominence. He had shown a propensity to hit for high averages (.349, .358, .316, and .315), as he progressed through the minors.

After posting a slash line of .340/.437/.598 with Triple-A affiliate Columbus in 1983, he was rewarded with a permanent job with the big-league Yankees by June 21. Splitting his time between first base and the outfield, he hit a respectable .283 in 91 games, with 4 home runs and 32 RBIs. The 23-year-old secured the full-time first-base job at the start of the 1984 season.

Winfield was in his 12th major-league season and fourth with the Yankees. He had been an All-Star in each of his three previous seasons, while capturing three Silver Slugger Awards. However, he was not known for high batting averages. He had hit over .300 only twice before, with back-to-back .308 seasons in 1978 and 1979 with San Diego.

Dave Winfield went 1-for-4 on the last day of the season to lose the batting title to teammate Don Mattingly, who went 4-for-5.

While Winfield and Mattingly were hitting well, the batting title race between them didn't become serious until the end of July.

Winfield had an exceptional month of June with a .476 average, which raised his season average to .368. He went hitless in only four games that month while he belted out multiple hits 15 times, including three games with five hits in each. By the All-Star break after July 8, he appeared to have an insurmountable 40-point lead over Mattingly (.370 to .330). Yet at the end of July his lead had diminished to only 7 points (Winfield dropped to .346 while Mattingly increased to .339.) Between August 17 and September 8, Winfield mounted another surge with a 20-game hitting streak that included a slash line of .427/532/.747. Yet on a calendar month basis, he had four months in which his batting average was below .300.

Mattingly was more consistent from month to month than Winfield throughout the season. His best came during August, when he hit .383. But then in September, both players experienced virtual slumps, when compared with the rest of their seasons. Mattingly hit .319, while Winfield hit .290.

By September 21, Mattingly had overtaken Winfield, .346 to .344, and they were nip-and-tuck through the rest of the season. The following table illustrates the closeness of the race and how the batting averages progressed during the week leading up to the final game.

Date	Mattingly	Winfield
9/24 (1)	.344 (1-for-4)	.341 (1-for-3)
9/24 (2)	.344 (2-for-5)	.341 (1-for-3)
9/25	.344 (1-for-3)	.342 (2-for-4)
9/26	.342 (0-for-4)	.342 (1-for-4)
9/27	.342 (1-for-3)	.341 (0-for-1)
9/28	.341 (1-for-4)	.342 (2-for-5)
9/29	.339 (0-for-3)	.341 (1-for-4)

The Yankees were tied with Boston for third place in the AL East going into the last day of the season. They had been out of contention for the division lead since April. Their opponent was the division-leading Detroit Tigers, who were completing the best season (104 wins) in franchise history.

A crowd of 30,602 showed up in Yankee Stadium for the season finale to see who would reign as the batting-average leader. Tigers rookie right-hander Randy O'Neal drew the starting assignment from manager Sparky Anderson. He had won his first two decisions

as a September call-up by the Tigers. Yankees manager Yogi Berra countered with rookie left-hander Dennis Rasmussen, who held an 8-6 record.

O'Neal was roughed up by the Yankees in the first inning; they scored three runs including one by Mattingly, who singled, and Winfield, who reached on a fielder's choice.

Mattingly led off the bottom of the third with a double and eventually scored, while Winfield drew a walk.

In the fourth, Mattingly again doubled for his third hit off O'Neal, scoring Andre Robertson, who had led off the inning with a single. Winfield got his first hit in the game, and Baylor doubled for the second time to score Mattingly and Winfield, making the score 7-1.

With the game seemingly well in hand in the fifth inning, attention turned toward the batting race. Mattingly batted in his third consecutive inning and was retired for the first time in the game by Tigers reliever Sid Monge on a fly out.

With the score 9-1 in the bottom of the sixth inning, Winfield flied out against Aurelio Lopez.

Mattingly got a bad-hop single to right off Willie Hernandez in his fifth at-bat in the eighth inning, while Winfield hit into a fielder's choice. The game ended with a final score of 9-2. Tigers second baseman Scott Earl, who thought he would catch the groundball on Mattingly's last at-bat, said, "I ranged over to get it, but at the last second it came up. I didn't have a chance to get my glove up, and it bounced over my glove. I was aware of their race, but it didn't matter to me who won it. If Winfield hit that same ball, the same thing would have happened. I just didn't have time to react. It took a bad hop."[1]

Mattingly's four hits increased his final batting average to .343, while Winfield finished at .340 on his lone hit.

"Someone said if I didn't get a hit the last time up and Winfield did, he'd have won by two-thousandths of a point," Mattingly said. "Right then I knew there was no way I could be a loser. Neither of us could be a loser. But I guess that's the American way – someone has to win and someone has to lose."[2] He added, "I never thought it would come down to the last at-bat. You couldn't write it any better. It's been a storybook year for me and it will be hard to duplicate.[3] However, if Mattingly hadn't made the last hit the correct calculation would have been .00053 (.34215 to .34162) difference in Winfield's favor.

When Winfield hit his groundball in his last at-bat in the eighth inning, forcing Mattingly out at second,

Mattingly first returned to the dugout and then re-emerged to meet Winfield at first base, where they shook hands and embraced. Berra sent Scott Bradley to pinch-run for Winfield, and the two hitting leaders walked off the field together. Mattingly said, "Dave has been a great person through this whole thing. He handled himself like a gentleman. I have great respect for him." Mattingly said he and Winfield had spoken a couple of weeks earlier and "agreed there was no need for friction" during their head-to-head battle.[4]

However, Bill Madden of the *New York Daily News* asserted that Winfield was not as amiable about the outcome of the batting race, noting that Winfield hastily checked out of his locker and exited a side door of the clubhouse in order to avoid teammates and reporters.[5]

The batting title was Mattingly's only one during his 14-year career, although he finished as runner-up (to Wade Boggs's .357) with a .352 mark two years later. It was the Yankees' first since Mickey Mantle's in 1956.

The Mattingly-Winfield duel was reminiscent of other years when teammates' competitions for the batting average title were settled on the last day of the season. Willie Mays won out over Giants teammate Don Mueller in 1954, and George Brett edged Royals teammate Hal McRae in 1976.

Mattingly followed his masterful 1984 season with an MVP year in 1985, when he batted .324 and led the league with 48 doubles and 145 RBIs. He was eventually named captain of the Yankees and was the face of the franchise until his retirement as a player in 1995.

SOURCES

In addition to the sources in the Notes, the author consulted:

Klein, Moss. "Will Berra Be Back in '85? Or Weaver?" *The Sporting News*, October 15, 1984: 23.

"Mattingly Nips Winfield for A.L. Batting Crown," *The Sporting News*, October 8, 1984: 32.

"Perfect Ending for Witt," *Detroit Free Press*, October 1, 1984: 1H.

NOTES

1   Murray Chass. "Mattingly Wins Title; Witt Pitches Perfect Game," *New York Times*, October 1, 1984: C1.

2   Chass.

3   Bill Madden. "Mattingly's Four Hits Nip Winfield for Title," *New York Daily News*, October 1, 1984: 41.

4   Chass.

5   Madden.

MATTINGLY SETS MVP TONE WITH WALK-OFF HOMER IN RECORD-TYING COMEBACK

May 13, 1985:
New York Yankees 9, Minnesota Twins 8,
at Yankee Stadium

By Jake Bell

In the days leading up to one of Yankee Stadium's most surprising comebacks, it was the visitors' ballpark that was making headlines. The previous week, the New York Yankees dropped a two-game series to the Minnesota Twins, and placed the blame on the Hubert H. Humphrey Metrodome's roof.

After New York fielders lost some routine fly balls against the unevenly lit dome, Yankees owner George Steinbrenner preemptively protested the second game.[1] Manager Billy Martin called the Metrodome a "Little League ballpark" and blasted Twins owner Carl Pohlad for being too cheap to "spend some money on some blue paint for the [expletive] ceiling."[2]

Martin's frustration was no doubt intensified because the losses broke a four-game winning streak that had lifted New York out of the American League East cellar. The disappointing start to the team's season had prompted the firing of manager Yogi Berra after 16 games, ushering in Martin's fourth stint as Yankees skipper. Martin wanted it made clear that the ballpark, not his team nor his "Billy-ball" approach, was at fault for the losses. "We were playing good baseball and we come in here and it looks like a circus," he complained.[3]

Another Yankee looking to prove that first Metrodome loss was a fluke was starting pitcher Ed Whitson. The high-priced offseason acquisition had been rocked for five runs on nine hits in only 1⅔ innings in Minneapolis, and two dome-induced hits were a key factor.

Looking for redemption in the Bronx, however, he quickly learned that the best-hitting team in the major leagues[4] could hit on the road as well.

The game had barely started when Whitson found himself down 1-0 with runners at the corners. The Twins' first three batters, Kirby Puckett, Mickey Hatcher, and Kent Hrbek, had all singled within his first six pitches The Twins scored a second run and a fourth single before Whitson escaped the inning.

Things got more grim for the Yankees when Minnesota starter Mike Smithson's first pitch smashed into Rickey Henderson's elbow. Once aboard, Henderson wasted no time in stealing second, then advancing to third on a Ken Griffey fly out. Henderson tried to score on a Don Mattingly fly ball to shallow center field, but was gunned down at home by Puckett.

Henderson then left the game for x-rays. His elbow had already been swelling, and on the attempt to score, he'd slammed it into the shin guard of catcher Mark Salas.[5]

In retaliation, Whitson opened the second inning by plunking Gary Gaetti in the hip, which cost him when Gaetti stole second and then scored on a pair of singles that ended Whitson's night.

Martin turned to former Twins reliever Don Cooper to stop the bleeding, but the righty struggled to locate his pitches. He allowed both inherited runners to score, including one on a wild pitch to Tom Brunansky, who then drew a walk. With two runners on, designated hitter Randy Bush clanged a deep fly off the right-field foul pole for his second home run in as many days[6] and an 8-0 Twins lead.

When the ninth batter of the inning, former Yankee Roy Smalley, mercifully slapped an inning-ending groundout toward first baseman Mattingly, many of the 15,136 in the stands were already taking up a taunting chorus of "Let's go Mets!" chants,[7] which intensified as the next three Yankee batters went down in order.

Martin made another call to the bullpen, where someone else had an axe to grind about the previous week's trip to Minnesota. The second game of the series was the reason right-hander Joe Cowley was available as a reliever in the first place. Much like Whitson before him, Cowley was shelled in the Metrodome, surrendering seven runs on six hits in 3⅔ innings. Martin was so upset by Cowley's performance that he wouldn't even come out of the dugout to pull his starter. "He showed me nothing. ... Cowley is going to the bullpen," Martin told reporters.[8]

Cowley held the Twins scoreless in the third, and then again in the fourth. Meanwhile, since drilling Henderson, Smithson had retired 10 straight batters before Mattingly finally got New York's first hit, a double to right field.

The defending AL batting champ had just three hits in his previous 25 at-bats, a slump that had dropped his batting average by almost 50 points, from .329 to .282, and started with a 1-for-10 showing at the Metrodome. Dave Winfield brought him home with a single, but Smithson seemed unfazed by his lead shrinking from eight runs to seven, and perhaps with good reason.

After all, a Yankees win on this night would require them to match the record for the team's greatest-ever comeback at Yankee Stadium.[9] In the ballpark's 62-year history, fans had seen their boys in pinstripes rally from an eight-run deficit only twice – both on consecutive Saturdays in 1933.[10]

After Smithson hurled a perfect fifth, momentum shifted drastically in the sixth. Bob Meacham, Omar Moreno, and Griffey strung together three singles to load the bases, and Meacham scored on Mattingly's fly ball. Winfield's second RBI single of the night drove home Moreno. But Smithson, still staked to a five-run lead, remained on cruise control.

Don Baylor knocked a grounder at third baseman Gaetti, who stepped on the bag for the unassisted out. Smithson only needed to retire Butch Wynegar, the light-hitting catcher who'd missed the previous night's game with the flu.[11]

Facing the right-hander, the switch-hitting Wynegar, who'd spent seven seasons in Minnesota,[12] batted lefty, allowing him to take advantage of Yankee Stadium's famous short porch in right field. He crushed a three-run homer into the bleachers, and suddenly New York was within two runs. Smithson took one more shot at ending the inning, but finally got the hook after walking Willie Randolph, which brought the tying run to the plate. Though reliever

Pete Filson got a quick groundout, the atmosphere in Yankee Stadium had changed.

Cowley responded by sitting down the Twins' 3-4-5 hitters on his way to retiring 12 straight. After the game, Martin would say the pitcher "did a complete 180"[13] in scattering five singles over seven scoreless innings, and reinstated him to the starting rotation.

New York mounted another threat after the seventh-inning stretch. Meacham reached first on a Gaetti throwing error, then got to second when pinch-hitter Henry Cotto singled. Both advanced on a groundout to first base by Mattingly.

With the tying run now in scoring position, Twins manager Billy Gardner pulled Filson for Ron Davis, the team's de facto stopper. The one-time Yankee All-Star silenced the Bronx crowd by striking out Winfield. In the eighth, he further crushed their hopes with a three-up-three-down inning.

Yankee fans got a glimmer of hope when Davis started the ninth by walking pinch-hitter Ron Hassey on four pitches.[14] He refocused and managed to get two more outs, but then walked Griffey, bringing Mattingly to the plate representing the winning run.

"I was just looking for a double, something to score Griff from first," Mattingly said later.[15] "The first pitch was a curve and it missed, so I just sat there waiting for a fastball."[16]

In the Twins dugout, Gardner grew concerned about his pitcher's control, but feared that pulling him could undermine Davis's confidence. He decided to give the veteran one more pitch, but pull him if it missed the strike zone.[17]

Davis didn't miss. He hurled a fastball right across the center of the plate.

"I had a pretty good feeling when I hit it," Mattingly recalled.[18] The ball rocketed over the right-field fence for a three-run, walk-off blast in a 9-8 comeback victory that also set the tone for what became an MVP season for Mattingly and proved a turning point for both teams.[19]

Mattingly batted .330 with a .972 OPS from that point forward, belting 33 more home runs[20] and getting 123 of his league-leading 145 RBIs. He won the American League MVP Award in a landslide.[21]

The win was the first of 85 that the Yankees earned the rest of the way, the most in the American League. Their 97-64 record, however, left them two games behind Toronto for the AL East pennant.

The Twins had come into the game questioning whether they were legitimate World Series contenders, and this loss seemed to be their answer. Minnesota won just five more times in May. Gardner was fired after they lost 21 of their next 32 games. Their 61 wins the rest of the season were fourth-worst in the AL.[22] They finished 77-85, tied with Oakland for fourth place in the AL West.

ACKNOWLEDGMENT

Katie Sharp of Sports Reference LLC provided indispensable help in finding the biggest Yankee Stadium comebacks.

SOURCES

In addition to the sources cited in the Notes, the author accessed Baseball-Reference.com, Stathead.com, and Retrosheet.org.

https://www.baseball-reference.com/boxes/NYA/NYA198505130.shtml

https://www.retrosheet.org/boxesetc/1985/B05130NYA1985.htm

NOTES

1   Steinbrenner's protest contended that the Metrodome wasn't up to major-league standards, and he demanded that American League President Bobby Brown launch an investigation and "straighten out this situation." The protest was rejected, but the Twins announced the next day that 49 new 1,000-watt ceiling lights would be installed. The Twins insisted that the Yankees' protest was not a factor in the renovation, that the $100,000 contract for the work had been signed two weeks earlier with the goal of completing the work in time for the All-Star Game. United Press International, "Let There Be Lights! Metrodome Adds 49," *New York Daily News*, May 10, 1985.

2   Bill Madden, "Yanks Find No Home in the Dome, 8-6," *New York Daily News*, May 8, 1985: 47.

3   Tom Pedulla, "Billy Blows His Top," *Yonkers* (New York) *Herald Statesman*, May 8, 1985: C5.

4   Before the May 13 game, Minnesota's team batting average was .297 with an OPS of .833, and Puckett and Hatcher ranked first and second in hits. For comparison, the Oakland A's were second in both categories, batting .274 as a team with a .770 team OPS.

5   Though the x-rays showed no break, Henderson's elbow would force him to miss three of the Yankees' next four games. He pinch-ran and scored the game-winning run against the Texas Rangers on May 16, but didn't return to the starting lineup until May 18 in Anaheim.

6   The previous night, he'd belted a grand slam against the Orioles, giving him seven RBIs in just over 24 hours.

7   Fred Kerber, "Mattingly Magic," *New York Daily News*, May 14, 1985: 59. Tom Pedulla, "Mattingly HR Stuns Twins," *Mamaroneck* (New York) *Daily Times*, May 14, 1985: C1.

8   Bill Madden, "HRs Put Cowley on Relief," *New York Daily News*, May 10, 1985: 59. Cowley was also an odds-on favorite for demotion to Triple-A Columbus to make room on the roster when reliever Rich Bordi came off the 15-day disabled list.

9   The Yankees had overcome nine-run deficits in their history, but those comebacks occurred in other ballparks.

10   In both cases, New York found itself down 11-3 before bouncing back to win, 15-11 over the Chicago White Sox on May 27 and 17-11 against the Philadelphia Athletics on June 3. The biggest comeback in Yankee Stadium's history was a nine-run turnaround by the White Sox, who'd found themselves down 12-3 after seven innings on July 28, 1931, but plated 11 runs in the eighth and won 14-12. The Yankees eventually matched that mark on June 26, 1987, overcoming a 9-0 Boston Red Sox start to win 12-11. They equaled the team record on May 16, 2006, with a 14-13 win over the Texas Rangers after trailing 9-0.

11   Tom Pedulla, "Yanks Beat Themselves," *Mamaroneck Daily Times,* May 13, 1985: D4.

12   As a Twin, Wynegar was a two-time All-Star and a runner-up to Mark Fidrych for 1976 Rookie of the Year.

13   Kerber, "Mattingly Magic."

14   Rex Hudler ran for Hassey.

15   Tom Verducci, "Yankees' Rally Wins Fans Over," *Newsday* (Long Island, New York), May 14, 1985: 102.

16   Kerber, "Mattingly Magic."

17   "[If] he threw one more ball … he was gone." Howard Sinker, "Twins Fall on Home Run in 9th Again," *Minneapolis Star Tribune,* May 14, 1985: 1D.

18   Kerber, "Mattingly Magic."

19   This was the fourth consecutive game in which the Twins' opponent hit a ninth-inning home run, and the third of which was a walk-off. The previous three all came off the bat of Fred Lynn in Baltimore. On May 10, Davis surrendered a solo shot to Lynn in a tie game, giving Baltimore a 6-5 win. On May 11, Davis was brought in to preserve a 2-1 lead, but gave up singles to Cal Ripken Jr. and Eddie Murray. Curt Wardle replaced Davis and gave up a home run to Lynn for a 4-2 Orioles victory. Then on May 12, starter Frank Viola took a 7-0 shutout into the ninth; Ripken doubled, Murray walked, and Lynn parked another one. In this case, the Twins held on to win 7-3.

20   A career-best 35.

21   Mattingly garnered 23 of the 28 first-place votes. George Brett received the other five. Henderson, who led the league in bWAR, finished third.

22   The teams with fewer wins were Milwaukee, Texas, and Cleveland, which finished second-to-last in the AL East, last in the AL West, and last in the AL East, respectively.

MATTINGLY'S RECORD SIXTH GRAND SLAM SINKS RED SOX

September 29, 1987:
New York Yankees 6, Boston Red Sox 0,
at Yankee Stadium

By Ray Danner

For a player who had excelled so consistently for the prior three seasons, Don Mattingly's 1987 was unusually streaky. After leading the American League in hitting in 1984 and finishing first and second respectively in the 1985 and 1986 MVP voting, Mattingly got out of the gate slowly, batting .175 without a home run in the season's first nine games.

On a getaway day in the Bronx, Thursday, May 14, against the Texas Rangers, Mattingly entered the game slashing .240/.318/.411 with just three home runs through 33 games. He hit his first career grand slam that afternoon, a fourth-inning blast off Mike Mason.[1] He hit a three-run home run the next night in Seattle, along with three hits and five RBIs, to get his season on track. With two hits at Yankee Stadium on June 1, he topped .300 to stay.

Mattingly's season was interrupted in early June by a 20-day stint on the disabled list, the first visit of the 26-year-old's career. The break divided his season into two halves, and when he returned to action on June 24, he resumed his annual pursuit of crushing American League pitching, batting .336/.371/.601 over his final 88 games with 24 doubles, 24 home runs, and 79 RBIs.[2]

His second grand slam came in Toronto on June 29, against John Cerutti in a 15-14 win. On July 8 Mattingly began one of the more remarkable hitting feats in baseball history when he went deep in eight straight games, matching Pittsburgh Pirate Dale Long's accomplishment in 1956.[3]

From July 8 to July 18, Mattingly went 17-for-37 (.460 batting average) with 10 home runs and 21 runs batted in. The streak included two more grand slams, in a July 10 victory against Joel McKeon of the White

Sox and a July 16 win in Texas against Charlie Hough and the Rangers.

The Yankees led the American League East into August, when they lost 8 of 10 on a road trip to Cleveland, Detroit, and Kansas City and settled into third or fourth place for the rest of the season. But Mattingly wasn't done hitting grand slams.

He tied the all-time single-season mark set by Ernie Banks (1955 Cubs) and Jim Gentile (1961 Orioles)

In addition to his six grand slams in 1987, Don Mattingly tied a major league record by homering in eight straight games earlier in the year.

with his fifth slam on September 25 in an 8-4 win in Baltimore against rookie José Mesa, leaving him with nine remaining games in the Yankees schedule. He would strike for a sixth and final time four days later back in the Bronx.

The defending American League champion Boston Red Sox came into New York playing out the string. Boston's 74-82 record put the Red Sox 21½ games behind Toronto in fifth place, while the Yankees' 86-70 record was a distant fourth, 9½ games back. In a disappointing sequel to their magical 1986, the Red Sox hadn't been a .500 club since late April.

The Yankees had pulled off a stunning comeback the night before. Trailing 7-3 in the bottom of the ninth, New York scored six runs off four Boston pitchers, capped off by Mike Easler's walk-off two-run home run off Calvin Schiraldi. Mattingly knocked in the first of the six runs with a bases-loaded sacrifice fly.

Boston sent veteran southpaw Bruce Hurst to the mound for his final start of the season. Hurst was 14-6 with a 3.76 ERA through mid-August when his season went into a tailspin. He lost six of his next seven starts with an ERA of 6.32, putting him at 15-12, 4.27 for the season.

New York countered with 28-year-old Charles Hudson, who was 10-6 with a 3.82 ERA. In his first season in the Bronx after a trade with the Phillies, Hudson had started the season 6-0 with a 2.02 ERA but had not won as a starter since May 15. He spent much of the season in and out of the rotation and even endured his first trip back to Triple A in four years.

Hurst and Hudson were sharp early, each allowing one baserunner in each of the first two innings. Marty Barrett singled for his second hit of the day but was stranded in the top of the third, and then the Yankees batters went to work in the bottom half of the inning.

Hurst struck out Joel Skinner to start the inning, but rookie Roberto Kelly and Rickey Henderson followed with singles and a double steal that put runners at second and third.[4] Hurst lost Willie Randolph on a non-intentional walk, loading the bases for Mattingly.

After falling behind in the count one ball and two strikes, Hurst tried to fool Mattingly with a changeup. "I just wanted to try to stay on the ball," Mattingly explained after the game. "I didn't want to pull off. He got me with two changeups the first time."[5]

Mattingly set the record in style, launching his sixth grand slam "11 rows deep into the third tier of the right-field stands," according to the *New York Times*.[6]

"I can't explain it," Mattingly mused after the game when asked about his newfound prowess with the bases loaded. "I haven't done anything different other than try to hit the ball hard. Before, I would hit a sacrifice fly with the bases loaded."[7]

The Yankees led 4-0 but the assault kept coming. Hurst sandwiched a Gary Ward single between two walks to load the bases again. Mattingly's grand slam was his sixth of the season and the Yankees' 10th, tying the 1938 Detroit Tigers' all-time team record.

Boston manager John McNamara replaced Hurst with right-hander Tom Bolton to face the switch-hitting Bob Meacham. Meacham grounded out to first, plating the Yankees' fifth run of the inning, before Skinner bookended the inning with a fly out to right.

Hudson kept the momentum as he allowed just one baserunner, a fifth-inning single to Ed Romero over the next four innings.

The Yankees had another shot at a grand slam in the fifth inning when singles by Ward and Royster and a walk to Meacham loaded the bases for the third time in three innings. Skinner popped out to first and Kelly grounded out to keep the Yankees off the scoreboard in the fifth.

Hudson allowed his final hit in the eighth as he cruised to his 11th victory of the season with a four-hit shutout. "That," manager Lou Piniella said after the game, "is as good a pitched game as we've had all year."[8]

New York tacked on one more run in the bottom of the eighth with a sacrifice fly, leading to the final score of 6-0 in front of 20,204 spectators.

It was a final highlight in a disappointing 1987 season for the Yankees. Mattingly hit his 30th home run in the season's next to last game, making him the first Yankee since Mickey Mantle (1955-62) and Roger Maris (1960-62) to hit 30 in at least three straight seasons. Despite his sluggish start and his 20-day visit to the DL, Mattingly finished with numbers in line with his prior excellent seasons: .327/.378/.559 for a 146 OPS+, slightly off his 158 OPS+ of 1984-86, along with 38 doubles and 115 RBIs, striking out only 38 times. He did not lead the league in any major categories and finished seventh in the American League MVP vote.

Mattingly did not hit another grand slam in his 14-year major-league career. "It feels good to do this, to do something nobody in the game has done," Mattingly said when asked about the record. "All the players who have played, it's surprising that nobody did it. You don't go after records. I just try to hit the ball hard."[9]

The Yankees finished the season a respectable 89-73 but a distant nine games behind Detroit, which swept Toronto in the final weekend of the season to take the American League East. Boston finished 20 games off the pace at 78-84, one of only two seasons in the 1980s that Boston did not reach .500.

SOURCES

In addition to the sources cited in the Notes, the author accessed Baseball-Reference.com for the box score and play-by-play as well as James Lincoln Ray's SABR biography of Don Mattingly.

https://www.baseball-reference.com/boxes/NYA/NYA198709290.shtml

https://sabr.org/bioproj/person/don-mattingly/

NOTES

1   Coming into 1987, Mattingly was 12-for-47 with one double with the bases loaded.

2   Mattingly's second half was more in line with his 1984-86 run when he batted .340/.382/.560 while averaging 48 doubles, 30 home runs and 123 RBIs per season. He batted .311/.390/.485 with six home runs before his stay on the disabled list in 1987.

3   The feat was matched by Ken Griffey Jr. in 1993.

4   The stolen base was the 40th of the season for Henderson and the 700th of his career. He was almost exactly halfway to his career total of 1,406 stolen bases, an all-time record which stood 468 steals ahead of second-place Lou Brock as of this writing in 2022.

5   Murray Chass, "Mattingly Breaks Slam Mark," *New York Times*, September 30, 1987: B7.

6   Chass.

7   Chass.

8   Bob Ryan, "Mattingly's Record Slam Sinks Hurst," *Boston Globe*, September 30, 1987: 52.

9   Chass, "Mattingly Breaks Slam Mark."

JIM ABBOTT'S NO-HITTER

September 4, 1993:
New York Yankees 4, Cleveland Indians 0,
at Yankee Stadium

By Dana Joseph Berry

It was 77 degrees with an overcast sky and occasional rain in New York, on September 4, 1993, when the second-place Yankees hosted the sixth-place Cleveland Indians.

The Yankees (76-60) were chasing down the Toronto Blue Jays (78-58) in the American League East. A series against the sub-.500 Indians (65-70) could be their chance to gain ground. But the Yankees had lost the previous night's series opener, 7-3.[1]

Jim Abbott, a left-handed pitcher famous for being born without a right hand, was the starting pitcher for the Yankees that afternoon. During a 1987 interview with *Sports Illustrated,* the then-sophomore at the University of Michigan had stated, "I've been blessed with a pretty good left arm and a not-so-great right arm."[2]

The no-hitter was Jim Abbott's only shutout in his two seasons with the Yankees.

Abbott had posted a career 26-8 record at the University of Michigan, earning the 1987 Golden Spikes Award and the 1987 James E. Sullivan Award as the nation's top amateur. He was named the 1988 Big Ten Conference Male Athlete of the Year, led the US National team to a Silver Medal at the Pan American Games, and pitched the 5-3 Gold Medal-clinching victory over Japan at the 1988 Olympics.[3]

He had started his career with the California Angels in 1989,[4] skipping over the minor leagues completely to go from college ball to the majors, and had come to the Yankees in a December 1992 trade for three players.[5]

But the southpaw entered his 27th start of 1993 with a 9-11 record and a rather lofty ERA of 4.31; his struggles were in part attributed to his somehow losing 2 mph off his fastball.[6] To this point in his career, Abbott was 2-4 with a 3.92 ERA against the Indians. Though Abbott's last start, six days earlier, against the same Indians roster at Cleveland Stadium, was a game he'd likely prefer to forget. Abbott was able to survive only 3⅔ innings, giving up seven earned runs and 10 hits.

Hence why he showed up to the ballpark that day wearing his "lucky" jeans. (They had an "X" in the waistband.) Warming him up before the game, bullpen coach Mark Connor suggested Abbott "work the outside more and mix in breaking pitches" to compensate for his flagging speed.[7]

Despite the Indians' record, their lineup could hit. Abbott faced six players that day batting at least .287.[8] But their starting pitcher, journeyman Bob Milacki, was making his first appearance with the big-league club, having recently been called up from a season in Triple A.[9]

The game opened with Abbott walking Kenny Lofton. Shortstop Felix Fermin, the next batter, grounded into a third-to-second-to-first double play.

Carlos Baerga ended the top of the frame by flying out deep to left field.

Abbott struck out Albert Belle to start the second frame. Randy Milligan worked a walk. Ramirez flied out to center, and Candy Maldonado wrapped up the top of the inning by striking out.

The third inning saw Jim Thome fly out to center, and both Junior Ortiz and Lofton ground out to second base.

In the bottom of the third, the home team provided some run support for Abbott. Mike Gallego led off with a walk off Milacki. Randy Velarde fouled out to catcher Ortiz. Gallego went to second on Wade Boggs's line-drive single to right field. Left fielder Dion James hit what seemed an innocent single to Lofton in center, knocking in Gallego, but it turned into Indians chaos as Lofton's throw handcuffed third baseman Thome. After he ran to pick up the ball off the ground near the Indians dugout, with Boggs sliding home, Thome made a throw that bounced past Ortiz and into the Yankees dugout, allowing James to score. The Yankees got three runs on the single and two Indians errors, and led, 3-0.

In the fourth inning the Indians' Fermin and Baerga grounded out to second, and Belle grounded to third.

Cleveland's Milligan led off the fifth with a base on balls. But Ramirez grounded into a 6-4-3 twin killing. Maldonado followed with an easy fly out to left field.

The Yankees padded their lead as Velarde led off the bottom of the fifth with a homer to deep right-center field, making the score 4-0.

Thome led off the Indians' sixth with a line drive to shortstop. Again Abbott walked Ortiz, but Lofton flied out to left field, and Fermin grounded out to third. Abbott had still not given up a base hit.

In the seventh, Baerga grounded out to first. On a 1-and-2 count, Belle appeared to take away Abbott's no-hit bid by grounding hard to the gap between third and shortstop. But Boggs dove to snare the ball, jumped to his feet, and threw a rocket to first to get Belle by a step.

It was Boggs who was struck out by Yankees hurler Dave Righetti in 1983 as the final out in Righetti's no-hitter, which was the Yankees' last before this game.[10] No doubt with tongue in cheek, first baseman Don Mattingly joked after the game, "I was definitely thinking Boggsie, making a great play in this one and striking out in that one back in '83. I guess he helped make both [no-hitters] possible."[11]

After Boggs's heroics on Belle's drive, he fielded a routine grounder by Milligan to complete the seventh.

Abbott struck out Manny Ramirez to start the eighth. He thus matched his career high of 7⅓ no-hit innings. On May 29, 1993, Bo Jackson of the Chicago White Sox had ruined Abbott's no-hit bid by lining a hit to center. Ron Karkovice followed with a home run. Abbott eventually earned a win but had lost his no-hitter with just five outs to get.

The Indians' Maldonado grounded out to shortstop for the second out of the eighth. Again Abbott walked Thome (his fifth base on balls of the game) before Sandy Alomar Jr., pinch-hitting for Ortiz, grounded out to third.

"The last couple of innings, I had these huge goose bumps on my forearms, and the hair on the back of my neck was standing up," said Mattingly. "Maybe that would have happened with someone else. Maybe I'd have the same feelings. But I think because it was Jim there was a little something extra."[12]

In the ninth inning, leadoff batter Lofton bunted trying to get the Indians' first hit (and his 17th bunt base hit of the season). It went foul. Lofton heard the wrath of all 27,125 fans, because he broke one of baseball's unwritten rules: "No bunting to break up a no-hitter."[13]

Boggs then positioned himself closer to home to deter Lofton. With umpire Ted Hendry behind the plate, Lofton stared at a fastball down the middle for strike two. Lofton watched Abbott's third pitch go by. It was a ball, just an inch or two outside. On the next pitch, Lofton bounced a ball over the leaping Abbott to second baseman Gallego, who threw out the speedy Lofton running to first. One out.

Fermin watched the first pitch, down the middle, called strike one. The next pitch was low for ball one. Abbott threw a changeup that Fermin weakly bounced foul down the third-base line. With all in attendance standing, Abbott pitched ball two inside. Fermin lined the 2-and-2 pitch foul into the left-field stands. Then Fermin hit a line drive into left-center. The speedy Bernie Williams chased it down, catching it a couple of strides away from the fence. Two out. One to go.

Baerga came up, the Indians' last hope for a hit. The cheering was at such a noise level that Baerga had to call time to regain his concentration. Baerga, to that point batting 5-for-26 against Abbott and .318 for the season, took strike one. On the next pitch he grounded to shortstop Velarde, who threw to Mattingly at first. Jim Abbott had his no-hitter.

After the game, a smiling Abbott said, "I felt a little tired in the seventh inning, but in the eighth and ninth, with the crowd, I didn't feel it at all."[14]

Speaking about being at bat during the history-making out, Baerga said, "He had a very good curve and slider. He was way different last weekend. He kept the ball down today."[15]

Abbott walked five and struck out three, and 17 of his outs were on groundballs.

A day after the no-hitter, the Yankees moved into a tie for first, though the ultimately finished second to the repeating World Series champion Blue Jays.

Abbott finished 11-14 for the Yankees in 1993 and 9-8 the following year. He wrapped up a 10-year major-league career with 87 victories.[16]

"How does it all happen?" Abbott said of the no-hitter in retrospect. "A guy, growing up in Flint, Michigan, to this? For a tiny second, you're outside yourself."[17]

SOURCES

In addition to the sources cited in the Notes, the author consulted Baseball-Reference.com, Retrosheet.org, and reviewed the broadcast of the game on YouTube.

https://www.baseball-reference.com/boxes/NYA/NYA199309040.shtml

https://www.retrosheet.org/boxesetc/1993/B09040NYA1993.htm

https://www.youtube.com/watch?v=VhdzG2Y9HUQ

I want to thank Bill Nowlin, who would cause me to yell at the monitor, at times, while pushing me to write better than I ever thought possible.

I'm truly inspired and grateful for Tara Krieger. Tara, behind the scenes, is literally a literature alchemist. She took my written words and turned them into polished words that you will read and hopefully enjoy.

NOTES

1   In that game, Cleveland rookie Manny Ramirez, called up two days earlier, hit his first and second career home runs.

2   Hank Hersch, "That Great Abbott Switch," *Sports Illustrated*, May 25, 1987: 28-29.

3   "Jim Abbott (2004) – University of Michigan Hall of Honor," University of Michigan Athletics, https://mgoblue.com/honors/university-of-michigan-hall-of-honor/jim-abbott/150. Accessed October 13, 2022.

4   At a postgame press conference after his major-league debut, Abbott patiently discussed his pitching/fielding motion. "I've been doing this since I was 5 years old. Now it's as natural as tying my shoes." Rick Swaine, "Jim Abbott," SABR BioProject, https://sabr.org/bioproj/person/jim-abbott/. The quotation comes from Rick Swaine, *Beating the Breaks: Major League Ballplayers Who Overcame Disabilities* (Jefferson, North Carolina: McFarland, 2004), 13. Swaine discusses how Abbott fielded his position and handled batting in his 24 plate appearances with the 1999 Milwaukee Brewers. (He hit .095, but with 3 RBIs.)

5   To acquire Abbott, the Yankees traded pitchers Jerry Nielsen and Russ Springer and first baseman J.T. Snow.

6   Tom Verducci, "A Special Delivery," *Sports Illustrated*, September 13, 1993, https://vault.si.com/vault/1993/09/13/a-special-delivery-that-was-no-ordinary-no-hitter-yankee-jim-abbott-threw-against-the-indians.

7   Verducci.

8   The six players were starters Kenny Lofton (.317), Carlos Baerga (.317), Albert Belle (.296), Randy Milligan (.287), and Jim Thome (.292), and pinch-hitter Sandy Alomar Jr. (.286).

9   A right-hander, Milacki had come to Cleveland after five years with the Baltimore Orioles. This was his first major-league appearance of 1993.

10   Righetti no-hit the Boston Red Sox on July 4, 1983, winning 4-0. Bill Nowlin, "Dave Righetti tosses a no-hitter of Fourth of July," SABR Games Project.

11   John Harper, "Shades of Rags for Don, Wade," *New York Daily News*, September 5, 1993: 52.

12   Verducci.

13   This unwritten rule was discussed on the website baseballcodes.com: "'The first hit of a no-hitter is not a bunt,' said Kansas City Royals pitcher Danny Jackson 15 years earlier, in 1986, after Angels rookie Devon White attempted to break up his no-hitter with a failed eighth-inning bunt attempt. 'I don't know how long he's been around,' Jackson said about the outfielder, 'but he's got to go down.'" Jason Turbow, "Tenth Anniversary of an Unwritten Rule Violation People Still Delight in Referencing," *The Baseball Codes*, May 27, 2011, https://thebaseballcodes.com/2011/05/26/tenth-anniversary-of-an-unwritten-rule-violation-people-still-delight-in-referencing/.

14   Jennifer Frey, "Abbott: Not a Hit, Not a Run, Not a Doubt," *New York Times*, September 5, 1993: 3.

15   Sheldon Ocker, "Yankees' Left-Hander Stifles Indians 4-0," *Akron Beacon Journal*, September 5, 1993: E1.

16   A free agent after the 1994 season, Abbott signed with the White Sox. He signed with the California Angels before the 1996 season and experienced a dismal 2-18 season. After being released, he sat out 1997 but mounted a comeback with the White Sox in 1998 and was 5-0, winning each of his five starts. A final season with the National League's Brewers was less successful (2-8, 6.91 ERA). He retired from baseball in 1999.

17   Anthony McCarron, "Former Yankee Pitcher Jim Abbott Still Delivering a Positive Message," *New York Daily News*, May 31, 2009, https://web.archive.org/web/20130911022845/http://www.nydailynews.com/sports/baseball/yankees/yankee-pitcher-jim-abbott-delivering-positive-message-article-1.412950.

SEVENTH-GRADER JEFFREY MAIER ASSISTS JETER'S TYING HOMER IN ALCS OPENER

October 9, 1996:
New York Yankees 5, Baltimore Orioles 4 (11 innings),
at Yankee Stadium
Game One of the 1996 American League Championship Series

By Malcolm Allen

New York's reception of Roberto Alomar was the major storyline before the 1996 American League Championship Series. Despite spitting on an umpire on September 27, the Orioles' second baseman was permitted to compete. New York City Mayor Rudy Giuliani recommended silent protests to his upset constituents, while vowing that spectators caught heaving projectiles would be arrested.[1] The police stationed 160 extra officers inside the ballpark. Four security personnel guarded the Baltimore dugout.[2]

October 8 was the original date for Game One, but a tropical storm forced postponement until the next afternoon.[3] Banged-up players appreciated the schedule change, as did one young Yankees fan from Old Tappan, New Jersey, whose family's friends wound up with an extra ticket.[4] Jeffrey Maier was invited to skip seventh-grade classes to attend his first playoff game.[5]

New York's 21-game winner, Andy Pettitte, delighted most of the 56,495 in attendance with a perfect opening inning that ended with Alomar taking a called third strike. Alomar "was subjected to a deafening chorus of obscenities every time he came up to bat."[6]

In the bottom of the frame, Orioles left fielder B.J. Surhoff lost track of a routine fly that became a leadoff double for Tim Raines. Baltimore's Scott Erickson – the most extreme groundball pitcher among AL starters – induced groundouts from the next three hitters, but Raines advanced on the first two and scored.

Both teams capitalized on second-inning leadoff walks. After Rafael Palmeiro advanced to third on Cal Ripken's one-out double, the Orioles' Eddie Murray drove him home with a groundout. But the Yankees regained the advantage with an unearned run in their half. Alomar, a perennial Gold Glover, misplayed Paul

O'Neill's chopper to put two aboard. Baltimore then failed to convert two potential double plays. First, Ripken's relay pulled Palmeiro's foot off first base. With runners at the corners, New York went ahead, 2-1, when Jim Leyritz's shot toward third baseman Todd Zeile was not fielded cleanly.[7]

The Orioles had come back all year, though. Under .500 on July 29, they claimed the AL wild card with a

Including the "home run," rookie Derek Jeter was 10-for-24 (.417) with five runs scored in the ALCS.

37-22 finish behind an offense that produced 257 homers – then the most in a single season.[8] Brady Anderson's 50 round-trippers were a single-season Orioles' record, and Palmeiro's 142 RBIs set another club mark.[9]

Anderson and Palmeiro both batted left-handed, though, and only one lefty had taken Pettitte deep all year. But Anderson hit one out to right in the third inning, and Palmeiro did likewise in the fourth to put the Orioles up, 3-2.

Meanwhile. Erickson found his groove, and Baltimore added another run against Pettitte in the sixth. Pettitte issued two walks around a single, and Surhoff's sacrifice fly made it 4-2.

The Yankees couldn't score after a pair of two-out singles in their sixth. The same thing happened in the Orioles' seventh. By game's end, the teams were a combined 1-for-23 with runners in scoring position, with two dozen teammates left on the basepaths.

After an Erickson walk in the bottom of the seventh, Bernie Williams's double gave New York the tying runners in scoring position with their leading RBI man, lefty-hitting Tino Martinez, up next. Baltimore manager Davey Johnson called on southpaw Jesse Orosco, who fanned Martinez and intentionally walked Cecil Fielder to load the bases. When Yankees skipper Joe Torre sent righty-hitting Charlie Hayes up to pinch-hit, Johnson countered with his flamethrowing righty Armando Benítez. Darryl Strawberry then batted for Hayes and walked on a full count to bring the Yankees within 4-3, but Mariano Duncan fanned to end the uprising.

The Orioles made two defensive changes after going down in order in the top of the eighth. Mike Devereaux replaced Surhoff in left field and right fielder Bobby Bonilla, who had injured his shoulder the previous inning,[10] yielded to Tony Tarasco, a roster addition the day before.[11] The Orioles were just five outs from victory after Leyritz struck out leading off. Including playoffs, Benítez had limited right-handed hitters to a .130 average over 46 at-bats to that point in '96.

Next, righty-swinging rookie Derek Jeter drove a 0-and-1 slider to the opposite field. Tarasco retreated to the warning track and, with his back to the nine-foot wall, he was so confident of catching the ball that he never leaped: "I was ready to close my glove, but the ball never made it to my hand. … It was like abracadabra."[12]

The 12-year-old Maier had stuck his mitt into the field of play and yanked Jeter's drive into Row A of Box 325 in Section 31.[13] Tarasco immediately pointed up to where the ball had disappeared, but right-field umpire Rich Garcia signaled home run, tying the score, 4-4.

Tarasco protested vehemently. Moments later, he was joined by Anderson and Benítez. Johnson was ejected for arguing, and some spectators hurled cups and hot-dog wrappers at the angry Orioles.[14] But the call was not changed. Garcia explained later, "I asked for help from the second base umpire, the first base umpire and the plate umpire. They said they couldn't tell from where they were."[15] (Umpires were not allowed to review replays until 2008.)

Two of the next three Yankees reached safely. While Baltimore changed pitchers, fans cheered Maier and chanted "MVP!" during his live television interview with NBC's Jim Gray. The boy described how he had lost the ball in the excitement. Arthur Rhodes retired Martinez to end the inning.

Anderson doubled in the top of the ninth against New York's John Wetteland, but he did not advance. In the bottom of the inning, Fielder drew a leadoff walk from Baltimore's Terry Mathews and departed for pinch-runner Andy Fox. With one away, Duncan was hit by a pitch. Torre initially sent lefty Mike Aldrete up to pinch-hit but opted for righty-hitting Joe Girardi after acting Orioles manager Andy Etchebarren brought in southpaw Randy Myers. Girardi lined out to Ripken at shortstop, and the inning ended when the "Iron Man" threw to Alomar to double up Fox.

Neither team scored in the 10th. Palmeiro reached safely for the fifth time with a leadoff single, but the Orioles stranded two against the Yankees' Mariano Rivera. Jeter's fourth hit – including three infield singles – started the Yankees' half of the inning, but Myers retired two other future Hall of Famers, Raines and Wade Boggs, on a double-play grounder and popup respectively.

Baltimore nicked Rivera for a two-out single in the top of the 11th, but Alomar followed by striking out for the third time.

Columnist Buster Olney noted the next day, "The way Tarasco kept looking over at Garcia and then away, in disgust, it was as if the Orioles were waiting for the decisive blow."[16] It came in the bottom of the 11th. Myers left a 1-and-1 slider up in the strike zone, and Williams ripped it just inside the left-field foul pole for a game-ending homer.

Most of the postgame questions were about Maier's assistance to Jeter's homer. Johnson remarked, "I always say that one play doesn't beat you in a ballgame, but this is about as close as you can come to one play beating you."[17] In the opposing locker room, Jeter said, "Do I feel bad? We won the game. Why should I feel bad?"[18]

Garcia, after viewing replays, acknowledged that he should not have ruled Jeter's hit a homer, but he maintained, "The fan did not reach down. He reached out, which in my judgment he did not interfere with the guy catching the ball."[19] Tarasco disagreed, insisting he was "absolutely positive" that he would have snared it.[20]

The Orioles filed a formal protest the next day after meeting with AL President Gene Budig.[21] Since umpires' judgment calls were not disputable, Johnson knew it stood little chance of being upheld, but he was disappointed by the extra security promised to prevent such incidents.[22] (One week earlier in the ALDS, another fan at Yankee Stadium had snagged a fair ball hit by the Rangers' Juan González by reaching around the left-field foul pole. The umpires ruled it a homer.[23])

The producers of *Good Morning America* brought Maier and his family to a Manhattan hotel overnight so that he could appear on the show in the morning.[24] His father left a voice message for Tarasco, who said, "I don't have anything against the kid. If it was me, I might have leaned out more trying to catch it."[25] The *New York Daily News* treated the Maiers to lunch and allowed them to sit in the newspaper's box seats for Game Two. But the Yankees were reluctant to celebrate the boy, with a spokesman explaining, "Joe Torre said it best. He said, 'I think it's glorifying the wrong thing.'"[26]

The Orioles took Game Two to even the series, but their protest was formally denied the next day. The Yankees swept three contests in Baltimore to win the pennant, beat the Braves in the World Series, and then won three of the next four World Series. As for Jeffrey Maier, after playing college baseball at Wesleyan University, he married a Boston Red Sox fan and started a family in New England.[27]

SOURCES

In addition to sources cited in the Notes, the author consulted Baseball-Reference.com and Retrosheet.org.

https://www.baseball-reference.com/boxes/NYA/NYA199610090.shtml

https://www.retrosheet.org/boxesetc/1996/B10090NYA1996.htm

The author also watched (again) NBC's original television broadcast of the game. John Z, *YouTube* posting, June 17, 2020, https://www.youtube.com/watch?v=q45oly1Lchg&t=5049s (last accessed December 3, 2022).

NOTES

1. Clifford J. Levy, "Giuliani Is Urging Fans to Give Alomar the Silent Treatment," *New York Times*, October 9, 1996: 13.

2. Dave Anderson, "From Alomar to a Kid, to 'Ber-Nie,'" *New York Times*, October 10, 1996: 17.

3. Murray Chass, "Rain Gives Yankees an Extra Day Game," *New York Times*, October 9, 1996: A1.

4. Jeffrey Maier, "How Catching a Derek Jeter 'Home Run' Changed My Life Forever," *Bleacher Report*, April 6, 2014, https://bleacherreport.com/articles/2017536-how-catching-a-derek-jeter-home-run-changed-my-life-forever (last accessed December 3, 2022).

5. George Vecsey, "A 12-Year-Old Legend Is Born in Right Field," *New York Times*, October 10, 1996: 17.

6. Peter Schmuck, "Yanks Catch a Break," *Baltimore Sun*, October 10, 1996: 1A.

7. Mark Maske, "Fan Runs Interference for Yankees in Game 1," *Washington Post*, October 10, 1996: B1.

8. The Orioles beat the Cleveland Indians in the American League Division Series, three games to one.

9. In 1922, when the franchise was the St. Louis Browns, Ken Williams collected 155 RBIs. In 2004 Miguel Tejada established a new Baltimore record with 150 RBIs. Chris Davis homered 53 times in 2013 to surpass Anderson's total.

10. Murray Chass, "'Magic Trick' Causes Orioles to Disappear," *New York Times*, October 10, 1996: 17.

11. Jason Lancanfora, "Alexander Is Dropped, Tarasco Added to Roster as Insurance for Surhoff," *Baltimore Sun*, October 9, 1996: 2E.

12. Schmuck.

13. Vecsey, "A 12-Year-Old Legend Is Born in Right Field."

14. Buster Olney, "Fan Has Hand in Yanks' Win," *Baltimore Sun*, October 10, 1996: 1E.

15. John Eisenberg, "Everyone Saw the Kid but One Man Who Counted," *Baltimore Sun*, October 10, 1996: 1E.

16. Olney.

17. Schmuck.

18. Roch Eric Kubatko, "To Delight of Yankees, 12-Year-Old Plays Catch," *Baltimore Sun*, October 10, 1996: 6E.

19. Chass, "'Magic Trick' Causes Orioles to Disappear."

20. Olney.

21. Section 3:16 of the *Official Baseball Rules* stipulate that a batter should be ruled out if fan interference prevents a fielder from catching a ball. Although Garcia opined that the ball Jeter hit would not have been caught by Tarasco, his admission that his home run ruling was incorrect prompted the Orioles to protest on the basis of Rule 3:11, which said an umpire's decision could be reversed "should he be convinced that it is in violation of one of the rules." Had Garcia ruled that interference occurred, but Tarasco would not have made the catch (i.e., that the ball would have hit the top of the wall), home-plate umpire Larry Barnett would have decided how many bases to award Jeter. Murray Chass, "Orioles File Protest on Game 1, Citing Possible Loophole," *New York Times*, October 11, 1996: 11.

22. Schmuck.

23. "A Fan Gets a Piece of the Action as González Hits Bleachers Again," *New York Times*, October 3, 1996: 12.

24. Bruce Weber, "Boy Who Saved the Yankees Becomes a Man About Town," *New York Times*, October 11, 1996: A11.

25. Ken Rosenthal, "Win, Protest Help Sweep Away Sting of Bad Call," *Baltimore Sun*, October 11, 1996: 1E.

26. Weber.

27. Maier.

GLORY RETURNS TO THE BRONX

October 26, 1996:
New York Yankees 3, Atlanta Braves 2
at Yankee Stadium
Game Six of the 1996 World Series

By Paul Semendinger

It had been a long time. Too long for most, an eternity for some. In fact, it had been 18 long years since the New York Yankees had been in a position to capture ultimate glory and win a world championship.

For Yankees manager Joe Torre, it had been a longer time – forever. His playing career began in 1960 and lasted through 1977, and he had also managed in 15 prior seasons. For 32 long seasons, he had never been part of a World Series championship.[1]

It was a dry night in the Bronx. The weather was a comfortable 57 degrees. It was a perfect night for baseball.

Game Six of the 1996 World Series pitted the Yankees against the Atlanta Braves, the reigning World Series champions. The Yankees held the advantage in the Series, three games to two, but it hadn't been easy. The Yankees had dropped the first two games at home before heading to Atlanta and sweeping the three games there. What at first seemed like an easy World Series for the Braves had suddenly changed. The Yankees had to win only one more game to be crowned champions. The Yankees were playing at home, in Yankee Stadium, and this could have been seen as an advantage, but to date in this Series, the home team had yet to win even a single game.

Taking the mound for the Yankees was Jimmy Key, a quality left-handed pitcher who had signed a four-year free-agent deal with the Yankees before the 1993 season. Key was a key contributor to the Yankees, especially in the first two years of the deal, when he went 18-6 and 17-4. But injuries had since taken their toll. In 1996 Key's 4.68 ERA spoke to the fact that he was not the pitcher he had once been.

Pitching for the Braves was one of the best pitchers of his time, Greg Maddux, the reigning four-time National League Cy Young Award pitcher. Maddux had also already defeated the Yankees in Game Two of this World Series, pitching eight innings and allowing no runs. In that same game, Key allowed four runs for the loss.

The Braves were down, but they were certainly not out. For the Yankees to win this game, they would have to defeat a pitcher who seemed all but unbeatable.

For the more than 56,000 fans in attendance in the grand old ballpark in New York, the hope was for a close game – there was little likelihood of the Yankees scoring often in this contest.

From the start, it seemed clear that both pitchers brought their best.

The Braves went down in order in the top of the first inning. The Yankees did the same.

Javy Lopez, the Braves catcher, worked a one-out walk in the second, but no other runners reached base. Maddux again retired the Yankees in order.

It was in the third inning that things began to get interesting. Terry Pendleton, the Braves third baseman, led off with a grounder to second base that Mariano Duncan booted. Duncan had enjoyed a stellar 1996 season, batting .340. His energy and enthusiasm, as well as his phrase "We play today, we win today, Dassit," inspired the club. He was not, though, a great defensive player. In a tight game, an error could be disastrous. Jeff Blauser, the Braves shortstop and a former All-Star, stepped to the plate. Terry Pendleton was quickly thrown out trying to steal second base. Yankees catcher Joe Girardi, brought to the team for his catching skills and leadership, made a great throw to erase the runner. Blauser then doubled. Key was able to retire the next two batters.

In the bottom of the third, the Yankees' bats came alive. Paul O'Neill, who had joined the Yankees the same year as Key, led off with a double. Duncan followed with a groundout to the right side that allowed O'Neill to move to third base.

Some players have legendary careers. Some have remarkable seasons. For others, it might be a singular game that is remembered forever. Girardi's heroics came down to a single inning. First, he threw out Pendleton. In the bottom of the inning, he hit a blast, not a legendary home run, but something even more unlikely – a long triple to center field, scoring O'Neill with the game's first run. Said Girardi, "When I got on third base, I almost started crying."[2]

The next batter, rookie Derek Jeter, singled home Girardi with the Yankees' second run.[3]

Jeter then accomplished what Pendleton could not; he stole second base. Next, after Wade Boggs popped out, Bernie Williams singled home Jeter to give the Yankees a 3-0 lead. Williams noted, "[Maddux] made a few mistakes and we took advantage."[4]

It didn't take long for the Braves to answer right back. With one out, All-Star Fred McGriff walked. Lopez then singled, and so did the bright young star Andruw Jones. Just like that, the Braves had loaded the bases. Key, battling for his life, then walked Jermaine Dye to force in the first of the Braves' runs.

And that brought up Terry Pendleton.

Pendleton had been the National League MVP in 1991 and the runner-up in 1992. He was now 35 years old, but still a dangerous hitter. The previous inning, Pendleton had been caught stealing to partly negate a scoring threat. This time, he did worse. Pendleton grounded into a double play to end the inning. Jimmy Key and the Yankees had escaped.

Maddux, who had bent, wasn't going to be broken. Seeing that victory could be on the horizon, he rediscovered his best stuff. The Yankees went down in order in the fourth.

In the fifth inning, the Braves had a single, but could do no other damage, partly because Marquis Grissom was called out at second base after he tried advancing on an errant pitch. Braves manager Bobby Cox argued the call and was thrown out of the game. Replays later showed that the umpire had missed the call.[5] After the game Cox noted, "We're not going to blame the umpires. … We got beat and that's the end of the story."[6]

Maddux kept cruising; the Yanks went down in order again.

One of the particular strengths of the 1996 Yankees was their deep bullpen. As the game headed to its final acts, that strength would be used. Chipper Jones began the top of the sixth with a double. Key stayed on to retire McGriff on a groundout, but Jones moved to third. In from the bullpen came David Weathers, who struck out Javy Lopez before walking Andruw Jones, bringing up power hitter Ryan Klesko, pinch-hitting for Dye. Torre again went to the bullpen and summoned Graeme Lloyd.

Klesko popped out. The threat averted. The Yankees' precarious 3-1 lead remained intact.

The Yankees went down again in the sixth.

For the seventh inning, Torre called upon his young set-up man, a player just starting his legend, the future Hall of Famer Mariano Rivera. After a leadoff walk to Pendleton, he retired three in a row.

The Yankees threatened, but did not score in their half of the seventh inning.

The Yankees had last won a World Series at Yankee Stadium in 1977.

The Braves proved no match for Rivera in the eighth. They went down in order.

The Yankees also did not score.

This brought the Yankees and the Braves to the ninth inning. In from the bullpen came their closer, John Wetteland.

The inning began with Andruw Jones striking out. But Klesko and Pendleton both singled. The tying runners were on base.

Rafael Belliard was sent in to run for Pendleton. Luis Polonia, pinch-hitting for Blauser, struck out.

Grissom then singled to right field, cutting the Yankees' lead to 3-2. This brought up Mark Lemke, a career .286 hitter in World Series play.

Wetteland started him off with a fast strike. It wasn't going to be that easy, though. Wetteland's next two pitches were balls … not close. Girardi came to the mound to talk with his pitcher. A second quick strike followed that exchange.

Ball three followed.

Lemke then popped the ball up, in foul ground, off third base. Charlie Hayes, who entered the game as a defensive replacement, drifted to the ball, approached the Braves dugout, stretched his arm out, and just missed the game-ending catch as he fell into the dugout.

Lemke would get another chance.

And so would Hayes.

Another popup to the left side. Hayes settled under it, made the catch, and the Yankees were once again baseball's champions. The Braves became only the third team in the history of baseball to lose four consecutive games after winning the first two games of a World Series.[7]

For Joe Torre, it was his first time on top. He shared, "I've never been so happy. I never thought this would happen to me."[8]

PERSONAL NOTE

The author was privileged and thrilled to be able to attend this game with his father, a lifetime Red Sox fan, who put his allegiance to his team from Boston to root his son's Yankees on. We will both never forget the joy and excitement in the Stadium as well as Wade Boggs riding on the police horse as the celebration ensued.

SOURCES

In addition to the sources cited in the Notes, the author consulted the Baseball-Reference.com website for pertinent material:

https://www.baseball-reference.com/boxes/NYA/NYA199610260.shtml

He also viewed the game footage on YouTube, at https://www.youtube.com/watch?v=bKxi6-jxbTo.

NOTES

1   Jack Curry, "A Return to Glory," *New York Times*, October 27, 1996: 1.

2   Marty Appel, *Pinstripe Empire* (New York: Bloomsbury USA, 2014), 497.

3   Derek Jeter was named American League Rookie of the Year in 1996.

4   John Harper and Bob Klapisch, *Champions: The Saga of the 1996 New York Yankees* (New York: Villard, 1996), 205.

5   Thomas Stinson, "'It Was Time to Say Something' Dejected by Second-Base Call, Cox Ejected by Third-Base Ump," *Atlanta Constitution*, October 27, 1996: E9.

6   Tim Tucker, "Yanks' 3-2 Victory Finishes Off Braves," *Atlanta Constitution*, October 27, 1996: A1.

7   Tucker.

8   Harper and Klapisch, 207.

HIDEKI IRABU BRINGS JAPAN TO YANKEE STADIUM

July 10, 1997:
New York Yankees 10, Detroit Tigers 3,
at Yankee Stadium

By Chad Moody

"[Hideki Irabu] literally took on a nation to come here. He said, 'I want New York,'" exclaimed New York Yankees owner George Steinbrenner after his new pitcher's successful debut in US major-league baseball.[1] Indeed, the road to the Big Apple for the nine-year veteran megastar of Japan's Pacific League was rocky; systematic restrictions inhibited Japanese player transfers to major-league clubs at that time. In January 1997, the San Diego Padres struck a working arrangement with Irabu's prior team, the Chiba Lotte Marines, granting them exclusive rights to the services of the "real deal" 27-year-old, whose velocity approached 100 miles per hour.[2] However, contract negotiations stumbled over Irabu's insistence on signing only with the Yankees, sending the frustrated right-hander back to Japan where he threatened to forgo the season. But after monthslong wranglings, the Yankees finally picked up Irabu's negotiating rights from the Padres in an April trade, culminating in a $12.8 million contract signed in late May.

In preparation for "The Show," Irabu was given a handful of minor-league tune-ups. Steinbrenner himself attended the 6-foot-4, 240-pounder's July 5 start for the Triple-A Columbus Clippers. Irabu did not disappoint, allowing only two hits over seven score-less innings against the Toledo Mud Hens. "He was impressive," the Yankees owner gushed.[3]

After Irabu pleased The Boss, the second-place Yankees penciled him in for the start against the middling division-rival Detroit Tigers on the evening of July 10. A circus-like atmosphere grew in anticipation of the fireballer's big-league debut. Likened to iconic moundsman Nolan Ryan, Irabu was welcomed to New York the day before his premiere by Mayor Rudy Giuliani with "posters waving and organ music

blaring at top volume" in a celebration at City Hall.[4] And game day brought added "hysteria," with "300 media members, a dozen satellite television trucks and one news helicopter" helping to give a "World Series feel to a midseason game."[5] With the soon-to-be sixth-ever Japanese major leaguer generating "even more hype" than fellow countryman Hideo Nomo did upon his arrival stateside two years earlier, a large contingent of media members from Japan was present.[6] They would have to wait, however, as Steinbrenner received special dispensation from acting Commissioner Bud Selig to close the Yankees' clubhouse prior to the game to protect his players from an impending media frenzy.

Before the game Steinbrenner commented that he had "never seen pressure on a rookie anywhere like there is on Irabu."[7] And Yankees manager Joe Torre admitted that his new pitcher would face an "intimidating atmosphere."[8] Perhaps fittingly, Irabu warmed up to the song "Welcome to the Jungle" by the rock band Guns N' Roses in front of 51,901 fans at Yankee Stadium.[9] Another 35 million people were expected to view the contest on Japanese television.

Early on, Irabu displayed pinpoint control in setting down in order the first six Tigers batters – four of them via strikeouts. "When I got out on the mound, all the things that I went through in the last six months came to me in a flashback," Irabu said after the game through a translator. "I really had that on my mind. I had to change the channel. I knew I was part of this team now, and I had to do what I could to contribute."[10] Detroit's journeyman starter Omar Olivares likewise held New York's potent lineup scoreless after two innings.

Irabu faced his first struggles in the top of the third, which caused his "famed temper" to briefly flare.[11] A walk to Curtis Pride followed by Raul Casanova's base hit set the table for an RBI single by Deivi Cruz. Despite allowing another free pass later in the inning, Irabu was able to pitch out of further trouble.

The Yankees' offense came alive in the bottom of the third. With one out, Irabu's batterymate Joe Girardi drew a walk, and Derek Jeter followed with an infield single. Olivares retired the next batter, but a costly two-out throwing error by catcher Casanova scored Girardi and gave the Yankees new life. Slugger Tino Martinez took advantage of Detroit's miscue by drilling a tiebreaking three-run round-tripper off the second-deck facing in right field.

Now working with a 4-1 lead, Irabu struck out power-hitting Tony Clark on a changeup to begin the top of the fourth. After Bob Hamelin followed with a single, the "hulking" hurler "turned the crowd delirious" when he used his "vicious splitter" to strike out the next two Tigers hitters and end the frame.[12] Olivares also settled down in the latter half of the inning to retire the bottom of the Yankees lineup without incident.

Casanova's leadoff double and Bobby Higginson's two-out RBI single in the top of the fifth shrank New York's lead to 4-2. After getting two quick strikes on the potential third out, Irabu reeled off eight consecutive balls to load the bases. This prompted a mound visit featuring pitching coach Mel Stottlemyre and a congregation of teammates. Evading the language barrier, "Girardi simply stared at Irabu and exaggerated his breathing motion, his way of instructing the pitcher to calm down."[13] The rookie hurler did just that, retiring Hamelin on a first-pitch groundout to end the shaky inning.

The Yankees bounced back in the bottom of the fifth. Jeter and Luis Sojo led off with back-to-back singles. A sacrifice fly from Bernie Williams scored Jeter. An intentional pass to Martinez to set up a potential double play backfired when Paul O'Neill's double brought Sojo home and sent Detroit starter Olivares to the showers. Before finally shutting the door on the offensive flurry, reliever Jose Bautista allowed an RBI infield single by Charlie Hayes that extended the Yankees' lead to 7-2.

After cruising through a one-two-three top of the sixth, Irabu watched his teammates blow the game open in the bottom half of the frame. Parlaying two hits off Bautista and four walks off his successor, Roberto Duran, into another three runs, New York

padded its lead to 10-2 before Doug Brocail took the mound to stop the bleeding. O'Neill, Hayes, and Chad Curtis each collected an RBI in the inning – all on walks.

Despite retiring the first two batters in the top of the seventh, Irabu saw his magical debut end after 99 pitches. In his 6⅔ innings of work, Irabu allowed two earned runs on five hits and four walks. He struck out nine, recorded by fans who posted large placards in the stadium using the Japanese word for strikeout, "providing a touch of Tokyo in the South Bronx."[14] Manager Torre was "booed slightly" when he called upon bullpen arm Jeff Nelson, "but that quickly turned to thunderous applause as Irabu trotted off"; the standing ovation continued until the rookie eventually took a curtain call.[15] The only scoring the rest of the way came via a solo home run off Nelson by the Tigers' Clark in the eighth.

"The experience was more than I dreamed about or imagined for this night," Irabu said after the 10-3 drubbing of Detroit. "I wouldn't sell this night for anything."[16] His teammates – several of whom were initially "unhappy" with the big money and roster spot handed to what they perceived as unproven talent – were won over by the fine performance.[17] Star Yankees hurler David Cone praised Irabu's intangible "knack" for pitching, while teammate Martinez thought he "showed a lot of composure out there and a lot of maturity."[18] And Girardi added that the newest Yankee was "everything they built him up to be – and maybe a little more."[19]

Curiously, the overmatched Tigers provided tepid reviews of Irabu's outing. Detroit manager Buddy Bell offered only a backhanded compliment in reference to his opponent's "stuff," while Higginson noted that he "didn't throw as hard as I thought he would."[20] And Tigers third baseman Travis Fryman had this to say of Irabu: "I was not impressed with his forkball. His fastball was straight as an arrow."[21]

Detroit's critique of Irabu may have been skewed by sour grapes, but it nonetheless proved to be quite prescient. After struggling in his next three starts, Irabu was briefly demoted to Columbus. Continuing to disappoint upon rejoining the Yankees, he finished the campaign with a bloated 7.09 ERA in 13 games. Never living up to the lofty expectations, he ultimately spent six lackluster major-league seasons with three different teams. Irabu's troubled post-baseball life was riddled with alcoholism, arrests, marital problems, and depression. He committed suicide at age 42.

Despite the tragic ending to his story, Irabu played a key role in the establishment of the modern Japanese posting system with his battle to join the Yankees. "He will go down in history for fighting for players' rights in Japan, by refusing to accept the Lotte trade to San Diego," author Robert Whiting, an authority on Japanese baseball, declared.[22] And at least for one special moment in time on July 10, 1997, Irabu's "lifelong odyssey from a Japanese industrial town to Yankee Stadium culminated with an extraordinary night in the Bronx."[23]

SOURCES

The author accessed Baseball-Reference.com (baseball-reference.com/boxes/NYA/NYA199707100.shtml) for box scores/play-by-play information and other data, as well as Retrosheet (retrosheet.org/boxesetc/1997/B07100NYA1997.htm). In addition to the sources cited in the Notes, the author also accessed GenealogyBank.com, NewspaperArchive.com, Newspapers.com, and Paper of Record.

NOTES

1   Jack Curry, "A Midseason Classic: Irabu Wins His Debut," *New York Times*, July 11, 1997, nytimes.com/1997/07/11/sports/a-midseason-classic-irabu-wins-his-debut.html, accessed August 3, 2022.

2   Jon Heyman, "Irabu the Class of His 'A' Debut," *Newsday* (Long Island, New York), June 11, 1997: A75.

3   Carlos Frias, "Boss: Irabu 'Impressive,'" *Cincinnati Enquirer*, July 6, 1997: C5.

4   Malcolm Moran, "Yankees Get Rights to Irabu in Deal With Padres," *New York Times*, April 23, 1997, nytimes.com/1997/04/23/sports/yankees-get-rights-to-irabu-in-deal-with-padres.html, accessed August 3, 2022; Paul H.B. Shin, "Land of Rising Sum," *New York Daily News*, July 10, 1997: 7.

5   Rita Ciolli, "Fans Flock to Irabu," *Newsday*, July 11, 1997: A81.

6   John Lowe, "Striking Debut," *Detroit Free Press*, July 11, 1977: 4C.

7   Ian O'Connor, "He's Still Boss Man," *New York Daily News*, July 10, 1997: 82.

8   John Giannone, "Inside Irabu," *New York Daily News*, July 9, 1997: 25C.

9   Jon Heyman, "A Countdown to Craziness," *Newsday*, July 11, 1997: A80.

10   Curry, "A Midseason Classic: Irabu Wins His Debut."

11   David Lennon, "Irabu Makes Believers Fast," *Newsday*, July 11, 1997: A71.

12   Curry; John Giannone, "Irabu Ks 9 in Stunning Debut," *New York Daily News*, July 11, 1997: 77.

13   Ian O'Connor, "Irabu Catches Break With Joe," *New York Daily News*, July 11, 1997: 78.

14   Curry.

15   Giannone, "Irabu Ks 9 in Stunning Debut."

16   Curry.

17   Joe Gergen, "Irabu Makes Believers Fast," *Newsday*, July 11, 1997: A83.

18   Lowe, "Striking Debut"; Lennon, "Irabu Makes Believers Fast," A82.

19   Lowe, "Striking Debut."

20   Tom Gage, "Irabu Caps Tigers' Bad Day," *Detroit News*, July 11, 1997: 1F.

21   Lowe, "Striking Debut," 1C.

22   Daisuke Wakabayashi, "Japan Baseball Players' Debt to Hideki Irabu," *Wall Street Journal*, wsj.com/articles/BL-JRTB-10441, July 29, 2011, accessed August 10, 2022.

23   Lennon, "Irabu Makes Believers Fast," A82.

YANKEES AND ATHLETICS COMBINE
FOR STADIUM SCORING RECORD
AT 1998 HOME OPENER

April 10, 1998:
New York Yankees 17, Oakland Athletics 13,
at Yankee Stadium

By Thomas Merrick

The New York Yankees were set to play their first home game of 1998. Joe DiMaggio, 83 years old, strolled from the dugout to the pitcher's mound, threw a strike to catcher Joe Girardi, waved with both hands to an adoring crowd, and walked off the field.[1] It might have been the best pitching performance of the day; before the final out went in the scorebook, a Yankee Stadium-record 30 runners crossed home plate.

The Yankees began the season on the West Coast. After dropping two games in Anaheim, and another in Oakland, they toppled the Athletics 9-7 for their first win. It was on to Seattle, where an 8-0 thumping by the Mariners dropped New York to 1-4.

The Yankees won the final two games in Seattle, and headed home – burdened by a team ERA of 6.90 and the barbs of an unhappy owner. With the season barely underway, George Steinbrenner questioned the team's focus and resolve,[2] but assured manager Joe Torre his job was safe.[3]

Yankees fans did not share Steinbrenner's gloom; they picked up tickets for the home opener. The attendance of 56,717 was the largest turnout at Yankee Stadium since it was remodeled in 1976.[4]

Both pitchers began well. David Cone (0-1) retired the first two Athletics on popups and, despite being tagged for two singles, held Oakland scoreless in the first. A's starter Jimmy Haynes (1-0) – who had beaten the Yankees with six effective innings in Oakland – retired the three batters he faced. But, as soon became evident, this game would not prove to be a pitchers' duel.

Cone began the second inning with a strikeout, but a walk and two singles produced Oakland's first run.

Cone fanned Rickey Henderson for the second out, then Ben Grieve singled, bringing home rookie A.J. Hinch and Rafael Bournigal to give Oakland a 3-0 lead. Matt Stairs doubled home two more, and the Athletics were up 5-0.

Cone, who had undergone shoulder surgery in December 1997, was enduring his second straight poor start. After the game, Cone admitted his pitching was awful, but denied that his rehabbed shoulder was the problem.[5] Indeed, the shoulder was healthy; he won his next nine decisions, and completed the season 20-7. Cone was the Yankees' biggest winner in 1998, and tied Toronto's Roger Clemens and Rick Helling of Texas for the American League lead in wins.

Haynes faltered in the bottom of the second. A walk, single, and walk filled the bases, and Chad Curtis's sacrifice fly to right put the Yankees on the board. Scott Brosius flied to center; Tino Martinez tagged up and sped home. It was 5-2, Oakland, after two.

Oakland did not score in the top of the third, and Haynes returned to the mound with a three-run advantage. Derek Jeter flied out; he was the last batter Haynes retired. Haynes walked the next two hitters and ran the count full to Martinez, who drilled the 3-and-2 pitch 355 feet – over the fence and just in front of the right-field bleachers. The game was tied, 5-5.

Haynes issued his fifth walk, and Oakland manager Art Howe took him out, later explaining to reporters, "[Haynes] just wasn't showing me any signs of being able to throw strikes."[6] After the game, Haynes took full responsibility for blowing the five-run lead, admitting, "I was trying to be too fine."[7]

Aaron Small came in from the bullpen, but supplied no relief. The next three New York hitters singled, bringing home two more runs. A double play ended the inning, but the Yankees were leading, 7-5.

The Athletics did not score in the fourth even though Henderson reached first on an error to start the inning. He went to second on a passed ball, and was sacrificed to third, only to be stranded there.

In the bottom of the fourth, New York appeared to put the game out of reach by adding five more runs. Small issued consecutive walks to Jeter, Bernie Williams, and Martinez, to load the bases. Daryl Strawberry doubled, scoring Jeter and Williams and sending Martinez to third. No one was out; the Yankees' lead had grown to 9-5, and runners occupied second and third.

Howe ordered Small to intentionally walk Curtis to load the bases, then called upon Jim Dougherty to pitch. Brosius greeted Dougherty with a single to left, tallying Martinez and Strawberry and moving Curtis to second. An error reloaded the bases, and on a groundout, Curtis raced home. The inning ended with New York on top, 12-5.

Cone went to work in the fifth with a seven-run cushion, needing three outs to be eligible for his first win of the season. He never got those outs. Jason Giambi singled and Dave Magadan followed with a double, beginning an Oakland onslaught.

Oakland's third batter, Scott Spiezio, grounded out, scoring Giambi. Hinch singled, bringing home Magadan, and cutting Oakland's deficit to five runs.

Bournigal followed with another single, putting Athletics on first and second with only one out; Cone was done. Torre summoned free-agent acquisition Darren Holmes to the mound.

Henderson, the first batter facing Holmes, singled to load the bases. Jason McDonald slammed a hit to center and two more runners scored, slicing the Yankees' lead to 12-9. Holmes then hit Grieve with a pitch, filling the bases.

With only one out, the bases loaded, and four runs in, Torre called to the bullpen, handing the ball to rookie Mike Buddie for the third time in eight games. Buddie had not pitched well on the West Coast, giving up five runs in 2⅔ innings, for a 16.88 ERA.

Stairs welcomed Buddie with a grounder to third that Brosius could not handle; Henderson scored on the error, and the bases remained full. Consecutive singles by Giambi and Magadan drove in two more, putting Oakland ahead, 13-12, before Buddie could record the final two outs. The Athletics had scored

eight runs on eight hits, and sent 13 batters to the plate. Magadan later remarked, "It was one of those days. It was 13-12, and the game wasn't even official yet."[8]

With Dougherty still on the hill for Oakland, the Yankees responded with a game-winning rally. It began with a walk to Paul O'Neill. Williams then bunted in front of the plate, and when Hinch made an off-target throw to second, O'Neill took third and Williams second. Martinez doubled to center field, scoring both runners, and putting New York back on top, 14-13. Strawberry lined a single to center, scoring Martinez with the Yankees' 15th run.

With Curtis batting, Hinch threw out Strawberry attempting to steal. That cleared the bases, but the rally continued. Curtis drew a walk, and after Brosius flied out, Curtis went to second on Girardi's single. Dougherty was done.

The new Oakland hurler, T.J. Mathews, faced Chuck Knoblauch, who singled home Curtis, making it 16-13. That was the score when the fifth inning ended.

Over the last four innings Buddie, Graeme Lloyd, and Jeff Nelson held Oakland without a run, while New York scored one more.

In the seventh, Curtis legged out an infield single, stole second, went to third on a groundout, and sprinted home with his fourth run of the game when Giambi singled.

New York won, 17-13. The total of 30 runs made it the highest-scoring game in Yankee Stadium history, surpassing by two the 28 runs scored on June 3, 1933, when the Yankees clubbed the Philadelphia Athletics 17-11. Oakland stranded 11 runners, and New York 9, preventing the score from climbing higher.

Steinbrenner enjoyed the record attendance, as well as the game's outcome, but The Boss had harsh words for Holmes, who in December inked a three-year deal worth $4.65 million. Holmes did not record an out, prompting Steinbrenner to say, "He has to start showing something. They say he was throwing 95 miles per hour all the time. I don't see it."[9]

Buddie logged his first major-league win; he added three more in 1998. Dougherty took the loss; in July – with an 0-2 record and a 8.25 ERA – Oakland sent him to the Pacific Coast League.

Oakland pitchers gave up 16 hits, and walked 12, of whom 10 scored; New York pitchers surrendered 16 hits (14 singles, 2 doubles) and six walks. The Yankees' team ERA jumped to 7.57.

Oakland's Magadan made this frank assessment: "We didn't play very good baseball."[10] Torre was more diplomatic, telling David Lennon of *New York Newsday*, "We haven't reached our potential pitching-wise. But it's nice to have an offense that can hold you until that happens."[11]

The win lifted the Yankees to 4-4; they were at .500 for the first time. New York rolled up five more wins before losing in Detroit, and by the end of April the Yankees' record reached 17-6.

New York's final 114-48 record – the greatest win total in franchise history – was followed by a World Series championship. The pitching staff did reach its potential, posting a 3.82 ERA – the AL's best.

SOURCES

In addition to the sources cited in the Notes, the author consulted Baseball-Reference.com and Retrosheet.org for pertinent information, including the box score. The author also relied on game coverage in the *San Francisco Examiner,* the *New York Daily News,* and *New York Newsday,* and SABR BioProject biographies for several players involved in the game.

https://www.retrosheet.org/boxesetc/1998/B04100NYA1998.htm

https://www.baseball-reference.com/boxes/NYA/NYA199804100.shtml

NOTES

1   Mike Lupica, "Yanks Open," *New York Daily News,* April 11, 1998: 40.

2   Jon Heyman, "'The Boss' Is Already Hitting the Panic Button," *The Sporting News,* April 13, 1998: 33.

3   Peter Botte, "Boss Lets Joe Know Job's Safe," *New York Daily News,* April 11, 1998: 46.

4   Frank Blackman, "Yanks Walk All Over the A's," *San Francisco Examiner,* April 11, 1998: 37.

5   Peter Botte, "Bombers Left Standing as Stadium Record Falls," *New York Daily News,* April 11, 1998: 41.

6   Blackman.

7   David Lennon, "Pitching Almost Costs Win," *New York Newsday,* April 11, 1998: 38.

8   "A's Beat," *San Francisco Examiner,* April 11, 1998: 42.

9   Peter Botte and Rafael Hermoso, "George: Holmes clueless," *New York Daily News,* April 11,1998: 46.

10   "A's Beat."

11   Lennon.

BENITEZ BEANBALL BEGINS BIG BRAWL BETWEEN BALTIMORE BIRDS, BRONX BOMBERS

May 19, 1998:
New York Yankees 9, Baltimore Orioles 5,
at Yankee Stadium

By Jake Bell

"I guess if you can't win ballgames, you gotta try to win fights," Yankees owner George Steinbrenner jokingly taunted after witnessing one of the uglier brawls in baseball history. "If I hadn't been upstairs, I would've tried to get [Armando Benitez], too."[1]

Despite having baseball's biggest payroll, the 20-23 Baltimore Orioles came into Yankee Stadium on a five-game losing skid,[2] alone in the American League East cellar, 11 games behind the 28-9 Yankees. New York not only had the best record in baseball, but was off to the franchise's best start since 1939[3] and the best of any major-league team since the 1984 Detroit Tigers.[4]

The stark differences between the two teams' seasons could be summed up by their previous games. The Orioles wrapped up a humiliating homestand with a 6-3 loss that capped off a four-game sweep for the upstart Tampa Bay Devil Rays.[5] Meanwhile, the Yankees were coming off a perfect game thrown by David Wells.

David Cone took the mound for New York, sporting a record of 5-1 on his way to a 20-win season. The Orioles countered with Doug Johns, a 30-year-old southpaw with a career 5.66 ERA, who'd spent all of 1997 in Triple A and had just been reactivated from a stint on the disabled list for insomnia.

The pitching matchup proved more competitive than anticipated, however. Both pitchers surrendered a single run in the second inning: Cone on a line-drive single by Harold Baines; Johns on a groundout by Joe Girardi that allowed Scott Brosius to trot home from third.

Baltimore took the lead in the third on an RBI single by Roberto Alomar. Baines collected two more RBIs on another line-drive single to center field. And in the fourth inning, Jeffrey Hammonds hit a sacrifice fly that tagged Cone with a fifth run.

With the Orioles up 5-1, rookie right-hander Sidney Ponson replaced Johns in what became a three-up-three-down sixth inning, but surrendered a leadoff double to Chuck Knoblauch in the seventh. Paul O'Neill drove Knoblauch home with a double, then scored when Tim Raines blooped a single into left-center field. Ponson got out of the inning still leading 5-3, but in the bottom of the eighth, he issued back-to-back walks, bringing Derek Jeter to the plate representing the go-ahead run.

Orioles manager Ray Miller called on Alan Mills, who got Jeter to fly out, then immediately went back to his bullpen for Norm Charlton to set up a lefty-lefty matchup against O'Neill, which didn't work in Baltimore's favor. O'Neill belted Charlton's second pitch for an RBI single. With two outs, the tying run at second, and the go-ahead run at first, Miller brought in a fourth pitcher in as many hitters, asking closer Armando Benitez to collect a four-out save.

The 25-year-old fireballer had developed into one of baseball's best set-up men in 1997.[6] But his impressive regular season gave way to one of the worst postseason series for any reliever. In the American League Championship Series against the Cleveland Indians, Benitez made four appearances, all in games that became one-run Orioles losses, and was on the mound when the game-winning runs were scored in three of them. He gave up just three hits, but those were two home runs and a walk-off single that left him with a record of 0-2, a blown save, and an ERA of 12.00.

When Bernie Williams connected on a 2-and-1 slider, many Baltimore players and fans had flashbacks to that Cleveland series. The ball soared down the right-field line and landed in the upper deck for a three-run homer, putting New York up 7-5. But as Williams rounded the bases, as his teammates congratulated him at home plate, and as Tino Martinez walked to the batter's box, a few other Orioles recalled a different game, on June 7, 1995.

As a rookie, Benitez entered that game against the Seattle Mariners down 3-2 with two runners on. He walked the first batter he faced on four pitches, loading the bases for Edgar Martinez, who smashed Benitez's first offering over the left-field wall for a grand slam. The frustrated rookie hurled a fastball into the next Seattle hitter's shoulder, emptying both benches.

That now-former Mariner whom Benitez had plunked three years earlier was Tino Martinez, and he was about to become a victim of history repeating. The reliever who regularly flirted with triple digits on the radar gun uncorked a fastball that buried itself between the numbers on the back of Martinez's jersey.

By his own account, home-plate umpire Drew Coble "ejected Benitez almost before the pitch got there."[7] The Yankees poured out of their dugout, led by Darryl Strawberry. The Orioles followed as their closer threw down his glove and gestured toward the oncoming Yankees as if taunting them into a fight. Benitez later claimed he was trying to innocently express confusion about the Yankees' anger. "Everyone was coming to me. I had to throw my glove off and say, 'What's going on?'" Benitez insisted.[8]

The teams converged around the mound, and for a moment it seemed that calmer heads might prevail. Orioles players didn't seem too enthusiastic about standing up for Benitez's actions. "You know it's bad when guys on their team in the middle of the brawl are saying it was [garbage]," Yankee infielder Dale Sveum noted.[9] Jeter and others restrained Strawberry while Miller pulled Benitez away from the scrum and toward the visitors' dugout.

That moment of calm was shattered the second relievers Graeme Lloyd and Jeff Nelson arrived on the scene. The two sprinted from the New York bullpen and attempted a pincer attack against Benitez with Lloyd circling behind Miller to hit Benitez from the right while Nelson followed from his left. As soon as punches were thrown, the gaggle surged toward the action with players falling over one another.

Meanwhile, several Yankees and Orioles held back Martinez, who yelled about the 1995 incident as he attempted to swim through the mob to get to Benitez.

As Benitez stood on the top step of the dugout, Strawberry sucker-punched him, leaping at the pitcher with a left hook, then falling into the dugout. Others followed and piled on, including Mills, who jabbed his right fist into Strawberry's face, leaving a mouse under the slugger's left eye.

"It was ugly," Orioles catcher Lenny Webster recounted, "especially once it spilled into the dugout. Someone could have broken a leg falling down the stairs."[10]

"This was the most afraid I've been during a baseball game," Cone confessed. "It got really violent."[11]

Once Yankees manager Joe Torre calmed Strawberry down and marched him back to the home side of the diamond, and Cal Ripken Jr. and Orioles coach Eddie Murray restored order in their own dugout, the umpires began sorting things out. Strawberry, Lloyd, Nelson, and Mills were all ejected, and the game resumed after a 25-minute delay.

With Martinez on first and Bobby Muñoz, the O's fifth pitcher of the inning, on the mound, Raines blasted the first pitch he saw 408 feet to add two more runs to what would be a 9-5 New York win.

Benitez insisted that hitting Martinez was unintentional, offering his 17 walks in 17⅔ innings as evidence of his lack of pitch control. "I try to throw inside. I tried to scare him a little bit. I'm sorry about that," he said. "I feel very bad for hitting Tino. ... I don't want people to think I'm a bad guy."[12]

Martinez rejected Benitez's repentance. "An apology doesn't mean anything to me. He knew what he was doing," he responded.[13]

Even some on Benitez's own team weren't convinced. Miller called him "an immature young kid" and "out of control."[14] One anonymous teammate described him as "25 going on 15," and another said, "He embarrassed the whole organization. ... He may be ready physically to be a closer, but he's not ready mentally."[15] Webster said the blame for the brawl fell squarely on Benitez because "he hit the guy"[16] and acknowledged that "if I was Tino, I'd be upset, too."[17]

The next day, the American League handed Benitez an eight-game suspension and fined him $2,000. He chose not to appeal.[18]

Martinez sat out the next two games with a "bruise on his back ... this big" (as diagnosed by

Steinbrenner).[19] In his return, he belted an RBI triple, but strained his shoulder sliding into third. He believed the injuries were related as the bruise limited his range of motion. After sitting another six games, he went into a prolonged slump. Martinez, who had been batting .326 with an OPS of .957 before getting drilled, hit just .165 through June.[20]

SOURCES

In addition to the sources cited in the Notes, the author also accessed Baseball-Reference.com. Video of the brawl is available on YouTube.

https://www.baseball-reference.com/boxes/NYA/NYA199805190.shtml

https://www.retrosheet.org/boxesetc/1998/B05190NYA1998.htm

https://www.youtube.com/watch?v=ZKIHNsf8O_A

NOTES

1 Peter Botte, "George Weighs In with Fightin' Words," *New York Daily News*, May 20, 1998: 60.

2 The Orioles' losing streak eventually extended to nine games, the team's longest since its infamous 0-21 start to the 1988 season. They'd exceed that with a 10-game losing streak in August-September.

3 The 1998 team was the fourth team in franchise history to still have a single-digit number in the losses column after 37 games. The 1928 and 1939 Yankees both started their seasons 30-7. The 1998 team's record matched that of the 1926 team and has since been matched by the 2022 Yankees. https://stathead.com/tiny/RGJNh.

4 https://stathead.com/tiny/4HeXe.

5 The Devil Rays finished the season 63-99. Their seven wins against Baltimore were the most against any opponent.

6 Benitez converted 29 of 30 save situations into 20 holds and 9 saves.

7 Joe Strauss, "Orioles Go Down Fighting," *Baltimore Sun*, May 20, 1998: 1E.

8 Ken Rosenthal, "Benitez's Immature Act Wears Thin," *Baltimore Sun*, May 20, 1998: 1E.

9 Roch Kubatko, "Steinbrenner: 'Worst I've Seen,'" *Baltimore Sun*, May 20, 1998: 1E.

10 Bill Madden, "Lay Blame on Benitez, Orioles Say," *New York Daily News*, May 20, 1998: 60.

11 Ian O'Connor, "Baseball Trips on Its Tradition," *New York Daily News*, May 20, 1998: 58.

12 Joe Strauss, "O's Benitez Remorseful," *Baltimore Sun*, May 22, 1998: 1D.

13 John Delcos, "Yankees Notebook," *Rockland* (New York) *Journal News*, May 24, 1998: 4D.

14 Strauss, "O's Benitez Remorseful."

15 Tom Verducci, "Fevered Pitch," *Sports Illustrated*, June 1, 1998: 61.

16 Strauss, "Orioles Go Down."

17 Kubatko, "Steinbrenner: Worst I've Seen."

18 Strawberry and Lloyd each received three-game suspensions and were fined $1,000, while Mills and Nelson each got two games and $500 fines.

19 Botte, "George Weighs In."

20 From May 29 to June 30, Martinez had 16 hits in 97 at-bats. https://www.baseball-reference.com/players/gl.fcgi?id=martiti02&t=b&year=1998#896-923-sum:batting_gamelogs.

MARTINEZ GRAND SLAM CAPS YANKEE RALLY TO WIN GAME ONE OF 1998 WORLD SERIES

October 17, 1998:
New York Yankees 9, San Diego Padres 6,
at Yankee Stadium

By Mark S. Sternman

The 1998 Yankees had 114 wins to set a since-broken American League record and took on the San Diego Padres in the 1998 World Series. New York started David Wells, who "before the Series [proclaimed] that the Yankees would beat his hometown Padres in five games."[1]

After leading the 1998 AL with only 1.2 walks per nine innings, Wells issued an atypical base on balls to leadoff hitter Quilvio Veras. Playing hit-and-run, Tony Gwynn, the marquee player in the first half-century of the San Diego franchise, singled.[2] With Padres on first and second and none out, Wells induced a double-play grounder from Greg Vaughn and fanned Ken Caminiti to escape the jam.

San Diego starter and future Yankee Kevin Brown retired the first four New Yorkers, and none of the

Before the grand slam game, Tino Martinez had batted .188 (18-for-96) as a Yankee in the postseason.

first eight Yankees batters hit the ball out of the infield. Like Wells, Brown also averaged fewer than two walks per nine innings in 1998, but in the bottom of the second with one out, Chili Davis had an infield hit, and Tino Martinez walked. With two outs, Jorge Posada also walked to load the bases for left fielder Ricky Ledee, the least formidable of the Yankees starters. A 24-year-old rookie who had played in just 42 regular-season games, Ledee had gone 0-for-5 in the ALCS against Cleveland. But he pulled a double down the right-field line to put New York up 2-0. Brown fanned Chuck Knoblauch to end the frame.

The Padres quickly rallied, likewise sparked by a bottom-of-the-order hit. Ninth-place batter Chris Gomez singled over leaping shortstop Derek Jeter. With one out, Gwynn hit sharply to Martinez, who boxed the ball and could only retire Gwynn at first. The failure to turn the double play cost New York as Vaughn sent a low-and-away offering by Wells over the 385-foot sign in right-center for a homer that tied the game, 2-2.

Both pitchers settled down after the early scoring. With two outs in the bottom of the fourth, Scott Brosius hit into the left-center gap. Steve Finley, the Padres' center fielder, made the defensive play of the game. After briefly playing hot potato with the ball, Finley recovered to unleash a strong throw to second that beat Brosius to the bag. With Veras waiting with the ball, Brosius tried a swim move into the keystone sack but was easily tagged to end the inning.

San Diego broke through in the top of the fifth. With two outs, Veras blooped a single over Jeter. The lefty Gwynn followed by pulling a homer to deep right and, on the next pitch, the righty Vaughn pulled a no-doubter to deep left. The back-to-back blasts put the Padres up 5-2. "He missed spots," Yankees manager Joe Torre said later of Wells.[3]

After the game, reporters seemed surprised about the power displayed by the usually singles-hitting Gwynn. Tom Verducci of *Sports Illustrated* asked the future Hall of Famer about the reaction, and Gwynn said, "It's not like it's the first home run I've ever hit. I've hit a few before and I've hit a few longer than that. Give me a break."[4]

Consecutive singles by Ledee and Knoblauch put two Yankees on in the bottom of the fifth. With Joey Hamilton and Mark Langston warming up in the bullpen, Brown got grounders from Jeter and Paul O'Neill to protect the three-run San Diego lead.

In the top of the sixth with one out, Wells walked Wally Joyner. Holding Joyner, first baseman Martinez had the ideal position from which to field a line drive off Finley's bat and step on the base for a double play before the runner could retreat.

Hamilton and Langston resumed warming up as the bottom of the sixth began, but Brown had a one-two-three inning that featured strikeouts of Bernie Williams and Martinez. Wells also had a one-two-three frame in the top of the seventh.

The bottom of the seventh began innocently enough as Brosius grounded to Veras. After the out, Fox ran a graphic showing that the Yankees had a league-leading 50 come-from-behind wins. On cue, Posada singled over Veras. At 102 pitches, Brown readied to face Ledee with Donne Wall getting ready in the bullpen. Manager Bruce Bochy faced his first crucial decision of the contest. Ledee had two line-drive hits off Brown, who probably had few effective pitches left.[5] Bochy stayed with Brown, who proceeded to walk Ledee on four pitches, none of which came close to the plate. "Bochy called for Donne Wall and he might as well have called for Phillip Morris."[6]

Wall threw only four pitches. Facing Knoblauch, Wall missed with the first two before grooving one that Knoblauch hit high and barely inside the foul pole and over the left-field wall to tie the game. On the next pitch, Jeter smacked a line-drive single up the middle. Bochy, who had Langston warm up the last three innings, finally brought him in to face the heart of the New York batting order.

O'Neill flied out to leave Jeter on first with two outs and a 5-5 score. But then Langston wild-pitched Jeter to second, walked Williams intentionally, and walked Davis to load the bases with two outs for Martinez. Fox showed a graphic entitled "No Mr. October." At that point, Martinez with New York had a .184 career postseason batting average with only 1 home run and 5 RBIs.[7] Fox also showed Martinez's career stats with the bases loaded, which looked much better: a .326 batting average with six grand slams.

The day before the game, Martinez had anticipated facing a high-pressure situation: "For this one week, everything is so magnified," he told a sportswriter. "… Every at-bat, every base hit. And that's all you need. One big at-bat at the right time in the Series, one big play in the field."[8]

Perhaps less sharp than usual after having loosened for so long, Langston fell behind Martinez 2-and-0 and then, surprisingly given his wildness and the location of the game, got the call on a borderline pitch to make the count 2-and-1. With a 2-and-2 count, Langston threw a similar borderline pitch, more over the plate but possibly a little low as catcher Carlos Hernandez jerked his glove up in the strike zone after receiving the ball. Home-plate umpire Rich Garcia "called a ball on what surely could have been called a third strike," a sportswriter observed.[9]

"It was obvious we would have liked to have had it [called strike three]," Bochy said. "Langston, he thought it was there."[10]

The argument about whether this borderline call or the one earlier in the at-bat appeared more egregious became moot when Martinez hit a grand slam on the full-count pitch that followed, making the 3-and-2 pitch famous and the 2-and-0 pitch forgotten.

The grand slam, the 17th in World Series history and the first since Atlanta's Lonnie Smith hit one on October 22, 1992, off Toronto's Jack Morris, gave the Yankees a 9-5 lead.

The formidable back end of the New York bullpen had a comfortable four-run lead to protect. Jeff Nelson yielded a Gwynn single under Martinez's glove. Nelson broke Vaughn's bat and got the force at second. Mariano Rivera warmed up for the Yankees. Caminiti walked to put the tying run on deck. The lefty specialist Graeme Lloyd joined Rivera in the New York bullpen. Nelson struck out former Yankee Jim Leyritz before yielding to Rivera.

The peerless Rivera prevented San Diego from hitting the ball out of the infield. Joyner grounded to Knoblauch, but the shaky second baseman booted the ball as Vaughn scored. Rivera then retired Finley on a grounder to Martinez.

Leading 9-6, the Yankees had a big opportunity to pad the lead after loading the bases without a hit in the bottom of the eighth, but Randy Myers struck out O'Neill and Williams to keep the score the same.

Rivera had an easy ninth. He struck out pinch-hitters Greg Myers and the future Yankee John Vander Wal before Veras fouled out to Brosius to seal the New York victory.

Fox named Knoblauch and Martinez co-players of the game, and their homers clearly proved pivotal toward the outcome. More than a decade later, the game-tying homer by Knoblauch was largely forgotten in favor of the winning swat by Martinez, who "will always be remembered as one of the Yankees' 1998 postseason heroes, his grand slam … setting the stage for a World Series sweep of the Padres."[11]

But the heroics of the unheralded Ledee really proved the difference in the game. Ledee went 2-for-3 in Game One and in Games Two and Four as well, helping to lead the powerful Yankees to another World Series sweep and making Wells look like a pessimist for predicting New York in five.

NOTES

1   Jon Heyman, "New York," *The Sporting News*, October 26, 1998: 60.

2   All observations of the game come from the author's reviewing a version of the Fox broadcast that lacked audio. That version is no longer available online, but a version with audio is at www.youtube.com/watch?v=74VvI6Yt38w.

3   Buster Olney, "An Inning of Power Puts the Yankees on Top," *New York Times*, October 18, 1998: section 8, 1.

4   Tom Verducci, "Tony Gwynn Was a Joy to Watch at the Plate, and in Life," *Sports Illustrated*, June 16, 2014.

5   "A weary Brown began sending up red flares in the fifth inning, when he told Bochy, 'You might want to have somebody ready [for relief].' Then, before the seventh, Brown told his manager to 'pay attention' to him." Tom Verducci, "Tourist Trap Awestruck – and Awful/On Their First World Series Visit to the Bronx, the Padres Had to Contend With Both the Yankees and History," *Sports Illustrated*, October 26, 1998.

6   Murray Chass, "As Bochy Knows, There Is Little Relief in Sight for the Padres," *New York Times*, October 18, 1998: section 8, 2.

7   Martinez had already played in 40 postseason games prior to the 1998 World Series beginning with the 1995 ALDS that most Yankee fans would prefer to forget. He would end up playing 99 such contests with an underwhelming .233/.321/.351 slash line.

8   Gordon Edes, "Padre HR barrage trumped by NY," *Boston Globe*, October 18, 1998: D11.

9   George Vecsey, "Yankees Themselves Raise Stakes," *New York Times*, October 18, 1998: section 8, 1.

10 Jack Curry, "Finally, for Martinez, His October Moment," *New York Times*, October 18, 1998: section 8, 3.

11 Mark Feinsand, "Yankees vs. Orioles ALDS: Nick Swisher Looks to Put Dismal Past Postseasons Behind Him as Bombers Begin World Series Chase," *New York Daily News*, October 6, 2012.

SOMEHOW, THE PHRASE "WORLD CHAMPION NEW YORK YANKEES" NEVER SEEMS TO GET TIRED

October 27, 1999:
New York Yankees 4, Atlanta Braves 1,
at Yankee Stadium
Game Four of the 1999 World Series

By Alan Cohen

"We're just like everyone else. When good things are happening, sad things happen as well."
– Joe Torre, October 27, 1999[1]
"Making good on your moves does make you seem smart. Getting help from everyone makes you even smarter."
– Writer Shaun Powell describing Joe Torre and his cast of heroes after the 1999 World Series[2]

It had been a very trying year for the New York Yankees, beginning with manager Torre being treated for prostate cancer and pitching coach Mel Stottlemyre being treated for multiple myeloma, a cancer of the blood cells. Darryl Strawberry had not joined the team until September, following treatment for colon cancer, a suspension for drug possession, and a 21-game rehab stint in Triple A.

Through this and even more adversity, the team from the Bronx had prevailed. On September 12, third baseman Scott Brosius had lost his father to prostate cancer, and on October 21, second baseman Luis Sojo had lost his father to an aortic aneurysm. Now, on the day when outfielder Paul O'Neill had lost his father to heart disease, the Yankees were on the precipice of their 25th World Series championship. O'Neill was stationed in right field, and, at the end of the game, he was teary-eyed, an equal measure of sadness and joy. His uniform, like those of the other Yankees, showed remembrances of two former Yankees who had died in 1999. Joe DiMaggio's number 5 was on one shoulder

after his death in March, and a black armband was added when Catfish Hunter died in September.

The starting pitcher for the Yankees was Roger Clemens, three years removed from the rival Red Sox. The prior October, he had not been in the postseason after registering a 20-6 record with the Toronto Blue Jays. Yankees owner George Steinbrenner, not content with 114 regular-season wins in 1998 and World Series championships in 1996 and 1998, sought to bolster his pitching staff. On the first day of spring training, the Yankees acquired Clemens from Toronto in a trade for David Wells, Homer Bush, and Graeme Lloyd. Clemens responded with a 14-10 record and pitched the Yankees to a win in Game Three as they swept the Division Series against the Texas Rangers. A win on this evening would mean another sweep and the first World Series championship ring for Clemens since he came to the major leagues in 1984.

The Braves countered with John Smoltz, whose record in the postseason was 12-3 coming into the game. In 1999 he had gone 11-8 with the Braves, posting a 3.19 ERA.

The pitching of Clemens and Smoltz was dominant in Game Four. However, while Clemens was putting down the Braves on a minimum of pitches (he averaged fewer than 13 an inning in the first five innings), the Yankees were making Smoltz work, showing patience at the plate. He threw 75 pitches in the first three innings, facing eight batters in a 34-pitch third when the Yankees manufactured a trio of runs on four hits. The opportunistic Yankees did not hit the ball particularly hard but, in the words of old Yankee Wee Willie Keeler, "hit 'em where they ain't." Walt Weiss fielded Chuck Knoblauch's grounder in the hole between short and third, but the Atlanta shortstop was unable to make a play. Derek Jeter's broken-bat single to right field advanced Knoblauch to third. The hit extended Jeter's record of hitting in postseason games to 17. Jeter stole second base as O'Neill struck out. Bernie Williams received an intentional walk, and Tino Martinez sent a single into right field off the glove of Atlanta first baseman Ryan Klesko to drive home Knoblauch and Jeter. After Strawberry struck out (in his next-to-last big-league at-bat), the last of the inning's three runs came in when Jorge Posada, on the second 3-and-2 pitch, singled home Williams.

Those were the only runs that the Yankees scored against Smoltz. The Atlanta starter came out when the Braves took the field in the bottom of the eighth inning. He had allowed six hits (only one coming after the third inning) and struck out 11 batters.

Defensively, the Yankees shined. Clemens spent the night pitching groundballs, and his infielders backed him up (not a single putout was earned by a Yankee outfielder while Clemens was in the game). They turned a double play – Brosius to Knoblauch to Martinez in the fifth inning – and the climax came in the sixth inning when Brosius made a brilliant play at third base, robbing Chipper Jones of a hit to end the inning. Clemens ran to the dugout leaping toward the sky with his arms held high. And Knoblauch, who had been having difficulties making routine throws to first base, was errorless, his three throws to first being right on the money.

Before leaving the game in the eighth inning shortly after a slight injury covering first base on an infield single by Weiss, Clemens had allowed only four hits, and not a runner had advanced past second base. Weiss had hit the ball to first baseman Martinez, who went to his right to field the ball. The ball, Clemens, and Weiss arrived at first base together and Weiss apparently stepped on Clemens' right foot.[3] Umpire Gerry Davis ruled Weiss safe, much to the disappointment of most of the crowd of 56,752.[4] After Gerald Williams singled, sending Weiss to second base, Clemens was replaced by Jeff Nelson, who faced only one batter. Bret Boone singled up the middle to drive home Weiss and send Williams to third base. With two out and runners on the corners, Atlanta was threatening to close the gap further when Torre emerged from the Yankee dugout, the bullpen door swung open, and Mariano Rivera jogged in to douse Atlanta's hopes.

Rivera, the World Series MVP, went about his business with his usual degree of cool and calm. In a sport in which pitchers often have had scoreless streaks measured in innings and games, Rivera's scoreless streaks are measured in months. He had not given up an earned run since July 21. That was 28 regular-season appearances and seven postseason games. On this evening, in this third appearance in the 1999 Series, he retired Jones on a grounder to end the eighth after Chipper, on a pitch early in the at-bat, had rifled a shot down the first-base line that just went foul.

Terry Mulholland replaced Smoltz on the mound for Atlanta in the bottom of the eighth. After he recorded two quick outs, Jim Leyritz was sent up to pinch-hit. Leyritz homered to extend the Yankees' lead to 4-1, and a double by Posada brought manager Bobby Cox to the mound to change pitchers. Russ Springer got Chad Curtis out on a popup, and then it was three-up and three-down in the bottom of the ninth. As designated hitter Keith Lockhart's fly ball was descending toward the waiting glove of Yankee left fielder Curtis, the celebration began with catcher Posada charging the mound to embrace Rivera, and the crowd joining Frank Sinatra in singing, "Start Spreading the News!"

The postgame celebration for the team that had thus won 12 consecutive World Series games in which they had played was relatively low key. Their manager, Torre, liked it that way. As noted by Dominic Amore in the *Hartford Courant*, the team "could be remembered as much for its manners as for its homers. Celebrations are kept low-key by Torre. Demonstrations (however) are unabashed when it comes to respecting the opposition or caring about their own."[5]

Nevertheless, the postgame celebration was, by Yankee standards, exuberant. Jeter put an end to a media interview with team owner Steinbrenner by dousing the Boss with champagne. The players made their way back to the field and were greeted with cheers by the fans who had stayed behind. In his time on the field, Jeter, who went on to play a season's worth of games (158) in the postseason, batting .308 with 200 hits, said, "This is what everybody plays for. This is when you want to do your best."[6]

The streak of wins in 12 consecutive World Series games tied the record sent by the Yankees of Babe Ruth and Lou Gehrig in 1927, 1928, and 1932. The Yankees would tack on two more wins at the beginning of the 2000 series to set a major-league record for the team and its manager, Joe Torre.

After the game, Smoltz expressed his belief that "in every facet of the game, [the Yankees] had an answer.

I don't believe we were outmatched; I do believe we were outplayed."[7]

SOURCES

In addition to the sources shown in the notes, the author used BaseballReference.com, Retrosheet.org, and the following:

Amore, Dominic, David Heuschkel, and Jack O'Connell. "Heavy Heart for O'Neill," *Hartford Courant*, October 28, 1999: C7.

Heyman, Jon. "His Saving Grace: Cool as Always, Rivera Deflects Praise in MVP Show," *Newsday* (Long Island, New York), October 28, 1999: 104.

Howard, Johnette. "Clemens Steps Up," *Newsday*, October 28, 1999: 107, 92.

Jacobs, Jeff. "From Ruth to Clemens, Monumental Dynasty," *Hartford Courant,* October 28, 1999: C-1, C-6.

Rocca, Lawrence. "Joy of Yankees Twinged with Sorrow," *Newsday*, October 28, 1999: 106, 92.

"Yankees Sweep Braves for 25th Title as Clemens Gets His Series Dream," *New York Times*, October 28, 1999.

NOTES

1   Steve Jacobson, "Torre Has Life Perspective," *Newsday*, October 28, 1999: 103.

2   Shaun Powell, "All in Pinstripes Deserve Award," *Newsday*, October 28, 1999: 105.

3   Peter Botte, "Yanks Notch Series Sweep: Stake Claim to Greatness," *New York Daily News* World Series Supplement, October 28, 1999: 3.

4   Bill Madden, "Boss Leads the Cheers for Roger," *New York Daily News* World Series Supplement, October 28, 1999: 7.

5   Dominic Amore, "Sweep, Glorious Sweep," *Hartford Courant*, October 28, 1999: A1, A13. In 1999, caring about their own was a very key theme. Tim Raines, who had been with the team from 1996 through 1998, was no longer with the team when he was diagnosed with lupus in early 1999. When he returned to get his 1998 World Series ring, the team collectively rushed from the dugout to the field to embrace their stricken teammate.

6   Mark Herrmann, "Jeter Comfortable as a Young Leader," *Newsday*, October 28, 1999: 104.

7   Bob Herzog, "Braves Agree: Yanks Superior Team," *Newsday*, October 28, 1999: 100.

ROGER CLEMENS FACES PEDRO MARTINEZ IN A GAME FOR THE AGES

May 28, 2000:
Boston Red Sox 2, New York Yankees 0,
at Yankee Stadium

By Alan Raylesberg

The game between the New York Yankees and the Boston Red Sox on May 28, 2000, was one of the most anticipated regular-season games of that era. As pitching matchups go, it did not get any better. Roger

Freddy "Sez" Schuman was a Yankee Stadium mainstay, bringing his cheery signs and shamrock pans to nearly every home game from the late 1980's until his death in 2010.

Courtesy of Bill Nowlin.

Clemens, the former Red Sox ace, squared off against Pedro Martinez, the current Red Sox ace, in a showdown between two pitchers who were then earmarked for the Hall of Fame. Yankee Stadium was sold out for this Sunday night nationally televised game, with the two teams tied for first place in the American League East Division. Those in attendance, and those watching at home, were about to see one of those rare instances where a game lived up to the hype.

During the 2000 season, the Yankees and the Red Sox were in the throes of one of baseball's greatest rivalries. The Yankees were the two-time defending World Series champions, having won the fall classic in three of the previous four years (1996, 1998, 1999). They finished first in the AL East in each of those seasons, and in 1998 and 1999 the Red Sox finished second. In 1999 Boston finished only four games behind New York in the regular season before losing to the Yankees in the American League Championship Series.

May 28 was the final game of a three-game series between the two teams. The Red Sox won the opener on Friday night, 4-1, to take a one-game lead over the Yankees. The Yankees took the Saturday game, 8-3, to restore the tie.[1] That set the stage for the deciding game of the series, with first place on the line and the Clemens vs. Martinez matchup taking center stage. The two had faced each other only once before, in Game Three of the 1999 American League Championship Series, a game won by the Red Sox, 13-1, as Martinez struck out 12 in seven innings and Clemens allowed five runs in two innings.[2]

Clemens began his career with the Red Sox in 1984 and pitched for them over 13 seasons. In that span, he won three Cy Young Awards.[3] Leaving Boston in free agency after the 1996 season, he pitched two seasons for the Toronto Blue Jays, winning two more Cy Young Awards, before joining the Yankees in 1999, at the age of 36.[4]

Martinez came to the Red Sox in 1998, after six seasons with the Dodgers and Expos. At age 25, he won the Cy Young Award in 1997, pitching for the Expos.[5] After winning 19 games for the Red Sox in 1998, Martinez led the league in wins, ERA, and strikeouts for the 1999 Red Sox, garnering his second Cy Young Award.[6] The 27-year-old Martinez was off to a great start in 2000, with a record of 7-2 and an ERA of 1.19 as play began on May 28.[7]

With two of the greatest pitchers of their generation going head-to-head at Yankee Stadium, Dan Shaughnessy wrote in the *Boston Globe* that "in this lifetime we are not likely to see a better early-season matchup."[8] The fact that Clemens was the former Boston ace and Martinez the current one only added to the drama. Shaughnessy characterized it as "Ali-Frazier on God's green grass."[9]

The game did not disappoint, as both Clemens and Martinez were nearly flawless. Both teams were scoreless through eight innings, with each pitcher allowing only three hits; Clemens struck out 13, and Martinez 8.[10] It was as if each pitcher was trying to outdo the other.

Scoring opportunities were few and far between. After Derek Jeter singled off Martinez with one out in the first, he was erased on a double play. Shane Spencer drew a leadoff walk in the third before Martinez retired the next three batters. In the fourth, Jeter got the Yankees' second hit, a leadoff double, but was stranded when the next three batters were retired on two strikeouts and a popup. Ricky Ledee singled with two out in the fifth and stole second but was left there when Martinez retired the next batter. Martinez retired the Yankees in order in each of the sixth, seventh, and eighth innings.

The Red Sox fared no better against Clemens. After he retired the side in the first, Carl Everett singled with one out in the second. Clemens picked him off first, then got the third out on a strikeout. Clemens retired the next 11 batters, striking out seven of them, before John Valentin singled with one out in the sixth. Valentin was caught stealing and the next batter struck out. In the seventh, Trot Nixon tripled with one out and the Red Sox had the best scoring opportunity of the game. Clemens struck out the next two batters to end the threat.

In the ninth, Clemens retired Valentin for the first out. Jason Varitek tried to bunt his way on, but Clemens made the play for out number two. Jeff Frye then singled, bringing Nixon to the plate. The count went to 2-and-1. With the crowd cheering Clemens on, Nixon hit one deep to right field. The ball sailed into the seats for a two-run home run as the Yankees fans suddenly got quiet, and it felt as though the air had come out of the Stadium.[11] Clemens retired the next batter, but the damage was done.

In the bottom of the ninth, the Yankees rallied. Chuck Knoblauch was hit by a pitch and Jeter singled to right (his third hit off Martinez), putting runners on first and second with nobody out. Martinez struck out Paul O'Neill for his ninth strikeout. Bernie Williams hit one deep to right field, but Nixon caught it in front of the fence, with Knoblauch taking third on the play. Jeter then stole second; Jorge Posada was hit by a pitch; and now the bases were loaded with two out for Tino Martinez. The fans were on their feet and the game was on the line. There was no Yankees comeback as Tino Martinez grounded out, second to first, and the game was over.

Boston had a 2-0 win to take over first place.[12] Martinez had pitched a four-hit shutout, with one walk and nine strikeouts. Clemens had allowed only five hits, walked none, and struck out 13, and was just one Trot Nixon swing away from a shutout of his own.[13]

After the game, both pitchers recognized the magnitude of what had just taken place. "It's good for baseball," Martinez said. "The fans came out and clapped for both of us. ... We were feeding off each other the whole game."[14] Clemens said, "That's the way it's supposed to be. ... It was a fun game to pitch in. The intensity was every bit what it was supposed to be."[15] On the ESPN telecast of the game, Joe Morgan[16] commented that a lot of people like to see home runs and high-scoring games, "but I'll tell you what this is a baseball game. You're seeing two pitchers at the top of their craft."[17]

As Yankees manager Joe Torre said, after the game, "It was a classic."[18] The *Boston Globe* described it as "one of the greatest regular season games in 100 years of American League play."[19] "That's the best regular-season game I've ever seen ... one for the ages," said Boston pitching coach Joe Kerrigan.[20] On the ESPN broadcast, Jon Miller and Joe Morgan compared the game to the "1912 duel of the year" between Walter Johnson and Smoky Joe Wood at Fenway Park.[21] When the game ended, Miller remarked that

Clemens and Martinez had given fans "baseball's version of a night to remember."[22]

The Yankees-Red Sox rivalry, the importance of the game, and the fact that the two pitchers were all-time greats, combined to make the May 28, 2000, game one of the most memorable regular-season games in the long and storied history of Yankee Stadium.

At season's end, the Yankees finished first, 2½ games ahead of the Red Sox. They beat Oakland, three games to two, in the Division Series, beat Seattle in a four-game ALCS, and needed just five games to beat the New York Mets in the 2000 World Series. Clemens finished the season 13-8 (3.70). Though he lost both games he pitched in the ALDS, he shut out Seattle in Game Four of the ALCS and won Game Two of the World Series.

AUTHOR'S NOTE

The author attended the game, with his family, in an Upper Tier Box at Yankee Stadium, in fair territory in left field. While far from home plate, the author had a clear view and still vividly recalls the moment when Trot Nixon hit his ninth-inning home run off Clemens to break the scoreless tie and silence the Yankees fans.

SOURCES

In addition to the sources cited in the Notes, the author consulted baseball-reference.com and Retrosheet.org.

https://www.baseball-reference.com/boxes/NYA/NYA200005280.shtml

https://www.retrosheet.org/boxesetc/2000/B05280NYA2000.htm

NOTES

1   Coming into the game on May 28, each team had a record of 27-18.

2   Clemens was disappointed about how that game transpired. When asked about it prior to the May 28 rematch against Martinez, Clemens said, "I just pitched poorly and we'll leave it at that." Buster Olney, "Martinez Stands and Delivers for the Red Sox," *New York Times*, May 29, 2000: D1.

3   Clemens won the Cy Young Award, while with the Red Sox, in 1986, 1987, and 1991. He was also the American League's Most Valuable Player in 1986. During his Red Sox years, he also led the AL (or tied for the lead) in wins twice, in ERA four times, in complete games twice, in shutouts five times, and in strikeouts three times. In his 1986 MVP season, he was 24-4 with a league-leading 2.48 ERA.

4   In his first season with Toronto, in 1997, Clemens led the league in wins (21-7), ERA (2.05), innings pitched (264, tied for lead), and strikeouts (292). He was sensational again in 1998, as he tied for the AL lead in wins (20-6) and led the AL in ERA (2.65) and strikeouts (271). After the 1998 season Clemens was traded to the Yankees. In his first season with the Yankees, 1999, Clemens was 14-10 with a 4.60 ERA, the highest ERA of his career. He went on to have some good seasons with the Yankees, including 2001, when he was 20-3 with a 3.51 ERA and won the Cy Young Award. He pitched five seasons for New York before leaving in free agency to join the Houston Astros in the 2004 season. In his first season with Houston, at age 41, he won another Cy Young Award to give him a career total of seven Cy Young Awards, the most by any pitcher in history. Clemens pitched four seasons for Houston before returning to the Yankees as a free agent in 2007, his final season. His career performance (which included 354 wins) would certainly appear to qualify him for the National Baseball Hall of Fame. However, his career was tainted by his alleged use of performance-enhancing drugs, a factor that has prevented him from being elected, at least as of October 2022.

5   Martinez was 17-8 with a league-leading 1.90 ERA. After the 1997 season, the Expos traded him to the Red Sox for Carl Pavano and Tony Armas.

6   In his 1999 Cy Young-winning season, Martinez was 23-4 with a 2.07 ERA and 313 strikeouts in 213⅓ innings. Martinez pitched seven seasons for the Red Sox before signing with the Mets as a free agent beginning with the 2005 season. He played for the Mets through 2008 before finishing his career with the Phillies in 2009. Martinez won the Cy Young Award three times (1997, 1999, and 2000). His performance from 1997 through 2003 was one of the most dominant stretches of pitching in history. During those seven seasons, he led the league in ERA five times. Martinez was inducted into the Hall of Fame in 2015.

7   Clemens came into the game with a record of 4-4 and an ERA of 4.26.

8   Dan Shaughnessy, "Pedro Bests Rival Again," *Boston Globe*, May 29, 2000: E1.

9   Shaughnessy.

10   At the time, Clemens held the major-league strikeout record of 20 in a nine-inning game, having done it twice for the Red Sox, on April 29, 1986, and September 18, 1996. Kerry Wood of the Chicago Cubs also struck out 20 on May 6, 1998. In 2016 Max Scherzer of the Washington Nationals became the third pitcher in history to strike out 20 in a nine-inning game. Clemens also had 18 strikeouts in a nine-inning game on August 25, 1998, for Toronto. Tom Cheney of the Washington Senators struck out 21 batters in 16 innings on September 12, 1962; Randy Johnson of the Arizona Diamondbacks struck out 20 in nine innings, in a game that went 11 innings on May 8, 2001.

11   There were plenty of Red Sox fans in the sellout crowd, who cheered loudly as the Yankees fans sank into their seats.

12   The Yankees would go on to win the AL East with a record of 87-74, with Boston second at 85-77. Boston did not make the postseason, as Seattle was the wild card with a 91-71 record.

13   Martinez improved his record to 8-2 and lowered his ERA to 1.05. With the defeat, Clemens was 4-5 while lowering his ERA to 3.97. Martinez threw 128 pitches, Clemens 127. Martinez finished the 2000 season with a record of 18-6 and a league-leading 1.74 ERA, together with a league-leading 284 strikeouts. Martinez won the Cy Young Award for the second straight year and the third time in four seasons.

14   Shaughnessy.

15   Shira Springer, "Clemens Sure Has Not Lost It," *Boston Globe*, May 29, 2000: E8.

16   Morgan, a Hall of Fame second baseman, was the commentator on the broadcast.

17   Chad Jennings, "Distant Replay: The Night Pedro Martinez Beat Roger Clemens in Duel for the Ages," *The Athletic*, April 17, 2020, https://theathletic.com/1753055/2020/04/17/pedro-martinez-roger-clemens-yankees-red-sox-2000/.

18   Olney, "Martinez Stands and Delivers for the Red Sox." Torre also said. "It was an inspired performance on both sides, and somebody had to lose, unfortunately. It was a great game. … It definitely was a playoff atmosphere. The players felt it. Everybody was pumped up." Shira Springer, "Clemens Sure Has Not Lost It," *Boston Globe*, May 29, 2000: E8.

19   Shaughnessy, "Pedro Bests Rival Again."

20   Shaughnessy.

21   Jennings. See also Emil Rothe, "The War of 1912: The Wood-Johnson Duel," published in SABR's 1974 *Baseball Research Journal*, https://sabr.org/journal/article/the-war-of-1912-the-wood-johnson-duel/.

22   Jennings, "Distant Replay: The Night Pedro Martinez Beat Roger Clemens in Duel for the Ages."

YANKEES DEFEAT METS TWICE IN RARE TWIN BILL IN SEPARATE BALLPARKS

July 8, 2000:
New York Yankees 4, New York Mets 2,
at Yankee Stadium

By Thomas J. Brown Jr.

It was a once-in-a-century event for baseball fans in New York. The Mets and the Yankees were facing each other in two different ballparks on the same day.[1]

The Yankees started the day a half-game in front of Toronto in the American League East. The Mets came into the "subway series" 2½ games behind the Atlanta Braves. Both teams were excited about the series. Mets pitcher Turk Wendell said it was special because the teams were doing "something that nobody has done in 97 years. It's pretty cool to be part of that."[2]

The Mets lost the first game of the four-game set on Friday when Paul O'Neill jumped up and stole a home run from Derek Bell in the bottom of the eighth to give the Yankees a 2-1 win.

Dwight Gooden started for the Yankees in the first game on Saturday. It was the first time Gooden took the field at Shea Stadium as an opposing pitcher. "It was surreal seeing him on the mound in a Yankee uniform," Todd Zeile said afterward. Gooden pitched five innings and surrendered the only two Mets runs in the Yankees' 4-2 victory.

The first game was not without some controversy. Chuck Knoblauch led off the game with a single to center. Jay Payton bobbled the ball and Knoblauch went for two. After he was thrown out, first-base umpire Rob Cook said that Zeile had interfered with Knoblauch and awarded him second. Mets manager Bobby Valentine argued the call, even pointing out Knoblauch's path on the dirt. His arguing got him thrown out of the game and the Mets played the game under protest.

To make the afternoon even stranger, Zeile was called for interference again in the fourth. The second-base umpire, Mark Carlson, said that Zeile had interfered with Knoblauch as he ran to second. Zeile said

later that the calls were "more than strange," adding, "How many times do you see an obstruction play in a game, let alone with the same two players?"[3]

The first game ended at 4:30, with the next game scheduled for 8:05. After eating a team dinner at Shea Stadium and changing into their away uniforms, both teams were given a police escort across town while fans fought traffic or maneuvered the subway system. The Mets were greeted "with a lavish welcome from fans behind the barricade inside Yankee Stadium. They chanted 'Let's Go Mets' as the team walked in."[4]

Thirty-seven-year-old Roger Clemens started the second game for the Yankees. The right-hander entered the game with a 5-6 record. He had lost his first three starts against the Mets since joining the Yankees in 1999. Clemens almost hit Lenny Harris with the second pitch of the game. "It missed me by inches,"

Yankees manager Joe Torre and Mets manager Bobby Valentine would meet in the World Series that fall.

Harris said. "I thought, 'Oh, God.' A guy could lose his career."[5] The next Mets batter, Bell, was also brushed back by Clemens.

After Clemens retired the Mets in order in the first, he faced Mike Piazza to start the second. The 31-year-old catcher entered the game with a .354 batting average, 24 home runs, and 72 RBIs. He had been successful against Clemens in the past with 7 hits in 12 at-bats that included three home runs. Clemens' first pitch was an inside fastball for a called strike.

The second pitch, a 92-MPH fastball, came high and inside. An observer described it: "Piazza realized the ball was coming at him and began ducking, but it hit him solidly on the helmet, just above the bill. He fell onto his back, eyes closed and then open, his expression blank."[6]

The entire Mets team raced to the top of the dugout with bench coach and former Mets catcher John Stearns shouting at the umpires. "I didn't hit Mike on purpose," Clemens said after the game. "I was going to pitch him inside. I don't know if I've pitched inside as much as I need to this year. Mike has obviously hit me well."[7]

While Piazza remained on the ground surrounded by the trainers, manager Valentine was furious as he shouted at Clemens. Piazza was forced to leave the game. He was later diagnosed with a mild concussion. "He threw at Lenny's head, he threw at Derrick's head and he hit Mike," Valentine said. "Clemens is going to the Hall of Fame. He doesn't have that bad control."[8]

While Piazza was being treated, Clemens stood in front of the mound, looking down. "I was shaken after I hit him," he said. "That was not the way I wanted to get him out." Meanwhile the Mets were shouting profanities at Clemens from the dugout steps. Todd Pratt, the Mets' backup catcher, said of Piazza. "He's our leader. You always want to watch out for a teammate, but he's the No. 1 guy. There's a lot of emotions with seeing him go down."[9]

After the dust settled, both teams got back to baseball. Clemens retired the next seven Mets. In the fourth inning the Mets put a runner in scoring position on singles by Edgardo Alfonzo and Matt Franco (who had replaced Piazza). But Clemens struck out Robin Ventura and got Zeile to ground out, keeping the Mets off the board.

Left-hander Glendon Rusch started for the Mets. The 25-year-old Rusch entered the game with a 6-6 record. He had faced the Yankees five times when he played for the Kansas City Royals and lost each time.

It was his first start against the Yankees since his trade to the Mets in 1999.

In the bottom of the second, Tino Martinez, who had homered in the first game, led off and Rusch hit him on the back with a fastball. Both teams were given a warning as "Martinez glanced at Rusch, flipped his bat away and jogged to first, while 55,821 roared."[10]

The Mets took a two-run lead in the fifth. Melvin Mora hit a two-out single and stole second. Clemens walked Harris. Singles by Bell and Alfonzo scored two runs before Franco's groundout ended the frame.

The lead did not last. David Justice and Shane Spencer singled to open the Yankees' half of the fifth. Chris Turner's sacrifice moved the runners up. Scott Brosius lined a single to right field to score Justice and advance Spencer to third.

Knoblauch then hit a liner to left. Harris drifted back toward the wall, jumped, and reached up. The ball landed in his glove for an instant but then the glove hit the wall and the ball bounced over the wall for a three-run homer. The Yankees were ahead 4-2.

"All those ghosts in left field, maybe they pulled the ball out of my glove," Harris said later. "I thought I had it. Unbelievable."[11]

Both pitchers were flawless the rest of the way. Rusch retired the next 11 batters but the damage was done. He struck out 10 batters and walked none in a losing effort. Clemens retired the next six batters. He left in the eighth inning with a man on base – Bell with a leadoff double – and one out. Clemens finished with four strikeouts and one walk. Yankees manager Joe Torre brought in Mike Stanton, who got the next two batters out on six pitches.

Mariano Rivera, who earned a save in the first game, came in to finish the second game as well. Payton reached base on an error but the Mets couldn't capitalize. Rivera retired the next two batters to give the Yankees a sweep of the doubleheader and earn his second save of the day.

Valentine was still angry at Clemens after the game. He told reporters that he "hoped Roger Clemens would pitch a Subway Series in a National League park so that he would have to come to the plate against the Mets." Torre, who defended his pitcher, said, "Bobby wants to get a bat against Clemens? Good, I'd like to see that."[12]

Piazza was angry about the incident when he talked to reporters the following day. But then the catcher brought some levity to the situation when he said, "The only positive thing that would have come out of it is I would have been remembered as the best defensive catcher in baseball history. ... You know how when someone is gone, how they always get pumped up? People would have said, 'You know, he wasn't that bad.'"[13]

Despite missing Piazza, the Mets won the final game of the series, 2-0, at Shea Stadium on Monday behind Mike Hampton's seven-inning, eight-strike-out performance. The two teams eventually met in the World Series and Piazza's and Clemens' paths crossed once again – with both players almost coming to blows.[14]

In the end, it was about a memorable once-in-a lifetime doubleheader.[15] Torre told reporters after the game that "the handful of fans who had tickets for both games – perhaps they rode the No. 7 train from Shea and transferred to the No. 4 to Yankee Stadium – put their stubs away for sons and grandsons perhaps yet unborn. Mets and Yankees, Shea and Yankee Stadium, all on one day and nostalgia for a lifetime."[16]

SOURCES

In addition to the sources cited in the Notes, the author used the Baseball-Reference.com and Retrosheet.org websites for box-score, player, team, and season pages, pitching and batting logs, and other pertinent material.

https://www.baseball-reference.com/boxes/NYA/NYA200007082.shtml

https://www.retrosheet.org/boxesetc/2000/B07082NYA2000.htm

NOTES

1   The teams were playing a doubleheader to make up for a June 11 rainout of the final game of the first three-game series that season. There had been only one previous time when two New York major-league teams had played each other in two different ballparks on one day. It happened when the Brooklyn Superbas played the New York Giants on September 7, 1903. The Brooklyn team was known by several names in its early history: the Bridegrooms, Grooms, Superbas, Robins, and Trolley Dodgers. They officially became the Dodgers in the 1932. The teams split the doubleheader. New York won the first game, 6-4, at Washington Park, Brooklyn's home field. Brooklyn won the second game, 3-0, at the Giants' home park, the Polo Grounds.

2   Mark Herrmann, "Baseball Is Twice the Fun in Two Parks," *Newsday* (Long Island, New York), July 10, 2000: C4.

3   Kit Stiers, "Mets Feel Obstructed by Umpire's Ruling," *White Plains* (New York) *Journal News*, July 9, 2000: 28.

4   Herrmann.

5   Roger Rubin, "Mets Take Aim," *New York Daily News*, July 9, 2000: 44.

6   Buster Olney, "Clemens Stirs the Pot by Beaning Piazza," *New York Times*, July 9, 2000: 290.

7   Ohm Youngmisuk, "Roger Says Pitch Was a Mistake," *New York Daily News*, July 9, 2000: 45.

8   Rubin.

9   Rubin.

10   Olney.

11   Olney.

12   Mike Lupica, "Subway Sweep," *New York Daily News*, July 9, 2000: 43.

13   Marty Noble, "Franco Calling Rocket Reckless," *Newsday,* July 10, 2000: A37.

14   October 22, 2000: Clemens and Piazza clash as Yankees win Game Two. SABR Games Project, https://sabr.org/gamesproj/game/october-22-2000-clemens-and-piazza-clash-as-yankees-win-game-two/.

15   The Mets and the Yankees played split doubleheaders again in 2003 and 2008. The Yankees won both games in 2003. The teams split the doubleheader in 2008 with the Mets winning the first game at Yankee Stadium and the Yankees taking the second game at Shea Stadium.

16   Steve Jacobson, "Doubleheader Provided Very Special Day," *Newsday,* July 10, 2000: C5.

DAVID JUSTICE POWERS YANKS TO 37TH AL PENNANT IN COMEBACK WIN

October 17, 2000:
New York Yankees 9, Seattle Mariners 7,
at Yankee Stadium
Game Six of the 2000 American League Championship Series

By Mark S. Sternman

Nearly a quarter of a century had passed since the New York Yankees had appeared in three straight World Series, a feat last accomplished by the 1976-1978 teams. The veteran 2000 squad (which nearly blew a big American League East lead in the last week of the regular season) matched this record thanks to a stirring rally over the Seattle Mariners.

The Yankees led the Mariners, three victories to two, in the best-of-seven American League Championship Series. For Game Six of the series, New York started Orlando Hernandez, who had a track record of pitching well in the regular season but wonderfully in the postseason. Hernandez struggled in this game. With one out in the first inning, he walked Al Martin, who scampered home on Alex Rodriguez's double. Yankees playoff nemesis Edgar Martinez doubled Rodriguez home, and the Mariners quickly led 2-0.

Brooklyn-born John Halama protected the Seattle edge with a one-two-three first, and Hernandez likewise faced just three batters in the second after walking Carlos Guillen, who "was caught stealing when the Yankees pitched out and trapped him between first and second."[1]

Bernie Williams singled to give New York a promising start to the bottom of the second, but Tino Martinez hit into a 4-6-3 twin killing.

The Mariners doubled their lead in the fourth thanks to another inning with multiple extra-base hits. John Olerud doubled and Guillen, "who homers about as often as Don Zimmer parts his hair,"[2] did just that to put Seattle up 4-0. "As he watched the ball land in the upper deck, Hernandez covered his face with his glove, peeking through it as if to confirm the damage,"

noted the *New York Times*. "'I covered my face because I made a mistake,' Hernandez said through a translator. 'I threw it over the plate.'"[3] Yankees manager Joe Torre could have hooked Hernandez at this point but stayed with his experienced righty.

New York rallied in the fourth. With one out, David Justice and Bernie Williams both singled. Tino

Midseason pickup David Justice hit .305 with 20 home runs and 60 RBIs in 78 regular-season games with the 2000 Yankees.

Martinez walked to load the bases. In what would turn out to be the second most critical play of the game, Jorge Posada doubled, scoring two and sending Martinez to third. The Yankees trailed 4-2, but had the tying runs in scoring position and Paul O'Neill coming up. O'Neill had only nine hits in his last 72 at-bats. The *New York Post*'s Joel Sherman wrote, "This [had] been the worst six weeks in O'Neill's otherwise glorious, eight-year Yankee run. His bat [had] looked lifeless."[4]

Reversing his misfortunes, O'Neill singled to plate Martinez and narrow the deficit to 4-3. Here, Seattle manager Lou Piniella made the move Torre had declined to make by yanking his starter. The move paid off in the short term as Brett Tomko extricated himself from Halama's jam by getting infield outs off the bats of Luis Sojo and Scott Brosius to protect the slender Seattle edge.

After multiple runs by both teams in the fourth, the pitchers put up zeros over the next five half-innings. New York had two walks (one intentional) and a steal in the fourth, but Tino Martinez could not cash in his mates. In the sixth, after a second Rodriguez double, the *New York Post* described the events: "El Duque fanned Edgar Martinez on a 2-2 breaking pitch [and] walked … Olerud intentionally with Mike Stanton warming up in the pen. Raul Ibanez hit what should have been an inning-ending, 6-4-3 double play but the one-hop smash glanced off Derek Jeter's glove as he dove for the ball. A heads-up … Sojo retrieved the ball and stepped on second to force Olerud for the second out."[5] Hernandez walked Guillen to load the bases, but Jeter redeemed himself by making a fine play on a Mark McLemore grounder to keep the Yankees deficit at one run.

The bottom of the seventh proved the most decisive in the ALCS. Seattle skipper Piniella upgraded his outfield defense by moving Stan Javier to left and inserting Mike Cameron in center. He pulled Tomko, who had walked a pair but had not given up a hit in facing 10 batters, in favor of Jose Paniagua, who went a perfect 3-0 in 2000 and had not given up a run in six prior playoff appearances. Torre countered the Piniella maneuverings by batting Jose Vizcaino for Brosius. "Vizcaino," according to the *New York Times*, "topped a slow roller to the right side, just out of reach of the first baseman … Olerud. Second baseman … McLemore gloved the ball and threw to Paniagua covering the bag – too late to get Vizcaino."[6]

Of such puny plays do big innings begin. Chuck Knoblauch sacrificed and Jeter singled. New York had

runners on the corners with one out. Seeking the platoon advantage, Piniella brought in Arthur Rhodes to face Justice although he observed after the game that Justice "hangs in there … against left-handed pitchers. He did in this series, especially tonight."[7] The logical move backfired in the worst way possible for the Mariners as Justice "launched a viciously swift and hard line-drive home run that sailed into the right-field upper deck. In an instant, the Yankees had turned a 4-3 deficit into a 6-4 lead."[8]

"I'll tell you what," said Justice. "I never thought I would hit a homer that compared to the one I hit to win [the 1995] World Series [for Atlanta 1-0]. But that just exploded. I don't think I ever hit a ball that hard in a game this big."[9]

Like many good teams, New York added to its lead. Williams singled and Martinez doubled him to third. Seeking the platoon advantage again, Piniella had Rhodes walk Posada, but O'Neill inflicted more left-on-left harm with a two-run single that pushed Posada to third and the Yankees' lead to 8-4. Rhodes had faced four batters and retired none of them in addition to blemishing Paniagua's line by allowing both of his inherited runners to score. Jose Mesa walked the light-hitting Sojo, and Vizcaino had his second productive plate appearance of the seventh with a sacrifice fly that put New York up 9-4. Knoblauch walked to reload the bases, but Mesa got Jeter looking to end the decisive frame.

With Sojo now playing third and Vizcaino at second, Seattle gamely rallied in the eighth. Rodriguez homered for his third extra-base hit to make the score 9-5. Martinez walked, and Torre replaced Hernandez with Mariano Rivera. *Boston Globe* columnist Dan Shaughnessy compared the Yankees starter to another Cuban righty, noting that Hernandez "has won with great stuff and with mediocre stuff, like he had [in this game]. But like Luis Tiant (163 pitches in Game Four in 1975), he stays in the game long enough to win."[10]

Usually untouchable, Rivera bent but did not break. While Olerud's double pushed Edgar to third, it appeared Rivera would emerge unscathed by retiring the next two batters without a runner scoring. But McLemore hit a clutch two-run double to pull the Mariners considerably closer at 9-7, before Rivera fanned pinch-hitter Jay Buhner to escape.

The Yankees went quietly in the eighth and needed just three outs to return to the World Series. In a final move, Torre brought in Clay Bellinger to replace Justice, who had delivered the mighty blow of the game, in left. Rivera got the first two batters, but

Rodriguez got his fourth hit of the game with two outs. He went to second on defensive indifference, with Edgar Martinez the terrifying (for Yankees fans) tying run at the plate. Of all the batters Rivera faced in his career, Martinez finished with the second highest OPS, but on this day, in a confrontation that involved three future members of the Hall of Fame, Rivera induced a groundball to Jeter, who threw out the slow-footed Martinez. The outcome, with the crosstown Mets having won the NL pennant the night before, sealed the Subway Series matchup that so many New Yorkers had sought.

Yankee fans recall this as the David Justice game, but the 2000 Yankees won this game and would win the World Series due to the performance of far less heralded bench warmers like Sojo and Vizcaino, both pressed into extended action due to the throwing troubles of Knoblauch, who had played only second base in the postseason prior to 2000 but would never again do so.

Torre had to tread especially carefully with Knoblauch, who had "caused a stir ... prior to the Yankees losing [ALDS] Game 4 ... when he didn't take ground balls ... during batting practice... Knoblauch pointed out that ... there was no reason to tax his less-than-100 percent right elbow."[11] Torre thus deserves great credit for the success of this team. Unlike the wildly talented 1998 and 1999 squads, the 2000 club played good but not great baseball (the team's .540 winning percentage was its lowest between 1993 and 2012). Torre needed to protect some of the fragile egos of key members of his squad while moving around many pieces of the player puzzle just

to get the Yankees past the Mariners and back to the World Series.

SOURCES

In addition to the sources cited in the Notes, the author consulted Baseball-Reference.com and Retrosheet.org,

https://www.baseball-reference.com/boxes/NYA/NYA200010170.shtml

https://www.retrosheet.org/boxesetc/2000/B10170NYA2000.htm

NOTES

1   Bob Hohler, "Yankees Derail Mariners to Set Up the Subway Series," *Boston Globe*, October 18, 2000: 81.

2   Wallace Mathews, "Yanks Nearly Missed Train – Now They've Gotta Watch Step," *New York Post*, October 18, 2000.

3   Joe Lapointe, "Hernandez Overcomes His Failings," *New York Times*, October 18, 2000: D4.

4   Joel Sherman, "Gritty, Not Pretty – Just Like the City," *New York Post*, October 18, 2000.

5   George A. King III, "Yanks Climb Aboard as Justice Is Served – David's Three-Run Dinger Puts Yanks Back in Series," *New York Post*, October 18, 2000.

6   Buster Olney, "Yanks Win 37th Pennant With a Comeback Effort," *New York Times*, October 18, 2000: A1.

7   Murray Chass, "New York, New York," *New York Times*, October 18, 2000: D1.

8   Tom Verducci, "N.Y., N.Y.: The Mets Dusted the Cardinals, Then the Yankees Extinguished the Mariners to Set up the First Subway Series in 44 Years," *Sports Illustrated*, October 23, 2000.

9   Jay Greenberg, "MVP Award True Justice – David's Done Nothing but Deliver in Postseason," *New York Post*, October 18, 2000.

10   Dan Shaughnessy, "New Yorkers Are All Aboard for Fall Classic," *Boston Globe*, October 18, 2000: 81.

11   George A. King III, "Knobby Gets Nod as Leading Man – Disgruntled Chuck Returns to Lineup as DH for Game 5," *New York Post*, October 9, 2000.

VIZCAINO WINS 12-INNING GAME ONE OF 2000 SUBWAY SERIES

October 21, 2000:
New York Yankees 4, New York Mets 3,
at Yankee Stadium
Game Six of the 2000 American League Championship Series

By Gene Gomes

In October 2000, for the first time in 44 years, two New York City teams faced off in the World Series. The New York Mets, who qualified for the postseason as the National League wild-card team, upended the San Francisco Giants and defeated the St. Louis Cardinals for the pennant. It was their fourth in franchise history. The New York Yankees stumbled badly in September, losing 15 of their last 18 games, but prevailed as the American League East champions. They survived a tough Division Series against Oakland and triumphed over Seattle to win their 37th pennant. Suddenly, New Yorkers had a long-awaited Subway Series.

The last all-New York City World Series was the Brooklyn Dodgers-New York Yankees match in 1956. It was won by the Yankees in seven games and was highlighted by Don Larsen's perfect game in Game Five. Historically, there were 13 Subway Series played when the Dodgers, Yankees, and Giants teams were all in New York. The Mets and Yankees played each other in every regular season since interleague play began in 1997, but the World Series championship was now at stake.

Game One took place before 55,913 fans on Saturday night, October 21, at Yankee Stadium. Don Larsen threw the ceremonial first pitch to Yogi Berra, and Billy Joel performed the National Anthem.

Managers Bobby Valentine (Mets) and Joe Torre chose their top winning pitchers to start. Left-hander Al Leiter, two days shy of his 35th birthday, won 16 and lost 8 for the Mets in the regular season. Southpaw Andy Pettitte, 28, had a won-lost record of 19-9 for the Yankees. In the first inning, Pettitte retired Timo Pérez, Edgardo Alfonzo, and Mike Piazza in order. Leiter

set down Chuck Knoblauch, Derek Jeter, and David Justice. Both starters remained in control through five scoreless innings, yielding only seven baserunners between them.

A baserunning blunder by Timo Pérez cost the Mets a run in the sixth inning. Pérez led off with a single to center. After two outs, first baseman Todd Zeile hit a long fly to left. The ball landed on the top of the padded wall and fell onto the warning track. Pérez, thinking it was a home run, slowed down near second base. There was no home-run signal by the umpire, and Pérez sped up trying to score. Jeter took the relay toss from Justice and made an off-balance throw to Jorge Posada, who tagged Pérez out at the plate. Valentine and others came forward to implore the umpires to rule the hit a home run, to no avail. Television replays showed it was the correct call.

In the Yankees' turn in the sixth, ninth-place hitter José Vizcaíno singled to deep short but was thrown out at second by Leiter on Knoblauch's bunt. Jeter drew a walk, and Justice doubled to deep left-center field, scoring both runners. Leiter worked out of the inning, but the Yankees had a 2-0 lead.

The Mets responded right away. In the top of the seventh inning, sixth-place hitter Benny Agbayani singled with one out, rookie center fielder Jay Payton singled to center, and catcher Todd Pratt walked to load the bases. Right-handed batter Bubba Trammell pinch-hit for shortstop Mike Bordick. Trammell had been 7-for-18 against Pettitte in his career, and he came through with a two-run single. Pérez was retired by Pettitte on a bunt and the runners advanced to second and third. Right-hander Jeff Nelson replaced Pettitte to face Alfonzo, who bounced a slow grounder toward third base and beat Scott Brosius's throw to first base, driving in Pratt. Piazza, in the DH role for this game, flied out to end the inning. The Mets were ahead, 3-2.

Leiter blanked the Yankees in their half of the seventh. Through seven innings Leiter allowed five hits and three walks, and struck out seven in a strong performance. Nelson retired the Mets in order in the eighth. John Franco protected the one-run lead as he set the Yankees down in the bottom half. The Mets had a chance to increase their lead in the ninth with Mariano Rivera on the mound. Rivera retired Payton but hit Pratt with a pitch. Shortstop Kurt Abbott hit Rivera's second pitch to deep right field for a double, moving Pratt to third. Pérez hit a grounder to Vizcaino at second, who bobbled it before throwing to first for the out. The slow-footed Pratt held at third, and Rivera struck out Alfonzo to end the inning.

Mets right-handed closer Armando Benítez came in to pitch the ninth. The 6-foot-4-inch Benítez had 41 saves in the regular season and was an imposing presence on the mound. He retired Posada for the first

out. Right fielder Paul O'Neill came up next. O'Neill recalled, "Going into that Series, I was a little banged up and hadn't felt good at the plate. Then, I got behind right away and felt as if I were in an emergency mode from pitch one."[1] Benítez quickly got ahead with a 1-and-2 count and O'Neill stepped out of the box to reset. The clamorous crowd urged him on during every pitch. O'Neill managed to foul off four fastballs and ultimately drew a walk in a memorable 10-pitch at-bat.

Luis Polonia pinch-hit for Brosius and kept the rally going with a single. Vizcaino lobbed a single to left to load the bases. The crowd roared when Knoblauch lifted a fly ball to left field; Joe McEwing made the catch, and O'Neill tagged up and scored to tie the score, 3-3. Benítez struck out Jeter, but the Yankees had perhaps gained the momentum.

Rivera shut down the Mets in the 10th. Mets veteran lefty Dennis Cook began the bottom of the inning by walking Justice and Bernie Williams. Left-handed reliever Glendon Rusch was summoned to face Tino Martinez, and he delivered a wild pitch that enabled

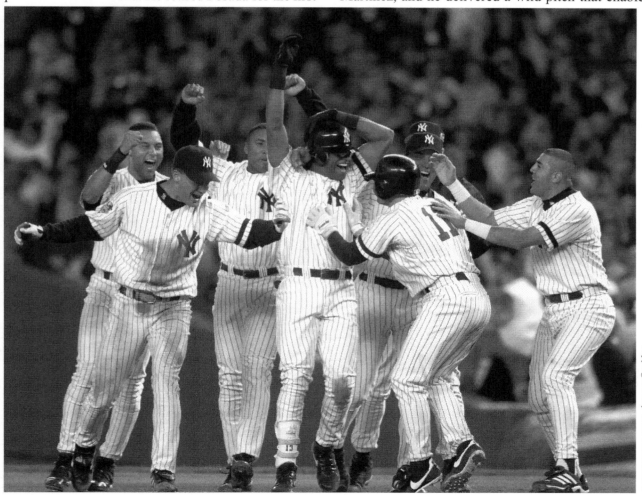

Yankees teammates mob Jose Vizcaino after his game-winning RBI single.

the runners to advance. Martinez popped out to short left field and Rusch intentionally walked Posada. With the bases loaded, Rusch induced O'Neill to hit into a double-play grounder, and that's how the inning ended.

Left-hander Mike Stanton kept the Mets at bay with a scoreless 11th inning. Turk Wendell came to the rescue of Rusch in the bottom half, retiring pinch-hitter Glenallen Hill with two runners on base for the third out. Stanton continued the stellar relief work by the Yankees bullpen (five shutout innings) as the Mets went down in order in the top of the 12th.

With one out in the Yankees 12th, Martinez singled and Posada doubled. Wendell walked O'Neill intentionally to load the bases. Third baseman Luis Sojo fouled out amid the tumult in the stadium. With two outs, Jose Vizcaino stroked an opposite-field liner to left on the first pitch, scoring Martinez to win the game. The Yankees embraced on the field as the crowd erupted.

The hit was Vizcaino's fourth of the game. The switch-hitter had been chosen by Torre over Sojo to play second base given his previous 10-for-19 hitting against Leiter.

The tense game lived up to all the fanfare and expectations. Benítez failed to slam the door in the ninth, while the Yankees relievers set down the last 11 Mets batters. Stanton was the winning pitcher and Wendell took the loss. It was the 13th consecutive World Series game victory for the Yankees.[2] This 12-inning affair was the longest World Series game by time in history, lasting 4 hours and 51 minutes, and ended at 1:04 A.M. Eastern time.[3]

The Yankees went on to capture their third consecutive World Series title four games to one, their 26th title. The Brooklyn-born 60-year-old Joe Torre was in his fifth season as Yankees manager and won his fourth title.

Derek Jeter was named World Series MVP. In an interview he said the Yankees fans would tell him, "Whatever you do, don't lose to the Mets." Jeter said, "We had a lot to lose. I'm serious: I would have moved right out of the city if we'd lost. You could have taken our three rings and thrown them out the window, as far as Yankees fans were concerned. I'm glad I played in a Subway Series, but maybe once is enough."[4]

Al Leiter felt that the key to the Yankees' winning the Series was the classic first game. Years later Leiter remarked, "If Paul (O'Neill) doesn't get that walk there, I think the Mets are high-fiving as we're walking off the field that night."[5] As of 2022, there hasn't been another Subway Series. It could happen one year, and if it does, the 4 Train in the Bronx and the 7 Train in Queens will be ready and running.

SOURCES

In addition to the sources cited in the Notes, the author consulted

https://www.retrosheet.org/boxesetc/2000/B10210NYA2000.htm

https://www.baseball-reference.com/boxes/NYA/NYA200010210.shtml

Quinn, T.J. "1st Yank Stop Extra Special: Win on Viz's RBI as Met pen fails to shut Subway door," *New York Daily News,* October, 22, 2000: 888-889.

"Jose Vizcaino vs. Pitchers," Stathead.com,

https://stathead.com/baseball/batter_vs_pitcher.cgi?batter=vizcajo01&pitcher=leiteal01&post=0.

"Bubba Trammell vs. Pitchers," Stathead.com,

https://stathead.com/baseball/batter_vs_pitcher.cgi?batter=trammbu01&pitcher=pettian01&post=0.

"2000 World Series New York Mets @ New York Yankees Game 1 – You Tube,"

https://www.youtube.com/watch?v=EXIJlOpSFNA, viewed September 28, 2022.

NOTES

1   Mike Lupica, "The Walk That 'Won' the Yanks the 2000 World Series," April 6, 2020, MLB.com, https://www.mlb.com/news/paul-o-neill-walk-in-2000-world-series , accessed September 6, 2022.

2   The Yankees won the final four games of the 1996 Series vs. Atlanta, swept all four games in 1998 vs. San Diego, and won all four games in 1999 vs. Atlanta. After winning the first two games in 2000, the streak was stopped at a record 14 games when they lost to the Mets in Game Three.

3   The length of this game has been surpassed three times: Game Three of the 2005 Series between the Chicago White Sox and the Houston Astros (14 innings, 5 hours 41 minutes); Game One of the 2015 Series between Kansas City and the New York Mets (14 innings, in 5 hours 9 minutes); Game Three of the 2018 Series between the Los Angeles Dodgers and the Boston Red Sox (18 innings, 7 hours 20 minutes). In comparison, Game Two of the 1916 Series between the Boston Red Sox and the Brooklyn Robins lasted 14 innings in 2 hours 32 minutes. This was the only other World Series game to last 14 innings.

4   Tom Verducci, "The Toast of the Town," *Sports Illustrated Vault,* November 6, 2000.https://vault.si.com/vault/2000/11/06/the-toast-of-the-town-after-leading-the-yankees-to-another-world-series-title-cool-yet-fiercely-competitive-derek-jeter-owns-yankee-stadiumand-the-rest-of-new-york-citythe-way-no-player-since-joe-dimaggio-has, accessed September 22, 2022.

5   Paul O'Neill and Jack Curry, *Swing and a Hit: Nine Innings of What Baseball Taught Me* (New York:Grand Central Publishing, 2022), 134.

GIAMBI GAME-ENDING GRAND SLAM GIVES YANKEES A 14-INNING WIN OVER TWINS

May 17, 2002:
New York Yankees 13, Minnesota Twins 12, (14 Innings), at Yankee Stadium

By Stew Thornley

With rain falling and the clock approaching 1:00 A.M., Yankees coach Don Zimmer wasn't even sure of the situation any more. He turned to Roger Clemens on the bench and asked, "If Giambi hits it out, do we win?"[1]

Such was the setting on a soggy Friday night-cum-Saturday morning in a back-and-forth game at Yankee Stadium. The Minnesota Twins had a 12-9 lead over the New York Yankees in the 14th inning as Jason Giambi came up with the bases loaded and one out.

The Twins were the darling team of baseball. Presumed to be one of the teams targeted for contraction after the 2001 season, the Twins were leading their division in 2002, not only surviving but thriving under new manager Ron Gardenhire.[2]

Beyond how much of a threat contraction really was, the Twins had started their comeback in the standings the year before. After eight straight losing seasons, Minnesota started strong in 2001 and held a five-game lead at the All-Star break. Even though they faded in the final months, the Twins still finished second by six games to Cleveland. The Indians were in a cost-cutting mode and lost some key players, including Roberto Alomar in a trade and Juan González to free agency, during the offseason. The Twins leading the pack in the Central Division wasn't as much of a miracle as some wanted to make it out to be.

However, it was still a splashier story than the Yankees, who had come within a half-inning of their fourth straight championship in 2001 and were 26-15 coming into a weekend series at home against the Twins.

For the series opener, New York went with Mike Mussina, who had dominated the Twins going back to his years in Baltimore. Against Minnesota, Mussina had an 18-2 career won-lost record with a 2.61 earned-run average. The Yankees staked him to a lead as Bernie Williams homered into the upper deck in right off right-hander Rick Reed in the bottom of the first.

But the Twins started the second with three hits, a double by Bobby Kielty, a bunt single by Jay Canizaro, and a run-scoring single by A.J. Pierzynski. Denny Hocking brought in Canizaro with the go-ahead run on a groundout, and Jacque Jones singled in Pierzynski for a 3-1 lead.

It lasted until the fourth inning. Jorge Posada started it by reaching base on an error by Reed, and Robin Ventura tied the score with a long home run to center. Singles by John Vander Wal and Rondell White continued the rally. After Nick Johnson struck out, Alfonso Soriano hit a long drive to left. Jones ran back, leaped, and momentarily had the ball in his glove before it popped out and dropped beyond the fence. Official scorer Bill Shannon said he thought about calling a four-base error on Jones. "I looked at it on replay very carefully," he said, but Shannon finally ruled it a three-run homer.[3]

Another home run, by Posada with Giambi aboard, in the fifth gave the Yankees an 8-3 lead, seemingly an insurmountable one for the Twins against a long-time nemesis. However, Mussina did not retire another batter.

Brian Buchanan opened the sixth with a pop fly to left. Miscommunication by shortstop Derek Jeter and left fielder Rondell White allowed the ball to drop for a double. More solid hits – singles by Kielty and Canizaro followed by a Pierzynski double – cut the lead to 8-5 and chased Mussina. Hocking greeted Mike Stanton with a single and Jones made the score even closer with a single to score Pierzynski. Cristian Guzman sacrificed the runners to third and second and, after an intentional walk to Torii Hunter, David Ortiz delivered a game-tying sacrifice fly. Ramiro Mendoza came in and tried to stop the carnage, but Buchanan came through with his second hit of the inning, a single to drive in Jones and put the Twins ahead, 9-8.

The lead held into the last of the ninth. Mike Jackson, who had struck out Soriano to end the eighth, stayed on to retire Jeter leading off the ninth. Gardenhire summoned Eddie Guardado – who was 14 for 14 in save opportunities – to finish it off, but Bernie Williams had other ideas. Batting right-handed this time, he drilled a homer to left to tie the score.

The Twins went down quietly against Steve Karsay and Mariano Rivera the next three innings, and the Yankees threatened but didn't score. With one out in the 13th, Giambi singled, and it looked as though the game might end when Posada blasted a drive over Hunter's head in center. Giambi was waved home but was nailed at the plate by Hocking's relay. The Yankees loaded the bases but White lined out to Jones, giving New York nine runners left on base over the last four innings.

Minnesota broke through in the 14th, starting with a walk by Casey Blake off Sterling Hitchcock. Buchanan beat out an infield single to third with Blake going to third on an overthrow by Enrique Wilson. Kielty singled Blake home. After a fielder's choice and fly out, Hocking and Jones singled to score Kielty and then Canizaro.

Mike Trombley was charged with finishing it off, but he allowed a single to Shane Spencer to open the bottom of the inning. After Soriano flied out, Jeter singled and Williams walked, bringing up Giambi. As the rain fell harder, Clemens answered his coach's question regarding Giambi hitting it out. "Yeah, Zim, that counts as four and we won't have to worry about the rain."[4]

Trombley's first pitch was a fastball on the outer part of the plate, just not far enough out. Giambi turned on the pitch and drove it into the right-center-field bleachers for a 13-12 win. As the Yankees mobbed Giambi and John Sterling yelled, "Yankees win. Thaaaa Yankees win," the remaining fans – still many of them remaining from the nearly 40,000 who

attended – were serenaded by Frank Sinatra's "New York, New York."[5] The time of game was 5 hours, 45 minutes.

The homer was Giambi's fourth hit of the game; Buchanan and Kielty had four hits for the Twins.

Giambi was in his first season with the Yankees, hitting well enough but still concerned about fitting in with the New York fans. With his grand slam, Giambi had earned his pinstripes.[6]

The Twins and Yankees both made the playoffs in 2002. Minnesota won its opening playoff round, against Oakland, and fell in the League Championship Series to the Anaheim Angels, the team that had beaten New York in the opening round.

As of 2022, the Yankees have made it to two World Series – winning one of them – since then, although this doesn't meet the standards of the Yankees of the twentieth century.

While the Twins continued winning division titles over the next eight years, their frustration has been worse, especially with the Yankees. In Ron Gardenhire's tenure with the Twins, his team went 26-64 in the regular season against the Yankees, 28-76 including the postseason. The New York dominance continued; through 2022, the Yankees were 98-38 and 114-40 including playoff games.

SOURCES

In addition to the sources cited in the Notes, the author consulted Baseball-Reference.com and Retrosheet.org.

https://www.retrosheet.org/boxesetc/2002/B05170NYA2002.htm

https://www.baseball-reference.com/boxes/NYA/NYA200205170.shtml

NOTES

1 Lisa Olson, "Yank Lore Gets to Grow Even More," *New York Daily News,* May 19, 2002: 58-59.

2 The Montreal Expos were the other team that were thought subject to contraction.

3 Bob Herzog, "What a Blast," *Newsday* (Long Island, New York), May 19, 2002: C3.

4 Olson.

5 Video of grand slam: https://www.youtube.com/watch?v=cQrVrAZSQaY.

6 Giambi's game-ending grand slam with his team down by three runs was only the second to occur at Yankee Stadium. The other was by Babe Ruth on September 24, 1925.

300 WINS AND 4,000 K'S AT NIGHT: FANS DELIGHT

June 13, 2003:
New York Yankees 5, St. Louis Cardinals 2, at Yankee Stadium

By Harry Schoger

For the second time in 18 days, a sellout crowd of over 55,000 came to Yankee Stadium hoping to witness right-handed starter Roger Clemens' 300th career win.[1]

Clemens, who had begun his career with the Red Sox and won three Cy Young Awards there, had won number 299 in Boston on May 21, beating Red Sox pitcher Tim Wakefield, a right-handed knuckleballer. On May 26 he had squared off against Wakefield again, in the House That Ruth Built, but lost, 8-4.

In the 18-day interim from May 26 to this Friday evening game in New York, he'd pitched twice. He had thrown six innings in Detroit, a no-decision on June 1 in a game the Yankees eventually won in the 17th inning.[2] On June 7 at Wrigley Field, he and the Cubs' Kerry Wood had treated the crowd to a good old-fashioned pitchers' duel. Clemens clung to a 1-0 lead going into the seventh inning, but he bore the loss after his reliever gave up a three-run homer.[3]

Clemens' strikeout totals had continued to grow, and it was likely he would record career strikeout number 4,000. He had 3,996 strikeouts coming into the night's game against the St. Louis Cardinals.

The weather for this evening's fourth attempt at 300 wins was marginal, but the crowd of 55,214 undaunted fans came prepared. The temperature was 59 degrees. It was a cloudy evening with persistent drizzle mixed with sporadic sprinkles, which were uncomfortable but not detrimental enough to suspend play. Such conditions would not help Clemens' battle with an upper respiratory infection.

The crowd included a Clemens entourage of some 40 to 50 family and friends, including Roger's wife, Debbie, and their four boys.[4] It did not include Roger's mother, who was in Texas, suffering from emphysema.[5] Her absence was discomforting for Clemens,

who lamented it on-air after the game.[6] The group had been assembled and in attendance at the three previous games on the 300th-victory trail. Debbie was the busy coordinator of the entourage,[7] many of them friends to whom Clemens felt he owed his success.

Roger Clemens became just the third pitcher to strike out 4,000 batters, behind Nolan Ryan and Steve Carlton.

The game was also notable because it was the homecoming of St. Louis first baseman Tino Martinez, who was a fan favorite during his six-year stint in pinstripes from 1996 to 2001, during which time Clemens was his teammate for three seasons. Handmade signs liberally peppered the stands heralding Tino's welcome back.[8] Yankees owner George Steinbrenner, "The Boss," took the evening off from attending the fifth game of the Nets-Spurs NBA Championship final in the Meadowlands to root his ace to victory and applaud the Yankee fans for turning out in such numbers despite the inhospitable weather.[9]

Clemens' batterymate this evening was Jorge Posada, who had caught him more than any other Yankees catcher. Clemens had asked him to catch his 300th game during spring training.[10] Posada was exhilarated by this profound honor in front of the Yankee fans. The opposing battery for the St. Louis Cardinals was right-hander Jason Simontacchi, a 29-year-old in his second major-league season. His catcher was veteran Gold Glover Mike Matheny, the Cardinals anchor at the position in his 10th major-league season.

The first inning started with the crowd on its collective feet in a vigil to cheer Clemens on to magic strikeout number 4,000. He rewarded their encouragement by striking out the side, dispatching Miguel Cairo, J.D. Drew, and 2003's major-league batting champion, Albert Pujols. In the bottom of the frame, Posada hit a double, driving in Derek Jeter, giving Clemens a one-run edge. Yankees 1, Cardinals 0.

Jim Edmonds evened the score in the Cardinals' half of the second with his 18th home run of the season. Scott Rolen followed with a double. He was stranded at second as Clemens proceeded to again strike out three batters. His first victim was Edgar Renteria, who, depending on one's perspective, gained the dubious distinction or the honor of being Clemens' 4,000th strikeout victim.

Clemens became the third pitcher to achieve a milestone only enjoyed then by Nolan Ryan and Steve Carlton.[11] There was a brief intermission while the crowd acclaimed the historic event. Posada stopped play to go to the mound and congratulate his pitcher. Clemens doffed his cap and then went back to work, punching out Martinez and Matheny. Hideki Matsui added a solo homer in the Yankees' half of the inning to regain the lead. Yankees 2, Cardinals 1.

Clemens held the Cardinals scoreless in the third while getting his seventh strikeout at the expense of Drew. However, the Yankees could do no better.

In the top of the fourth, the Cardinals knotted the score with a sacrifice fly by Martinez, driving in Rolen, who had led off the inning with a single. The tie was short-lived, as Ruben Sierra hit a two-out solo home run deep into the right-field stands for the Yankees in the bottom of the inning.

There was no scoring in the fifth or sixth inning. Clemens added two more strikeouts as he moved further beyond the 4,000 milestone. In the sixth inning, both teams went down in order.

In the seventh, Kerry Robinson and Cairo hit consecutive fly outs to center. Suddenly manager Joe Torre popped out of the dugout, signaling for Chris Hammond out of the bullpen. The crowd vehemently expressed its disfavor for the decision to lift Clemens at the threshold of Valhalla. However, he had already thrown 120 pitches and did not protest his manager's strategy, turning the ball over without incident. He walked coolly to the dugout to celebrate with his mates, tipping his hat twice to the formerly booing but now wildly cheering crowd. He took a seat between Torre and his pitching coach, Mel Stottlemyre, who was battling cancer. Hammond did his job, getting Edmonds to ground out and end any Cardinals threat.

In the bottom of the inning, Yankees hitters padded their one-run lead to provide some insurance for a Clemens win. Sierra singled to center and Raul Mondesi followed with a home run. Juan Rivera singled to left. Cardinals manager Tony La Russa lifted Simontacchi for Esteban Yan, who dispatched three of the four batters he faced, giving up a harmless walk to Posada. Yankees 5, Cardinals 2.

Antonio Osuna replaced Hammond to start the eighth inning. The Cardinals went down in order. Steve Kline replaced Yan on the mound for the Cardinals. Robin Ventura singled to right as did Matsui, holding the former to second base. Sierra flied to left, Mondesi lined to third, and Rivera forced Ventura at third.

Closer Mariano Rivera relieved Osuna. The Cardinals went down in order in the top of the ninth to end the contest. Clemens' 300th victory was secured.

It was the first time in 13 years that a new member had entered the hallowed circle of 300-game winners. The most recent to do so was Nolan Ryan in 1990. Clemens joined Phil Niekro, who did it as a Yankee in 1985, as the only players to reach the lofty milestone in pinstripes. But Clemens was the only one to achieve it at home.[12]

Clemens had gone to the showers and shaved while the Yankees relief corps dispatched the Cardinals. He returned to the dugout. After the final out, he emerged onto the field as the audio team played Elton John's "Rocket Man." Clemens happily and good-naturedly greeted each of his teammates and coaches with hugs, back slaps, and fist bumps. His two elder sons acknowledged their triumphant father, and the two younger jumped into his arms. He sent them off to gather dirt from the mound as a memento of the occasion. Debbie then gave him a long hug. At last, she was free from her duties as commander of the entourage.

The fans were in no hurry to exit. Most stayed to celebrate with the hero of the night and savor the iconic moment. Clemens, grinning from ear to ear, took off his cap and waved it to the fans as they cheered and chanted from the still-packed stands. He made no signs of leaving early.

The game was arguably pedestrian by many standards but momentous in the accomplishments it heralded, a game to be no doubt treasured in the memories of many.

SOURCES

In addition to the sources cited in the Notes, the author consulted Baseball-Reference.com, Retrosheet.org, SABR.org, and YouTube.com.

https://www.baseball-reference.com/boxes/NYA/NYA200306130.shtml

https://www.retrosheet.org/boxesetc/2003/B06130NYA2003.htm

https://www.youtube.com/watch?v=0EsGlYUQkqA

NOTES

1. Only 20 major-league pitchers had reached 300 wins as of that date. As of 2023, that number, including Clemens, was 24.

2. The Tigers game drew 44,095 fans to Comerica Park, an attendance record for the ballpark, which opened on April 11, 2000. The 17-inning, 5-hour and 10-minute game also was a ballpark record. Gene Guidi, "Tigers Deny Clemens, but Lose in 17th," *Detroit Free Press,* June 2, 2003: 25.

3. Clemens had been "huffing and puffing" from a respiratory infection, manager Joe Torre lifted him for Juan Acevedo, who immediately served up a three-run homer to Eric Karros, leaving Clemens with the loss, 5-2.

4. Krista Latham, "Chicago Next in Clemens' Quest," *Detroit Free Press,* June 2, 2003: 25.

5. Ronald Blum, "Clemens makes History with Career Win No. 300," *Scranton Times-Tribune,* June 14, 2003: 32.

6. Blum.

7. T.J. Quinn, "Mrs. C, Fans Miss Out," *New York Daily News,* June 8, 2003: 70.

8. Video: https://www.youtube.com/watch?v=0EsGlYUQkqA. Accessed September 30, 2022.

9. Peter Botte, "Rocket Has Boss Beaming," *New York Daily News,* June 14, 2003: 51.

10. Don Amore, "Bullpen Doesn't Fail Him," *Hartford Courant,* June 14, 2003: 187.

11. Randy Johnson became the fourth to join the 4,000 club, on June 29, 2004.

12. Niekro got his win, 8-0, on the road against the Toronto Blue Jays in the last game of the season. In the process, at age 46, he became the oldest major-league pitcher to throw a shutout, passing Satchel Paige. It was also Niekro's final game as a Yankee. He achieved his 300th on his fifth try.

AARON BOONE'S HOME RUN WINS THE PENNANT FOR THE YANKEES

October 16, 2003:
New York Yankees 6, Boston Red Sox 5 (11 innings),
at Yankee Stadium
Game Seven of the 2003 American League Championship Series

By Tom Naylor

A rivalry between the New York Yankees and the Boston Red Sox has existed in various states of contentiousness since at least December 26, 1919, when Red Sox owner Harry Frazee infamously sold Babe Ruth to the Yankees. Subsequent deals between the teams spurred the creation of the Yankees' first championship-caliber teams.

It was during the late 1970s, however, that tensions between the fan bases rose to a higher level of ferocity. In 1976 the Yankees succeeded the Red Sox as American League champions. A brawl between the teams on May 20, 1976, raised the level of personal enmity between some of the players, and heightened the disdain of the fans for their opponents. A one-game tiebreaker between the teams on October 2, 1978, at Fenway Park, won by the Yankees, had hardened the rivalry for generations. Red Sox fans readily acknowledged irritation at the numerous World Series championships won by the Yankees in the years since 1918, the last time the Red Sox had won.

History, both distant and recent, provided a rich background as the Yankees and Red·Sox met at Yankee Stadium to begin a deciding best-of-seven playoff series for the 2003 American League pennant. In the regular season New York had won the American League East Division title, finishing six games ahead of Boston and spending nearly the entire season in first place. It was the sixth consecutive year that Boston had finished second to New York. In the AL Division Series, the Yankees bested the Minnesota Twins and the Red Sox topped the Oakland A's, setting the stage for the Championship Series showdown.

The teams split the first two games in New York, and Game Three brought the Series and rivalry to an impassioned state of pugnacity. The game featured a pitching matchup of two three-time Cy Young Award winners, with Pedro Martinez starting for the Red Sox and Roger Clemens taking the assignment for the Yankees. Clemens had established himself in Boston as one of the game's greatest pitchers, winning three Cy Young Awards and a Most Valuable Player Award there before moving on to Toronto and, from 1999, New York. Martinez joined the Red Sox in 1998 and in his six Boston seasons to that point had been easily the best pitcher in the American League, capturing two Cy Young Awards of his own.

In the fourth inning of Game Three, immediately after surrendering an early lead, Martinez threw a pitch up and in, hitting Karim Garcia in the shoulder. "There's no question in my mind that Pedro hit him on purpose," said New York manager Joe Torre. "He was probably frustrated with the fact that we hit some balls hard. ... I didn't care for that."[1] Players exchanged angry words, but peace momentarily held. In the bottom of the inning, however, Manny Ramirez was angered by a high pitch from Clemens and approached the mound with bat in hand. This emptied the benches and led to 72-year-old Yankee coach (and former Red Sox manager) Don Zimmer being thrown to the ground by Martinez. Somehow, the umpires did not see fit to eject any of the participants, and eventually a smoldering sense of order was restored. The Yankees won the game, and the tension between the teams had become fevered.

The teams split the next two games and Boston won Game Six, coming from behind to take the lead with three seventh-inning runs off José Contreras, a Cuban free agent the Yankees had swooped in to sign after the Red Sox thought they had a deal with him (the signing being the proximate cause of Red Sox executive Larry Lucchino famously labeling the Yankees the "Evil Empire.") "When this series began, everyone knew it was going to be quite a battle," [Boston manager Grady] Little said after Game Three. "I think we've upgraded it to a war."[2] The stage was set for a tense and climactic Game Seven at Yankee Stadium.

Martinez and Clemens were again the opposing pitchers, a matchup befitting the historic significance of the contest. The Red Sox took a lead soon after the game began. In the second inning, Trot Nixon hit a two-run home run, scoring Kevin Millar. Another Red Sox run came in on a throwing error by Enrique Wilson, starting at third base in place of the slumping Aaron Boone, to provide a 3-0 lead. In the fourth inning, Millar homered as well, putting Clemens

and the Yankees behind, 4-0. Two batters later, Mike Mussina was brought in to relieve an ineffective Clemens. For Mussina it was the first relief appearance of his career after 386 regular-season and 14 postseason starts, and he performed admirably, shutting out the Red Sox for three innings.

Martinez kept the Yankee bats quiet until the fifth inning, when Jason Giambi touched him for a solo home run, cutting the Red Sox lead to 4-1.

The score was unchanged as Giambi came to the plate with two out and none on in the seventh. This time he took a Martinez fastball to center field, where it dropped over Johnny Damon's outstretched glove for Giambi's second home run of the night, bringing the Yankees to within two runs at 4-2. The next two Yankees singled before Martinez fanned Alfonso Soriano for the fourth time, closing out the seventh

Aaron Boone brought the Stadium to its feet (and teammates such as Jason Giambi and Jorge Posada off their feet) with his game-winning home run to left field.

inning. As he returned to the dugout, Martinez accepted traditional "game well-pitched" congratulations from his teammates, with body language indicating his work was finished for the night.

In the eighth inning, another Yankee starting pitcher, David Wells, was brought in with one out to face David Ortiz, one of the game's most dangerous hitters. Ortiz jumped Wells's first pitch and hammered it over the right-field wall to restore Boston's three-run cushion, 5-2.

As the Yankees came to bat in the eighth, Red Sox manager Grady Little had left-hander Alan Embree and right-hander Mike Timlin warming in the bullpen, but all were surprised to see Martinez return to the mound. After retiring Nick Johnson, Martinez surrendered a double to right field by Derek Jeter. Bernie Williams followed with a line single to center field, scoring Jeter. Now having thrown 115 pitches, Martinez was visited by Little for a brief conversation. Although Embree was warm, Little chose to stay with Martinez as left-handed hitter Hideki Matsui came to the plate.

Little's confidence was misplaced: Matsui ripped an 0-and-2 pitch into the right-field corner for a double, sending Williams to third. Jorge Posada then flared a fly ball to short center field where it dropped in to score the tying runs. The Yankee Stadium crowd erupted in joyous bedlam. After the game, Little defended his decision to keep Martinez in the game: "Pedro Martinez has been our man all year long and in situations like that, he's the man we want on the mound over anybody we can bring out of the bullpen."[3]

In the top of the ninth, the Yankees brought in closer Mariano Rivera to replace Wells, and Aaron Boone, having pinch-run in the eighth, took over for Wilson at third base. Rivera proved to be his usual indomitable self as he shut down the Red Sox for the next three innings. For the Red Sox, Timlin, who had closed out the eighth inning effectively, held the Yankees at bay in the ninth inning also. Tim Wakefield succeeded Timlin and retired the Yankees one-two-three in the 10th.

In the bottom of the 11th, Wakefield faced Boone, who swatted Wakefield's first offering into the left-field stands and triggered pandemonium in the Bronx, as his home run gave the Yankees their 39th pennant. Boone was mobbed at the plate as the fans erupted in joy. "I knew it was out, I finally put a good swing on it," said Boone after the game.[4] Teammate Jeter spoke

of the famed Yankee mystique. "I believe in ghosts," Jeter said when asked if there was something to the Curse. "And we have a lot of ghosts in this Stadium."[5]

The Yankee-loving segment of New York fell into delirium as they savored the dramatic victory. A notable exception was the editorial page of the *New York Post's* late city edition, which, due to a transmission error, published a piece prepared in advance in anticipation of a different outcome. "Looks like the Curse of the Bambino boomeranged this year. Despite holding a 3-2 lead in games over the Boston Red Sox, the Yankees couldn't get the job done at home; their season ended last night." The piece lamented opportunities missed by the Yankees, but urged a consoling "Wait'll next year!"[6]

Snake-bitten Red Sox fans everywhere took it as just the latest manifestation of the Curse.[7]

The Yankees were unable to take the 2003 World Series, losing in six games to the Florida Marlins, but the thrilling jubilation of the Championship Series victory is a momentous episode in Yankee history.

SOURCES

The author accessed Baseball-Reference.com for box scores/play-by-play information and other data, as well as Retrosheet and the video of the game at YouTube.com.

https://www.baseball-reference.com/boxes/NYA/NYA200310160.shtml

https://www.retrosheet.org/boxesetc/2003/B10160NYA2003.htm

https://www.youtube.com/watch?v=St3WF3_xaWk

NOTES

1   Dan Shaughnessy, "Sox Lose Game 3 Melee – Yanks frustrate Boston in Wild Playoff, 4-3" *Boston Globe*, October 12, 2003.

2   Tom Verducci, "Baseball Gets Rowdy," *Sports Illustrated*, October 20, 2003: 44.

3   Bob Ryan, "End result? Manager All But Finished," *Boston Globe*, October 18, 2003: D2.

4   George A. King III, "Boone HR Puts Yanks in Series: Empire Comes Back to Win on Blast in 11th." *New York Post*, October 17, 2003.

5   King.

6   A screenshot of the editorial is available at: https://legendsrevealed.com/sports/2009/04/29/not-quite-dewey-defeating-truman/. Retrieved October 13, 2002.

7   On October 28 Grady Little was fired as manager of the Red Sox. It was portrayed as "due to his insistence on a long-term contract and not his controversial decision" in Game Seven. Mark Asher, "Little fired as Red Sox manager," *Washington Post*, October 28, 2003. https://www.washingtonpost.com/archive/sports/2003/10/28/little-fired-as-red-sox-manager/95d1862f-e678-4094-9c82-5848af895066/. Accessed October 9, 2022.

DEREK JETER'S DANGEROUS DIVING CATCH SAVES GAME AS YANKEES COMPLETE SWEEP OF RED SOX

July 1, 2004:
New York Yankees 5, Boston Red Sox 4, at Yankee Stadium

By Tim Odzer

In the middle of an instant classic between the Red Sox and Yankees, Derek Jeter made the most dangerous catch of his career, hurtling headfirst into the stands to catch a popup off the bat of Trot Nixon. The play kept the score tied in a game New York went on to win on a walk-off single by backup catcher John Flaherty, completing a three-game sweep of their rivals.

The rivalry between the Red Sox and Yankees had never felt more intense than it did in the middle of 2004. After Aaron Boone crushed a fluttering knuckleball from Boston's Tim Wakefield into the upper deck of Yankee Stadium to win the 2003 pennant for the Yankees, Boston sought to improve its team. In the 2003-04 offseason, the Red Sox were close to acquiring 2003 American League MVP Alex Rodriguez, only for the Players Association to block the trade at the last minute. When Boone tore his ACL in the offseason, the Yankees pulled off a shocking move and acquired Rodriguez.

As the season neared the halfway point, the Red Sox and Yankees came together for a midweek three-game series in the Bronx. New York came into the series with a 5½-game lead in the AL East. In the first game, on June 29, Gary Sheffield's three-run home run in the bottom of the fourth gave New York a 7-2 lead en route to an 11-3 Yankees victory.[1] In the second game, on June 30, the Red Sox led 2-0 in the bottom of the seventh behind a strong pitching performance from Wakefield. But in the seventh, with the bases loaded and Wakefield out of the game, Tony Clark hit a groundball that squeezed through an opening in first baseman David Ortiz's glove, allowing two runs to score and tying the game. Ortiz found company in the error column in the bottom of the eighth when Yankees center fielder Kenny Lofton reached on an infield single and took second on a throwing error by Boston shortstop Nomar Garciaparra. Sheffield drove home the winning run on a double, and New York won, 4-2.

The pitching matchup for the final game appeared to be a mismatch on paper. It pitted three-time Cy Young Award winner Pedro Martinez against Yankees rookie Brad Halsey, who was making only his third major-league start. Martinez had started 2004 at 8-3 with a 3.73 ERA. Halsey, meanwhile, had pitched well in his first start, against the Dodgers, but struggled in his second start, against the Mets.

After Halsey retired Boston on one hit in the first, Martinez took the mound for his second start of the season against the Yankees. He quickly reintroduced himself to the Yankee Stadium crowd. Facing Sheffield with two outs, Martinez intentionally drilled Sheffield in the back after Martinez took umbrage at Sheffield's tardy time-out call. Sheffield yelled at Martinez as he walked to first but went no further. "Play the game right," Sheffield said he told Martinez."[2]

In the bottom of the second, the Yankees scored the first runs of the game on a two-run home run by Clark to right-center field. Both Halsey and Martinez settled into the game for the rest of the early innings, allowing no runs until Jorge Posada took Martinez deep in the fifth inning. At the end of five, New York led, 3-0.

Boston quickly mounted a rally in the sixth. After Halsey struck out Mark Bellhorn, Ortiz blooped a ball near the left-field line that Hideki Matsui was unable to catch. The ball bounced into the left-field stands for a ground-rule double. The next man up, Manny Ramirez, hit his 21st home run of the season to bring Boston within one run. Yankees manager Joe Torre lifted Halsey from the game and replaced him with Paul Quantrill, who retired the next two men.

The Red Sox tied the game in the top of the seventh. First baseman Dave McCarty doubled to deep center on a ball just out of Lofton's reach. A single by Kevin Youkilis put men at the corners with no outs. Pokey Reese, getting the start at shortstop in place of Garciaparra, grounded into a double play, scoring McCarty and tying the game, 3-3. Martinez worked around a walk to Posada and a single by Enrique Wilson to hold the Yankees scoreless in the seventh in his last inning of work. Martinez went seven innings, giving up three runs.

After nobody scored in the eighth, the Yankees loaded the bases with one out in the bottom of the ninth. The crowd of 55,265 was electric, anticipating a Yankees walk-off win. But Keith Foulke, the All-Star closer signed by Boston from Oakland before the season, struck out pinch-hitter Ruben Sierra and induced a groundball from Lofton to send the game into extra innings.

Yankees closer Mariano Rivera entered in the 10th and retired the Red Sox in order. Mike Timlin replaced Foulke in the bottom of the inning and hit Jeter leading off. Sheffield, the next man up, hit into a double play. Rodriguez doubled and stole third, putting the winning run on third with two outs. Alan Embree replaced Timlin and walked Bubba Crosby, who had entered the game as a pinch-runner for Matsui in the ninth. Bernie Williams lined out to Youkilis, sending the game to the 11th.

Still facing Rivera, the Red Sox loaded the bases with nobody out. The next man up, Kevin Millar, hit one sharply to Rodriguez at third. Rodriguez dove to his right to grab Millar's groundball, tagged third, and threw home side-arm to Posada to get the runner trying to score. McCarty then flied out to left, and Rivera escaped a perilous jam to keep the score tied. Embree retired the Yankees in order to send the game to the 12th.

Tanyon Sturtze replaced Rivera and found himself in trouble with runners at second and third and two men out. Nixon, pinch-hitting for Gabe Kapler, lofted a shallow fly near the left-field line. Sprinting full speed, Jeter made a spectacular catch to grab the ball. Jeter's momentum carried him headfirst into the third row of seats, and he sustained a laceration of his chin and bruises. "Those are the things I keep saying that don't show up in the stats," said Torre. "To make a play like that, with the game on the line, is pretty damn special."[3] "That's why he's Derek Jeter," said Yankees first baseman Jason Giambi. "He's a winner and that's why you want him on your team."[4] "Greatest catch I've ever seen," said Rodriguez. "It was unbelievable. He's just so unselfish. He put his body in a compromising spot. It was hard to watch."[5]

The play also juxtaposed Jeter with Garciaparra, Boston's star shortstop, who sat on the bench with the day off because of an injured right Achilles' heel.[6] With blood on his uniform, Jeter walked off with the trainers to a loud ovation. He left the game to get checked out at a local hospital.[7]

Curt Leskanic entered for Boston and gave up a leadoff triple to Miguel Cairo and loaded the bases with one out. On a 3-and-2 pitch to Bubba Crosby, Leskanic got him to hit a groundball to shortstop and Pokey Reese threw home for the force out.[8] With the bases loaded and two outs, Leskanic struck out Williams, and the game remained tied after 12.

In the top of the 13th, Ramirez hit his second home run of the evening to give Boston a 4-3 lead. With the Yankees down to their final out in the bottom half against Leskanic, Sierra singled up the middle. Cairo, down to his last strike, doubled to the right-center-field alley to score Sierra and tie the game. Flaherty singled to deep left field to score Cairo and win the game for the Yankees. New York had an 8½-game lead over Boston in early July.

"This game was just as exciting, if not more exciting, than Game 7 [of the 2003 ALCS]," said Embree.[9] Despite the outcome, Boston remained optimistic about its chances. "They got the better of us in this series," said Johnny Damon. "But this is going to be our worst dip in our year. We still believe we're going to go off and win the World Series."[10]

Damon proved prophetic. Though it certainly felt as though the Yankees would always find a way to beat the Red Sox, the tables eventually turned. In the AL Championship Series, the Red Sox rallied from a three-games-to-none deficit to beat the Yankees, then swept the St. Louis Cardinals in the World Series to win Boston's first championship since 1918.

SOURCES

In addition to the sources cited in the Notes, the author consulted Baseball-Reference.com and Retrosheet.org.

https://www.baseball-reference.com/boxes/NYA/NYA200407010.shtml

https://www.retrosheet.org/boxesetc/2004/B07010NYA2004.htm

The author also watched the game on YouTube: https://www.youtube.com/watch?v=aeejzvQzLWM&t=11s

NOTES

1 Boston also made three errors through the first four innings.

2 Tyler Kepner, "Dust Settles in 13th, and Yankees Sweep," *New York Times*, July 2, 2004: D3.

3 Ben Walker (Associated Press), "Catch Proves Why Yankees, New Yorkers Love Jeter," *Marysville* (Ohio) *Journal-Tribune* July 2, 2004: 11.

4 Walker.

5 Kepner.

6 Garciaparra came into the game hitting .235 with 5 errors in 17 games. Later in the month the Red Sox traded him to the Chicago Cubs at the trade deadline.

7 When Jeter left the game, Rodriguez moved over to play shortstop, and Sheffield moved to third base for the first time since 1993.

8 The Red Sox got the out in part by using five infielders (including a left-handed second baseman in McCarty) and leaving Ramirez and Damon to cover the outfield.

9 Bob Hohler, "Sox Falter Again as Yankees Rally to Complete Sweep," *Boston Globe*, July 2, 2004: 77.

10 Hohler.

THE LONGEST ALL-STAR GAME

July 15, 2008:
American League 4, National League 3 (15 innings),
at Yankee Stadium

By Cecilia Tan

As the construction timeline for the new Yankee Stadium emerged, speculation that New York would host the 2008 All-Star Game ran rampant. Mayor Mike Bloomberg and Commissioner Bud Selig confirmed the rumors on January 31, 2007, at a press conference announcing that the 2008 midsummer classic would take place during the Stadium's final season. Selig called Yankee Stadium "the most famous cathedral in baseball, and, I think, the most famous stadium in the world," that day, starting a hype train that would run full speed until the game itself.[1]

"Plenty of All-Stars talked about a pilgrimage to Monument Park this week, the historic site ... where some say the ghosts of Ruth, DiMaggio and Gehrig still reside," enthused one pregame item.[2] Before Opening Day, 3.8 million seats (of 4.4 million available) for the season had been sold, and tour attendance swelled.[3] All season, Fox TV hosted polls on the top moments in Yankee Stadium history during their Saturday baseball broadcasts. "House That Ruth Built Is Game's Biggest Star," proclaimed one headline.[4] Another agreed: "[Stars] Past and Present Gather to Bid Farewell to the Biggest Star of Them All: Yankee Stadium."[5]

Of course in the "Big Apple" – as well as any time George Steinbrenner was involved – only the biggest and best would do. The "largest red carpet in history" – 95,000 square feet – covered Sixth Avenue for a parade featuring the largest number of former All-Stars ever.[6] MLB and Bloomberg's office trumpeted one million "expected" spectators at the parade. (Actual attendance appeared far lower.[7]) The ticket price was also the highest ever for an All-Star Game: Lower deck seats set at "$525-$725, and bleacher tickets for $150. ... And that's the list price."[8]

But news more dire than Barry Bonds' lack of free-agent offers or players' public gripes over the game's effect on the World Series threatened to cast a pall over things.[9] Steinbrenner had been in poor health and hadn't attended a game all season.[10] Neither had announcer Bob Sheppard, who had been too ill to call a game since September 5, 2007.[11] And just days before the game, a new ghost might have joined those in Monument Park when longtime Yankee and YES announcer Bobby Murcer died from brain cancer.[12]

The pregame hype came with a tinge of rivalry: Boston Red Sox manager Terry Francona would helm the AL squad, and speculation was rife that he might "start" Mariano Rivera. Francona quashed the rumors. "You're expected to take a starter because that's the [unwritten] rules you play under," he told the media, while declining to answer whether he would go to Mo or Boston's closer, Jonathan Papelbon, in a save situation.[13]

Ultimately, Steinbrenner made it to the game and played a part in the pregame pomp, delivering baseballs via golf cart to the dignitaries who would toss the ceremonial first pitches: Yogi Berra, Whitey Ford, Goose Gossage, and Reggie Jackson.[14] They weren't the only former All-Stars on the field. The 49 "Living Immortals of Cooperstown" – not just All-Stars but Hall of Famers – assembled at each position before the starters joined them.[15]

Announcer Joe Buck also went "off script" during the pregame introductions to exhort the crowd to send well wishes to Bob Sheppard.[16] All told, pregame ceremonies went on so long that the first pitch didn't take place until 8:47 P.M. After so much historic, epic buildup, how could the actual game possibly live up to the hype?

By being the longest All-Star Game in history.

When the game began, of course, no one knew it would still be going in the wee hours. Cleveland left-hander Cliff Lee started for the AL and Milwaukee Brewers right-hander Ben Sheets for the NL.

When Derek Jeter stole second base in the first inning, the cheers from the hometown crowd were lusty. But the game was a scoreless affair through four innings, parading through the lineups as steadily as a convertible up a red-carpeted avenue.

Then came a speed bump. Matt Holliday led off the fifth for the NL. Holliday was only in the starting lineup because the Cubs' Alfonso Soriano had suffered a broken hand. The AL's fourth pitcher, the Angels' Ervin Santana, brought 98 mph heat, but Holliday lined a fastball deep into the right-field lower deck: they call that section the "short porch," but there was nothing short about the homer. The AL-partisan crowd grumbled a bit.

The National League added another run in the sixth, off Oakland's Justin Duchscherer, who gave up back-to-back singles to Florida's Hanley Ramirez and the Phillies' Chase Utley, and then a sacrifice fly to the Astros' Lance Berkman.[17] A single by once-and-future Cardinal Albert Pujols followed, and a big inning threatened to develop. The question simmered: Could the NL finally break the AL's 11-year unbeaten streak? But Duchscherer struck out Chipper Jones and then retired Holliday on a popup to second, limiting the damage to one run.

In the bottom of the inning, the Rangers' Josh Hamilton led off, sending a buzz through the crowd. Hamilton, the feel-good comeback story of the year, had electrified the Stadium the night before with an epic Home Run Derby performance in which several balls reached the back row of the bleachers, with estimated travel distances of over 500 feet. Though he didn't actually win, Hamilton's performance remains an indelible one. Now facing Dan Haren, he singled and stole second but was stranded.

The American League didn't give the opposition any more leash, tying the score in the bottom of the seventh. Justin Morneau – the actual Home Run Derby winner – doubled off Edinson Volquez. Volquez then got Ian Kinsler to ground out on one pitch and caught Dioner Navarro looking at strike three. To a smattering of anti-Boston boos, J.D. Drew then stepped into the batter's box. Drew had earned Player of the Month honors in June for hitting 12 homers while filling in for the injured David Ortiz. He quickly earned cheers by lining a 2-and-1 pitch right into the first row of the short porch to tie the game, 2–2.

The leagues traded blows again in the next inning, with the NL nicking Papelbon for an unearned run on a

Courtesy of Todd Radom.

Fans who stayed for the entire All-Star Game saw nearly five hours of baseball.

Miguel Tejada single-stolen base-throwing error-sacrifice fly (hit by Adrian Gonzalez). The AL answered right back. With two outs, pitcher Billy Wagner came in to face Grady Sizemore, who singled, then stole yet another base, and scored on a ground-rule double from Evan Longoria. (The AL tied an ASG record with six stolen bags.[18])

With the game tied 3-3 in the ninth, fans wondered if Mariano Rivera would pitch in a nonsave situation. The bullpen door swung open, but Francisco Rodriguez took the mound. He walked the leadoff man, Aramis Ramirez, then gave up a fly-ball out to Corey Hart. Then Francona called for Mo, who induced a double play from Ryan Ludwick to snuff the threat.

After Ryan Dempster struck out the side in the bottom of the ninth, Francona went back to Mo for the 10th. Although he did give up two singles (to Russell Martin and Tejada), he got out of the inning with another double play. Francona had used his entire bench of hitters, but thanks to the rule adding more pitchers to the rosters – enacted after the 2002 All-Star Game ended in an 11-inning tie due to lack of arms – there were still pitchers in the bullpen ... right?

Concerns simmered as the game stretched past midnight that many pitchers who had made the roster were unavailable because they had started on the Sunday before the game. NL manager Clint Hurdle was supposedly unable to tap Dempster, Brandon Webb, or Tim Lincecum, but used Dempster in the ninth and had to go to Webb for the 14th after the AL had left men at third in the 10th, 11th, and 12th innings. Meanwhile, Francona texted Tampa Bay general manager Andrew Friedman: Could he use starter Scott Kazmir? Friedman said no – Kazmir had thrown 104 pitches that Sunday.[19]

A second round of "Take Me Out to the Ball Game" was sung in the 14th, and Francona was running out of options. After 1:00 A.M., the 15th inning arrived, and Kazmir was summoned despite the Rays' wishes. He pitched a scoreless 15th.[20]

Brad Lidge took the hill for the NL. Lidge was having a stellar season, with 20 saves in 20 chances and a 1.13 ERA to that point. But Morneau singled, Navarro singled, and J.D. Drew walked to load the bases. All it would take to send everyone home would be a long fly ball, and Michael Young finally hit one to Hart in right. Morneau slid across the plate safe, just ahead of the tag, at 1:37 A.M. The game had lasted a record 4 hours, 50 minutes.

Drew was voted MVP. A record total of 63 of the 67 players on the rosters had been used, also setting records for most strikeouts (34) and runners left on (28). Longtime AP writer Ronald Blum's postgame article summed up the epic perfectly, titling it "The Long Goodbye."[21]

SOURCES

In addition to the sources cited in the Notes, the author consulted Baseball-Reference.com and Retrosheet.org.

https://www.baseball-reference.com/allstar/2008-allstar-game.shtml

https://www.retrosheet.org/boxesetc/2008/YAS_2008.htm

NOTES

1   Jack Curry "Yankee Stadium Gets One Last All-Star Game," *New York Times,* February 1, 2007. (Accessed November 5, 2022: https://www.nytimes.com/2007/02/01/sports/baseball/01base.ready.html).

2   Associated Press, "NY on their Minds," *Ellwood City* (Pennsylvania) *Ledger,* July 16, 2008: 9.

3   Tony Morante, Yankees former head tour guide, personal email and phone call, November 7, 2022. Tour demand in 2007 topped 100,000 visitors for the first time, and in 2008 over 150,000 took the Stadium tour.

4   Ronald Blum (Associated Press), "House That Ruth Built Is Game's Biggest Star," *Indiana* (Pennsylvania) *Gazette,* July 15, 2008: 15.

5   Joel Duplessis, "Yankee Stadium to Host 79th MLB All-Star Game (Cover Story)," *Greenwood* (South Carolina) *Index-Journal,* July 13, 2008: 51.

6   Duplessis.

7   "A total crowd of several thousand people could be made to look like hundreds of thousands. Even a million, if one were bold enough to make such a claim," wrote Jim Dwyer in a sarcastic, critical article. "In All-Star Parade, Playing Games Before Ball," *New York Times,* July 16, 2008. (Accessed November 7, 2022: https://www.nytimes.com/2008/07/16/nyregion/16about.html).

8   Scalpers were asking even higher prices, of course. Ronald Blum (Associated Press), "All-Stars Fighting for Attention in New York," *Greenwood Index-Journal,* July 13, 2008: 81.

9   Ben Walker (Associated Press), "No One Wants Bonds, Slugger's Prospects Look 'Bleak,'" *Indiana* (Pennsylvania) *Gazette,* July 15, 2007: 16; Associated Press, "Players Rip All-Star Format," *Indiana Gazette,* July 13, 2007: C-4.

10 Ronald Blum (Associated Press), "All-Star Game Site Is Rife with Memories," *Indiana Gazette,* July 14, 2008: 13.

11 Steve Politi, "Bob Sheppard Not Able to Be at All-Star Game," *Newark Star-Ledger*/NJ.com, July 9, 2008. (Accessed November 7, 2022: https://www.nj.com/yankees/2008/07/bob_sheppard_not_able_to_be_at.html).

12 Dan Graziano, "Bobby Murcer, 62, Dies of Brain Cancer," *Newark Star-Ledger*/NJ.com, July 12, 2008. (Accessed November 7, 2022: https://www.nj.com/yankees/2008/07/bobby_murcer_62_dies_of_brain.html) In an unusual coincidence, two years later, Bob Sheppard and George Steinbrenner would die within two days of each other, Sheppard on July 11 and Steinbrenner on July 13, 2010.

13 Associated Press, "Don't Expect Yankees' Rivera to Start All-Star Game," *Huntsville* (Alabama) *Times,* July 11, 2008. Papelbon and the other Red Sox were predictably booed during the parade and ceremonies.

14 On the receiving end of the ceremonial tosses were four current Yankees: Derek Jeter, Alex Rodriguez, Mariano Rivera, and manager Joe Girardi.

Girardi was also seen (without protective gear on) helping to warm up pitchers in the AL bullpen during the game.

15   National League starting pitcher Ben Sheets confessed that he was "nervous" to meet the likes of Bob Gibson, Bob Feller, and Steve Carlton, but he couldn't miss the moment: "[I] probably should have been in the bullpen. The pregame ceremony was amazing [and] I wanted to be part of it." Associated Press, "Hall of Intro: New, Old All-Stars Take Places," *Ellwood City* (Pennsylvania) *Ledger,* July 16, 2008: 9.

16   MLB, "2008 All-Star Game at Yankee Stadium," YouTube video, streamed live on April 29, 2020, https://www.youtube.com/watch?v=obTBHlo6aQM.

17   The Astros were in the National League through the 2012 season.

18   "All-Stars vs. All-Stars – MLB Game Recap," ESPN.com, July 16, 2008. (Accessed November 7, 2002: https://www.espn.com/mlb/recap/_/gameId/280715131).

19   As told to sideline reporter Ken Rosenthal and reported on the broadcast. See MLB, "2008 All-Star Game at Yankee Stadium," YouTube video, streamed live on April 29, 2020, timestamp 3:55-4:00, https://www.youtube.com/watch?v=obTBHlo6aQM.

20   The previous record for longest All-Star Game had been 1967's: It also ran 15 innings, but the time of game was 3:41.

21   Ronald Blum (Associated Press), "The Long Goodbye," *Indiana* (Pennsylvania) *Gazette*, July 16, 2008: 13.

THE FINAL GAME AT YANKEE STADIUM

September 21, 2008:
New York Yankees 7, Baltimore Orioles 3,
at Yankee Stadium

By Alan Raylesberg

It was a night like no other. A night to say farewell to an old friend. A night full of memories. A night that would go down in history. And so it was, on September 21, 2008, that more than 54,000 people showed up for the final game to be played at the old ballpark in the Bronx. Yankee Stadium, where so much of baseball history was written, would be torn down, and across the street a new, modern edifice would replace it in time for the 2009 season. But first, one last game,

one final night to remember what made the place so special.

The Baltimore Orioles were in town to play the Yankees, but this night was about the Stadium. It was built in the third decade of the twentieth century, and captain Derek Jeter often spoke about the ghosts that inhabited the catacombs during the twenty-first century. The ghosts that came out to give the Yankees magical moments such as their two comeback wins in the

In the Stadium's final game, Yankees fans were treated to a parade of legends and a come-from-behind victory.

2001 World Series and their extra-inning win in Game Seven of the 2003 American League Championship Series. It was only fitting that, on this very special night, the Yankees would bring those ghosts to life in a pregame ceremony that combined the elements of an All-Star Game with Old-Timers Day and the Field of Dreams.

The festivities started with the recorded voice of Bob Sheppard, the Yankees longtime public- address announcer, welcoming everyone to The Final Game.[1] The Yankees then unveiled, in the center-field bleachers, the original 1922 American League pennant that was raised on the day the Stadium opened on April 18, 1923. To connect the present to the past, the 1923 Opening Day lineup was announced, with actors wearing vintage uniforms running onto the field from behind the outfield fence and lining up in center field. [2]

Longtime Yankees broadcasters Michael Kay and John Sterling[3] took over as emcees, evoking memories that had the sellout crowd roaring from start to finish. Attention was directed to the giant video screen on the center-field scoreboard as clips of the greatest players in Yankees history were shown, one position at a time.[4] With dramatic music playing, the fans were treated to a video montage of some of the many memorable moments that had occurred at the Stadium over its 85-year history. There was Lou Gehrig's "Luckiest Man" speech in 1939; Babe Ruth's home-run trot; Mickey Mantle hitting his 500th home run into the right-field stands; Roger Maris hitting number 61 in 1961; Chris Chambliss hitting a walk-off home run to win the 1976 American League pennant; Reggie Jackson hitting three home runs in Game Six of the 1977 World Series; Ron Guidry setting the Yankees' single-season strikeout record in 1978;[5] Tino Martinez hitting a grand slam in the 1998 World Series; Scott Brosius hitting a game-tying home run in Game Five of the 2001 World Series;[6] the fans chanting Paul O'Neill's name as he stood in right field in his final game at the Stadium in the 2001 World Series; Don Larsen pitching the only perfect game in World Series history; and David Wells and David Cone pitching the only other perfect games in Yankees history.[7]

The video clips brought back memories, yet it was the introduction of those former players in attendance that made one feel chills on this historic night. As Kay and Sterling announced them, the former greats came out of the Yankees dugout one by one and took their place at their position on the very ground that had been their home for so many years. Perhaps the most popular Yankee of them all, 83-year-old Lawrence Peter

"Yogi" Berra, was introduced to a thunderous ovation as he walked slowly to his familiar spot behind home plate. Introduced as the greatest Yankees pitcher ever, 79-year-old Edward Charles "Whitey" Ford strolled to the pitcher's mound. From the great Yankees teams of the 1950s and early 1960s, on to the field came Bill "Moose" Skowron, along with Bobby Richardson and Gil McDougald. From the most recent Yankees dynasty came Martinez, Brosius, O'Neill, Jorge Posada, and Mariano Rivera. Jackson, Larsen, Cone, Wells, and Goose Gossage were there;[8] Mantle's look-alike son, David, took his place in center field, joined in right field by Randy Maris, the son of the man who broke Ruth's single-season home-run record in 1961.[9]

There was an outpouring of love when the family of Bobby Murcer was introduced. The heir apparent to Mantle, and a longtime popular Yankees broadcaster, Murcer had died two months earlier at the age of 62.[10] The late Thurman Munson's son, Michael, bearing a striking physical resemblance to his father, took his position behind the plate.[11] He was joined there by the daughter of another catcher, Elston Howard.[12] The widow of Catfish Hunter joined the other former pitching stars. The noise level in the Stadium got louder and louder as the parade of Yankees greats and relatives continued.[13] When Michel Kay introduced "the final guest," the Stadium rocked as Bernie Williams ran out to center field to stand next to the families of Mantle and Murcer and the ghosts of Earle Combs and Joe DiMaggio.

As the fans settled down to watch a game that seemed like an afterthought, the Yankees had another surprise in store. Kay announced that, since Babe Ruth had opened the Stadium with a home run, it was only fitting that the Stadium "close with a Ruth," as 92-year-old Julia Ruth Stevens, the daughter of The Babe, walked out to the area in front of the pitcher's mound to throw out the first pitch.[14] She threw a strike to Posada and it was time to play the Final Game at the old ballpark in the Bronx.

Throughout the ceremonies, the present-day Yankees and Orioles stood at the top of the dugout steps,[15] enthralled at what they were witnessing. They watched as Don Larsen scooped up dirt from the pitcher's mound with assistance from Whitey Ford, as Willie Randolph ran out of the dugout and slid into second base[16] and as the voice of Yogi Berra declared, "Only this time when it's over, it's over."[17]

The drama of the evening continued with a unique introduction of the Yankees starting lineup. The voice of Bob Sheppard announced the lineup as each player, one by one, ran on to the field to their position and joined the former Yankees greats already standing there.[18] With the Yankees one loss away from being eliminated from the postseason, the game itself, against the last-place Orioles, was not significant.[19] Yet, as Orioles manager Dave Trembley said, the atmosphere "was kind of like the seventh game of the World Series, the Super Bowl, the Mardi Gras … everything rolled into one."[20]

Staving off elimination, the Yankees won the game, 7-3. Andy Pettitte started and pitched five innings for the victory.[21] Chris Waters started for the Orioles and took the loss. Johnny Damon and José Molina homered for the Yankees. Molina's fourth-inning home run was the last one hit in Yankee Stadium.[22] In the ninth inning, the fans got to see what they anticipated and hoped for, when Rivera came in to pitch for the final time at the Stadium.[23] After Rivera retired the first two batters, Jeter was called in off the field to a tremendous ovation, before coming out for a curtain call.[24] Rivera then completed a one-two-three inning and the game was over.[25]

The celebration was not. As the game ended, and the fans said goodbye to The Cathedral of Baseball, the entire Yankees team came on to the field and gathered at the pitcher's mound. Jeter had a microphone and the fans sensed they were about to witness one of those great moments in Yankee Stadium history.[26] Jeter, poised as usual, remarked that the Stadium had been home for 85 years and that there was a lot of tradition and memories. He told the fans that "we are relying on you to take the memories from this Stadium, add them to the new memories to come at the new Yankee Stadium and continue to pass them on from generation to generation."[27] He closed by saluting "the greatest fans in the world," before the entire Yankees team took a lap around the field, waving their caps to their adoring fans. Frank Sinatra's "New York, New York" played for one last time as the crowd roared in a final goodbye to the House that Ruth Built.

AUTHOR'S NOTE

The author, a lifelong Yankees fan, sat with his son in an Upper Tier Box near third base that night. The evening brought back many memories and created a new one that will last a lifetime.

SOURCES

In addition to the sources cited in the Notes, the author also viewed the broadcast of the ceremonies on YouTube, https://www.youtube.com/watch?v=qTIT-7WCv3qU and consulted Baseball-Reference.com.

https://www.baseball-reference.com/boxes/NYA/NYA200809210.shtml

NOTES

[1] Known as "The Voice of God," Sheppard started as the public-address announcer for the Yankees during the 1951 season. A speech teacher with impeccable diction and a voice to match, Sheppard remained as the PA announcer for an incredible 57 seasons, through 2007. Illness prevented him, at the age of 97, from announcing during 2008. Still too ill to attend the Final Game, but hoping to return as PA announcer in 2009, Sheppard recorded the announcements played at the Stadium for the Final Game. Sheppard died in 2010, three months shy of his 100th birthday. Even after his passing, his recorded announcement of Jeter coming to bat ("now batting for the Yankees, number two, Derek Jeter, number two") was played when Jeter came to bat for many years afterward. Sheppard is honored with a plaque in Monument Park.

[2] The Opening Day lineup was Whitey Witt in center field, Joe Dugan at third base, Ruth in right field, Wally Pipp at first base, Bob Meusel in left field, Wally Schang at catcher, Aaron Ward at second base, Everett Scott at shortstop, and Bob Shawkey pitching. Also announced was the manager, Miller Huggins. Some of the players who are in Monument Park were then recognized, with actors running onto the field in vintage uniforms to represent them. Those players included Gehrig, Lefty Gomez, Red Ruffing, Bill Dickey, DiMaggio, Allie Reynolds, and managers Joe McCarthy and Casey Stengel.

[3] Kay, a former sportswriter, began announcing Yankees games in 1992, initially partnering with Sterling on radio. Beginning in 2002, Kay became the Yankees' primary television announcer and still had that role as of October 2022. Sterling has been a Yankees radio broadcaster since 1989 and, at age 84, was still their primary radio voice as of October 2022.

[4] Left fielders were shown first, followed by shortstops, third basemen, right fielders, second basemen, first basemen, catchers, pitchers, and finally center fielders.

[5] Guidry struck out 248 batters in 1978. He won the Cy Young Award with a record of 25-3 and an ERA of 1.74. In October 2022, Gerrit Cole broke Guidry's strikeout record, doing so on the same night that Aaron Judge hit his 62nd home run of the season to break Roger Maris's Yankees and American League single-season home-run record.

[6] The video also showed Martinez's dramatic game-tying home run the night before, in Game Four of the 2001 World Series, a home run that Kay said made the Stadium "shake."

[7] Other moments shown on the screen included Jeter's "Mr. November" game-winning home run in Game Four of the 2001 World Series; Alex Rodriguez's 500th home run; Bucky Dent's pennant-winning home run against the Red Sox in 1978 (which took place at Fenway Park); Mantle celebrating his 1956 Triple Crown; Dave Righetti's no-hitter; and Jim Abbott's no-hitter. Phil Rizzuto was seen speaking about what it meant to be a Yankee.

[8] When O'Neill went out to right field, the fans serenaded him with the same "PAUL O'NEILL" chants that shook the Stadium in the 2001 World Series. When Jackson went to right field, the fans chanted "REGGIE-REGGIE-REGGIE" just as they had done during the 1977 World Series when Jackson hit three home runs in one game, a feat that at the time had been accomplished by only one other player in baseball history – Babe Ruth (twice).

[9] Randy Maris wore his father's number 9 uniform. Roger Maris's 61 home runs in 1961 were the American League single-season record until 2022, when another Yankees right fielder, Aaron Judge, broke the record, with 62.

[10] Murcer was represented by his wife, Kay, and his children, Tori and Todd.

[11] Munson was 32 years old, and the Yankees captain, when he was killed in the crash of his private plane during the 1979 season.

[12] Howard died in 1980, at the age of 51. He played in 13 seasons with the Yankees and later was their first-base coach for 11 years.

13　In addition to the players mentioned in the text, others who were introduced to the crowd and took their positions on the field included left fielders Roy White and Dave Winfield (left field was his original position as a Yankee); shortstop Rizzuto, represented by his widow, Cora; third basemen Graig Nettles and Wade Boggs; second baseman and Yankees manager Billy Martin, represented by his son Billy Martin Jr.; and catcher and then Yankees manager Joe Girardi. Many former greats who were not there in person, as well as some current Yankees, were highlighted during the position-by-position video presentation. They included outfielders Ruth, DiMaggio, Combs, Tommy Henrich, Hank Bauer, Lou Piniella, Bobby Abreu, Rickey Henderson, Johnny Damon, and Hideki Matsui. The infielders included Dugan, Clete Boyer, Mike Pagliarulo, Rodriguez, Randolph, Joe Gordon, Snuffy Stirnweiss, Jerry Coleman, Chuck Knoblauch, Dent, Alfonso Soriano, Robinson Cano, and Jeter. First basemen included Gehrig, Hal Chase, Pipp, Joe Pepitone, Don Mattingly, and Jason Giambi. Catchers included Dickey. Pitchers included Herb Pennock, Ruffing, Gomez, Joe Page, Reynolds, Eddie Lopat, Bob Turley, Luis Arroyo, Al Downing, Mel Stottlemyre, Sparky Lyle, Ed Figueroa, Tommy John, Righetti, Abbott, Jimmy Key, Andy Pettitte, Dwight Gooden, John Wetteland, Orlando "El Duque" Hernandez, Mike Mussina, and Chien-Ming Wang. Conspicuous by their omission were pitcher Roger Clemens and manager Joe Torre. Clemens was in the midst of a scandal involving performance-enhancing drugs, a fact that may have explained his lack of mention. Torre's omission was more puzzling. Jason Zillo, a Yankees spokesman, later said, "A lot of great Yankees weren't mentioned. There was no slight intended. Perhaps in hindsight, they should have been mentioned." Richard Sandomir, "Finale Had Too Much Familiar and Too Much Missing," *New York Times*, September 23, 2008: D4.

14　Stevens wore a Yankees jacket and waved to the crowd as she walked slowly to the mound accompanied by her son, Tom.

15　The dugout was so full that some of the Yankees sat on the dugout roof to watch the ceremonies. Rookie pitcher Phil Coke said after the game, "Totally and completely blows my mind. I turn around and look and see Goose Gossage walking around our clubhouse. Wow." Tyler Kepner, "A Long Goodbye to an 85-Year Run," *New York Times,* September 21, 2008: SP8.

16　Randolph grew up in Brooklyn and played 13 seasons at second base for his hometown Yankees before becoming a Yankees coach and then manager of the crosstown Mets. After the game, Randoph described his slide, saying, "I just wanted to get my uniform dirty one more time. That's how I played." Michael S. Schmidt and Joshua Robinson, "Night of Reflection for Sons of Two Yankees Greats," *New York Times*, September 22, 2008: D2.

17　Berra was emotional about the Stadium's closing. "It will always be in my heart, it will," he said, "I'm sorry to see it over. I tell you that." Kepner, "A Long Goodbye to an 85-Year Run."

18　The starting lineup was Damon in center field, Jeter at shortstop, Abreu in right field, Rodriguez at third base, Giambi at first base, Xavier Nady in left field, Cano at second base, Matsui at designated hitter, Jose Molina at catcher, and Pettitte pitching.

19　The Yankees had not been eliminated from the postseason since 1993. They came into the game in third place in the AL East, with a record of 84-71, nine games behind Tampa Bay. Baltimore was last in the division, 25 games out of first. The Yankees were eliminated from the postseason two days later when the eventual wild-card team, Boston, beat Cleveland, while the Yankees were winning their sixth straight against Toronto. Before being eliminated in 2008, the Yankees had made the playoffs every season from 1995 through 2007. They also finished first in 1994 when the season ended due to the players strike. The Yankees opened the new Yankee Stadium, in 2009, by finishing first in the AL East and winning the World Series. They made the playoffs each season after that through 2012, finishing first in the division in all but one of those years.

20　Associated Press, "For Final Game at Yankee Stadium, Yanks Win to Prevent Playoff Elimination," ESPN Gamecast Recap, https://www.espn.com/mlb/recap/_/gameId/280921110. Yankees manager Joe Girardi also compared the atmosphere to the seventh game of the World Series. Kepner, "A Long Goodbye to an 85-Year Run."

21　After the game, Pettitte said, "The way I feel emotionally right now, and just physically so drained, it feels like a huge postseason win for us. I kind of feel embarrassed saying that, because unless a miracle happens, we're not going to the postseason. But it was special." Kepner, "A Long Goodbye to an 85-Year Run."

22　Molina, a career backup and the brother of Cardinals great Yadier Molina, played 15 seasons in the majors. Molina started more games at catcher that year than any other Yankee. A lifetime .233 hitter with only 39 home runs in 2,795 plate appearances, Molina will always be the answer to the trivia question of who hit the last home run in the old Yankee Stadium. When asked about where his home run stood among his career highlights, Molina said, "Right at the top. It can't be better than this." He added, "You have a lot of players, great players, Hall of Famers, a lot of catchers that came through here. Just to be a part of that, knowing that your name is written right by theirs, it's amazing." Tyler Kepner, "In the Afterglow, Yankees Cling to Hope," *New York Times*, September 23, 2008: D4.

23　Rivera is generally considered the greatest closer of all time. Inducted into the National Baseball Hall of Fame in 2019, he pitched 19 seasons for the Yankees (from 1995 through 2013). He saved 652 games in the regular season and 42 in the postseason.

24　Pettitte had a curtain call earlier, when he was removed from the game during the sixth inning.

25　Rivera held on to the final ball and told reporters that he would give it to 78-year-old Yankees owner George Steinbrenner, who watched the game from his home in Florida. "Mr. George, he gave me the opportunity and he gave me the chance," Rivera said. "The least I can do is give the ball to him." Kepner, "A Long Goodbye to an 85-Year Run."

26　Yankee Stadium was the site of memorable speeches before the one that Jeter gave that night. Among them was Lou Gehrig's "Luckiest Man" speech on Lou Gehrig Appreciation Day in 1939; Babe Ruth saying goodbye to his fans in his final visit to the Stadium in 1948, when his number 3 was retired; and Mickey Mantle addressing the crowd on Mickey Mantle Day in 1969, when his number 7 was retired. After the game, Yankees general manager Brian Cashman said, "What I was thinking as Derek was speaking was that it was going to be one of those moments that will play over and over for the next 100 years, like Lou Gehrig." Harvey Araton, "A Quiet Captain's Stirring Epilogue," *New York Times*, September 23, 2008: D1. Jeter's speech can be viewed on YouTube, https://www.youtube.com/watch?v=HJrlTpQmoto.

27　Jeter had said that the ghosts from the old Stadium would simply move across the street but some of the fans had other ideas. One fan told the *New York Times,* "I don't know if the ghosts are going to be there. You can feel that, standing here – Babe Ruth, Joe DiMaggio. It's not going to be the same." Kepner, "A Long Goodbye to an 85-Year Run."

APPENDIX: MORE GREAT GAMES
AT YANKEE STADIUM

If the editors had infinite space, we would have included more memorable games at Yankee Stadium. With a few exceptions, we opted mostly for game stories that had yet to be told by SABR writers. Many more of those historic moments at Yankee Stadium – the good, the bad, and the ugly – have already been published and are available to read via the SABR Games Project, at https://sabr.org/gamesproject.

June 15, 1923 – Lou Gehrig plays his first game in Yankee pinstripes –Yankees 10, Browns 0
The future Iron Horse was a ninth-inning defensive replacement for the guy he permanently replaced two years later, Wally Pipp.

June 1, 1925: Babe Ruth returns from 'Bellyache Heard 'Round the World' – Senators 5, Yankees 3
The Bambino plays his first game of the year after being hospitalized following a preseason collapse on a train. Lou Gehrig pinch-hits in the first of his 2,130 consecutive games.

June 2, 1925: Gehrig replaces Pipp as Miller Huggins shakes up Yankees lineup – Yankees 8, Senators 5
With the Yankees floundering in seventh place, Miller Huggins replaces three regulars with newcomers – including Pipp for Gehrig. The rest is history.

September 24, 1925: Babe Ruth beats White Sox with extra-inning walk-off grand slam – Yankees 6, White Sox 5
In the bottom of the 10th, The Babe hits the first "ultimate grand slam" in Yankees history (a walk-off with the team down by three). Not until 2002 – featured in this book – would it happen again.

October 10, 1926: Pete Alexander saves the day – Cardinals 3, Yankees 2
In Game Seven of the World Series, aging St. Louis pitcher Grover Cleveland Alexander comes on in relief after pitching a complete game the previous day and plays hero in the Cardinals' first World Series championship by striking out Yankees rookie Tony Lazzeri. Babe Ruth gets caught stealing to end the game.

September 11, 1927: Browns avoid the skunk as Milt Gaston earns "brilliant victory" over mighty Yankees – Browns 6, Yankees 2
Milt Gaston, and his ERA above 5.00 went the distance for the St. Louis Browns' only win in 22 games against the mighty Murderers' Row. He also gave up Babe Ruth's 50th home run.

September 29, 1927: Babe Ruth hits grand slam in second consecutive game for No. 59 – Yankees 15, Senators 4
The Babe ties his previous season record with the bases loaded in the fifth, spoiling Paul Hopkins' major-league debut.

September 30, 1927: Babe Ruth hits record 60th home run – Yankees 4, Senators 2
Tom Zachary becomes a trivia question as the pitcher off whom Ruth broke his own home-run record.

October 8, 1927: New York Yankees win World Series on a wild pitch – Yankees 4, Pirates 3
The Yankees cap their season of dominance with a four-game sweep of Pittsburgh for their second World Championship. But it doesn't quite end in typical Murderers' Row fashion.

April 18, 1929: Babe Ruth celebrates "honeymoon" with a home run – Yankees 7, Red Sox 3
The new Mrs. Claire Ruth – having just married the day before – watches her husband go long in the first inning on Opening Day. The Yankees debut numbers on their backs.

May 26, 1930: Goose Goslin, Joe Judge first in twentieth century to hit back-to-back homers twice in a game – Senators 10, Yankees 7
Washington's number 3 and cleanup hitters put up straight jacks twice, and the Senators put up a seven-spot in the fifth inning.

July 28, 1931: Bob Fothergill leads White Sox in 11-run rally to beat Yankees – White Sox 14, Yankees 12

An 11-run eighth inning turned a 12-3 deficit into a 14-12 win for Chicago, as Bob Fothergill went 4-for-5 with a home run, two doubles, and a triple.

May 27, 1933: Yankees score 12 runs in eighth for big comeback win – Yankees 15, White Sox 11

The Yankees roughed up future Hall of Famer Ted Lyons for nine runs, part of a historic late rally that erased an 11-3 deficit. Every position player scored a run, and Bill Dickey homered with five RBIs.

October 1, 1933: Lefty Ruth all right in final mound appearance – Yankees 6, Red Sox 5

In his only mound appearance at Yankee Stadium, the Bambino goes the distance for the win over the team for which he once regularly pitched. He also homered.

June 10, 1934: Doc Cramer hits for the cycle, but Lou Gehrig's grand slam wins game – Yankees 7, A's 3

The A's pulled their starter in the first inning after the opening three batters loaded the bases, and Gehrig took reliever Bill Dietrich deep. That was all the Yankees needed, rendering A's centerfielder Doc Cramer's cycle a mere footnote.

October 4, 1936: Monte Pearson outduels Carl Hubbell as Yankees take commanding 3-1 lead in World Series – Yankees 5, Giants 2

Offseason pickup Monte Pearson earned his Pinstripes by outpitching the National League MVP, who had won his last 16 starts of the season.

July 9, 1937: Joe DiMaggio hits two homers as part of cycle – Yankees 16, Senators 2

The Yankee Clipper went 5-for-5 with 7 RBIs, and the Yankees scored in every inning but the second.

August 1, 1937: Gehrig hits for the cycle but DiMaggio's home run grabs headlines – Yankees 14, Browns 5

Less than a month after DiMaggio's cycle, Lou Gehrig had the second one of his career, but DiMaggio's seventh-inning homer put him three games ahead of Babe Ruth's pace in 1927.

May 31, 1938: Lou Gehrig plays his 2,000th consecutive game – Yankees 12, Red Sox 5

The Iron Horse, in a season-long slump, ignored his wife's advice to stop The Streak at 1,999 games and had an RBI single in the eighth.

April 25, 1939: Lou Gehrig shows final flash of brilliance with two-hit game for Yankees – Yankees 8, A's 4

With the effects of what was discovered to be ALS now showing, Gehrig had his last multihit game, with two singles, as well as the last of his 1,995 RBIs.

April 30, 1939: Lou Gehrig plays his final game with Yankees – Senators 3, Yankees 2

The Yankees' captain went 0-for-4 in his 2,130th consecutive game; batting .143, he benched himself two days later and never played in the majors again.

September 6, 1939: Gomez beats Grove in duel of Hall of Fame lefties – Yankees 2, Red Sox 1

The Yankees padded their double-digit game lead over second-place Boston. Starter Lefty Gomez went the distance, allowing one run on six hits; Red Sox moundsman Lefty Grove allowed two runs (one earned) on seven hits.

October 5, 1939: Yankees' Monte Pearson flirts with no-hitter in dominant Game 2 performance – Yankees 4, Reds 0

In another dominant World Series start, Monte Pearson took a no-hitter into the eighth and finished with a shutout.

June 16, 1941: DiMaggio ties Yankee record with 29-game hitting streak – Yankees 6, Indians 4

DiMaggio's fifth-inning double surpassed a team record held by Earle Combs and Roger Peckinpaugh.

October 5, 1942: Cardinals clinch World Series on Kurowski's ninth-inning clout – Cardinals 4, Yankees 2

Whitey Kurowski's two-run homer off Red Ruffing in Game Five broke a ninth-inning tie and gave the Cardinals the championship, and the Yankees their first World Series loss since 1926.

YANKEE STADIUM 1923-2008

September 22, 1946: Yogi Berra and Bobby Brown shine in major-league debut with Yankees – Yankees 4, A's 3

In the first game of a doubleheader, Berra, the starting catcher, went 2-for-4, his first major-league hit being a home run. Brown went 1-for-2 with a run scored in the number 3 spot at short.

September 30, 1947: Yankees score 5 in 5th inning to beat Dodgers in World Series opener – Yankees 5, Dodgers 3

Johnny Lindell's two-run double, Bobby Brown's bases-loaded walk, and Tommy Henrich's two-run single off Brooklyn's Hank Behrman in the fifth were all the Yankees needed to take Game 1 of the fall classic.

October 5, 1947: Dodgers beat Yankees to send World Series to decisive seventh game – Dodgers 8, Yankees 6

The Dodgers' win in Game Six to stave off elimination for one more day was marked by left fielder Al Gionfriddo's one-handed catch in the sixth inning to rob Joe DiMaggio of a game-tying hit.

October 6, 1947: Joe Page leads Yankees to Game 7 win over Dodgers – Yankees 5, Dodgers 2

Joe Page limited the Dodgers to one hit in pitching the final five innings in relief, and the Yankees won their 11th championship.

June 13, 1948: Babe Ruth makes final visit to Yankee Stadium – Yankees 5, Indians 3

Ravaged by cancer, the Bambino made a final, ceremonial appearance for the Stadium's 25th anniversary. In the game that followed, Eddie Lopat outpitched Bob Feller to hold off the first-place Indians.

September 11, 1949: Four Senators pitchers set major-league record with 11 walks in one inning – Yankees 20, Senators 5

In a 50-minute third inning, the Yankees batted around twice and 12 runs on four hits, the result of a record 11 free passes handed out by the last-place Senators.

October 5, 1949: Allie Reynolds two-hitter, Tommy Henrich home run give Yankees a 1-0 win in World Series opener – Yankees 1, Dodgers 0

Reynolds rebounded from a poor final regular-season start with a gem, outpitching the Dodgers' Don Newcombe to give the Yankees a 1-0 Series lead.

October 6, 1949: Preacher Roe shuts out Yankees in Game 2 to even World Series – Dodgers 1, Yankees 0

Now it was the Dodgers' turn for a 1-0 shutout, as Brooklyn starter Preacher Roe limited the Yankees to six hits. Yankees righty Vic Raschi allowed an RBI single to Gil Hodges in the second for the only run.

July 18, 1950: Johnny Mize homers twice, Yankees crush Browns – Yankees 12, Browns 1

The Big Cat, approaching the twilight of his career, had the first of three multihomer games in 1950, with two off St. Louis's Don Johnson.

October 6, 1950: Jerry Coleman's walk-off single lifts Yankees to 3-0 lead in World Series – Yankees 3, Phillies 2

Jerry Coleman both scored the tying run in the eighth and drove in the winning run in the ninth to put the Yankees one game away from a World Series sweep of the Whiz Kids.

October 7, 1950: Yogi Berra delivers knockout blow as Yankees sweep Phillies in World Series – Yankees 5, Phillies 2

The Yankees broke out the brooms against Philadelphia and captured their 13th championship. Yogi Berra had a homer and two RBIs and rookie starting pitcher Whitey Ford did not allow an earned run in 8⅔ innings.

September 28, 1951: Allie Reynolds throws his second no-hitter of the season – Yankees 8, Red Sox 0

In addition to becoming the first Yankee to throw two no-hitters, Reynolds also became the second Yankee to pitch a no-hitter at the Stadium.

October 4, 1951: Monte Irvin steals home as Giants take Game 1 over Yankees – Giants 5, Yankees 1

The Giants' Monte Irvin took advantage of Allie Reynolds' slow delivery for a clean theft of home in the first inning of the World Series opener, and unlikely Giants starting pitcher Dave Koslo held off the Yankees' bats for the duration of the game.

October 5, 1951: Eddie Lopat's hurling, hitting lead Yankees to Game 2 win over Giants – Yankees 3, Giants 1

Eddie Lopat scattered five hits over a complete game and drove in a run himself in the eighth inning as the Yankees evened the Series at one game apiece.

October 10, 1951: Yankees edge Giants in Game 6 to win third straight World Series – Yankees 4, Giants 3

Hank Bauer's three-run triple in the sixth made the difference as the Yankees held off a late Giants rally to capture their third straight championship – and 14th overall.

August 25, 1952: Virgil Trucks hurls his second no-hitter of the season – Tigers 1, Yankees 0

Virgil Trucks became the second opposing pitcher to pitch a no-hitter at Yankee Stadium, and the third pitcher to throw two no-hitters in a season – and somehow finished the year with a 5-19 record.

October 4, 1952: Allie Reynolds' 4-hit shutout in Game 4 evens World Series – Yankees 2, Dodgers 0

Allie Reynolds struck out 10 in the Yankees' only win at Yankee Stadium en route to their fourth straight championship. Johnny Mize homered, and Mickey Mantle tripled and scored on an errant throw.

April 13, 1955: Whitey Ford pitches and hits Yankees to lopsided Opening Day win – Yankees 19, Senators 1

Buoyed by three home runs and driving in four runs himself, Whitey Ford allowed just two hits against the Senators to start the Yankees' new pennant drive. The Senators' lone run scored on a balk.

September 28, 1955: Jackie Robinson steals home for Dodgers in Game 1 of World Series – Yankees 6, Dodgers 5

Until the day he died, catcher Yogi Berra would emphatically insist he tagged Robinson out. The Yankees won.

September 29, 1955: Tommy Byrne's pitching gives Yankees 2-0 lead in World Series – Yankees 4, Dodgers 2

Tommy Byrne went the distance and added a two-run single as the Yankees scored all their runs in the fourth inning.

October 3, 1955: Yankees' Whitey Ford shuts down Dodgers to send World Series to deciding game – Yankees 5, Dodgers 1

The Yankees were pushed to the brink after three losses in Brooklyn, but Whitey Ford's gem (one run, four hits, eight strikeouts) and the Yankees' five-run first, capped off by Moose Skowron's three-run homer, forced a Game Seven.

October 4, 1955: Brooklyn Dodgers win first World Series as 'Next Year' finally arrives – Dodgers 2, Yankees 0

Having been on the losing end of seven World Series, including five against the Yankees, the Brooklyn Dodgers captured their only championship, ending a seven-game thriller with a victory in the Bronx.

October 8, 1956: Don Larsen throws a perfect game in the World Series – Yankees 2, Dodgers 0

Don Larsen became the only man to throw a perfecto in the fall classic against the Dodgers in Game Five.

September 1, 1961: Skowron's single launches Yankees on 13-game winning streak – Yankees 1, Tigers 0

The Yankees started the night 1½ games ahead of Detroit for the AL pennant. But Moose Skowron's walk-off hit in the ninth sent both teams on a run; New York won its next 13, and the Tigers lost their next eight.

October 1, 1961: Roger Maris surpasses Babe Ruth with 61st home run – Yankees 1, Red Sox 0

In Game Number 162, Roger Maris broke Babe Ruth's record for home runs in a season with a fourth-inning blast to right field that also proved the game-winner.

October 4, 1961: Whitey Ford pitches third consecutive World Series shutout as Yankees win Game 1 – Yankees 2, Reds 0

Whitey Ford ran his scoreless World Series innings streak to 27, just 2⅔ innings short of Babe Ruth's record (which he would break in Game Four), with a complete-game two-hitter. Moose Skowron and Elston Howard went deep.

October 5, 1961: Underdog Reds win first World Series game in 21 years – Reds 6, Yankees 2

The Reds recorded their only win of the World Series – and their first since 1940 – behind Joey Jay's complete game.

August 4, 1963: Mickey Mantle returns to Yankees in a pinch – Yankees 11, Orioles 10

After two months on the injured list, the Mick pinch-hit a game-tying home run in the bottom of the seventh. Yogi Berra's sacrifice fly won it in extra innings

October 2, 1963: Sandy Koufax sets World Series strikeout record, fanning 15 Yankees – Dodgers 5, Yankees 2
Brooklyn native Sandy Koufax fanned 15 Yankees as the LA Dodgers took the World Series opener.

October 3, 1963: Johnny Podres extends Dodgers' World Series lead in Game Two – Dodgers 4, Yankees 1
Podres may not have been as emphatic as Koufax in shutting down the Yankees, but the Dodgers went up two games to none thanks, in part to a home run from ex-Yankee Moose Skowron.

September 19, 1964: Yankees grab the lead for good in AL pennant race – Yankees 8, A's 3
In a heated pennant race with the White Sox and Orioles, the Yankees grabbed sole possession of first place for the first time since July… and for the remainder of the season.

October 10, 1964: Mickey Mantle's record World Series home run wins it in 9th – Yankees 2, Cardinals 1
In what turned out to be the Mick's last World Series, he also hit the only walk-off home run of his record 18 Series round-trippers.

May 18, 1965: Tresh, Yankees tame Boston's "Monster" with extra-inning win – Yankees 4, Red Sox 3
Red Sox starter Dave Morehead took a no-hitter into the seventh – albeit seven walks – but off reliever Dick "The Monster" Radatz, the Yankees tied the game in the ninth, then won it on Tom Tresh's RBI triple in the 12th.

April 14, 1967: Red Sox' Billy Rohr misses no-hitter by one out in debut – Red Sox 3, Yankees 0
Before Boston's "Impossible Dream" season took off, there was rookie Billy Rohr outdueling Whitey Ford, holding the Yankees hitless save for Elston Howard's single with two outs in the ninth.

May 14, 1967: Mickey Mantle smacks his 500th home run – Yankees 6, Orioles 5
On Mother's Day the Commerce Comet took Stu Miller of the reigning World Series champion Baltimore Orioles deep in the seventh inning for the milestone homer.

August 29-30, 1967: Yankees, Red Sox play 40 innings in 24 hours – Red Sox 2, Yankees 1; Yankees 4, Red Sox 3; Red Sox 2, Yankees 1
The Yankees and Red Sox split a Tuesday doubleheader, with Horace Clarke's RBI single winning the second game in the bottom of the 20th. Less than 12 hours later, the teams played another extra-inning match; Yankees starter Al Downing went all 11, but lost on a home run by Carl Yastrzemski.

October 1, 1967: Kansas City Athletics play their last game – Yankees 4, A's 3
Somewhat fittingly, the team that was dubbed the Yankees' "farm club" for many years ended its last season in Kansas City with a loss to New York, with future Yankees star Catfish Hunter picking up the "L."

September 20, 1968: Mickey Mantle's 536th and final home run marks end of an era – Red Sox 4, Yankees 3
Mantle's final home run of his career came in the third inning of a game in which the team's late rally, with runs in the eighth and ninth, fell just short.

June 15, 1969: "One big wet blanket" for Seattle's Pilots on Bat Day at Yankee Stadium – Yankees 4, Pilots 0
A game delayed, then shortened by rain in the sixth inning saw young fans swarm the field during delays, slipping and sliding through the mud with their free giveaway bats. The Pilots protested afterward, but the score held.

July 20, 1969: Yankees win an ordinary game on an ordinary day on Planet Earth – Yankees 3, Senators 2
In the midst of a tie game eventually won on Gene Michael's 11th-inning walk-off single, fans learned that Apollo 11 landed on the moon.

June 7, 1970: White Sox edge Yankees in 12 innings on Bat Day at Yankee Stadium – White Sox 4, Yankees 3
The Yankees' annual promotion may have worked against them, when a young fan's free giveaway bat deflected an otherwise playable ball hit by Chicago's Tom McCraw in the top of the 12th for a ground-rule double that would ultimately score the deciding run.

May 17, 1973: Graig Nettles' walk-off homer lifts Yankees in 11 innings – Yankees 4, Brewers 2
In front of a crowd of just 7,116, the Yankees' new third baseman capped a two-run ninth with a game-tying RBI single, then went deep in extra innings for the win.

May 20, 1976: Spaceman brawls with Yankees' Graig Nettles – Red Sox 8, Yankees 2
Boston catcher Carlton Fisk incited a historic bench-clearing brawl after Lou Piniella ran him over at the plate, in which Bill "Spaceman" Lee emerged with a torn shoulder ligament and a black eye courtesy of the Yankees' Graig Nettles.

October 21, 1976: Big Red Machine sweeps Yankees for second straight World Series championship – Reds 7, Yankees 2
The Yankees' first season in their renovated Stadium ended with another team celebrating, due in part to Cincinnati catcher Johnny Bench's two dingers. The next two years would be better.

June 24, 1977: Reggie Jackson's single in the 11th inning leads Yankees over Red Sox – Yankees 6, Red Sox 5
Roy White's game-tying two-run homer in the bottom of the ninth set the stage for Jackson's walk-off in extra innings.

August 27, 1977: Rangers hit inside-the-park homers on consecutive pitches at Yankee Stadium – Rangers 8, Yankees 2
Toby Harrah's and Bump Wills's back-to-back inside-the-park round-trippers in the seventh inning off Yankees rookie Ken Clay were only the second time in history two inside-the-park home runs had been hit in succession.

June 17, 1978: Ron Guidry strikes out 18, sets new Yankee record – Yankees 4, Angels 0
Word had it that the Gator setting a team record for strikeouts in a game begat the fan tradition of standing and cheering with the count at two strikes.

October 1, 1978: Cleveland's Rick Waits handcuffs Yankees, forces playoff with Red Sox for AL East title – Indians 9, Yankees 2
The Yankees' 14-game comeback ended in a tie with Boston atop the AL East when New York lost Game number 162. The indirect result was that Bucky Dent hit a home run at Fenway Park the next day.

October 13, 1978: Graig Nettles' defense leads Yankees in Game 3 win – Yankees 5, Dodgers 1
Nettles' quick reflexes at the hot corner saved at least four runs from scoring and gave the Yankees their first win of the Series, which ultimately resulted in a 22nd championship.

August 3, 1979: Somebody's missing: Heartbroken Yankees play first game after Thurman Munson's death – Orioles 1, Yankees 0
A mere 24 hours after the Yankees captain perished in a plane crash, his stunned teammates were shut out in spite of Luis Tiant's eight innings of two-hit ball.

August 6, 1979: Yankees bury Thurman Munson, win emotional game against Orioles –Yankees 5, Orioles 4
The Yankees returned from Munson's funeral with a walk-off win off the bat of Bobby Murcer.

June 28, 1980: Legend of "Super Joe" Charboneau launches at Yankee Stadium – Yankees 11, Indians 10
The Indians' highly touted Rookie of the Year launched an upper-deck home run in the second inning, but the Yankees ultimately won on a walk-off in the ninth, on Rick Cerone's two-run single.

October 10, 1980: Royals advance to first World Series after sweeping Yankees in ALCS – Royals 4, Yankees 2
George Brett's three-run seventh-inning homer clinched Kansas City their first pennant, and the Yankees lost their first ALCS.

July 4, 1983: Dave Righetti tosses a no-hitter on Fourth of July – Yankees 4, Red Sox 0
Righetti beat rival Boston for the first no-hitter at the Stadium since 1956.

July 24, 1983: The Pine Tar Game – Royals 5, Yankees 4
The Royals' George Brett exploded from the dugout upon learning the pine tar was too high on his bat for his ninth-inning home run to count. Kansas City initially lost the game, but ultimately won the protest. When play resumed on August 18 (with Yankees pitcher Ron Guidry in center field and first baseman

Don Mattingly playing second), the Royals proved victorious.

August 2, 1985: Catcher Carlton Fisk tags out two baserunners on same play – White Sox 6, Yankees 5
The Chicago backstop became just the fourth man to accomplish the feat, tagging both Dale Berra and Bobby Meacham at the plate in the bottom of the seventh to preserve a tie score. The White Sox won in 11 innings.

August 4, 1985: Tom Seaver wins his 300th game in New York – White Sox 4, Yankees 1
Ex-Mets legend Tom Seaver returned to the city that made him famous and went the distance to make his case for Cooperstown.

July 17, 1990: Bo Jackson clouts three home runs in Royals' victory over Yankees – Royals 10, Yankees 7
After his trio of jacks, only a sixth-inning shoulder injury could stop Bo; he sustained it chasing unsuccessfully after an inside-the-park home run by the Yankees' Deion Sanders.

September 6, 1992: Kamieniecki fires eight shutout innings as Yankees rally late – Yankees 7, Rangers 0
Scott Kamieniecki (5-11) threw eight innings of three-hit ball, and the Yankees put up a six-spot in the bottom of the eighth.

October 4, 1995: Jim Leyritz's homer in the 15th lifts Yanks in ALDS – Yankees 7, Mariners 5
The high point of the Yankees' first return to the postseason since 1981 saw them take a two-game lead against Seattle when soon-to-be perennial playoff clutch hitter Jim Leyritz went deep in the 15th inning.

May 14, 1996: Dwight Gooden pitches no-hitter for Yankees – Yankees 2, Mariners 0
After being suspended for cocaine use the entire previous season, Doctor K completed his comeback by shutting down a lineup that included Ken Griffey Jr., Alex Rodriguez, Edgar Martinez, and Jay Buhner.

June 16, 1997: Mets win their first regular-season game against Yankees – Mets 6, Yankees 0
The first regular-season interleague game at Yankee Stadium didn't go the home team's way, as Dave Mlicki pitched a complete-game shutout. The Yankees would take the next two games against the Mets.

May 17, 1998: David Wells pitches first perfect game in Yankee Stadium since Don Larsen – Yankees 4, Twins 0
An infamously hung-over David Wells becomes the second Yankee to go 27-up, 27-down. It also happened to be Beanie Baby Day at the Stadium.

May 9, 1999: Mike Stanton's "bullpen game" start leads Yankees to win – Yankees 6, Mariners 1
When Sunday afternoon starter Ramiro Mendoza fell ill before the game, Mike Stanton and Jason Grimsley stepped in for four innings apiece of one-run ball. Mariano Rivera closed it out.

July 18, 1999: With Don Larsen watching, David Cone channels perfection for Yankees – Yankees 6, Expos 0
With Don Larsen throwing out the ceremonial first pitch to Yogi Berra, and Yogi's number 8 emblazoned behind home plate, David Cone threw the Yankees' third perfect game in 88 pitches.

October 26, 1999: Chad Curtis whacks a World Series walk-off home run for Yankees – Yankees 6, Braves 5
The Yankees chipped away at an early 5-1 deficit against the Braves and won the game on Chad Curtis's 10th-inning walk-off home run to bring them within a game of an eventual World Series sweep.

October 22, 2000: Clemens and Piazza clash as Yankees win Game 2 – Yankees 6, Mets 5
The Yankees went up 2-0 in the Series against the Mets in a game unfortunately remembered for when Roger Clemens threw a broken bat toward Mike Piazza.

September 25, 2001: Yankees return to Yankee Stadium after 9/11 – Devil Rays 4, Yankees 0
An emotional pregame ceremony before the Yankees first home game after the terrorist attacks almost rendered the final score inconsequential. As Tampa Bay winning pitcher Tanyon Sturtze said, "We may have won the game, but we were all just out there trying to play for the fans of New York."

October 30, 2001: Clemens closes the door on Diamondbacks in Game 3 – Yankees 2, Diamondbacks 1
The Yankees' bats were lukewarm after being ice cold the first two games of the World Series, but Roger

Clemens limited the Arizona lineup to three hits for the win, and Mariano Rivera recorded a two-inning save.

October 31, 2001: Jeter becomes Mr. November – Yankees 4, Diamondbacks 3
Tino Martinez's game-tying ninth-inning home run off Arizona closer Byung-Hyun Kim sent the game to extra innings and set the stage for Derek Jeter's walk-off home run at the stroke of midnight (November 1).

November 1, 2001: Scott Brosius deja vu in the Bronx – Yankees 3, Diamondbacks 2
Lightning struck twice as the Yankees again tied the game in the ninth against Byung-Hyun Kim, this time off the bat of Scott Brosius. Alfonso Soriano's RBI single in the 12th gave the Yankees a 3-2 Series lead.

June 11, 2003: Six Astros pitchers combine for no-hitter at Yankee Stadium – Astros 8, Yankees 0
Astros starter Roy Oswalt left with a groin injury two pitches into the second inning, but his bullpen bailed him out, for the first and only combined no-hitter at Yankee Stadium.

August 31, 2004: Indians set AL shutout record with rout of Yankees – Indians 22, Yankees 0
The only question for fans watching the most lopsided loss in Yankees history was how high the score would go.

October 12, 2004: Late Red Sox rally falls short in ALCS Game 1 – Yankees 10, Red Sox 7
The Yankees battered Boston starter Curt Schilling for six runs in the first three innings, and Hideki Matsui had five RBIs to lead them to victory in the ALCS opener.

October 13, 2004: Yankees win something of a pitching duel in the Bronx – Yankees 3, Red Sox 1
New York's Jon Lieber outpitched Boston's Pedro Martinez, and John Olerud hit a two-run homer to put the Yankees up 2-0 in the ALCS.

October 19, 2004: Curt Schilling keeps Red Sox alive in "Bloody Sock Game" – Red Sox 4, Yankees 2
With his injured ankle barely sutured together and "K ALS" written on his shoe, Boston's Curt Schilling somehow pitched seven innings of one-run ball, and suddenly the ALCS had a Game Seven.

October 20, 2004: "Hell freezes over"; Red Sox complete historic ALCS comeback over Yankees in Game 7 – Red Sox 10, Yankees 3
Kevin Brown had nothing on a night most Yankee fans would prefer to forget happened in their house.

June 27, 2008: Carlos Delgado sets Mets record with 9 RBIs in opener at Yankee Stadium – Mets 15, Yankees 6
In the first game of a doubleheader that started at Yankee Stadium and concluded at Shea, Carlos Delgado drove in more runs in a game than any other Met on two homers and a double. (The Yankees won the nightcap in Queens, 9-0.)

August 3, 2008: Xavier Nady drives in six as Yankees score 10 unearned runs to beat Angels – Yankees 14, Angels 9
The Yankees capitalized on four Anaheim errors, and Xavier Nady went 4-for-5 and had a career-high six RBIs.

CONTRIBUTORS

Malcolm Allen moved to New York City in 2000, where he met his wife, Sara, fathered two daughters, and joined SABR. Born and raised in Baltimore – and still an Orioles fan – he attended more than a dozen games at Yankee Stadium, including July 29, 2008, when George Sherrill fanned Wilson Betemit to finish off the Orioles' final victory in that hallowed ballpark.

For four decades and counting, umpire **Perry Barber** has been establishing a lot of "firsts" and "onlys" in baseball. She's the only woman so far to umpire major-league exhibitions in both the United States and Japan, and one of very few women to umpire major-league spring-training games in the United States. She's the first winner of the SABR Women in Baseball Lifetime Achievement Award, nicknamed "The Dorothy" after Dorothy Seymour Mills, and is also a *Jeopardy!* champion, a Mensa member, a lone identical twin, a published author in her own right as well as the subject of numerous magazine articles, newspaper profiles, and books, and in her former life as a singer/songwriter/guitarist, she was the opening act for Bruce Springsteen, Billy Joel, Hall and Oates, and other music luminaries. In 2008 Perry assembled the first and (so far) only four-woman crew to umpire a major-league spring-training game. She was selected as an alternate umpire for the 1996 Olympics in Atlanta, taught umpiring to public-school students in New York City while securing paying assignments for them with local associations, and is the only woman so far to umpire in the Cape Cod League. She's a New York State Baseball Hall of Fame inductee, and her photograph is displayed at the National Baseball Hall of Fame in Cooperstown with her name on a plaque on the wall next to it, but rather than resting on her laurels, she's still working tirelessly to recruit and train other women as umpires in order to render the phrase "woman umpire" as redundant as "female president" or "woman astrophysicist." After more than 40 years, Perry is still fighting *not* to be in a league of her own.

John Bauer resides with his wife and two children in Bedford, New Hampshire. By day, he is an attorney specializing in insurance regulatory law and corporate law. By night, he spends many spring and summer evenings cheering for the San Francisco Giants, and many fall and winter evenings reading history. He is a past and ongoing contributor to other SABR projects.

Jake Bell, a government contractor who used to be a TV sports anchor many years ago, visited Yankee Stadium only once, for a 5-3 win over Kansas City in 1999.

While growing up in a small town in Ohio during the 1970s, **Dana Berry** followed the Cincinnati Reds. He spent many summer days throwing a ball against the family shed while imagining announcers Marty Brenneman and Joe Nuxhall describing his pitching the Big Red Machine to another title. While he was only 6 at the time, Dana remembers that fateful day of November 28, 1978, when Sparky Anderson was fired. Deep inside, he secretly blamed his dad because that was the same day he purchased *The Main Spark: Sparky Anderson and the Cincinnati Reds.* When not pitching in front of the hometown fans, in his imagination, Dana remembers every Saturday tuning into *The Baseball Bunch* (with Johnny Bench, Tommy Lasorda, and The San Diego Chicken; followed by *This Week in Baseball* (hosted by Mel Allen), concluded by *The Game of the Week* on NBC (broadcast by Vin Scully and Joe Garagiola). Unfortunately for Dana, he never pitched for the Reds. He has spent many years in therapy, blaming his parents for knocking down the shed. Currently, he lives in the same small town, but now with his wife, two dogs, and two cats.

Luis A. Blandon, a Washington D.C. native, is a producer, writer, and researcher in video and documentary film production and in archival, manuscript, historical, film, and image research. His creative storytelling has garnered numerous awards, including three regional Emmys®, regional and national Edward R. Murrow Awards, two TELLY awards, and a New York Festival World Medal. He worked as a producer and/or researcher on several documentaries including *Jeremiah*; *Feast Your Ears: The Story of WHFS 102.3*; and *#GeorgeWashington*. Most recently he was co-producer of the documentary *The Lost Battalion*. He is serving as a consultant on a documentary film project for the United States Naval Academy's Stockdale Center for Ethical Leadership and Maryland Public Television on the Vietnam War POWs and leadership. He was senior researcher and manager of the story development team for two national programs for Retirement Living Television. He has worked as a historian for two public-policy research firms: Morgan Angel & Associates and MLL Consulting LLC. He served as the principal researcher for several authors including for *The League of Wives* by Heath Hardage Lee and her current biography project on First Lady

Pat Nixon. He has a master of arts in international affairs from George Washington University.

Thomas J. Brown Jr. is a lifelong Mets fan who became a Durham Bulls fan after moving to North Carolina in the early 1980s. He was a national board-certified high-school science teacher for 34 years before retiring in 2016. Tom taught science to ELL students in the last eight years of his career and still mentors many of them. He has been a member of SABR since 1995, when he learned about the organization during a visit to Cooperstown on his honeymoon. Tom became active in SABR after his retirement, writing biographies and game stories, mostly about the New York Mets. He loves to travel with his wife, always visiting major-league and minor-league ballparks whenever possible. Tom also loves to cook and writes about the diverse recipes he makes on his blog, Cooking and My Family.

Dr. John J. Burbridge Jr. is professor emeritus at Elon University, where he was both a dean and professor. While at Elon he introduced and taught Baseball and Statistics. He has authored several SABR publications and presented at SABR conventions, NINE, and the Seymour meetings. He is a lifelong New York Giants baseball fan. The greatest Giants-Dodgers game he attended was a 1-0 Giants victory in Jersey City in 1956. Yes, the Dodgers did play in Jersey City in 1956 and 1957. John can be reached at burbridg@elon.edu.

Frederick C. "Rick" Bush has written articles for over two dozen SABR books and, together with Bill Nowlin, has co-edited five SABR books about the Negro Leagues, including *The First Negro League Champion: The 1920 Chicago American Giants* (2022) and *When the Monarchs Reigned: Kansas City's 1942 Negro League Champions* (2021), which received the 2022 Robert Peterson Recognition Award. Rick lives with his wife, Michelle, their three sons – Michael, Andrew, and Daniel – and their border collie mix, Bailey, in the Houston metro area. He has been an educator for nearly 30 years and has spent the past two decades teaching English at Wharton County Junior College's satellite campus in Sugar Land, Texas, which is home to the Astros' Triple-A franchise.

Vincent J. Cannato is a professor of history at the University of Massachusetts Boston. He is the author of *The Ungovernable City: John Lindsay and His Struggle to Save New York.*

A lifelong White Sox fan surrounded by Cubs fans in the northern suburbs of Chicago, **Ken Carrano** works as a chief financial officer for a large landscaping firm and as a soccer referee. He has been a SABR member since 1992 and has contributed to several SABR publications and the SABR Games Project. Ken and his Brewers' fan wife, Ann, share two children, two golden retrievers, and a mutual distain for the blue side of Chicago.

Alan Cohen chairs the BioProject fact-checking committee, serves as vice president-treasurer of the Connecticut Smoky Joe Wood SABR Chapter, and is a datacaster (milb first-pitch stringer) for the Hartford Yard Goats of the Double-A Eastern League. His biographies, game stories, and essays have appeared in more than 65 SABR publications. The subject of his earliest *Baseball Research Journal* article was the Hearst Sandlot Classic, the last seven games of which were played at Yankee Stadium. His most recent contribution to the *BRJ* catalogued Josh Gibson's feat of hitting home runs in 17 big-league ballparks, including seven at Yankee Stadium. He included the first game back at Yankee Stadium after the 9/11 attacks in SABR's web-based project, First Games Back. He has four children, nine grandchildren, and one great-grandchild and resides in Connecticut with wife Frances, their cats, Ava, and Zoe, and their dog, Buddy.

Richard Cuicchi joined SABR in 1983 and is an active member of the Schott-Pelican Chapter. Since his retirement as an information technology executive, Richard authored *Family Ties: A Comprehensive Collection of Facts and Trivia about Baseball's Relatives.* He has contributed to numerous SABR BioProject and Games Project publications. He does freelance writing and blogging about a variety of baseball topics on his website, TheTenthInning.com. Richard is a regular contributor to CrescentCitySports.com, where he writes about New Orleans baseball history. Richard lives in New Orleans with his wife, Mary.

Rich D'Ambrosio has been a member of SABR since 1997. He is the author of several biographies and game accounts, many of which have appeared in SABR publications. A lifelong resident of Philadelphia, Rich is a graduate of Temple, La Salle, and St. Joseph's Universities and teaches English at St. Hubert Catholic High School for Girls, also in Philadelphia. A serious baseball memorabilia collector, Rich has a special research interest in the Philadelphia Phillies and the first and last games played in major-league ballparks.

Ray Danner lives in Cleveland Heights, Ohio, and works at the Greater Cleveland Aquarium as part of the dive team. He was on the sports beat for *The Cauldron* at Cleveland State University and was a contributing writer at the website "It's Pronounced Lajaway" and a member of the ESPN SweetSpot Network. Ray also plays rover on a vintage base ball club, the Whiskey Island Shamrocks. A SABR member since 2012, he is a lifelong Strat-O-Matic fan and enjoys contributing to SABR's Games Project and BioProject.

Larry DeFillipo is a retired aerospace engineer who worked on numerous spacecraft and launch vehicle projects in his career, including the Cassini mission to Saturn, the New Horizons mission to Pluto, and the Antares launch vehicle, which delivers cargo to the International Space Station. He lives with his wife, Kelly, a retired geologist, in Kennewick, Washington, near their two young grandchildren. He joined SABR in the late 1990s, digitized Deadball Era box scores for Retrosheet and wrote his first baseball article for the 2005 edition of *The National Pastime*. He has written several articles for SABR's BioProject and over 20 stories for SABR's Games Project. In addition to his baseball research efforts, he is a volunteer tax return preparer for AARP.

Bryan Dietzler has been a professional sportswriter for the last 23 years, writing mostly about football and baseball, but he has dabbled in hockey and basketball in the past. He currently lives in North Liberty, Iowa, and attends as many Iowa Hawkeye football and basketball games as he can. Go Hawks! He is a huge fan of the Chicago White Sox and the Chicago Bears and has attended many games for both. His dream is to retire and travel to every baseball and football stadium in America.

Daniel R. Epstein is a teacher, writer, musician, and union leader in Central New Jersey. He writes for Baseball Prospectus, Off the Bench Baseball, and Bronx Pinstripes. He also serves as co-director of the Internet Baseball Writers Association of America. By day, he is an elementary-school special-education teacher and president of the Somerset County Education Association.

Scott Ferkovich is the author of *Motor City Champs: Mickey Cochrane and the 1934-1935 Detroit Tigers*. His work has appeared in numerous SABR publications.

Brian Frank is passionate about documenting the history of major- and minor-league baseball. He is the creator of the website The Herd Chronicles (www.herdchronicles.com), which is dedicated to preserving the history of the Buffalo Bisons and professional baseball in Buffalo. His articles can also be read on the official website of the Bisons. He was an assistant

editor of the book *The Seasons of Buffalo Baseball, 1857-2020*, and he's a frequent contributor to SABR publications. Brian and his wife, Jenny, enjoy traveling around the country in their camper to major- and minor-league ballparks and taking an annual trip to Europe. Brian was a history major at Canisius College, where he earned a bachelor of arts. He also received a Juris Doctor from the University at Buffalo School of Law.

John Fredland, an attorney and retired Air Force officer, grew up in a suburb of Pittsburgh. As an undergraduate at Rice University, he covered Rice's nationally ranked baseball teams for the school newspaper, the *Rice Thresher*. John received his law degree at Vanderbilt University, then served as an active-duty attorney in the Air Force's Judge Advocate General's Corps for 20 years. He currently lives in San Antonio, Texas, and chairs SABR's Baseball Games Project Research Committee. His only visit to Yankee Stadium was on July 17, 1986, when he and his family saw the Yankees' 5-4 win over the Chicago White Sox, highlighted by Don Mattingly's home run off the upper-deck façade.

Craig Garretson is a lifelong New York Yankees fan. He was in Yankee Stadium for Don Mattingly's final home game, in the 1995 ALDS win in Game Two over the Seattle Mariners, and Doc Gooden's 1996 no-hitter against the same team. He lives in New Jersey with his wife, two daughters, and a dog named Bernie (after the Yankee center fielder). A member of SABR since 2019, he makes his rookie debut as a SABR publication contributor.

Gordon J. Gattie is a lifelong baseball fan and a SABR member since 1998. Currently a civilian US Navy engineer, he includes among his baseball research interests ballparks, historical trends, and statistical analysis. Gordon earned his PhD from SUNY Buffalo, where he used baseball to investigate judgment performance in complex dynamic environments. Ever the optimist, he dreams of a Cleveland Guardians World Series championship. Lisa, his wonderful wife, who roots for the Yankees, and Morrigan, their beloved Labrador retriever, enjoy visiting ballparks and other baseball-related sites. Their lifelong adventure visiting all major-league ballparks started with Yankee Stadium. Gordon has contributed to several SABR publications, including books, *The National Pastime*, and the Games Project.

Michael Gibbons served as executive director of the Babe Ruth Birthplace and Museum from 1983 to 2017 and has continued working with the organization as director emeritus/historian. During his tenure, the museum's mission expanded to include Baltimore's Orioles, Colts, and Ravens, the Maryland Terrapins, and local athletes including Michael Phelps, Carmelo Anthony, and Kimmie Meissner. He developed Sports Legends Museum at Camden Yards to house the museum's expansive collection of state sports memorabilia. A native Baltimorean, Gibbons earned his undergraduate degree at the University of Maryland Baltimore County and a graduate degree from Johns Hopkins University. He taught writing for 23 years at the University of Baltimore.

Bob Golon is a retired manuscript librarian and archivist at Princeton Theological Seminary library. He also spent three years as labor archivist at Rutgers University Special Collections and University Archives. Bob is past president of the New Jersey Library Association History and Preservation section and a member of the Mid-Atlantic Regional Archives Conference. Prior to getting his MLIS from Rutgers University in 2004, Bob worked 18 years in sales and marketing for the Hewlett-Packard Company, working with the group that established the successful dealer distribution channel for HP printers and personal computers. A baseball historian and SABR member, Bob has been a contributor to various publications, can be seen prominently on the YES Network's *Yankeeography – Casey Stengel,* and is the author of *No Minor Accomplishment: The Revival of New Jersey Professional Baseball* (Rivergate Books/Rutgers University Press, 2008).

Gene Gomes has a family connection to professional "base ball" in his great-grandfather Abner Powell, who was a nineteenth-century player, manager, owner, and innovator – primarily of the New Orleans Pelicans. Gomes was born in New Orleans and coached his children's baseball teams both there and in Minneapolis after moving in 2000. He became active in the Halsey Hall SABR Chapter in 2012 and has written a few articles for SABR since he retired from dental practice. His wife, Ginger, is supportive of his baseball hobby, and he hopes to pass on his love of the game to each of their seven grandchildren.

Jim Griffin is a lifelong baseball fan with experience writing for Yankee-specific blogs since 2010. His first book, *The New York Yankees All-Time All-Stars,* was published by Lyons Press in August 2019. He resides in Glenside, Pennsylvania, with his wife, Amanda, and two children, Josephine and Seamus.

Ed Gruver is a native of Kearny in northern New Jersey, 10 miles from NYC. A longtime sportswriter,

he's covered major-league baseball, the NFL, NBA, hockey, and boxing. He's the author of 10 books and a contributing writer to 27 books, and his work has appeared in various national magazines. His books on baseball include *Hairs vs. Squares: The Mustache Gang, the Big Red Machine, and the Tumultuous Summer of '72,* and *Koufax.*

Vince Guerrieri is a journalist and author in the Cleveland area. He's the secretary/treasurer of the Jack Graney SABR Chapter, and has contributed to the SABR BioProject, the SABR games project and several SABR anthologies. He's written about baseball history for a variety of publications, including *Ohio Magazine, Cleveland Magazine, Belt Magazine,* and *Deadspin.* He can be reached at vaguerrieri@gmail.com, or found on Twitter @vinceguerrieri.

Donna L. Halper is an associate professor of communication and media studies at Lesley University in Massachusetts. She joined SABR in 2011, and her research focuses on women and minorities in baseball, the Negro Leagues, and "firsts" in baseball history. A former radio deejay, credited with having discovered the rock band Rush, Dr. Halper reinvented herself and got her PhD at age 64. In addition to her research into baseball, she is also a media historian with expertise in the history of broadcasting. She has contributed to SABR's Games Project and BioProject, as well as writing several articles for the *Baseball Research Journal.*

Sharon Hamilton is the chair of the Society for American Baseball Research's Century Research Committee, which celebrates important milestones in baseball history. She served as project manager for the special 100th-anniversary SABR Century 1921 project at SABR.org as well as for web projects on Jackie Robinson's Re-integration of Baseball and on Baseball and the Supreme Court.

Bruce Harris has been a SABR member since 2006. A New Yorker, he became a Cubs fan after seeing the Cubbie patch on the sleeve of Lou Brock's 1964 Topps card. He still thinks about his beloved 1969 Cubs and wishes things had turned out differently. He is fortunate to have watched Roger Maris hit number 61 and Aaron Judge hit number 62. He has contributed to SABR's BioProject, Games Project, *Metropolitan Stadium: Memorable Games at Minnesota's Diamond on the Prairie,* and the *Baseball Research Journal.* He has also published in *Hobart's* annual online baseball issue.

Paul Hofmann has been a SABR member since 2002 and contributed to more than 25 SABR publications. Paul is the assistant vice president for the International Center at the University of Louisville and teaches in the College of Management at National Changhua University of Education in Taiwan. A native of Detroit, Paul is an avid baseball card collector and lifelong Detroit Tigers fan. He currently resides in Lakeville, Minnesota.

Jeff Howard grew up on the Northwest side of Chicago and currently resides in Elk Grove Village, Illinois. He was born and raised a Cubs fan. One of his first recollections of attending a baseball game was on May 15, 1960, when his mom took him to a Sunday doubleheader at the friendly confines of Wrigley Field to see Ernie Banks get his MVP trophy for the 1959 season. Don Cardwell pitched a no-hitter that day. He hasn't seen a live no-no since, which reinforces a fundamental credo to capture and embrace every moment when it happens. Jeff visited Yankee Stadium for a Sunday doubleheader in the '60s at the age of 10 or so during a family vacation and still remembers the glamour and mystique of the historic venue.

Mike Huber joined SABR in 1996, when he first co-taught a Sabermetrics course at West Point. In the many years that followed, he would often take his class to Yankee Stadium, to meet with the Yankees' staff, tour the Stadium, sit in the dugout and appreciate all that the Yankees have accomplished. He enjoys writing for SABR's Games Project and has been rooting for the same American League East team since 1968.

Lew Insler is a semiretired attorney now living in Asheville, North Carolina, after spending 40 years in New York's Westchester County. He grew up around the corner from Yankee Stadium and saw his first game there at age 3, and is a lifelong Yankees fan and collector. This is his first article for SABR. He is also teaching an adult-education course on baseball's origins and early days called "Baseball Before the Babe" at UNC-Asheville's Osher Lifelong Learning Institute.

Kirk C. Jenkins practices appellate and constitutional law in San Francisco. A dedicated childhood fan of the Cincinnati Reds, he switched his allegiance in 1994 to the San Francisco Giants. He regularly publishes on a variety of subjects, including Civil War history, classic-era baseball history and many areas of law.

Don Jensen is a longtime member of the Society for American Baseball Research and has written or co-authored many books and articles on the sport. He was the 2015 winner of the Chairman's Award of the SABR Nineteenth Century Committee. From 2018 to 2021 Jensen was editor of the award-winning annual book series *Baseball: New Research on the Early Game* (McFarland). He is currently editor of *The Inside Game*, the newsletter of the SABR Deadball Era Research Committee, and a member of the selection committee for SABR's Larry Ritter Book Award, which recognizes the best new baseball book primarily set in the Deadball Era that was published during the previous calendar year.

Bill Johnson has contributed over 40 articles to SABR's Biography Project, and presented papers at the 2011 Cooperstown Symposium on Baseball and American Culture, the 2017 Jerry Malloy Negro League Conference, and the inaugural Southern Negro League Conference. He has published a biography of Hal Trosky (McFarland and Co., 2017) and most recently an article about Negro American League All-Star Art "Superman" Pennington in the journal *Black Ball*. Bill and his wife, Chris, currently reside in Georgia.

Stephen Keeney is a lifelong Reds fan. He graduated from Miami University in 2010 and from Northern Kentucky University's Chase College of Law in 2013. He lives in Dayton, Ohio, with his wife and two children, and works as a union-side labor lawyer. He has contributed to several SABR publications, and his article "The Roster Depreciation Allowance: How Major League Baseball Teams Turn Profits into Losses" was selected for *SABR 50 at 50: The Society for American Baseball Research's Fifty Most Essential Contributions to the Game.*

Thomas E. Kern was born and raised in Southwest Pennsylvania. Listening to the mellifluous voices of Bob Prince and Jim Woods in his youth, how could one not become a lifelong Pirates fan? Arriba Roberto! He now lives in Silver Spring, Maryland, and sees the Nationals and Orioles as often as possible. He is a SABR member dating back to the mid-1980s. With a love and appreciation for Negro League Baseball, he has written SABR bios of Leon Day, John Henry Lloyd, Willie Foster, Judy Johnson, Turkey Stearnes, Hilton Smith, Louis Santop, Andy Cooper, and Buck Ewing. Tom's day job is in the field of transportation technology.

David Krell is the author of *Our Bums: The Brooklyn Dodgers in History, Memory and Popular Culture, 1962: Baseball and America in the Time of JFK,* and *Do You Believe in Magic? Baseball and America in the Groundbreaking Year of 1966.* He has edited the anthologies *The New York Yankees in Popular Culture* and *The New York Mets in Popular*

Culture. David is the chair of SABR's Elysian Fields Chapter.

Tara Krieger first fell in love with Yankee Stadium in 1993, in a game that Jim Abbott pitched and Don Mattingly homered, but the home team lost. She had dreams of one day working there, but when that didn't work out, she figured writing about it was the next best thing. She has been on staff as a sportswriter at *Newsday* and as an editorial producer for MLB Advanced Media. Her current day job is as an attorney for the City of New York.

For over 20 years, **Kevin Larkin** patrolled the highways and byways of the roads in his hometown of Great Barrington, Massachusetts. When not at work keeping the citizens of his hometown safe, inevitably Larkin was listening to a baseball game on the radio. He has been going to baseball games since he was 5 years old. His baseball life is the only thing he loves more than his children and grandchildren. One day while browsing through the local bookstore, the owner of the bookstore asked him if he was interested in writing a book about baseball. Larkin's first effort was *Baseball in the Bay State: A History of Baseball in Massachusetts*. He then took quite an interest in the history of the game, authoring a book on one of his heroes, Lou Gehrig, called *Gehrig: Game by Game*, a look at every game that the Iron Horse played during his major-league career. He has since written a number of other books and articles on the sport and has others ready for future publication. His latest book, *Big Time Baseball in a Small Berkshire County Town,* led to his heading a project to erect a historical marker in the town where this semipro team played a number of major-league teams, Black baseball teams, and the House of David touring team, with the plaque being dedicated on July 6, 2022. Kevin and Jesse Stewart also co-host a monthly radio show on WSBS that talks about baseball history with a focus on Berkshire County baseball and its players. He writes and fact-checks for SABR, an experience he considers the best decision he has ever made. He also hosts a baseball history show on a local radio station. According to Larkin, writing about baseball is a great way to keep the memory of the sport alive and he will continue to delve into sports history with more to come

Len Levin is a longtime newspaper editor in New England, now retired. He lives in Providence with his wife, Linda, and an overachieving orange cat. He now (Len, not the cat) is the grammarian for the Rhode Island Supreme Court and edits its decisions. He also copyedits many SABR books, including this one.

He lives just down the interstate from Fenway Park, where he has spent many happy hours.

A graduate of the New School for Social Research with an MFA in creative writing and from New York University with a B.A. in journalism and history, **David H. Lippman** is an award-winning journalist on three continents, for 45 years. Mr. Lippman has been a senior press information officer for the City of Newark, New Jersey, for the past 25 years. He is a member of SABR, serving on the BioProject, Games Project, and Black Sox research committees, and as an officer of the Casey Stengel Chapter.

Nick Malian lives with his wife and daughter in LaSalle, Ontario, Canada, where he was born and raised. Growing up in a border city, he idolized Detroit Tigers greats Cecil Fielder and Alan Trammell. As an impressionable 12-year-old, his allegiance shifted from the Tigers to the New York Yankees following their postseason dominance in 1996. He still attempts the "Derek Jeter jump-throw" (with limited success) at his weekly softball games. Nick is a pharmacist by day and amateur home chef by night. He enjoys reading anything about baseball and getting lost in science-fiction and fantasy novels.

Mitchell Manoff is a proud member of SABR, where he gets to blend his finance and business background with his passion for baseball. His focus within SABR is historical statistics and the Business of Baseball Research Committee. He has written a couple of articles for the committee newsletter. For 17 years he also taught entrepreneurship/new business development at Baruch College in NYC. He and his wife are lifelong New Yorkers. As are his three children and two grandchildren.

Scott Melesky has been a sports journalist for over 20 years. He graduated from Syracuse University with a bachelor's degree in history in 1995. Melesky earned his master's degree in education from Pacific Oaks College in May 2021. He has worked as a sports editor and writer for 18 publications and websites, including the *Los Angeles Daily News*, the *Quincy Patriot Ledger*, and the *Syracuse Herald Journal*. Melesky has also worked in four collegiate sports information departments highlighted by Marquette University. Melesky has contributed to four baseball books and is currently co-authoring *Take Back Your Power* with Marla McKenna and contributing to Nick Del Calzo's *My Baseball Story: The Game's Influence on America* and SABR's book on the 20th Anniversary of the 2004 Boston Red Sox' World Series championship.

YANKEE STADIUM 1923-2008

Thomas Merrick is a retired North Dakota district judge and an Air Force veteran now living in Buffalo, Minnesota. He has been a SABR member since 2000 and is a frequent contributor to the SABR Games Project. He and his wife, Pamela, recently celebrated their 45th wedding anniversary, and they have been blessed with three children and two granddaughters.

Andrew Milner joined SABR in 1984 and has written for *The National Pastime, Baseball's Biggest Blowout Games,* and, most recently, *From Shibe Park to Connie Mack Stadium.* He is mentioned in the acknowledgments to the latest editions of *The Dickson Baseball Dictionary* and *The New Bill James Historical Baseball Abstract,* and was quoted in the 2022 book *Once Upon a Time in Queens: An Oral History of the 1986 Mets.* A graduate of Syracuse University, he lives in suburban Philadelphia.

Chad Moody is a nearly lifelong resident of the Detroit area, where he has been a fan of the Detroit Tigers from birth. An alumnus of the University of Michigan and Michigan State University, he has spent 30 years working in the automotive industry. Chad has contributed to numerous SABR and Professional Football Researchers Association projects. He and his wife, Lisa, live in Plymouth, Michigan, with their dog, Daisy.

Tony Morante says, "I was fortunate to have witnessed some of the best that baseball had to offer for over 70 years in the mecca, Yankee Stadium. A symbiotic relationship evolved early in my life including many of the Yankees' watershed moments, until now, capped off by being inducted into the New York State Baseball Hall of Fame. Still involved with SABR, MLBPAA, and the IABF ... 'a lot to live for'"!

Tom Naylor was born in New York City and grew up there and on Long Island. He is a lifelong Yankee fan now residing in southern New Jersey. Having recently retired from a Wall Street career, he continues in his role as an arbitrator for the Financial Industry Regulatory Authority. He volunteers with Save Ellis Island, leading photography tours of the unrestored buildings on the island. Tom has also worked extensively as a volunteer with the National Kidney Donor Organization.

A lifelong Yankees fan, **Dan Neumann** lives in Crofton, Maryland, with his wife, son, and dog. With his brother Andrew, he co-hosts the *Hello Old Sports* podcast on the Sports History Network, covering any and all topics related to sports history from the 1869 Red Stockings to the 1990s NBA. He is a member of SABR and the Professional Football Researchers Association. During the day, he works for the Federal Aviation Administration and teaches part-time for the Boston University Washington Internship Program.

Bill Nowlin has perhaps logged 1,000 games at Fenway Park and maybe 20 or so at Yankee Stadium (wisely enough, never wearing a Red Sox cap) – both the original one and the newer one, and including the 2001 weekend series before 9/11. He preferred the old ballpark for its greater grittiness and narrower concourses, which seemed to better amplify the passion. After 50 years in the record business, most of his time is spent writing and editing for SABR.

Tim Odzer visited Yankee Stadium for two games in August 2007. He vividly remembers sitting in the center-field bleachers on a sweltering summer day watching Roger Clemens struggle through 1⅔ innings against the White Sox. A baseball fan since 1998, Tim enjoys contributing to the SABR Games Project. A graduate of the University of Chicago Law School, Tim is a practicing attorney who lives in Miami with his rescue dog, Paco.

James Overmyer writes and lectures on baseball history, primarily African American. He is the author of *Queen of the Negro Leagues: Effa Manley and the Newark Eagles; Black Ball and the Boardwalk: The Bacharach Giants of Atlantic City, 1916-1929*, and *Cum Posey of the Homestead Grays: A Biography of the Negro Leagues Owner and Hall of Famer*.

Ralph Peluso was born in New York City and remains a loyal Yankees fan. Since becoming a member of SABR in 2009, he has been a contributing member of the Overlooked Legends committee. Ralph holds an MBA in finance from Bernard Baruch College and is now retired after 45 years in corporate finance and management consulting. His book *512*, a fictional re-imagination based on Babe Ruth, was published in 2014. His latest work, a psychological thriller titled *Back Stories,* was released in November 2022. Several of Ralph's short stories are published. He began contributing to SABR projects in 2018. Ralph trekked to Mount Everest base camp in April 2019. He serves as the literary editor for the Zebra Press, a monthly newspaper serving Northern Virginia and the DC Metro area, and writes the "Book of the Month" series. Ralph and his spouse, Janet, enjoy retirement in an active 55+ community near the Delaware beaches.

Zac Petrillo has a BA from Hunter College and an MFA from Chapman University's Dodge College of Film and Media Arts. He has directed multiple short films and produced shows for *Comedy Central* and *TruTV*. In 2016 he launched Vice Media's 24/7 cable network, *Vice TV*. As a Society for American Baseball Research member, he focuses his work on post-1980s baseball and the intersection between the game and the media industry. He is currently the director of post production at A+E Networks and teaches television studies at Marymount Manhattan College.

Jack Pfeifer, an Orioles fan since childhood, is president of the Track and Field Writers of America and a retired editor for the *New York Times.*

Scott Pitoniak is a nationally honored journalist and the author/co-author of more than 35 books. His first game at the House That Ruth Built was on September 17, 1966, Bobby Richardson Day. A Syracuse University graduate, Scott has worked as a sports columnist for the *Rochester* (New York) *Democrat & Chronicle, USA Today*, and Gannett News Service (150 newspapers nationwide), and has written scores of magazine and website articles, often focusing on the human side of sports. The recipient of more than 100 journalism awards, Scott has been named one of the nation's top columnists by the Associated Press Sports Editors. In 2013 he was inducted into the Rochester Red Wings Hall of Fame with Mike Mussina. Scott regularly contributes articles to the National Baseball Hall of Fame's *Memories & Dreams* magazine. His books include *Memories of Yankee Stadium* and *Remembrances of Swings Past: A Lifetime of Baseball Stories.*

Bill Pruden has been an educator, primarily a teacher of American history and government and mostly at the high-school level, for almost 40 years. A SABR member for over two decades, he has contributed to both SABR's BioProject and Games Project as well as some book projects. A lifelong baseball fan, he also loves to read, research, and write about American history of all kinds, passions undoubtedly fueled by the fact that as a 7-year-old, at only his second major-league game, he witnessed Roger Maris's historic 61st home run.

Todd Radom is a designer, sports branding expert, and writer. His work includes the official logos for Super Bowl XXXVIII, the 2009 NBA All-Star Game, the 2014, 2016, and 2018 MLB All-Star Games, the graphic identities of multiple major-league baseball teams – including the Washington Nationals and Los Angeles Angels – and league, team identity, and branding for Ice Cube's BIG3 basketball league. His work was included in the Worcester Art Museum's 2021 exhibition "The Iconic Jersey: Baseball x Fashion," the first exhibition in an art museum solely devoted to the baseball jersey. Radom is the author

of *Winning Ugly: A Visual History of Baseball's Most Unique Uniforms*, and co-author of *Fabric of the Game: The Stories Behind the NHL's Names, Logos, and Uniforms.*

Alan Raylesberg is an attorney in New York City. He is a lifelong baseball fan who enjoys baseball history and roots for the Yankees and the Mets. Alan also has a strong interest in baseball analytics and is a devotee of baseball simulation games, participating in both draft leagues and historical replays. Alan has written a number of articles for SABR, including other biographies. Before going to law school, Alan was the sports director of his college radio station and dreamed of a career in sports broadcasting or journalism. Now, after many years practicing law, he is grateful for the opportunity that SABR has provided to allow him to realize at least some of that dream from many years ago.

Mike Richard is a lifelong Red Sox fan, a retired guidance counselor at Gardner (Massachusetts) High School and a longtime sports columnist. He has written for the *Gardner News, Worcester Telegram & Gazette,* and *Cape Cod Times*. A Massachusetts high-school sports historian, he has authored two high-school football books: *Glory to Gardner: 100 Years of Football in the Chair City* and *Super Saturdays: The Complete History of the Massachusetts High School Super Bowl.* He has also documented the playoff history (sectional and state championships) of all high-school sports in Massachusetts. He lives in Sandwich on Cape Cod with his wife, Peggy, and is the official historian of the Cape Cod Baseball League. They are the parents of a son, Casey, and a daughter, Lindsey, and have two grandchildren, Theo and Grace.

Carl Riechers retired from United Parcel Service in 2012 after 35 years of service. With more free time, he became a SABR member that same year. Born and raised in the suburbs of St. Louis, he became a big fan of the Cardinals. He and his wife, Janet, have three children and he is the proud grandpa of two.

Harry Schoger is a Hoosier transplanted to the Buckeye State, where he now lives with his wife of 63 years, Eleanor. In his professional career he worked in management roles in the primary steelmaking industry. His fifth-grade teacher brought in his radio so the class could listen to the 1948 World Series between the Cleveland Indians and Boston Braves. The experience made him an Indians/Guardians fan to this day. By coincidence he now lives in Canton, Ohio, home of the Pro Football Hall of Fame, near Cleveland. He has been a history aficionado, including baseball, all his life and a SABR member for the past few years. He has contributed both bios and games to several books.

Paul Semendinger, Ed.D., a lifetime educator currently serves as a college professor after retiring following a 32-year career as a teacher and principal. Paul has authored numerous books including *The Least Among Them* and *Scattering the Ashes.* Paul recently collaborated with Yankees great Roy White on his autobiography, *From Compton to the Bronx,* scheduled for release in April 2023. Paul runs the Yankee site "Start Spreading the News," still plays competitive baseball, and runs marathons. He is a proud dad and has been happily married for more than 30 years.

Lyle Spatz has been a SABR member since 1973. He served as chairman of the Baseball Records Committee from 1991 to 2016.

A fan of the Yankees since the 1970s, **Mark S. Sternman** grew up in New York before settling in Boston in 1995. He still roots for the Yankees. Sternman has never had a favorite Yankee player, but his beloved stepfather Mickey (Charlie Keller) and sister Cheryl (Lou Piniella) both did. Sternman's most memorable Yankee Stadium moment came when he saw Nelson Mandela speak at the Big Ball Orchard in the South Bronx (hat tip to sports talk radio legend Art Rust Jr.) on June 22, 1990.

Aaron Tallent is a writer whose work has appeared in the *Washington Post, Washington Times, Advocate & Democrat, Athlon Sports,* The Sweet Science, Oncology Business Review, and FOX Sports' Outkick the Coverage. He writes extensively about sports history and lives in the Washington area with his wife and two cats.

Cecilia Tan has been writing about the Yankees since a fourth-grade book report on Reggie Jackson. She has written for *Yankees Magazine, Yankees Xtreme, Gotham Baseball,* and Baseball Prospectus, and still occasionally updates her blog, "Why I Like Baseball." She has been SABR's publications director and the editor of the *Baseball Research Journal* since 2011.

Stew Thornley is a lifelong Yankees fan who has lived in Minnesota most of his life-long. He also loves all things about New York (even the Mets a little bit). He has been a SABR member since 1979.

Doug Vogel is a lifelong baseball and golf fan. He has made a living as a golf-course superintendent for the past 32 years. Doug is a credentialed press member of the PGA Tour, the PGA of America, and the United States Golf Association and covers major golf tournaments with an emphasis on golf course tournament preparation. He is a past editor of *The Greenerside,* an award-winning newsletter published by the Golf Course Superintendents Association of New Jersey. Doug is well known for writing articles that have combined golf and baseball story lines. He recently published his first book, *Babe Ruth and the Scottish Game – Anecdotes of a Golf Fanatic.* The New York Mets and the New Jersey Jackals are his teams.

Joseph Wancho has been a SABR member since 2005. He resides in Brooklyn, Ohio, and serves as the vice chair of the Baseball Index.

Bob Webster grew up in northwest Indiana and has been a Cubs fan since 1963. After relocating to Portland, Oregon, in 1980, Bob spends his time working on baseball research and writing and is a contributor to quite a few SABR projects. He has worked as a stats stringer on the MLB Gameday app for three years, is a member of the Pacific Northwest Chapter of SABR, and is on the board of directors of the Old-Timers Baseball Association of Portland.

Upon realizing that he couldn't hit the curveball, **Mike Whiteman** turned to reading and writing about the national pastime. He is a regular contributor to the Yankees-themed blog *Start Spreading the News* and has contributed to five SABR book projects. He enjoys summers on his porch in Lancaster, Pennsylvania, listening to baseball on the radio. His home team includes his wife, Nichole, and their two daughters.

Tim Wiles is the library director at the Guilderland (New York) Public Library. He was the director of research at the National Baseball Hall of Fame library from 1995 to 2014. He co-authored *Baseball's Greatest Hit: The Story of Take Me Out to the Ball Game* in 2008. He co-edited *Line Drives: 100 Contemporary Baseball Poems* in 2002. His blog on women and girls in baseball can be read at grassrootsbaseball.org.

The SABR Digital Library

Available wherever books are sold

Friends of SABR

You can become a Friend of SABR by giving as little as $10 per month or by making a one-time gift of $1,000 or more. When you do so, you will be inducted into a community of passionate baseball fans dedicated to supporting SABR's work.

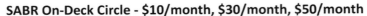

Friends of SABR receive the following benefits:
- ✓ Annual Friends of SABR Commemorative Lapel Pin
- ✓ Recognition in This Week in SABR, SABR.org, and the SABR Annual Report
- ✓ Access to the SABR Annual Convention VIP donor event
- ✓ Invitations to exclusive Friends of SABR events

SABR On-Deck Circle - $10/month, $30/month, $50/month

Get in the SABR On-Deck Circle, and help SABR become the essential community for the world of baseball. Your support will build capacity around all things SABR, including publications, website content, podcast development, and community growth.

A monthly gift is deducted from your bank account or charged to a credit card until you tell us to stop. No more email, mail, or phone reminders.

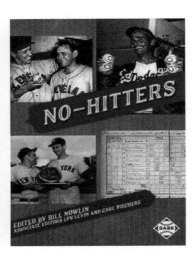

Join the SABR On-Deck Circle

Payment Info: _____Visa _____Mastercard

Name on Card: _____

Card #: _____

Exp. Date: _____ Security Code: _____

Signature: _____

○ $10/month

○ $30/month

○ $50/month

○ Other amount _____

Go to sabr.org/donate to make your gift online

Made in the USA
Monee, IL
07 June 2023